*New Jersey Politics and
Government*

New Jersey Politics and Government

THE SUBURBS COME OF AGE

THIRD EDITION

BARBARA G. SALMORE

STEPHEN A. SALMORE

RIVERGATE BOOKS
An Imprint of Rutgers University Press
New Brunswick, New Jersey, and London

LIBRARY OF CONGRESS CATALOGING-IN-PUBLICATION DATA

Salmore, Barbara G., 1942–
   New Jersey politics and government : the suburbs come of age /
Barbara G. Salmore, Stephen A. Salmore. — 3rd ed.
          p. cm.
   Includes bibliographical references and index.
   ISBN 978-0-8135-4285-0 (hardcover : alk. paper) — ISBN 978-0-8135-4286-7
(pbk. : alk. paper)
       1. New Jersey—Politics and government.   I. Salmore, Stephen A.   II. Title.
JK3516.S35 2007
320.9749—dc22

                                                                    2007024982

A British Cataloging-in-Publication record for this book is available
                        from the British Library.

Visit our Web site: http://rutgerspress.rutgers.edu

Manufactured in the United States of America

For our daughter, Elizabeth Hiatt Salmore
A native New Jerseyan and a citizen of the world

Contents

List of Tables

ACKNOWLEDGMENTS

LIKE MANY RESIDENTS OF NEW JERSEY, both authors of this book were born in New York City, but we have been privileged to be observers, participants, and analysts of New Jersey politics for all of our adult lives. Our greatest debts are to the countless members of the state's political community who have observed, participated, and analyzed along with us. Without the insights so many of them shared over many years, this book truly could not have been written. Some demand special mention.

Former Governor Thomas H. Kean shared his insights on both politics and government and was a careful reader of the entire manuscript of the first edition of this work, without ever trying to influence our assessments in any way.

New Jersey's statehouse press corps is rich in talent. As we worked on this volume over time, we learned a great deal from listening, reading, and conversing with Michael Aron and Kent Manahan of New Jersey Network, Jim Goodman of the *Trenton Times*, Sal Paolantonio and Dick Pohlman of the *Philadelphia Inquirer*, Joe Sullivan and Jerry Grey of the *New York Times*, Alan Guenther of the *Cherry Hill Courier-Post*, and Joe Donohue of the *Newark Star-Ledger*.

Democratic consultants Barry Brendel, Don Herche, and Steve DeMicco (a former executive director of the party) were also our teachers, as were lobbyists Roger Bodman, Harold Hodes, and Jim McQueeney. It was a special pleasure to learn about New Jersey politics from former students who are now active participants in New Jersey politics, particularly Drew alumni Lysa Israel and Larry Purpuro and Rutgers alumni Gregg Edwards and Bill Palatucci.

A number of experts gave us the benefit of their wisdom on particular subjects and what we wrote about them. We acknowledge with thanks the contributions of Ross Baker, Andrew Baron, Stanley Friedelbaum, Mary Annie Harper, Frederick Hermann, Peggi Howard, Perry Leavell, Frank LoBiondo, Eve Lubalin, Maureen Moakley, Gerald Pomper, Ingrid Reed, and Alan Rosenthal. Fred Hermann and Steven Kimmelman at the Election Law Enforcement Commission responded to special requests with graciousness and alacrity. We also benefited greatly from the many thoughtful suggestions by Daniel Elazar, Russell Harrison, John Kincaid, and Steven Schechter, who read the original manuscript. Grants of released time and administrative support from Drew University and the Eagleton Institute of Politics at Rutgers University were essential for getting us started on our work. We also thank the team at Rutgers University Press for believing in this book, and especially our copy editor, Willa Speiser, for her many contributions to both style and substance.

The Eagleton Institute has long been a place where practitioners and scholars gather together to discuss and study New Jersey politics. In a reflection of this commitment, Eagleton has since 1975 sponsored three edited volumes on New Jersey politics and government. This book can be considered as the latest in this series. Since it is not an edited volume, it reflects the particular opinions and idiosyncrasies of the authors, a bipartisan team.

Stephen Salmore died suddenly in the midst of our work on this third edition, but his extraordinary understanding of his adopted state infuses every page.

New Jersey Politics and Government

Chapter 1

Prologue

Countin' the cars on the New Jersey Turnpike....
[T]hey've all gone to look for America . . .

—Paul Simon

In 1923, Ernest Gruening edited a delightful guide
for armchair travelers, *These United States*. Edmund Wilson Jr.—distinguished literary critic and native of Red Bank, New Jersey—contributed
the essay entitled "New Jersey: The Slave of Two Cities." He offered the
following thesis: "It is precisely its suburban function which gives New
Jersey such character as it has. It is precisely a place where people do not live
to develop a society of their own but where they merely pass or sojourn on
their way to do something else. Its distinction among eastern states is that it
has attained no independent life, that it is the doormat, the servant, and the
picnic-ground of the social organisms that drain it."[1]

In 1971, Gruening wrote a new preface to a reprint of his 1923 work.
It was important, he told a new generation of readers, to know "a different
America." He offered but one caveat: "I doubt that Edmund Wilson, Jr. . . .
would find much to change in his "New Jersey, the Slave of Two
Cities."[2]

Gruening reflected a common view of New Jersey, but one already
becoming out of date. More than three decades later, it is almost entirely
wrong. It is not that New Jersey is no longer a suburban state. It is that the
United States has become a suburban society, and in so becoming, it has
enabled New Jersey to develop a society of its own.

A current New Jersey resident, Yogi Berra, once remarked, "You can
observe a lot just by looking." New Jersey looks different than it did in
1923, or even in 1971. To be sure, there are still pockets of "the cramped
smudgy life of industry" that Wilson described. Parts of the southern
Pinelands are still "desolate wilderness." And certainly a journey to
Princeton still means that "one seems to have at last reached a place where

no one cares what is happening in New York."[3] Yet much of blue-collar Jersey City is now a yuppie haven; retirement communities encroach on the Pinelands; and many New Jerseyans all over the state no longer care what is happening in New York.

THE "NEW" NEW JERSEY

Today, the symbols of change are everywhere. Among the places George Washington slept is eighteenth-century Liberty Hall, ancestral home of William Livingston, New Jersey's first governor, and of Thomas Kean, its forty-eighth governor. Liberty Hall is now a museum, its grounds given over to luxury apartments and offices. The stately Chalfonte-Haddon Hall Hotel "on the boardwalk in Atlantic City" has become the Resorts Casino Hotel, the first legal gambling salon on the east coast. A Newark synagogue, built at the turn of the century, is now a Pentecostal church. Hoboken's Irish saloons have been replaced by restaurants serving young professionals who have renovated the city's brownstones and commute to Wall Street. A sports and entertainment complex and golf courses are built atop the swampy landfills of the northern Meadowlands.

A traveler seeking contemporary New Jersey should visit Toms River, seat of Ocean County. In 1950, the population of Toms River was 7,000, and Ocean County, with 50,000 people, was the second poorest and second most sparsely populated county in the state. In 1955, the Garden State Parkway opened, and "for the first time, everybody in North Jersey could get to the shore without spending half the day in the car. And everybody did."[4] Some stayed to buy the development houses being built a few miles away in Toms River. By 1970, its population had grown to 43,000, Ocean County's to more than 200,000, and the huge Ocean County Mall opened in 1972. Echoing Edmund Wilson, Joe McGinnis wrote: "A suburb, in fact, was what Toms River was becoming. The only peculiar thing was that there wasn't any 'urb.' Toms River was 60 miles from anywhere, not part of the social or cultural or economic orbit of either New York or Philadelphia. It was a town with no connection to anyplace else."[5]

On this last point, McGinnis was wrong. Toms River was connected to all the other rapidly suburbanizing places in Ocean County. During the 1970s, as McGinnis himself noted, Ocean County's population grew at the rate of one person every four minutes. Only Orange County, California, grew as fast. During the 1980s, Ocean was the fastest growing county in the state. In the state, as in the nation, the population was moving south and west. By 2005, there were 95,000 people in Toms River, and 560,000 in Ocean County.

Many of Ocean County's new residents left New Jersey's cities. The "Big Six"—Camden, Elizabeth, Jersey City, Newark, Paterson, and Trenton—were home to one in four New Jerseyans in 1950, but only one in twelve by 1990. Newark's losses were especially dramatic. It had been the nation's sixteenth largest city in 1905, but its population fell by 16 percent during the 1980s, dropping below 300,000 for the first time in the century. Superhighways, office parks, single-family homes, and shopping malls had created Toms River. The nation's Newarks were "places built for another kind of world."[6]

Overall, New Jersey's population during the 1980s grew by about 5 percent, to 7.8 million, but the state's minority population increased by over 30 percent. The sort of middle-class whites who were leaving the cities and moving to Toms River made up less than 1 percent of the net increase. It was, rather, African Americans, Hispanics, Pacific Islanders, Indians, other Asians, West Indians, and a dozen other nationality and ethnic groups that helped New Jersey grow. These new arrivals allowed some cities to hold their own, but New Jersey's minority citizens were moving to the suburbs too. Bergen, composed entirely of seventy suburban towns, overtook Essex, dominated by Newark, as the state's most populous county. The newest of the shopping malls dotting Bergen was Edgewater's Yaohan Plaza, where the video rental shop specialized in Japanese-language films. It was the first large Asian specialty mall outside California.

Many of Bergen's Asians and other émigrés were professionals who worked for the numerous foreign subsidiaries doing business in the state. Concentrated in high-technology fields like consumer electronics and pharmaceuticals, these firms were the leading edge of an economic transformation that began in the 1970s and gained steam in the 1980s. In 1950, New Jersey's jobs were evenly divided between the industrial and service sectors. By 1990, the service sector dominated by a three-to-one ratio.

In 1950 North Jersey offered half as many jobs as New York City did, but by 1990 it was closing in on parity. The new white-collar occupations were higher paying than the factory jobs they replaced, and this was soon reflected in New Jerseyans' income. Per capita income growth tracked the national average through the 1960s and 1970s but exceeded it substantially during the 1980s. It made New Jersey's always relatively well-off population on average the second wealthiest in the nation. There were new demands on their personal income, however. Median single-family home prices in the state, which were at the national average in 1970, were a third higher than the average in 1990.

Growth and development had other costs too. New Jersey's students scored high on national mathematics tests—skills critical to jobs in the state's new high tech economy. But the range of scores was among the widest in the nation. Students in urban schools were most likely to do poorly. Yet Paterson textile mills, Jersey City rail yards, Trenton pottery factories, and Camden assembly plants that might once have employed the less educated were almost all gone. Commuters to suburban office parks suffered some of the worst traffic congestion anywhere. Combating air and water pollution and disposing of the state's garbage as open space dwindled became leading public questions. As they entered the new century, New Jerseyans recognized that growth at the pace of the 1980s was unlikely, and might "even be undesirable in view of the environmental consequences."[7]

Politics and Government in the "New" New Jersey

The issues that drive New Jersey politics today, and which have transformed its politics and government, grow directly out of the population dispersion that began after World War II. More than any other populous American state, New Jersey politics in the past was dominated by those generally unfriendly to cities—rural interests before 1970, and suburban ones thereafter, and its echoes remain today. Aside from that, state politics and government have been almost entirely reshaped since 1970, and that transformation is at the center of virtually every chapter of this book.

Chapter 2 provides a brief introduction to the state's history, from early European settlement to the turn of the twentieth century. Chapters 3 and 4 offer an overview of New Jersey's political history and the forces that shaped it. Edmund Wilson's biting portrait describes a conservative, parochial state that seemed to have no function but to serve New York City and Philadelphia. What identity New Jersey citizens had was with their own towns—more of them per square mile than anywhere else in the country. This was a potent recipe for strong home rule, strong local political machines, and weak statewide institutions. This New Jersey grew more slowly than its neighbors and resisted social and political innovation.

The catalysts for the changes that became widely apparent in the 1970s, and dominant thereafter, were largely external—a postwar population boom fueled by federal highway and housing policies and U.S. Supreme Court decisions ending legislative malapportionment. These forces destroyed the "unholy alliance" of Republican rural-based machines and Democratic urban ones that had dominated New Jersey politics for 150 years. The partners' only common interest was maintaining their individual power bases. As they disappeared, a new political system could emerge. Chapters 4 and 5 describe the volatile, candidate-centered elections that replaced party-dominated contests and were increasingly decided by politically independent suburbanites. Chapter 6 details an interest-group universe that changed correspondingly, as new interests appeared along with the scattering population and increasingly complex economy and were more difficult for political parties to broker or aggregate.

A state's constitution sets out its government's structures, limits, and powers, as well as its aspirations. New Jersey's first two constitutions, of 1776 and 1844, were, like its citizens, already somewhat behind the times when they were promulgated. In contrast, the current constitution of 1947 anticipated the future. It was written by New Jersey's "moralistic" reform element, never dominant but always present. New Jersey's three constitutions and the political forces that produced them are described in chapter 7. After actively fighting it for years, the political traditionalists agreed to the 1947 constitutional convention because, in line with their usual mode of thinking, they believed they could extract parochial advantage as the price of cooperation. The urban Democrats indeed got concessions on local railroad taxes, the southern Republicans retained control of the state agriculture department, and both won continuation of the malapportioned state senate that was the foundation of their power. The traditionalists won their battles but did not realize they had lost the war.

Out of the constitutional convention emerged state executive and judicial institutions that were among the most powerful and far-reaching in the nation. Within twenty years, the federal courts would dismantle the traditionalists' base in the legislature. Railroads and agriculture became afterthoughts in the wake of the developers and the superhighways. Suburbanization moved people out of the cities and transformed the countryside, and both elements of the uneasy alliance thus lost power in the voting booth. For a brief period, the legislature, which had ruled politics and policy since New Jersey became a state, was so weakened as to be almost irrelevant. However, a new breed of independent and entrepreneurial legislators soon gave it the capacity and resources to deal as an equal partner with the governor and the courts. Chapters 8 through 11 trace the development of the state's political institutions.

All these changes in state government—one might almost say the creation of a genuine state government—also brought vast changes in other relationships within the state and outside it. As service in Washington became more important to talented politicians than a stint in the legislature or county and municipal government, New Jersey's congressional delegation became more distinguished and active. Trenton adopted a far more confident and assertive posture toward New York City and Philadelphia. Bewildered local officials found themselves caught between the Scylla of new state aid and the Charybdis of new state mandates. Chapters 12 and 13 describe Trenton's uneasy new relations with its neighboring states, the federal government, and to New Jersey's 566 municipalities and 21 counties.

Massive alterations in political and governmental structures bring massive alterations in public policy, and so they have in New Jersey. As stronger state institutions developed, bent on forceful intervention in the state's life, New Jersey became one of the last states to adopt broad-based taxes. So intense was public aversion to an income tax that only the state supreme court, backed by the governor, could mandate its passage in 1976. When Trenton proved that the modest new tax actually lowered local property taxes (at least temporarily), New Jerseyans gave it grudging acquiescence. Hikes in the broad-based taxes as the economy took off in the early 1980s produced undreamed of revenue, and the state budget quadrupled over fifteen years. The spending spree that transpired left the state deep in debt in the new century. The evolution of state taxing and spending, a metaphor for the contest between state and local forces, is described in chapter 14.

Expenditures for public education consume a third of the state budget, and New Jersey has ranked first or second in spending for elementary and secondary education among the states for some years (although somewhat lower when spending is related to per capita income). Despite that, the state's proportional fiscal contribution is still below the fifty-state average, and local property taxes in New Jersey remain among the highest in the nation. Nowhere else is the state's home rule tradition more apparent than in the realm of public education. Almost all New Jersey municipalities have their own elementary schools, and high schools of barely five hundred students are the rule rather than the exception. Arguments for curricular enrichment or economies of scale pall when they mean eliminating the institution most central to the identity of New Jersey's towns, where high school football is practically a ritual. New Jerseyans are barely inclined to redistribute their school tax dollars outside their own communities, much less to redistribute their children. Battles over public education—who should control it and how to fund it—have devoured more debate time in New Jersey in the last four decades than even the tax system to which they are intimately connected. Chapter 15 tells this long-running tale.

If there is anything about which residents agree, it is that their quality of life is threatened. The cars they drive to their suburban jobs bring air pollution and traffic gridlock. Stormwater runoff from land paved over for development, illegal dumping, and overburdened municipal sewage systems pollute too many streams and rivers and threaten the beaches New Jerseyans prize. Citizens will thus do almost anything to protect the environment, remaining open space, and natural wonders—except welcome restrictions on how they use their own property or on the way their own towns develop. Trenton's increasing ventures into environmental, transportation, and land use regulation, and the response from citizens and local governments, are the subject of chapter 16.

In the new century, providing quality education, protecting the quality of life, and accommodating a multicultural society while sustaining growth and opportunity were central domestic issues as the United States moved inexorably toward becoming a nation of suburbs. America's most suburban state is, for those who know it, a continuously fascinating place. Its complexity and diversity can never be fathomed by those who race down the Turnpike. New Jersey is a place more Americans should get to know, because of what it may tell them about their own future.

CHAPTER 2

Foundations

NEW JERSEY, 1600–1900

It was Alexander Hamilton who discovered the uses of
New Jersey.

—Lincoln Steffens

WHEN CHILDREN STUDY THE AMERICAN REVOLUTION, they
read of its opening and closing chapters in Massachusetts and Virginia, and
they tour Lexington, Concord, Philadelphia, and Yorktown. But few travel
to New Jersey, the scene of more battles than any other state. All Americans
learn about the Boston Tea Party and count Massachusetts's Paul Revere a
hero. Few know of New Jersey's Greenwich Tea Party, which took place
a year later, or about New Jersey's Nathaniel Scudder. He rode all night on
July 1, 1776, to warn the Provincial Congress when the Sandy Hook militia
spotted an approaching British naval fleet. The Provincial Congress alerted
the Continental Congress sitting in Philadelphia, which proclaimed the
Declaration of Independence three days later.

It was across New Jersey that George Washington was thrown back
from New York to Pennsylvania and fought the battles of New Brunswick,
Monmouth, and Princeton. It was in Morristown and Somerville that the
ragtag Continental army spent three bitter winters, and at the Battle of
Monmouth that Molly Pitcher's name became immortal. The tide of the
war turned when Washington crossed the Delaware River and captured the
Hessian garrison at Trenton. The man who would be the nation's first
president wrote his farewell address to his troops in a house in Rocky Hill.

In this early history are clues to what New Jersey would become, and
in critical respects remain, for centuries thereafter. As it was for the Revolutionary armies, New Jersey was long "a region that one traverses to go
somewhere else, a kind of suburb and No Man's Land between New York
and Philadelphia."[1] The immense consequences of New Jersey's location

between two of the nation's most important cities led Benjamin Franklin to call New Jersey a "valley between two mountains of conceit" and a "cask tapped at both ends." New Jersey's most famous governor, Woodrow Wilson, would complain more than a century later, "We have always been inconvenienced by New York on the one hand and Philadelphia on the other."[2]

Location contributed powerfully to the lack of a clear state identity, and other factors reinforced it. One was the division of the original British royal land grant into East Jersey and West Jersey. Throughout the colonial period, New Jersey maintained two capitals at which the provincial legislature met alternately—Perth Amboy for East Jersey and Burlington for West Jersey. The counties that had originally made up West Jersey would still be threatening to secede from the state two hundred years thereafter.[3]

Ethnic and religious diversity complicated the regional cleavage. By the early eighteenth century, there were Dutch settlements in Bergen and Middlesex counties, Scots in Perth Amboy and Freehold, and Germans in Hunterdon County. Puritans from New England founded Newark, Elizabeth, and Woodbridge. Quakers lived along the Delaware River. Presbyterians dominated Princeton and its college, while the Dutch Reformed Church founded New Jersey's other colonial college, Queen's College (later Rutgers), at New Brunswick. Among all the colonies, only Pennsylvania's population was as diverse. Later waves of immigration made the New Jersey of 1910 the state with the fifth highest proportion of foreign-born residents.

Domination by its larger neighbors, parochialism, and social cleavages fostered suspicion of centralized authority. The state's earliest political "parties" were East Jersey versus West Jersey factions organized by county and concerned mainly with filling patronage jobs.[4] The counties would remain the state's most powerful political units for almost two centuries, and some of America's hardiest political machines blossomed there.

The first state constitution, of 1776, assigned virtually all powers to a legislature dominated by county interests and made the governor little more than a figurehead. In this respect, New Jersey was little different from the other original states, but weak state government had incredible persistence. The second constitution, of 1844, in force until 1947, still limited the governor to one three-year term, gave the "chief executive" almost no appointment powers not shared with the legislature, and only the weakest of vetoes. None of these officials had much to do; counties and localities raised almost all the money for the limited public purposes citizens saw fit to support.[5] In 1960 New Jersey was still one of only three states without a state sales or income tax.

It also took a long time for New Jersey to accept its role in the federal union. The local militia's tendency to melt away early in the War of Independence led General Washington to write in exasperation, "The conduct of the Jerseys has been most infamous."[6] During the Civil War, draft riots in New York overshadowed similar events in Newark. New Jersey was the only northern state to deny a plurality of its popular vote to Abraham Lincoln in 1860 and 1864, and that era's momentous amendments to the U.S. Constitution were, variously, rejected or rescinded by the state's legislature.

Thus, the keys to understanding New Jersey's politics from its earliest days forward lie in how profoundly its location and social and political fragmentation worked against identity with state or nation. This chapter describes how these factors shaped the state's early politics. The next chapter carries the story through the twentieth century. For almost two hundred years, the lineaments of New Jersey's politics, government and policy remained almost frozen. The cast of characters changed; the drama's basic plot did not.

COLONIAL NEW JERSEY

New Jersey's original inhabitants, the Leni-Lenape Indians, were the first to repel an invasion from New York. In 1618, Dutch settlers ventured across the Hudson River to establish a trading station but were driven back to Manhattan by 1643. The British gained control of the area two decades later, and King Charles II gave James, Duke of York, all the lands between the Connecticut and Delaware rivers. They were named Albania, after James' Scottish title, Duke of Albany. Fortunately, this appellation was short-lived. Like so many after him, James focused his attention on the northeastern portion of the territory and gave the region between the Hudson and the Delaware to Lords John Berkeley and George Carteret. A map error led the new owners to believe they had acquired an island; thus they named the tract after Carteret's native island of Jersey.

Before the end of the century, Berkeley had sold the western portion to a group of Quakers headed by William Penn. The Quakers' proprietorship was also brief. After buying East Jersey from Carteret's widow in 1680, the Quakers rapidly sold it off in sections and transferred West Jersey to a society of London merchants. East and West Jersey formally became one colony in 1702 but retained two capitals until after the Revolutionary War.

Queen Anne also had little interest in the colony. In 1703, she appointed Lord Cornbury royal governor of New York—and as an afterthought, also governor of New Jersey. Perhaps this was because there was so little to govern. Only 10,000 souls lived in the entire province (7,500 in the East and 2,500 in the West), compared with the 20,000 residents of New York City and the 15,000 in Philadelphia. After much agitation by the colonial assembly, Lewis Morris was named New Jersey's first separate governor in 1738.

New Jersey's early inhabitants were overwhelmingly rural, living on small farms in East Jersey and larger ones in the West. Immigration in the eighteenth century was largely from Britain and the German states, although one particularly notable nineteenth-century arrival was Napoleon's brother, Joseph Bonaparte. Fleeing France after the Battle of Waterloo, he lived "in regal splendor" on an estate near Bordentown until he returned to Europe in 1832.[7]

Aside from good farmland, the colony had few resources. A small iron-mining industry centered in the northwestern hills quickly failed for lack of timber to drive the furnaces and forges.[8] Among those laboring on the farms were indentured servants and African slaves—the Duke of York, president of the Royal Africa Company, had directed Governor Cornbury to oversee "a constant and sufficient supply of merchantable negroes, at moderate rates."[9]

With the West Jersey Quakers' distaste for the "peculiar institution," West Jersey's population in the first half of the eighteenth century was about 4 percent black, compared to 12 percent in East Jersey. Bergen County led the way, with 20 percent of its inhabitants in bondage.[10] The original inhabitants of the colony, the Leni-Lenape, had numbered a few thousand when whites first arrived, but had been reduced by warfare, disease, and bad land sale bargains to a few hundred. Herded on to a reservation in Burlington County, the last few left to join the Mohegans in upstate New York in 1801.[11]

Location was New Jersey's most valuable resource, and the first regular transportation services in North America became an early bulwark of the economy. "Jersey wagons," or stagecoaches, first ran on old Indian trails from Burlington to Philadelphia in 1733, from New Brunswick to Trenton in 1738, and from South Amboy to Bordentown in 1740. At the end of each route, ferries transported travelers across the Hudson, Raritan, and Delaware rivers. By 1765, New Jersey had more roads than any other colony, and most of those roads led to New York and Philadelphia.

With no large seaport of its own, the colony's trade passed through these cities, draining New Jersey of cash. Tensions rose when the British banned the colony from issuing paper money. Debtors stormed the Monmouth County courthouse and clashed with creditors in Newark riots. Rebellious sentiments were strongest among the Baptists and Presbyterians, who were headquartered at the College of New Jersey at Princeton. Opposing them were the West Jersey Quakers, who condemned war as against the Gospel and civil harmony. The Anglican and Dutch Reformed communities were divided. Even the most vociferous objectors were somewhat leery of independence, for they saw the British Parliament as their protector from domination by New York.

Ignoring pleas from their last colonial governor (Benjamin Franklin's illegitimate son, William), New Jersey's delegates to the First Continental Congress in early 1775 supported a boycott of British goods and other resolutions hostile to Britain. Rebels dominated the Provincial Congress meeting in Trenton in May. The Presbyterians successfully intimidated Tory sympathizers to keep them from casting ballots for members of the congress. Despite virtually universal male suffrage, two-thirds of the eligible electors did not vote. The Provincial Congress sent four Presbyterians and a Baptist to the Second Continental Congress in Philadelphia, including Princeton's John Witherspoon, the president of the college. When war broke out, the Provincial Congress ordered William Franklin deported to Connecticut as a prisoner of war. The rebels selected William Livingston of Liberty Hall in what was then Essex County as their first provincial governor. Livingston ordered mass arrests of Tory sympathizers and their deportation to the colony's interior.

Historians estimate that at least a third and perhaps half the population was active or covert Tories when the war came to New Jersey. At the war's midpoint, there were more inhabitants serving as British troops than in the Continental army. One regiment was led by a British brigadier general who had been speaker of the colonial assembly.[12] The largest segment of the population changed allegiance "with the tide of battle, being loyal subjects of King George today and fervent admirers of George Washington tomorrow."[13]

Linking New England and New York with the South, New Jersey felt the full force of the struggle for independence. Washington spent a quarter of his generalship in New Jersey. His armies crossed the colony four times, spending the winters of 1778 in Somerville and 1777 and 1779 in Morristown. After bidding farewell to his troops, Washington met with the independent nation's first Congress at the College of New Jersey's Nassau Hall.

BETWEEN THE REVOLUTIONARY AND CIVIL WARS: "THE STATE OF THE CAMDEN AND AMBOY"

After independence, New Jersey continued to languish in the shadow of New York and Philadelphia. By 1820, the population had barely doubled, to 227,500. In comparison, by 1820 New York State boasted a million inhabitants. In 1830, there were 242,000 residents of New York City and 80,000 in Philadelphia, compared with 11,000 in Newark, New Jersey's largest city. Thanks largely to Alexander Hamilton and his associates, promising urban locales in the northern part of the state remained under the control of New Yorkers. Hamilton sought to achieve his dream of great industrial cities by founding the Society for Useful Manufactures at the Great Falls of Paterson, and drawing the charter for the Associates of the Jersey Company at the site of what is now Jersey City.

The Society for Useful Manufactures was given a "perpetual monopoly" on manufacturing activities in Paterson in 1791 and acted as its effective government until 1830. The 1831 Paterson city charter gave its government minimum powers, and the Society tax-free status. When the City of Jersey was chartered in 1838, rights to the valuable Hudson River waterfront remained with the Jersey Company. Until the state government signed a treaty with New York State in 1833, New Jersey had no rights to use the waters of the Hudson.

Just as all New Jersey roads led to New York, waterborne transportation was also dominated by its powerful neighbor. In 1807, the New York legislature granted a monopoly on steamboat transportation between the two states to inventor Robert Fulton and his partners. Thomas Gibbons, an Elizabethtown entrepreneur, challenged the New Yorkers' monopoly with one granted him by the United States Congress. His rival boat, piloted by New Brunswick's Cornelius Vanderbilt, "puffed about New York Harbor" flying a streamer proclaiming, "New Jersey must be free!"[14] The dispute led to a landmark U.S. Supreme Court case, *Gibbons v. Ogden* (1824), which affirmed the federal government's authority to regulate traffic on navigable waterways under the interstate commerce power. Daniel Webster argued the case for the victorious Gibbons.[15]

The century's most important form of transportation did boast local ownership, however. In 1811, the state legislature had rejected as "visionary" the petition of Hoboken's John Stevens to build a rail line. The persistent Stevens family was finally granted a charter for the Camden and Amboy Railroad in 1830. In return for a thirty-year monopoly of a route between the Hudson and Delaware rivers, forbidding any competing line "between the cities of New-York and Philadelphia," the Stevens family gave the state one thousand shares in the railroad, and a guarantee that their annual dividends would never fall below thirty thousand dollars.[16] The Camden and Amboy was quick to involve itself in politics: "Railroads from Maine to California played an important role in state politics during the nineteenth century, but in no state was that role assumed earlier or more pervasively than in New Jersey."[17]

This suited both the corporation and the state very well. The railroad's monopoly permitted it to overcharge hapless travelers between New York and Philadelphia. The Camden and Amboy's second-class fare was $2.50, at a time when $1 was the average laborer's weekly wage. The benefit to the state was that transit levies, imposed on out-of-state travelers rather than on the company, "neatly eliminated the need for statewide taxes."[18] In 1850, Trenton's entire operating fund totaled only $128,600, and the transit tax alone contributed $86,000, with other railroad taxes making up most of the rest.[19]

The Federalist Party in New Jersey was formed in 1789 to contest the first congressional elections. It remained an important force, never garnering less than 48 percent of the vote through 1814, when, as elsewhere, it effectively disappeared. New York Federalists, migrating across the Hudson River as they lost control of New York City to the Democrats of Tammany Hall, were an important element of its support. In 1798, the Federalists controlled the New Jersey legislature by a margin of thirty-eight to twelve. In that year, in reaction to the Alien and Sedition Acts, followers of Thomas Jefferson formed the Democratic-Republican Party and elected three of the state's five at-large U.S. congressmen. The heavy concentration of their support in the northern counties of Sussex, Essex, and Morris, however, hampered their progress. The Jeffersonians won statewide victories such as the at-large congressional elections, but only a small minority in the Trenton legislature.

Early voting in New Jersey was as enthusiastic, widespread, and corrupt as elsewhere, and it was grounded principally in religious and regional antipathies—as when West Jersey Quakers were urged during New Jersey's first congressional election "to keep out the bloodthirsty Presbyterians and to prevent War, Blood and Slaughter."[20] A 1790 law forbade voters to come to the polls with any "Weapons of War, or Staves, or Bludgeons." Most polling places were in taverns, producing the scenes described in the *New Brunswick Guardian*: "Lo! a voter brimful of freedom and grog, marching up to the election box, guided by two or three staunch patriots, lest the honest soul should mistake, lose his way, or be surprised by the other party and lost."[21] The state's 1776 constitution briefly permitted truly universal suffrage, for "all inhabitants . . . of full age," including women and blacks. After women hustled to the polls made the difference in a fierce fight between Newark and Elizabethtown over the location of the Essex County courthouse, an 1807 law confined the franchise to free, white, property-owning males.[22]

From 1828 until the Civil War, state politics settled into close contests between the Jacksonian Democrats and the Whigs. Both parties had well-organized get-out-the-vote operations, centered in the counties. Election rules designed to benefit one party or the other changed often, as the alliances traded legislative majorities in Trenton. Until an 1842 federal law required U.S. representatives to be chosen from congressional districts, whichever party was dominant opposed such district elections and favored statewide at-large choices. Similarly, the Whigs favored stricter taxpayer and citizenship qualifications and closing the polls at sunset, while the Democrats, with greater support among immigrants and the lower classes, pushed for fewer restrictions on the franchise and extended polling hours.

State politics meant legislative politics; the 1776 constitution made the governor "a convenience occasionally employed by the legislature to carry out a mandate it did not see fit to direct to some other officer or body."[23] Chosen annually by the legislature, and with no appointment or veto powers, the governor was more a judicial than an executive official. He served as the presiding officer of the legislative upper house, which acted as the highest court. New Jersey's governors of the first half of the century thus held a mostly honorific position and were usually members of prominent families.

About the time the Camden and Amboy Railroad was established, New Jersey politics became "democratized" in a number of ways that led the railroad to involve itself ever more heavily in political activities. Immigrants, especially from Ireland, were flooding into the northern part of the state and swelling the Democrats' ranks. A new constitution in 1844 made the governorship an elective office and removed property qualifications for the franchise, although voting was restricted to white males until 1875.

Even if inspired to some degree by the national fervor for Jacksonian democracy, the new constitution hardly constituted a revolution. The governor, while gaining modest appointment and veto powers, was limited to one three-year term—an election schedule that also effectively insulated state politics from national politics. Members of the legislature's upper house continued to be elected one from each county, and the upper house selected or ratified all officers of the executive branch, save the governor and state auditor. Assemblymen were elected for terms of only one year, their nominations firmly in the hands of county party organizations. Although Dorothea Dix led a successful campaign for a state mental hospital in 1848, and a state normal school was established to train teachers in 1855, the government's largest operation was a prison, whose keeper was appointed by the legislature.

Moreover, the white Protestants still leading the Democratic Party remained suspicious of strong central government in state or nation. The 1844 constitution banned the creation of any state debt in excess of one hundred thousand dollars without a public referendum. This provision made it almost impossible for the state to take over the Camden and Amboy by purchasing it. It was thus to the Democrats that the railroad entrusted its fate. State elections became contests between its supporters and opponents. The railroad's local agents mobilized the Democratic faithful, often paying them for their votes; it "extended if not practically introduced" the role of money in elections.[24] Great electoral exertions were necessary because after 1840 "New Jersey was at all times a doubtful state."[25]

Starting in 1852, New Jersey voters endorsed every Democratic presidential candidate for the next four decades, except for split electoral votes in 1860 and 1872. Twelve of the fifteen governors in this period were also Democrats, but victory margins in all these races never reached 54 percent. With the railroad dominating the Democratic party, "New Jersey became known as the state of the Camden and Amboy, and that is what she was, and as such she was execrated and ridiculed throughout the Union."[26]

THE CIVIL WAR AND AFTER: "NEW JERSEY, THE TRAITOR STATE"

Just as many New Jerseyans had opposed the War of Independence, many sympathized with the southern cause as the nation moved toward civil war. South Jersey Quakers, however, were key participants in the "underground railroad" that sheltered escaping slaves. Three principal routes and nine smaller ones ran into New Jersey from Maryland and Delaware.[27] New Jerseyans' chief concern was not slavery but the state's economic links to the Confederacy and, especially, the principle of states' rights—a sore point in New Jersey since colonial times.

Although still overwhelmingly a rural state in 1860, with 56,000 factory workers, New Jersey ranked sixth among the states in industrial production. Many of its factory workers were Irish immigrants, who started arriving in large numbers as a result of the famine of the 1840s and who made up more than half of the state's foreign-born population. Industry depended heavily on southern markets; a popular contemporary saying was that "the South walks on Newark shoe leather." A budding tourist industry relied on southern visitors; Cape May, on the Jersey Shore below the Mason-Dixon line, hosted many visitors from Maryland and Virginia. The College at Princeton drew over one-third of its students from the Confederacy.[28]

Even more powerful than these economic concerns was the widespread sympathy for the states' rights argument. Support for the Democratic position on states' rights was so great that the nascent New Jersey Republican Party chose to call itself the Opposition Party throughout the Civil War era. Despite tapping the state's William L. Dayton as his running mate, John Fremont ran a poor second to the Democrats' James Buchanan in the 1856 presidential election and barely outpolled the American Party's Millard Fillmore, candidate of the nativist Know-Nothings. Buchanan's runaway margin of victory in New Jersey was more than triple that of the greatest victor in the previous three presidential elections despite the three-way race.

In the same year though, a coalition of Republicans and Know-Nothings gave a razor-thin victory to the Opposition Party gubernatorial candidate, as they did again in 1859. This latter governor, Charles Olden of Princeton, was almost single-handedly responsible for persuading New Jersey not to secede. The state's critical balancing act between North and South also was evident when the U.S. House of Representatives in 1860 chose a first-term Republican congressman from New Jersey as its compromise candidate for Speaker of the House.

Although the Republicans' defeat in New Jersey's presidential balloting was narrower in 1860 than 1856, with the war looming the state continued to deny Abraham Lincoln's electors a complete victory, and it repeated this choice in 1864. Mixed feelings about the military campaign were evident throughout the conflict. Although Brigadier General Philip Kearney became a hero who could rightly brag, "I can make my men follow me to Hell," the secretary of war ordered the arrest of another New Jersey officer, Peace Democrat Colonel James Wall. Outrage over Wall's arrest carried a Democrat to a landslide win in the 1862 gubernatorial contest, and Wall himself to a seat in the U.S. Senate in an 1863 special election.

That year was the height of the Peace Democrats' influence. In March, both houses of the Democratic-dominated legislature passed resolutions opposing the Emancipation Proclamation and the Thirteenth Amendment to the U.S. Constitution and urged peace talks with the Confederacy. In July, draft riots broke out in Newark. Vast numbers of draftees sought to purchase substitutes; of the 6,981 men drafted in March 1864, only 380 actually served.[29]

In the years that followed, Republicans and Democrats traded control of the governorship and the legislature. A total Republican takeover in 1865 led to the legislature finally ratifying the Thirteenth Amendment to the U.S. Constitution and also the Fourteenth; when the Democrats prevailed in the 1867 legislative elections, they rescinded the Fourteenth Amendment's ratification and, in 1870, refused to ratify the Fifteenth Amendment. When a Republican majority replaced them the following year, the legislature reversed course on ratification once again. All of the landmark Civil War–era amendments garnered enough support from the other states to become part of the federal Constitution before New Jersey accepted them.

If the Civil War brought acrimony, it also brought growth. The population rose by 50 percent during the 1860s, then reached 906,000 in 1870, 1,000,000 in 1875, and almost 2,000,000 by 1900. Its geographic distribution changed markedly. Before the war, the largely rural populace was divided evenly among the state's counties. By 1880, two-thirds of the twenty-one counties still did not have a community with a population as large as 10,000, and only 9 of the state's 270 municipalities were that large. Almost three-quarters of all New Jerseyans lived in eight cities along the Camden and Amboy rail line snaking from the northeast to the southwest between Jersey City and Camden. Factories, whose numbers more than doubled between 1870 and 1900, were located in these railroad-oriented cities. Newark, with 72,000 residents in 1860, grew to 137,000 a decade later, and Jersey City mushroomed from 29,000 to 121,000 people. In contrast, areas farthest from the railroad and New York or Philadelphia were often more thinly settled than they had been at the time of the Revolution.

Politics now reflected the political aftermath of the war and the demographic and economic changes. A crucial event occurred in 1871, when the Camden and Amboy leased all of its property and rights-of-way to the Pennsylvania Railroad, destroying the "local ownership" justification for its monopoly in the New York–Philadelphia corridor. The *New York Herald* editorialized, "The halo of New Jersey's glory has left her. Her Ichabod hath departed. The Camden and Amboy Road, the pride of the state and the ruler of her Legislature, has been ceded to Pennsylvania."[30]

By 1873, a Republican-dominated legislature ended the Pennsylvania Railroad's monopoly, and other lines expanded or were built. Between 1870 and 1880, trackage in New Jersey increased from 1,125 miles to 1,684; eventually there would be 2,500 miles of track in a state that only extended 166 miles from north to south and 57 miles from east to west. Industrial and urban growth exploded as the railroads reached every corner of the state.

Three competing lines along the Atlantic coast turned the Jersey Shore town of Atlantic City into the nation's premier middle-class vacation resort. A wealthier clientele summered in Long Branch, the summer residence of presidents from Grant through Garfield—who died there some months after an attack by an assassin. The extensive rail lines swelled the ranks of New York and Philadelphia commuters who went home to bedroom suburbs in New Jersey.

Most affected by the rail explosion was Hudson County, and especially Jersey City, its largest municipality. Across the Hudson River from Manhattan, Jersey City had suffered indignities at the hands of transportation companies and the government in Trenton from its earliest days. After the state finally won the right to use the Hudson waters, it gave a private company rights to much of the city's waterfront. The state courts denied Jersey City the right to run a ferry line competing with the Jersey Company, and its lack of control over its own waterfront was reaffirmed by the legislature in a new city charter in 1851.

Shortly thereafter, the Jersey Company sold its waterfront rights to a local railroad, which transferred them to the Camden and Amboy in 1867. Another part of the waterfront was acquired by the Jersey Central Railroad, which, in 1868, over the loud and futile protests of local residents, made it suitable for rail construction by importing New York City garbage to fill in mudflats extending a thousand feet into the river. Jersey City's mayor vainly protested that his city was "hedged round about, cut up and run over by the great monopolies; her commercial facilities cut off; her natural energies crushed; her public spirit smothered; her growth retarded; the very air she breathes as a city dealt out to her in small quantities by one or the other of these gorged institutions that have no souls and no eye for anything that does not fill up and protect their own plethoric purses."[31]

More indignities were to come. Hudson County, anchored by Jersey City and heavily Irish and Roman Catholic, accounted for much of the state's Democratic vote, and for the narrow Democratic gubernatorial victories in every election between 1873 and 1892. The Republican stronghold was the legislature, where rural counties retained dominance of the upper house through the proviso that each county be represented by one senator. Republican domination of the assembly was less secure. Thus in 1871, when the GOP gained control of the legislature, it gerrymandered Hudson County into six tiny assembly districts that were home to most Protestant voters and one huge, oddly shaped district taking in most of Jersey City. Dubbed the Horseshoe, it contained most of the Democrats and Catholics in the county.

Not content with exempting much of the city's wealth from taxation and emasculating its role in state politics, the final Republican coup was ending Jersey City's self-government with a so-called ripper law. In reaction to the 1870 Democratic legislature's appointment of a state-controlled police commission for Republican Newark, the 1871 Republican legislature stripped Democratic Jersey City of all public functions and appointed a series of state commissions to handle all governance matters. The low point of the ring controlling Jersey City was reached when the state-appointed city treasurer (ironically, named Alexander Hamilton) absconded to Mexico with the city's funds. Finally, in 1876, the state's highest court returned governance to the city's residents after a constitutional amendment prohibited legislative regulation of the internal affairs of municipalities.

Before the Civil War, state politics had revolved around the Democratic supporters and Republican opponents of the Camden and Amboy. Now, with many competitor lines appearing, the railroads collectively continued to run state politics. There were enough lines—thirty-five different ones by 1900—to bankroll and control every political organization in the state. William J. Sewall, the undisputed Republican boss and U.S. senator for the last three decades of the nineteenth century, was a Pennsylvania employee who "held court" in the railroad's Camden office.[32] His Democratic counterpart from 1870 to 1897, Secretary of State Henry Kelsey, masterminded the election of railroad vice president George McClellan (former Union general and Peace Democrat presidential candidate) to the governorship in 1877. McClellan's predecessor, Joseph D. Bedle, became counsel to the Jersey Central upon leaving office. The Democratic boss of Middlesex County was an agent of the Lehigh Valley Railroad. An especially close 1880 gubernatorial election, which the Democrats won by less than seven hundred votes, was a battle between candidates representing the Pennsylvania and the Jersey Central railroads.

With most gubernatorial elections decided by less than 2 percent, the larger railroads now found it prudent to have agents in both parties. Along with the Republican Sewall of South Jersey, the Pennsylvania was also allied with the Catholic and Democratic Essex County boss, James Smith of Newark, elected U.S. senator in 1892. Even the Democratic leader of beleaguered Hudson County controlled local railroads and utilities within the county in the 1890s. With increasing use of gas, electricity, and motorized public transportation, public utilities like Elizabeth Gas and Light and the Public Service Corporation played a role similar to that of the railroads—seeking exclusive and perpetual franchises from the legislature and placing their agents inside state government.

As the nineteenth century wore on, state government remained weak and undeveloped. There was no governor's mansion in Trenton, and many chief executives continued to work in New York City. Journalist William Sackett nicely captured the flavor of the period: "'Governor's Day' [Tuesday] . . . was marked by 'Cabinet meetings,' at which the Department heads laid before the Governor the things they had done—or rather had not done—during the week past for the public weal, and the programmes for the week ahead were laid out. And they all flitted out of town into seclusion again until the next week's gathering was due."[33]

Gradually, however, state government took on more responsibilities, particularly in education. When an 1871 legislative act compelled all municipalities to offer a nine-month school term and prohibited tuition charges, New Jersey became one of the last two states to guarantee free public education.[34] An 1875 constitutional amendment reinforced the commitment by calling for a "thorough and efficient" public school system for all children between the ages of five and eighteen. These initiatives eventually required the state to raise more revenue, because reliance on the local property tax to finance public schools increasingly beggared municipalities, especially those where much railroad property was exempt from local levies. Fully one-quarter of the property in the state was tax-exempt. By 1883, New Jersey had the fifth highest public debt and second highest average property taxes in the nation, but it was last in the amount of income derived from them. In neighboring New York City, local tax rates were under 1 percent of assessed valuation, whereas in Jersey City, with one-third of its property tax-exempt, they were almost 3 percent.[35]

New Jersey was fortuitously saved once again from tapping residents' pocketbooks by the push in most of the rest of the country for antitrust legislation. In 1889, the legislature allowed companies to hold stock in other companies—commonly known as holding corporations or trusts. Only West Virginia and Delaware had similar laws, and New Jersey's proximity to Wall Street got it most of the business. One Jersey City office building near the ferry landing was the official "headquarters" for more than twelve hundred companies, and another in Camden hosted more than seven hundred.[36] The price to corporations for this favored treatment was a state tax of twenty cents on each thousand dollars of capitalization.

Thus, for example, when the U.S. Supreme Court dissolved the Rockefellers' Standard Oil Trust in 1892, the company quickly reincorporated in New Jersey and was able to achieve domination of the domestic oil industry. Standard Oil's example was followed by many others, leading the former "State of the Camden and Amboy" to be called the "Mother of the Trusts," the "business Tenderloin of the United States," and "the Traitor State." In giving New Jersey this last appellation, muckraker Lincoln Steffens wrote, "Every loyal citizen of the United States owes New Jersey a grudge. The State is corrupt; so are certain other states. . . . The offense that commands our special attention, however, and lifts this state into national distinction is this; New Jersey is selling out the rest of us. . . . [O]ur sister State was not prompted by any abstract consideration of right and wisdom. New Jersey sold us out for money. . . . And she gets her revenue. Her citizens pay no direct State tax. The corporations pay all the expenses of the State, and more."[37] Steffens's final observation captured what most New Jerseyans saw as ample justification for friendliness to the trusts. The $292,000 earned for the state by the capitalization tax in its first year rose to $707,000 by 1896 and by 1902 the state's debt had been eradicated.[38]

New Jersey's politics in the twenty-five years after the Civil War shows how the state tracked national events and how it diverged. As was true nationally, both major political parties were dominated by their conservative, business-oriented wings. The state's Republicans had opposed the GOP's abolitionists during the Civil War era and were favorably inclined to the "captains of industry" who dominated the party after the war. New Jersey Democrats also identified with their party's conservative wing. The Populist movement of the 1880s onward, later absorbed by the Democratic Party and personified by its three-time presidential candidate William Jennings Bryan, never made headway in New Jersey. Prosperous farmers, many of them Quakers, did not share the Populists' discontent. Agricultural interests became less important in the late nineteenth century anyway, as industry and urban areas boomed. Some Democrats, especially the party elite, were business people; many of the rest were urban, Catholic, immigrant laborers—unlikely to be attracted by the fundamentalist Protestant Populists in the nation's hinterlands who agitated against liquor and lenient immigration policies.[39]

New Jersey Republicans thus became more amenable to the national direction of their party in the late nineteenth century; New Jersey Democrats were comfortable with the "Gold Democrat" wing headed by Grover Cleveland and considerably less so with the Bryan wing. The conservatism of both parties' adherents thus made state politics counter-cyclical to national trends until almost the end of the century. National politics from 1860 through 1892 was competitive with a Republican tilt; New Jersey politics was competitive with a Democratic tilt.

Scholars who study late-nineteenth-century voting behavior debate its nature and meaning. Walter Dean Burnham characterizes it as a time of intense participation, high turnout, and issue-based partisanship. Others ascribe the turnout to corruption and vote buying, and the strong partisanship to patronage jobs and party-prepared ballots that made split-ticket voting difficult.[40] New Jersey provides some evidence for both interpretations.

Turnout was high, averaging close to 90 percent in presidential elections, and only about 10 percent lower in the usually off-year triennial gubernatorial contests. On the other hand, an 1883 legislative commission estimated that one-fifth to one-quarter of the vote was for sale. With annual assembly elections as well as other frequent state and national contests, these citizens could rely on payment for their ballots as a "regular source of income."[41]

THE BIRTH OF A NEW POLITICAL ORDER

The national election of 1896, which presaged the almost unbroken domination of the conservatives in both parties for the next three decades, was a watershed election in New Jersey as well. The Republicans began a long string of victories in state and federal elections, and major changes occurred in the leadership of both parties, even though there were few significant policy differences between them.

Democratic governors elected in 1889 and 1892 had some reform instincts, but this was not true of their partisans in the legislature, many of whom were supported financially by increasingly influential racetrack owners and gamblers. The 1893 legislature passed a set of notorious laws legalizing betting at a rapidly growing number of tracks. When Democratic Governor George Werts vetoed this legislation, his fellow partisans in the legislature led the way in overriding it. Along with other related scandals, these events led voters to hand the Democrats a massive defeat in 1895, and the Republicans elected their first governor in nine terms and twenty-seven years. The new Republican legislature overturned the Democrats' gambling legislation and amended the state constitution to prohibit book-making, pari-mutuel betting, and lotteries.

The defeat of the ring that had reigned in Trenton for three decades left the Democrats mired in factionalism. The divisions were not ideological, because the party had no "reform" wing. There were, rather, loyalties to different local bosses in the northern counties producing most of the Democratic vote. The two principal figures were Robert "Little Bob" Davis of Hudson County and James C. Smith of Essex. Instead of making common cause, Davis and Smith fought over preferments such as choosing the U.S. senator the legislature would elect in 1892. Smith was successful in getting himself named over Hudson County's candidate, popular outgoing governor Leon Abbett. Abbett's bitterness, and his death soon thereafter, intensified the enmity between the Democratic factions.[42]

On the Republican side in the later 1890s, party boss William J. Sewall of the Pennsylvania Railroad expanded his links to other sections of the state's corporate elite, especially after they became more important in financing the operations of state government. At his behest, the legislature elected to the U.S. Senate John F. Dryden, president of the Prudential

Insurance Company, and John F. Kean, president of Elizabeth Gas and Light. Sewall himself went to the Senate twice. Not forgetting his own employer, Sewall also arranged the appointment of the Pennsylvania Railroad's chief legislative lobbyist as the state commissioner of banking and insurance in 1895. Yet divisiveness also came to the newly triumphant GOP. Sewall died in 1901, just as Progressivism was emerging in the party nationally. As elsewhere, the New Jersey Republicans splintered—along both ideological and geographic lines.[43] The business-oriented, conservative faction, however, generally prevailed.

Officeholders in both parties were engaged in less genteel corruption or impropriety. Walter Edge, later an outstanding Republican governor, was a young state senate journal clerk in 1898. His memoirs describe an exciting legislative investigation of local Democratic officials in Hudson County, "including grand jury packing by the sheriff to protect what were alleged to be Democratic-sponsored vice-rings; but this died quickly when the opposition suggested an inquiry into Republican activities in Camden County where conditions appeared to be at least as bad."[44]

Most New Jerseyans were more than willing to trade off the state's unsavory reputation for the financial benefits. At his inauguration in 1905, Governor Edward C. Stokes spoke for many when he declared: "Of the entire income of the state, not a penny was contributed directly by the people. . . . The state is caring for the blind, the feeble-minded and the insane, supporting our prisoners and reformatories, educating the younger generations, developing a magnificent road system, maintaining the state government and courts of justice, all of which would be a burden on the taxpayer except for our present fiscal policy."[45]

Still, voices began to be heard, and they would gather force, protesting a system that supported the small Trenton government handsomely but favored huge and powerful employers over their employees, and utility cartels over municipal governments. As Stokes made his pronouncement, a young Irish Catholic resident of the Jersey City Horseshoe was beginning a career in Hudson County Democratic politics, which he would dominate for four decades. About fifty miles southwest of Jersey City, a Virginia minister's son had recently assumed the presidency of the renamed Princeton University, and would be elected governor of New Jersey in 1910. The first of these men was Frank Hague. The second was Woodrow Wilson. Together, they would embody the conflicting strains in New Jersey's political culture for the next half-century.

As the period described in this chapter drew to an end, the moralistic impulses that were arising nationally, symbolized by the Progressive movement, washed over New Jersey. Although Wilson's extraordinary governorship would leave lasting marks, it was Frank Hague, the embodiment of the machine politics that still dominated, who would have much the stronger effect on the state's politics for the next half century.

CHAPTER 3

"The Statesman and the Boss"

How the hell do I know whether he'll make a good
governor? . . . [H]e will make a good candidate, and that
is the only thing that interests me.

—"Little Bob" Davis, Democratic machine leader, on
Woodrow Wilson's gubernatorial nomination, 1910

If the reform side of him is twice as efficient as reform
ever was, the Tammany side is twice as efficient as
Tammany ever was.

—journalist's assessment of Jersey City Mayor
Frank Hague

TWO TOWERING FIGURES, Woodrow Wilson and Frank
Hague, symbolize the divergent strains in New Jersey's politics in the twentieth century. The early part of the period saw the state's first political
reform movement. By the 1920s, the movement's force was spent, but it
would reemerge five decades later. The later part of the era was a period of
archetypical county machine–dominated government, not seriously challenged until the 1970s. Vestiges of it still remain.

To comprehend this period, one must begin again with demography.
The state's population almost doubled between 1890 and 1915. New Jersey
ranked eighteenth among the states in population in 1890 and tenth in
1910. Nineteenth-century settlement patterns were further reinforced. In
the first decades of the next century, nearly two-thirds of municipalities had
fewer than two thousand residents, but 75 percent of the population was
concentrated in seven of the twenty-one counties—six in the New York
City metropolitan area and one bordering Philadelphia.[1]

Two of the northern counties—Hudson and Essex—each contained
about one-fifth of the state's residents in 1910. Half of Hudson's were in
Jersey City, and two-thirds of those in Essex lived in the state's largest city,
Newark. The county next in population, Passaic, was less than half the size

of Hudson or Essex, just as its largest city, Paterson, was similarly dwarfed by
Newark and Jersey City.

New Jersey's cities were not very large and would never get much larger.
Newark's population was 347,000 in 1910, and Jersey City's was 268,000.
The citizens of Camden, on the Philadelphia border, numbered only 95,000.
Thanks to the dominance of New York and Philadelphia, New Jersey was
already assuming a suburban character. As Edmund Wilson observed in
1923, these metropolises kept New Jersey's "minor cities from rising above
their flatness and drabness. They are content to leave to New York and
Philadelphia ambition, liveliness and brilliance."[2]

By the late nineteenth century, immigrants from other countries and
other states had begun to flood into New Jersey, another trend that intensified in the succeeding decades. By 1920, almost a quarter of the state's three
million inhabitants were foreign-born, and another fifth had been born in
another state—the highest proportion of nonnatives in any state save
Delaware.[3] Foreign-born immigrants were not evenly distributed; they were
concentrated in the New York–area counties. Hudson County's peculiar
geography produced the classic ethnic neighborhood in its purest form. Its
Irish, German, Slavic, and Italian communities were clearly delineated by
their churches, saloons, and local shops but often further separated from
other parts of the cities by the ubiquitous railroad tracks.

Geography also ensured that Hudson County would not develop spa-
cious suburbs. The Meadowlands, a vast marsh to its west, forced development into a narrow strip along the Hudson River. Upwardly mobile citizens
seeking suburban homes thus went north to Bergen, south to Middlesex
and Monmouth, or west across the wetlands into Essex.[4] Hudson's residents
remained newer, poorer immigrants, or those who did not want to leave old
ethnic neighborhoods.

Neither the suburban commuters nor the insular ethnics felt much
identity with the state. Thus, New Jersey's politics remained local, parochial,
and based in county organizations. Indeed, one might say there was no state
politics to speak of. Political attention always focuses on where public
money is raised or distributed. In the New Jersey of the early 1900s, Trenton continued to raise its modest budget almost entirely from the corporations and the railroads, and to spend it on the penal system and skeletal social
services. In contrast, localities raised and spent four times as much, almost
all of it coming from the highly visible local property tax and going to visible services such as roads and public schools. State government, with 2,900

employees in fiscal year 1916–1917, was not nearly so rich a source of patronage jobs as were counties and municipalities. Still, the price exacted by this system, especially in Hudson County, made possible a surge of reform. Its exemplar became Woodrow Wilson.

THE STATESMAN: WOODROW WILSON AND NEW JERSEY PROGRESSIVISM

In the early 1900s, New Jersey was "one of the last strongholds of an industrial-feudal order that was the object of violent attack by progressive leaders throughout the country."[5] As a Hudson progressive who became an intimate of Woodrow Wilson described it, "Every election was, in its last analysis, a solemn referendum upon the question as to which corporate interest should control legislation—whether the Pennsylvania Railroad, whose mastermind was the Republican leader of the state, U.S. Senator Sewall, or the Public Service interests, whose votaries and friends were [Democratic] Senator Smith of New Jersey and Milan Ross Sr. of Middlesex County."[6] Consequently, a small band of reformers could be found in each party, for neither was hospitable enough to attract them as a group.

The first major reform victory occurred in beleaguered Jersey City. Because of its Democratic machine's close ties to local railroads and utilities, reform initially found its home in the Republican party. In the 1901 mayoral election, a young Irish reformer, Mark N. Fagan, assisted by Maine native and recent party convert George L. Record, swept to victory on a platform demanding "equal taxation" of the railroads.

For five years, the reformers won important battles, moving on from the railroad issue to an attack on the tax preferences and perpetual franchises of the public utilities. Fagan was reelected in 1903, and with other Republican reformers, notably in Essex County, launched the New Idea movement, with a standard progressive platform. Led by Everett Colby, the Essex reformers defeated the Republican regulars in the 1905 state primaries for delegates to county party conventions.[7] By 1907, however, the Republican New Idea movement had disintegrated. To Fagan's disappointment, Progressive Republican President Theodore Roosevelt refused to withdraw federal patronage from the Republican regulars, although he had similarly helped Wisconsin's Robert LaFollette and New York's Charles Evans Hughes.

Fagan lost the mayoralty in 1905 when his financial support of the public schools and lax enforcement of Sunday blue laws led the Jersey City

Catholic hierarchy to withdraw its support. Abandoning their coreligion-
ist, the church supported his Democratic German Protestant opponent,
Otto Wittpenn. The movement's other major leader, Colby, declined to
run for governor in 1905 and lost a bid for the state senate to an
Essex Democratic progressive. With the Republican Party back in the
hands of the regulars, the reform-minded shifted their attention to the
Democrats.

Some Hudson Democratic reformers, such as Joseph P. Tumulty,
gained election to the legislature. They achieved some further success,
including passage of the direct primary for local elections in 1907 and the
institution of civil service hiring for state government and for municipalities at their option. New Jersey's reformers emphasized the aspects of the
progressive agenda related to bossism and corruption. More radical ideas
that made headway in progressive strongholds in the West—woman suffrage, the initiative, referendum and recall, and direct election of U.S.
senators—received scant attention in New Jersey.[8]

The reformers had less success in electing statewide candidates. In
1907, when he garnered 47 percent of the vote, Trenton Mayor Frank
Katzenbach made the Democrats' best gubernatorial showing since 1892,
but the Republicans had won five straight gubernatorial elections since
1895, and control of the state legislature also gave them command of U.S.
Senate elections. With Republican legislators electing U.S. Senate candidates until direct Senate elections began in 1913, Democratic Senate aspirants were sacrificial lambs. Reformers were thus sometimes able to
nominate the party's candidates for an office of little interest to the conservative regulars.

The counties' preeminent political role made even the reformers center
their attention there. Lincoln Steffens wrote of the New Jersey progressives
in 1906, "such citizenship as they have is mean, narrow, local. Jersey, in the
minds of the average Jerseyman is a group of counties, and his concern, if
he worries at all, is with the petty evils of his own sordid surroundings."[9]

Thus, when it came time for the Democrats to select a U.S. Senate
candidate who would face certain defeat in 1908, the progressives backed
one of their own and paid little attention to Woodrow Wilson, the candidate touted by the regulars. The Virginia-born Wilson had been president
of Princeton University since 1902, arriving there as a professor in 1890
when it was still the College of New Jersey. So far as the reformers knew,
Wilson was just an articulate version of the typical regular. He opposed

regulation of the trusts, labor legislation, and other favorite progressive themes, calling them "confused thinking and impossible points of law."[10] A strong supporter of the Cleveland wing of the party, Wilson refused to let William Jennings Bryan speak at Princeton and declined to appear with him anywhere.[11]

Tiring of battles with the university's faculty and trustees, Wilson began to think about a political career—but in national politics rather than state government. Like so many of New Jersey's outstanding citizens, there was no evidence "that he concerned himself one whit about New Jersey politics before 1907."[12] An early champion and confidant of Wilson's was journalist George Harvey, a power in the Cleveland wing of the party. Harvey's association with New Jersey dated from 1883, when he became New Jersey bureau chief of Joseph Pulitzer's influential Democratic organ, the *New York World*.

By 1899, Harvey had bought the *North American Review* and become editor of *Harper's Weekly*, but he summered at an estate in the Jersey Shore town of Deal and maintained interest in New Jersey Democratic politics and a friendship with James Smith, leader of the Essex County Democratic organization.[13] Smith was president of a Newark bank, publisher of the *Newark Evening Star*, a friend of Public Service, and had served as U.S. senator from 1892 to 1898. His nephew, James R. Nugent, was state party chairman.

Harvey urged Wilson to seek the Democratic Senate nomination to gain credibility for a presidential run in 1912 and offered to intercede with the Smith-Nugent faction, which had little interest in who got the "empty" designation. Wilson permitted his name to go forward but did not seem to have his heart in the enterprise. Joseph Tumulty, who proposed the eventual designee, described events in the legislative nominating session: "The speech nominating Woodrow Wilson . . . was the shortest on record. It was delivered by one of the Smith-Nugent men from Essex County. . . . No applause greeted the name of the man he nominated. It seemed as if the college professor had no friends in the Legislature except the man who had put his name forward."[14]

Wilson eventually withdrew his name, but his failure to endorse the progressives' nominee seemed further proof that Wilson was not one of them. Tumulty was thus unenthused when the Princetonian surfaced again as a gubernatorial candidate in 1910: "We suspected that the 'Old Gang' was up to its old trick of foisting upon the Democrats of the state a tool . . .

who, under the name of the Democratic party would do the bidding of the corporate interests which had, under both the 'regular' organizations, Democratic and Republican, found in New Jersey their most nutritious pastures." At a strategy meeting (held, typically, in a New York City club), Tumulty and the other "Young Turks" pledged their "undying opposition" to Wilson's candidacy.[15]

Unknown to them, however, Wilson had become converted to the progressive agenda between 1908 and 1910, and more convinced that he wanted to seek national office. The governorship became a means to that end. As he wrote to a friend and Princeton trustee,

> The question of my nomination for the governorship of New Jersey is the mere preliminary of a plan to nominate me in 1912 for the presidency. . . . Last evening I dined with Colonel Watterson of the Louisville Courrier [sic] Journal, Colonel [George] Harvey, of Harper's Weekly, and James Smith, the reputed Democratic boss of New Jersey. . . . Whatever one may think of Colonel Watterson, there can be no doubt of his immense political influence. . . . [B]efore the evening was over [Watterson] said that, if New Jersey would make me Governor, he would agree to take off his coat and work for my nomination in 1912. The opportunity really seems most unusual.[16]

With Harvey's advice to stay out of the party's internecine battles and his own sharp political instincts, Wilson at first steered a cautious course. He declined to take any public position on contentious issues like regulation of the utilities, direct U.S. Senate elections, or workmen's compensation. To an intermediary, he wrote, "I would be perfectly willing to assure Mr. Smith that I would not, if elected Governor, set about 'fighting and breaking down the existing Democratic organization.'"[17] This confirmed progressive opinion that Wilson was the regulars' catspaw. The *Trenton Evening Times* editorialized that his failure to answer the questions directed to all the candidates was "conclusive proof of his hypocrisy."[18]

Still, most of the regulars were also suspicious. At the June meeting of the state committee, twenty of the twenty-one county leaders, including Smith's nephew, Nugent, favored Frank Katzenbach, the 1907 nominee. But Wilson had the most crucial party leaders, Smith and "Little Bob" Davis of Jersey City, in his corner. Smith, who had sent three sons to Princeton, liked the idea of being a president maker and backing a winner who could deliver state and then federal patronage. Davis favored Wilson because he could ensure the defeat of Otto Wittpenn, Davis's local neme-sis and another gubernatorial hopeful.

Smith and Davis prevailed, and so, on September 15, 1910, the unwill-ing delegates assembled in Trenton to make their nomination: "They were arriving all day . . . to renew old friendships with men they had not seen in years, to smoke awful convention cigars and to talk and talk and talk . . . 'Frank's entitled to it and he's going to have it!' is a declaration I heard over and over again. And a disquieting question I heard, too, many times: Where does Wilson come in? Do *you* ever see him."[19] Wilson's acceptance speech to the distrustful convention delegates truly began the reform era. He proclaimed his independence from the bosses, strong support for equal taxation of corporations, and advocated a regulatory public utilities com-mission. All around him, Joe Tumulty heard the cry, "Thank God, at last, a leader has come!"[20]

As the campaign went on, Wilson's criticisms of the "bosses" of his own party became even more trenchant. The campaign's turning point was provided by Republican progressive George L. Record, who had labored in the trenches of reform since the days of the Fagan mayoralty in Jersey City. In his Jersey City newspaper column, Record challenged Wilson to a debate on progressivism. Wilson declined to debate a noncandidate but said he would answer questions in writing. Record then addressed nine-teen probing questions to Wilson. The candidate's responses, published in most of the state's newspapers in the last week of October, determined the election's outcome.

In answer to Record's query, "Do you admit that the boss system exists as I have described it?" Wilson replied, "Of course I admit it. Its existence is notorious. I have made it my business for many years to observe and understand that system, and I hate it as thoroughly as I understand it. You are quite right in saying that the system is bipartisan." When Record asked how "such Democratic leaders as Smith, Nugent and Davis" differed from a number of Republicans, including the last three governors, Wilson said, "They differ from the others in this, that they are in control of the govern-ment of the State, while the others are not and cannot be if the present Democratic ticket is elected."[21]

Record concluded, "That letter will elect Wilson governor," and his-torian Arthur Link has compared its importance to the Lincoln-Douglas debates.[22] Wilson's 54 percent margin was the most decisive win for a New Jersey Democrat since the institution of an elected governor, and equal to the best Republican performances. So great was his victory that the assembly also passed into Democratic hands for the first time since 1893. Once in office, the former professor fulfilled his campaign promises, mostly in the extraordinary 1911 legislative session. Wilson achieved passage of the direct primary for all offices, establishment of a regulatory public utilities commission, and workman's compensation legislation.

From a political standpoint, however, the most stunning event was the opportunity to elect a Democratic U.S. senator—an event beyond the Democrats' "wildest dreams or vain imaginings."[23] It was here that Wilson's mettle was truly tested. Boss Smith was staggered by the governor's legislative agenda, but his most important personal agenda was to return to the U.S. senate, from which he had been swept after the Democratic legislative debacle in the 1890s. Support of Smith would give the lie to everything Wilson had pledged. The situation was further complicated by the results of a preferential primary, won by a perennial candidate and buffoon, the "farmer-orator" James Martine. Martine had run unsuccessfully eleven times for various state and federal offices. His selection by the small number who bothered to vote in the preferential primary underscored the Democrats' disbelief that they could actually be in a position to select the next U.S. senator.

Many thought Wilson's best strategy was to stay out of the race and claim it was the legislature's problem. However, the new governor defended the hapless Martine against both Smith and the Republican incumbent, utility magnate and former gubernatorial candidate John Kean. In a statement to the *Trenton True American*, Wilson observed, "So far as the voters of the state are concerned and the state's essential interests, there is no reason why a change should be made from Mr. John Kean to Mr. James Smith, Jr. They are believed to stand for the same influence and to represent the same group of selfish interests. . . . If Mr. Smith is sent back to the United States Senate, the Democratic party and State itself is once more delivered into the hands of the very influence from which it had struggled to set itself free."[24]

The governor-elect's conversion to reform was genuine, but he also had in mind the effect of the Senate election on the national future of his party and his own prospects in 1912. As Wilson wrote to George Harvey, "ridiculous though it undoubtedly is,—I think we shall have to stand with Mr. Martine. After all that has been said and done, we shall be stultified if we do not." Addressing the larger issue, he continued, "It is a national as well as a State question. If the independent Republicans who in this state voted for me are not to be attracted to us they will assuredly turn again to Mr. Roosevelt, and the chance of a generation will be lost to the Democracy: the chance . . . through new leaders . . . to constitute the ruling party of the country for the next generation."[25]

When the new legislature turned its attention to the choice for Senate, Martine received forty votes on the first ballot (one short of the number needed for election) and Smith only ten. With the outcome clear, Smith released his supporters, and Wilson exulted to a friend, "My victory was overwhelmingly complete."[26] It only remained to remove Nugent as party chairman. A drunken encounter with New Jersey national guardsmen at a Shore restaurant contributed to Nugent's political demise. Raising his glass, Nugent told the appalled officers, "I propose a toast to the governor of New Jersey, the commander-in-chief of the Militia, an ingrate and a liar. Do I drink alone?"[27] To keep his chairmanship, Nugent refused to convene the state committee, which then held a rump meeting in Asbury Park in August. Nugent arrived at the conclave with a "strong-arm mob of petty gangsters from New York" and "kidnapped" a committee member to deny the group a quorum. When another member arrived to reestablish the quorum, the committee promptly voted to remove the Essex boss.[28]

After the brilliant successes of 1911, Wilson's momentum slowed. In the legislative elections at the end of the year, the Republicans recaptured control of the assembly despite the governor's plea that the election be seen as a referendum on his record. In large measure, he was thwarted by his nominal fellow partisans, Smith and Nugent. The bosses sat out the election in their Essex County redoubt. The Essex vote was barely half that of 1910 and resulted in a complete Republican victory there. Wilson became increasingly preoccupied with his presidential quest, leaving the state for long periods and making little effort to conciliate the legislature's Republican majority. Although he carried New Jersey in the three-way presidential contest of 1912, his 41 percent share of the vote was down 13 percentage points from his gubernatorial showing only two years earlier, and slightly behind his national performance.

In March 1912, Wilson resigned the governorship to take up his new duties in Washington. He took with him Joe Tumulty, the progressive Democrats' most effective political tactician. Two and a half years, as dazzling as they were, could not obliterate the state's traditional political patterns: "New Jersey did not have Wilson long enough."[29] With the progressives' commander gone, the regulars reasserted themselves.

Political energy quickly passed from Trenton back to the county satraps. Hudson's "Little Bob" Davis had died in 1911, leaving the Smith-Nugent Essex organization even more dominant in the party's perennial internal struggles. However, Hudson County would soon produce a new leader whose skills and staying power would far surpass those of Wilson.

THE BOSS: FRANK HAGUE AND THE "GIBRALTAR OF DEMOCRACY"

Woodrow Wilson began public life as a sympathizer of the regulars, then blazed an extraordinary career as a reformer. Frank Hague, the state's other legendary political figure, followed precisely the opposite path. He rose to prominence as a purported reformer and spent a long career as the apotheosis of the regulars.

In 1875, the year Jersey City rid itself of the "ripper" laws giving Trenton Republicans control of its government, Hague was born in Jersey City's Irish Catholic Horseshoe. The Horseshoe's political life was organized around its saloons, and Hague got his start in politics when one of the saloon keepers backed his run for constable in 1896. Hague rose steadily through the Hudson Democratic organization, becoming a deputy sheriff in 1898, a precinct leader in 1901, and a ward leader in 1906. He was thirty-six when Davis died in 1911, and he became an important warlord among the factions that emerged thereafter. By 1916, Hague was able to name two county freeholders, the county surrogate, and two state assemblymen.[30] In that year he was elected Jersey City's commissioner of public safety, giving him command of the police and fire departments. This post had rich political payoffs—control of many patronage jobs and the very public employees charged with "enforcing" election laws.

Political reform movements often produce outcomes opposite to what the reformers wish. New Jersey in this period provides an example. Hague achieved power by using some of the progressives' most cherished policies for his own ends—in particular the direct primary and government reorganization schemes aimed, like the primary, at sapping the strength of party bosses and their allies.[31]

After a series of half-measures, New Jersey fully adopted the direct primary with passage of the Geran Act in 1911. Its intended consequence was clear: to take nominations out of the hands of party organizations and give them to "the people." The reality, however, especially in the Democratic Party, was to increase the power of organizations in the populous counties that were able to dominate primaries because of their large numbers of voters.

Malapportionment made it difficult to end Republican legislative control, especially in the state senate, whose twenty-one members each represented one county, regardless of population size. On the other hand, the large populations of the few reliable Democratic counties made it possible for Democrats to prevail in gubernatorial elections—at least after political independents and Republicans with reformist tendencies learned with Wilson the habit of voting for mildly progressive Democratic candidates.

As long as the Smith-Nugent regulars dominated the Essex County Democracy, such candidates were likely to come from Hudson County, and about half the Hudson vote came from Jersey City. Thus, Hudson and Jersey City became the key players in Democratic gubernatorial politics just at the time Hague's influence in the Hudson organization was growing.

Municipal reform was another progressive idea that Hague turned to his own purposes. The 1913 Walsh Act permitted municipalities to adopt commission-style government, and Jersey City chose to do so. This form of government, entailing election of commissioners who head specific administrative departments and are accountable for their performance, gave Hague control over the most politically sensitive and useful organ of city government—the police.

Similar reorganization schemes for state government were also transformed into a source of power for the Hudson organization. By the time Wilson became governor, state boards and commissions were proliferating. Their members, appointed by the legislature, were a fertile source of patronage for county party leaders. When Wilson appointed a commission to study reorganization in 1912, his legislative message inquired quizzically, "Why should every oyster bed have a commission of its own?"[32]

Although it would be another thirty-five years before Trenton's administrative quagmire was overhauled by a new constitution, a number of agencies were consolidated between 1915 and 1920, with appointment powers given to the governor. These became additional patronage resources for the county leaders to whom Democratic governors owed their election—and most of these leaders, like Frank Hague, were in Hudson County.

Finally, external events also aided Hague in unanticipated ways. The traditional opponents of Hudson's Irish Catholic politicians were German Protestants. The outbreak of World War I damaged the political careers of

German American politicians. Even the national movement for Prohibition was a boon for the politicians then in power. Prohibition, or its selective enforcement in Hudson County, closed down saloons that were the organizational hubs for the opposition.

All these things came together for Hague in the years between 1917 and 1920. In 1917 Hague was elected Jersey City's mayor, which began his preeminence in the Hudson County organization. He consolidated his power over the state party when the Smith-Nugent machine was defeated decisively in the 1919 gubernatorial election and progressive Republicans took control in Essex.

In the 1919 Democratic gubernatorial primary, Nugent was opposed by Hudson's Edward I. Edwards, a progressive who had been the Democrats' U.S. Senate candidate in 1908 when Woodrow Wilson first considered entering state politics. Edwards defeated Nugent by a margin of about 14,000 votes. Nugent won Essex by 13,000 votes, but thanks to Hague, he lost Hudson by 25,000.

Edwards went on to a narrow win in the general election. A beneficiary of enhanced gubernatorial patronage, he gifted Hague with the power to name the president of the state civil service commission, a third of the members of the public utilities commission, the state highway engineer, and the members of the Hudson County tax board and board of elections. Hague's success in this election also gave him a role in the national party. He led New Jersey's delegation to the 1920 Democratic national convention and became the state's national party committeeman, a position he held for almost thirty years. The 1922 Democratic gubernatorial victor, George S. Silzer, added to Hague's authority the appointment of the county prosecutor and many judicial nominations.[33]

The 1919 and 1922 elections solidified Hague's domination of state politics. Through 1940, the partisan vote in the rest of the state was balanced closely enough that massive Democratic majorities in Hudson (which earned it the sobriquet the Gibraltar of Democracy) could produce a Democratic gubernatorial victory most of the time.

Between 1916 and 1940, Democrats won six of the nine gubernatorial contests, and their victories were usually attributable to Hudson landslides. For example, Silzer in 1922 won by 46,000 votes statewide, and by 80,000 in Hudson. His successor, Hudson County's A. Harry Moore, ran 38,000 votes ahead of his Republican opponent statewide, and an astonishing 103,000 votes ahead in his home bailiwick. Moore would go on to win twice more in nonconsecutive contests in 1931 and 1937, and still holds the state record for years of service—nine—in the elected governorship.[34]

Not only did Hague produce victories for Democratic governors, but he put Republicans in his thrall as well. The Hudson "dictator" was perfectly willing to collude with Republicans to secure his home base and maintain control of Hudson's patronage. In 1916, Hague assured the election of Republican Walter E. Edge because Edge's opponent was Hague's Hudson archenemy, Otto Wittpenn. The Democratic majority in Hudson, compared with that in the previous election, was cut by almost two-thirds: "Organization Democrats were not urged to vote Republican in that election; they simply were urged not to vote."[35]

Edge returned the favor. One of his major goals was improved transportation links to New York and especially, given his South Jersey home base, Philadelphia. Northern New Jersey was then connected directly to New York City only by rail links. Pedestrians and automobiles still traveled on ferries, as they did to Philadelphia. To win approval of a bridge to Philadelphia that North Jersey had long opposed, Edge paired the South Jersey project with a vehicular tunnel to New York, conveniently entering the state in Jersey City.[36] The two proposals were submitted to the legislature simultaneously and passed with Hudson County's backing.

The 1928 and 1934 elections also demonstrated Hague's ability to profit from inevitable Republican victories. As in 1916, the Democrats were hard-pressed in the 1928 gubernatorial race because of the flood of Republican presidential voters. Hague therefore backed the most "cooperative" Republican, Morgan S. Larsen of Middlesex County, who won the general election. A 1929 inquiry established that 22,000 Hudson Democrats participated in the Republican gubernatorial primary. In 1934 Hague faced the prospect of an extraordinarily popular Republican gubernatorial candidate, Harold G. Hoffman of normally Democratic Middlesex County. As a Middlesex Democratic newspaper editorialized, "We were opposed to his election but. . . . He swept through the District even in strong Democratic sections with an ease that made one fairly gasp for breath."[37] The charismatic Hoffman had the same effect statewide. He won office in the only federal midterm election year to that date when a sitting president (and one not of Hoffman's party) had ever gained congressional seats, and despite an 80,000-vote plurality in Hudson for his opponent.

However, it was not long before Hoffman too found himself in the debt of the Hudson County boss. Like the rest of the nation, New Jersey faced a staggering Depression-era welfare burden. True to their heritage, voters remained adamantly opposed to a revenue-producing statewide tax. To meet a $2 million-per-month relief bill, much of which emanated from Jersey City, the governor proposed a statewide sales tax. Hoffman managed to guide it through the assembly by a vote margin of thirty-one to twenty-seven, although outraged voters obtained its repeal four months later. Only eleven of his fellow Republicans supported it; the other twenty votes came from Hague-controlled Democrats. Immediately after the vote, Hoffman named the Democratic assembly minority leader to the state's highest court and other Hudson figures to many boards and commissions.

Hague's patronage resources were not limited to New Jersey. Although a firm supporter of his fellow Irish Catholic Al Smith in both 1928 and 1932, Hague was willing to back Franklin D. Roosevelt just as strongly in exchange for New Jersey's share of federal patronage. Smith won a 61 percent to 39 percent victory over Roosevelt in New Jersey's 1932 presidential primary. Yet once Roosevelt defeated Smith (and Hague's second choice, John Nance Garner) at the Democratic national convention, the mayor produced one of the largest turnouts in history for Roosevelt's kick-off campaign rally. It was held at Governor Moore's summer home in Sea Girt in August.[38] Hague gifted Roosevelt with a 118,000 margin in Hudson County in November, enabling the Democrat to carry New Jersey by 38,000 votes. Roosevelt carried the state all four times he ran, but only in 1936 could he have done so without Hudson County. It was Hague and Chicago boss Ed Kelly who were largely responsible for Roosevelt's unprecedented third term nomination in 1940.

Hague himself had suffered near electoral defeat in 1929, when the ungrateful Republican governor, Morgan Larsen, launched a legislative probe of political corruption in Hudson County and of Hague's personal finances. Although Hague had never earned more than $8,000 a year, an investigating committee discovered $393,000 in transactions by dummy corporations connected to Hague that handled real estate and bank stock. When the mayor refused to answer the committee's questions, he was arrested for contempt. A Hague-selected justice quickly granted him habeas corpus, and the state's highest court, also populated with his designees, upheld the writ.

Fortuitously, the onset of the Great Depression revived the mayor's popularity. New Deal relief programs gave Hague access "to huge amounts of *legal* money and jobs."[39] His affronted constituents forgot their moral scruples in their need for Hague's patronage. By 1939, one out of every twenty Hudson County adults depended on it for their livelihood.[40]

By 1940, however, the mayor's statewide power was slipping, and cities had begun the population decline from which they would never recover. In the 1940s New Jersey gained seven hundred thousand people, most of them suburban commuters to New York and Philadelphia. Charles Edison (son of inventor Thomas), elected governor in the first year of the decade, was a reform-minded New Deal official whom FDR imposed on the county boss. Consciously echoing Woodrow Wilson's attack on "the bosses," Edison declared, "if you elect me, you will have elected a governor who has made no promises of preferment to any man. . . . You can be sure that I'll never be a 'yes-man' except to my own conscience." One of Edison's first official acts was to disconnect Hague's private telephone line to the governor's office.[41]

The next gubernatorial election, in 1943, was won by Republican Walter E. Edge who, after years in the U.S. Senate, diplomatic service, and retirement returned to the office to which he had been elected in 1916. A 97,000 vote Democratic plurality in Hudson was now offset by an almost identical advantage for Edge from the Essex and Bergen suburbs.

Hague's decline through the 1940s was only gradual, however. Although unable to prevent Republican gubernatorial victories for Edge or his successor, Albert Driscoll in 1947, the mayor extracted the same sort of concessions he had exacted from Edge back in 1916. The signal New Jersey political battle of the 1940s, described in detail in chapter 7, was the struggle for a new constitution to replace the antiquated 1844 state charter. It was Hague's last major victory.

For the mayor, the important matters in the constitutional campaign were protecting the judicial patronage that kept him free of investigation and obtaining concessions on railroad taxes, still a major issue in Hudson County. Edge, who pledged in 1943 to end Republican cooperation with Hague, could not be budged. Their combat over the constitution in 1944 overshadowed all other political happenings: "The presidential duel between Roosevelt and Dewey was a matter of secondary importance."[42]

To win this final victory, Hague reached into the primal psyches of his supporters. He began with extensive newspaper advertising claiming the new constitution's tax provisions were a front for lower railroad taxes and the opening wedge for a state income tax, and that the new charter also threatened the tenure and pensions of public employees. The fatal blow, however, was Hague's charge in the last days before the election that the document was anti-Catholic. Rumors spread that church property would be taxed under the new constitution and priests forced to reveal the secrets of the confessional. The Newark archdiocese ordered all priests to speak against the constitution the Sunday before the election. Despite formation of a group of prominent Catholic laity (including a U.S. senator and the editor of the *Trenton Times*) to combat the hysterical rumors, Hague's denunciation of the referendum as a tool of the railroads and the Protestant Republicans was primarily responsible for the 54 percent to 46 percent defeat of the proposed constitution.[43]

Governor Driscoll, Edge's successor, took a more pragmatic approach to the Hudson leader. He first negotiated a change in railroad taxes that produced a $5 million annual windfall for Jersey City, then supported constitutional revision that would leave much of the county court system intact. Finally, instead of a Republican-dominated legislature sitting as a convention, as proposed in 1944, Driscoll suggested a bipartisan elected body.

Hague's reversal of position was dramatic. He told his followers, "I cannot too strongly urge all of you to support it on election day. . . . With this new constitution, we forgive everyone—because we won."[44] This time, the constitutional convention referendum passed easily. In response to cries of a sellout, Driscoll remarked with considerable foresight that "equal treatment . . . would remove one of the major issues on which Hague has flourished—that he was Hudson's only savior."[45]

Driscoll's characterization of Hague explains how a man called a dictator and an American fascist maintained power for more than three decades. No amount of electoral chicanery can yield margins like the 111,000 to 7,000 victory he achieved in 1937. Governor Edge wrote in 1948 of his long-time antagonist, "He is a cold, calculating and ruthless political boss, but he is at the same time an able administrator with strong humanitarian qualities, and Jersey City is in many ways a well-managed municipality."[46]

Where one stood on Hague depended on where one sat. From a good government perspective, Hague was a loathsome creature, ruling through criminality and intimidation. His control of civil service regulatory bodies made the merit system a sham, as Hague dismissed opponents on grounds of economic necessity or job abolition. Willingness to pay the organizational "mace," or "voluntary political contribution" of from 3 to as much as 40 percent of the annual take from patronage jobs and city contracts was the chief qualification for their award. Hague's command of the criminal justice system allowed him to seek or quash criminal indictments as he pleased.[47] Supervision of the police had many uses. At election time,

> It was relatively easy for Hague's people manning the polls to erase ballots, change ballots, destroy ballots, miscount ballots—while Hague-controlled policemen looked the other way or pressured inspection officials to stand aside. . . . [a state election superintendent said of the 1925 gubernatorial election] "We know it is futile to arrest anyone belonging to the Democrat organization in Hudson County on Election Day. The accuser usually finds himself in jail as the arrested party by the time he gets to the station house.[48]

The police were on the job for the mayor every day of the year, protecting businesses, both legal and illegal, that enriched the machine and its leader and intimidating those who did not. Jersey City became the illegal betting capital of the nation. Illicit wagering on races at every major track in the United States and Canada earned the city the title of the Horse Bourse.[49] Famed gangster Joseph "Newsboy" Moriarity operated a $10 million-a-year numbers racket under police protection. Friendly mobsters and cooperative AFL (American Federation of Labor) unions controlled the Jersey City waterfront, while CIO (Congress of Industrial Organizations) organizers were called Communists and driven out.[50] By conservative estimate, these varied activities brought in $1 to $1.5 million per year for the Hudson Democrats, and the constabulary received their share. A study of police forces in U.S. cities of similar size found that the average Jersey City police salary was 65 percent higher than its closest competitor.[51]

Yet from the perspective of the mayor's Catholic and working-class constituents, Hague was a savior. Christmas turkeys, coal for winter heating, and summer picnics for thousands of children accompanied the patronage employment. New Deal money built Hague's proudest monument, the two-thousand-bed Jersey City Medical Center. Offering free care to residents, it was then the third largest hospital in the world. An art deco treasure now on the National Register of Historic Places, the hospital buildings were replaced by a new facility in 2004 and are being converted to luxury condominiums. His penury for public education did not concern those who sent their children to parochial schools. If garbage collection still depended on horse-drawn carts into the 1940s, failure to mechanize preserved many jobs.

Illegal betting was "clean graft"; the abstemious mayor who neither smoked nor drank was diligent in keeping drugs and prostitution out of Jersey City, and women were barred from public taprooms. Yet this most traditional of men gave women political opportunities long before they were available elsewhere. Hudson women served in the state assembly and county governing body from the early 1920s, and U.S. Representative Mary T. Norton was sent to Washington for thirteen terms beginning in 1925.[52]

Hague embodied the resentment of Catholics and workers toward Protestants and corporations. His crusade against these enemies began in 1917, when as the new mayor he announced he was raising municipal taxes on Standard Oil from $1 million to $14 million, on the Public Service Corporation from $3 million to $30 million, and on the railroads from $67 million to $160 million. The state board of taxation's cancellation of this edict was seen as proof of Hague's charge that Republican Governor Edge and his board were the tools of the interests.

Detractors were appalled when Hague made his famous pronouncement, "I am the law." His supporters put it in context—Hague made the remark when he gave jobs to young delinquents without legal working papers, a plan he regarded as more effective rehabilitation than a term in reform school.[53] When critics demanded "reform" of the Hague organization, Hudsonites recalled that "reform was often a code word for Protestant hegemony and Catholic disenfranchisement."[54] It was this worldview that Hague used in his shameful attack on the constitutional referendum. As Thomas Fleming has observed of the sectarianism of the 1870s, "only by grasping its persistence as a motive force can the political and social history of the state for the next several decades be understood."[55]

In 1947, Hague, who spent increasing time at his homes in New York City and Florida, resigned the mayoralty he had held for thirty years and installed his nephew, Frank Hague Eggers, in his place. He still retained his seat on the Democratic National Committee, control of federal patronage, and selection of county officials and the 1949 Democratic gubernatorial nominee. Yet Hague's political life was closing. Returning war veterans with a broader view of the world recoiled from machine politics, high tax rates, and declining public services.

Other ethnic groups—Italians and eastern Europeans—were now a majority in Jersey City. They became restive at their exclusion from the organization's upper echelons when Hague continued his traditional practice of awarding city council nominations to four Irish Catholics and a token Protestant. John V. Kenny, the most senior of Hague's ward leaders (who were known as "the twelve apostles"), resented being passed over in favor of the mayor's nephew. He allied himself with Poles and Italians and ran as a "reform" opponent against Eggers in 1949. The torchlight parade celebrating the Kenny ticket's victory "resembled nothing less than the liberation of Paris five years earlier."[56] A tightly controlled Hudson County organization was dying. Discipline disintegrated, as fifty-one county freeholder candidates contested a few seats in 1950.

Hague, who finally resigned the last of his positions after the 1949 rout, and whose allies lost local Hudson battles thereafter, died in his New York City apartment in 1956 at the age of eighty-one. His mausoleum still dominates Jersey City's Holy Name Cemetery. Hague was unable to build a strong statewide Democratic organization, and he had little interest in doing so. His departure accelerated political change and made development of a statewide Democratic party possible for the first time.

The Democrats were aided by one of the state's frequent political scandals. In the spring of 1953, the Republican state chairman testified that gamblers had made large contributions to Governor Driscoll's reelection campaign. There were also allegations that the governor had personally collected protection money. Driscoll forcefully denied the charges, and the alleged go-between was tried and acquitted. Still, the damage was done, and Democrat Robert Meyner of Warren County, candidate of the party's anti-Hague forces, coasted to victory in 1953 even as the Republicans maintained control of both houses of the legislature. Meyner carried only three counties besides his native Warren: Mercer, Camden, and Kenney's Hudson.[57]

Warren County was a Democratic stronghold, but it was small, largely rural, and on the banks of the Delaware River, far from ethnic and boss-controlled Hudson and Middlesex. Meyner distributed patronage to counties where Democrats were traditionally weak but whose local leaders had backed his campaign. The traditional bosses' displeasure was an overall plus for the governor, contributing to an image that pleased many voters. As the state's leading newspaper commented, "He came to terms with party bosses, while preserving a reputation for independence. He has so thinned out his image that he won over the progressive concerned with human welfare and the conservative concerned with property. His youthful energy delighted the young, his marriage [while in office] enchanted the romantic, his concern about the aged, the disabled, the underpaid and underprivileged touched the public conscience."[58]

POLITICS AFTER HAGUE

The 1947 constitution made Meyner the first Democratic governor who could run for reelection. He achieved a resounding victory in 1957 over well-known financier and Republican state senator Malcolm Forbes, and the Democrats gained control of the assembly for the first time since 1937. They would remain dominant or highly competitive in state politics thereafter, although New Jersey continued to tilt Republican in presidential elections until 1992.

The Republicans' own long-standing factionalism also helped the Democrats. One of its sources was regional competition between the party's northern and southern wings, usually led by Essex and Atlantic counties respectively. A second was ideological disagreement between the GOP's progressives and regulars. This intense feud resulted in two relatively centralized and competing sources of Republican campaign funds for candidates representing the party's two wings.[59]

Because legislative control (especially of the state senate) was so crucial to the Republicans' power base, its county party leaders, unlike the Democrats, regularly sought legislative election. The Republican analogue to Frank Hague was Atlantic County state senator Frank "Hap" Farley, who served for thirty years between 1941 and 1972. Through control over other Republican senators from small southern counties, Farley dominated the legislature. Like Hague, the patronage-minded Farley had little desire or ability to build a statewide party.

It might thus appear that Meyner's governorship ushered in a new political era. The new constitution created one of the strongest state executives in the country. The governor could now run for two four-year terms; he was the only statewide elected official; he appointed all high-level officials to a greatly reduced number of more powerful cabinet departments and courts; and he had a variety of strong veto powers. Further, although Meyner's first victory and that of his successor, Richard J. Hughes, depended on the Hudson County vote, both won easily without Hudson in their second races, as did a later Democratic governor, Brendan Byrne (1974–1982), in both his contests. The Hudson organization was no longer essential to Democrats' statewide success, and it had also degenerated into factionalism. After Kenney, no Jersey City mayor of the next sixty years would complete two terms in succession.

On the other hand, although party organizations now counted for less in general elections, until the 1970s they remained central to nomination contests. Governor Byrne, a superior court judge whose primary victory was assured when a wiretapped mobster called him a man who "couldn't be bought," has admitted he would not have sought office in 1973 without Hudson County's endorsement.[60] The same was true of his predecessor, Richard Hughes. William T. Cahill (1970–1974), the lone Republican victor between 1949 and 1981, and a man loath to deal with Republican county leaders, was denied renomination when those leaders withdrew their support.

County organizations also continued as arbiters of governors' legislative success well into the 1960s. In the state senate, malapportionment favoring the smaller Republican counties meant that Meyner and Hughes faced a Republican senate dominated by "Hap" Farley for fourteen of the sixteen years they served. For many years, the Republicans required eleven votes (a majority of the entire senate) in their caucus before any bill would be released. Thus, as the *National Municipal Review* pointed out in 1950 when there were fourteen Republicans in the senate, only four Republican senators representing 3 percent of the state's population could hold a proposal hostage. The *Review* asked rhetorically, "What is the essential difference between the Russian system and the New Jersey system?"[61]

Even a partisan majority was no guarantee of gubernatorial success. In 1945, a second attempt to revise the 1844 constitution failed because of the opposition of Essex Republican leader Arthur T. Vanderbilt to elements of his own governor's proposal. Comparing Vanderbilt to Hague, Governor Edge later wrote of this impasse, "Vanderbilt, in a benevolent way, was as absolute a political boss in the Republican Party as Hague was in the Democratic organization. While these two men used their power to different ends . . . his control over the thirteen Essex legislators was just as absolute. . . . For the second year in succession, New Jersey had lost the opportunity to modernize its archaic constitution."[62]

The new powers in the revised charter still did not give the governor reliable control over county-controlled legislators. Meyner met regularly "with his political cabinet of Democratic county leaders when the Legislature [was] in session to decide on the action to be taken on major legislative policy questions." Their periodic rebellion suggested that "no New Jersey political party can ever be more than a confederation of county organizations, more or less held together by the glue of patronage."[63]

Emboldened by a 1965 landslide victory and the twentieth century's first Democratic legislative majorities in both houses, Meyner's successor,

Governor Hughes, proposed the abiding "third rail" of New Jersey politics, a state income tax. The urgent need for more state aid, especially for hard-pressed cities, was all the more evident because of the recent major riot in Newark. The tax went down to defeat when the Essex Democratic leader withdrew his support. Republican Governor William Cahill received almost no backing from his party's legislative majorities for a similar proposal in the next administration.[64] Although county leaders were more likely to attend to parochial issues affecting their own powers and patronage resources than to broader public policy, these instances demonstrate the power they could exert when they so chose.

Yet internal forces already threatened the dominance of the county party organizations—especially the decline of the cities and the growth of middle-class suburbs. Between 1940 and 1960, New Jersey's population swelled by almost half—from about four million to six million residents. Only California grew faster. Almost all of the population increase was in the suburbs. Counties which doubled in size in this period included Bergen and Morris in the north, Middlesex and Somerset in the central part of the state, Monmouth and Ocean along the shore, and Burlington and Gloucester in the south. In contrast, Hudson's population declined, and Essex only held steady. By 1970, the "Big Six" cities (Camden, Elizabeth, Jersey City, Newark, Paterson, and Trenton) had lost half their total population of 1930, and contributed but 11 percent to the statewide vote.[65]

Many of the new suburban residents had little interest in state politics. Large numbers worked in New York and Philadelphia, and their political information came from sources in those cities. New Jersey and Delaware were (and remain) the only states without their own network television stations.[66] Residents thus listened to out-of-state "local news" on television, as did more than half of those who used radio as a major source of political information.

Of the ten newspapers with the largest circulation, four were published in New York or Philadelphia. New Jersey—based papers were locally oriented, serving small central cities and their surrounding areas, or covering sprawling suburbs. The leading Newark papers circulated fairly widely but served only a limited number of readers in the northern half of the state. Although they did reach much of the narrow political elite, they could not reflect or shape public opinion. Thus, New Jersey residents remained notoriously ignorant, apathetic, and cynical about state politics. In October 1973, more residents in the northern part of the state could name a candidate in

New York City's mayoral election than could identify a New Jersey gubernatorial candidate.[67]

We cannot know when this archaic system would have fallen of its own weight, for its end came from an external source—the U.S. Supreme Court's 1964 decision in *Reynolds v. Sims*. Noting that the Supreme Court's mandate of "one person, one vote" was flagrantly violated in the state senate, the New Jersey Supreme Court enjoined further legislative elections and called for an interim election plan and constitutional revision. It further rejected an attempt to retain a county-based senate using weighted voting.

In 1966, a constitutional convention created a forty-member senate and an eighty-member assembly, whose districts were to be composed of "contiguous territory, as nearly compact and equal in the number of their inhabitants as possible." Another state supreme court decision in 1972 specifically directed that county boundaries be ignored in the drawing of district lines, in favor of more attention to population equality and contiguity.[68] In thus destroying the county organizations' control over legislative nominations, the court did much to destroy their overall political role.

Other developments completed the job by ending much of the county organizations' influence on gubernatorial nominations as well.[69] By the early 1970s, campaign finance reform was on the national agenda because of the Watergate scandal, and its appeal was strengthened in New Jersey by scandals in the Cahill administration. Governor Byrne, the "man who couldn't be bought," took advantage of the climate and pushed through the first public finance scheme for gubernatorial elections in the United States. Not only did the state provide proportionally more generous public funding than the federal program for presidential contests, but, as with the federal plan, money was funneled through candidate committees rather than party organizations.

Byrne himself was the first beneficiary of these developments. In 1977, county leaders withdrew their support of his renomination and ran five different county organization candidates against him in the Democratic primary. Byrne conducted the first statewide campaign heavily dependent on television. His victory with 28 percent of the vote in a large field of candidates, and his subsequent landslide general election win, truly ushered in New Jersey's modern political era. Individual candidates' appeal, television, and money replaced the county organizations as the driving forces in gubernatorial campaigns.[70]

The 1977 gubernatorial election was a genuinely pivotal event, for the content of Byrne's campaign was just as significant as its conduct. In 1973, the state supreme court had overturned the state's public school funding formula based on the local property tax. For three years, the governor and legislature wrangled over the issue. Faced with an injunction shutting down all the public schools in the state, the legislature in 1976 finally passed a statewide income tax.

Yet it was the governor whom voters held chiefly responsible for the income tax. The tax legislation was the major reason that Byrne's approval ratings at the start of the 1977 campaign plummeted to 19 percent. Byrne made his reelection quest a referendum on the need for the income tax. Byrne's opponent could not make a persuasive case that New Jersey could get by without it. The voters demonstrated their respect, if not affection, for the governor by giving him a fourteen-point victory margin.[71] The revenues the income tax generated for state projects went far in making a state politics possible for the first time in New Jersey.

With the end of county party domination, the rise of candidate-centered politics, and an assured flow of money for state initiatives, a genuinely new era for New Jersey politics and policy began in 1977. The new era produced an ironic twist of fate. Governor Byrne was succeeded in 1982 by a Republican who neither sought nor received many county endorsements. He expressed concerns about the role of money in politics and business's social responsibilities; courted and won Hudson County Democratic voters; and significantly expanded the reach and role of state government.[72] One can only wonder what New Jersey's first governor, William Livingston (1776–1790), and its Old Guard Republican senators, John Kean (1898–1910) and Hamilton Fish Kean (1928–1934), would make of their descendant—governor from 1981 to 1989, Thomas H. Kean.

One of the strangest periods in New Jersey's political history began with the end of the Kean governorship. Over the next fifteen years, New Jersey was to have four governors, only two of them elected. As Hague had foreseen, "reform" can have unintended consequences. Kean was succeeded by Democrat Jim Florio, the candidate he had barely defeated in 1981. When Florio became the state's chief executive, with majorities of his partisans in both houses of the legislature, he seemed poised to be another Brendan Byrne. Yet the 1990s were not to be the Florio decade, for the governor badly misread his state's history and culture. After a campaign predicated on the premise that New Jersey's fiscal problems were rooted in excessive expenditures rather than insufficient revenues, Florio used his authority to force an enormous state tax increase through a nervous Democratic legislature. The voters' massive reaction produced midterm veto-proof Republican majorities in both the assembly and the senate. The Republicans' control of the legislature for the next twelve years proved to be Florio's most enduring legacy, as in 1985 he became the only sitting governor since the adoption of the 1947 to be defeated for reelection.

The victor was Republican Christine Todd Whitman, New Jersey's first woman governor. Sometimes referred to as "Tom Kean with pearls" because of her similar aristocratic and political pedigrees, Whitman had an agenda—or perhaps the lack of an agenda—that allowed the legislature to continue regaining more equal stature. She entered office promising little other than to cut taxes and to be the antithesis of the activist Florio, and she succeeded. Reelected in 1997 with the narrowest of margins, she resigned from office nine months before her term ended to become the head of the federal Environmental Protection Agency during the first term of the George W. Bush administration. Following the succession plan prescribed by the state constitution, Republican senate president Donald DiFrancesco became acting governor and readied himself to run for a full term that fall.

When corruption charges compelled DiFrancesco to end his campaign, Democratic candidate Jim McGreevey, the Woodbridge mayor and state senator who had almost defeated Whitman four years earlier, was more successful in 2001, or so it seemed. Elected along with a new Democratic majority in the assembly and a tie in the senate, he came to be identified with the remnants of his party's county machines and brought New Jersey international attention in 2005 when he resigned, proclaiming that he was a "gay American" who was being blackmailed by his alleged lover. For the second time in four years, the state senate president, this time Democrat Richard Codey, stepped in as acting governor to serve the remaining fifteen months of McGreevey's term.

U.S. Senate politics in the state in this period were almost as chaotic. The state's senior U.S. senator, Democrat Frank Lautenberg, announced that he would not run for reelection to a fourth term in 2000. He was replaced by a political neophyte, Jon Corzine. Like Lautenberg when he first ran in 1982, Corzine was a wealthy business executive with no political biography who spent liberally from his own fortune to make himself known to voters. Shortly thereafter, the state's other Democratic U.S. senator, Robert Torricelli, who had tried and failed to get the Democrats' gubernatorial nomination in 1997, became caught in his own corruption scandal and withdrew from his 2002 reelection campaign against Republican Doug Forrester—another wealthy political newcomer. Forrester's only elective office had been as mayor of West Windsor, a Mercer County suburb. Republicans, sensing victory because of Torricelli's problems, were outraged when the Democrats persuaded Lautenberg (who needed little persuading) to come out of retirement and run for the seat. He defeated Forrester by a 10-point margin.

This confusing story did not end there. As acting governor Codey mulled a race for a full gubernatorial term in 2005, Senator Corzine announced that he was once again prepared to reach into his own deep pockets to acquire the Democrats' nomination for chief executive, and Forrester promised to match him in a quest for the Republican nod. Both were successful in their parties' primaries, and thus the first gubernatorial contest in which the candidates renounced available public funding took place, ending with a Corzine victory.

Many of the signal events in New Jersey state politics since the 1970s may thus be described as a continuing dialogue between "the statesman and the boss."[73] Governor Byrne and Governor Kean bring Woodrow Wilson to mind. Governors Cahill and McGreevey, like Frank Hague, did not seek to personally enrich themselves but were charged with cronyism and collusion with machine politicians. Senators Torricelli and Corzine were seen, respectively, as contributing and distributing campaign funds in a manner that once again made irony of political "reform." In his 2006 inaugural address, Governor Corzine told his constituents, "It is simply inexcusable that we have a state government that again and again ranks low in public trust and esteem. . . . We must change how our government does business. . . . To do that we will need real reform. . . . So I call on all my fellow public servants to join in an historic effort to end the toxic mix of politics, money and public business—at every level of New Jersey government." Somewhere, no doubt, Woodrow Wilson applauded and Frank Hague yawned, as their dialogue continued.

CHAPTER 4

Contemporary Political Patterns

I have eaten everything from sauerbraten to pirogies to
tacos, because New Jersey has only about ten fewer
ethnic groups than the U.N. has countries.

—Former Governor Tom Kean

FROM THE TIME OF FRANKLIN ROOSEVELT'S NEW DEAL
until the recent past, New Jersey's partisan voters were aptly described as rag-
ing moderates. The state's Democrats were never prominent in the ascendant
Roosevelt "liberal" wing of their party when "liberal" had a principally economic definition. Frank Hague, New Jersey Democrats' long-time leader,
had a strong antipathy to the labor unions that were a major force among
Democratic liberals. New Jersey's many small cities, located from one end
of the state to the other, also did not inspire the kind of upstate-downstate,
liberal-conservative, Democratic-Republican split of California, Illinois, or
New York. The reform-minded "amateur democrats" who blossomed in
those states in the 1950s had no counterpart in New Jersey.[1]

Conversely, the majority of the state's successful Republicans were in
its moderate wing. Although, there were dueling Republican organizations
in the north (representing the moderates) and the south (representing
the conservatives), all of the GOP's victorious candidates (governors from
Walter Edge early in the twentieth century to Christine Todd Whitman at
the century's close) were centrists. Conservative activists have become more
prominent of late in the GOP, but much less so among those who win general elections.

By the 1960s New Jersey was poised for transformation. The old-style
party system remained in place, continuing to dominate state politics because
there was no way for the new independent-leaning suburban majority to
communicate, or for politicians to reach them. They read local newspapers,
or the Philadelphia and New York press, and listened to out-of-state radio
and television stations. The United States and New Jersey Supreme Courts

finally smashed the old political structure based on county party organizations with the reapportionment decisions described in chapter 3. With that external blow, a new system could finally begin to emerge. But the traditional underpinnings did not entirely disappear, and demographic and geographic vestiges still remain.

DEMOGRAPHY

To understand the state's politics, one needs to understand its demography. Ethnicity, religion, population change, and the structure of the economy all contribute to shaping New Jersey's politics.

Ethnic and Religious Patterns

New Jersey has always been a multicultural state. Early Dutch, British, and German settlers were joined in the mid-1800s by the Irish and shortly thereafter by, among others, large numbers of Italians, Poles, Hungarians, and European Jews. The state's Jewish population of slightly over 5 percent is proportionally second only to New York, and Catholics, making up about two-fifths of the state's residents, represent the second highest Catholic population share in the nation. The 5 percent of New Jersey's population that was African American in 1940 has tripled in the past fifty years and at 1.3 million is the fifteenth largest among the fifty states. The size and proportion of the Hispanic population are almost identical, a figure that ranks New Jersey seventh in the nation in numbers and ninth proportionally.[2]

Since 1990, the number of residents who report that they speak a language other than English at home has grown from 1.4 million to 2 million, or one-quarter of the state's population. The Census Bureau estimates that almost 550,000 international immigrants entered New Jersey legally between 1995 and 2005. Their origins were primarily Asian and Latino. They were accompanied by about 135,000 undocumented aliens—bringing the "best guess" approximation of the number of illegal aliens in the state to about 350,000.[3] Since the number of native-born residents decreased during this period, New Jersey's population would have declined if these newcomers had not arrived. Annual population growth, which in 2005 was thirty-ninth among the fifty states, has dropped steadily since 1950, leaving New Jersey "riding in the caboose of the national demographic train."[4]

Like earlier immigrants, many of the newer ones have settled in urban areas, particularly the Newark and Jersey City metropolitan areas. Of late, however, they have been following the rest of the population to the suburbs.

Both the Middlesex-Somerset-Hunterdon and Bergen-Passaic PMSAs (primary metropolitan statistical areas) are now home to more of the foreign-born than is the Jersey City PMSA, and together they far exceed the numbers in the Newark PMSA.

African Americans and Hispanics, the largest minority groups, are concentrated in particular areas. Atlantic, Burlington, Camden, Cumberland, Essex, Mercer, Salem, and Union counties all have populations that are more than 15 percent black, while the northwestern counties and Ocean County along the Shore are less than 3 percent black. Similarly, more than 15 percent of the residents of Essex, Hudson, Passaic, Union, and Cumberland are Hispanic; few Latinos reside in most of the southern and western counties. In 1950 Newark, at 17 percent, had the largest proportion of black residents of any city. Now, more than half of Newark, Camden and Trenton residents are African-American, and Hispanics are a majority in Elizabeth, Passaic and Paterson.

Until recently, voters chose statewide officeholders from the earlier arriving ethnic groups. New Jersey did not elect an Irish Catholic to the governorship until the 1960s and did not choose one of southern European extraction until 1989. Its first Jewish senator, Frank Lautenberg, was thought by many to be a German Protestant. Robert Menendez, appointed to fill a U.S. Senate vacancy in 2005 and elected to a full term the following year, was the first Hispanic to hold statewide office. In 2002 Cuban-born Alberto Sires became the state's first Hispanic assembly speaker. Three years later, Bonnie Watson Coleman would become the first black and female assembly majority leader. All of these officeholders were Democrats and reflect the party's strongest voting base, in contrast to the Republican base, which is most strongly English, Irish, and German in ancestry. Among the other larger ethnic groups, those of Italian and Polish background are the most likely to be swing voters.

In local politics (see chapter 13), New Jersey's "tribalism" still holds sway. Hudson County's local races involve mortal combat between Irish, Italian, Polish, African American, and Cuban candidates, among others. Arabs are seeking a place in Passaic politics, and a Middlesex County assemblyman is of Indian ancestry. Statewide candidates can rise above ascriptive identifications. Republican Governor Tom Kean, for example, won a majority of the black vote in 1985 and defeated Democratic opponent Peter Shapiro among Shapiro's Jewish coreligionists. Yet, when one looks at their base areas of strength, there are still significant differences in the demographic makeup of New Jersey's parties.

The Demography of the Partisan Vote

A significant change in the composition of the "partisan base vote"—defined as the vote in those municipalities that consistently supported candidates of the party defeated in statewide elections—began in New Jersey in the 1990s, and the evolution of the ethnic and religious patterns just described contributed to this development.

In the period from 1973 through 1988, the GOP base vote remained stable at 43 percent. During this time, the Democratic base—those areas carried by their losing presidential candidates from 1976 through 1988—dropped from 44 to 41 percent. "Swing" localities with mixed records rose at the Democrats' expense from 13 to 16 percent. The almost equal partisan base votes and the growth of swing areas accounted for New Jersey's political volatility. For example, running in the same elections, both Republican President Ronald Reagan and Democratic Senator Bill Bradley won in landslides in 1984; Republican President George H. W. Bush and Democratic Senator Frank Lautenberg both triumphed comfortably in 1988. Democratic Governor Brendan Byrne's record-setting gubernatorial vote of 67 percent in 1973 was eclipsed by Republican Tom Kean's 70 percent victory in 1985.

In the parlance of political pundits, however, since the 1990s New Jersey has become routinely deep blue. In 1992, presidential candidate Bill Clinton became the first Democrat to carry New Jersey since Lyndon Johnson did so in 1964. Clinton repeated that statewide victory in 1996, as did Al Gore and John Kerry in 2000 and 2004. Between 1978 and 2004, Democrats won every U.S. Senate election, and Republican Governor Christine Whitman's two anemic plurality victories during the 1990s were the only successful statewide contests for the GOP between 1986 and 2005. By 2005, the Democratic base vote had risen to 47 percent, while the Republican base dropped to 40 percent and mixed areas to 13 percent.

Geographically, the Republican base is centered in counties with concentrations of its demographic loyalists—Hunterdon, Morris, Warren, and Sussex in the north and west, and Cape May, Monmouth, and Ocean along the Shore. It has decreased in Bergen, Essex, Passaic, and Union counties, which have large populations of recent immigrants and those of southern and eastern European stock.

Areas where the Democratic base declined in the 1980s showed two different patterns. One inclined voters toward the Republican side, and one moved them toward the "swing" category. Democratic declines in the

Shore counties, Hunterdon, Warren, and Burlington, represented even weaker performances in traditionally Republican areas with growing populations. Most of the new residents of these areas come from groups favorably disposed to Republicans, and thus they became even more strongly Republican. This pattern has generally persisted through the present, with little change in the large GOP majorities.

The other pattern in this period was the Democrats' loss of support in older, less wealthy suburbs in the northern counties. These areas often had large southern and east European ethnic populations who were shedding traditional Democratic loyalties but who soon demonstrated that they were not yet reliably Republican voters either. Much of the Democratic dominance since the early 1990s is due to the return of some "Reagan Democrats" to their ancestral party home. In comparing the results of the four statewide elections from 1993 through 1997 (two for governor and two for the U.S. Senate) to the four similar elections between 2001 and 2005, the later period shows a net shift away from the Republicans of at least 5 percentage points in Middlesex, Mercer, and Union and even larger shifts in Essex and Hudson, where the GOP's already weak performance has become steadily weaker.

Suburbanization and Population Change

The U.S. Census Bureau classifies every New Jerseyan as an urban dweller. Population density is slightly over 1,100 per square mile—the highest in the United States. It is three times higher than the average for the Northeast; fourteen times higher than the average for the entire nation. Yet these figures mask broad internal variations. Density is an astonishing 13,000 per square mile in Hudson. On the other hand, some western counties have fewer than 300 people per square mile.

New Jersey is overwhelmingly suburban rather than urban. Only Newark and Jersey City have populations over 200,000. Cities like Camden and Trenton have fewer residents than suburban townships like Edison and Woodbridge in Middlesex County or Hamilton in Mercer County and are barely larger than Brick in Ocean County or Cherry Hill in Camden County. These suburban townships have no identifiable "downtowns" or other traditional urban features. Even more New Jerseyans live in prototypical small towns in the northern half of the state, which merge into each other. As *National Geographic* magazine observed of New Jersey as early as 1933, "Once isolated villages have expanded so rapidly that outsiders cannot tell where one ends and the other begins."[5] All these suburbanites meet not downtown, but in vast shopping malls along the major highways.

The Appalachian foothills of the northwest and the southern Pine Barrens were traditionally the New Jersey of sparse population and unspoiled natural beauty. Thanks to protective legislation in the 1970s and 1980s, the Pine Barrens—with great stands of forest, blueberry and cranberry bogs, and grassy wetlands—will remain one of the most ecologically pristine areas in the entire Boston-Washington corridor. Although the Delaware Water Gap, a magnificent twelve-hundred-foot gorge through the Kitatinny Mountains, and other scenic places in the northwestern part of the state retain their grandeur, interstate highways have brought them "closer" to population centers. Each year, as one travels west, shopping malls, research parks, and condominium developments march further into the "country," replacing scattered lakeside summer cottages.

The Economy

The foremost analysts of the state's economy have written, "New Jersey rides an economic roller coaster."[6] Since the 1980s New Jersey has had three economic expansions and three recessions. The first expansion, from 1982 through 1989, during Republican Governor Thomas Kean's tenure, produced the largest job gains in the state's history. His successor, Democrat Jim Florio, was greeted with a recession that was, in terms of job losses, the deepest in the state's history. By 1992 the economy had begun to recover, but Florio, vilified for imposing large increases in the state income and sales taxes, was defeated for reelection in 1993. Republican Christie Whitman arrived in the governor's office to preside over most of the second period of economic growth, which continued until 2000. A relatively mild downturn ended as 2003 began, and by November 2004 New Jersey had reclaimed all the lost jobs of what has been termed a "recessionette."[7]

There were, however, disturbing differences as these cycles of growth and decline progressed. Compared to the state's long-term trend line of annual job creation, the expansion of the 1980s was 126 percent higher, that of the 1990s was 69 percent higher, and the "recovery" that began in 2004 was, eighteen months later, 22 percent lower. During the 1980s, New Jersey's rate of job creation ranked eighteenth among the fifty states and fourth among the eleven most industrialized states. By 2005, it lagged behind rather than surpassed the national average. No longer the engine of growth in the Northeast, it fell behind the performances of neighboring New York and Pennsylvania.

The consequences and explanations of these patterns are many. Turning first to explanations, New Jersey has continued to hemorrhage manufacturing jobs, losing about 130,000 (more than one-fifth of its manufacturing base) during the 1990s and another 100,000 between 2000 and 2005. But the creation of almost 600,000 jobs in the service sector during the 1980s had brought virtually full employment. Hotels real estate, legal services, and business services jobs increased by a third to a half. Employment grew dramatically in the securities and commodities industry as Wall Street moved back office jobs across the Hudson. During that decade, New Jersey became the fifth largest office market in the nation, "leaping out of nowhere."[8]

With the exception of once-grimy Hudson County towns like Hoboken and parts of Jersey City, which are now outposts of Wall Street and have become trendy yuppie havens as a result, these new jobs were in the suburbs rather than the cities. During the 1990s, the job loss in the cities was almost identical to the number gained in the suburbs. By the turn of the twenty-first century, the suburbs for the first time claimed the majority of jobs in the state. Towns at the interchanges of major highways like Parsippany-Troy Hills in Morris County, South Brunswick in Middlesex County, and Mount Laurel in Burlington County experienced explosive growth.[9] Parsippany-Troy Hills, for example, was the sixth most frequently named employment location in the state in the 2000 U.S. Census. It offered more employment opportunities than the cities of Elizabeth and Paterson, despite having considerably less than half the population of either.

Joel Garreau calls such growth zones "edge cities." Edge cities have at least five million square feet of office space, six hundred thousand square feet of retail space, more workers than residents, and were largely residential or rural less than thirty years ago. He counts ten edge cities in New Jersey, second only to California's twenty-six. They represent a "third wave" of suburban migration—a movement of corporate employers to the suburbs that has followed the earlier movement of first people and then retailers.[10]

Consequently, when the new century brought the third recession with it, for the first time an economic downturn affected the suburban office parks. The bursting dot com bubble took with it half of New Jersey's telecommunications jobs. Pharmaceutical companies, whose New Jersey jobs in 1990 had provided a fifth of all U.S. employment in that industry, saw their employees in the state dwindle by one-quarter over the next fifteen years. The numbers of those working in finance, business, and professional services stagnated or declined. Job creation was concentrated primarily in the public sector and the lower reaches of the service sector, such as restaurant workers. One analyst estimated that of the nearly sixty thousand new jobs created between 2000 and 2006, almost fifty-four thousand were in the public sector.[11]

Perhaps symbolically, the brightest star in the New Jersey technology firmament may now be Cognizant Technology Systems, which in 2006 reported annualized earning increases of 44 percent over the previous five years. It ranked at the top of *Forbes* magazine's list of the top ten small businesses in the nation and was named to the Standard and Poor's 500 Index in 2007. Begun as an in-house technology center at Dun and Bradstreet headquarters in Princeton in 1994 and spun off two years later, 70 percent of its twenty-five thousand workers are in India. It recruits more new Indian MBAs than any other IT company in the world, along with thousands of engineers, and pays its highly skilled offshore workforce an average yearly salary of less than 10 percent of U.S. wages for comparable jobs. Pharmaceutical companies with major New Jersey facilities, like Novartis and Pfizer, are also turning to India, where their ongoing clinical trial programs are expanding to R&D projects.[12]

There are many consequences of the changing global and national economy for New Jersey. With its onset, "New Jersey's always undistinguished cities have been left as monuments to advanced industrialization. . . . Indeed, there are few states of equivalent size within which major cities play so small a role."[13] A shifting employment profile that advantages the highly educated and disadvantages those without the needed skills has had a major impact on income inequality. During the past two decades, the average income of the wealthiest fifth of New Jerseyans rose 79 percent, while that of the bottom fifth grew only 24 percent. The state now ranks ninth nationally in the size of the gap between the top and bottom quintiles of income earners. Rising unemployment among computer programmers and research chemists as well as factory workers has played havoc with the state's budget, which built in the rising revenues of the 1980s in a permanent fashion.

Economic climates also affect population growth, as vibrant economies act as a magnet for mobile workers. During the 1980s, New Jersey's population increased far less than that of many states in the South and West, but much more than the other large northeastern states of Massachusetts, New York, and Pennsylvania. In contrast, growing internal out-migration since 2000 is related to an economy that has become less vibrant. Surpassed by Georgia in the 2000 census, the state slipped from ninth to tenth in population size. The U.S. Census Bureau estimated that in 2005 New Jersey fell behind North Carolina as well, dropping out of the top ten for the first time since the 1920s and on track to lose a congressional seat after the 2010 census.

In considering these blows to the New Jersey economy, though, its enduring strengths should be remembered, for it starts from a very high platform. The state remains second only to Connecticut in per capita income, and first in family income. Four of its counties rank among the fifteen wealthiest in the United States. If New Jersey were to secede from the union and become an independent country, it would be the second richest nation on earth after Luxembourg.[14] New Jersey still has a leading edge economy and a lot of talent that wants to keep it that way. An early innovator in the information and research-based market sectors, New Jersey's future economic performance will be an indicator of how the entire nation meets the challenges of the new global economy.

POLITICAL OFFICE AND THE GEOGRAPHY OF THE NEW JERSEY VOTE

Population distribution and the new economic structure interact with the traditional political focus on counties and more recent developments like the power of incumbency to produce New Jersey's voting patterns. These patterns used to vary considerably for different political offices but have recently become more similar.

Presidential Voting

In the years between the departure of Franklin Roosevelt and the arrival of Ronald Reagan, presidential voting in New Jersey showed considerable stability. Republican strength was greatest in the rural northwestern reaches of Hunterdon, Morris, and Sussex counties and along the southern portions of the Shore, in Ocean and Atlantic counties. The Democrats did best in Camden and Cumberland, the counties bordering Pennsylvania and Delaware; in heavily urban Essex and Hudson counties near New York City; and in the state capital's county of Mercer, with its many government workers. The parties alternated presidential victories through 1964.

Republicans won every election thereafter until 1992, although the 1968 and 1976 contests were relatively close, as they were nationally.

After Gerald Ford's narrow win in New Jersey in 1976, Republican victories became more substantial, as GOP presidential candidates ran 3 to 4 percentage points ahead of their national showings through 1992. Almost all of the state shifted fairly evenly in a Republican direction. Strongly Republican counties became even more Republican; strongly Democratic ones less so. Between 1948 and 1976, the average Democratic presidential vote in the banner Democratic counties was over 50 percent. In the three presidential contests between 1980 and 1988, it dropped below 50 percent in all except Essex. There, the black population of 37 percent, more than twice that of any other county, produced a Democratic increase. New Jersey's "lunch bucket Democrats" applauded Ronald Reagan and George H. W. Bush.

A dramatic change began in the 1990s, however. Although the first President Bush, in losing the state by 2 percent to Bill Clinton, still did 4 points better than he did nationally, the 16 percent of the vote that went to Ross Perot was the first sign that New Jersey's "Reagan Democrats" were becoming dubious about the leanings of a Republican Party dominated nationally by southerners, Mountain State westerners, and social conservatives, and increasingly impressed by independent mavericks like Perot or "New Democrats" like Bill Clinton. They confirmed this decision in 1996, when the Perot vote dropped in half and New Jersey awarded Clinton a margin 5 points greater than his national victory. The election of 2000 was even more lopsided, with Al Gore running 10 points ahead of his nationwide showing. Despite some voters' inclination to support the incumbent Republican president in wartime and in the face of the World Trade Center attacks (many of whose victims were Garden State commuters), John Kerry also carried the state in 2004, running 5 percent ahead of his national totals. Reversing the trends of the 1980s, Democratic counties became even more Democratic and Republican counties a bit less so.

Senate Contests

A somewhat different pattern had characterized U.S. Senate contests. In post–World War II Senate elections until the mid-1970s, the Senate vote closely tracked the presidential vote. The statewide average for the period was only about 2 percent more Democratic for Senate races than presidential ones. In all of the Senate races in that period, candidates or current issues resulted in only two counties swinging more than 5 percent in their average partisan division in presidential as opposed to Senate contests. In contrast, in the four Senate and three presidential races between 1978 and 1988, the state voted an average of 16 percent more Democratic in the Senate elections. Only five of the twenty-one counties had an average presidential-Senate partisan swing under 15 percent. Even Essex, the most strongly Democratic county in this later period, had an 11 percent deviation favoring the Senate candidates.

The separation of voters' presidential and Senate choices was seen most directly when elections were concurrent. In 1984, Bill Bradley ran 25 points ahead of Democratic presidential candidate Walter Mondale statewide and at least 20 percent ahead in every county. In 1988, Frank Lautenberg ran 11 points ahead of Michael Dukakis statewide and at least 9 percent ahead in every county. In the 1996 and 2000 Senate elections, however, the victorious Democratic Senate candidates actually ran behind their party's presidential candidates' landslides.

Congressional Contests

A vast academic literature documents the increased importance of incumbency in voters' choices since 1970.[15] In New Jersey, the lack of statewide media, coupled with the disruption of political recruitment by county party organizations, created conditions made to order for incumbent success. Incumbency and the advantages it brings—name recognition, the ability to raise campaign funds, free mailings to constituents and other such perks—is a major reason that Democrats have almost continuously maintained the majority of New Jersey's House delegation that they achieved in 1964.[16]

Congressional redistricting had an unusually strong impact on the House delegation in 1992, when three senior Democrats unexpectedly announced their retirements—the result of a unique combination of factors. These included the state's loss of a seat, court orders to draw "majority-minority" districts, House members' final opportunity to keep unspent campaign funds for personal use; and the sour atmosphere surrounding Congress.[17] The redistricting process had no such effect in 2002, which was aptly described as "dealing incumbents an inside straight."[18] The twelve who ran and won raised the number of New Jersey House incumbents standing for reelection to 116 out of 120 over the past two decades; the thirteenth winner replaced a retiring Republican and left the delegation's balance unchanged, as it remained through 2008.

When nominally competitive House seats open, the common pattern is a narrow victory followed by large reelection margins. Consider the example of New Jersey's Twelfth District, scene of one of the few defeats of a sitting incumbent. Meandering through several counties, the long-time Republican stronghold has been represented since 1998 by Democrat Rush Holt. Holt defeated a first-term Republican incumbent, Michael Pappas, after Pappas took to the House floor to sing a ditty he had composed to praise the special counsel in the Clinton presidential impeachment investigation: "Twinkle Twinkle Kenneth Starr. Now we see how brave you are." His moderate constituents were not amused, and Holt eked out a 51 percent victory.

Convinced that the Pappas loss was a personal fluke in a "safe" district, in 2000 the Republicans fielded the Twelfth's former congressman, Dick Zimmer, who had regularly garnered close to two-thirds of the vote but left the House to run unsuccessfully for the U.S. Senate in 1996. After a spirited campaign and a recount, Holt prevailed over Zimmer by 651 votes. Helped substantially by redistricting, he has won by about 20 percentage points ever since.

Another way to illustrate the incumbency effect in House elections is to look at the difference between presidential and congressional voting patterns in the twenty-one counties.[19] Before 1972, split-ticket voting for president and Congress was rare, except when large numbers of partisans crossed over to vote for an exceptionally popular presidential candidate (such as Democrats voting for Eisenhower in 1956), or against an exceptionally unpopular candidate of their own party (such as Republicans voting for Johnson in 1964), and returned home to vote for the rest of the ticket.

Through the 1970s and 1980s, split-ticket voting tripled to between 10 and 15 percent, which primarily reflected Democratic House incumbents' ability to withstand the substantial margins rolled up by Republican presidential candidates. As Democratic presidential candidates started winning the state at the presidential level in the 1990s, split-ticket voting declined almost to the levels before 1972. Fewer Democrats were splitting their tickets, but as the Democrats had done earlier, Republican incumbents easily survived their presidential candidates' losses. Although the delegation is almost evenly balanced, with few exceptions the margins of

Republican incumbents have recently been lower than those of the Democrats, leading to less split-ticket voting overall.[20]

Governors' Races

In contrast to the Democrats' strength in Senate races and incumbents' strength in House races, gubernatorial contests have shown more twists and turns, and previously reliable strategies for analyzing their outcomes have become less useful. In considering the patterns in the gubernatorial vote, three points must be borne in mind.

First, the governorship has been the only elected state office. New Jersey did not have the elected lieutenant governors, attorneys general, or high-ranking judges that launch gubernatorial bids in other states after gaining public recognition in their runs for other offices.[21] It was also difficult for ranking state legislators to build recognition and organizational support because of a tradition, broken only in recent decades, of rotation of the legislative leadership after each election. These attributes gave incumbent governors an extra leg up since their opponents were generally unknown; they also meant that open seat races generally featured candidates who were unfamiliar to the public. It remains to be seen if a constitutional amendment creating a lieutenant governor, to take effect for the 2009 gubernatorial election, puts a meaningful rung on the political ambition career ladder.[22] Second, the 1947 constitution allowed New Jersey governors to run for two consecutive terms for the first time in the state's history. Until the 2005 election, all of the incumbents who could do so sought renomination; all but one, who lost his party primary, won reelection.[23] Five of these seven governors came to office from careers in the state legislature and the U.S. House of Representatives, as did most of their opponents.

Conspicuously missing compared with other states were the nonexistent inhabitants of other statewide elected offices, and "amateur" business executives. The New Jerseyans in the latter category were more likely to be oriented toward New York, Philadelphia, the nation, or the world, rather than Trenton. Well-known financier Malcolm Forbes ran for the governorship in the 1950s but had previously "served his time" in the state legislature. Political neophytes like Senators Bradley, Lautenberg, and Corzine chose to run for the U.S. Senate, where there was less competition and interest from those who focused on the governor's chair. Governor Corzine's eventual move from Washington to Trenton was relatively uncommon for both New Jersey and the nation; election traffic between the state and national capitals more often goes in the other direction.

A third focus in analyzing New Jersey gubernatorial elections has been the traditional role of powerful county party organizations who cared little about federal races with no patronage payoffs. As the only elected official at the statewide level with thousands of jobs to dispense, the gubernatorial nominee was of intense interest to the county parties, who played their most important role in the primary elections.

On the Democratic side, even after the demise of the Hague organization, Hudson County's support was usually essential for Democratic candidates. Hudson's control of gubernatorial nominations explains why there were no significant Democratic primary battles for the governorship between 1933 and 1946. On the Republican side, nomination contests were frequently rivalries between candidates of the strong county organizations in South Jersey and those of the northern and western parts of the state. Thus there was a stronger regional cast to gubernatorial elections than those for other offices.

Television and court reapportionment decisions at first did not succeed in erasing the stronger regional flavor of these elections, particularly those with no incumbent. Public financing of governors' races, which began in 1977 and was accepted by all of the major party candidates until 2005, put a fairly tight cap on campaign expenditures. This prevented candidates, particularly in the nomination phase, from getting well-known outside their home regions through television in the way that Senate candidates did.

The nomination-phase budget allowed for, at most, two or three weeks of heavy buys in the Philadelphia and New York TV media markets during the primary season—not nearly enough for candidates to paint detailed positive pictures of themselves, or negative ones of their opponents. "Free" TV coverage, in the guise of news reports and interview appearances, was and remains limited by competition for air time from New York City and Philadelphia politicians. Despite taking place in odd-numbered off-years, the governor's contest always competes for news time in the heavily populated northern part of the state with the usually more colorful and entertaining mayor's race in New York City.

When many county party organizations became less important, gubernatorial candidates' own organizations and recognition levels still had regional bases, and the common mode of electoral analysis was geographical. In short, a prediction in any election that the winning primary candidates and the governor would have served in the state legislature or the House of Representatives, would be of moderate ideological coloration, would run best in their home county and regions, would have support from the stronger county party organizations, and would accept state matching funds and their expenditure limits was not likely to be far off the mark. Finally, a forecast that an incumbent governor would win a convincing victory seemed virtually a given.

Beginning in the 1990s, however, all of these indicators became less reliable, as a brief analysis of the traditional races of the 1980s with those that followed makes clear.

Camden-area Congressman Jim Florio was the Democratic candidate in both 1981 and 1989. Both were open-seat contests. Florio won the 1981 primary with 26 percent of the vote in a thirteen-candidate field by piling up huge margins in seven South Jersey counties. Fully 60 percent of his statewide vote came from these counties, more than one-quarter of it from Camden County alone. The potential counterweights to Florio's southern juggernaut, Essex and Hudson, divided their votes among multiple "hometown" candidates, and Florio was thus able to run second in these counties, as well as in vote-rich Middlesex and Mercer, which also had their "own" candidates. When Florio lost to Tom Kean by a hair's breadth in 1981 and passed on the chance to run against the popular incumbent in 1985, he was quickly assumed to be the Democrat's leading contender for 1989.

On the Republican side, both Kean, the 1981 nominee, and Representative Jim Courter, the 1989 standard-bearer, constructed regional bases that won them each about 30 percent of the primary vote in fairly large fields. Each constructed a northwest-Shore axis including Morris, Monmouth, and Ocean counties and did respectably in the largest county, Bergen.

In the 1981 and 1989 general elections, the distribution of the candidates' votes also had a regional coloring, despite the fact that Florio lost narrowly in 1981 and won in a landslide in 1989. In 1981, Florio led by two to one in the southern counties that made up his congressional district and had a similar margin in the flagship Democratic county of Hudson. Kean had big leads in the Republican redoubts of Hunterdon, Morris, Somerset, and Warren and did well in the Shore counties. Florio's narrow loss resulted from lackluster wins in traditionally Democratic Middlesex and Mercer. The weakening ability of those county Democratic organizations to "deliver" in governors' races and Kean's own skills in cutting into the Democratic base gave him his victory.[24]

In winning the general election in 1989, Florio piled up similar margins in Camden, Gloucester, and Hudson. Unlike 1981, he achieved large majorities in Mercer and Middlesex and carried the usually Republican bastions of Ocean, Monmouth, and Somerset. Despite losing by the third largest margin in the history of state gubernatorial contests, Courter still won the northwestern Republican counties of Morris, Warren, Hunterdon, and Sussex.

Changes in these patterns started to become evident in the 1993 elections. Jim Florio, running for reelection and redemption, had seemed a ripe target for the Republicans since his first year in office when enraged voters believed he had broken a campaign promise not to raise taxes. The first to feel their wrath was the state's most revered political figure, U.S. Senator Bill Bradley, who was up for reelection in 1990. After Bradley refused to take a position on the tax increase, calling it a "state issue," he came within a point of defeat by Christie Whitman, then an unknown who was a second-level member of the Kean cabinet and a former county official. If there was any doubt that 1993 would be the GOP's year to recapture the governorship, it disappeared after the Republicans wrested control of both houses of the legislature from the Democrats in the 1991 legislative elections, achieving veto-proof majorities as they did so.

The 1993 gubernatorial primary contests had several rather unusual aspects. First, as the incumbent, Florio had no opponents, but Republicans had to choose between two major candidates, both of whom had unusually strong claims on the nomination. The winner, with 41 percent of the vote, was Whitman. Although a national celebrity after she almost defeated Bill Bradley, she had not been the choice of New Jersey's Republican establishment. They favored Cary Edwards, a candidate in the classically successful Republican mold. A veteran state assembly member from Bergen County, he later served as both chief of staff and attorney general in the Kean administration, and was the second place finisher to the more conservative Jim Courter in the 1989 GOP primary. When Edwards and Whitman both stumbled with a series of campaign gaffes, they were joined in the fray by a former state senator who was a 1981 primary candidate and conservative business executive. He hoped to capitalize on the sizable Perot vote in the 1992 presidential election.

Whitman's novel traits as a serious gubernatorial contender were a second unusual feature. She was the first woman to make a significant bid for statewide office, and one of the few gubernatorial candidates who had served in neither the legislature nor the U.S. Congress. With the exception of the assembly speaker, the GOP's leading officeholders were absent from her inner circle, which consisted largely of other Republican women and family members.

Third, because both candidates were unusually well-known to party activists, the northwest-Shore coalition of counties that produced wins for the primary election victors in the 1980s did not appear in the 1993 contest. Whitman and Edwards carried their important home counties of Somerset and Bergen respectively, but the other Republican bastions split between them. Whitman won in Monmouth and Ocean, Edwards prevailed in Morris and Sussex, and Warren was almost a dead heat.

More challenges to the conventional wisdom transpired in the general election. Coming off a big win in the heavily Republican legislature to ban assault weapons, and with the economy improving, Governor Florio had fought his way back from the political graveyard; he actually led Whitman in polls taken shortly after the primary election. Geography proved to be a less potent indicator of the vote than in the past. Whitman won the standard big victories in the northwestern Republican counties, but she also narrowly carried the typically Democratic strongholds of Middlesex, Mercer, and Passaic and cut into Florio's customary margins in the smaller South Jersey counties. On the other hand, Florio combined a typical Democratic landslide performance in Essex and Hudson with surprisingly strong showings in the Shore counties of Monmouth and Ocean.

The 1997 elections seemed at first a return to type. Running for reelection, Whitman was unopposed in the GOP primary. However, she faced problems even within her own party for replacing lost tax revenue with a "borrow and spend" strategy that hugely increased the state's bond indebtedness. Botched plans to deal with the highest auto insurance rates in the nation and long waits at auto inspection stations exasperated the many voters whose love of their cars almost matched their distaste for higher taxes, and her approval ratings were sinking. Now that it was her fiscal policy rather than Jim Florio's that was at issue, the Democratic aspirants multiplied rapidly to seven, including Florio himself.

In a throwback to the past, the Democratic county chairs met in January to try to agree on a candidate, force most of the gubernatorial aspirants out of the race, spend less time and money on a bruising primary, and target Whitman from the start. The strategy failed, but by April the field was down to three, who symbolized "the battle of the county bosses" with which New Jerseyans were so familiar. The endorsed candidate of twelve counties, mostly in the northern and central parts of the state, was Woodbridge Township mayor and state senator Jim McGreevey. The other nine counties, mainly in the south and west, were behind Congressman Rob Andrews, who had followed his mentor, Jim Florio, into the U.S. House. Reflecting their traditional rivalry for gubernatorial patronage, Essex endorsed McGreevey while Hudson backed Andrews. The joker in the pack was Michael Murphy. A former state prosecutor from Morris County and stepson of the popular former governor and chief justice of the state supreme court, Richard Hughes, he had no organizational support and was not expected to affect a close race between the frontrunners. Election Day delivered the first surprise in this otherwise classic contest. It was not startling that McGreevey bested Andrews by only about five thousand votes. What was startling was the 21 percent of the vote received by Michael Murphy, who carried not only his home areas of Hunterdon and Morris, but also Mercer. It was another sign of weakening organizational strength.

As in 1993, the 1997 general election contest did not go by the usual playbook. The first peculiarity was the first third-party candidate to qualify for state matching funds, Libertarian Murray Sabrin. Sabrin was able to raise enough money through a national direct mail effort to Libertarians all over the country to qualify for public funding. This allowed him to mount a fairly serious television ad campaign and also meant that he had to be included in the three televised debates mandated by the public funding law. An economics professor at a state college, Sabrin was clearly enjoying himself and had a gift for the well-turned phrase. As a "certified" candidate and a fresh new face, the media gave him considerable coverage.

Sabrin also contributed substantially to the second interesting characteristic of the race, which was incumbent Whitman's victory by a mere twenty-six thousand votes. Receiving 5 percent of the vote statewide, Sabrin garnered twice that proportion in Hunterdon, Sussex, and Warren, cutting into the GOP margins in those counties, and did well enough in Mercer and Middlesex to turn Whitman's victories there in 1993 into routs in 1997. Whitman became the first two-term governor never to win a majority of the vote.

Thus, while not eradicating them completely, the gubernatorial elections of the 1990s had a number of twists on the usual roles of geography, candidate career ladders, the role of the county organizations, and the powers of incumbency. That left the effects of public financing and candidates who moved to the center in the general election, if not already there, as the only reliable touchstones for election analysts. In the next two gubernatorial elections, they too would be challenged.

The Republicans began 2001 assuming that New Jersey senate president Donald DiFrancesco would be their candidate. "Donnie D," as he was known in the political community, had become acting governor in 2000 after Christie Whitman resigned in 2000 to head the federal Environmental Protection Agency. Similarly, the Democrats were coalesced around Jim McGreevey, who had almost slain the incumbent dragon four years earlier. On the Republican side, DiFrancesco's only opponent for the nomination was Brett Schundler, the first GOP mayor of Jersey City since World War I. Schundler was of the populist conservative mold—an evangelical Christian who opposed legalized abortion and gun control and favored school vouchers and abolishing the tolls on the Garden State Parkway. A charismatic figure who could expect financial support from interests doing business with Jersey City and from national conservative groups, he threatened to reject public financing to avoid its primary election spending limits.[25]

The race took its first unexpected turn in April, when revelations mounted about some of DiFrancesco's questionable personal business dealings and activities as a municipal attorney. Two months before the June primary election, the acting governor withdrew from the race, ending a political career that had spanned twenty-five years in the legislature and nine years as senate president.

The GOP establishment believed that it had the perfect replacement in Bob Franks. An affable moderate who had entered politics in the 1981 Kean campaign, Franks had previously served in the state legislature, the House of Representatives, and as chair of the Republican State Committee. In a run for the U.S. Senate in 2001, he lost narrowly to the Democrats' Jon Corzine, who outspent him ten to one. Franks had more recognition among primary voters than most gubernatorial challengers, proven abilities as a statewide campaigner, and the ability to raise money quickly. The party leaders in twenty of the twenty-one counties had supported DiFrancesco against Schundler, and nineteen of those twenty fell in line behind Franks.[26]

In a poll of registered Republicans a month before the June primary, Franks led Schundler by almost two to one. It was, therefore, astonishing to almost everybody when days before the primary election the same polling organization found the race to be a dead heat, with the Jersey City mayor actually ahead among the most likely voters by 54 to 39 percent.[27] Schundler went on to win by a 57 to 43 percent margin. Although he handily carried his home county of Hudson (not exactly a powerhouse in GOP primaries) and Franks took his home county of Union, the conventional geographic explanations otherwise went by the boards. In addition to Union, Franks won only four counties in the south. Schundler triumphed in all the others, including the genteel "hunt country" in Hunterdon, Somerset, and Morris, and had a big victory in Bergen, which alone produced about 10 percent of the total vote.

The key reason for his victory was his ability to mobilize the party's conservative activists, who had long felt shut out and patronized by the moderate GOP hierarchy, and to do so with the first widespread and imaginative use of the Internet. In the year preceding the election, Schundler amassed an "e-army" of thirty-five thousand supporters who were linked to the campaign by e-mail and received daily talking points, press coverage, and contact information for conservative talk radio programs. He was also the first candidate to raise significant campaign donations eligible for state matching funds over the Internet, garnering one hundred thousand dollars in this fashion.

Thus the GOP victor seemed an oddity in modern New Jersey politics—an articulate and proudly conservative ideologue with no discernible geographic base, and mayor of a premier Democratic-voting city. As Schundler faced Jim McGreevey, it remained to be seen how this persona would be greeted by the more than two million voters in general elections as opposed to the three hundred thousand or so who participated in the GOP primary.

In November, Jim McGreevey defeated Brett Schundler by a convincing 56 to 42 percent margin. In the most basic sense, geography remained an important variable in the general election, as both candidates did best in their bedrock counties. McGreevey garnered at least 60 percent of the vote in Camden, Essex, Mercer, Middlesex Union, and Hudson, where he dealt Jersey City's mayor a crushing two-to-one defeat. Schundler came close to 60 percent in Hunterdon and Sussex but did not do as well in other traditionally Republican territory. He lost in both Monmouth and Ocean, and ran significantly behind the usual Republican vote in Morris, Somerset, and Warren.

Schundler's loss brought into sharp relief the heretofore muted conflict between the moderate Republicans who dominated the party hierarchy and the growing number of grassroots conservatives who shared the views of the national party's dominant wing. The state's conservatives had produced GOP gubernatorial primary victors before, but only in races with virtually assured Democratic winners.

The 2005 gubernatorial campaign season began for activists even before the votes were counted in the 2004 federal elections. It appeared that it would echo 2001, in that the Democrats would once again be represented by a presumptive nominee, the incumbent governor, and the Republicans would face an internecine battle for the winner of the June 2005 primary. These expectations proved to be the case only on the Republican side, but with its own new twists.

Beginning with the Democrats, Governor McGreevey threw the race into turmoil with his announcement in August 2004 that he would resign in the fall because of his extramarital affair with another man. Surveys indicated that being a "gay American," as he described himself in his resignation speech, would not have been fatal in tolerant New Jersey. Rather, McGreevey's falling approval ratings prior to his announcement were related to widespread corruption charges in his inner circle. These included awarding his male friend well-paid positions for which he had no apparent qualifications. McGreevey was replaced for the last fifteen months of his term by Richard Codey, the state senate president.

It was then assumed that like DiFrancesco before him, Codey would choose to run for a full term in 2005. However, this scenario was disrupted when U.S. Senator Jon Corzine announced his candidacy. Corzine, who had spent more than sixty million dollars of his own personal fortune to win the Senate race in 2000, and bestowed millions on county party organizations, was prepared to forgo public funding and once again self-finance his campaign. Codey, who would remain in the second most powerful office in the state if he did not run for governor, withdrew, and Corzine entered the Democratic primary virtually unopposed.

Corzine's move did not dissuade seven Republicans from seeking their party's gubernatorial nomination. They were led by Brett Schundler, undeterred by his general-election defeat in 2001. His principal opponent was Doug Forrester, the former mayor of suburban West Windsor in Democratic Mercer County, who had run and lost to Frank Lautenberg in the 2002 U.S. Senate contest. From the perspective of the beleaguered

Republicans, now shut out of control of the governorship, both houses of the legislature, and the campaign contributions that flow to the majority party, Forrester had two persuasive claims to the nomination. He promised to wage his campaign with his personal fortune, and he was not Brett Schundler.

The traditional regional flavor of Republican gubernatorial primary campaigns before 2001 was largely absent. Three of the other six candidates were from Bergen County and two from Morris County. Between them, Forrester and Schundler carried all but one of the twenty-one counties and garnered about two-thirds of the total vote.[28] Forrester prevailed with 36 percent of the vote to Schundler's 31 percent. Analysts ascribed Forrester's victory to the record ten million dollars he spent, primarily on television advertising, and the conviction of some GOP primary voters that Schundler could not win a general election. Another factor in the outcome, however, was the presence on the ballot of Steve Lonegan. Mayor of the small Bergen County town of Bogota, Lonegan shared almost all of Schundler's issue positions and indeed had been one of his key supporters in 2001.[29] His twenty-four thousand votes were more than the margin of Schundler's loss to Forrester.

The battle of the self-financed millionaires ended in November when Corzine triumphed with just over 55 percent of the vote, and Forrester ran only about 2 percent ahead of Schundler's 2001 showing. Corzine bested his percentages in the 2000 Senate race in twenty counties, and carried twelve. Forrester ran ahead of Schundler in the GOP heartland—Hunterdon, Morris, Somerset, Sussex, and Warren—and narrowly carried the Shore counties of Monmouth and Ocean, which Schundler had lost four years earlier.

This performance was not nearly enough to withstand the tidal wave of Corzine votes in Democratic bastions. Corzine supporters in just Essex and Hudson—both of which awarded him three-quarters of their vote—were greater in number than Forrester votes cast in all of the five Republican banner counties. The Democrat's vote total in the swing counties of Bergen and Burlington offset almost exactly Forrester's showing in the two large Shore counties.

The elections of the past three decades show that few counties are impregnable for the local "minority party" candidate, even in governor's races. However, regionalism still makes some more difficult than others. Any Democrat will find the far northwestern counties very tough going, and any Republican will have major obstacles in Camden, Essex, and Hudson. Bergen, the most populous county, remains a crucial battleground. Kean and Whitman both carried it twice for the Republicans; Schundler and Forrester were less fortunate.

Legislative Contests

If gubernatorial elections still somewhat reflect old regional partisan lines, one might expect that contests for the state legislature would be even more likely to show these patterns. To some extent they do, although even at this level the candidate-centered campaign has taken hold and incumbency has become a significant factor.

In postwar legislative elections prior to the mid-1970s, the "usual suspects" were arrayed in familiar patterns. The Shore counties and most of the northwest fell firmly in the Republican column; the "railroad counties" constituting the spine between New York and Philadelphia, led by Hudson, were the areas of Democratic strength. From the mid-1970s to 1991, there was a Democratic trend. Five counties moved from the competitive or Democratic to Democratic or strong Democratic categories, and four more shifted from Republican categories into the competitive range. The only countertrend was in the northwest, with Sussex becoming even more strongly Republican, and Warren moving almost all the way from Democratic to strong Republican.

To some extent, these changes reflected underlying shifts in partisan strength. Increased Democratic voting in Atlantic, Camden, and Essex was a product of growing black populations. Bergen gained a large number of liberal New Yorkers, who moved to huge apartment complexes on the Palisades with spectacular views of the New York skyline and easy access to the city. The Republican shift in Warren (the one northwestern county that had been historically Democratic) resulted from the declining vote share of the county's single urban center of Phillipsburg (hometown of former Governor Meyner) and the growth of exurban development in that county. More important for these legislative races than underlying partisan changes, however, was the impact of gubernatorial elections in the later period.

Most of the earlier period just described consists of years when county organizations controlled nominations and practiced rotation in office. But when districts crossed county lines as a result of *Reynolds v. Sims*, legislative candidates had to construct personal organizations. With county organizations less of a factor, the legislative vote began more strongly to reflect gubernatorial landslides and, somewhat later, the effects of incumbency.

We can demonstrate this by looking at the statistical relationship between the gubernatorial vote and the assembly vote since 1969. Between 1969 and 1981, there was a consistent relationship between the governor's vote and the total vote for his party's assembly candidates. For every 1 percent of the vote over 50 percent the governor received, the total assembly vote over 50 percent for his party increased by one-half of 1 percent. Each 1 percentage point increase in the statewide partisan assembly vote resulted in three additional legislative seats. For example, Governor Byrne's 67 percent landslide in 1973 produced a total Democratic assembly vote of 58 percent, and the Democrats captured sixty-six of the eighty assembly seats. Many independents and Republicans who chose the Democratic gubernatorial candidate chose Democratic assembly candidates as well.

In contrast, the Kean and Florio landslide victories of 1985 and 1989 illustrated the continued but declining power of gubernatorial coat tails in assembly voting. Kean's 70 percent share of the vote should, in accord with past voting patterns, have resulted in 60 percent of the assembly vote for his party, and 70 seats. Instead, Republican assembly candidates received 57.5 percent of the total vote and only fifty seats. By the previously established formula, 57.5 percent of the vote should have produced sixty-two or sixty-three seats rather than fifty.[30] In 1989, Florio's 62 percent share should have produced 56 percent of the total assembly vote for the Democrats, and fifty-eight seats; the Democrats won only 53 percent of the vote and forty-four seats. Beginning in the 1990s, the relationship broke down completely, as in each election legislative incumbents in both parties did substantially better than the model would have predicted. Indeed, despite Governor McGreevey's 40 percent approval rating, by running on local issues his party picked up six seats in the 2003 midterm election, the first time the majority party had done so in fifty years.

In the early 1970s, Neal Peirce, writing of New Jerseyans' fondness for incumbents, noted, "Only state legislators, more faceless and thus nameless to the general public, tend to get shunted in and out of office rapidly in Jersey. It may be that those fickle suburban voters, once they get the name of an officeholder in their heads, simply vote the familiar until some cataclysmic event propels them to change their habits."[31] In the case of legislators, at the time Peirce wrote, being on the wrong side of a gubernatorial landslide was a sufficiently "cataclysmic event" to get them dislodged from office. By the 1980s, they were well on their way to achieving the incumbency effects pioneered by their legislative brethren in the U.S. House.

The prisms of census data and election returns explain many aspects of New Jersey's politics. But as the failure of long-accurate models to predict statewide election outcomes shows us, it can only be fully understood by also studying the attitudes and opinions of its voters. That is our next subject.

CHAPTER 5

Voters, Elections, and Parties

Attack of the Human ATM machine.

—journalist's description of
Jon Corzine's 2000 Senate campaign

IN AN ERA of "negative political campaigns," those in New Jersey are state of the art. Consider the strategies of the 2005 gubernatorial candidates. U.S. Senator Jon Corzine opposed Republican Doug Forrester, who in 2002 had lost to Frank Lautenberg in his bid to join Corzine in Washington as New Jersey's other U.S. senator. The campaign illustrated New Jersey swing voters' most pronounced qualities—prickly sensitivities about the state and its politicians' motivations; pragmatism and independence; low levels of political knowledge; a tendency to make judgments based on candidates' personal qualities; and last-minute voting decisions.

As the campaign season began, Democratic state senate president Richard Codey, who began serving as acting governor in November 2004 after the resignation of Jim McGreevey, was expected to run for a full term. New Jerseyans' judgment of Senator Corzine's performance was also positive, but more modestly so. Yet Corzine had advantages in a primary contest with Codey. In January 2005, after more than two months as the state's chief executive, 35 percent of registered voters still did not recognize Codey's name, and 44 percent of those who did were unable to offer an opinion of his job performance. By April—six weeks before the primary—22 percent still said they did not know who he was.

In contrast, in both January and April, 90 percent could identify Corzine, and only one-quarter could not evaluate his performance in office. The senator also enjoyed a 44 to 30 percent lead over Codey among poll respondents who reported voting in a recent Democratic primary.[1] Finally, Corzine had the endorsement of Democratic county leaders thanks to the millions he had contributed to their party coffers, as well as that of the statewide Black Ministers' Council, who received two million dollars from the senator that year. Lacking the support these organizations could supply in a primary and the sixty-two million dollars of his own money that Corzine had spent on his Senate victory, Codey decided not to run.

Because of his previous campaign for the U.S. Senate, by April, 80 percent of voters also recognized Forrester's name. However, name recognition was the extent of many voters' knowledge. Although four out of five of his potential constituents said that they had heard of Forrester, half of those were unable to say whether their view of him was positive or negative.[2]

The candidates kept a relatively low profile over the summer, largely reacting to unflattering press reports. Democrats charged that Forrester's insurance company, which did business with many municipal and county governments, had made illegal campaign contributions to Republican candidates over the years. Corzine had to deal with the revelation that he had forgiven a "loan" of $470,000 to a former romantic interest so that she could cancel a house mortgage. The woman, Carla Katz, happened to be president of the largest state employees' union local. Perhaps fortunately for the candidates, many voters were still not paying attention to the race.

The focus of both campaigns became more apparent in September. Polls showed that the major issue on voters' minds was their ever-increasing property taxes—the highest in the nation—followed by concern over corruption involving members of the McGreevey administration and Democratic county officials and party leaders. Forrester pledged that he would lower local property taxes 30 percent over three years and bring an end to the scandals. Corzine at first focused on these two issues as well, promising ethics reform and his own tax plan. He maintained a lead of about 20 points over Forrester into the early fall, but the independents who determine statewide election outcomes were still mostly undecided.

Corzine reintroduced himself to voters who knew his name but not much about him by first airing a sixty-second biographical ad. It recounted how from humble beginnings in rural Illinois he had moved to New Jersey, become the head of a premier investment bank, and was elected to the United States Senate. He had "lived the American dream," the ad said, but never forgotten his roots. A second ad extolling his fights in Congress to adjust the federal tax code in favor of the middle class and families with children soon followed. Both messages conveyed to New Jerseyans that the multimillionaire candidate was at heart "one of you." As long as his lead held up, Corzine could run a positive campaign.

Forrester faced a more challenging situation. In two months, he had to introduce himself to an electorate that knew little about him and, given the Democrats' substantial advantage in party registration and identification, provide independents and some Democrats with a reason to vote for him rather than for Corzine. His first two TV ads addressed these problems. One featured a group of dissident Democrats expressing their support for Forrester because of their disgust with high taxes and official corruption. The other, hailed as one of the most effective ads of any political season, featured Forrester's wife, Andrea. Seated in her living room as soft music played, she confided to viewers, "I want to tell you about the Doug Forrester I know. We met in sixth grade and just celebrated our thirtieth wedding anniversary. What is Doug like? Well, he's compassionate, honest, and has a great sense of humor. And nothing's more important to Doug than our family. The politicians in New Jersey have really let us down: the corruption, the deception. But Doug is going to change that. He'll be a breath of fresh air. He'll never let New Jersey families down, because he never let ours down."

This ad did several things effectively at the same time. It espoused the family values so important to Forrester's base, particularly conservative Republicans. It homed in on the official corruption that was a major concern of independent voters. It finessed his lack of political experience by concentrating on his personal traits rather than his limited public service. And although Republicans denied it, many thought it also implied a comparison with his opponent. It was a reminder that in 2002, after thirty-three years of marriage, Jon Corzine had divorced the woman he met in grade school, become romantically involved with the president of a state employees' union, and given her a half-million-dollar gift. If the Forrester ad was subtle, another running at the same time on the cable news networks was not. Sponsored by Taxpayers for Change, an independent group including Brett Schundler's campaign manager, it urged its listeners to "tell Jon Corzine that bribing union officials is wrong."

Soon after Andrea Forrester began appearing on New Jersey's television screens, the race began to tighten, and the Corzine camp felt compelled to begin its own "comparative" advertising. Polls during mid-October showed that Forrester had cut Corzine's margin to single digits. The state's volatile swing voters are famed for their late decisions and tendency to surge in one direction in the last days of campaigns. Both campaigns pursued them with a barrage of negative advertising, spending seventeen million dollars in the last three weeks of October to remind those still undecided what they didn't like about "the other guy."

The most attention-getting Forrester ad depicted Corzine at the center of a twirling roulette wheel, surrounded by pictures of Democrats implicated in the corruption scandals. Labels on the pictures such as "now in prison" and "payoff" helpfully cued viewers about their nefarious deeds. The opposition's retort was to tie Forrester ever more tightly to the culturally conservative positions of President Bush and the congressional Republicans, which were anathema to two-thirds of the state's voters. Their most discussed ad featured a quadriplegic former star high school athlete in a wheelchair who, looking directly into the camera said, "Doug Forrester doesn't support embryonic stem cell research. Therefore I don't think he supports people like me and doctors who say a cure is coming." Another Corzine message reminded voters that the allegedly corruption-fighting Forrester was enmeshed in "fraud" charges related to his insurance company's business with county and local governments.

Both campaigns also trotted out their most iconic supporters to attest to their candidate's worth. Former Republican governor Tom Kean, fresh off his stint as co-chair of the 9-11 Commission (National Commission on Terrorist Attacks Upon the United States), whose best-selling report was critical of the Bush administration, told voters, "Like me, Doug is his own man. He's a moderate who supports a woman's right to choose. And Doug Forrester is one of the most honorable men I've ever known." Former president Bill Clinton applauded Corzine's leadership and reminded them that the Democrat had fought in the Senate against everything that the unpopular national Republicans represented.

As the contest entered its final week, Corzine appeared to be the winner of the war of words, with most polls showed his margin widening. Media coverage began to focus on the extraordinary nastiness of the campaign, of which the worst was still to come. Less than a week before the election, the *New York Times* published lengthy profiles of the candidates. The Corzine analysis incorporated statements from an interview with his former wife, including her reaction to watching Andrea Forrester's paean to her husband: "When I saw the campaign ad where [she] said, 'Doug never let his family down and he won't let New Jersey down,' all I could think was that Jon did let his family down, and he'll probably let New Jersey down, too."[3]

Buried three-quarters of the way down a three-thousand-word piece, this observation attracted much more media attention than earlier and longer comments in the article about Ms. Corzine's distaste for the Democratic bosses and her ex-husband's relations with them, which were "old news." Responding to reporters' questions that evening, Forrester said that his opponent's marital problems were not a public issue and did not belong in the campaign. By the next day, however, a fifteen-second Forrester commercial was blanketing the airwaves. It laid out Ms. Corzine's observations in white letters against a black background with no sound track, and ended any possibility of an issue-oriented end to the campaign. When the candidates met on Saturday for their final televised debate, the media reportage about the candidates' bickering over the propriety of the ad overshadowed any discussion of its substantive content.

Three days later, New Jersey voters went to the polls and elected Jon Corzine their governor by a 9-percentage-point margin. The most expensive race in New Jersey history, in which the candidates had spent seventy-three million dollars of their own money, had another distinction: the lowest voter turnout ever for a gubernatorial election.

THE CONTEXT OF PUBLIC OPINION: IMAGES AND ISSUES

When native son Samuel Alito was being coached for his U.S. Supreme Court confirmation hearings in 2006, one of the participants in the exercise approvingly said of him, "He will have a couple of hairs out of place. . . . He might not wear the right color tie. He won't be tanned. He will look like he's from New Jersey, because he is. . . . That's a very useful look. . . . He's able to go toe to toe with senators, and at the same time he could be your son's Little League coach."[4] These observations again suggest New Jerseyans' view of their state and themselves: aware of New Jersey's checkered reputation, street smart, and, while cynical, perversely fond of their home. When Governor Codey asked them to send him suggestions for a new state slogan, they obliged with self-deprecating humor:

"New Jersey: You Got a Problem With That?"

"Leave Your Heart in San Francisco and Take Your Wallet to New Jersey"

"Great Place to Visit, You Just Can't Afford to Move Here"

"Most of Our Elected Officials Have Not Been Indicted"

"If Living Here Were Easy, It Would Be Another State"

"Three Quarters of the State Is Really Nice"[5]

Since 1977, Rutgers University's Eagleton Poll has conducted four more-quantitative studies of how its residents view the state.

As table 5.1 details, perceptions of the quality of life in New Jersey closely track the performance of the economy. They shot up during the boom years of the 1980s, declined in the face of the recession and the Florio tax increase in 1990, and started inching up as the economy began to expand again. Citizens did not perceive greener pastures elsewhere; in 2003, 71 percent thought New Jersey was better or the same as other states as a place to live, and only 16 percent thought it was worse. Many believed, however, that their favorable view was not widely held elsewhere: 48 percent said they thought outsiders had a negative perception of the Garden State.

For the past thirty years, three issues—the economy and taxes, education, and the environment—have dominated the list of what New Jerseyans consider to be the most important issues facing the state. Taxes lost a long-standing position at the top of public concern during the flush 1980s, and residents then focused increasingly on the environmental problems accompanying economic growth. Imposition of a huge state tax increase in the midst of recession in 1990 returned that subject to the fore. During the 1997 and 2001 gubernatorial campaigns, education was the chief concern, and, by 2005, vexation about property taxes and their link to the cost of education was back at the top of the list.

Despite the historic distaste for state taxes detailed in chapter 15 New Jerseyans grudgingly accept increases when a good case is made for

TABLE 5.1.

Percentage Rating New Jersey as a Good or Excellent Place to Live

Year	Percentage
1977	62
1980	68
1984	80
1988	78
1990	59
2003	72

SOURCE: Eagleton Polls, specified years.

them. In 1977, 57 percent agreed the state could not be run effectively without the recently passed income tax, and 56 percent approved of the 1982 increases in the sales and income taxes.[6] Unlike the wildly unpopular 1990 tax hike, both of the earlier increases were preceded by long periods of debate during which the legislature, and eventually the public, was gradually persuaded they were necessary. In 2006, when Governor Corzine proposed an increase in the sales tax, he had begun to warn residents about the reasons it might be necessary even before he was elected, and he challenged the legislature to find other solutions. In contrast to the Florio era, voters were divided over the necessity of the proposed tax hike, but, after it finally passed in July 2006, they awarded Corzine the highest approval ratings of his six months in office.[7]

The picture which thus emerges is of an electorate capable of making judgments, but difficult to reach with detailed political information and arguments. New Jerseyans know the state's major problems and are willing to use their wealth to solve them in good economic times. They are eager to shed a historical inferiority complex, especially in relation to their larger neighbors. This is the broad context in which New Jersey elections take place.

The Level of Political Knowledge

Unless candidates have run before, less than half of the voters can actually name a candidate without prompting when statewide campaigns begin. Although more claimed to have at least "some" knowledge about Governor Tom Kean in 1985 than any other candidate in the previous decade, more than two in five still said they knew little or nothing about him. As Kean ran for reelection in 1985, the state tourism agency began a heavy TV advertising campaign featuring him. Ostensibly targeted at potential vacationers, the ads ran through Election Day, concurrent with Kean's political ads. Roger Stone, one of the governor's political strategists, observed that all the TV messages were intended to "flesh out Kean. People knew him, but nothing about him."[8]

Kean's use of early media messages paid for by the state government was adopted by his successors. Jim Florio and his wife, both one-time high school dropouts, extolled the value of education. Christie Whitman made "public service" ads in which she declared, "New Jersey is open for business." Jim McGreevey and his wife praised the virtues of reading to children, and he was featured in state radio ads about traffic safety and tourism. For several months around the 2003 midterm elections, his picture took up most of the space on the homepage of the state Web site.

As campaigns progress, the electorate learns more about candidates' personal qualities than their issue positions. Candidate advertising in New Jersey, as in other places, stresses valence rather than positional issues. Positional stances "for" or "against" specific programs and policies can be electorally dangerous. The more complex or controversial the issue, the more difficult it is to lay out a reasoned position in a thirty-second ad, and the more voters the candidate may antagonize. Valence issues, in contrast, are subjects about which everyone agrees. Economic opportunity, a safe and healthy environment, and building a good future for children are all common valence issues. Campaigns emphasizing valence issues ask the voter to choose the candidate who seems most likely, based on personal qualities, to achieve desired ends.[9]

Political commentators decry "issueless" campaigns focused on valence issues, but they accord with life experience. People learn that taking a position is not enough to ensure a desired outcome; success depends on the proponent's integrity, force of personality, negotiating abilities, and resolve. Campaign messages thus do not use issues primarily to present a policy agenda, but rather to make a statement about what kind of people they or their opponents are.

In the Corzine-Forrester race, as we have seen, the advertising focused less on positional issues than on why the candidates did, or more often did not, have the personal qualities to deal with them successfully. By the end of the campaign, this strategy resulted in about half of likely voters dividing evenly on who could deal better with lowering property taxes and fighting corruption, and the other half saying "neither one" or having no opinion. About one-fifth thought that neither candidate was "honest and trustworthy." By a margin of 45 percent to 25 percent, they perceived Corzine as having more experience, and a smaller plurality chose him as the candidate who better understood "the average person" or "people like you."[10] Thus, voters did not give Corzine a policy mandate. Instead, those who did not stay home rather grudgingly chose the candidate they felt had the personal qualities to address current problems most effectively, or who shared their political party preference. But if voters cannot learn much about difficult issues from paid messages, why don't they get that information from print and television news?

THE ROLE OF THE MASS MEDIA

New Jersey's media patterns still hinder learning about state politics, even now when politicians try to be more visible and government in Trenton is doing more things of interest. New Jersey did not have a commercial VHF television channel licensed to the state until 1984.[11] It finally gained (from New York City) WWOR-Channel 9, an independent station that later successively became part of the UPN, WB, and CW networks. WWOR maintains offices as close to New York City as possible and has no full-time Trenton correspondent. Its evening news program covers the entire region and runs to "happy talk."[12] The station has a tangled history, having been sold three times since 1986. In the turmoil surrounding it for the past twenty years there has been one constant: it is a "New Jersey station" in name only. Its evening news broadcast ran fewer stories about the 2005 gubernatorial election than did any of the New York-based network affiliates.[13]

Coverage of New Jersey political news is also meager on New York's major network stations even during the campaign season, as studies of the coverage of the 2001 and 2005 governor's races demonstrate. Although not directly comparable, each demonstrates the paucity of information about elections available to New Jersey viewers of local news broadcasts.[14] In the thirty days preceding the 2001 election, the three most-watched New York network affiliates (ABC, CBS, and NBC) devoted 17 percent of 489 minutes of election coverage to New Jersey, despite the fact that the state's viewers made up about 30 percent of the audience, and its gubernatorial candidates bought 40 percent of campaigns' commercial time on the three stations in that period. The study of 2005 election coverage, which was based on the number of stories rather than the time allotted to them, was somewhat broader in that it also included the New York Fox network affiliate as well as WWOR and three New Jersey cable stations that emphasize news and public affairs. This analysis found that 41 percent of the election coverage on the four New York network affiliates was devoted to New Jersey, with almost all of the rest being reports on the concurrent New York mayor's race. This apparent "improvement" was presumably due to the fact that New York City Mayor Michael Bloomberg faced little meaningful opposition in 2005.

Beginning in the 1990s, however, other broadcast options appeared for those seeking New Jersey news, and many of its media organizations underwent a major shakeup. The emergence of a radio station calling itself New Jersey 101.5 (WKXW-FM) was the first noteworthy development. Based in Trenton, its signal reaches north to Bergen County. In 1990, WKXW changed its format to call-in segments on New Jersey affairs, trumpeting itself as "Proud to be New Jersey!" The change catapulted it from seventh to first place in Arbitron's Trenton market ratings, and it became the nerve center of the statewide tax revolt. Talk-show emcees broadcast the telephone numbers of protest leaders, whipped up attendance at mass demonstrations in the capital, and played host to Governor Florio, who identified himself as "Jim from Drumthwacket"—New Jersey's governor's mansion. Still the state's top-rated station, 101.5 is also still involved in political controversy, most often generated by the "Jersey Guys," who host the station's evening drive-time program. In the past few years, they have caused an uproar with vulgar comments about Asian Americans in general and a Korean mayoral candidate in Edison Township in particular and made fun of Governor Codey's wife's bouts with depression. A campaign urging listeners to turn in illegal immigrants was introduced with mariachi music and scheduled to end on the Mexican holiday of Cinco de Mayo. Not surprisingly, the general public's sympathy is usually with the Jersey Guys' targets.

As cable TV and access to the Internet became ubiquitous, other news sources emerged. New Jersey Public Television (NJN) had for many years aired an award-winning nightly news program and other public affairs shows on four regional UHF stations that were difficult to access without powerful antennas. The state's political activists were attentive viewers, but these UHF stations in a VHF-dominated market drew minuscule audiences. As cable penetration became prevalent and the UHF–VHF distinction almost meaningless, NJN programming became more accessible, and it is now estimated that about 110,000 households watch its evening news program.[15] The growing cable audience potential produced a commercial competitor to NJN in 1996, when Cablevision established News 12 New Jersey. News 12 is a 24/7 news station whose slogan is "as local as local news gets."

Four years later, in 2000, the Web site PoliticsNJ.com was launched. This site offers in-depth reportage and commentary, as well as links to the coverage of politics and government in all of the state's daily newspapers. According to its operators, by 2006 the site was receiving four million hits per month. This impressive figure, however, should be considered in tandem with their estimate that PoliticsNJ attracts about forty thousand individual regular visitors, and more than twenty thousand who read it every day. They include New Jersey's political players at all levels of government but, like the cable news and weekend public affairs programs on NJN and News 12, PoliticsNJ barely makes a dent in the general population.

Serious students of politics and policy can also call up the Web sites of think tanks of all ideological persuasions and browse the links on the state's Web page to every institution and agency of state government. But for the average citizen, New Jersey remains "a newspaper state in a television world."[16] About half the population says they rely on the print press for "most of their information about politics and public affairs," as opposed to less than one-third who cite television.[17]

As recently as the mid-1980s, New Jerseyans could read twenty-six daily newspapers, compared with nineteen two decades later. A telling characteristic of New Jersey newspapers is that most do not have locational mastheads. As the population moved out of the cities into the burgeoning suburbs, the *Newark Star-Ledger* became the *Star-Ledger*; the *New Brunswick Home News* became the *Home News Tribune*, and so on. These papers now cover surrounding suburbs more heavily than they cover their original places of publication.

Three chains (Newhouse, Gannett, and Macromedia) control three-quarters of daily newspaper circulation. The leading organ by far is the Newhouse flagship paper, the *Star-Ledger*.[18] It ranks sixteenth in circulation among all newspapers in the country, commands over one-third of the newspaper readership in the state, and is the first or second most frequently read paper in eleven of the fourteen counties in central and northern New Jersey. The *Ledger*, as it is familiarly known, has enjoyed this status for the past three decades, but it is a very different paper now than it was through the mid-1990s.

In 1995, editor Mort Pye, who had joined the *Ledger* in 1957, retired. Pye was noted for preaching state boosterism, providing exhaustive coverage of state politics and government at every level, exchanging the paper's uncritical support of the political establishment for the promise of "scoops," and endorsing incumbent officeholders. Some veteran reporters of the Pye era, particularly on the important education and environmental beats, were regarded as extremely influential. Beat reporters frequently wrote multipart, front-page series on current issues. The drumbeat was taken up on the editorial page, and action, or at least talk, followed in Trenton. With Pye's departure and the arrival of Jim Willse, former editor of the tabloid *New York Daily News*, the *Ledger* acquired a new look and tone. Trendy graphics and color photographs replaced staid typography, and the editorial page took on a more liberal, critical, and populist cast. Although the paper no longer reports on every planning board meeting in its coverage area, the many full-time reporters in the *Ledger's* Trenton bureau make up nearly one-third of the entire statehouse press corps, allowing for considerable specialization.[19] Although some of the *Ledger's* statehouse coverage appears in the other six Newhouse dailies, it has been the chain's style to run the papers as separate newsroom and editorial board entities.

At about the same time as the *Ledger* shakeup, a major competitor was emerging in central and southern New Jersey. After a brief period of local newspapers there merging with each other, the Gannett chain bought several of them. From owning only two papers in the 1980s, which had less than 7 percent of the state's total circulation, Gannett acquired five more, and its seven dailies now draw one-quarter of New Jersey's newspaper readership.[20] Gannett's flagship paper, the *Asbury Park Press*, circulates primarily in Monmouth and Ocean counties, and has about one-third of the circulation of the *Ledger*.

Before Gannett acquired the papers in 1997, some of them had banded together to establish a highly regarded statehouse bureau that rivaled that of the *Ledger* in size and influence. The chain was noted for making deep staff cuts after such takeovers, and in short order it established a single statehouse bureau for all seven papers with fewer than half the reporters they had individually fielded. Circulation of the flagship *Asbury Park Press* plummeted as Gannett cut back on news in favor of features and revenue-generating tactics like publishing paid obituaries of both people and their pets. In 2002, a new editor, William "Skip" Hidlay, arrived at the *Press*, and set about branding the paper as a champion of investigative journalism. His novel strategy was to assign reporters from all of the Gannett papers to work together on important regional or statewide stories, which were then distributed on the chain's newswire.[21]

The last major local player in the New Jersey newspaper world is the Macromedia group, which publishes *The Record*, a Bergen County-based paper, and the *Herald News* of Passaic County. With 11 percent of the circulation in the state, largely confined to the two populous northern counties where it dominates, its readership is equivalent to that of the *Asbury Park Press*. It supports a statehouse bureau equal in size to that of the Gannett chain.

Finally, about 10 percent of New Jersey's newspaper circulation is claimed by the *New York Times*, which is the fourth most frequently read news organ in the state. In fifth place at 5 percent is the *Philadelphia Inquirer*. The *New York Times* is among the most widely read newspapers in Bergen, Mercer, Morris, and Somerset counties, while the *Philadelphia Inquirer* enjoys a similar position in the southern counties of Burlington, Camden, Gloucester, and Salem. The circulation these two out-of-state papers command is magnified by the wealth and influence of their readership.[22]

The changes in the media landscape have both helped and hindered citizens' understanding of state politics and policy. The changes in editor-ship have brought more hard-hitting journalistic inquiry, whose quantity and quality are new to the state. Consolidation has produced sizable bureaus that are highly competitive and have the resources to pursue stories. Since 2001, the *Star-Ledger* has twice won Pulitzer Prizes, the first in its history. Its 2005 award honored the paper's coverage of Governor McGreevey's abrupt resignation. An influential series of investigative articles produced by the Gannett chain, titled "Profiting from Public Service: How Many N.J. Legislators Exploit the System," won numerous prizes, including the Asso-ciated Press Managing Editors award for public service, besting entries from the *Washington Post* and the *Los Angeles Times*. Consisting of seventy-two articles published over eight days in September 2003, and taken up for discussion by New Jersey 101.5's shock jocks, it was credited with defeat-ing several legislators in that year's elections, including the copresident of the state senate.

If there is a downside to this new style of journalism, it is its unrelieved attention to scandal and the misdeeds, alleged or real, of political personal-ities. During the 2005 gubernatorial campaign, countless newspaper stories reiterated that the voters' top concern was the state's high local property taxes, and that both major candidates had plans to lower them. Most often these articles offered "he said/he said" reportage about the two tax plans, frequently in the context of the five televised debates. But in contrast to the frequent articles fully describing the negative TV ads and analyzing their veracity, there was little analytic coverage of the competing tax proposals or their likely effects.[23]

CHANGING PATTERNS OF PARTISAN IDENTIFICATION

Just as New Jersey voters often know little about candidates initially, candidates face uncertainty about voters. The clearest finding in table 5.2 is the volatility in self-reported party identification over time.

Between the early 1980s and the early 1990s, the GOP erased a 10 percentage point lead for the Democrats and achieved virtual parity. By 2002, the Democrats had regained a 10 point lead. The initial shift toward the Republicans did not occur evenly throughout the electorate. Among certain groups—whites, Catholics, those aged eighteen to twenty-nine, and those in blue-collar occupations, the number of self-identified Republicans at least doubled. It was some of the members of the same demographic groups whose return to the Democratic fold ended party parity.

Catholics, who had split 32 percent to 27 percent in favor of the GOP in 1995, preferred the Democrats by 36 percent to 21 percent by 2002. Those aged eighteen to twenty-nine reversed course even more dramatically. In 1995 the Republican margin in this group was 34 percent to 19 percent, while in 2002 38 percent called themselves Democrats and only 22 percent identified with the Republicans.[24] Even whites, who are the most Republican of the standard demographic groups, shifted 5 points more Democratic. Since 2002, these volatile groups' partisan leanings have at times moved a few points away from the Democrats, but that movement has been toward the independent column rather than toward the GOP.

These are the swing voters in the suburbs. They are middle-middle class residents of the older suburbs, the sort of voters political strategists refer to as "Joe Six-Pack." Democratic voter-contact specialist Barry Brendel characterizes them as belonging primarily to two groups. The first holds skilled blue-collar jobs, are mostly Catholic, of Italian and East European extraction,

TABLE 5.2.
Party Identification in New Jersey (by percentage)

	1971	1978	1985	1992	2002
Democrat	30	35	32	27	35
Republican	20	19	26	28	24
Independent	38	40	38	34	30
Other, don't know	12	6	4	10	5

SOURCE: Eagleton Polls, relevant years.

and over forty-five. The second are their children—often more affluent, but not wealthy. They work at white-collar middle-management jobs, play golf on public courses, and worry about being able to afford housing in the towns where they grew up.[25] The swing vote (and for that matter much of the partisan vote) is not notably ideological. During the Republicans' political high watermark in the mid-1990s, 54 percent of all New Jerseyans said they were neither liberal nor conservative but "somewhere in between," and that figure has changed little in the more recent period of Democratic dominance. On average, Democratic identifiers have been about 10 points more likely to be among the one-fifth of New Jerseyans who call themselves liberals, but usually about twice as many of them fall into the "in between" category. In contrast, Republican identifiers have been about 20 points more likely than the one-fourth of voters in the 1990s, and the one-fifth since then, who say they are conservatives.[26]

Since the independents who decide elections are more likely to place themselves in the moderate or "somewhere in between" category than the general population, successful candidates in statewide elections must devise campaign themes that appeal to them, rather than appealing to political philosophy or party loyalty. Certain types of issues and images—those that are mainstream and pragmatic and without strong ideological baggage—are the most persuasive. As we shall see, for the past two decades this has posed a particular dilemma for Republican candidates.

THE EFFECT OF CONTEXT ON STATE ELECTIONS

Low levels of political information, the unique media environment, lingering sensitivities about New Jersey's image, a changing issue mix, high levels of political independence, and weak party ties have many effects on election contests. All other things being equal, they advantage incumbent and moderate candidates. They also make competitive races very expensive and often centered on personal and negative themes.

Advantaged Candidates

With strong partisanship in decline and a media climate that makes it difficult for newcomers to become known, voters usually choose the only candidates they have heard much about—the incumbents. The incumbency advantage feeds on itself. Challengers who might have run in the past because they enjoyed party organization support or sensed an advantage from the trends of the times are more loath to do so now.[27] They know how difficult it is to defeat an incumbent. Consequently, many incumbents do not face their strongest potential challengers.

Like challengers, most candidates who think of themselves or can be painted by their opponents as cultural conservatives face an uphill battle. New Jersey voters who call themselves "something in between" conservative and liberal tend to be moderate or conservative on economic issues (particularly taxes) but liberal on social issues. Decisive majorities favor legalized abortion, embryonic stem cell research, environmental regulation, gun control, and rights for homosexuals. Charges of cultural conservatism are not a problem for Democrats, whose statewide candidates are usually perceived as the moderates even their own partisans prefer. GOP governors Tom Kean (1982–1990) and Christie Whitman (1994–2001), the only Republicans to win statewide office since the 1980s, were also seen as the kind of moderates that the majority of New Jerseyans consider themselves to be.

For the past three decades, however, almost all of the other GOP candidates seeking to represent the entire state have had to grapple with this ideological problem, which begins when they seek nomination. Republican identifiers, who are presently greatly outnumbered by Democrats and independents, are considerably more conservative than the population as a whole. Their grassroots activists, who comprise a disproportionate proportion of primary voters, incline even more to the right. Sometimes this results in the nomination of avowed conservatives like 2001 gubernatorial candidate Brett Schundler, who was pilloried in the general election campaign for his pro-life and pro-gun positions and who lost decisively.

More often, the Republican nominee is a relative moderate who has to move to the right to succeed in the primary election and encounters trouble finding the way back to the center in the general election. Doug Forrester, the GOP candidate for both the U.S. Senate in 2002 and the governorship in 2005, is an example. His campaign spending, the presence of six other candidates, and sufficiently "correct" positions on cultural issues allowed him to defeat Bret Schundler in the 2005 GOP primary. When the results were known, conservative assemblyman Guy Gregg, a Schundler supporter, observed, "This group that ran in 2005 may have been the most conservative we've had in a primary. . . . The difference is that we'd normally have one purist in the race and a couple of other Republicans who might call themselves conservatives. This race had everyone trying to be Bret."[28]

By late October however, after Forrester had accepted the endorsement of Republican Majority for Choice, a GOP group which supported
a woman's right to abortion, the schisms in the party broke out once again.
Steve Lonegan, the most conservative of his primary opponents, told the
Star-Ledger, "I was going to keep biting my tongue, but this is just off the
charts. . . . You can't spit in our faces." The organizer of the endorsement
press conference, a Republican moderate, responded, "Corzine wants to
scare people into thinking that Doug Forrester is not a mainstream Republican. These are mainstream New Jersey values and Doug represents those values."[29] Conservative activists in the GOP are convinced that their candidates
lose statewide general elections because the party's moderate establishment
abandons them. The party's moderates and most commentators believe they
lose because they are too conservative for New Jersey.[30]

Some even argue that until the national party adopts a more moderate
face, no one in New Jersey with a Republican label can be elected
statewide. In 2006, running unsuccessfully for the U.S. Senate, a centrist
Republican with a revered name—Tom Kean Jr.—did all he could to distance himself from his national party. He called for the resignation of
Defense Secretary Donald Rumsfeld and even arranged to show up at a
fund-raiser featuring Vice President Cheney after Cheney had left so that
he would not be photographed with him. In the wake of Republican congressional ethics scandals, he painted his opponent, Bob Menendez, as the
ethically challenged candidate in the race. Three weeks before the election,
a Democratic campaign poll asked likely voters "which generic candidate
they would prefer: A Democrat with some baggage on ethics—or a
Republican who usually supports President Bush. The verdict was over-
whelming. By a margin of 54 to 31, the voters of New Jersey preferred the
slippery Democrat."[31]

Campaigns and Money in New Jersey

Substitution of money-intensive campaign technology for labor-
intensive party organizations accounts for the hyperinflation of campaign
costs in New Jersey and began in federal races. The combined expenditures
of $16 million by the 1988 candidates for the U.S. Senate raised eyebrows.
No one could then foresee the $70 million contest of 2000, in which Demo-
crat Jon Corzine self-financed a campaign in which he outspent his opponent by ten to one. It was by far the most expensive such race in U.S. history.
In the somewhat more normal U.S. Senate election of 2002, combined

major party spending totaled $20 million, which at the time was the second most expensive campaign ever waged for that office.[32] A hotly contested House race in 1990 saw combined spending of more than $2.5 million. By 2006, in the most competitive such race thereafter, that figure doubled.

Relatively speaking, public financing used to make gubernatorial races less spendthrift. Starting with the 1977 election, New Jersey became the first state to adopt public financing of gubernatorial campaigns.[33] Its goals were to remove special interests and their money from gubernatorial elections, allow candidates of modest means to run credible contests, and keep a realistic cap on spending. As with the federal law providing for public financing of presidential campaigns, gubernatorial candidates are not required to accept public financing and abide by spending limits, but there was a strong incentive to do so. Until 2005, all the major party general election candidates participated, as did almost all primary election candidates.

Originally, the public finance law covered only the general election campaign and limited each candidate to a $2.2 million spending ceiling. Candidates became eligible for public funding after raising $40,000 privately. Contributions from individuals could not exceed $600. Once a candidate became eligible, the state matched every private dollar raised on a two-to-one basis until the limit was reached. For the 1981 election, the law was amended to include public financing of party primary contests— following the same scheme as for the general election, but with a spending limit of $1.1 million. The individual contribution limit was raised to $800, and candidates were required to raise $50,000 to qualify.

By 1989, the spending caps seemed inadequate in the face of $8 million campaigns on each side in the 1988 U.S. Senate race. Even in 1985, Governor Kean's staff had indicated he might opt out of the public finance system if a serious challenge developed. There was also a growing feeling that the $50,000 trigger wasted too much of the taxpayers' money on fringe primary election candidates.

Accordingly, in 1988, the legislature (which contained several gubernatorial aspirants) raised the 1989 spending limits to $2.2 million in the primary and $5.5 million in the general election. The limit on individual contributions rose to $1,500. Candidates had to raise $150,000 to qualify for public financing, and the first $50,000 raised was exempted from the two-to-one match. Those accepting public funds were required to participate in at least two televised debates in both the primary and general elections. The state Election Law Enforcement Commission was also empowered to raise future spending caps by the inflation rate.[34] As a result, by 2005 the primary election spending limits had reached $6.4 million, and $9.6 million could be spent for the general election campaign. Candidates would now have to raise $300,000 to collect public funding, with the first $96,000 exempt from the match.

Although the new limits kept nominal costs somewhat below those for competitive U.S. Senate races, the numbers must be placed in broader perspective. In Michigan, the only other state with extensive public financing of governor's races, candidates get by with general election budgets of roughly one-third of what New Jersey provides its candidates. Michigan's population is larger, but its media markets are much cheaper. Further, a "soft money" loophole, similar to the one in presidential contests, permits New Jersey's state party committees to spend additional millions for party-building activities and generic party advertising.

Thus, the public finance law substantially understated real expenditures in gubernatorial campaigns. Despite the legal avenues for financing a campaign with significant amounts of taxpayer dollars, in the 2005 "battle of the billionaires," Jon Corzine and Doug Forrester became the first major party candidates to reject public funding and its limits since the law was passed in 1974. Now it is not clear what will happen to New Jersey's noble experiment.

Contribution limits in the gubernatorial public finance law diverted large individual and special interest contributions to legislative candidates and state party entities. Before the television and direct mail age, these contests were mostly cheap and largely invisible affairs, driven by party identification and organizations and by coattails in gubernatorial election years. By 2003, however, when the entire legislature was last up for reelection, the major party candidates spent $40 million, evenly divided between the forty-member senate and the eighty-member assembly. In the decade between 1995 and 2005, both years in which only assembly members were running, spending doubled from $10.6 million to $22 million. In four assembly districts, combined spending in 2005 exceeded $1 million. These included the second district in Camden and Atlantic counties, where the four major candidates for two seats spent $4 million—the most expensive assembly race in state history—to achieve a split partisan decision.

The spending boom followed a law that took effect in April 1993. It limited individual, corporate, and union contributions to nongubernatorial candidates to $1,500 per election (that is, $3,000 for the primary and general elections of one cycle), and political action committee (PAC) contributions to $5,000 per election (or $10,000 per election cycle). In contrast, designated party committees—the Democratic and Republican state committees, the four committees controlled by the Democratic and Republican leaders in the assembly and senate, and the forty-two Democratic and Republican county committees—could each receive $25,000 annually from any of these contributors. Most of these limits are adjusted periodically for inflation, so that by 2007 individual contribution limits to candidates for each election had risen to $2,600, PAC contributions to $7,200, and contributions to the forty-two county party committees to $37,000 each. Additionally, both individuals and PACs could still contribute $25,000 per election to the state party committees and the legislative leadership committees. Each of these party committees can make unlimited direct contributions to candidates, or expenditures on their behalf.

The intent of this legislation was to strengthen the role of the political parties versus the special interests. A by-product was to increase the fully reported and legal money flowing into legislative campaigns, and it did exactly that: total spending in legislative races increased by 40 percent from 1993 to 1997.[35] Most of the increase in 1997 occurred in senate races, where spending was up 74 percent from four years earlier, as opposed to an 8 percent increase in assembly spending. Democrats had little hope of retaking the assembly that year, but a senate takeover seemed possible. Thus large sums were expended in a few hotly contested races targeted by the state party committees and the legislative leadership, a strategy that has continued ever since. Although contributions and expenditures keep rising, the size and allocation of the increases depends on the number of seats perceived to be competitive in a given year, and where they are.

Negative Campaigns

New Jersey's expensive campaigns, we have noted, are also often negative. These phenomena are not unrelated. Statewide candidates must purchase broadcast time in the first and fourth most expensive markets in the country—New York City and Philadelphia—and it accounts for most of their expenditures. The state election law enforcement commission reports that "mass communication" has accounted for more than 80 percent of gubernatorial campaign spending since 1988. Most of this goes for TV advertising, with direct mail costs a distant second. A single thirty-second spot on a top-rated show like *60 Minutes* cost the 2006 U.S. Senate campaigns $22,000 in New York and $14,000 in Philadelphia.[36]

With only about one-third of the viewers in both media markets being New Jersey residents—the rest live in New York, Pennsylvania, Delaware, or Connecticut—there is a tremendous but unavoidable waste of candidates' resources. These costs cause television campaigns to start later than in most states. A New York buy of two ads on a top-rated program is roughly equivalent to the price of a whole week's buy in sparsely populated markets. Thus, a statewide candidate in Montana or North Dakota can be on the air for several months at less expense than a three-week buy in New York or Philadelphia.

These facts help explain New Jerseyans' low level of political knowledge and the especially negative tone of many campaigns. Voters usually "meet" statewide candidates barely two months before election day, while residents of most other states have been getting to know their aspiring officeholders and listening to their appeals much longer. Even the best-financed New Jersey candidates cannot afford a TV ad campaign that starts before mid-September, with perhaps a week or two of introductory advertising around the June primaries. Repetition is a key to effective advertising. People must hear a message several times before it sinks in. Because New Jersey campaigns start so late, candidates can transmit fewer different messages than in most other states. A well-financed campaign can only air seven or eight different messages with sufficient repetition to be assimilated, while candidates in states with cheaper media markets can run twenty or thirty different spots.

Additionally, a credible negative message penetrates a viewer's consciousness more quickly than a positive one. For positive messages to be convincing, voters must know quite a bit about candidates and be favorably disposed to them to begin with. This is rarely the case in New Jersey, particularly for challengers. The limited number of messages candidates can air tempts them to spend more time and money criticizing opponents rather than promoting themselves. With little knowledge about most political aspirants, voters are prone to accept negative information that seems to have a kernel of truth. However, they also dismiss charges that are clearly preposterous, a point often lost on the many critics of negative ads. Further, despite assertions that voter disgust with negative ads contributes to decreasing voter turnout, analysis of national turnout patterns gives this hypothesis little support.[37]

Negative advertising has also become a major factor in legislative races, where the messages more often get delivered in the mail rather than on television. Just as candidate advertising must cut through all the other advertising on TV, political direct mail must compete with the glossy catalogues from L. L. Bean or Land's End. As a California-based creator of Democratic legislative direct mail described his product, "We call it TV mail . . . Good graphics count quite a bit."[38]

Many mail pieces feature pointed personal attacks on opponents or tie them to unpopular figures. In 1991, GOP mail was shaped by the continuing suburban outrage over Governor Florio's $2.8 billion tax hike. Pieces pouring into every suburban district were almost identical, varying only in the wording tying local candidates to the tax hike and to Florio. Strategists on both sides saw the campaign environment the same way. Dave Murray, architect of the Republican mail assault, asserted, "The Republicans owe their success to Jim Florio, pure and simple. New Jersey ignored the Bush recession because Florio glowed in the dark." Democratic consultant Frank Robinson reported long discussions about a "generic" Democratic response, but concluded, "The problem was, what could we say?"[39] The tables were turned in 2005 when Democratic mail linked Republicans to George W. Bush and his hot-button stands on cultural issues.

The Role of Political Parties in Elections

For 150 years, from the emergence of the Jacksonian Democrats to the rise of television, American political parties were social formations whose organizational strength was at the state and county levels. These organizations subsisted on patronage, enjoyed a strong psychological tie to voters, chose the candidates and decided when to rotate them out of office, ran campaigns, and got the vote out.

The first blows to their dominance came in the Progressive era, with the spread of the direct primary and the civil service. Primary elections gave rise to insurgent candidates who could capture the party label from the organization's favorites. Later technological developments, from the television to the computer, allowed candidate organizations to replace most of the other functions of the traditional party organizations. In populous states like New Jersey, statewide campaigns became technologically driven. Professional political consultants and the fund-raisers who paid the consultants' bills replaced the traditional party bosses and precinct captains.

In politics as in architecture, however, form follows function. Rather than continuing to decay, what political scientist John Aldrich called "parties in service" emerged, designed around the ambitions of office seekers and their candidate-centered campaigns.[40] If technology-based mass communication was the new bedrock of campaigns, the "party in service" could raise the money to pay for it and to hire the vendors. This assistance was particularly useful for legislative candidates, more numerous and less well-known than aspirants for executive office and spread from the national to the state level. The state party system now consists of three increasingly interrelated entities, all devoted primarily to raising the money and providing or paying for professional campaign services: the legislative campaign committees; the county party committees; and the state party organizations.

THE LEGISLATIVE CAMPAIGN COMMITTEES. A key element of the party in service at both the state and national levels is the greatly magnified role of legislative campaign committees, overseen not by the party organizations but by the officeholders themselves. By the 1980s, successful candidates for the U.S. Congress gratefully accepted this assistance, but they had also become adept at raising their own money and building their own organizations. It did not take long to realize that this model could be adopted for campaigns for the state legislature, and a series of court decisions and campaign finance legislation buttressed its development.

Each of the state's leading political figures—the governor, the senate president, and the assembly speaker—now controls a separate political organization. Each has its own staff for political activities and for raising and allocating money. New Jersey is one of about twenty-five states where the leaders of the legislative party caucuses play a major role in the direction and financing of legislative campaigns, and one of perhaps a dozen where leaders' power and continuation in office depend heavily on fund-raising abilities.[41] Table 5.3 shows the expenditures of the legislative campaign committees during the last four years in which both houses were up for reelection, as well as the figures for 2005 when only the assembly stood for election.

The most obvious finding in this table is the huge increase in expenditures over time. The level of competition explains much of it, for this decade saw control of both houses and the governorship pass from the Republicans to the Democrats. In 1993, the Republicans enjoyed an almost three-to-one majority in the assembly, a two-to-one majority in the senate, and held the governorship. Donors eager for state business, advantageous legislation, and

TABLE 5.3.

*Legislative Campaign Committee Expenditures, 1993–2005
(in millions of dollars)*

	1993	1997	2001	2003	2005
Democrats					
Assembly	0.473	0.791	2,101	5,120	6,796
Senate	1,153	2,393	3,116	4,008	No election
Republicans					
Assembly	1,523	1,484	2,582	1,780	2,514
Senate	1,756	3,401	4,380	3,299	No election
Grand total	4,905	8,147	12,179	14,207	

SOURCE: New Jersey Electoral Law Enforcement Commission.

favorable regulatory decisions opened their wallets to the GOP. Strong Democratic challengers and their party were deterred by their inability to raise the money to run effective campaigns. By 1997, the GOP still had a twenty-seat edge in the lower house, and the parties' spending figures continued to reflect that. In the senate, victories in five districts would have given the Democrats a majority. In tandem with the close governor's race that outcome seemed possible, and contributors began to hedge their bets. In the event, despite the Democrats' greater spending in senate races, the GOP retained its eight-seat edge.

By 2001, the Democrats' fortunes were improving. The senate was still within reach and the Republicans' majority in the assembly had been cut in half. With the increasingly Democratic complexion of the state, a governor's race they seemed likely to win, and favorable redistricting outcomes, the Democrats were able to raise and spend much larger sums than they had four years earlier. Republicans countered this genuine threat to their ten years of legislative domination by escalating their spending as well. In their battle for control of the senate, the combined spending of the two senate legislative campaign committees almost equaled party investments in all of the legislative races in both houses in 1997. The Democrats picked up only one seat in the assembly, but fought their way to an unprecedented twenty–twenty tie in the upper house. They entered the 2003 election season with a governor of their party in control for the first time in two decades except for the four years of the Florio debacle of 1989–1993 and emerged with control of both houses.

As compared with the Republican majorities ten years earlier, the Democratic margins in both houses were much slimmer, accounting for the continued spending frenzy evident in the 2005 assembly elections. Table 5.3 also demonstrates the obstacles a party faces when it does not control any elected branch of government, as was the case for the Republicans in 1993. Although the sums involved are much larger, the Democrats' proportional advantage in 2003 was equivalent to that of the Republicans in 1993.

THE COUNTY PARTY COMMITTEES. Along with the 1993 campaign finance legislation, an important impetus to building parties of service in the states was the U.S. Supreme Court's 1989 decision in *Eu v. San Francisco*, which found California's ban on preprimary endorsements by political parties an unconstitutional infringement of the First Amendment rights of voters to free speech and free association.[42] Following the *Eu* decision, the state superior court ruled that it was applicable to New Jersey, and overturned the 1981 open primary law requiring statewide candidates (that is, for U.S. senator and governor) to run on a separate ballot line rather than on a party organization slate. The right to make preprimary endorsements also allowed party organizations to expend money on behalf of their endorsed candidates during the primary election season.

Although the state party organizations have not issued formal endorsements in state-level contests, numerous county and municipal organizations have, thus rendering legal what had long been standard practice.[43] Many counties now hold preprimary conventions that determine local endorsements and provide forums for statewide candidates seeking county support and a favored ballot position. The *Eu* decision, along with the state campaign finance law that awarded county party organizations the most generous contribution limits, brought about vastly greater fund-raising by the forty-two Democratic and Republican county party organizations. Their combined receipts of $7 million in 1993 reached $27 million in 2003—about twice the amount raised by the legislative campaign committees.

Fund-raising is up all over the state, but there are sharp variations among the counties related to the talents of the county party leadership. Bergen, Camden, Hudson, and Middlesex lead the way for the Democrats. Among the Republicans, the county organization in bucolic Burlington County is a Republican financial powerhouse, raising and spending at a similar level. Each of these county organizations raised between $2 million and $4 million in 2003. Unlike the fabled county leaders who preceded them in the first half of the twentieth century, most of those described as the powerful "bosses" in these counties do not presently hold elective office (although some have in the past) and most of them are also not now the county party leaders of record (although most were in the past). Rather, their continuing influence stems from their ability to raise prodigious amounts of money even absent a formal position.

STATE PARTY COMMITTEES. The third leg of the party fund-raising triad is the state committee of each party, which serves as the crucial mechanism in coordinating all of their campaign activities and those of their respective national party organizations. Oversight falls to the state party chairs. Particularly when the party holds the governorship, the chair is likely to be a sitting member of the legislature. Thus, Christie Whitman's initial appointment was Republican Assembly Speaker Chuck Haytaian, while Jim McGreevey and Jon Corzine appointed, respectively, Democratic assembly members Bonnie Watson Coleman and Joseph Cryan.

The party that does not hold the governorship often chooses a non-officeholder without ties to any of its gubernatorial aspirants. Examples are Tom Byrne, the Democrats' chair from 1994 to 1998, who operates a financial services firm in Princeton and is the son of a former governor and Tom Wilson, a former partisan staffer in the legislature and Trenton lobbyist, elected as chair by the Republican state committee in 2003 and reelected in 2005 and 2007. Both Byrne and Wilson served while their opponents had complete control of state government and were regarded by the statehouse press as the public face and voice of the party on political matters.

In the wake of the *Eu* decision and the campaign reform legislation, both parties also made extensive changes in their bylaws that emphasized the coordinated nature of fund-raising and campaign activities and were more explicit about the role of the state party in providing various forms of campaign assistance.

The Republicans' bylaws specify that the officers of the state party committee are its chair, vice chair, secretary, and treasurer, elected by the state committee for two-year terms on the second Thursday after the party primary in odd-numbered years (that is, the year of gubernatorial and midterm legislative elections). The bylaws also describe a Legislative Steering Committee, whose four permanent members are the state party chair, the senate and assembly leaders, and the (nonvoting) legal counsel to the state committee.

Two permanent and independent divisions within the Legislative Steering Committee are the Senate Republican Majority (SRM) and Assembly Republican Majority (ARM). Each of these divisions is headed by the party's legislative leader or the leader's appointee, who are responsible for all personnel, both paid and unpaid, of their respective divisions, and who select the staff and determine its compensation. The legislative steering committee establishes policy and collects and expends funds for legislative campaigns, with ARM and SRM maintaining separate state committee accounts. This set of arrangements, inspired by the need to conform to Postal Service regulations regarding reduced rates for political direct mail formalizes the merger of the state committee and the legislative leadership PACs into a unified state party.[44]

The two-year term of the Democratic state chair now begins on January 1 following the November gubernatorial and midterm legislative elections. However, in years in which a gubernatorial term ends, there is an interim appointment from the time of the primary until January 1 of the following year. This provision gives the gubernatorial nominee the ability to select the party chair. If the gubernatorial candidate loses the election, the party chair can be replaced. The state committee chair, vice chair, secretary, and treasurer are elected by the state committee, but the state chair appoints the chair and members of the state party finance committee. He or she is also empowered to select, hire, and pay campaign consultants.

The Democrats' state party bylaws also specify a coordinated campaign committee, appointed by the party chair. Its members are the state committee's executive director (a full-time, paid position), one representative from among the statehouse entities (the governor and the leadership of the two houses of the state legislature), all elected members of the federal House and Senate delegations, the county chairs, and others designated by the chair.[45]

Resurgent State Parties?

Since 1989, the New Jersey Election Law Enforcement Commission (ELEC) has produced several comprehensive analyses of the financing of state legislative campaigns.[46] The successive reports first trace "deterioration of a strong party system" in which "the state's storied history of legendary party leaders and dominant county organizations" had become "a thing of the past." By 2003, however, the analyses find that thanks to the *Eu* decision and the 1993 reform legislation, the party organizations had risen phoenix-like from the ashes, and "become as influential, if not more so, than ever before." They tell of a transformed "electoral landscape" and "a monumental shift in New Jersey electoral politics from a system that was candidate-centered to one that is now party-dominated."[47]

Political parties play many roles, but they can be broadly classified in terms of their functions for the electorate, as organizations, and in government. We will consider these in turn. First, the volatility in party identification over the past two decades indicates that the parties' role in structuring the voters' ultimate choice of candidates is limited. And if the eventual party nominee is chosen in a competitive primary that anyone can enter, we have the very definition of candidate-centeredness. In gubernatorial races, which the ELEC reports do not address, the candidate-centered model certainly continues to hold sway. Although the Corzine and Forrester self-financed campaigns of 2005 may be an extreme example, the public financing law that has applied in all previous gubernatorial races since 1977 is predicated entirely on the fund-raising success of individual candidates.

The major roles of the party as organization are to recruit candidates and run their campaigns. As we have seen, money is now the key to performing both these functions. The ELEC reports' argument for revived party dominance is based on the fact that close to two-thirds of all the funds raised in the 2003 legislative elections were contributed by "party entities." It could hardly be otherwise, given the 1993 reforms that severely limited individual and "special interest" contributions to candidates, and permitted much larger contributions to any, or hypothetically all, of the two state committees, four legislative leadership committees, and forty-two county committees that constitute "the state parties"—not to mention the state parties' federal accounts. The real question is if it makes any difference to candidates that the parties are now the recipients of the "special interest" and other funds that used to flow to them.

Consider first the fund-raising totals for incumbents and challengers. In 1991, the last election before imposition of the new contribution rules, incumbents collected 61 percent of all legislative campaign contributions. Twelve years later, the figure was 60 percent. Next, consider the role of special interest contributions from businesses and PACs. In 1991, they accounted for 26 percent of all contributions directly to candidates.

By 2003, those direct contributions had dropped to 11 percent of candidate treasuries but accounted for almost 40 percent of the money raised by party entities, which then passed it on to the candidates.

Political scientist David Menefee-Libey has called this an "Accommodationist" model, in which the parties have accepted "the candidate-centered order as inescapable and devised a means to accommodate its central features."[48] The most "central feature" of a "candidate-centered order" is getting candidates the funds and the services needed to win elections. Ambitious officeholders' quest for higher office is a second feature of a candidate-centered order, and thus they seek to gain or retain the legislative control that brings them leadership roles, additional staff, and public notice. The Accommodationist New Jersey parties perform these functions admirably for legislators. Incumbents have not suffered any greater competition, and some challengers have benefited from the parties' practice of pouring huge amounts into targeted districts.

Finally, we come to the role of the party in government. It is the conventional wisdom that parties are most powerful when they control both the executive and legislative branches, which enables them successfully to enact their policy agendas. It might then seem ironic that the opposite has often been true in New Jersey of late. It was Governor Whitman's Republican colleagues in the legislature who sank her proposals to reform auto insurance, Governor Florio's fellow Democrats who dismantled his education program, and Democratic legislative leaders who were among the loudest critics of Governor Corzine's first budget plan. Different perspectives on the content of good public policy doubtless played some role, but underlying all of these debates were legislators' calculations about how these issues would play when they next individually faced the voters. The ability to raise their own money and weakened or absent gubernatorial coattails gave them considerable freedom of action.

Thus, if there has been a "monumental shift" in the New Jersey political universe, it would seem to consist entirely of the maturation of the "parties in service" and their functions as organizations that provide candidates with what they now most need, which is money. In the mind of the public, political money has long been associated with official corruption. With so much of it now flowing from the special interests to the party organizations, it was not long before New Jersey reformers took aim against "pay to play"—a shorthand name for the belief that contributions to the parties gained the special interests the access and the favors heretofore sought from contributions to well-placed officeholders. By 2004, reformers once again were trying to plug the holes in the dike through which political money flows by attempting to sharply curtail pay to play.

Specifically, this legislation prohibited any entity with a state government contract worth more than $17,500 from donating more than $300 to the politicians who awarded the contracts or to their political party committees. As always seems to be the case with campaign finance "reform," however, enterprising officeholders quickly found ambiguities in the law to exploit. A typical example was an event planned by the chief fund-raiser for Victory 2005, the state Democrats' coordinated campaign committee. Ostensibly held to raise money for the Democratic National Committee rather than for the state election contests, it offered hors d'oeuvres and cocktails for purchase of a $2,500 ticket and, for $25,000, a chance to have a meal and mingle with an assortment of Democratic celebrities like DNC chairman Howard Dean and U.S. senator and gubernatorial candidate Jon Corzine.

Several attorneys whose firms held major state contracts were among those who enjoyed a very expensive seared-tuna dinner. That the Democratic National Committee was pledged to pour at least as much money into the state elections as the $2 million raised at this dinner was irrelevant from a legal perspective. Although state Republicans claimed that the Democratic-controlled legislature had prevented them from closing this loophole, this did not deter them from noting on the invitations to a state GOP fund-raiser for Doug Forrester that contributors could avoid the pay-to-play ban by contributing to the legislative campaign committees.[49]

The widespread practice of transferring funds donated to one party committee to another is known as "wheeling." Depending on one's perspective, wheeling is either among the worst or the best aspects of the campaign finance system. On the one hand, it makes a mockery of contribution limits if donors "maxed out" at one party committee can find numerous others willing and able to accept their donations. On the other hand, it allows the parties to deploy money more efficiently and where they think it counts, such as in targeted districts rather than safe incumbents' war chests.

In January 2006, the same formal prohibitions against pay to play were extended to county and municipal governments. For these entities, the most gaping loophole is the exemption for contracts awarded in a "fair and open" process. This provision mandates that contracts being offered be publicly advertised in a newspaper or on a Web site, granted with a public announcement, and decided not on the basis of competitive bidding, but according to a "predefined" process whose definition is left up to the particular governing body.

The very month the law went into effect, the Middlesex County Improvement Authority (MCIA) advertised $1.5 million in contracts that required qualified applicants to have "knowledge of the authority's operations." They were given "to the same politically connected law firms, financial advisors and other professionals who have always gotten the work" and who had contributed almost half a million dollars to the Democratic county party organization over the past six years.[50] The MCIA is an obscure agency with a varied portfolio including the county recycling program, bonding authority for county infrastructure projects, and redevelopment of low-income housing, all of which have little in common except the opportunity to dole out contracts. It is one of hundreds of such governmental entities in the state, which are perceived as the revived power bases of the county party organizations and their "bosses."

There is no doubt that the most successful of the county "bosses" have exercised great authority in their home bailiwicks, principally through their control of patronage and the fund-raising that goes along with it. Documenting it has become a favored pastime of investigative reporters.[51] Evidence suggests, however, that their alleged power over important state policy was confined to the early years of the McGreevey administration. Unlike most of his recent predecessors, who had strong personal images when they ran and were elected, McGreevey, as a suburban mayor and rather junior legislator, relied heavily on the more notorious Democratic "bosses" in large counties—particularly George Norcross in Camden and John Lynch in Middlesex—just at the time they had regained statewide influence as a result of the *Eu* decision and the 1993 campaign finance law. Their own aggrieved testimony, however, is that their influence was short-lived.[52]

Ultimately, the debate about whether elections have become "party-centered" rather than "candidate-centered" may be of the "is the glass half-full or half-empty?" variety. Political scientists spend much time on these questions. Politicians intent on winning do not care much.

CHAPTER 6

The Representation of Interests

If a group is wise, it goes to the party leaders and not to
the committee members in charge of a bill.
—New Jersey state legislator, 1935

In the old days . . . you needed a majority of the majority
party. . . . Now you have to worry about committees and
even second committees. There are a lot more players in
the process with life and death power over your bill.
—lobbyist, 1987

TWO DESCRIPTIONS OF NEW JERSEY'S interest group sys-
tem convey its essential features. From a veteran legislator's perspective,
"Every issue around here has more than two sides. They are more a cube
than a coin." From a leading lobbyist, "It's like eighteenth century Europe.
There are no friends or enemies, just shifting alliances."[1] Interest group tactics are many, and one cannot tell who is on the same side at a particular
time without a current scorecard. The myriad groups now bringing their
problems to Trenton are all the more remarkable because half a century ago
there were so few of them.

In the 1930s, Dayton McKean, a Princeton political scientist and
Mercer County assemblyman, estimated there were about twenty lobbyists
plying their trade at the state capitol. Most represented the business enterprises central to state politics, and their strategy was simple—purchasing
officeholders. McKean noted of his fellow lawmakers, "It is perfectly well-
known that some members represent certain interests"—including roughly
one-quarter of the entire legislature rumored to be on retainer by the Public
Service Corporation, a holding company for most of the state's utilities
and bus and trolley companies. Aside from a few other large corporations,
interests then resident in Trenton included the labor, education and local
government groups present in most state capitols.[2]

The recent changes are due to the same factors affecting almost every aspect of politics and government in New Jersey after the 1960s—declining localism, growing state identity, and government activism. Yet just as traces of the past remain in New Jersey's electoral politics, so too are they found in interest group politics. Home rule is wounded but not dead; the media environment still limits the ability of general public opinion to compete with narrow interests in setting policies. Every state has seen the explosion of interests that has occurred in New Jersey, but few experienced it so rapidly.[3]

THE INTEREST GROUP UNIVERSE

In 2007, there were more than 1,000 "government affairs agents" or registered lobbyists in Trenton, with about 1,500 clients, as compared with the 20 McKean identified in the 1930s, the 70 who registered in 1964 when it was first required, and the 254 who registered in 1976. About 15 percent of all the registered agents represented the health care industry, and another 10 percent lobbied for utilities and energy companies, or for commerce and industry associations. About half as many represented, respectively, builders, developers, and other real estate interests; banks and other financial institutions; education groups; pharmaceutical and chemical companies; transportation interests; "good government" or "public interest" groups; and insurance concerns. They were followed in number by agents for labor unions, local governments, the communications industry, food and agricultural interests, regulated occupations (for example, beauticians and morticians), and environmental groups. Lists of groups tell little about particular organizations or how their power has changed over time, however. Since the 1930s, four studies of varying precision have examined these questions. Although they are not directly comparable, significant shifts can be detected.

In 1938, McKean offered an informed if impressionistic judgment. He cited the New Jersey State Teachers Association (later renamed the New Jersey Education Association), the Chamber of Commerce, the New Jersey Manufacturers' Association (later renamed the New Jersey Business and Industry Association), the Public Service Corporation, the New Jersey Taxpayers' Association, and the American Federation of Labor (AFL) as the state's most influential groups. These groups had different resources and sources of power. Teachers, the Manufacturers' Association (representing smaller companies than the Chamber of Commerce), and unions were present in almost every legislative district. Unions engaged mostly in electoral reprisal or support, while teachers and businesses also lobbied effectively in Trenton. The other three groups—large corporations or institutions representing them—contributed money to the parties and were thought to have lawyer-legislators on retainer. McKean also noted that business groups were more often fragmented and in conflict than mutually supportive. Finally, he praised the New Jersey Municipal Association and the Association of Freeholders for useful assistance with technical statutes affecting local government.[4]

A more systematic survey in 1962 confirmed McKean's impressionistic analysis. Scholars asked legislators in four states an open-ended question about "the most powerful groups" (termed "generalized power") in their states, and which groups' "advice *ought* to be considered whether they happen to be powerful or not" (termed "group merit").[5] Table 6.1 presents the results for New Jersey.

New Jersey legislators named thirty-eight organizations, but only nine were mentioned by at least 1 percent of the respondents. Only the three groups with members in every legislative district—the state teachers' organization and the largest business and labor groups—were fairly widely regarded as "powerful." New Jersey legislators were also least likely to assign generalized power to business groups, most likely to say educational groups were powerful in their own constituencies, and named the lowest number

TABLE 6.1.

Interest Groups Most Frequently Cited by New Jersey Legislators, 1962 (by percentage of legislators interviewed who mentioned the group)

	Generalized power	Group merit
New Jersey Education Association	30	11
Chamber(s) of Commerce	20	25
AFL-CIO	23	10
New Jersey Municipal League	7	17
New Jersey Taxpayers Association	5	21
New Jersey Manufacturers Association	7	2
League of Women Voters	3	12
New Jersey Farm Bureau	4	2
PTA	1	–

SOURCE: John Wahlke et al., *The Legislative System* (New York: Wiley, 1962), 318–319.

NOTE: All groups mentioned by at least 1 percent of the respondents are included.

of groups.[6] The results led to a widespread conclusion that New Jersey was a weak interest group state.

In 1979, Philip Burch conducted the next wide-ranging study, based on in-depth interviews with legislators, lobbyists, reporters, and former governors and cabinet officers. Respondents were asked "a series of questions ranging from an appraisal of the strength of interest groups and an assessment of the various major kinds . . . to a more detailed evaluation of all organizations."[7]

Burch singled out the New Jersey Education Association (NJEA) "as unusually effective," and the Chamber of Commerce and the New Jersey Business and Industry Association (NJBIA) as the most important business groups. He described the AFL-CIO membership as so large that it "cannot help but be a major force in New Jersey politics" but noted that, "unlike the NJEA, it has never been able to translate most of its vast personnel and financial resources into any kind of equivalent political power."[8] The League of Municipalities was cited for technical expertise within its special domain. Burch also noted the latent influence of the legal profession because of the many lawyer-legislators, rather than their organizational clout. He also identified a number of other groups not mentioned in earlier studies, including senior citizens, builders and realtors, and the health professions. Although Burch did not rate them as particularly active or effective, their inclusion signaled the broadened scope and activity of New Jersey state government, which had already begun by 1979.

In 1987, the Gallup Organization, retained by several clients, conducted a survey of the New Jersey legislature and made some of its results available to the public. Although they were not the study's major topic, legislators were asked to rate "the effectiveness and credibility" of thirteen interest groups. Why these particular groups were chosen is not certain. However, they account for much of the PAC money contributed to legislative candidates and parties and figure prominently in journalistic coverage of New Jersey's lobbyists and interest groups.[9] The relevant results of this survey appear in table 6.2.

The table shows the continuing strength of the New Jersey Education Association, whose impressive five-story headquarters is located across the street from the state capitol. The NJEA has two hundred thousand active and retired members and runs one of the state's best-financed political action committees, sends candidate endorsement letters to all of its members, and conducts effective Election Day get-out-the-vote operations. Legislators

TABLE 6.2.

Effectiveness and Credibility of Selected Interest Groups, Ratings by New Jersey Legislators, 1987

Group	Effectiveness rating	Credibility rating
NJEA (teachers)	4.3	3.5
NJBIA (business)	4.2	4.0
Dental Association	4.0	3.7
Builders' Association	3.9	3.3
Auto Dealers Association	3.6	3.4
Trial Lawyers Association	3.6	2.8
School Boards Association	3.6	3.8
AFL-CIO	3.5	3.1
Cable TV Association	3.3	3.2
FAIR (Insurance)	3.2	2.9
Casino Association	3.2	3.1

SOURCE: Gallup Organization, *The 1987 Gallup Survey of the New Jersey State Legislature* (Princeton, NJ: Gallup Organization, 1987), 2.

respect NJEA for its political clout and professionalism. As one legislator observed, "They represent a large constituency. They have a good research division. Good publicity; personal meetings; periodic information; luncheons; visible representatives in Trenton." Another put it this way: "Some legislators are so afraid of the NJEA they quake."[10]

The NJBIA, founded in 1905 by Paterson silk mill owners to oppose workman's compensation laws, matches NJEA in perceived effectiveness and has the highest credibility rating of any association listed. Like NJEA, the New Jersey Business and Industry Association is respected for its knowledge, presence, and ability to help in campaigns. Another important similarity is the pervasive presence of both groups in legislators' districts. NJEA has twenty-two field offices and fifty-seven field representatives. NJBIA, with more than twenty-three thousand member companies, is the nation's largest statewide employer association. It has employer legislative committees (ELCs) in each of the state's twenty-one counties. County business leaders on these committees hold monthly meetings with association lobbyists to share information and concerns. Compared to the NJEA, the NJBIA is more often cited as an "honest broker."[11] One legislator described NJBIA as having "a good research staff that provides detailed reasoning. They don't just say I'm for this or that." Another noted, "They give me both sides of the coin."[12]

The Gallup survey also showed the continuing (but lesser) influence of the AFL-CIO, whose members are also present in many districts. Yet as Burch commented, organized labor has never played the political role their numbers might suggest—even in labor's boom times. New Jersey's unions have been unusually factious and often politically inept. Although their numbers are dwindling, almost 20 percent of New Jersey workers are still unionized, the sixth highest total in the United States.

Discord in the labor movement stretches back to the bloody and prolonged strikes of Paterson silk mill workers and Passaic factory hands. The 137 strikes in Paterson between 1881 and 1900 amounted to "a virtual state of war."[13] The international anarchist movement made Paterson its U.S. headquarters. A five-month walkout by Paterson weavers in 1913 was taken over by the radical International Workers of the World (IWW), colloquially known as Wobblies. The IWW brought in leading leftists like Elizabeth Gurley Flynn, John Reed, and Upton Sinclair to inspire the strikers. A similar year-long work stoppage, involving between ten and twelve thousand workers, occurred in Passaic in 1913. One reason leftists gained influence with these workers was that the conservative state AFL, dominated then and now by the building trades, supported the successful strikebreakers.

The relatively conservative bent of the largest labor federation and its uneasy relationship with other elements of organized labor continue to the present. The New Jersey AFL supported Jersey City Mayor Frank Hague's successful efforts to keep CIO organizers out of Jersey City (see chapter 3). When the AFL and CIO merged in 1955, only one state—New Jersey—refused to go along. Federation President George Meany forced the warring New Jersey unions to unite in 1961, but the old CIO unions withdrew again in 1964.

Today, there are two AFL-CIO organizations in New Jersey; sometimes they cooperate and sometimes they do not.[14] For more than fifty years, Louis and Charles Marciante, father and son, led the older and larger body. When "Big Charlie" finally retired in 1997, he was succeeded by "Little Charlie" Wowkanech, assistant to the president since 1989, and a man "always at [Marciante's] side as he works Statehouse hallways."[15] Although the federation tends to endorse Democrats, it has a long history of also working with Republicans, seventeen of whose assembly members it endorsed in 2005. Charles Marciante served on the labor advisory council of the Republican National Committee, and Wowkanech, his successor, worked with Republican legislators to form the Republican Labor Legislative Caucus in 2006—a group that attracted more than one-third of the GOP members of the senate and assembly. Over the past decade, the AFL-CIO has aggressively sought to elect union members to office, and almost four hundred now serve at the various levels of government, including the chairs of the labor committees in both houses of the legislature.

The Industrial Union Council (IUC), originally a CIO union, is the smaller and more liberal of the two union bodies. Its longtime head, Joel Jacobson, was a fervent liberal Democrat active in the Vietnam-era antiwar movement and the civil rights movements. While Marciante concentrated on pocketbook issues, Jacobson led labor's fights for right-to-know legislation and plant closing notification. Upon his death, he was succeeded by Bill Kane, who shared Jacobson's political views—as early as 2002, the New Jersey IUC executive board had unanimously passed a resolution condemning U.S. involvement in Iraq. The IUC, although smaller, has an active and well-financed PAC and a technologically advanced campaign operation for its endorsed candidates (almost always Democrats, who sometimes run against Republicans endorsed by the AFL). Its affiliates include the Teamsters, the International Brotherhood of Electrical Workers, and the Communications Workers of America, which represents many state government employees.

The Gallup study documents the appearance of many new groups, including several Burch described as politically feeble in the late 1970s—senior citizens, bankers, dentists, builders, and the organized trial lawyers. Others, such as the casino association and the cable television association, had barely come into existence at the time Burch wrote. Their rankings are further testimony to the expanding role of the state government. In sum, a few New Jersey interest groups have been continuously influential for at least fifty years—the largest business groups, the major labor federation, and the teachers' organization. They have been joined by other groups whose economic interests are now more affected by state action. With the establishment of political action committees (whose dramatic growth we discuss later in this chapter), more interest groups have greater access to legislators.

Large individual corporations, once the rulers of the legislature, now play a more limited role because their principal concerns are usually dealt with by the federal government rather than state government. Unless they are of great magnitude, their issues are most often handled by umbrella associations like the state Chamber of Commerce. Large corporations with

New Jersey headquarters, such as Johnson and Johnson, the Prudential Insurance Company, and Public Service Electric and Gas (PSE&G), also make their presence felt more informally. As sources of campaign funds, employment, and managerial and fiscal expertise, they are important to New Jersey's political leaders and often take a benevolent interest in the state. Johnson and Johnson spearheaded redevelopment and revitalization in downtown New Brunswick, where its international headquarters are located. Prudential's willingness to underwrite bonds for the New Jersey Sports and Exposition Authority was a key component in the development of the Meadowlands. PSE&G has underwritten state agency advertising promoting New Jersey business and bond issue referenda.

Some interests important in other states do not play a weighty role in New Jersey. The federal government is not a significant presence as landowner or source of employment, and the state sends more money to Washington than it gets back. New Jersey's religious organizations are denominationally diverse, predominantly mainstream, and liberally inclined. Although maintaining Trenton representatives to lobby on issues like state aid to parochial schools, they generally adhere to the principle of separation of church and state, and seldom get actively involved in broader social policy.[16] So-called good government groups such as the League of Women Voters and Common Cause often receive approving lip service for their activities, but they do not have the numbers or financial resources to lobby their issues effectively. They are, however, frequently quoted in the state's media as reporters seek to present "the voice of the public."

Political developments have enhanced the lobbying role of state agencies. State intervention in so many new policy fields forced agencies to develop their own agendas and appoint legislative liaisons. With more issues on the state government's docket, governors concentrated their own lobbying efforts on a few priorities, leaving the agencies to deal with lesser ones. Many laws must be implemented by administrative rules, and the agencies that promulgate them are another venue for lobbyists. Agency rules must be published in the *New Jersey Register* twenty days before they take effect. Joseph Gonzales, the former executive director of the NJBIA, explains the effect of regulations from an interest group's point of view: "A department is likely to take the bare bones of a bill and put meat, gristle and fat on it. As a result, you may be faced with something completely different than what the legislature intended, and that's a tough fight in itself. That's why it's important to develop a good relationship with people in the executive branch."[17]

One experienced lobbyist has estimated that there are more than eighty state government departments, divisions, commissions, boards, agencies, councils, and authorities empowered to issue regulations.[18] It is in this arcane and publicly invisible implementation phase that the experience of lobbyists who have served in the executive branch is most useful: "There are lobbyists who are extremely influential in this phase of the process. They tend to be highly skilled experts who are well-funded and knowledgeable about how to play an insider's game. They help to shape rules and regulations by providing research and background material to appropriate executive branch officials *before* a rule is promulgated."[19]

LOBBYISTS: A PORTRAIT

Most New Jersey lobbyists are employed full-time as government affairs specialists by individual businesses or associations or are contract lobbyists representing several clients.[19] Large concerns often have sizable in-house lobby operations. The NJBIA and NJEA, for example, both have more than a half-dozen full-time lobbyists. In recent years, the role of contract lobbyists has increased dramatically. Joseph Katz, the first such "hired gun," set up shop in 1966. In 1983, there were twenty-two registered individuals or firms with multiple, unrelated clients. By 1990 this had mushroomed to forty-five different individuals or firms. Fifteen contract lobbyists had at least ten clients, and three had more than forty. By 2005, there were sixty-one lobbyists or firms with ten clients or more, and five of those represented forty or more interests.[20]

Clients are not confined to enterprises without their own government affairs agents; many hire contract lobbyists to augment in-house staff. Some firms without in-house personnel also retain more than one contract lobbyist. In 2005, twenty-five corporations and associations, almost all with their own in-house lobbying capacity, each reported spending more than $100,000 on additional lobbyists. Many contract lobbyists have held high positions in the executive branch of state government or on the legislative staff, while others are ex-legislators or former newspaper reporters. The major firms are bipartisan, including principals from both parties. In 1990, contract lobbyists reported collecting fees of $7.7 million, more than a third of which was earned by seven firms. Fifteen years later, their receipts totaled $28.9 million, and the three largest firms accounted for fully half of that total.

Leading the list was Princeton Public Affairs, whose founder, Dale Florio, is the chair of the Somerset County GOP; the firm also employs John

Russo, a former Democratic state senate president. The second and third largest firms have undergone a dizzying number of mergers and reorganizations, which is the major reason that a smaller number of groups now collect a larger portion of lobbying fees than in the past. Public Strategies/Impact, number two in revenues in 2005, is a result of the 1986 union between companies headed by Harold Hodes, chief of staff to Governor Byrne in the 1970s, and Roger Bodman, who headed two cabinet departments during the Kean governorship in the 1980s. In 2002, this company merged with the GluckShaw group, which is led by Hazel Gluck, twice a cabinet head in the Kean administration and a close advisor to Governor Whitman, and Judy Shaw, Whitman's first chief of staff. This arrangement collapsed within a year, and GluckShaw's subsequent merger with yet another major lobbying group to create MBI-GluckShaw, put it third on the fee collection list in 2005.

A likely reason contract lobbyists keep increasing their client rosters is that legislators regard them favorably. The Gallup legislative survey included a question about whether "in general," contract personnel, staff, or organizational volunteers were "most effective in communicating issues to you." Of the three-fifths of respondents indicating a preference, 47 percent chose contract lobbyists, 27 percent said staff lobbyists, and 26 percent picked the nonprofessionals.[21]

Another reason for the growth of contract lobbying is greater use of transient multigroup alliances to lobby major issues. Often, one of the participants' lobbyists assumes the lead role. During a successful two-year battle to prevent the merger of PSE&G with Illinois-based Exelon Corporation to create the nation's largest utility company, the Service Workers' International Union led an unusual alliance of business, labor and public interest groups which contended the deal would stifle competition and raise rates.[22] Another example is PatientGUARD ("Groups United Against Reprocessing Dangers"), a coalition seeking legislation to prohibit hospitals from recycling single-use medical devices because of infection risks. Most of its twenty-two institutional members are patient advocacy groups, such as the American Diabetes Association and the Arthritis Foundation, but it is led by the Healthcare Institute of New Jersey, the trade association for the New Jersey pharmaceutical and medical technology companies that manufacture such devices. The president of the Healthcare Institute is Bob Franks, the former state legislator, U.S. senate candidate, and head of the Republican state committee.

Generally speaking, therefore, the growth in the number and functions of lobbyists mirrors the growth in the complexity of issues, and the processes needed to resolve them.

Regulation of Lobbyists

New Jersey was one of the last states to regulate lobbyists. Not until 1964 were lobbyists required to register with the secretary of state's office, disclose clients, report their interest in bills quarterly, and wear a badge while at work in the capitol. In 1973, when the state Election Law Enforcement Commission (ELEC) was established to monitor party and campaign expenditures, the enabling legislation also provided that lobbyists would have to file annual spending reports with the commission. This portion of the law was immediately challenged in court by twenty lobbyists led by the Chamber of Commerce, and was tied up in legal wrangles for six years. The legislature took up the financial reporting requirement again in 1981, when it became the most heavily lobbied bill of the year. The focus of debate was on a provision that expenditures be reported for any contacts with a legislator "without limitation."[23]

The session-long battle came to a mysterious end at literally the last moment. In the wee hours of the morning just before a new governor and legislature were to take office in January 1982, the outgoing legislature struck out the bill's "without limitation" wording and substituted language that only expenses connected "expressly" with discussions of specific legislation would have to be reported. The outgoing governor, Democrat Brendan Byrne, who had previously vetoed several similar wordings, signed it at 8 a.m. on his way to the inaugural. All the participants later claimed surprise that the final bill was so favorable to the lobbyists. Most legislators said they did not realize what they were voting for in the year-end legislative blizzard, and the Chamber of Commerce lobbyist who had led the fight for seven years claimed it was a "Hail Mary" bill—one hoped for but never expected to happen.[24]

After a series of scandals during 1990, a blue-ribbon Commission on Legislative Ethics and Campaign Finance, appointed by the senate president and assembly speaker and headed by the director of the Eagleton Institute of Politics at Rutgers University, recommended that lobbyists be required to report any spending intended to influence public policy. In 1991, the legislature finally passed a reform package removing the "expressly" wording, extending reporting requirements to lobbying directed at executive agencies, and centralizing all reporting at ELEC. The 1990–91 reforms strengthened what some observers still regarded as rather weak regulation of lobbyists. Many loopholes were closed in 2004 by eight separate laws that were part of a large package of ethics reforms. Beginning in 2006 lobbyists, who previously were not required to report their expenditures on grass-roots campaigns or their attempts to influence state agencies on contracts, rate setting, penalties, and permits, now had to do so. The new laws also prohibited legislators from accepting any gift worth more $250 from an individual lobbyist, or subsidies of more than $500 for travel.

ELEC's 2006 annual report on lobbying expenditures demonstrated the dramatic effect of the new disclosure provisions. Reported expenditures almost doubled over those of 2005, to $54.8 million, and the number of entities required to register rose from 647 to 1,010. New Jersey, which had ranked eleventh among the states in lobbying expenditures in 2005, had climbed to fourth a year later. In something of an understatement, ELEC's executive director, Frederick Herrmann, observed that the new law had "been very effective in terms of improving transparency in the lobbying process in New Jersey."[25]

Interest Group Tactics

New Jersey's interest groups spend most of their time and resources cultivating access to legislators and executive branch officials. Two assured ways to gain access are supplying campaign money and providing reliable technical information. Seasoned lobbyists hope to delay action in the legislature or executive agencies so as to maintain the status quo for as long as possible, insert amendments in bills or regulations that make unwanted legislation more palatable, or persuade the governor to exercise one of several different types of veto power.[26]

Technical information has long been the lobbyist's stock in trade. When the legislature met only once a week for a few months a year, had almost no staff, and was populated by amateurs with high turnover rates, lobbyists had a near-monopoly on information and bill drafting.[27] Because of the increase in the number of complex issues, more staff and a more professional legislature have not diminished the value of lobbyists' information. As legislators' comments about the NJEA and NJBIA indicate, they are quite willing to listen to lobbyists with reputations for knowledge and probity. The expertise of credible lobbyists is important in making it possible for legislators to understand many of the several thousand bills that cross their desks in a typical session.[28] However, as the backgrounds of the leading contract lobbyists make evident, political connections count for at least as much, and probably more, than technical knowledge. The leading players may depend on staff for data, but former officeholders and appointed officials do the important contact work.

Lobbyists' increased reliance on political contributions to secure access to lawmakers, and the growth in those contributions, is a more recent development. Interest groups certainly contributed to campaigns in the past, but the amounts were much smaller. As discussed in chapter 5, campaigns in New Jersey's pre-media age, which extended well into the 1970s, were relatively inexpensive. The era of high-tech candidate-centered campaigns dramatically escalated costs, and PACs have footed much of the bill. ELEC, which makes PAC reports available on its website, sorts them by type such as "labor union" or "trade association" but the available data makes it difficult to determine apparently simple information, such as how many PACs are registered, the specific interests they represent, the largest givers, or what percentage of campaign spending they contribute. Some PACs choose names not easily associated with a company or industry, making the identity of the givers something of a treasure hunt.[29]

In 2004 the *Bergen Record* deployed a small army of reporters, computer specialists, editors, and other staff to try to answer some of these questions. In a weeklong "Special Report" about campaign money in the 2003 elections, they informed readers that organized labor groups provided $5.6 million in contributions, and real estate and construction companies donated $9.3 million. To ascertain the identity of a PAC which gave only a Washington, DC, post office box as its address, made fourteen separate contributions totaling $24,000, and was listed in the ELEC data base under four different acronyms ("MAPAC," "MAPAC 2," "IMPAC," and "MOPAC 2"), the team resorted to a Google search of the post office box number. That led them to a campaign finance watchdog site which posts the tax returns of political donors who are not required to register with the Federal Election Commission.

This document revealed that the uninformative full name of the group was the Mid-Atlantic Political Action Committee. Further research indicated that it had been founded by officers of the United Food and Commercial Workers (UFCW) Union, which represents supermarket workers. Altogether, a variety of PACs affiliated with the UFCW contributed about $175,000 to New Jersey legislative candidates in 2003.[30]

Overall, these findings reflect the general conclusions about the current role of interest groups in the states. A more complex state economy does not lead, as was once thought, to weaker groups because of increasing pluralization. Rather, there are just more groups and continuing dominance, albeit even more fragmented, by business. The greater need for campaign money is met substantially by increased interest group contributions, although the lion's share now goes to the state party entities rather than to individual candidates.

Of the traditional pressure groups, education, labor, and business remain strong. Some of the most important new actors are developers, the health care industry, and single-issue groups (for example, tort reform advocates or supporters and opponents of legalized sports betting) whose particular concerns land on the state's policy agenda from time to time. Less wealthy or well organized groups must, as they always have, depend on the kindness of strangers.

Although journalists and public interest groups regularly accuse the PACs of "buying" votes, the givers and recipients do not see it that way. The 1987 Gallup survey found that 45 percent of legislators thought PAC contributions had a positive effect on their relationship with interest groups, 7 percent thought it had a negative effect, and 48 percent expressed no opinion. Legislators cited good personal relations, more awareness of issues, and support for their own personal positions as the major positive effects.[31]

Legislators freely admit that they give "access" to big contributors, but argue that all it brings them is a sympathetic ear. In the words of senate president Richard Codey, "If you give me a contribution, you get a thank-you. That's it. . . . Some of them might say, 'Codey doesn't agree with us on these issues, but maybe down the road there'll be another issue where he might,' so they give a contribution because they want to have an entree, to build a rapport." John Torok, the lobbyist for the state's optometrists agrees: "It's not as simple as saying if I [raise] $100,000, somebody will do this bill for me. I wish it were that simple."[32]

Some of the crusaders against the PACs grudgingly agree that it is more image than actual malfeasance that is of real concern. Staci Berger, program director of New Jersey Citizen Action, the state's largest watchdog coalition, observed, "I don't think every special interest gets what it wants . . . most of the time you have corporations fighting other corporations. . . . What it buys you is the ability to have your idea floated in the first place, or the ability to stop things from happening."[33]

Although campaign contributions and legislative activity remain lobbyists' chief stock in trade, on issues that affect the broader public there is greater use of strategies that seek to bring external pressure on the legislature. Grassroots lobbying—in the form of organized mail and phone campaigns—is an increasingly common tactic. There are also frequent public relations campaigns on major issues that involve newspaper, radio and television advertising, commissioning of public opinion polls, and distribution of their results. Cable television legislation provides examples of both techniques.

Under a 1972 law passed when cable TV was in its infancy, New Jersey required providers to negotiate individual franchises with each of New Jersey's 566 municipalities. The expenses involved in the initial wiring eventually resulted in two companies—Cablevision and Comcast—controlling 93 percent of the market of about 2.5 million households. When Governor Florio proposed extending the state sales tax to monthly cable television bills in 1990, the New Jersey Cable Television Association orchestrated the mailing of "more than 125,000 anti-tax postcards, which were bundled in bags and delivered to the Statehouse in a wheelbarrow."[34] The cable tax was the only one of the governor's several unpopular sales tax extenders to be rejected by the legislature.

Fifteen years later, as a result of technological developments and a regulatory environment that favored competition, much more was at stake for both cable providers and their subscribers. The advent of the Internet led cable companies to offer many other products, including telephone service. Verizon, which was New Jersey's largest provider of landline and cell phone service, countered by seeking a share of the cable television market. By the end of 2005, it had wired 123 of the state's 566 municipalities with its own advanced fiber optic system, and was seeking legislation awarding them a statewide franchise, rather than requiring the town-by-town negotiations dictated by the 1972 law.

Cablevision and Comcast swung into action. The stakes were high for both the warring corporations and the state's consumers, who spent $2.2 billion for telephone and Internet service in 2004 and had seen an increase of 80 percent in the price of premium channels since their price was deregulated in 1999. In a public relations campaign of unprecedented scope, the opponents reported spending $3 million in a two year campaign during 2004 and 2005. It was waged in media advertising and direct mail as well as in the halls of the legislature, with Verizon and the cable companies hiring twenty-three different contract lobbying firms to supplement their in-house staff. In 2006, when the final law was passed and the stiffer disclosure requirements had gone into effect, Verizon alone report lobbying expenditures of $4.7 million. Its opponents said they spent only about a quarter of that, but this figure excluded about $4 million in advertising on the cable channels they owned, which did not have to be reported.[35]

MORE REFORM? THE INITIATIVE AND REFERENDUM AND "CLEAN ELECTIONS"

New Jersey, like most other eastern states, has not had the primary vehicle to advance the public's role in policy making—statewide initiatives or referenda placed on the ballot by petition, and known familiarly as "I&R." Nor does the state that pioneered public financing of gubernatorial elections provide, as a few other states do, taxpayer funding of legislative contests to lessen the need for special interest campaign money.[36] Both proposals have some history in New Jersey, with that of "I&R" much longer.

The Movement for I&R in New Jersey

Although its proponents were never successful in their own state, New Jersey played a major role in the early national movements for adoption of initiative, referendum, and recall elections in the states. During the 1890s, the New Jersey Direct Action League, in concert with the AFL, was among the first in the United States to call for a state constitutional amendment to permit I&R. Despairing of it ever passing, the League then unsuccessfully sought legislation to allow citizens to put nonbinding, advisory initiatives on the ballot. Once again with the support of organized labor, the next serious effort to adopt I&R was in 1947, when delegates convened to rewrite New Jersey's state constitution. It also failed, and the constitution permits the legislature to authorize ballot referenda dealing only with the state's bonded indebtedness or constitutional amendments.[37]

I&R remained a dormant issue until the mid-1970s, when the state chapters of Common Cause and the League of Women Voters revived it. In both 1981 and 1983 the state senate overwhelmingly approved an I&R bill, but it never came to a vote in the assembly. The two houses reversed course in 1986 when the assembly supported an I&R bill but it lost in the senate.[38] In 1989, public exasperation over high auto insurance rates produced a drive to put a nonbinding referendum on forcing down rates on the ballot in all twenty-one counties. The state supreme court ruled it unconstitutional. In

1990, Hands Across New Jersey, a citizens' group irate over large tax increases, launched a million-signature petition drive to promote statewide initiative, referenda, and recall elections. Vocal support by New Jersey 101.5, the Trenton talk radio station, and *The Trentonian* newspaper magnified their message. Over thirty county and municipal governments also authorized nonbinding referenda urging repeal of the taxes, but the state supreme court again declared almost all of them unconstitutional.

To date, I&R has not been seriously revisited, and the only referenda or public questions appearing on the ballot in New Jersey fall within the narrow parameters set by the state constitution. Most proposed constitutional amendments address procedural issues such as the length of sheriffs' terms or the residency requirement for voting. However, because the constitution specifically prohibits all forms of gambling not approved by the voters, it must be amended to permit major changes like legalizing casino gambling in Atlantic City (approved in 1976, after a referendum to allow casinos anywhere in the state failed in 1974), and also minor ones like changes in the rules for bingo, raffles, and boardwalk games of chance.

Voters have also passed judgment on numerous bond issues for public land acquisition, farmland preservation, wastewater treatment facilities, hazardous waste cleanup, and the like. Some bond issues, however public spirited, mean a great deal to particular interest groups. The construction industry, for example, is especially enthusiastic about frequent bond questions on state building projects.

Public Funding of Legislative Elections

The history of the "clean elections" movement to provide public funding for legislative elections is briefer. Just as official corruption scandals in both the state and federal capitals during the 1970s produced taxpayer-supported gubernatorial campaigns in New Jersey, the same sorts of outrages in the early 2000s generated interest in extending it to legislative contests. The 2005 assembly elections featured a pilot project based on existing programs in Arizona and Maine, crafted principally by Democratic assemblyman Joseph Roberts (then majority leader and later speaker). It required each party to select one from a list of three competitive or moderately competitive districts to participate.

After raising twenty thousand dollars in small contributions, candidates who voluntarily chose to be included would receive a state subsidy, based on 75 percent of the average amount spent in the district by the assembly candidates from both parties in the two previous general elections, and additional public funds if they became targets of independent expenditures or if an opponent opted out of the plan or raised money above the subsidy. Republicans chose the Thirteenth District in Monmouth County and the Democrats the Sixth District in Camden County. At that time, the two assembly seats in each of these districts were both held by the party choosing them and involved only one incumbent; the rest of the candidates were challengers.

The experiment could not be called an unqualified success. None of the candidates in the Thirteenth District met the contribution threshold, and both Democrats opted out of the program in frustration over its burdensome regulatory requirements. In the Sixth District the Democratic candidates, aided by their efficient county party organization, raised far more in small donations than was required. Trying to save the experiment, the Sixth District Democrats actually contributed their excess funds to their opponents. Although applauding this goodwill gesture, some noted that identifying even moderately "competitive" Democratic assembly districts was so difficult that the Sixth made the list—despite regularly producing 20 percent margins for their party's candidates, one of whom was then the chair of the chamber's budget and appropriations committee.

In reviewing the outcome of the project (which produced no change in the partisan makeup of the districts' representatives), both participants and observers faulted its complex ground rules. The "small contributions" had to be made in specified numbers of $5 and $30 donations, payable only by check or check card, and documented with voluminous paperwork. Candidates who failed to collect the threshold amounts for participation had to return whatever funds they did raise and drop out of the program. After they did so, "the rich got richer," as their better financed opponents became eligible for additional subsidies.

Thirteenth District Republican challenger Amy Handlin, who eventually raised almost $100,000 from the usual suspects when freed from the Clean Election regulations, and who won with 53 percent of the vote, summarized the mixed reaction to the program: "Having knocked on doors in 105 degree heat begging for $5, I know this program is very, very flawed and essentially has to be recreated. I hope the success in a second try will be as spectacular as the failure was in the first go-round."[39]

The Clean Elections idea got another test in 2007 after its sponsors revamped the program to address some of the shortcomings of the 2005 version. The program was expanded to three districts and this time included the senate candidates, who had not been up for reelection in 2005. The legislative leadership of the two major parties was each to choose one district in which their candidate for governor had received a majority of the vote in 2005 and the three incumbents were all members of that party. The Democrats selected the Thirty-Seventh District and the Republicans picked the Twenty-Fourth, both considered safe for their respective parties.

The third district, to be agreed upon jointly by the leaders, was to be among the six where partisan representation was split. If they could not reach agreement, which proved to be the case, the decision was to be made by a committee of five members: two citizens appointed by each party's leaders, and one former governor chosen by the majority party. The majority Democrats nominated Jim Florio. The choice of District Fourteen (parts of Middlesex and Mercer counties) was made on a party-line vote, with the three Democrats in favor and the two Republicans preferring District Twelve in Monmouth County. With the Republican senator in the Fourteenth retiring and an assemblywoman in the Twelfth giving up her seat to run for the senate, both districts had open seats.

Simplified contribution rules required that participants raise at least $10,000 in contributions not exceeding $500. A candidate who received $10 donations from eight hundred individuals qualified for the full amount of public funding. This sum was set at $100,000 for the Democratic and Republican districts; in the split district it was to be calculated on the basis of average spending in the two previous elections. ELEC, which supervised the program, was empowered to as much as triple the amount of public funds to the candidates in the Democratic and Republican districts if their opponents chose not to participate or they became targets of independent expenditures.[40]

Although the legislation passed by sizable majorities in each house (58–18–3 in the assembly and 23–7–5 in the senate), the unusual number of abstentions provided a clue to misgivings about it, particularly among senators, Republicans, and former state senator William Schluter, who headed a bipartisan commission that reviewed the 2005 program and made recommendations for 2007.

Schluter and the Republicans had several concerns, but foremost among them was the act's failure to include primary elections. The real action in the many noncompetitive districts in the state was for the majority-party nomination, and some of these districts were still controlled by county party organizations. For example, internecine warfare in the Hudson

County party organization led Senator Bernard Kenney, the Democratic majority leader, and Senator Joseph Doria, a former assembly speaker, to resign their seats in 2007 rather than face difficult primaries.

Although the final version of the legislation specified that primary elections would be included in 2009 if the 2007 pilot was "deemed a success," this did not satisfy Schluter, who testified against the measure, calling it "a sham" and "a lousy bill."[41]Many of the Democratic senators who voted for it grudgingly had another worry, which was that there was insufficient protection against unlimited independent expenditures. Ray Lesniak, who finally provided the vote that broke a stalemate on the senate floor, warned that he would not vote for a third iteration of Clean Elections if the 2007 trial was as unsuccessful as that of 2005, saying, "for me, it's two strikes and you're out."[42]

Regional neighbors with political cultures similar to New Jersey provide mixed signals about the possible future of the Clean Elections experiment. Massachusetts passed a similar program in 1998, only to abolish it in 2003 in the wake of state budget shortfalls. After the arrest and conviction of its Republican governor on corruption charges, in December 2005 Connecticut's legislature provided for full public funding of its statewide and state legislative elections, to take effect for the 2008 elections. It remains to be seen whether New Jersey legislators and their constituents will ultimately care more about "clean elections" or lower state budgets.

CONCLUSION

Amidst vast changes in New Jersey's interest group politics, there are also elements of continuity. They are all related to the state's enduring localist orientations. The interest groups that have remained important over the past fifty years—education, labor, and small business—are those with large and relatively cohesive representation in legislators' districts. To explain oddities like New Jersey's status as the only state that until 1992 did not license physician's assistants (although its state medical school trained them), or as one of only two states still without self-service gas stations, one need look no further than the many nurses, physicians, and independent gas station owners who are all legislators' vocal and well-organized constituents.[43]

Most of the issues state government deals with remain narrow and distributive in character, or at least are defined that way. The newest groups with a Trenton presence are the targets of greatly increased state regulation—developers, the financial community, insurance interests (and their frequent nemeses, the lawyers), and the health care industry (and their largest clientele, senior citizens). Rarely, aroused public opinion may intervene in debate on these "special interest" issues. However, the continuing absence of true mass media in the state—particularly its own mass audience television stations—makes it difficult for public, rather than special interest, opinion to form. Today, unlike the heyday of the Camden and Amboy Railroad and the Public Service Corporation, no small number of interest groups dominates the state. Rather, there are a myriad of small fiefdoms. Influence in Trenton, in the words of a local wag, has passed from the hacks to the PACs.

CHAPTER 7

The Constitution

The American constitutions were to liberty, what a
grammar is to language: They define its parts of speech,
and practically construct them into a syntax.

—Thomas Paine

It shall be lawful . . . to conduct, under such restrictions
and control as shall from time to time be prescribed by
the Legislature . . . the specific kind of game of chance
sometimes known as bingo or lotto, played with cards
bearing numbers or other designations, 5 or more in one
line, the holder covering numbers as objects, similarly
numbered are drawn from a receptacle and the game
being won by the person who first covers a previously
designated arrangement of numbers on such a card.

—Article IV, Section 7, New Jersey Constitution

NEW JERSEY'S THREE CONSTITUTIONS—of 1776, 1844,
and 1947—successively emphasize each of the three strains of American
constitutionalism identified by Daniel Elazar: communitarian, federalist and
managerial.[1] The 1776 charter reflected early American faith in a weak
executive and a strong legislature. The 1844 constitution responded haltingly
to the emerging needs of an industrializing society and incorporated some
aspects of Jacksonian populism. The 1947 charter stimulated development
of an activist state government.

It has been said that "political decisions made by constitutional conventions are really temporary truces in a never-ending conflict between
social, economic, political, and sectional forces in the state."[2] This chapter
describes how New Jerseyans worked out those truces in each constitution.

THE CONSTITUTION OF 1776

On May 15, 1776 the Continental Congress requested the colonies to
prepare constitutions. New Jersey's Provincial Congress issued a call for

delegates to a constitutional convention on May 28. They convened in Burlington on June 10 and on July 2 approved a document drawn from colonial texts.[3]

Only thirty-five of the sixty-five delegates were present to vote on the charter, which was never formally engrossed, signed, nor submitted for popular ratification. New Jersey's first governor, William Livingston, announced at his inauguration that "by tacit acquiescence and open approbation," the constitution "received the assent and concurrence of the good people of this State."[4]

Provisions of the 1776 Constitution

The brief charter, of about two thousand words, was mostly devoted to the selection and duties of a legislature combining judicial, executive, and legislative functions. The vote was granted to "all Inhabitants of this Colony of full Age who are worth Fifty Pounds proclamation Money." Article 19 required officeholders to profess "a Belief in the Faith of any Protestant sect," but prohibited "Establishment of any one religious sect in this Province in Preference to another." Quaker influence made New Jersey one of the four original states that never had an established religion.

Citizens annually chose members of a bicameral legislative council and assembly, who had to meet stiffer property requirements than did voters (£500 for the assembly; £1,000 for the council). Each county elected one member to the upper house and three members to the assembly, with the legislature authorized to adjust the composition of the Assembly over time to reflect "more equal Representation."

The legislature, in joint session, appointed all other state officers (the governor, an attorney general, a secretary, and a treasurer), and members of the supreme court and inferior courts. Its upper house, the council, served as the highest appeals court. Although the governor, chosen annually, was granted supreme executive power, he had no appointment or veto authority. The governor was commanding officer of the state militia, presiding officer in the council, and "Ordinary or Surrogate-Officer"—the highest officer of the courts. The 1776 constitution was, therefore, a brief restatement of colonial governance documents, revised to account for independence and distaste for a strong executive. "The center of gravity was legally changed from governor to legislature, with as little change in form and familiar landmarks as possible."[5] This first fundamental law served the state for sixty-eight years.

Deficiencies of the 1776 Constitution

Attorney William Griffith, writing as "Eumenes," set out most fully the rapidly apparent deficiencies of New Jersey's first constitution.[6] They included its ambiguous status as fundamental law, lack of an amending mechanism, absence of a formal bill of rights, questions about representation, and, most critically, failure to provide for separation of powers.[7] Griffith's analysis served as the revisionists' bible for the next seven decades.

The document's status was ambiguous because public officials did not have to swear to defend or uphold it. They were limited only by the prescription of religious freedom, the provision for annual elections, and a guarantee of jury trials—which was violated many times during the charter's life.[8] Early acceptance of judicial review somewhat allayed concern about unbridled legislative authority. Judicial review was implied in *Holmes v. Walton* in 1780 and stated emphatically in *State v. Parkhurst* in 1802 when New Jersey Chief Justice Andrew Kirkpatrick wrote, "Now to say that the legislature can alter or change such a constitution, that they can do away with that very principle which at the same time gives and limits their power, is in my view a perfect absurdity. It is making the creature greater than the creator. It is establishing despotism without limitation and without control."[9]

However, this still left the question of how to alter a constitution without an amending procedure. Practical questions quickly arose, particularly about the franchise. Voters could simply state they met the property requirement "by proclamation." As Griffith put it, "Our polls swarm . . . with the worst sort of people from the neighboring States, fugitives from justice, absconding debtors." Griffith's ire, however, was directed primarily at the female vote. Women, he wrote, were not "fitted to perform this duty with credit to themselves, or advantage to the public."[10]

In 1807, female voters played a critical role in an electoral dispute over the location of the Essex County courthouse. Unable to amend the constitution's grant of the franchise to "all inhabitants of full age," legislators decreed they could "interpret" or "explain" the document—and passed laws limiting the vote to adult white males on the tax rolls.[11] The immediate issue was resolved, but the fundamental problem remained.

Lack of a comprehensive bill of rights was another oft-cited deficiency. Colonial documents' promise of rights to life and property was absent. An 1816 writer asked, "What is there to prevent the majority from suspending the habeas corpus act, and practicing a system of tyranny against the minority?"[12] The framers likely believed such rights were subsumed in Article 22, which stated that "the common law of England heretofore practiced in this colony, shall still remain in force."[13] Still, concerns remained.

Representation was another issue. There was little discussion about allocating one seat in the upper house to each county regardless of population—a proviso that survived for two hundred years, with profound effects on state politics—but there was debate about the assembly's composition. Reapportionment based on population occurred periodically, but the charter included neither a schedule nor detailed rules for making such changes.[14]

The most glaring deficiency was the failure to provide for separation of powers, a widely approved doctrine by the late eighteenth century. James Madison wrote, "The accumulation of all powers, legislative, executive, and judiciary, in the same hands . . . may justly be pronounced the very definition of tyranny." Madison then observed, "The constitution of New Jersey has blended the different powers of government more than any of the preceding [states examined]."[15]

Griffith echoed Madison and described the legislature as "a scene of intrigue, of canvassing and finesse, which baffles all description, and is too notorious to require proof, and too disgusting for exhibition. The members of a county in which an office is to be disposed of are beset by partisans and friends of the candidates . . . one grand scene of canvass and barter ensues."[16] Local justices of the peace were too often, in the words of Governor Livingston in 1786, "partial," "groggy," and "courting popularity to be chosen Assemblymen."[17] Most power resided with these numerous local officials.

Attempts to Revise the 1776 Constitution

Despite sporadic discussion of its deficiencies, legislators concluded that the constitution enjoyed public acceptance, that they had no authority to call a constitutional convention, and that tinkering might make it worse. A state constitutional convention became an issue in 1800, by which time seven states had already revised their original charters. The newly formed Democratic-Republican Party successfully opposed a convention because it suspected the motives of the Federalists supporting revision. Dissatisfaction continued to surface periodically. In 1827, citizens from nine counties composed a memorial requesting constitutional change. Lawmakers buried the appeal in committee. In his 1840 and 1841 messages to the legislature,

Governor William Pennington argued that the increase in judicial business required separating the supreme executive and judicial offices. The legislature rejected Pennington's request because of "the hazards of a radical change."[18]

Thoroughgoing constitutional reform thus never generated widespread clamor. Rather, dissatisfaction with various provisions (or the lack thereof) bothered different politically active citizens at different times. The constitutional convention of 1844, which drew up New Jersey's second charter, probably came about because of the Whig Party's political ineptitude. During the 1842–1843 legislative session, the Whigs defeated a compromise bill to submit the convention question to popular referendum. In all likelihood, the referendum would have lost. However, the Whigs' decision mobilized enough antagonists to elect a Democratic legislature in 1844, which passed a bill calling for a convention. Thus ended the sixty-eight-year life of New Jersey's first charter. Although imperfect, it served the society for which it was written. "Small, rural and conservative, the state drifted into and through the age of Jackson with her fundamental law intact."[19]

THE CONSTITUTION OF 1844

Although three times longer than its predecessor, New Jersey's second constitution, which endured for 103 years, did not depart dramatically from the 1776 document. It ameliorated some significant shortcomings, but the changes were modest compared to those in other states.[20]

The 1844 Convention and Its Delegates

Delegates to the 1844 constitutional convention, divided almost exactly between Whigs and Democrats, met in Trenton between May 14 and June 29. The fifty-eight participants included three former governors, three state supreme court justices, two attorneys general, and seven congressmen. Two other delegates later became governors and fifteen more would serve on the state supreme court. Almost half were lawyers, and a slightly larger number were officers or owners of corporations or businesses.[21] The framers spent seven weeks in session and thirty-seven days in debate and approved their handiwork by a vote of 55 to 1. Newspapers in each county published the proposed text once a week for six weeks. In a special election on August 13, the document was ratified by a vote of 20,276 to 3,526.[22]

Modest alterations and bipartisan amity contributed to the over-whelmingly favorable vote. New Jersey's Whigs and Democrats divided on national rather than state issues. "The one State and local issue constantly between the parties . . . was the distribution of jobs."[23] In 1844, the largest state enterprise was still the state prison, and the transit tax on through-state railroad passengers financed Trenton's modest needs. New Jersey's domination by New York and Philadelphia still "conditioned its economy, denatured its politics, and restricted the scope of its government."[24]

Constitutional Provisions

With little discussion, delegates wrote a bill of rights and extended the franchise to all white males save "pauper idiots," "insane persons," and unpardoned criminals.[25] The convention also adopted almost verbatim an amending article from the 1838 Pennsylvania constitution. It provided for submission of amendments to the people for ratification, but no more often than every five years and only after passage by two successive legislatures.

The convention's most important work dealt with separation of pow-ers. An assembly committee on constitutional revision had noted in 1840 that "the governor of New Jersey has less power than is conferred by the constitution of any other state upon its executive."[26] The convention made the governor a popularly elected official. He was given a three-year term and could not run for a second successive term. New appointment powers allowed him to nominate high court judges, the attorney general, and the secretary of state, subject to approval by the renamed upper house, the sen-ate. The governor's judicial role was ended. A new court of errors and appeals replaced the senate as the court of last resort. Its unique member-ship consisted of a chancellor appointed by the governor as the presiding officer, the justices of the supreme court, and six lay judges appointed for six-year staggered terms. The lay judges preserved a role for non-lawyers, as had been the case when the senate was the highest tribunal. Otherwise, the judiciary remained a complex system grounded in English common law.

The new charter did not eliminate fused powers. The legislature con-tinued to appoint, in joint meeting, the most important state officers—the treasurer, prison keeper, and the local common pleas judges. The same simple majorities in each house that passed a bill could override a guber-natorial veto. Members of the assembly continued to be elected annually. Senators, like the governor, were elected to three-year terms. The gover-nor's new power to nominate judges stemmed partly from distaste for an elected judiciary, an idea gaining currency elsewhere. Finally, the upper house continued to have one member from each county—one of the few provisions with obvious political implications. As a delegate from a small county said of proposals to apportion the senate by population, "I should be unworthy to represent the people of Cape May if I did not resist this in its incipient stage. They will never submit to it."[27] The treatment of separation of powers therefore "represented no fundamental or drastic break with the past" and "indicated the conservative nature of the new structure of government."[28] The constitutional convention's delegates indicated they might "trust the legislature less," but they were "not disposed to trust the governor much more."[29]

Contemporary politics shaped the 1844 constitution. New Jersey's Democrats did not provide a populist, Jacksonian cast to the debate as they did in other states. Disputes over the franchise did not arise because of the provision for virtually universal male suffrage in 1807. The Democrats, allied with the dominant railroad, were hardly less friendly to business than were the Whigs. Strict limits on what the state could borrow reflected recent bank failures and skyrocketing public debt but had no effect on special business legislation. The increasingly common "long ballot," with election of judges and many state officials, was never seriously considered. Unlike other state charters of the day, New Jersey's constitution did not become a policy compendium. It said little about the relationship between state government and county or local bodies. It remained a fundamental law, "containing only the bare outlines of a frame of government."[30]

Deficiencies of the 1844 Constitution

This new charter also soon proved inadequate for an increasingly urban and industrial state. The constitutional convention did not foresee the social and political changes that were looming on the horizon. These included alterations in the state's political patterns, a growing role for state government, and massive pressures on the court system. New Jersey was, in Elazar's term, becoming a "commercial republic," but its fundamental law barely recognized it.[31]

At the center of new political debate was the senate made up of one member from each county. A motion in the 1844 convention to elect senators from five equally sized districts had failed by a more than two-to-one margin. None of the counties was overwhelmingly dominant in 1844; the convention's delegates perceived themselves as "a family of little communities."[32] By the end of the century, the northern counties contained most of the population, most of the heavily Catholic recent immigrants, and most of the Democrats. Most southern and western counties were thinly populated, heavily Republican, Protestant, and "native." The population ratio between the largest and smallest counties was less than seven to one in 1840. It was twenty-seven to one by 1910.[33]

Although New Jersey politics was competitive throughout the nineteenth century, only toward the century's end did that competition produce divided government. The Democrats of the populous north could elect the governor, but the numerous rural counties gave Republicans control of the senate. Republican senators regularly rejected Democratic governors' nominees for judicial and executive office. With few limits on their intervention in municipal affairs, legislators could emasculate Democratic city governments.

The state's weak chief executive and the urban Democratic majority were thus held hostage to the Senate Republican caucus and the rural minority. In 1844, former Democratic governor and convention delegate Peter Vroom had expressed satisfaction that with newly elected local officials, the legislature would "come to make laws and not justices of the peace." Now the legislature made judges, state commissioners, and prosecutors on a scale beyond what Vroom could have dreamed.[34]

Amendments to the 1844 Constitution

During its 103-year life, the 1844 constitution was amended only four times. Five times between 1881 and 1913, the assembly called for a constitutional convention, as did three governors. The senate blocked all these appeals, fearing a convention would reapportion the upper house. Nineteen proposed amendments that did pass both houses were defeated in public referenda.[35] The four occasions on which voters did amend the constitution involved Catholics and Democrats lined up against Protestants and Republicans.

The first and most thoroughgoing revision—twenty-eight amendments affecting four of the constitution's ten articles—took place in 1875. In his 1873 inaugural address, Governor Joel Parker, a Democrat, had called for an end to proliferating special and private laws. He noted that general public laws passed in the last legislative session occupied about 100 pages in the statute books, while 1,250 pages were devoted to special legislation—mainly business incorporations. A bipartisan commission appointed to devise appropriate constitutional amendments quickly turned to other topics as well. These included absentee voting for members of the armed services; assessment of property at true value and under uniform rules; free public schools providing a "thorough and efficient education"; increasing the governor's appointive powers to include common pleas judges and the keeper of the state prison; prohibition of legislative intrusion into internal municipal affairs; and an end to white-only suffrage.

The most controversial amendments—taxation at true value and municipal government autonomy—most affected heavily Catholic Hudson County, particularly Jersey City. The debate was sectarian and ugly. In revulsion, voters in a rare moralistic mood individually approved all twenty-eight amendments in a special election on September 7, 1875.[36] The victory was "incomplete and costly."[37] The legislature continued passing theoretically prohibited private laws, throwing them into the overburdened courts. Between 1875 and 1944, the courts overturned more than three hundred statutes, two-thirds of which were special, private, and local laws. "Thorough and efficient" public education and uniform taxation at true value remained items of hot dispute for decades.[38]

Constitutional reform became dormant for almost seventy years. In the 1890s, a period of Republican (and hence rural) dominance began, with five successive Republican governors elected between 1895 and 1907. Voters endorsed an 1897 amendment prohibiting gambling by a margin of 801 in a total vote of 140,000; at the same time they approved a limit on the governor's recess appointments. The first amendment was a Protestant and Republican slap at Catholics and Democrats; the second a restraint on Democratic governors. Gambling also figured in a 1939 amendment legalizing pari-mutuel horse betting, which was supported by tourist interests in the Republican Shore counties. In between, the only other amendment approved (in 1927) gave municipalities the power to zone.

By the time Democratic governors started again winning frequently between 1920 and 1940, Hudson County boss Frank Hague had assumed control of the party. He had no interest in disturbing the status quo assuring his power. The 1927 and 1939 amendments met his qualifications. Hague's excesses and the eventual decline in his influence fueled a new movement for constitutional reform, which in turn resulted in New Jersey's third and current constitution of 1947. The 1844 constitution was born of earnest nonpartisanship, but the government it created became the underpinning of partisan battles. In contrast, the 1947 constitution arose from fierce partisan battles but became a fundamental law admired for its non-partisan integrity.

Prelude to the 1947 Constitution: The Reform Drive of the 1940s

By the 1940s, the 1844 constitution was the despair of half New Jersey's political establishment, and the source of power for the other half. Each of its deficiencies—a weak executive, an archaic court system, a malapportioned legislature, and a difficult amending procedure—had immense political implications. They were particularly resistant to change because important political cleavages crossed party lines.

A coalition of Hudson County Democrats and rural Republicans ruled New Jersey in the first half of the twentieth century. It derived its power from the system of weak state government and strong county government. As long as the governor was weak, the judiciary populated by county party appointees, and all legislation controlled by a senate safeguarding county interests, this ruling coalition could endure. It was in the interest of the Hague Democrats and the rural Republicans to form a winning alliance. Opposed to this coalition were "reform" Republicans and anti-Hague Democrats. Reform Republicans controlled Essex, which rivaled Hudson as the most populous county. During most of the 1930s and 1940s, Arthur T. Vanderbilt led the Essex County Republican Clean Government Association. A distinguished attorney, Vanderbilt eventually became dean of New York University's law school, president of the American Bar Association, and chief justice of the New Jersey Supreme Court.

Vanderbilt sought to make the Clean Government faction, which had some southern allies, a statewide counterweight to Hague and his confederates. He favored constitutional reform because of its potential to modernize the court system. The Clean Government Association also wanted to rationalize the tangled state bureaucracy and make state government more efficient. This aim allied them with influential groups like the Chamber of Commerce and the New Jersey Taxpayers Association.[39] The Clean Government group had little success outside Essex County during the 1930s. It lost primary elections to the rural Republicans (who nominated and elected Governor Harold Hoffman in 1934) and general elections to the Hagueites (who elected T. Harry Moore governor in 1925, 1931, and 1937). However, their prospects improved with the election of Democratic Governor Charles Edison in 1940.

Edison, navy secretary under President Franklin Roosevelt, was imposed by Roosevelt on a reluctant Hague. Once inaugurated, Edison denounced Hague and called for constitutional revision.[40] A blue ribbon citizens' group, the New Jersey Committee for a Constitutional Convention (NJCCC), formed within a month. It embraced the League of Women Voters, the New Jersey Educational Association, the Chamber of Commerce, the Taxpayers Association, the CIO, and the Vanderbilt Clean Government Organization.

The 1941–1942 Hendrickson Commission

The new drive for constitutional reform stalled when Edison suggested that a constitutional convention should make legislative apportionment its first order of business. The Republican legislature took no action. In a token gesture, it appointed a seven-member commission to study constitutional reform in late 1941. The majority was Republican, and all were opponents of Frank Hague. They were led by Arthur Vanderbilt and Robert Hendrickson—commission chairman and the Clean Government gubernatorial candidate that Edison had defeated in 1940.

The commission's closed sessions, beginning just after the bombing of Pearl Harbor, attracted little attention. Most members intended to compose "merely a few innocuous amendments," but Vanderbilt convinced them otherwise.[41] The commissioners emerged from seclusion with a full-blown draft constitution and suggested the legislature organize itself as a constitutional convention to ratify the draft and submit it to the public. Their document provided for a simplified court system, a four-year term for a governor with increased appointment powers, abolition of most dedicated funds, and reorganization of all state agencies into nine departments. These measures reflected Vanderbilt's reform agenda. Other provisions, continuing the legislature's appointment of the state treasurer and chief budget officer and the override of gubernatorial vetoes with a simple majority, embodied the preferences of Hendrickson and the other legislators on the panel. Most notably, no changes were proposed for the senate.[42]

The commission explained its failure to act on frequent criticisms of the 1844 charter and its plan to move the document through the legislature rather than an elected convention as acquiescence to "political realities." Legislators would never release a document that tampered with the senate. An elected constitutional convention dominated by delegates from the large counties would try to alter the senate, endangering the prospects of the other proposals.[43] The concern for "political realities," however, did not extend to how the Hague Democrats and their Republican allies would receive the draft constitution. Instead, the commission went out of its way to enrage the Hudson boss. Requiring all high court judges to have graduated from a law school at least ten years prior to appointment was a provision clearly aimed at Hague's son, a lay member of the court of errors and appeals. Frank Jr. had finally passed the New Jersey bar exam, but he never won a degree from any of the several law schools he attended. Another provision authorized the legislature to investigate local officials. It would have overturned *In re Hague*, which quashed a legislative examination of Hague's affairs.[44] Even the gambling clause took a slap at Hague and his supporters. It permitted racetrack betting but banned the bingo games that were a favored Catholic fund-raising device.

These heavy-handed stipulations guaranteed Hague would move to thwart the commission's recommendations.[45] His chances were improved by failure to give rural Republicans any reason to support reform. A stronger governor with more appointive powers would diminish their legislative patronage and end legislative control of the agriculture department. Once the proposal was transmitted to the legislature, the bipartisan coalition opposed to Vanderbilt and Edison took control. An eight-member committee appointed to study the draft constitution included two Hudson members and four rural Republicans. In the summer of 1942, it voted six to two to take no action until the end of the war.[46]

As 1943 opened, Edison was a lame duck, and politicians turned their attention to that year's gubernatorial election. Believing a new constitution important enough to "plant the seeds even if he was not around to reap the harvest," Edison made constitutional reform the centerpiece of his January legislative message.[47] In a calculated appeal to the heavily Republican legislature, he told them, "If we are honest with ourselves we cannot expect that the haphazard, inefficient and irresponsible State government that we have under the Constitution of 1844 will be half-way competent to deal with the new problems it will have to face. Washington will once more be compelled to act."[48] His words fell on deaf ears, but other political considerations eventually moved the Republican lawmakers.

First, annual rotation of the legislative leadership gave North Jersey Republicans command of the assembly and the senate. The new leaders were the two members of the 1942 joint legislative committee who had opposed its decision to abandon constitutional reform. Second, after years of Democratic gubernatorial dominance, Republicans were hungry for victory in 1943. Walter Edge—governor during World War I and former U.S. senator and ambassador to France—agreed to be their standard-bearer. Active in the NJCCC, Edge's price was Republican support for constitutional reform. Once Edge promised to retain county-based senate representation, a bill for a referendum on the legislature sitting as a constitutional convention sailed through both houses in May 1943.

Reformers were active between spring and Election Day. They were led by the umbrella citizens' group, now renamed the New Jersey Committee for Constitutional Revision (NJCCR). An offshoot, the New Jersey Constitution Foundation, distributed "educational" materials, and had a weekly statewide radio program. It was said that "if three men stopped for a traffic light, someone would run up and make a speech for a new constitution."[49]

Opponents were less visible. Rural Republicans were silent in fear of Edge's wrath and possible damage to their chances in the simultaneous governor's contest. The Democratic gubernatorial candidate, Newark mayor and AFL leader Vincent Murphy, was a trustee of the New Jersey Constitutional Foundation, but he was also aware of Hague's hostility to the measure and needed a huge Hudson vote. Murphy thus blamed the Republicans for past failures and otherwise avoided the subject. Hague himself decided to await the outcome of the referendum.

On Election Day, voters gave both Edge and the constitutional convention solid victories. The referendum won in nineteen counties, losing only in Hudson and Ocean. However, a lack of real interest in reform was evident; only 55 percent of gubernatorial voters bothered to vote on the public question. Having achieved victory, Edge moved quickly and decisively—in the opinion of many, too quickly and too decisively. The day after the election, he issued a "must list" for the new constitution—a reformed court system, a stronger governor, and an easier amending process. By mid-November, an unofficial legislative "committee of thirty" was constituted to go over the Hendrickson Commission draft.

Desiring speed and secrecy so that interest groups could not sabotage the document, Edge decreed that enough public hearings had been held. To criticism that the members of the committee of thirty were all Republicans, he replied they were simply an advisory committee to the governor-elect. As a last-ditch effort, opponents contended in court that the constitution could only be amended by the cumbersome procedure in the 1844 charter. A supreme court justice agreed with Arthur Vanderbilt, who had been deputized by Edge to argue for the state, that it was a "political question" between the people and the legislature, and declined to hear the case.

Thus, a draft constitution, almost identical to that recommended by the Hendrickson Commission, was sent to both houses of the legislature on January 24, 1944, a few days after Governor Edge assumed office.[50] Edge refused to make patronage appointments or allow lawmakers to embark on their usual mid-winter recess until they acted. On February 25, both houses agreed to put the document before the people at the November 1944 elections.

Opponents, led by Hague, now swung into action. Events over the past two years had made the Jersey City mayor even more determined to defeat his political enemies. With Edge's support, Governor Edison had pushed through a measure lowering the tax bill of New Jersey's railroads. It also retroactively relieved the railroads of $39 million in taxes—73 percent of which was due Hudson County, and 53 percent to Jersey City alone.[51]

Edge had also won several "ripper" laws—requiring use of voting machines in Hudson County but not in the solidly Republican rural counties, removing Hague appointments to the county election board and jury commissions, and reforming the county civil service system. The state's largest newspaper wrote that Edge had delivered "more smashing blows" to Frank Hague "than all the other New Jersey governors combined during the last generation. . . . The final blow will be delivered in November if the voters approve a new constitution."[52]

Supporters were confident of victory. Polls during the summer showed a comfortable lead. The Hudson voter rolls had declined by seventy-one thousand since 1940. The presidential contest would bring out the "good-government" commuter vote that usually skipped other elections, and the 1943 referendum had passed easily. Republican presidential candidate Thomas Dewey taped radio spots endorsing the new constitution. However, the Republicans underestimated the Hudson County boss.

Mayor Hague proceeded to organize the opposition on a "magnet issue" basis. Hudson voters were whipped up on the railroad tax issue and the "Edison-Edge-Railroad conspiracy." Labor unions were warned the constitution did not provide collective bargaining rights, and women and minorities were told it had no specific antidiscrimination provisions. Abolition of the chancery court, conservative lawyers were advised, would turn

New Jersey into a divorce mill. The Grange worried about loss of control of the Agriculture Department and uniformed employees about the end of dedicated funds for their pension systems. Finally, in the last days, Hague characterized the whole document as anti-Catholic. Most of the charges had little merit, but there were so many that they were impossible to answer fully. Also, the proponents' attention, and that of the critical independent voters, was centered elsewhere. Edge was distracted by wartime responsibilities and by national politics (he was thought to be a leading contender for the 1944 Republican vice presidential nomination). D–Day and the Normandy invasion deflected the media's interest, particularly that of the New York and Philadelphia newspapers read by commuters.

On Election Day, the constitution was defeated, 54 percent to 46 percent. One in four presidential voters cast no vote on the charter. South Jersey Republicans rejected both Thomas Dewey and the constitution, and Hudson County buried both of them. The proposal was defeated in twelve of the twenty-one counties.[53] By presenting the constitution as a partisan issue, organizing the campaign for it in a partisan manner, and failing to lead that campaign, Edge suffered an embarrassing defeat. He was unable to mobilize the Republican-leaning commuter vote, reluctant rural Republicans, or enough Democrats.[54]

Edge declined to lead further reform efforts. The victorious Hague announced that he would support a popularly elected constitutional convention. The legislature preferred a piecemeal amendment route. The NJCCR, still led by Vanderbilt, decided to concentrate on court reform by amendment. When the legislature devised an eighteen-amendment package, Vanderbilt, opposed to provisions for county courts that were a concession to Hague and the rural Republicans, instructed the Essex legislative delegation to block them. Edge's term ended with the constitution unchanged.

Governor Driscoll and Constitutional Politics

The choice of Alfred Driscoll as the 1946 Republican gubernatorial nominee revived reform efforts. Driscoll, from Camden County, had served in the Edge administration and had good relations with both the Clean Government and Hague Republican factions. He defeated a Hague Republican, former Governor Harold Hoffman, in the Republican primary and won Clean Government support by secretly promising Vanderbilt he would support constitutional reform. Both gubernatorial candidates had ignored the issue in their campaigns, but in his inaugural address Driscoll called the 1844 constitution "hopelessly out of step with the requirements of our modern industrial age."[55] He then sought support for a popularly elected constitutional convention from all the important political factions.

Driscoll first mollified Mayor Hague by removing the Edge-appointed Hudson County election supervisor, ending a state investigation of Hudson bookmaking operations, appointing Hague nominees to Hudson County courts, and supporting bipartisan selection of convention delegates in each county—which would increase the number of Democratic delegates relative to their numbers in the legislature. He also promised to let Hague select the chair of the convention committee on the legislative article. Rural Republicans won agreement that convention delegates would be apportioned among the counties on the basis of their numbers in the legislature—giving the small counties an "unrepresentative" delegate based on their senate representation. The governor also assured small counties that the wording of the new constitutional referendum question would disallow tampering with the senate during the convention.

Driscoll's bargains infuriated Clean Government Republicans. Edge deplored the concessions to Hague, which undid his own attacks on the Boss. Vanderbilt called Driscoll's actions a "grand double-cross."[56] In an April speech, the Clean Government leader said of the delegate composition, "Every day the convention goes on, the people from the larger counties will be wondering what it is that they have done that should have led to their being treated as a politically inferior race. . . . In one Republican county after another we have been treated to the spectacle of the Republican county committee accepting the recommendations of the Democratic county chairman, in each case the direct representative of the Hague machine. . . . The beaches are strewn with the bleached bones of Republican politicians who have listened to the siren voice of Mayor Hague."[57]

Knowing that Vanderbilt's main concern was that rural Republicans and Hagueites would undermine court reform, Driscoll won Vanderbilt's support by endorsing Vanderbilt's court reform plan and giving him the choice of the chair and vice chair of the convention committee on the judiciary. He also promised to make Vanderbilt chief justice of the new high court if the constitution was ratified.

With all factions on board, the second referendum for a constitutional convention in four years passed by a five-to-one vote on June 3, 1947. The major antagonists assured a smooth convention opening by departing the scene of battle. In a surprise move, Mayor Hague resigned on June 4, anointed his nephew, Frank Hague Eggers, as Jersey City mayor, and left for a summer in California. Vanderbilt departed for his Maine vacation home to recuperate from a stroke. Edge withdrew to a hunting lodge in Canada.

THE 1947 CONSTITUTIONAL CONVENTION
AND THE NEW CONSTITUTION

With a somewhat anticlimactic air, eighty-one delegates convened in the Rutgers University gymnasium in New Brunswick on June 12, 1947. After a century of attempts, there was finally wide agreement on the need to produce a modern frame of government. The challenge was how to do it while protecting all major political interests.

The convention delegates numbered fifty-four Republicans, twenty-three Democrats, and four independents. They included twenty-five with legislative experience (including ten incumbent state senators), twenty with judicial experience, twelve business executives, eight women, one black, two farmers, and one labor leader.[58] Rutgers President Robert C. Clothier was elected convention president. For the first seven weeks, the delegates met in committee, convening periodically for progress reports. A small number of committees with complex charges kept members focused on their particular tasks. Lobbyists were banned from the floor, which helped delegates concentrate on major issues.[59]

Although the major committee chairs were strategic choices, representation for all factions prevented assignments from being a source of conflict. Many bipartisan county delegations and alphabetic rather than county roll call votes contributed to a purposeful atmosphere. Even the Hudson Democrats did not vote as a bloc on important issues. A firm September deadline for completion of their work also moved the process along. Each major committee reached quick agreement on once contentious issues and spent most of their time on one or two points with weighty political implications.

For the Committee on the Executive, the question was "not whether the office should be strengthened, but to what degree."[60] Once it was agreed the agriculture secretary would remain a farm group nominee approved by the governor, there was almost no debate about reorganizing the state bureaucracy into no more than twenty cabinet departments otherwise headed by gubernatorial nominees. The committee's toughest issue was gubernatorial succession. The one-term governors of the 1844 constitution were unable to become party leaders—to the satisfaction of the rural county organizations. However, even on this issue, the "conservative" position, which carried the day, was for a four-year term with one immediate reelection try permitted, as opposed to no limit on successive terms.

The committee on the legislative article began work with its major bone of contention—senate reapportionment—declared off the table. It rapidly agreed on longer legislative terms (four years for senators instead of two; two years for the assembly instead of one); limiting legislative appointment power to the state auditor; and retaining annual sessions instead of moving to biennial ones. Its only difficult charge had nothing to do with legislative structure or process—it was handed the hot potato of legalized gambling.

Several factors contributed to the complexity of this issue and its appearance in the constitution. First, gambling was a traditional way to entice New York and Pennsylvania money into an economic area where New Jersey could compete. Second, Jersey Shore resorts desired horse racing and boardwalk games attractive to tourists. Most critically, gambling policy was a metaphor for Catholic–Protestant and Democratic–Republican conflict. The committee could not resolve the conflicts; in its report, it passed on a number of options to the convention as a whole.

The most technically complex work of the convention took place in the committee on the judiciary. The New Jersey court system was the most complicated in the nation, with overlapping jurisdictions at every level that confused even members of the bar. Everyone agreed on the need for reform, but lawyers were hopelessly divided on its shape.[61] There were two principal stumbling blocks. The first was New Jersey's separate equity courts—present in only two other states. Younger attorneys wished to abolish them. Older ones pointed to the state bar's distinguished contributions to equity law. Judges on these courts feared for their jobs. The second issue was what to do about the county courts, beloved of patronage-minded (and prosecution-avoiding) county politicians. They were defended as "close to the people."

The judiciary committee began by hearing forty expert witnesses, who conducted "law school seminars" on state court systems.[62] The teachers included eminent outsiders like Dean Roscoe Pound of Harvard and Judge Learned Hand, as well as New Jersey's governor, chancellor, chief justice, and leaders of the state bar. The choice of Vanderbilt allies as the committee's leaders tilted the committee toward massive reform. The celebrated visitors' impressive arguments for reform, and the less convincing ones by local jurists against it, persuaded the committee's lay members reform was necessary. Consequently, the committee recommended a unified and simplified court system. Hudson County delegates served notice that they would oppose the plan on the floor.

The two other substantive committees also wrestled with predominantly political problems. The committee on taxation and finance quickly agreed on a uniform fiscal year, a single appropriations bill, abolition of all constitutionally protected dedicated funds except the school fund, and the borrowing and spending language of the 1844 constitution. It then had to face the interminable problem of railroad taxation, the only issue about which Hague seemed willing to wreck the convention. From his outpost in California, he warned that the people would "never permit Railroad influences to dominate the preparation of a new constitution."[63] On hearing of Driscoll's recommendation for uniform property taxation, a Hudson County delegate wrote in his diary, "This was about equivalent to His Excellency asking us to jump off the Empire State Building. . . . What the irate taxpayers would do to us delegates if we were to agree to such a proposal is too horrible to contemplate."[64]

The tax issue was clearly headed for the convention floor. However, other potentially dangerous subjects—property tax exemptions for religious organizations and state aid for parochial school busing—passed easily, and another round of religious warfare was avoided. Patriotically inspired delegates also recommended a property tax break for recently returned veterans.

The last of the substantive committees—on rights, privileges, and amendments—had only a few charges, but serious disagreements about them. Most important were the provisions for constitutional amendment. A Hudson County–rural county coalition quickly dispatched a provision, supported by the NJCCR, for automatic referenda on constitutional revision every twenty or twenty-five years. As a Hudson delegate observed, the small counties "thoroughly distrust Essex and Bergen Counties and believe that their fellow Republicans in those counties will liquidate them the first chance available. . . . I too believe it is folly to believe that once turned loose the remainder of the State could be depended upon to decline to liquidate Hudson County . . . the fears of rural Jersey and our own are, in principle, similar."[65]

The small counties also wanted retention of the cumbersome 1844 amending procedures, but in a six-to-five committee vote, their opponents

won amendment ratification by a three-fifths vote of the legislature, gubernatorial assent, and public approval. While hardly radical (amendment by
public initiative, for example, was never considered), the amending process
was greatly simplified.

The committee also had to consider contentious changes in the 1844
bill of rights. First was labor's demand for constitutional protection. The
committee approved the right of private employees to bargain collectively
but did not extend it to public employees. It also drafted a general antidiscrimination statute but rejected pleas of blacks and women for special
protection.

The convention began general sessions on August 10. The changes in
the legislative and executive articles were quickly accepted and produced one of the strongest governorships in the nation. A poorly crafted
Hudson amendment to save the equity courts was defeated easily, but the
Hudson–rural Republican coalition was able to retain the county courts.
Otherwise, the committee's design of a unified and simplified court system
became the convention's major triumph.[66]

Still outstanding were the most "political" decisions—on gambling
and taxes. Compromises were reached on both. Delegates voted to prohibit
all gambling unless approved by public referendum or permitted in the
1844 constitution. However, they also endorsed a referendum on an
amendment permitting games of chance conducted by charitable organizations. This satisfied Hudson County, and thus did bingo, lotto, and raffles
achieve sanctification in New Jersey's fundamental law.

Delegates left negotiations on the tax article to those with the only
hope of achieving an agreement—Governor Driscoll and Jersey City
Mayor Eggers. The convention recessed for several days while Driscoll,
Eggers, and convention president Clothier worked out a complicated deal
to preserve uniform property assessments for all property but ensure legislative action to provide more railroad tax money for Hudson County. Once
this was done, "there was great rejoicing in Jersey City," and "for all intents
and purposes, the constitution of 1947 was 'home.' "[67]

The draft constitution was then approved with only one negative vote,
and the convention adjourned on September 10, ten days ahead of schedule.
Two months later, voters approved it by a margin of five to one. The southern rural counties were least supportive, but the heavily populated northern
and central areas of the state—led by a 131,000 plurality in Hudson—
confirmed it overwhelmingly.

Constitutional Developments Since 1947

Since 1947, the constitution has been significantly altered only with respect to the pivotal issue of legislative apportionment. A constitutional convention limited to that subject was held in 1966 because U.S. Supreme Court rulings in *Baker v. Carr* and *Reynolds v. Sims* required change. The legislature was enlarged from 81 to 120 members, and senate districts, based on population, now cross county lines. In 1978, with many party machines enfeebled, voters also terminated the county courts. Adjustments have been made three times in how long a governor may consider bills and use the pocket veto. Otherwise, the frame of government created in 1947 has remained.

The framers succeeded in keeping New Jersey's charter a fundamental law. At about seventeen thousand words, including all amendments, it is one of the shorter state constitutions.[68] The constitution grants broad statutory powers to the legislature. It is silent on detailed regulation of county and local government—a legacy of the home rule tradition. Interest group provisions cluttering other state constitutions are confined to special property tax exemptions for veterans and senior citizens. Gambling's peculiar constitutional status has also produced several amendments. Well over half of all amendments since 1947 relate to legalized gambling and minor changes in taxation.

New Jersey's latest adventure in constitution writing contains a number of lessons. Good timing contributes to success. The times were right in 1947. The end of World War II encouraged the state to look to its future. The waning power of the Hudson–rural county coalition made it possible to address previously intractable problems. Political leadership is also crucial. Governor Driscoll conciliated the various political factions while never abandoning fundamental principles. Others who could have upset the process—Frank Hague, Arthur Vanderbilt, and former Governor Edge—ultimately showed restraint and statesmanship.

The 1947 constitution blends revolution and evolution. It has been described as a pathbreaking document that "became a model for other states" and as having been "framed strongly by the past."[69] New Jersey's framers saw that the state was ready for far-reaching reform of the executive and the judiciary, and they seized the opportunity. Yet they also understood that assaults on legislative structure and home rule would doom the entire process. Their achievement was a fundamental law that would not shackle the state in the future, as did the earlier charters of 1766 and 1844.

CHAPTER 8

The Governor

In the states the executive power is vested in the hands
of a magistrate, who is apparently placed upon a level
with the legislature, but who is in reality nothing more
than the blind agent and the passive instrument of its
decisions.

—Alexis De Tocqueville, 1830

I have almost total control over the policy-making
apparatus in the state. I am not unhappy about it. A good
governor should absolutely dominate the political debate
in the state and set its agenda.

—Governor Thomas Kean, 1988

The Legislature has had a pretty free hand in how it
manages affairs in the state of New Jersey for the better
part of a decade, and we're going to have to reassert, in a
reasonable way, the authorities of the governor for
leadership in a lot of these areas.

—Governor Jon Corzine, 2006

IN THIS CHAPTER, after reviewing the development of
gubernatorial powers and profiling the people New Jerseyans have chosen
to lead the state, we will look at how recent governors have attended to
their fundamental tasks—achieving support for policy priorities and organizing their offices to seek those priorities effectively. Because the governor
is now so central to almost every aspect of the state's politics, we also discuss the chief executive's role in many other places in this book. Chapters
4 and 5 discuss gubernatorial elections and the governor's role as party
leader; chapter 7 describes the constitutional development of the office and
governors' role in constitutional revision; chapter 10 addresses management
of the executive branch; chapter 12 discusses the chief executive's growing

participation in the federal system; and chapters 14, 15, and 16 deal with gubernatorial policy formulation.

THE POWERS OF THE NEW JERSEY GOVERNOR

When John Adams described the U.S. vice presidency as the most insignificant office ever conceived, he might have included the state governors of the time. In the postcolonial era, memories of the British sovereign and the colonial governor were a powerful argument for a dominant legislature. New Jersey's 1776 charter devoted five articles to the qualifications, election, and duties of legislators. Only one article dealt solely with the governor. As to the chief executive's qualifications, the constitution specified only that the legislature should "elect some fit Person within the colony to be a Governor for one year."[1] As noted in chapter 7, the governor was given the "Supreme executive power," but that power was nowhere defined.

New Jersey's governor was apparently better placed than his contemporaries, however. "It is a notable circumstance," wrote one commentator, "that the powers of the governor of New Jersey under the constitution of 1776 exceeded those of any officer of the same rank in the United States."[2] The legislature often chose distinguished citizens to fill the post. William Livingston, the state's first governor, was reelected fourteen times and sufficiently respected that he "even elevated to a position of influence the impotent office he held."[3]

The new constitution of 1844 provided for popular election of the governor to a three-year term, a weak veto, and some appointment powers. Still, some delegates at the constitutional convention feared that removing the governor from the judiciary would make the position so unattractive that distinguished citizens would shun it. One delegate worried, "I don't think the Governor ever will be a lawyer again. I mean a practicing Lawyer, for the office will not be worth the acceptance of a man with a good practice."[4]

The 1844 constitution did, however, contain the provision that Coleman Ransone suggests opened the way to gubernatorial participation in policy making: "[H]e shall communicate by message to the legislature at the opening of each session, and at such other times as he may deem necessary, the condition of the State, and recommend such measures as he may deem expedient." Eventually, like the president's state of the union address, the governor's annual message became the vehicle for laying out a legislative program. Alan Ehrenhalt argues that Governor Woodrow Wilson (1910–1912) was the first chief executive of an American state to do so.[5]

Under the 1844 constitution, governors were, for a century, subservient to the legislature. This meant first subservience to the railroads and later to county party organizations. Still, a few chief executives such as Wilson were able to affect the course of the state dramatically. What is true of presidents is also true of governors; force of personality, political skills, and the "power to persuade" often count as much as official powers.[6] The executive did gain major advantages under the state's third constitution of 1947, however. Governors could now succeed themselves, hold longer terms, and exercise strong veto and appointment powers.

With these new powers, New Jersey's chief executive is among the strongest in the nation.[7] The governor has wide latitude to initiate by issuing executive orders—a prerogative of only nine of the nation's fifty governors—and broad powers to reject. Along with more than forty other governors, he or she can veto entire pieces of legislation or exercise a line-item veto. Like only fourteen others, the governor may also issue a conditional veto, rejecting portions of a bill and suggesting new language.

The New Jersey governor has been one of only three that are their states' only elected official. New Jersey has not had a lieutenant governor, or an elected secretary of state, treasurer, or attorney general, although the state's voters amended the constitution in 2005 to create a lieutenant governor who will run conjointly with the chief executive beginning with the 2009 election. In twenty-seven states, elected officials hold all of these positions. The governor also appoints, and may remove, most members of his or her cabinet.[8]

If these are "sticks," New Jersey's chief executive also has many "carrots"—powers to provide. Each year, he or she dispenses about five hundred appointments to boards and commissions, and as chief party fundraiser, doles out generous campaign funds. If enjoying the informal power derived from widespread popularity, New Jersey's governor seems almost, as columnist George Will suggested, "an American Caesar."[9] It is thus not surprising that most of New Jersey's post-World War II governors have achieved many of their stated objectives.

Yet these achievements have not come easily. Before the 1970s, the governor's imposing formal powers were still circumscribed by the informal realities of state politics. These were, in particular, the power of the county party organizations, the state's limited fiscal resources, and the governor's public invisibility. As late as 1973, Republican county leaders disenchanted with their sitting governor, William Cahill, could engineer his defeat in the party's nominating primary. Cahill's support for a state income tax was a prime cause of his downfall, and a similar proposal by Cahill's Democratic predecessor, Richard Hughes, was also thwarted by his own legislative partisans. Locally oriented newspapers paid little attention to Trenton and denied the governor a reliable communication channel to the public.

Many of these impediments disappeared in a remarkably short period during the 1970s. The U.S. Supreme Court's reapportionment decisions sapped the powers of the county organizations. In 1977 Democratic county leaders were unable to unseat Governor Brendan Byrne, an incumbent they intensely disliked, as the Republicans had done to Cahill only four years earlier. The New Jersey Supreme Court handed down decisions on school financing that virtually forced the legislature to enact an income tax in 1976.

These developments were crucial to making the governor the genuinely formidable chief executive envisioned by the framers of the 1947 constitution. However, some historic obstacles still remain, and new ones have arisen. Since the elected governorship began in 1844, chief executives have faced legislatures with at least one house under opposition control more than half the time, a figure that has varied little since inception of the constitution in 1947.

Although divided government now occurs more frequently everywhere, it has been common in New Jersey, because there has never been a period when either major party was a helpless minority. Legislators have increasingly independent power bases, and less to fear from gubernatorial "punishment." Until recently, the governor's staff was too small to be "commensurate with the additional authority granted the office."[10] Further, New Jersey's chief executive continues to have the most difficult media climate in the country—with not a single commercial television station oriented primarily to New Jersey, and no statewide newspaper.

THE GOVERNORS: A PERSONAL PROFILE

The ten persons who have won New Jersey's highest office since the 1947 constitution transformed it are similar in many ways to their counterparts across the country. Most were married and in their late forties or early fifties when elected, and all have been white. The last of the few governors who was not a college graduate served in the 1930s; since the 1950s, all but one has had postgraduate education, and seven were lawyers. Until the 1950s, every governor identified with a mainstream Protestant denomination, despite the state's large Catholic population. Since then, more Catholics—five of the ten most recent elected chief executives—have been elevated to the governorship. Four of them were Democrats and all were at least partly of Irish ancestry.[11]

There is a striking difference between New Jersey governors and their colleagues elsewhere in the career paths they follow, and what they do afterward. New Jersey's governors have always been more likely than average to come from the state legislature or the U.S. Congress. Almost all who were not in the legislature or the U.S. Congress when elected had served there earlier in their careers. Among the post–World War II governors, only Christine Todd Whitman broke this mold. Important recruitment channels in other states—elected statewide offices other than the governorship, and elected judgeships—have been absent.

Administrative officials were more likely to run for governor in the early part of the century, when they were chosen by the legislature and were often past members themselves. Since the 1947 constitution made their positions gubernatorial appointments, administrative officials have less often had office-seeking backgrounds. Such recent gubernatorial hopefuls—most often attorneys general—have thus lacked the public recognition or political base to run successfully. Governor Whitman, a former president of the state board of public utilities, is once again the lone exception, but it was her surprise near-victory in the 1990 U.S. Senate race against Bill Bradley rather than her cabinet position that elevated her to top-tier candidacy.

On leaving office, New Jersey's governors, like those in other states, have rejected downward political mobility. They are unlikely to seek lower state office or to enter the U.S. House of Representatives. Otherwise, however, the pattern in the state has been the reverse of the national one. Nationally, retired governors are now more likely than they were early in the century to go on to other high offices, particularly appointive ones, and about as likely to seek U.S. Senate seats as they were in the past. In New Jersey, however, no governor has sought a Senate seat since the 1920s, nor have any ascended to the federal bench or served as an elected federal official, all common aspirations in earlier years. A few have sought or been sought for federal cabinet positions, but only one has yet ended up there.

Governor Whitman, after briefly considering a run for the U.S. Senate in 2000, accepted appointment as commissioner of the federal Environmental Protection Administration on the condition that it be elevated to a cabinet position. Like Whitman, Governor Kean came close to seeking a U.S. Senate seat or accepting a cabinet position, but he made negative decisions about both options more than once while serving as Drew University's president from 1990 to 2005. His habit of floating his name as a possible candidate at every possible opportunity convinced many in the political community that the former governor "preferred agonizing about possible races to actually running for office."[12] Kean's most important postgubernatorial public service came with his appointment as the chair of the national 9–11 Commission after former Secretary of State Henry Kissinger declined the position. Going on the averages, a New Jersey governor is now likely to return to private life upon leaving Trenton.

THE GOVERNOR AND POLICY MAKING: POWERS AND PROBLEMS

New Jersey's modern governors command many advantages in setting the state's agenda and determining major policies. Broad veto powers, domination of the budget process, use of executive orders, wide-ranging appointment powers, and the likelihood of reelection constitute formidable weapons for the chief executive. Additionally, several recent governors have followed up rather systematically on many of their predecessors' chief concerns: "When few others thought the task was worth the trouble, the state's governors have had to struggle to build support for the recognition of statewide needs."[13] Through the 1960s and 1970s, three governors from both parties stubbornly persisted, at considerable political cost, in seeking approval of the statewide income tax finally enacted in 1976. The same three governors sequentially pursued the development of the Meadowlands. Their successors emphasized integrity in state government and politics, protection of the state's environment, and adequate funding of education.

A number have also honored their predecessors or gubernatorial opponents in remarkable ways. Republican William Cahill (1970–1974) appointed his predecessor, Democrat Richard Hughes (1962–1970), as chief justice of the state supreme court. Democrat Brendan Byrne (1974–1982) appointed Republican Thomas Kean (1982–1990) a commissioner of the State Highway Authority after Kean had left the Republican legislative leadership to run unsuccessfully for his party's gubernatorial nomination against Byrne in 1977. When Kean assumed the governorship four years later, he supported the life-tenure appointment by Byrne of Robert Wilentz (a former Democratic legislator and son of a leading Democratic county leader) as state chief justice against the opposition of many in his party. One of Kean's last official acts was to name Byrne a commissioner of the New Jersey Sports and Exposition Authority. Despite palpable hostility between Kean and his successor, Democrat Jim Florio, Florio bestowed Kean's name on a new state aquarium in Camden.[14]

Accomplishments, we have noted, have not always come easily for these "American Caesars." Victory on the income tax was achieved only when court decisions forced it, and the state underwent another major tax battle in the early 1990s. Initiatives in several administrations to help the state's decaying cities have made slow progress. Implementation of land use regulations has moved glacially. Each governor has at least a short list of individual aspirations that went unrealized, and a longer list of initiatives that underwent major modifications. The principal obstacles to gubernatorial success are the increasingly assertive state legislature and the peculiar difficulties in mobilizing public opinion in New Jersey.

The Governor and the Legislature

With mounting staff and personal resources, longer incumbency, and more continuous leadership (subjects addressed in chapters 4 and 9), state legislators have been able to oppose the governor more effectively in recent years. The most important elements affecting governors' abilities to deal with the legislature have been its partisan makeup, the personalities and styles of individual governors, and the nature of the times in which the governor serves.

All other things being equal, a governor does best with the legislature when his own party controls both houses by comfortable but not enormous margins, and when he or she has won a convincing electoral victory.[15] Between 1954 and 2007, Republican William Cahill (1970–1974) and Democrats Brendan Byrne (1974–1982), Jon Corzine (2005–), and Jim McGreevey had these advantages through most of their terms. Republican Thomas Kean (1982–1990) was the only governor since the 1950s who did not enjoy a single year in which his party controlled both legislative houses. Kean also served in the period when the legislature's structural resources increased most markedly. A veteran of the state assembly and its former speaker, his ability to realize his centrist agenda stemmed from his skill at keeping conservative Republicans happy with his positions on crime, taxes, and deregulation while garnering Democratic support for environmental and education initiatives. As the then-assembly speaker described it, "If you didn't know the internal politics of the state, you would swear Tom Kean was a liberal Democrat."[16]

Governor Jim Florio (1990–1994) had early legislative success with auto insurance, gun control, and tax proposals immediately after a landslide gubernatorial victory when his party controlled both houses by only a few votes. Governor Christie Whitman (1994–2000) found that majority control of both houses often did not convince her fellow partisans to back a governor who won with less than 50 percent of the vote both times she ran. Her lack of experience also contributed to her problems. Judy Shaw, who served as Whitman's first chief of staff, reported, "When we came in, we didn't understand this co-equal branch of government stuff. We said, 'Hey, she's the governor, this is what she wants to do.' Then when they started to assert their co-equalness, we realized it was something we had to deal with."[17]

Whatever the partisan makeup of the legislature, the governor's relationship with lawmakers is affected by personal style and political experience. Some governors have been reserved, even taciturn or arrogant in their dealings with legislators and others; other executives have been gregarious, affable, and eager to be liked. There have been pragmatists willing to cut political deals or play political hardball to achieve major ends; others have rejected that strategy.[18]

Democrats Richard Hughes and Jim McGreevey represent one end of the spectrum. Hughes loved people and as a long-time county party politician could cut a patronage deal with the best of them. As Hughes described himself, "My overall thrill at being governor was the relationship with the people. . . . My wife says that if I got an invitation to see three Public Service Electric and Gas men open a manhole in Teaneck I would go . . . to cheer them up as part of our labor force." Hughes decided to run for a second term because there were "so many hundreds and thousands of people depending on you for jobs." Of his dealings with Republican senate leader (and three-time gubernatorial candidate) Charles Sandman, Hughes recalled, "We worked well together on patronage . . . and let's-get-this-bill-up-front stuff." McGreevey depicted his own political persona in language similar to that of Hughes: "I went to every Carpenters Union and Operating Engineers Union local; to the electricians and the laborers; to the women's groups, Latino festivals and almost every African American church in New Jersey. I went to street fairs and picnics and ethnic festivals and flag raisings. The people there really charged my batteries. . . . I loved meeting people from one end of the state to the other, listening to what people wanted and figuring out how to provide it." Like Hughes, he was an experienced county politician who could see patronage in a positive light: "it can have some social benefits. Even Supreme Court Justice Antonin Scalia has extolled patronage as a tool for promoting political stability and easing the integration of marginalized groups." McGreevey admired mayors who could "run their domains like magnanimous despots, taking care of the citizens, keeping the trains running on time, and maintaining cool heads through careful appointments."[19]

At the other end of the spectrum, Brendan Byrne's style was a sharp contrast to that of Hughes. Governor Byrne seemed unconcerned about his low popularity ratings, particularly after the passage of the landmark income tax. As he said of his second victory in 1977, "They probably didn't like me, but they recognized we were making decisions that had to be made. . . . I wanted to get some things done, and I thought in the long run people would appreciate they had to be done. That was more satisfying to me than having people happy with me."[20]

Unlike Hughes, Byrne was not previously active in elective politics. As a veteran Democratic legislator observed of Byrne's prior experience, "He never had to deal in a compromise setting. He was always in a position to call the tune, as a county prosecutor, or on the Public Utilities Commission, and ultimately as a judge."[21] Uncomfortable bargaining with legislators, he relied on staff to do it. One described the preferred method: "I used to see them hiding under their desks. I'd go in and say 'Himself would like to speak to you,' and they would whine, and then you'd drag them into the hall."[22] Once the unhappy lawmakers arrived there, they would find not the governor, but his chief of staff or other major aides, ready to describe the governor's wishes and, perhaps, cut a deal.

Governor Corzine's style had similarities to those of both Byrne and Hughes. Like Byrne, his background—in this case, twenty-six years at the Goldman Sachs investment bank, where he rose to be chairman and CEO—let him call the tune: "[W]hat he said, they got done, and sometimes they worked all night to get it done."[23] And also like Byrne, he seemed unconcerned about his own popularity: "I'm not going to define myself only in life by whether I get reelected, and I'm just not going to make decisions in that context. I'm not sitting around quivering in my boots because

my poll numbers are going to go down." During a standoff with his own
party's assembly leadership over his proposal to add a point to the state sales
tax in 2006, senate president Richard Codey observed, "He [Corzine]
should have realized early on that it's not Goldman Sachs. You can't do a
budget by yourself."[24] On the other hand, like Hughes, Corzine knew how
to cut a deal. When the sales tax imbroglio was finally resolved in his favor
after he shut down state government for the first time in history, he signed
a budget bill that included a record-breaking $350 million in "Christmas
tree" items for Democrats' districts, despite Republicans' call to eliminate
them at a time of severe fiscal distress. He also enjoyed mingling with his
constituents, if it was the many town meetings he held to sell his budget
plan, or spending a day at an elementary school "talking with parents, listening to a group of students sing 'It's a Grand Old Flag' and sharing lunch
in the cafeteria." At the end of his first year, in agreeing that being governor was the best job he had ever had, Corzine himself said, "It's got a policy level, a human context and an overlay of strategy. . . . This job is
unbelievably fun."[25]

    In addition to the legislature's partisan balance and the governor's per-
sonal style, the nature of the times—especially the state of the economy—
affects the governor's success with the legislature. When the economy is
good and there is more money to spend, governors have an easier time with
their initiatives and can afford to let the legislature be more proactive.
When times are tougher and the public is protesting inflation or tax burdens, the governor needs more creativity and resourcefulness.

    How the nature of the times interacts with the governor's own
predilections is important as well.[26] Democrat Robert Meyner (1954–1962)
was a fiscal conservative who fit well into the Eisenhower era. His successor, Richard Hughes, had an expansive view of government's role in tune
with the Kennedy–Johnson era in which he served. Kean's tenure coincided
with the Reagan presidency; like the president, the governor had a gift for
espousing a convincing rhetoric of fiscal conservatism while taking advantage of a boom economy during most of his term to engage in record
spending. Whitman served during Democrat Bill Clinton's presidency, but
both were perceived as moderates within their respective parties and agreed
on many issues.

    In contrast to these happy matches were the tenures of Republican
William Cahill during the economically difficult 1970s and Democrats Jim
Florio and Jim McGreevey, whose terms coincided with that of the first

and second Bush presidencies. Cahill's view of government's role was similar to that of Hughes, but he got caught in the conservative shift among Republicans nationally. Additionally, as the Watergate scandal unfolded nationally, Cahill's own administration suffered scandal. All this contributed to his being the only postwar governor whose renomination bid failed. A combative person, Cahill called his greatest satisfaction in office "the battles I lost. I thought that what I was doing was necessary and right."[27]

Shortly after the first President Bush famously declared "Read my lips—no new taxes," Florio campaigned for governor on the theme that New Jersey had an expenditure problem rather than a revenue problem; shortly thereafter he rammed through the biggest increases in state levies in history. Renominated nonetheless, he became the only post-1947 governor to be denied reelection. McGreevey sought to maintain programs cut by the second President Bush's administration by borrowing rather than taxing. The vast increases in New Jersey's structural deficit that followed posed a major problem for his successor.

State Media and the Role of Public Opinion

As governors seek to guide their agendas through the legislature, they are both helped and hindered by the difficulty of mobilizing public opinion. Through the 1960s, few citizens identified with the state. Its economic leaders did not see New Jersey as a cohesive market, and county bosses dominated political life. "Public opinion" on state issues barely existed and was thus not a terribly important concern for the governor. If the bosses got their patronage, the chief executive had broad flexibility in setting state policy. He only had to deal with a small elite—in politics, the media, and the business community—who were all personally well acquainted. The reverse side of that coin was that without widespread public support, the scope of his policy agenda could not be very ambitious.

Before the 1970s, therefore, a governor's most valuable attributes were extensive knowledge of the state's narrow power structure, a strategic sense of how its members would react to proposals, and, perhaps most importantly, skills at persuasion and negotiation. Consequently, it was not surprising that of these governors, "none were charismatic folk."[28]

State leaders have always known the power of public opinion aroused in support of the governor's priorities; the problem was how to arouse it. Republican Walter Edge, who served two terms separated by almost thirty years (1917–1920, 1944–1947), was a public relations executive by profession. He used his business experience to advance his policy aims and wrote, "Much of the credit for any success my legislative programs may have had belongs to the press of New Jersey . . . the newspapers of New Jersey were extremely helpful in molding public opinion in support of administration policies."[29] A few other earlier governors, notably the elegant orator and writer Woodrow Wilson, were also able to use the press to good effect. However, the locally oriented newspapers and lack of statewide radio or television stations led to the conclusion that "[i]t naturally follows that no Governor except one with the most unusual qualities or remarkable good luck can make or keep himself the dominant factor in state government."[30]

In the 1970s, just as state government expanded, television became the dominant medium, and New Jersey, divided between the New York and Philadelphia media markets, did not have a single commercial TV station. Governor Cahill stated the problem facing its chief executive: "The state comes up short in affording a governor the opportunity to utilize the media properly. There is really no way that you can talk to all the people through any television medium. We do not . . . have the opportunity to get on television and speak to all the people at once. We also do not have a statewide newspaper. . . . The regrettable part about it is that our citizens are not fully informed and therefore do not understand the problems and needs of the entire state."[31] Even if Cahill had enjoyed easy access to television, he was not the sort of warm or articulate person who could use it effectively. Neither was his successor Byrne, who described his own speaking style as "the oratorical equivalent of a blocked punt," and his monotonic voice as resembling a "dial tone."[32] Not until the arrival of Governor Kean in the 1980s did New Jersey's governors move into the media age.

Kean had considerable experience with television before taking office in 1982. Upon losing his first bid for the Republican gubernatorial nomination in 1977, he became a political commentator for the state public television network. After chairing President Gerald Ford's 1976 New Jersey campaign organization, he declined a similar post in the 1980 New Jersey Reagan campaign, preferring to cover it as a reporter. These experiences gave him exposure to the national media and leading Republican media consultants, and further insight into how to use television effectively.[33] Once elected, Kean became New Jersey's first "media governor," displaying considerable ingenuity in getting around the state's special media problems.

Kean believed that "[t]he most important power the governor has is the power of communicating. If that isn't done properly, you lose your power very fast." He saw the problem of mobilizing the public in much the same way Cahill had: "It's more difficult in New Jersey. You haven't got TV—you can't go on TV like you can in forty-eight other states. In other states, if the governor wants something, he'll go on and do a message like the president. There are five TV stations in the state that will give him the time. You can do it [in New Jersey] but it's more difficult. It's more difficult to rev up the newspapers than to go on TV and get out a message."[34]

Kean used a variety of strategies to get his message out. He held hundreds of town meetings all over the state, giving his constituents a chance to make their concerns known, and at the same time experience personally the governor's persuasiveness and charm. He sought opportunities to participate in New York and Philadelphia radio and television programs. His frequent appearances on Sunday morning public affairs shows got him the attention of the attentive public, while less politically aware citizens could often hear him on mass audience call-in programs and see him making public-service announcements on television. (Embroidering on Kean's strategy, Governor Whitman recorded a weekly radio address. Its script was sent to all of New Jersey's numerous suburban weekly newspapers, which greatly magnified its impact.)[35]

Kean's days as a part-time reporter and as a legislative leader gave him a sure sense of media relations; as a reporter commented of each year's most important state news headline, "His years of experience in the political trenches of Trenton have taught him what sells in a budget. He knows exactly what ingredients the press looks for in those first budget stories, which are probably all that most people read."[36]

Some of his successors went further, using television time to defend their budgets without a reportorial filter. In 1990, Governor Florio pleaded his case for his unpopular tax increases on "two commercial stations, the state's entire public-television network and five radio stations, with almost as much fanfare as an Oval Office address . . . hauling his desk and state flag from Trenton to the studio to add the right touch of gubernatorial pomp and circumstance."[37] He was the first (and to date, the last) New Jersey governor to make a statewide television address. In 2007, Governor Corzine, the day after presenting his FY 2008 budget, participated in a prime-time call-in show on the New York City and Philadelphia public television stations, and then continued the program *Ask the Governor* on a monthly basis.

Thus, as governors pursue support for their policy agendas in the legislature and with the public, their methods depend on the climate of public opinion, the political climate in the legislature, and their own personal styles. Governor Hughes in the 1960s and Governor Kean in the 1980s were both veteran legislators with conciliatory styles, and both faced long periods of opposition-dominated legislatures. But Hughes did not enjoy Kean's access to mass television audiences, and Kean did not enjoy Hughes's ability to succeed simply by persuading a few county bosses to get their legislative troops in line. In the 1970s, Governors Cahill and Byrne could both guide their party's legislative majorities with a heavy hand, as unknown legislators with few independent resources feared the governor's wrath or sought future executive branch appointments. Governors Florio, Whitman, McGreevey, and Corzine had to contend with a more independent and assertive legislature and with state media organs that increasingly practiced "gotcha" journalism.

ORGANIZING FOR SUCCESS: THE GOVERNOR'S OFFICE

When Brendan Byrne began his second term in 1977, there were about 60 staff in the governor's office. In 1979, according to the National Governors' Association, the average number of such employees nationally was 34, with a range from 6 to 262.[38] The number of New Jersey staffers increased moderately in Byrne's second term but ballooned to about 150 during the Kean administration. It was not until 2006, when Governor Corzine fired 41 of them and did not fill 21 vacant positions, that the "front office" shrunk appreciably.

Until the second Byrne administration of the late 1970s, the governor's office was run by a small and loosely organized collection of top aides. The chief counsel, assisted by a few lawyers, tracked legislation and prepared "passed-bill" memos advising the governor on appropriate action. A press secretary coordinated relations with reporters, overwhelmingly from the print press and usually the press secretary's former colleagues. An executive secretary dealt with the governor's daily schedule, hiring in the office and, perhaps most crucially, the allocation of gubernatorial patronage. Often the secretary of state, a cabinet official, served as the governor's chief arm-twister in the legislature. Occupants of this position, such as Paul J. Sherwin in the Cahill administration and Robert J. Burkhardt in the Hughes administration, seemed to have a propensity for getting indicted for various forms of corruption.

During the Byrne years, the enactment of the state income tax, the collapse of county party organizational power, and development of new institutional resources for the legislature occurred almost simultaneously. These developments made politics and policy making more complex, and that was soon manifested in the organization of the governor's office. In his second term, Byrne was the first governor to appoint a chief of staff and a director of public information. His chief legislative counsel in the first term was named director of policy and planning, a new office intended to coordinate policy initiatives that crossed traditional departmental lines. The new arrangements reflected widespread opinion in and out of the statehouse that the governor's nominal constitutional powers had "always been limited by the lack of staff to oversee what was going on."[39]

Byrne's successor, Tom Kean, expanded the new components of the office and added some others. Staff in both the counsel's office and the office of policy and planning was greatly augmented. More help was needed in the counsel's office because of the increasing number of bills churned out by the legislature, and also because Kean was the first governor not to enjoy an informal kind of pocket veto known as gubernatorial courtesy. Although the state constitution called for the governor to act on a transmitted bill within ten days, the clock did not officially start running until the governor "called for" the bill. Many of the bills the legislature enacted were dispensed with by never being called for. A constitutional amendment at the end of 1981 ended that practice. More assistant counsels were needed to write more passed-bill memos and veto messages in a short period of time, especially at the end of legislative sessions.

In the case of policy and planning, the growing complexity of state policy made many issues too convoluted for one cabinet officer to deal with and slowed down the whole policy process. The number of cabinet departments grew from fourteen to twenty between 1950 and 1980, and their subdivisions mushroomed. Increasing fragmentation predictably produced duplication of effort, cross-purposes, and more things falling between the cracks. As a Kean cabinet official described it, coordination was needed in the growing instances when, for example, "the policy of the environmental commissioner is radically different from the transportation commissioner's, or from Treasury, where revenue growth is affected. It's a hell of a lot worse than ten years ago."[40] The office of policy and planning also helps a governor decide which current issues should become thematic priorities, receiving close attention and the full weight of the governor's support. Other governors created similar offices at about the same time, but the New Jersey office is one of the strongest and most wide-ranging.[41]

Kean's reorganization of the governor's office also included a massive increase in its outreach capacities. The director of public information was replaced with a director of communications and a larger staff to coordinate public relations. In the Byrne administration, one secretary was in charge of vetting the governor's mail from the public, and Kean's staff arrived to find a closet stuffed with unopened correspondence. Along with Kean's own expanded outreach activities like town meetings and media appearances, an office of constituent communications was instituted to answer every piece of mail. Elaborate word-processing systems replaced the previous adminis-tration's typewriters.

The front office under Kean's successor, Jim Florio, further expanded on the Kean innovations, devoting even more resources to planning and coordina-tion, legislative relations, and public outreach. The Policy and Planning office, renamed the Office of Management and Planning, served as a clearing house for the activities of all state agencies as well as being a policy development body. The head of the office devoted herself to management and coordination, while a director of policy worked on programmatic initiatives.

The director of communications, while responsible for speechwriting, public communication and event planning, also supervised the press secre-tary. Florio's Office of Constituent Relations had a staff of twenty-three to deal with hundreds, sometimes thousands, of letters and phone calls daily. The advent of computer-generated correspondence increased the load, although also making it somewhat easier to address. Governor Corzine got by with a staff of thirteen who created generic responses to "hot button" issues. Specialized audiences had specialized writers, like the woman who did nothing but responding to children's letters.[42]

In her first term, Governor Whitman neither dispatched skillful liaisons to the legislature nor mounted the kind of public relations campaigns that were the hallmark of the Kean administration. She seemed more often to comment on legislative initiatives than to advance her own. As her second term began, Whitman fired her Washington-based consultants, mobilized her staff to focus more on "message discipline" and grassroots communica-tion, and sought tight coordination between her policy, media, and sched-uling staff. "Message months" and "message weeks" became frequent occurrences. In weekly senior staff meetings, the first item on the agenda was matching the governor's event invitations to the current primary initiative. For example, a billion-dollar program to buy land for permanent open space in the nation's most densely populated state was the most important initiative of her second term. October 1998 was Open Space message month, and the only events in which Whitman participated were geared toward pushing the Open Space proposal through the legislature.[43]

All governors now must grapple with a more complicated policy agenda, an assertive legislature, and a more interested public. In some ways, their staffs tend to be similar, made up primarily of policy generalists and old political acquaintances. Mobility and authority within the office are fluid, depending as much on political acumen and skills as formal titles. But each governor's office also reflects the individual.

Byrne's distaste for personal bargaining, and the presence of some top aides whom legislators viewed as being as arrogant and unfamiliar with Trenton folkways as Byrne was, led to poor relations with the legislature in his first term. Things improved somewhat in his second term when the top staffers changed and the governor distanced himself more. Throughout his tenure, however, Byrne limited personal access and kept a tight rein on the agenda. No administration official went to a committee meeting or to the floor of the legislature without clearance from the counsel's office, and the administration bill list was always very large and very clear.

In contrast, Kean had an open door to a larger number of staff. Throughout his eight years as governor, the chief of staff, chief counsel, and director of policy and planning were a troika, equally important in the office hierarchy. His press secretary also participated fully in policy debates. Kean welcomed written arguments and information from many sources explaining, "I like information, I like to hear what's going on. . . . People have different perspectives. It's not efficient and you do run into problems, but you don't get blindsided; somebody will bring everything to your attention. I like that, but most executives would not like it. Every governor has to design it for themselves. . . . Eventually you know your own style. It took me a year or two until I had exactly the office I wanted."[44] Although Kean's top legislative priorities were clear, other issues were dealt with less tightly than in the Byrne administration. Cabinet officers had latitude to develop programs outside Kean's central agenda. It was not uncommon for commissioners to espouse different positions on cross-cutting issues. The governor's office took no position on bills of this kind as long as they were still in committee. It was only when they reached the floor that an assistant counsel would be dispatched to announce Kean's position to the Republican legislative caucuses, and attempts would ensue to keep unwanted bills from being posted or to get amendments.

Governor Corzine had a similarly deliberative style. In 2006, because of his concerns about the financial ability of New Jersey's Public Service Electric and Gas Corporation to manage the state's aging nuclear power plants, he initially supported a merger between the Illinois-based Exelon company and PSE&G to create the nation's largest utility corporation. When Exelon threatened to cancel the deal because of regulatory requirements proposed by the Board of Public Utilities and the opposition of the Department of the Public Advocate, Corzine admitted, "I'm out of sync with my administration on this one." He went on to say, however, "There needs to be serious analysis of the financial terms and conditions for the ratepayers in this state. And I don't think it needs to be done on a crash-course basis just because the board of directors of one of the companies decides that Friday on some day in August is the day that they want a decision." Although the deal had been approved by Connecticut, New York, Pennsylvania, and the Federal Energy Regulatory Commission, Corzine's tepid support and the opposition of the BPU led to its collapse.[45]

Governor Florio combined aspects of the Byrne and Kean styles. Even more than Byrne, Florio exercised tight control over cabinet departments. Even more than Kean, he was concerned with strategic planning for the future and domination of the media. Florio used his personal staff to monitor a wide variety of initiatives, ending what he regarded as the Kean cabinet's style of freelancing. Cabinet officers became extensions of the Governor's staff, a distinct change from the traditional standing of them being an extension of the Governor. Cabinet meetings were used to communicate Florio's agenda, rather than being the briefing sessions of the Kean era—leading Labor Commissioner Raymond Bramucci to tell Florio in exasperation at the end of one such meeting, "You treat us like mushrooms. You keep us in the dark and cover us with bull . . ."[46]

Florio extended even further the use of the Policy and Planning Office that Kean had institutionalized. The Florio Office of Management and Planning was not only a policy incubator but a vehicle for coordinating cross-departmental programs in a manner Florio described as horizontal rather than vertical. His managerial model was small groups of cabinet officers working with senior staffers in the governor's office to develop policies affecting several departments. It reflected both Florio's preference for centralized management and the growing complexity of issues. Governor

Whitman organized her policy staffers similarly, assigning each of them to department portfolios, and holding cross-agency meetings.

Governors and State Policy: A Summary Assessment

We end this chapter as we began it. The governor is a powerful official and can expect to leave office with many accomplishments. Yet victories are harder won and more extensively compromised than they would have been a few decades ago—even when the governor enjoys the most favorable combination of public opinion, partisan advantage, and external events. There are simply more people to satisfy, more complexities to overcome, and more players with more of their own resources than there have ever been before. This is particularly true of the legislature, which we examine in detail in the next chapter.

Because legislators know that their careers depend more and more on their own efforts and less and less on the governor or partisan considerations, neither gubernatorial threats nor rewards have much effect on their long-term propensity to cooperate. One former gubernatorial aide has said of the legislature, "Every governor has to understand they may say, 'This is fine for you governor, but how is it going to play in Woodbridge,' or another part of their constituency. . . . If you've got a tough agenda . . . then you know you're going to be in for a long, very rocky road."[47]

In the end, achieving difficult policy priorities now depends most on the governor's own persistence and ability to mobilize public opinion and persuade the legislature that what is good for the governor is good for them as well. As the Republican assembly budget officer observed of the legislative maneuvering around Governor Corzine's first spending plan, "You're going to see a lot of scrambling and a lot of posturing. It's not about the people running around the supermarket. It's what the meal looks like at the end of the cooking."[48]

CHAPTER 9

The Legislature

Speaker: Why do you rise?
Assemblyman: Mr. Speaker, I rise to aerate my shorts.
>   —colloquy in the New Jersey Assembly, 1976

The truth is that without a strong governor, the New
Jersey legislature is out to lunch.
>   —Duane Lockard, 1976

The legislature today insists on sharing not only in the
credit for state policy, but also its formulation. It no
longer tolerates being excluded from the initiative and
planning part of the process.
>   —Alan Rosenthal, 1986

IF NEW JERSEY BARELY had a state politics before the
1970s, until then it also barely had a state legislature. Before the adoption
of the 1947 constitution, the legislature's powers far surpassed those of the
governor, but before 1947 there was not much any element of state government was expected to do. State representatives, for annual salaries of five
hundred dollars, did the public's business at Monday night meetings five
months of the year.

When the constitution granted the governor important new powers,
and nothing about the legislature changed, its institutional role became even
less significant. Today's stronger and more competent legislature arose from
external forces that compelled change—U.S. Supreme Court rulings ending
malapportionment, and the decline of most of the county party organizations that recruited legislators and rotated most of them out of office quickly.

John Wahlke's 1962 description of the New Jersey legislature makes the
scope of change apparent. Its "essential features," Wahlke noted, were small
size, extreme partisanship, dominance by the (Republican) majority

caucus, an irrelevant committee system, the impersonalism of rotation, and a shut-out (Democratic) minority.[1] None of these "essential features" survive. The New Jersey legislature of today is an almost new institution—highly professionalized and with much greater capacity.

LEGISLATIVE STRUCTURE BEFORE THE 1970s

Until 1968, the legislature had eighty-one members, and was the sixth smallest in the nation. The assembly still had the sixty members specified in the constitution of 1844. Members were elected at large until 1852, when multimember, county-based districts were created. At-large elections within the districts continued, enhancing the strength of a county's majority party. In 1953, for example, Republican candidates running for Essex County's twelve assembly seats received an average of 125,000 votes, while their Democratic opponents averaged 117,000. Due to the at-large system, the Republicans won all of the Essex seats, although they received only about 52 percent of the vote.[2]

Assembly districts were apportioned by population, but each county was guaranteed at least one—a provision benefiting the Republicans who dominated most small, rural counties. Assembly members were elected annually, and most were rotated out after two single-year terms. As it had been since 1776, the legislature's upper house was composed of one member from each county, regardless of population. In 1954, New Jersey was one of only six states using counties as the basis for representation in the upper house; the other five were thinly populated and lacked urban concentrations.[3] The senate's size changed only as new counties were formed, and stabilized at twenty-one after Union County's creation in 1857. The senate was severely malapportioned. In the 1930s, members representing 15 percent of the state's population—fewer than the residents of the single county of Hudson—could put together a senate majority. Even by 1963, when migration to the suburbs had produced more even population distribution, an eleven-member majority could be made of senators representing about 41 percent of the public.[4] New Jersey senators served three-year terms.

A county-based system of representation advantaged the Republicans, especially in the senate. So did elections in odd-numbered years, when there were no federal contests to draw casual voters to the polls. By the 1960s, the Republicans had controlled the upper house for all but three years of the entire century and the assembly for all but thirteen, despite frequent statewide election of Democratic governors.

LEGISLATIVE STRUCTURE: 1970 TO
THE PRESENT

"One person/one vote" court decisions in the 1960s almost annihi-
lated the counties as the basis of representation in both houses. As a result,
a 1966 constitutional convention produced a new 120-member legislature
of 40 senators and 80 assembly members, two in each senate district. Members of the assembly are now elected in odd-numbered years for two-year
terms, while senators are elected in odd-numbered years for nonstaggered
terms, usually of four years.[5] Many districts cross county lines. Although
about half the forty senate districts now include municipalities in only one
county, only in small, rural Cape May are all county municipalities still represented by one senator.

County lines do, however, continue to influence political thinking and
organization, creating problems for the politicians whose districts cross
them. As a particularly unfortunate lawmaker whose district covered parts
of five counties observed, "The result is five Lincoln Day fundraisers, five
NJEA legislative dinners, and five of almost everything else, a needless waste
of time and expense for a part-time legislator."[6]

When the census requires legislative redistricting, a ten-member bipartisan commission named by the state party chairs is charged with drawing
new district lines. If the commission cannot reach agreement within thirty
days of receipt of official census figures, the state's chief justice appoints a
neutral tiebreaker. In both 1980 and 1990, political scientist Donald Stokes,
dean of the Woodrow Wilson School at Princeton University, was the
tiebreaker who cast the deciding vote. Stokes's integrity is best demonstrated
by complaints in both years that he was "unfair"—from the Democrats in
1980 and the Republicans in 1990.

In 1982, amendments to the federal Voting Rights Act mandated creation of "majority minority" districts where possible. They were an important factor in the 1990 redistricting process. Republicans and the NAACP
called for two districts in Essex County with minority voting populations
of over 60 percent. Tiebreaker Stokes agreed with the Democrats' proposal
for three districts with minority populations of about 55 percent. The immediate effect was to protect white Democratic incumbents. The new map
also contained a Hudson County district with a Hispanic majority.[7]

The lines drawn for the 1991 legislative elections created a new district
in the southern half of the state, combined two in the north, and generally
shifted districts south and west, reflecting population shifts. The same

majority-minority districts were also the center of debate after the 2000 census, when Princeton political scientist Larry Bartels served as the tiebreaker. The Republicans contended that the existing majority-minority districts, now totaling five, should be increased to six. The Democrats, upon discovering that every legislative district with a black population of at least 22 percent had at least one African American legislator, and that eight of the fifteen black lawmakers represented districts whose populations were less than 30 percent black, proposed instead to "unpack" the majority black districts to add some white voters and to move enough black voters to an adjacent district to make it likely that a white Republican senator would be dislodged. Bartels accepted the Democratic plan, asserting that it best met the criteria of partisan fairness, responsiveness, and accountability.[8]

In response to the Democrats' charge that their opponents were "packing" minority voters into districts to protect a white Republican legislator, the Republicans replied that the Democrats were "cracking" traditional communities apart. Four of the five GOP members refused to attend the redistricting commission's last meeting to vote on the plan (which then passed by a majority of six to one, with Bartels siding with the Democrats), and the next day they took their complaints to federal court.

The arguments in the expedited trial for *Page v. Bartels* centered on contending partisan interpretations of the intent of the Voting Rights Act. The Republicans' attorneys continued to maintain that the plan violated it. The Democrats' lawyers, supported by the state's entire minority political establishment, argued instead that the Voting Rights Act sought not the highest possible number of minority voters in a district, but rather their effective representation. Thus, a plan that could diminish their underrepresentation in the legislature relative to their population best reflected the intent of the law. In a unanimous decision the three judge panel agreed.[9]

LEGISLATORS: A PORTRAIT

A few county or municipal party chairs still serve in the legislature, but most local party organizations can no longer single-handedly choose their delegations, nor rotate them out of office after a term or two. However, lawmakers still have deep local roots. In both houses, large majorities are New Jersey natives, and many represent at least portions of the county where they were born. Most of the nonnatives arrived long ago from neighboring states.

Although legislators are firmly embedded in their communities, not all of the state's communities are firmly embedded in the legislature. As with

most other American legislatures, New Jersey's is heavily white and male
and includes a narrow range of professions. A new high of 23 women (19
percent) among the one 120 legislators in 2007 placed New Jersey thirty-
fifth among the states in terms of female representation.[10] Twenty-three
lawmakers were persons of color, and both women and persons of color
remain underrepresented relative to their proportion of the population.

About one-third of the members of the 212th legislature of 2006–2008
were attorneys. More than half the state senators of the 1930s were lawyers,
and about three-quarters were in 1955. Almost half the assembly members
that year were also from the legal profession, compared to 22 percent nationally.[11] Thus, the national decline of lawyer-legislators has also occurred in
New Jersey, but the state had more of them to begin with. An increasing
number (22 percent in 2006–2008) identify themselves as full-time lawmakers. In descending order, the other most common occupations of New
Jersey lawmakers are in business, local government, education, and the
health professions.[12] A 2003 national survey of state legislators found that
the New Jersey respondents reported spending an average of 70 percent of
the time requirements of a full-time job on legislative work, including session time, interim work, constituent service, and campaigning.[13]

A stiff conflict-of-interest law affects attorneys' ability to serve. Not
only are legislators banned from doing legal business with the state themselves, but they are also banned from membership in a firm in which other
partners do such business. Although well intended, the law bars many distinguished, politically active lawyers from legislative service. One example
is former assemblyman Robert Wilentz, scion of a prominent political
family, and later chief justice of the state supreme court. Wilentz voted for
the conflict-of-interest bill that ended his legislative career and left the
assembly at the end of that term. The remaining attorneys are of the "Main
Street lawyer" variety, whose practice often includes work for municipal
and county governments.

Handsome salaries in many states lead an increasing number of lawmakers to make officeholding a full-time career. Once New Jersey raised its
long-standing annual stipend of $500 to $5,000 shortly after passage of the
1947 constitution, legislators began approving regular salary increases—to
$10,000 by 1976, $18,000 in 1980, $25,000 in 1984, $35,000 in 1990, and
$49,000 in 2005. The pay of the leaders of both houses is one-third higher.

In the 2006–2008 legislature, fifty-two of the members (42 percent) held
at least one other salaried position on a state or local payroll, a practice

known as double dipping. A 2004 study by the Center for Public Integrity found that New Jersey led the nation in dual officeholding, which is illegal in thirty-eight states.[14] A number of legislators were employed in the public educational or health systems, but twenty-one were also elected local officials, primarily mayors or county freeholders (the New Jersey term for county legislators). Senator Nicholas Sacco of Hudson County was a triple dipper, serving also as mayor of North Bergen and its assistant superintendent of schools. Senator Wayne Bryant of Camden County, who at one time held four government jobs simultaneously, was forced to resign as chair of the budget committee in 2006 when a state grand jury began a study of his records that resulted in his indictment the following year. The resulting furor led to passage of a 2007 law prohibiting legislators from being newly elected to more than one office after February 2008. It thus grandfathered nineteen current lawmakers who held more than one elected position and who would be returning for the next legislative session.

Almost all the dual officeholders come from one-party strongholds and are part of a long-standing tradition in the state.[15] In 1947, delegates to the constitutional convention considered banning the practice, but took no action. In the early 1960s, the New Jersey Supreme Court handed down three successive decisions dealing with the "incompatibility" of holding multiple government positions. The legislature swiftly passed a law exempting concurrent service in local or county office and the legislature from the court's dicta. Its constitutionality was quickly affirmed by the same court, which held that "if the lawmakers acting . . . as the architects of the structure of government ordain that one person may or may not hold two public offices, the judiciary cannot interfere."[16]

The legislature's unusual meeting schedule makes it relatively easy to pursue another occupation while serving in Trenton. A few other geographically compact states have a commuter legislature, but only New Jersey's is technically in session almost all year yet meets as a body only twice weekly—on Mondays and Thursdays. There are usually long breaks for committee hearings after the governor's February budget message, few sessions during the summer, and an election-time recess in the years legislators are running.

Members can travel to the capital in less than two hours from anywhere in the state and return home the same day. With recent scheduling improvements, many can make it home in time for dinner. Trenton thus largely lacks the hangout hotels, restaurants, and other components of legislative life common to most state capitals. After late sessions, legislators are as likely to stop for a hasty meal at one of New Jersey's ubiquitous highway diners on their way home as they are to go to a Trenton watering hole to talk shop with their colleagues.

Having once gained election, lawmakers were prone to stay in their seats. Turnover in the assembly dropped steadily through the 1970s and 1980s. Most of the new members were not successful challengers but rather won seats that opened because of voluntary resignation (often to run for the senate) or death. Although departures also dropped steadily in the upper house, it took a while longer for the senate to reach the assembly's level of continuity. In both houses, incumbents running for reelection in most of the last several contests had about a nine in ten chance of being returned. The pattern of low turnover was only disrupted in elections immediately following redistricting, but the most recent such contest was rather different. In 1983, forty-seven incumbents did not return to the legislature, and in 1993, fifty-two incumbents did not return. In 2003, however, only seventeen members did not return.

While this post-redistricting changing of the guard was very modest, the 2007 primary elections saw an unprecedented number of departures in the senate. Of the 40 members of the upper house, 13 chose to retire, taking with them about three hundred years of legislative experience. There was a ripple effect in the assembly as 15 of its members sought to move up to the senate. All told, 260 candidates sought seats in the 120-member legislature. The reasons for the senators' voluntary departures varied, but some patterns can be discerned. As a consequence of the low turnover of previous years, almost all of those departing were more than sixty years old; a number were over seventy and had significant health problems. Several would have faced tough contests in either the primary or general elections. Many were disgruntled about cultural changes like expensive, ideological campaigns and close scrutiny by the media. Nine of the thirteen were Republicans, frustrated by the Democrats' lock on all three branches of state government.

LEGISLATORS' WORK ENVIRONMENT

In the days of the amateur, part-time legislature, desks in the legislative chamber comprised most New Jersey lawmakers' work environment. Only the senate president and assembly speaker had offices in the statehouse, and there were no rooms for committee meetings. A 1963 study observed,

"Their present practice of considering important public business in the gallery during recesses is deplorable."[17] Former governor Thomas Kean, who was elected to the assembly in 1967 and served ten years, recalls an early experience there: "My first year, there was some bill where I said, 'We've got to discuss this in committee before we even take it to caucus.' We had to go and negotiate for the ladies' room. They had a lady's cloakroom that was right across from the assembly chamber—so we sat in there, across from the chamber, because there was no other space."[18]

The legislative staff consisted of some part-time patronage employees performing the most basic administrative and secretarial functions at the behest of the leadership. This staff increased modestly in the 1950s, and acquired the impressive-sounding appellation of Legislative Services Agency. The staff increases were partly the result of the recommendations of a legislative commission and partly due to the tendency to ignore legal limits. In 1957 for example, the rules called for twelve assembly clerks and four in the senate. The actual numbers of such employees were forty-four and nineteen respectively.[19]

Little changed until the early 1970s, when a new breed of legislator less tied to party organizations began to arrive and assume leadership positions. Dramatic increases in all kinds of staff support followed quickly.[20] In the space of a few years, full-time, nonpartisan, professional staff, partisan staff, and personal staff were all created or grew markedly.

A 1971 Commission to Study the Legislature (spearheaded by, among others, then-Assembly Majority Leader Tom Kean) called for full-time staff to support the work of committees. The Legislative Services Agency, shortly renamed the Office of Legislative Services (OLS), assumed its current organizational structure in 1979—consisting of divisions of State Auditing, Legal Services, Legislative Information and Research, and Budget and Program Review. The first two offices perform the traditional tasks of postaudits of state agencies (constitutionally assigned to the legislature) and bill drafting. However, the divisions that have grown the most are those providing research and budget analysis.

These staff additions gave lawmakers independent information and support and reduced their dependence on interest groups and the governor's office.[21] Governor Kean, in comparing the legislature in which he served in the 1960s and 1970s to the current body has observed, "The legislature had no fiscal capacity, and if we wanted anything, we had to go to [the state budget director]. If the governor didn't want us to do that, they'd just say no . . . [Now] they have the capability to do real research. They have the capability to know what they're talking about. They have the capability to look at the budget with a fine-tooth comb and ask really penetrating questions. . . . That's what a legislative body should have, even if you have to question how they're using it." As governor, Kean personally experienced the contribution of the budget-reviewing Office of Fiscal Affairs to legislative autonomy, which as a legislative leader he had helped to create. He ruefully recalled, "I sometimes wonder if [Governor] Cahill wasn't right. I had to bargain with him to sign it—he said no governor should sign this bill."[22]

In 1968, the Information and Research Division consisted of nine professionals supporting a few committees. By 1971, the professional personnel had grown by half, so that five could be assigned to support key committees and the rest worked for two committees each. By the late 1970s, every committee had its own nonpartisan full-time professional staffer. The OLS budget grew from $3.3 million in FY 1975 to $11.3 million in FY 1984, $20.9 million in FY 1991, and $29.9 million in FY 2007, when it had 350 employees.[23]

At about the same time that members strengthened the nonpartisan staff, they also began to turn the patronage employees into a more professional operation. Both parties appointed executive directors for the partisan staff in 1970. Most of the growth of this more overtly political operation, however, occurred in the 1980s, after the beefed-up OLS showed legislators how useful staff could be. As the OLS head put it, lawmakers developed "the sense that our function was too important not to be a political function."[24]

Whereas OLS staff provides committee chairs with legal, research, and bill-drafting assistance, the partisan staff serves at the pleasure of the party leadership in each chamber. Its highest officials are a useful "institutional memory," especially on the Democratic side, with longer tenure than many legislators. Although developing party policy and providing support to committees are part of their job, the partisan staff spends much time running an elaborate press operation for leaders and members and serving as a more or less permanent campaign organization. Partisan workers compile voting and attendance data on the opposition for use in campaigns, write statements and speeches for members, and manage many campaigns.

The partisan staff's political activities became unusually public in 1990. The attorney general launched an investigation of a Republican assembly staffer who had "spied" on the Democrats by breaking into their data files on the legislature's computers. After admitting he knew of the staffer's activities and had done nothing about them, the GOP assembly staff director was forced to resign. Democrats could take little pleasure in their opponents' discomfort, however, because the files in question included records of Democratic campaign contributors—an obvious misuse of state property and possible official misconduct.[25]

After six months of study, a state grand jury found that while legislative employees of both parties improperly performed campaign work on state time, there were no "uniform guidelines" to provide grounds for criminal indictments. It proposed a draft law prohibiting the use of public funds "in furtherance of the nomination, election or defeat of any candidate for public office."[26]

Along with all the aides that legislators share, each lawmaker has a budget for personal staff and a district office. By the mid-1970s, to enhance communication with constituents, each member already received funds to rent and furnish a district office, a telephone credit card, stationery, and five thousand stamps. The allowance of $15,000 for personal staff aides in 1976 has grown steadily, increasing fastest in recent years. The $25,000 members awarded themselves for this purpose in 1985 became $45,000 by 1987, $70,000 in 1991, and $110,000 in 2005. The nature and use of personal aides varies widely. Generally speaking, legislators from competitive suburban districts turn district office staff into a well-honed constituency service and personal political organization. Some district representatives pool their funds to pay a relatively small number of full-time staff, who run professional and smoothly functioning offices. On the other hand, some legislators from safe districts with remnants of a county party organization hire large numbers of "very part-time" or no-show employees whose offices are hard to find and seldom open. Many "aides" receive annual "salaries" of $500 to $1,000, whose real value is to the employee's eventual state pension. Pension payments are dependent on the number of years of state, county, and municipal employment, and these small stipends count toward those years.

Overall, New Jersey ranks high in its provision of legislative staff of all varieties. In 1979, it was one of only three states providing full-time personal staff to members of the lower house and one of ten allotting such staff to senators. New Jersey then ranked thirteenth nationally in the size of its state legislative staff, and by 1988, when there were 780 staffers, it was ninth. By 2003, a staff of 1,265 put New Jersey sixth among the states.[27]

THE ORGANIZATION OF THE LEGISLATURE:
COMMITTEES AND LEADERSHIP

In the era when New Jersey legislative committees had no staff, their absence was unremarked. Although formally numerous, committees were merely paper organizations. Rules called for weekly committee meetings, but they were seldom held. Many committees had no bills referred to them, and no records were kept of attendance or actions. Although the forty-five senate committees and fifty-four assembly committees of 1953 were soon severely reduced, the smaller number was not much more effective. The twenty-one senators were still nominally assigned to nine to twelve committees each, leading the authors of one survey of legislative work to comment, "One can only wonder what would happen if in fact the Senate committees did attempt to meet regularly."[28]

The legislature's work, such as it was, got done not in its committees but in the majority party caucuses, particularly in the senate—which is to say, by the Republican senators. As it was described in the early 1960s, "When Senators arrive on Monday morning, the Republicans go into caucus and the Democrats wait around wondering what is going to come out of caucus."[29] The senate Republican caucus of this epoch, as we noted in chapter 3, was similar to the despotic U.S. House Rules Committee of the same era and was called the "most powerful majority party caucus in any state legislative chamber."[30]

When the senate doubled in size and the Democrats assumed control in 1974, the Republican caucus lost its power to delay or defeat. With no alternative institutions to play the caucus's role, control of the legislative agenda passed for a brief time to the governor's office. New Jersey's legislative committees, compared to those in other states, were described as "very passive"—with light work loads, few bills referred, and even fewer amended. The committees had "little to do with policy and program formulation."[31] However, the 1971 Commission to Study the Legislature, which had launched the development of a professional staff, also began the process of constructing a genuine committee system for the staff to serve. Over the next few years, the commission's recommendations to establish committee rooms, record committee actions and attendance, open meetings to the public, refer bills routinely to reference committees, and hold legislative sessions two days a week were all adopted.

In the 212th legislature (2006–2008), there were thirteen standing reference committees in the senate and twenty-two in the assembly, numbers that have varied somewhat since committees were reduced to twelve in both houses in 1954. Since the severe pruning of the 1950s, the trend has been toward increased numbers, especially in the assembly. Traditionally, the membership and chairmanships of the various committees resembled a game of musical chairs, with new players constantly entering the game. High turnover ensured a lot of new members and open slots, and continuing legislators migrated to "better" committee slots and then to the leadership ladder. At least half the members of the "desirable" and important committees dealing with taxation, finance, and judicial appointments changed from one session to the next between 1948 and 1967.[32]

Turnover is usually lower now, especially on the committees dealing with financial affairs, and changes occur less often because of members' departure from the legislature. Rather, they are occasioned more by alterations in party balance (and thus parties' respective proportions of committee members) and the creation of new committees on which to serve. All bills of any import now go through committee screening and public hearings, and a growing number of committee meetings and public hearings are held on non-session days so there is time for more careful consideration.

All these logistical alterations and the proliferating staff would still not have given the legislature more control over its own affairs if it had not, at roughly the same time, begun to develop more continuous leadership. Before the 1970s, there was a long tradition of leadership rotation in both houses and both parties. The few lawmakers who stayed around more than two or three years followed a preordained leadership ladder—one year as chair of the appropriations committee, then one year each as assistant majority leader, majority leader, and finally, assembly speaker or senate president. Occupants of these positions often achieved them less because of political or legislative skills than because of their county of residence. The most powerful county organizations in each party saw to it that they shared in the leadership spoils, as a look at the Democratic leadership as late as the end of the 1970s and into the early 1980s demonstrates. The senate presidents were from the politically potent counties of Mercer and Essex successively, the assembly speakers from Hudson and Middlesex.

Republican leaders in the early 1970s began ending the tradition of annual leadership change when Senate President Raymond Bateman (GOP gubernatorial candidate in 1977) held office for an unprecedented three years between 1970 and 1972, and Assembly Speaker Thomas Kean (governor from 1982 to 1990) served for two years in 1972 and 1973. It briefly appeared that a tradition of one leader per legislature (a two-year term), was developing. However, beginning in 1978, successive senate presidents and assembly speakers from both parties established a "new tradition" of two-term leadership, or four years.

This two-term rule held sway through 1990, after which it was completely shattered. On the Democratic side, Joseph Doria of Hudson County led his members in the assembly as speaker and minority leader for ten years, while John Lynch of Middlesex County served eight years as senate president and minority leader until he retired. Richard Codey succeeded Lynch, and will lead his party for at least ten years. Governor McGreevey displaced Doria, who shortly thereafter was appointed to the state senate and went on to win a full term. His successor, Albio Sires, left after two terms upon winning a congressional seat. His replacement, Joseph Roberts of Camden County, gave South Jersey's members a long-absent voice.

Republican leadership during the 1990s was also affected by leaders' ambition for higher office. Assembly Speaker Chuck Haytaian (1990–1994) voluntarily retired from the legislature to run unsuccessfully for the U.S. Senate. His successor, Jack Collins, served for six years—the longest incumbency of any Republican assembly speaker—and after considering a race for governor, joined a lobbying firm. Collins' replacement, Paul DiGaetano, became minority leader when his party lost its assembly majority; after the GOP's dismal showing in 2003, the caucus deposed him in favor of Alex DeCroce of Morris County. DeCroce's opposite number in the senate is Leonard Lance of Hunterdon County, elected at the same time to replace the defeated senate copresident, John Bennett.

For the most part, the current legislative leadership is composed of veterans who have more interest in politics in Trenton rather than Washington. If they step down anytime soon, it will likely be the result of internecine warfare within their caucuses rather than voluntary departure. It seems clear, though, that the time-honored means of ascent to the top posts has changed in important ways. Many leaders in both houses in recent years represent partisan bastions, but they need virtues other than place of residence. Rather, their skills at public relations, political strategy, and especially campaign fund-raising play the most critical role.

Legislative Work: The Nature of the Product

The first thing one notices in considering the work of the legislature is that it is doing a lot more of it than it used to. The increase in the legislature's staple product—bills—is due to its new resources, growing autonomy, and need for credit taking in campaigns. The effect of more control over the "means of production" is apparent in a huge upsurge in the number of bills introduced. Between 1931 and 1935, on average of 1,000 bills were introduced per session, and the average number passed was slightly over one-third of that total. By the 1978–79 sessions, 5,142 bills were introduced, and only 13 percent made it into the books. By 2005, the number of bills introduced was 8,177, but only 5 percent became statutes.[33]

To be sure, many laws produced in recent years—those about issues not part of the governor's legislative agenda—are unlikely to change the life of New Jersey citizens. Other chapters of this book (particularly 14–16) describe the legislature's growing role in shaping the state's more important public policies; we concentrate here on the rest of the legislative output. Among the less-than-earthshaking measures the legislature has solemnly considered are banning computer-assisted hunting, prohibiting the detention of homing pigeons, and reimbursing a motorist for $662.65 worth of damage caused by an escaping state prison inmate who stole the citizen's car.

As these examples suggest, special-interest concerns take up much of the legislature's time. If there are vocal proponents, no opposition, and little cost, the legislature will acquiesce to their desires. But if there are determined groups on both sides, such issues can haunt lawmakers year after year. Some recent perennials include battles to allow self-service gas stations, which are permitted in forty-eight other states (independent station owners vs. the oil companies), regulation of leghold traps (hunters vs. animal rights activists), and prohibition of disposable soft-drink containers (soft drink manufacturers and South Jersey glass manufacturers vs. environmentalists). When faced with this kind of dispute, the legislature often assumes the role of referee. Requests for new or expanded functions for licensed professionals are a frequent example. When occupational therapists, for instance, sought licensure, they were bidden to strike a deal with hospitals and physical therapists, the other interested parties.

The governor rarely intervenes in such matters. A rare exception was Governor Cahill's 1972 rejection of a bill designating a melody called "I'm From New Jersey" as the official state song. Cahill dismissed this composition, approved after its author sang it from the assembly gallery accompanied by a six-piece musical group, with a succinct veto message: "It stinks."

A veteran analyst of the legislature ascribes its style of dealing with special interest legislation to the crush of bills, the limited time to deal with them on sporadic Mondays and Thursdays, and the fragmented sessions: "For the legislator, life in Trenton is discontinuous, and the legislative process moves by fits and starts. It is almost impossible to give anything much attention for any significant length of time."[34] The nature of the legislative day illustrates the problem. Members leave home early in the morning to get to the committee sessions scheduled for ten. Around noon, party conferences on the day's agenda begin. About two in the afternoon, floor action is supposed to start. All the while, there are constituents and visiting schoolchildren to greet, lobbyists to consult, and calls to make from one's floor desk phone since there are still no offices for the rank and file.

Because all these activities constantly run behind schedule, the body operates on what is known as "legislative standard time"—about an hour behind scheduled clock time. Members may not know until the last minute what bills the leadership will post that day, or in what order they will come up. Assembly members who wish to gain the floor are at the mercy of the speaker, who controls not only recognition but also the chamber's microphones. As sessions draw to a close, there is always a last-minute blizzard of "must-pass" legislation, and the thirty-bills-per-day official limit is often waived. Furthermore, until recently it was difficult for legislators (or anyone else) to reflect back on what they had done, because, despite the presence of the necessary equipment, legislative sessions were not recorded. When the state supreme court, and later the U.S. Supreme Court, ruled on an important New Jersey school prayer case requiring "a moment of silence," judges had to rely on newspaper clippings to assess legislative intent.[35] Now, lawmakers as well as the general public can watch video of sessions and important committee meetings on the state Web site, and in 2007 the legislature voted to post voting records there as well.

THE LEGISLATURE: AN ASSESSMENT

We began this chapter with a description of the legislature of fifty years ago—a small body composed of a few distinguished public servants and a large number of party hacks who left quickly; an institution almost without structure; a formally coequal branch of government that did little when it had constitutional power and willingly ceded that power to an executive branch eager to seize it when the constitution changed—just as state government began to develop into a vital instrument.

Remnants of that old legislature remain. Commuting lawmakers, discontinuous meetings, and "off-off year" elections keep the old parochial political culture going to a considerable extent. Although the number of members living off county organization patronage has declined, there are other ways of making a living from a long-term political career. Former governor Kean has described them graphically: "They parlay the [money for staff and from salary] into another two hundred thousand dollars they get from representing a couple of towns. . . . The same applies to an insurance agent or a real estate person who gets local business. It's all based on the assembly seat and therefore they'll do anything to keep it. If they lose the assembly seat, they're liable to lose all the rest too."[36]

Yet much has changed. There is, first, the nature of the membership. Legislators today come to Trenton with more officeholding experience, usually stay longer, and get to know their jobs better. Buffoons and hacks are fewer; substantive experts and persons of thoughtful mien may be more numerous. If they are more personally ambitious, they are also more likely than they were to build careers based on policy accomplishments or constituency service, rather than service to corporations or political machines.

The thread of personal ambition and political entrepreneurship runs through all the other changes in the legislature. More staff positions were created so that legislators could help formulate policy rather than rubber-stamp it. Nonpartisan staff was supplemented—some say elbowed aside—by partisan and personal staff that could better serve ambitious members' political ends. The director of the Office of Legislative Services complains that his personnel are overwhelmed by a system that allows every member to request research, legal opinions, or bills. He suggests that, as in many other states, some clearance—perhaps from the leadership—should be required.[37] "Good-government" types look askance at the no-show "district aides" and political operatives on the state payroll. Yet thanks to the staff, as a former Republican staff director points out, "Today, even unspectacular legislators can be incredibly well-informed on issues in bills coming up." A Democratic counterpart agrees, saying that legislation goes "to a more argumentative fate, but better argued than ever before."[38]

Similarly, committee chairs and senior members stay in place longer because of policy interests and expertise, and because their path to house leadership is slowed by colleagues serving longer there. Effective legislative leadership has long been a vehicle for a serious gubernatorial candidacy. In recent years, however, those candidacies have been deterred or aborted by opponents willing to spend their personal fortunes on television advertising (Jon Corzine and Doug Forrester in 2005), charismatic ideologues (Brett Schundler in 2001), or political celebrities (Christie Whitman in

1993). The emergence of such gubernatorial nominees testifies again to the decline of the party organizations.[39]

While they are serving, legislative leaders have an independent power base derived from the gratitude of their partisan colleagues for fund-raising prowess and other campaign assistance. They are thus less likely to work in harness even with a governor of their own party. A recent stark example was the budget standoff between Assembly Leader Joseph Roberts and Governor Corzine. Roberts's extended refusal to support a sales tax increase to balance the FY 2007 state budget shut the government down for a week in July 2006.[40] Further, almost every member of the majority party in each chamber has some claim to be a "leader," for all of them in the last few legislatures have been chairs or vice-chairs of some committee—the impetus for the growth in the number of committees.

What have been the effects of the careerist, professional legislature on the institution and its performance? The answer to those questions is complex.

The Institution

Political scientists have analyzed the development of state legislatures from three perspectives: legislative reform in the 1960s and 1970s, professionalization in the 1980s and, most recently, institutionalization.[41] The continuing effects of the first two approaches on New Jersey's legislature are the subject of much of this chapter. Reform was focused on the legislature's capacity to do their jobs—expanding the space in capitol buildings for committee rooms and staff, for example. That allowed both the partisan and nonpartisan staff to grow and to provide legislators with information that had once been available only to the executive branch and to lobbyists. More information made legislators more powerful players in crafting policy and required more of their time. More time spent at their tasks with more information led to members' professionalization. Increased expertise and influence intensified their interest in staying on the job and turnover dropped. More lawmakers became full-time legislators who viewed politics as a career ladder. With a career on the line, their new resources became instruments of successful campaigning as well as governing.

The strength of an institution can be defined by its separation from its environment. In applying this concept to state legislatures, Alan Rosenthal offers three measures of legislative institutionalization—continuity of personnel, shared norms, and managerial autonomy.[42] Through the 1980s and 1990s, all became increasingly present in New Jersey.

Like legislators elsewhere, those in New Jersey began serving for longer periods and, unlike their colleagues in thirty-nine states, were not subject to term limits. They developed shared rules of the game, of which perhaps the most important was cooperation on critical elements of both governing and campaigning. The majorities of moderates in both parties struck deals to pass important legislation that would redound to everyone's electoral benefit. Lawmakers implicitly agreed to turn a blind eye to practices that served their careers, such as dual officeholding and "Christmas tree" budgetary items for their districts. The greatest threat to managerial autonomy—externally generated ballot initiatives that could limit their control over policy and their own procedures, or impose term limits—was absent in New Jersey.

Rosenthal's analysis of these stages of legislative development was written in the mid-1990s and concluded that most state legislatures were beginning a reversal into institutional decay and less insulation from the external environment. Closer monitoring by the public and a "gotcha" attitude among the press corps were chiefly responsible. That was not the case in New Jersey then, but there is more evidence for it now.

The voluntary departure of almost one-third of the members of the upper house and half of the Republican senate caucus was unprecedented. With fifteen members leaving the assembly to run for the senate, there would be less continuity in the legislature's 2008 membership than at any time since 1993. Several of the departing veterans were victims of the loss of shared norms, particularly of the legislative and political comity that had often characterized the body. On the Republican side, some of the most senior members faced serious primary challenges from those in the emergent right wing of their own party, who gleefully called themselves "the mountain men." They preferred ideological purity and sharp elbows to negotiation. Democrats from counties like Camden, Essex, and Hudson (and even a Republican or two from Burlington) learned that building pensions from no-show government jobs and steering "Christmas tree" budget ornaments to their employers, friends, and relatives were no longer acceptable rules of the game to a crusading press corps and the most active federal prosecutor since the Watergate era. Oversight of legislative ethics was no longer an internal managerial prerogative.

Legislative Performance

Much of the "deinstitutionalization" of the New Jersey legislature has occurred too recently to determine its effects on how the legislature functions, and perhaps it should not be overstated. Well over half the membership of 2006–2008 will be back in Trenton in 2008–2010. Thus, an assessment of the body's performance viewed through the prism of its recent past may still be an accurate prediction about its future.

The genesis of the legislative reform movement that began in the late 1960s is widely ascribed to the analysis and recommendations of the Citizens Conference on State Legislatures, published in 1971. In that study of performance, New Jersey's governing body ranked thirty-second overall among the fifty states. Even then, however, it was graded fourteenth in its capacity for legislative and administrative oversight, and eighteenth in terms of information resources. Much lower ratings on independence from the governor and interest groups (thirty-first), representativeness (thirty-fifth), and public accessibility to its documents and proceedings (forty-second) pulled down the overall rank.[43] New Jersey legislators themselves, in a seven state survey, confirmed this general picture.[44]

If that study were to be repeated today, the available data, albeit scattered and incomplete, demonstrates that New Jersey would score much higher. One scholar has calculated that from the 1960s to the 1990s, New Jersey advanced from being the thirty-second most professionalized legislature in the nation to the seventh.[45] Another national study using different measures also ranks New Jersey seventh, and it finds that the ambitious politicians of professionalized legislatures are the most responsive to aggregate constituency concerns.[46]

This last finding brings us to the issue of performance—and its definition. One longtime student of state legislatures, Ronald Weber, chooses to focus on the dark side of professionalization: legislators' use of their resources to advance themselves personally and politically rather than attending to the proper representation of their constituents. He calls for radically "purging the state legislative process of the pursuit of self-interest." Harking back to the Progressive era, he recommends that "neutral" state commissions take over the legislature's role in redistricting, regulation of campaign finance and lobbyists, and the setting of lawmakers' compensation.[47] Frank Hague, who used the commission form to build one of the most notorious political machines in U.S. history, might applaud Weber's idea, but students of the long history of unintended consequences of political reforms would be more dubious.[48]

Rosenthal approaches the question more pragmatically and dismisses some frequent measures of legislative performance. Its product—for example, the "right" balance of taxes assessed vs. services provided in a state budget—is a matter of individual values. Structural improvements and professionalization brought on by the era of legislative reform increased legislative expertise on the one hand and the self-serving behavior and ethical issues that Weber decries on the other. Rather, Rosenthal suggests, we should focus on the body's key roles: representation, lawmaking, and balancing the power of the executive branch. A "good" legislature is one that manages these critical tasks in proper equilibrium. This is not an easy assignment, leading him to call his study *Heavy Lifting*.[49] His general conclusion that legislatures do better at the first two than the third applies to New Jersey.

The business of representation has two principal components. The first is assisting constituents with their myriad idiosyncratic issues. It ranges from the district staff helping individuals make their way through the bureaucracy to the vast amount of special interest legislation of great import to a particular group and of little or no interest to anyone else. The second is that subset of legislation that is of greater significance and visibility to large numbers of the general public. When one considers the major issues facing the state, the legislature has more often than not been responsive and responsible, even if the governor at times has had to drag it kicking and screaming to that point.

The experienced legislative leadership on both sides of the aisle that New Jersey enjoyed for most of the past three decades has been critical to the development of major public policies in the state. Leaders' negotiating skills, and their willingness to use them, have mattered a great deal. Effective lawmaking may suffer if the exodus seen in 2008 continues over time and the ideological temperature of the body rises. Senator Joseph Doria, a former assembly speaker who retired in 2008 after thirty years in the legislature, has said, "In the present political atmosphere, it's difficult to deal with issues. Political dialogue needs to be more thoughtful and less contentious." A Republican colleague, Leonard Connors, also retiring after twenty-five years of service, made the same point in recalling the bipartisanship that obtained when Republican Governor Thomas Kean dealt with a Democratic legislative majority: "We talked to one another. We went out and had dinner and discussed the issues of the day. There just seemed to be a lot of harmony."[50]

This brings us finally to the legislature's role in balancing the power of the chief executive. Governors have many tools at their disposal to work their will, and the New Jersey governor has more than most. Yet, as we saw in chapter 8, a combination of the particular political environment and the styles of both the governor and the legislative leadership powerfully affects representatives' ability to perform this function. Through the 1990s, they were aligned in a positive way for the majority party's lawmakers. Neither Governor Whitman nor Governor Florio was particularly adept at dealing with them. The Republicans' veto-proof majority left Florio on the sidelines for most of his term. Whitman saw many of her initiatives deflected or rewritten by GOP legislative leaders with their own gubernatorial ambitions. Governor McGreevey was a creature of the legislature, more interested in what would sell than its consequences.

Governor Corzine entered office determined to change the balance. He had the determination of a former corporate chief executive to get his way, along with the informed prudence and gambling instincts of the accomplished bond trader he once was. To the surprise of some he worked well with the Democratic senate president, Richard Codey, who had wanted Corzine's job, but Codey was that increasingly rare leader who put the good of the state and the institution above his own ambitions. Assembly Speaker Joseph Roberts was new at his job and determined to protect his caucus's authority and reelection prospects. His clashes with Corzine over the sales tax increase in the FY 2007 budget, which shut the government down for a week, were ascribed in large measure to their mutual stubbornness and lack of experience in their new positions. It was left to Codey to guide them toward a compromise resolution.[51] Republican Bill Gormley, known for giving Democrats his vote on contentious issues in return for favorable legislation for the Atlantic City casinos in his district, explained the "three basic rules" for legislative success: "Get along with the governor. Get along with the governor. Get along with the governor."[52] Thus, if the legislative process is not as pure and legislators are less high-minded than "good government" requires, still the improvements over the past half-century are striking. Legislatures "reflect fundamental tensions of political life and fundamental contradictions in political institutions, not just human failing."[53]

CHAPTER 10

The State Bureaucracy

The governor's ability to exert control over the state government has remained his most difficult challenge.

—Donald Linky, former director, State Office of Policy and Planning

The skilled career bureaucrat knows thousands of ways to stall a project.... Stalling is a piece of cake in an election year, for the political appointees are busier than ever over-reacting to crises erupting daily from unfavorable press coverage. Any bureaucrat worth his salt can wait out a political hack.

—anonymous bureaucrat, "The Trenton Rulebook"

CREATING A STRONG AND EFFICIENT EXECUTIVE branch was a major accomplishment of New Jersey's 1947 constitutional convention. Since then, executive agencies have grown at a pace the framers could hardly have envisioned. Bureaucracies by nature are concerned less "about the overall architecture of government" than they are with "the narrow sliver they believe they represent."[1] This chapter looks at the factors that shape New Jersey's executive branch—constitutional, cultural, historical, and political.

To reinforce a newly powerful chief executive, the 1947 constitution limited the number of cabinet departments to no more than twenty. They were to contain "all executive and administrative offices, departments and instrumentalities of the State government" and be "under the supervision of the governor."[2] The charter's framers took aim at the myriad departments, boards and commissions that had begun to multiply after 1900. No one oversaw their work. Governor Franklin Murphy (1902–1905) thought about reestablishing a governor's mansion in Trenton because, if he were in town regularly, "the department chiefs might be shamed out of their apparent notions that the State was paying them big salaries only to have them serve as State House ornaments. . . . [T]he chiefs of the State House had gone to their offices in Trenton only—well, they were always there on paydays, at any rate. The work of their departments—even the supervision of them—was left entirely in the hands of their deputies and clerks and assistants."[3]

In 1929, a National Institute of Public Administration (NIPA) study found that New Jersey state government consisted of "a grand total of ninety-four agencies. . . . many are practically independent of the governor, either because of the nature of their appointment or the length of their terms of office. The seventy-two boards and commissions consist in the aggregate of approximately five hundred members."[4] The report recommended abolishing many of these bodies and putting the rest into twelve cabinet departments responsible to the governor. It recognized that strong executive leadership was at least as important for successful state government as the "neutral competence" exemplified by independent commissions.[5] In his 1932 inaugural address, Governor A. Harry Moore endorsed the recommendations. As they usually did, the legislature ignored the governor. Unusually forceful chief executives like Woodrow Wilson (1911–1912) and Walter Edge (1917–1919, 1944–1947) achieved some administrative consolidation, but the chaotic and antiquated bureaucracy remained largely in place until 1948.

Although the 1948 constitution permitted twenty cabinet departments, only fourteen were established. Within thirty years, however, the department limit was reached de jure and breached de facto. To maintain it, authorities and operating commissions "in but not of" cabinet departments proliferated—formally assigned to departments but operating virtually autonomously. Thus, for example, the New Jersey Meadowlands Commission, which regulates development in fourteen municipalities in two counties, is "in but not of" the Department of Community Affairs, and the Motor Vehicle Commission is "in but not of" the Transportation Department. The five hundred appointments to boards and commissions that NIPA decried in 1929 are about the same number as today.

Today's complex bureaucracy differs sharply from that of the 1930s, however. The governor now appoints and removes almost all top officers at will, and almost all leave office when the governor does. It is now the governor who controls the patronage appointments to boards and commissions, rather than legislators or county party officials. Although the senate must confirm many gubernatorial appointments, rejection is virtually unheard of.[6] Obstacles to executive leadership are now logistical and political rather than statutory. Still, the career employees just below the top layer of gubernatorial appointments, who actually run agencies, have considerable resources. These "be-heres" ("when this governor and his appointees are gone, we'll still be here") command civil service protection, technical expertise, and the agency's institutional memory.[7] State government is so vast that a thin layer of political appointees can never entirely master the larger departments. Moreover, career managers' knowledge, close relationships with clientele groups, and their own short tenure tempt political appointees to join subordinates in opposing gubernatorial programs with negative effects on the agency. The tension between control and cooperation, as the governor and cabinet officers strive to lead the state's permanent government, is a major theme of this chapter.[8]

State Bureaucracy: Size and Structure

To begin with the basics, it is difficult to provide a deceptively simple figure—how many workers the state employs. In 2006, the state workforce in the executive, legislative, and judicial branches numbered about 84,000, up from 67,500 in 1992 and 76,000 in 2002. To complicate matters, 14,000 of these workers are paid with pass-through funds from the federal government, counties, and other non-Trenton sources. Finally, there are more than 55,000 other employees whom the public considers "government workers," although most of them are paid with the fees, tolls, and similar revenues they generate rather than with state appropriations. Some of the larger entities in this group are employees of New Jersey Transit, the state's public college and university systems, and the Turnpike Authority.[9] When commuter fares, tuition, or tolls go up, it is state government that gets the blame.

Departments of State Government

During the Corzine administration, New Jersey had eighteen cabinet departments.[10] Table 10.1 shows their dates of creation or most recent major functional reorganization, and their number of employees.

As table 10.1 indicates, only four of the eighteen departments—Agriculture, Treasury, Law and Public Safety, and State—remain as they were created in 1948. These departments perform essential state government functions. Most of the remaining departments have been collapsed, spun off, or reorganized—sometimes repeatedly—since 1948. The Banking

TABLE 10.1.

Cabinet Departments of New Jersey State Government (listed alphabetically)

Department	Date of creation or reorganization	Number of employees, 2006
Agriculture	1948	271
Banking and Insurance	1970	511
Community Affairs	1966	1,169
Corrections	1976	10,461
Education	1967	982
Environmental Protection	1970	3,473
Health and Senior Services	1948	2,216
Human Services	1976	23,897★
Labor	1981	4,040
Law and Public Safety	1948	10,430
Military and Veterans Affairs	1987	1,575
Personnel	1986	379
Public Advocate	1974	NA★
State	1948	586
Transportation	1966	6,970
Treasury	1948	6,167

SOURCE: New Jersey Department of Personnel, 2006 Workforce Profile.

★Data do not include reinstatement of the Department of Public Advocate and the creation of the Department of Children and Families in 2006, both staffed with transfers from other departments.

and Insurance and Labor departments cover areas once part of a single Department of Labor and Industry. Another spin-off from Labor and Industry was a Commerce Department that was created in 1981 and converted to a Commission on Economic Growth and Tourism in 1998. In 1987 it had absorbed the now defunct Department of Energy, which itself existed for only a decade. In 2007, Governor Corzine moved central oversight of economic enterprise—a growing concern in all states—to a new Office of Economic Growth and downgraded the Commission, moving its tourism functions to the Department of State.[11] Corrections and Human Services are two of the largest departments. They were created by a breakup of the original Department of Institutions and Agencies. Governor Whitman added Senior Services to the Department of Health, and

Children and Families migrated from Human Services in 2006, when repeated scandals and tragedies befalling children under the state's care led Governor Corzine to create it.

The other departments that existed in some form in 1948—Military and Veterans' Affairs, Personnel, and Transportation—have been renamed and reorganized since then to reflect new emphases or missions. The old Defense Department was renamed Military and Veterans' Affairs in 1987 when veterans' offices in other agencies were transferred there. The old Civil Service Department was restyled as Personnel in 1986, when some hiring and management functions were transferred to individual departments. Transportation grew out of the old Highway Department; the new name reflected growing state responsibilities for mass transit.

Only three departments represent genuinely new cabinet-level areas of state activity. The oldest, the Department of Community Affairs, was established in 1966 to manage programs for local communities and clientele groups spawned by the War on Poverty in the 1960s. As these initiatives lost favor in Washington, New Jersey continued many as state programs.[12]

The Department of the Public Advocate was unique to New Jersey when it was created in 1974 in the midst of the Watergate reform climate. Its largest component was the Office of the Public Defender, a conventional state function. Its more innovative offices included the divisions of Public Interest Advocacy, Citizen Complaints and Dispute Settlement, Rate Counsel, Mental Health Advocacy, and Advocacy for the Developmentally Disabled; they represented the public at regulatory hearings and regularly sued other cabinet departments on behalf of the poor, the disabled, and prisoners.

At the time it was formed, many Republicans viewed the Public Advocate as hostile to business and did not believe the state should have an agency that frequently sued other state agencies. Their irritation grew when the Public Advocate became involved in efforts to force towns to provide affordable housing during the 1980s and to consolidate schools to achieve racial balance in the early 1990s. Having achieved veto-proof majorities in both houses of the legislature in 1992, the GOP removed the funds for all of the department's services except the Public Defender's office from the FY 1993 budget, and abolished it as a cabinet agency after Christie Whitman became governor in 1994.[13] When it was restored by Governor Codey and the Democratic-controlled legislature in 2005, the enabling legislation asserted that "the abolition of the Public Advocate and the transfer of some of its functions to various departments has resulted in diffuse, ineffective representation of the rights of those unable to effectively advocate for themselves."[14] Finally, the Department of Environmental Protection, created in 1970, expresses the state's resolve to deal aggressively with harmful aspects of its industrial past.

REORGANIZATION SCHEMES: PANACEA OR PLACEBO?

Since the 1960s, each governor has rearranged some of the cabinet departments and agencies, seeking stronger executive direction of policy.[15] Among the Democratic chief executives, Richard Hughes created the Department of Community Affairs and reorganized the old Highway Department into the broader Department of Transportation. Brendan Byrne focused on better management of health and welfare services. He broke up the huge Department of Institutions and Agencies, separating it into Human Services and Corrections. Byrne also created the Department of the Public Advocate because of his concerns about public representation when he served on the Board of Public Utilities in the 1960s.

Jim Florio proposed substantial reorganization to create "a smaller and smarter" state government. In the face of recession and budget deficits, he called for consolidations to eliminate three departments and reduce the state work force by eight thousand. The legislature did not support his proposals. Jim McGreevey took on two related issues that exasperated almost all New Jerseyans: their dreaded visits to the Division of Motor Vehicles (DMV) and the highest auto insurance rates in the country. Modifying burdensome regulations, McGreevey brought back the auto insurance companies that were fleeing the state and turned the old DMV into a surprisingly responsive and efficient Motor Vehicle Commission. Jon Corzine entered office with the Public Advocate restored to the cabinet and addressed the issue of safeguarding vulnerable children by moving those functions to a new Department of Children and Families Services.[16]

Republican governors have tended to reorganize agencies dealing with economic development and to introduce private-sector management techniques. This latter effort goes back to 1913, when Governor Walter Edge ran on the slogan of "A Business Man With a Business Plan." In 1970, in the Edge spirit, Governor William Cahill appointed a blue-ribbon Government Management Commission led by a vice president of the Prudential

Insurance Company. The commission suggested ways to save eighty million dollars through administrative orders and consolidation of the then-seventeen existing cabinet departments into six superagencies. The legislature declined to pass this plan, and Cahill instead increased the number of cabinet offices. He separated the Banking and Insurance departments and inaugurated the Department of Environmental Protection.

When Tom Kean became governor in January 1982, he launched the most ambitious of the Republican management studies—the Governor's Management Improvement Program, known familiarly as GMIP. GMIP was headed by executives from AT&T, Johnson and Johnson, and First National State Bancorporation. They raised $2.6 million from New Jersey's business community to fund the project and recruited 250 executive volunteers to help run it. Opinions vary about GMIP's success in cutting government spending and introducing increased efficiency.[17] It was, however, given more credit for increasing gubernatorial control of programs through a new budget process.

Before GMIP, division and bureau managers made budget recommendations to department heads, who transmitted them to the governor. Traditionally, requests would range about 10 to 15 percent above the pool of available money. Working with the Treasury Department's Bureau of the Budget, the governor would balance the budget, as required by the state constitution. Under the new process, an Office of Management and Budget (OMB) in the Treasury Department and the governor's office work together to set mandatory budget targets for all agencies. Previous budget powers had looked impressive on paper, but the governor had "never had the staff, the administrative apparatus, to exercise that power within the bureaucracy. The creation of the OMB gives him the potential to probe the operation of the departments."[18]

New Jersey's other recent Republican governor, Christie Whitman, made the structure of state government an early symbol of her determination to downsize the public edifice in Trenton. In short order, she eliminated the departments of Higher Education and the Public Advocate and combined the departments of Banking and Insurance, reducing the nineteen cabinet departments she had inherited to sixteen. Later on, she also converted the Department of Commerce and Economic Development into a commission. These agency reductions were accompanied by highly publicized programs of privatization of government services such as the state motor vehicle offices and the temporary disability insurance fund.

Despite their frequent reorganization, the size and complexity of cabinet departments still work against executive control. Similar events in the sprawling Department of Human Services (DHS), separated by two decades, provide an example.

One of DHS's most difficult tasks is placing the developmentally disabled in community care facilities overseen by its Division of Developmental Disabilities. After being sued by the Public Advocate during the Kean administration, the division pledged that waiting lists would be erased by July 1987. When the deadline arrived, there was still an official waiting list of 1,800, and 1,500 more who were ready to leave state institutions. The following year, it was discovered that Eddie Moore, the career head of the division, had "resolved" the wait list problem by overspending his budget for community care by at least $21.5 million. Moore knew the paper forms used to submit data on over 1,000 contract accounts were not compatible with either DHS or OMB computer systems.[19] Richard Codey, who was then a frequent legislative critic of the DHS (and who got himself hired as an attendant at a state mental institution, using the name and address of a convicted sex offender and the social security number of another felon convicted of armed robbery and drug violations), observed, "DHS may very well be unmanageable. It is just too big and too vast to really have a handle on it. It's a cabinet position, but you never hear of political leaders who are going to kill to get that job."[20]

In the words of New Jersey's Yogi Berra, when Codey himself left the acting governorship in 2005, it was "déjà vu all over again." A national advocacy group for the disabled was suing the state on behalf of 3,100 people on a community care wait list because the Division of Developmental Disabilities had insufficient funds to place them; the director of the state Office of Information Technology testified that despite an expensive revamping, he still did not have a list of all of the state's computer systems because he lacked "management authority over the various departments and agencies."[21]

Although an extreme example, the continuing troubles at DHS demonstrate that despite reorganization schemes and elaborate monitoring systems, management problems can still become political crises.

THE POLITICS OF THE BUREAUCRACY

Bureaucratic functioning depends ultimately on political processes. They include the governor's relationship with political appointees, the appointees' relationships with career officials, and the role of clientele groups.

Selection of Cabinet Officers

An appointed official heads each of New Jersey's cabinet departments. Almost all are nominated by the governor and confirmed by the state senate. Some departments are traditionally led by policy experts, others by politicians, and some by persons from a variety of backgrounds. Policy professionals always head the departments of Education, Corrections, Health, Human Services, Military and Veterans' Affairs, and the Public Advocate. New governors sometimes continue expert incumbents in office, as Governor Corzine did when he reappointed his predecessor's military adjutant general and acting commissioner of education. Other departments in this group change leadership when a new governor arrives, but their commissioners are seldom principally known as political activists. Since the Public Advocate's post was established, for example, all its occupants have been members of prominent minority groups (two African Americans, two Hispanics, and an Asian) with prior careers in public service law or legal education.

Historically, at the other end of the spectrum were the heads of the departments of Law and Public Safety, Community Affairs, Labor, and State. Their leaders were the governor's political associates, representatives of department clientele groups, or both. Until the 1970s, the attorney general and the secretary of state were the executive's chief political agents, coordinating relations with the legislature and dispensing patronage. With the development of the counsel and chief of staff roles in the governor's office during the Byrne and Kean administrations, these officeholders' political roles became diminished, although echoes of the past surface from time to time. In 1992, Governor Florio appointed a longtime political ally as secretary of state, whose job was defined once again as "chief political operative."[22] Governor McGreevey followed suit, appointing a Democratic political consultant who specialized in get-out-the-vote operations. Governor Whitman named her personal lawyer as attorney general after he served for a brief period as her chief counsel and chief of staff. His previous political experience consisted of heading the ill-fated Courter gubernatorial campaign of 1989 and "puppy-like" devotion to Whitman.[23]

Career politicians are most regularly found at the Department of Community Affairs (DCA), which dispenses money and advice to localities. When

Governor Hughes created the DCA in the days of the Great Society, he nominated noted social scientist Paul Ylvisaker as its first commissioner, but that did not begin a tradition. Governors Cahill and Byrne appointed mayors to head the agency. Governor Kean chose first the Essex County Republican chair, and last a seven-term Republican assemblyman. Between them was the only echo of Commissioner Ylvisaker, a black Republican with a graduate degree from Harvard's Kennedy School. Governor Florio's first appointment was the Democratic mayor of Camden. Governor Whitman first chose a Republican assemblyman, and a former mayor of Cherry Hill served both governors McGreevey and Corzine.

Departments whose commissioners shift back and forth between politicians and professionals—notably Labor, Banking and Insurance, Transportation, Treasury, and Environmental Protection—handle issues that are technically complex but politically potent. Governors place at their head technical experts with strong political skills, or skilled politicians who can control the department's career technical experts.

While Tom Kean's first treasurer was a professional economist and nominal Democrat, and Jon Corzine appointed a former colleague from the Goldman Sachs investment bank, Governors Byrne and Florio chose their campaign managers (a former professor of public policy and an attorney, respectively) to head this department. Governor McGreevey named the former Woodbridge Township finance officer who had served him during his nine years as that township's mayor. Labor commissioners usually come from the state's union leadership or its lobbying arms in Democratic administrations, while Republicans appoint political supporters or business executives with personnel backgrounds.

The governor's party and own political style influences the balance of career professionals and politicians in each administration. Commissioners with political backgrounds are more numerous in Democratic administrations. This difference is partly due to Republicans' stronger links to the business community, but also to the Democrats' dominance of the governor's office and the large county governments. Six Democrats held the governorship more than 60 percent of the time between 1953 and 2009. Thus, when a new Democratic governor arrives, many Trenton veterans are available.

Republican Tom Kean became chief executive in 1982 by the smallest margin in the state's history, and there had been only one other GOP governor in the prior three decades. Thus there was no large pool of experienced statehouse hands at the ready. An election recount did not confirm his victory until the end of November—barely six weeks before he would assume office. Kean had also promised to base major appointments on merit alone. His solution was to employ an executive search firm to seek out talented cabinet officers. It screened candidates and recommended finalists to his transition team, who forwarded names to the governor. The first commissioners of health, insurance, education, environmental protection, commerce and economic development, and the state treasurer all emerged from this process. They were professionals the governor had not known personally.

Governor Whitman retained several Kean appointees and made a point of choosing many women for high-level positions. They initially headed five of the sixteen cabinet departments (Banking and Insurance, Community Affairs, Law and Public Safety, Personnel, and State), and included Deborah Poritz, the state's first female attorney general. Members of minority groups—two African Americans and a Hispanic—were also unusually prominent in a Republican cabinet. Governor Whitman perceived herself (and was perceived) as "not one of the boys." Unlike Kean's leadership body, which contained several former lawmakers, only one male legislator captured a position in Whitman's first cabinet. An unusual number of cabinet members were civil service experts who had risen through the ranks or were holdovers from previous administrations.

The Democratic governors who preceded and followed Tom Kean used different strategies. His predecessor, Brendan Byrne, drew heavily on a talent pool from the Hughes and Meyner administrations, in which he had served himself. Among these veterans were his first appointments as treasurer, attorney general, labor commissioner, and public advocate. With polls showing Byrne on the way to a landslide victory, the administration could make a quick start. As his treasurer (and campaign manager) Richard Leone commented, "We had the advantage of a few people who knew exactly what they were going to do 24 hours after the election."[24] Florio enjoyed somewhat similar conditions in 1990. His first commissioners of environmental protection and human services had also served in the Byrne administration, and Richard Leone resurfaced as chair of the Port Authority of New York and New Jersey, and then as the head of the Corzine transition team.

In comparison with earlier Democratic administrations, there were fewer political people in the McGreevey and Corzine cabinets. Both those governors entered office at times when state government was in the throes of various political scandals, and both made changing the way Trenton does business the hallmark of their election campaigns. It was somewhat ironic that much of the mess that Corzine pledged to clean up had been perpetrated by McGreevey, but the McGreevey scandals primarily involved the governor's office and his relationship with party bosses rather than his cabinet. A leading scholar of state government described his cabinet appointees as "qualified individuals who do not raise any eyebrows."[25]

The earlier professional and political experience of cabinet members is not a reliable guide to how successful they will be. Some business leaders and others with executive backgrounds have had trouble learning "that the frustrating circumstances with which they must contend—lack of formal authority, meddling by legislators, pressure from interest groups—are features of the duly constituted political order."[26] Some political appointees are unable to match the infighting skills of high-ranking and experienced civil servants. In one such instance, Governor Byrne dispatched someone from the governor's office to act as deputy commissioner in an agency whose leader was uncooperative. The governor's operative reported the results: "The governor said, 'Go over and be deputy commissioner for six months.' Well, I arrived, and the night before, [the commissioner] took the [deputy commissioner's] office and cut it in half, put up a wall literally, so the size of the office I was going into was half of what [his predecessor] had. . . . [T]he message was clear. I had only spent three days there when I fully realized that I was going to be less valuable to the governor enmeshed in the bureaucracy than I could be with some independence back in the governor's office, and I called and begged to get back."[27]

Other appointees lack adeptness at public relations. Governors McGreevey and Corzine were both embarrassed by Zulima Farber, whose competence as an attorney surpassed her political talents. Farber was an Afro-Cuban woman with an inspiring life story and distinguished legal career, who had served as public advocate in the Florio administration. She was described as the ultimate diversity appointment when McGreevey proposed her as a justice of the state supreme court—a plan that went awry when it was discovered that a bench warrant had been issued for her failure to respond to a traffic violation. In the messy aftermath, McGreevey said Farber had shown disrespect for the law, while Farber accused the governor of character assassination. Latino leaders were furious and lobbied Corzine to appoint Farber as the first Hispanic attorney general. Despite the doubts of some of his advisers, Corzine did so, and Farber drew smiles

at her confirmation hearing when she thanked the governor for offering
her a job that came with a car and driver. It was thus particularly unfortunate when a few months later, the attorney general and her car and driver
showed up at the site of a traffic stop where her companion had been cited
for driving without a license or registration. When it became public that
the citations had been canceled, Farber was forced to resign.[28]

The Role of Politics and Clientele Groups

Whatever the process used to select cabinet officers, their political skills
and styles and those of the governor are critical in determining their effectiveness. Governor Kean, who had equally impressive executive and political
skills, did elevate merit over patronage in some important appointments.
He surprised many by naming a Democratic economist as his first state
treasurer. (One of the most surprised was the Republican senator representing the treasurer's home county, who learned of it in the newspapers.)
But Kean ignored advice to dismantle or reorganize the patronage-heavy
departments of State and Community Affairs, for all administrations must
"find a place to bury your most loyal but least talented supporters. . . .
They don't have much talent but they have a lot of persistence."[29]

If it has the support of influential clientele groups, dismantling an entire
department may be impossible. The successes and failures of governors
who have tried it yield instructive lessons about the role of clientele groups
in bureaucratic politics. Brendan Byrne was unable to abolish the Department of Community Affairs, while Tom Kean did succeed in eradicating
the Energy Department. Christie Whitman did away with the Public Advocate, but a decade later it was restored. She was more successful at eliminating the Department of Higher Education.

Governor Byrne, citing an end to federal funding for many of its programs, sought abolition of the Department of Community Affairs in January 1976.[30] Local officials and legislators protested vociferously. Despite
large majorities in both houses, Byrne could not find a legislator to sponsor his initiative. He withdrew the proposal and transferred the key Division
of Local Government Services to the Treasury Department by executive
order. Overturning an executive order requires a two-thirds vote in each
house of the legislature. Despite the Democrats' dominance, the assembly
easily mustered the votes, and Byrne was forced to concede failure.

Quite the opposite was true of the Department of Energy—an agency
similar to the federal cabinet department created in response to the rise of

the OPEC oil cartel—which Byrne created late in his first term. Its mission was "perceived as unnecessary by many people and as boring by most."[31] The department's chief promoter, however, was an important state senator from the governor's home county of Essex, who was critical to the governor's difficult campaign for a second-term nomination. That, along with federal subsidies for most of the department's costs, persuaded Byrne to endorse its establishment. A decade later, weak leaders had still not defined a mission for the department. The department was perceived as "doing little or nothing at all. At the same time, it has incurred the wrath of the utilities and the segments of the business community it has attempted to regulate."[32] At Kean's suggestion, its functions were absorbed by the Board of Public Utilities and the Department of Commerce and Economic Development, whose mission and clientele guaranteed that regulations would be scrutinized for their economic impact. Few mourned its passing. As the Democratic assembly speaker said of Energy, "The department doesn't have a constituency."[33]

Byrne's inability to eliminate or emasculate DCA and Kean's success in abolishing Energy might seem surprising, since Byrne's fellow Democrats controlled the legislature, which had to pass the DCA reorganization plan, while Republican Kean had Democrats in charge in the senate and the narrowest of Republican majorities in the assembly when Energy disappeared. The explanation lies in the difference in the departments' clienteles. Business interests most affected by the Energy Department were hostile to its basic mission. In contrast, Community Affairs "comes closer to being all things to all people than any other department of state government."[34] It dispenses technical assistance to municipalities preparing their budgets or writing grant proposals; funds to pay for police and firefighters; and underwrites public works projects benefiting bankers and developers. DCA's supportive clientele has all the hallmarks of a strong constituency base—it is large, geographically dispersed, prestigious, committed, knowledgeable, and well organized.[35]

Clientele groups also played critical roles when Christie Whitman embarked on her downsizing initiatives. As with the Department of Energy, the clientele of the Department of Higher Education (DHE) shared the governor's desire to eliminate it. When DHE was created in 1966, New Jersey lagged far behind most other states in its development of a higher education system. Three decades later, the department was a victim of its own success in converting former teachers' colleges to large comprehensive institutions, establishing a statewide community college system, and launching public medical and dental schools. Their presidents complained that the department had outlived its usefulness and overregulated and interfered in campus affairs. They proposed that its oversight functions be replaced by a council consisting of themselves. Democratic legislators and teachers' unions protested that the change would lead to higher tuition, program duplication, and political interference, but in 1994, the regulation-averse Republican legislative majorities, with the support of the strongest interested parties, passed the proposal easily.[36]

At about the same time, a coalition of those targeted by the Public Advocate's lawsuits also backed Whitman's proposal to eliminate that department. In fact, the legislature had already done most of the job by removing the agency's funds from the budget the summer before Whitman entered office. As described earlier, Republicans were opposed in principal to state support of a "public interest law firm," as well as the agency's habit of suing regulated businesses, and its intervention in civil rights matters such as de facto school segregation and affordable housing. Whitman's own opinions were made particularly clear when the shrunken office of the ratepayer advocate, representing consumer complaints, was moved to the Commerce Department and given "a new mandate: to try to accommodate the needs of utilities."[37]

In contrast, much of the bedrock Democratic vote was supportive of the Public Advocate's mission. As early as 1996, Wilfredo Caraballo, a newly elected Democratic assemblyman and head of the Office of the Public Advocate in the Florio administration, introduced a bill to restore the agency. It went nowhere in the Republican-controlled legislature. When the Democrats reclaimed the governorship in 2001, Governor McGreevey not only called for the agency's revitalization but even named the person he proposed to head it. He was thwarted at the time by budget shortfalls and the Republicans' continuing, if diminished, majority. Upon regaining control of both houses of the legislature in 2003, however, the Democrats reinstated the agency, with Governor Codey proclaiming it a "champion of ordinary people with real needs but without political capital."[38]

Do these changes actually accomplish what governors intend, or do they bring about the problems opponents predict? Democrats can point to a massive scandal at the University of Medicine and Dentistry in 2005 that might not have been happened had the DHE been there to keep watch; Republicans can counter that Governor Corzine's appointment of a Public

Advocate when the agency was reestablished was instrumental in preventing a utility merger in 2006 that Corzine favored and that had been approved by several other states and the federal government. By and large, however, reorganizations in and of themselves have more political than policy implications. As one respected pundit observed when Governor Codey signed the Public Advocate back into law, "people can at least see that he is responding to their demands to do something."[39]

The "Other Governments": Authorities and Commissions

Although the number of cabinet departments has remained at or below the constitutionally mandated limit, there are still myriad boards, commissions, and authorities—many buried "in but not of" cabinet departments. In 2005, a study counted 476 such entities—operating commissions, temporary commissions established by the governor or the legislature, and boards, authorities, and other special purpose agencies.[40] They include permanent multistate agencies (such as the Port Authority of New York and New Jersey), temporary bodies that satisfy clientele groups (such as the Holocaust Victims Memorial Commission, the Commission on Italian or Italian-American Heritage Cultural and Educational Programs, and the Martin Luther King, Jr. Commemorative Commission), and managers of large state enterprises (such as the New Jersey Sports and Exposition Authority, the New Jersey Transit Authority, and the New Jersey Turnpike Authority).

The important authorities and commissions present an interesting paradox. On one hand, their functions and funding are insulated from the vagaries of budgetary politics because most issue their own bonds and do not have to depend on tax revenue and legislative appropriations. On the other hand, they have been accused of being unaccountable empires and patronage dens. Their leaders are appointed by the governor, serve at his or her pleasure, and enjoy both power and substantial salaries. In both Democratic and Republican administrations, authority commissioners have hired the politically well-connected for executive positions and to do the lucrative bond and legal work which, under a "professional exemption," does not have to be put out for bid.

When Governor Kean's first chief of staff was seen as stumbling after a year in the job, Kean appointed him to a newly created position as executive director of the Sports and Exposition Authority, and Governor Whitman gave him a similar post overseeing the Garden State Parkway.

Claiming that it would eventually save money, Governor McGreevey merged the Parkway and Turnpike authorities and the Garden State Arts Center (an entertainment space on the Parkway). At the same time, the merged authority created, among others, two new positions with six-figure salaries; they were filled by the finance chair of the Democratic State Committee (as director of development for the arts center) and a former McGreevey campaign treasurer and director of administration and personnel in the governor's office (as deputy director of human resources).[41]

It is, however, the state's politically active law firms that have reaped the largest rewards from the authorities when party control of the governor's office changes. Firms with strong connections to one party have collected enormous fees when it is in power, then seen them disappear when the other party assumes control. For example, a major contributor to Republican campaigns, the Morristown firm of Riker, Danzig, collected twenty-one million dollars as counsel to the Turnpike Authority during the Whitman administration. When Governor McGreevey took office, that job was awarded to Wilentz, Goldman, Spitzer of Woodbridge. Founded in 1919 by David Wilentz, a legendary Middlesex County boss, the firm was the largest contributor to McGreevey's campaigns over the years, and its building was the site of McGreevey's campaign headquarters.

Powerful partisan law firms expect this rise and fall in their fortunes, but a few survive administrative changes by hedging their bets. The largest firm in the state, McCarter and English, with headquarters in Newark, has calibrated its campaign donations to the prevailing political winds and kept its state business. While Jim Florio was governor, Democrats received about twice as much in campaign contributions from the firm as did Republicans, and the ratio was reversed during Christie Whitman's term in office. The firm's managing partner explains, "The firm is active in the political life of the state and the communities. We have always supported the candidates of both parties. "We support the office and institution regardless of which party holds it at any given time."[42]

A similar philosophy obtains at the Teaneck firm of DeCotiis, FitzPatrick, Gluck & Cole of Teaneck, the names of whose founding partners read like a bipartisan honor roll.[43] When McGreevey took over from Whitman, he simply moved oversight of the firm's New Jersey Highway Authority bond work from Republican attorney Michael Gluck to the Democrat Robert DeCotiis. Of the eleven state authorities that spent the most on outside legal counsel, ten firms lost their business in the first months of the McGreevey administration. The DeCotiis firm was the sole exception.[44]

While still a candidate in 2005, then-Senator Corzine convened a task force to study the independent authorities, calling them an "invisible government." The task force's recommendations formed the basis for an executive order issued in September 2006. In this executive order the governor directed that authorities establish "pre-set transparent procedures" for awarding contracts, advertise their availability, and, with the continuing exemption of "sophisticated professional services," give contracts to the low bidder. Contracts falling under the exemption (such as legal services) are to be awarded by a staff evaluation committee with expertise, which has been screened for conflicts of interest using an approved scoring system. Further, "for professional services rendered in connection with bond sales, related financial instruments, and litigation matters, where similar services are expected to be required on numerous occasions over a period of time, the procedures and criteria . . . may be used to create a pre-qualified group or 'pool' of potential contract partners for a term not to exceed two years. The establishment of such a pool may not be used to circumvent a genuine competitive process that ensures that quality service is being obtained at the best possible value."

At a press conference at which he signed the executive order, the governor proclaimed, "The days that people take political appointments as a way to advance private activities, personal gain, should be—and are—over;" and added that contracts would henceforth be awarded on the basis of "competence and quality, not contributions and corruption."[45]

The executive order should put an end to long-standing practices that Corzine described as "wasteful, sometimes outright unethical and even potentially criminal practices."[46] No one would accuse the state's large politically connected law firms, who employ many of the state's most distinguished lawyers, of engaging in such practices, and doubtless they all will be in the prequalified pool. Whether authority commissioners in a Democratic administration will award major contracts to Riker, Danzig, or one whose leaders are appointed by a Republican government will choose Wilentz, Goldman, and Spitzer, remains to be seen.

The Career Personnel System

Toilers in the bowels of the bureaucracy rarely affect major state policies. It is possible for "the fourth level bureaucrat whose life depends on being able to shut down the War Memorial or whatever to come in and destroy everything that everybody else is trying to do."[47] More critically, however, civil servants' pay, pensions, and other benefits swallow up over one-fifth of the general fund and contribute to the state's budget woes and high local property taxes. For that reason alone, the career civil service deserves scrutiny.

The Structure of the Civil Service System

New Jersey's public personnel system has more than seven thousand job titles. A large number have a single occupant, often to reward and retain desirable employees who have "maxed out" on the salary scale for their previous titles. The state's rigid seniority-based "bumping" system when downsizings occur has resulted in situations where middle managers are paid less than some of the staff they supervise.

The Kean administration's GMIP exercise brought about the first major civil service reform act in eighty years, replacing the old Civil Service Commission with a Department of Personnel. The act was intended to make merit the sole basis for hiring, firing and promotion; give managers more authority to carry out program responsibilities; enhance equal opportunity in state employment; and guard against political coercion and protect employee bargaining rights.[48] A powerful clientele kept the absolute veterans' preference in place and unchanged. To assist in realizing the first two goals, the Civil Service Reform Act of 1986 created a Senior Executive Service (SES). The SES was established to "enhance State government by fostering and developing a cadre of high-level potential managers and executives" and to provide "an appropriate avenue of mobility and influence for those who have demonstrated their dedication and ability in the Career Service."[49] It resembled similar programs in about a dozen other states and the federal government.

By the time Kean left office, the Senior Executive Service had 564 members, averaging seventeen years of government service and working in twelve of the nineteen cabinet departments and the Board of Public Utilities. At least 85 percent had to be career personnel, and all were to have "substantial managerial, policy-influencing or policy executing responsibilities."[50] In return for higher base salaries, more vacation days, continuing education opportunities, and that greatest of perks—a reserved parking space—SES members had to agree to possible transfers and salary adjustments entirely dependent on annual merit evaluations.[51] Most members of the SES (85 percent) occupied "key positions" identified by department leaders and were "encouraged" to join the SES. Other positions were posted, and their current occupants moved to regular civil service jobs. A bipartisan Merit Systems Board had to approve each SES position, and the commissioner of personnel had to approve each nominee.

When Jim Florio took office in 1990, the SES was one of the first programs examined by the new Governor's Management Review Commission. State employee unions, hostile to "merit" schemes and facing layoffs due to budget shortfalls, charged the Senior Executive Service contained "unnecessary layers of management" and too many political appointees receiving inflated salaries.[52] The Management Review Commission found the number of SES unclassified employees to be well below the statutory limit, and saw little evidence of salary inflation. However, it criticized a "departmental focus" that permitted each cabinet unit to determine its own participation level, implementation strategy, and positions to include in the SES. The commission concluded that, while of value, the Senior Executive Service was "fragmented, decentralized, diffused and unstructured." Reflecting Florio's preference for centralized control, it recommended that the SES serve as a mobile "SWAT team," guiding policy "in a manner consistent with the goals and objectives of the Administration, and with full loyalty to the Chief Executive and his key unclassified appointees." Shortly thereafter, Florio removed 385 positions from the SES, bringing the total number of participants to only 179.[53]

By 2006, there were 307 positions in the SES. They were heavily concentrated in a few departments, with Human Services, Transportation, and Treasury accounting for more than half of them, and five departments having no members at all.[54]

As noted, the SES addressed two civil service reform goals: enhancing the role of merit in career advancement, and strengthening managerial personnel and processes. Significant progress was also made on the third goal—equal opportunity. Between 1982 and 1989, the number of minority employees increased from 26 percent to almost 32 percent of the state work force, and by 2006, it was 41 percent nonwhite.[55]

From the viewpoint of public employees, the record on the fourth goal—removing apparent political preferences and protecting collective bargaining rights—is more mixed. The number of "provisionals," often patronage appointments, has dropped dramatically. The myriad job classifications—also alleged to have political implications—have been reduced from more than 12,000 to fewer than 8,000. A Labor Advisory Board, meeting bimonthly, has routinized communication between the personnel commissioner and union leaders.

Yet there are still concerns. Rank and file and administrators alike find the mechanism for shrinking classifications and titles difficult and time-consuming. Employees fear downgrading and salary reductions. Moratoria on new titles are frustrating, as new programs requiring new skills come on line. Unions worry that the Department of Personnel will become even more of a management tool than it was in the past. They also see conflicts between merit provisions and collective bargaining. The outcome of these issues remains to be seen.

The Pension and Benefits Dilemma

Beginning in the 1960s, public employees negotiated increasingly favorable pension and benefit arrangements. State pensions became vested in ten years, and a method of calculating pensions based on the five highest earning years was lowered to three. Annual pension COLAs were raised to 60 percent of the consumer price index. Retirees retained full health benefits for themselves and their families, and the cost of their fully paid health insurance quintupled in two decades.[56]

Less well-known were some other provisions in the state's pension plan, particularly the practice of including part-time municipal and county professional employees in the pension system. Attorneys in particular have become adept at a strategy known as "tacking," practiced primarily at the municipal and county level. Tacking enables those providing professional services to local governments to qualify for large state pensions by cobbling together several part-time jobs. The tacking champion in 2006 collected almost $300,000 year as a municipal judge for eight towns in Ocean County, and if he had retired that year at the age of fifty-seven, he would have received an annual state pension of $135,000. Close behind him was a tax assessor for eight towns who earned more than $250,000 from his collection of part-time jobs. Altogether, in 2006 there were eleven individuals who, with decades of such employment, were eligible for state pensions paying at least $100,000 annually.[57]

New Jersey's nine separate pension and health benefits systems affect the one in seven families that include state, county, and municipal employees (including employees of the public education system). Despite expressions of concern in the GMIP study and Governor Kean's warnings about spiraling pension and benefit costs, they were not addressed during his tenure, leaving his successors to grapple with an ever worsening problem.

Governor Florio began his term in office by threatening the unions with legislative action to remove many benefits that were then written into law as not subject to negotiation. In exchange for leaving them largely untouched, he won a fifteen-month wage freeze for state employees (although leaving in place cost-of-living adjustments that vitiated the freeze). In 1992, his administration changed the method of valuing the state pension funds from book value (the original cost) to market value (current worth), instantly acquiring $769 million to help balance the state budget and to pay for the cost-of-living adjustments granted in the 1970s but never put into the funds' payment schedule.

Governor Whitman went Florio one better in several respects. The administration hung tough in contract negotiations with the Communications Workers of America (CWA), the largest union, whose settlements provide the model for many of the others. When the talks collapsed, a mediator called for a four-year contract rather than the usual two years, a two-year wage freeze, and the first co-payment requirements for health benefits. Incentives encouraged beneficiaries to choose managed care plans over the most expensive ones with freedom to select any health care provider, which had been chosen by two-thirds of those eligible. Free life-time health benefits after twenty-five years of service were now extended only to employees rather than also including their dependents. (The police union, favored by many legislators, escaped several of these provisions and won some new special concessions.)

These gains came with possible dangers. Like Florio, Whitman engaged in accounting smoke and mirrors to meet payment obligations to the pension funds. In Whitman's first year in office, the state treasurer, by changing assumptions about the funds' growth, declaring that the state had overestimated necessary payments in previous fiscal years, and extending the payment period for shortfalls, "found" $1.3 billion to balance the governor's first budget and expedite her promised tax cuts. By FY 1995, however, it developed that in fact the state had underestimated the required payments to the funds, and the gap between assets and future payments had risen from $800 million in FY 93 to $4.7 billion in FY 95; put another way, assets represented only 89 percent of the pension benefit funding level in the latter year, as opposed to 98 percent in the former year.

This led, in the last year of Whitman's first term, to a more radical and innovative gimmick to balance the FY 98 budget. To maintain services, pay for large increases in court-mandated educational aid to poor districts, and balance the budget without making program cuts or dismantling any tax cuts, Whitman proposed the largest state bond issue ($2.75 billion) in history, borrowing the money to close the future payments gap in the pension funds. She argued that these borrowed funds, deposited in the pension fund accounts, would earn interest income at a higher rate than the 7.4 percent interest payments on the bonds, thus permanently solving the problem. As another short-term advantage, the state did not have to make any payments in the year the money was borrowed, freeing those funds up for other purposes in FY 98.

Whitman's supporters argued that the plan made excellent sense, and the bond rating services implicitly agreed with them. Moody's Investors' Service calculated that the state's total debt after the bond issue stood at $1,588 per capita, up from $781 at the end of 1993, against a national median for all states of $422. However, Moody's pronounced the New Jersey debt figures "not unmanageable" and left the state's bond rating unchanged at AA1. Opponents, including the longtime Republican chair of the senate appropriations committee, argued that the plan depended upon the uncertain fortunes of the stock market.

Not long after, he was proved correct. During the remainder of Whitman's term, the stock market soared and investment returns far exceeded the interest payments on the bonds. The state (and local governments) started suspending their annual payments into the pension system, but, led by the Republicans who still dominated the legislature, in 2001 they gave state workers a series of gifts to be delivered just before the November elections. They included a 9 percent across-the-board increase in pension benefits for retirees and, for current employees, dropping the retirement age from sixty to fifty-five and vesting state pensions after five years rather than ten. The effect was to increase the portion of the state budget allocated to public employee benefits from less than 9 percent in 2002 to 16 percent in 2006, and a projected figure of 20 percent in 2010— just as the stock market bubble burst in 2000, plunging the state into an ever-worsening structural deficit. By 2006, state workers' pensions were funded at only 79 percent of future obligations.

The strategy of replacing "tax and spend" with "borrow and spend" had many other ramifications that were ignored in the heady days of the

stock market run-up. First, the annual payments due on the pension obligation bonds increase steadily over their thirty-year lifetime so that the
$170 million annual payment of 2006 will gradually rise to $500 million by
the time they expire. Second, to quell public workers' fear of precisely
what did happen to the stock market in 2000, lawmakers tied the hands of
future administrations by granting state employees a "non-forfeitable right
to receive benefits" when their pensions vested after five years. Hence, the
benefits of all but workers with less than five years of service cannot be
altered in the future. Finally, the bond rating services that had applauded
the deal in 2001 changed their minds, and by 2004 lowered the rating of
New Jersey's general obligation bonds from AAA to AA- or AA1 to AA3,
making it more expensive for the state to borrow money.

While Governor McGreevey used tax increases on corporations and
cigarettes along with "one-shot" revenue enhancers to cope with this situation, Acting Governor Codey and Governor Corzine took the bull at least
gingerly by the horns. In 2005, Codey appointed a study commission to
make recommendations for paring pension and benefit expenses, and in
2006, Corzine, along with Assembly Speaker Joseph Roberts and Codey
(returned to the senate presidency), set up four legislative panels to study,
in a special session, public worker pensions and benefits and three other
interlocking issues: education aid, shared county and local services, and
property tax reform. The results of their efforts are discussed in chapters
14 and 15.

As his second term drew to a close, Governor Kean reflected on his
experience managing the vast state executive branch. Kean had achieved
the first meaningful civil service reform in a century. He had brought some
oversight of independent authorities into the governor's office. The
reformed budget process gave the governor unprecedented control of state
policies and programs. In pondering his jousts with the bureaucracy, Kean
thought first of an anecdote about another chief executive: "There's a
quote by Truman where he said, talking about the transition [from the
Truman to Eisenhower presidencies] and the administration, 'Poor Ike—
he's used to being in the Army where he said something and it got done.
He's going to get into this office, and he's going to say something—and
nobody's going to pay any attention to him!' "[58]

CHAPTER 11

The Courts

If you want to see the old common law in all its
picturesque formality, with its fictions and its fads,
its delays and uncertainties, the place to look for them
is not London, not in the Modern Gothic of the Law
Courts in the Strand, but in New Jersey. Dickens, or any
other law-reformer of a century ago, would feel more at
home in Trenton than in London.

—D. W. Brogan, 1943

New Jersey's [judicial] system embodies a combination of
the features proposed as models. . . . [They] have placed
New Jersey in the vanguard of the states.

—Sheldon D. Elliott, 1959

THE 1947 CONSTITUTION brought change to all of New
Jersey's political institutions, but especially to the courts. The popular
phrase "Jersey justice" was a pithy description of the pre-1947 judicial system. It was a contemptuous allusion to "the most complicated scheme of
courts existing in any English-speaking nation."[1] Based on a model Britain
abandoned in the nineteenth century, an archaic structure of separate law
and equity courts and a welter of inferior courts reflected the state's
parochialism and hostility to change.

Yet "Jersey justice" also had a positive meaning. Politics infused the
judiciary as it did everything else, but a certain propriety obtained in
choosing high-court judges. When making nominations, governors followed a tradition of bipartisan balance. Even reformer Arthur Vanderbilt—
first chief justice under the new constitution and longtime opponent of
the Hudson County machine—admitted that county party organizations
lifted up talented jurists. Vanderbilt thought it wrong to foresee "a governor and a senate appointing bad judges to the court of last resort" because
"with a very few exceptions over the last hundred years" this had not happened.[2] Indeed, even in 1920, a scholarly study ranked New Jersey tenth in

reputation among the then forty-eight state supreme courts.[3] Structural deficiencies rather than the caliber of the justice dispensed were the major impetus for the 1947 judicial reforms.

CHIEF JUSTICE VANDERBILT AND COURT REFORM

The new constitution's judicial clause called upon the new chief justice to implement massive organizational reforms. The job fell to Arthur T. Vanderbilt—dean of the New York University School of Law, longtime Essex County political leader, and nationally known court reform scholar. Vanderbilt's ten years as chief justice left an indelible mark on the organization and administration of the courts. His successors—Joseph Weintraub, Richard Hughes, Robert Wilentz, Deborah Poritz, James Zazzali, and Stuart Rabner—have followed his lead.[4]

The State Court System

Before 1947, New Jersey had separate law and equity courts; several county and state courts with overlapping roles; a misleadingly named "supreme court"; and a court of errors and appeals, to which cases from the supreme court and some other courts could be appealed. The court of errors and appeals had sixteen members, including ten lay judges. A 1947 constitutional convention delegate described it as "little larger than a jury, little less than a mob."[5]

The new constitution abolished the separate law and equity courts that required resort to the law courts and their adversarial process for assessing damages and to the equity courts for fact-finding, injunctions, and other court orders. Instead, it created a single three-tier court system, with equity and law divisions. The system was also reorganized functionally and geographically.

The superior court has jurisdiction over all matters originating in the state courts. Its law division handles civil and criminal actions, including small claims cases assigned to the Special Civil Part. The equity division deals with requests for injunctions, orders compelling performance of contracts, probate of contested estates, and family concerns (for example, juvenile delinquency, domestic violence, adoptions, and divorces). Superior court judges sit in fifteen vicinages, headquartered in county courthouses. Eleven counties have separate vicinages. There are two multicounty vicinages in the south (Atlantic and Cape May; Gloucester,

Cumberland, and Salem) and two in the west (Morris and Sussex; Somerset, Hunterdon, and Warren). In each vicinage, an assignment judge devises the calendar for all its judges. Judges generally hear cases of a single type (civil, criminal, or equity). Superior court cases are heard by a single judge, and only murder cases must have jury trials.

The thirty-five judges of the appellate division of superior court sit in Atlantic City, Elizabeth, Hackensack, Morristown, Newark, and Trenton. Two- or three-judge panels hear appeals of lower court and administrative law decisions and publish written opinions. The appellate division may not overturn such decisions but can reduce sentences or damages. Appellate judges review procedures, jury instructions, and statutory interpretations.

Atop the system is the seven-member supreme court, sitting in Trenton. It is the sole New Jersey court in which all the member judges hear cases en banc. The high court only accepts cases with substantial constitutional questions, a dissent in an appellate court decision, or the imposition of a death sentence. At least three justices must agree to hear a case. Because of the court's strict interpretation of its jurisdiction, it hears fewer cases than most state supreme courts.[6]

The supreme court's procedures put a heavy burden on the appellate division of superior court, since each loser in the lower courts is permitted one appeal. Deciding cases in a timely manner has been a high priority in recent years, as it was in Vanderbilt's time. In 1988–1989, the appellate division disposed of 6,500 appeals, and had 5,100 pending—21 percent of them for more than a year. By 2004–2005 however, the backlog of cases, which had dropped steadily for more than a decade, reached its lowest point in twenty years.[7]

The state's forty-two administrative law judges, sitting in Atlantic City, Newark, and Trenton, hear about 12,000 cases a year. They are housed in the Office of Administrative Law, which is "in but not of" the Treasury Department and "independent of any supervision or control by the department or any personnel thereof."[8] The Office of Administrative Law was established in 1979 to systematize the work of hearing examiners assigned to investigate complaints against state agencies. Administrative law judges make recommendations to agency heads, which can accept or reject them. A complainant dissatisfied with the final agency decision can appeal to the courts.

The only post-1947 blot on this simple organization was the general-purpose county court, a concession by the constitutional convention to powerful county political organizations. A 1978 constitutional amendment abolished the general-purpose county courts, and county juvenile and domestic relations courts were similarly terminated in 1983. These county courts were absorbed into superior court (hence its name, although there are no state courts below it).

Bearing most costs of the state court system remained the most important vestige of the counties' judicial role, and a constant source of friction between state court administrators and county governments.[9] Disparate population size and crime rates produced an inequitable distribution among the counties of the cost of running the state courts. When Essex County filed suit in 1991 to force Trenton to assume all costs of the state court system, Essex taxpayers were subsidizing it at a rate more than twice that of Bergen County residents. In November 1992, voters approved a constitutional amendment to phase in the state's assumption of all court costs. By 1995, all court employees had been moved to the state payroll; the Administrative Office of the Courts (AOC) had assumed oversight of all of the system's functions, and resource allocations to the vicinages reflected their workload.

Despite the pressures on it, simple and rational organization makes the court system a prototype for court reformers in other states. Aside from a tax court established in 1979 to hear appeals of property tax assessments, there are no special courts outside the basic system.[10] Most states have many more special courts.

Judicial Rule Making and Administration

When Arthur Vanderbilt became the new system's first chief justice, he saw his administrative role as important as deciding cases. Vanderbilt established the first state Administrative Office of the Courts.[11] Its rules required that cases be decided within four weeks of submission. Vanderbilt personally kept track of the rate at which judges were clearing cases, and he rode herd on dilatory jurists. He personally admonished a judge who took a day off to drive his son to college and wrote another, "I am considerably concerned to note that you have five undecided cases, the oldest of which dates back to August 25th. There is no other county judge in the state who has a single undecided case back of September tenth."[12] His concern for speedy trials led him to advocate removing or even disbarring justices who falsified their weekly reports. This efficiency campaign prompted Felix Frankfurter to describe the New Jersey chief justice as "a pompous martinet who treats his court as a factory where men punch clocks."[13] However, Vanderbilt's stringent rules addressed the defects of a system in which twenty years could pass before a case was settled. In the first year of the new system, the superior court law and chancery (equity) divisions doubled the average number of cases heard by each judge. The appellate court heard 70 percent more cases, and the supreme court 50 percent more.[14]

Thanks to Vanderbilt, in addition to their administrative powers New Jersey's chief justices also have unusual control over the rules of judicial procedure.[15] The 1947 constitution appeared to divide this power between the chief jurist and the legislature when it stated, "The supreme court shall make rules governing the administration of all Courts in the State *and, subject to law, the practice and procedure in all such Courts*" (emphasis added).[16] At the start of his tenure, Vanderbilt precipitated a constitutional crisis by testing the limits of statutory law on the courts' rules of conduct. The contest went on for almost a decade. It involved both constitutional law and politics, particularly the historic clash between the "moralist" forces Vanderbilt represented and their perennial antagonists in Hudson County and the rural counties.

Two weeks before the new constitution's judicial article was to take effect, the legislature passed a bill that limited the supreme court's right to make rules for other courts and permitted judges to continue private legal practice. Governor Driscoll vetoed the bill, as well as another measure recreating the equity courts. Soon thereafter, in a contentious opinion in *Winberry v. Salisbury*, the court asserted its right to determine time limits for filing appeals. The case became a symbol of the conflict between the judiciary and the legislature.

Winberry generated critical articles in seven law reviews, including those of Harvard, Rutgers, and Vanderbilt's own New York University. A bipartisan legislative coalition, led by Democratic state senator Robert Meyner of Warren County, threatened a constitutional amendment to reverse it. Politicians and legal scholars alike agreed that *Winberry* did violence to even the most expansive reading of the constitution. The public, however, supported Vanderbilt, even if he did not have a legal leg to stand on. For them, it was not a question of legal niceties, but suspicion of the political forces—Hudson County and the rural Republicans—arrayed against him. Senator Meyner's proposed constitutional amendment died in committee, and he was defeated for reelection in 1951 when his opposition to Vanderbilt became a major issue.

The legislature abandoned attempts to control the court's procedural rules, but the underlying dispute soon flared anew. Meyner won the 1953

Democratic gubernatorial primary by fifteen hundred votes and went on to defeat Vanderbilt ally Paul Troast in the general election. Troast sued to overturn the results, based on irregularities in the Hudson County primary vote. A superior court judge threw out the case. On appeal, the supreme court decided 6–1 for Meyner, with Vanderbilt the lone dissenter. This "left the implication that [Vanderbilt's] motives were blatantly political."[17]

Governor Meyner renewed his conflict with the chief justice in 1955, when he insisted that the legislature had the constitutional power to determine rules of evidence. Vanderbilt appeared before the legislature to argue the contrary, saying his visit did not violate separation of powers because the legislature had invited him.[18] Although Vanderbilt contended that rules of evidence were procedural, the U.S. Supreme Court had treated them as matters of substance. The issue remained unsettled until Vanderbilt's sudden death in 1957. Meyner's appointment of his former counsel, Joseph Weintraub, as the new chief justice improved the court's relationship with the legislature. In a three-branch compromise, New Jersey in 1960 became the first state to adopt nationally proposed uniform rules of evidence.[19]

Death did not end the long debate about whether Vanderbilt was a "leader" or a "boss." Vanderbilt was devoted to the law and the advancement of the courts, but his behavior also reflected years of battle with Hudson County's Boss Hague when Vanderbilt was leader of the Essex County Republicans. Looking back, Governor Meyner observed, "I am sure he felt that the end justifies the means. Vanderbilt in the *Winberry* case was so fearful of legislative action that he was willing to distort the language of the constitution." A Vanderbilt biographer concluded he was "a moralist who used less than moralistic means to attain his goals."[20] In any case, there is wide agreement that only Vanderbilt could have institutionalized the 1947 reforms, because other candidates were less than forceful personalities or outright opponents of reform. Twenty-five years after Vanderbilt's death, a leading judicial scholar ranked New Jersey first among the states in judicial power over rule making, and third in centralized management of the courts.[21] This is Arthur Vanderbilt's legacy.

NEW JERSEY JUDGES AND HOW THEY VIEW THEIR WORK

New Jersey's judges have long been noted for the high quality of their professionalism. The new judicial system made this characteristic even more prominent, and by 1975 the state judicial system's reputational rank had risen to third, behind only California and New York.[22] Under Vanderbilt's leadership and thereafter, the state supreme court also developed a reputation for activism and innovative decisions.

In part, this distinctive ethos results from the "moralistic" aspect of the state's political culture finding its strongest expression in the courts. Under New Jersey's first constitution of 1776, the governor was chief magistrate, and the legislature gave this role to the state's most distinguished citizens. Even during the heyday of the party machines under the second constitution of 1844–1947, there was respect for the role of judges. The court has continued to "insulate itself from the prevailing political culture in the state and created a distinctive state legal culture."[23]

If history institutionalized the tradition of a high-quality judiciary, recent developments have advanced the newer tradition of activism. Since 1947, each of New Jersey's chief justices has previously served as an elected or appointed official, and none has disdained "the political thicket." As party organizations weakened and the legislature's power centers fragmented, the courts were increasingly called on to resolve difficult political issues. Further, as the legislature gained independence from the governor, both branches looked to the courts to resolve disputes between them.

JUDGES: SELECTION, CREDENTIALS, AND PROFESSIONALISM

All New Jersey judges must have been members of the bar for at least ten years when named to the state bench. All are nominated by the governor and confirmed by the senate. After a seven-year probationary period, judges reconfirmed by the senate receive tenure and may serve until mandatory retirement at age seventy. The system is unusual in several respects. Only seven other states have no judges elected by the public or the legislature. In most states, judges undergo periodic review. Only Rhode Island grants life tenure initially; only Massachusetts and New Hampshire, in addition to New Jersey, grant tenure after a probationary period until age seventy.[24]

Despite their diminished role, county party organizations are still active in naming judges. Vacancies in the lower courts are first identified as "belonging" to the Democrats or Republicans, in accord with bipartisan tradition. Informal negotiations among county party organizations, bar organizations, and local state senators produce names to submit to the governor, who may also have other candidates in mind. In this competition for judgeships, "rarely does the individual without 'connections' and without a record of partisan political activity do well."[25] Despite the politics involved in their selection (or perhaps because of it), judges are proud of a strong code of ethics, which they follow de facto as well as de jure. Unlike federal judges or those in forty-six other states, no sitting judge may teach in a law school or accept lecture fees or book royalties, much less have a private practice.[26] A survey of supreme court justices in four states found New Jersey's most likely to emphasize the importance of "proper judicial behavior."[27] In publicly reprimanding two superior court judges for accompanying politically active spouses to Governor Jim Florio's 1990 inaugural ball, Chief Justice Robert Wilentz acknowledged many jurists' past political activity, but asserted, "[T]hat stops completely and without exception on becoming a judge. . . . The prohibition is absolute."[28]

The court also takes seriously its policing of the state bar. In many states, disbarred lawyers are actually only suspended. Only in New Jersey and Ohio can they be permanently prohibited from practice in the state. More than two hundred New Jersey attorneys were disbarred during the 1980s. Only three of those expelled from the state bar in the twentieth century won reinstatement—the last in the 1950s. Policing of the bar has become even stricter since then. In the 2004–2005 term, the court's Office of Attorney Ethics announced that it would disbar previously sanctioned attorneys for actions that would previously have only resulted in suspension, and thirty-one lawyers—up from eleven in 2001–2002 and twenty in 2002–2003—had their licenses to practice revoked.[29]

Traditionally, "senatorial courtesy" allowed state senators to delay or kill judicial nomination or reconfirmation, but after the furor over three such efforts by Republican senators between 1983 and 1993, the use of this practice for reconfirmation was disallowed. Senator Gerald Cardinale's 1983 attempt to deny tenure to Judge Sylvia Pressler, before whom he had personally appeared (and lost) twice, was a watershed event. Chief Justice Wilentz held his first press conference to denounce Cardinale's action, calling it "the most important thing that has happened during my tenure."[30] The *New Jersey Law Journal* published an extraordinary front page editorial criticizing senatorial courtesy. The senate voted 35–2 to reconfirm Pressler, and Cardinale's previous victory margin of 11,000 votes fell to about 1,200 when he ran for reelection that year.[31]

The issue arose again when Chief Justice Wilentz came up for tenure in 1986. Senator Peter Garibaldi, from Wilentz's home county of Middlesex, opposed reconfirmation—nominally because Wilentz did not actually live at his legal residence in Perth Amboy, but rather in an apartment in New York City. The chief justice explained that he was in New York to be with his wife, who was receiving advanced medical treatment there.

Some senators were clearly using the residence issue as an excuse to deny confirmation to a judge whose "liberal" and "activist" opinions they abhorred. Furthermore, to live in New York for any reason was political dynamite. Republican Governor Tom Kean, who gained respect for Democrat Wilentz when they served together in the legislature and who renominated him, wrote of the furor, "beneath the patina of new [state] pride lay a two hundred-year-old case of insecurity. To have the chief justice live out of state was bad enough. But in Manhattan! To listen to some senators, one got the impression that it was grounds for impeachment."[32] After Kean's last-minute intervention, the senate reconfirmed Wilentz by the narrowest of margins, 21–19. Garibaldi was the only incumbent to suffer defeat in the 1987 elections.

The matter arose for a third time in 1993 when Senator (and Majority Leader) John Dorsey used it to oppose the granting of tenure to Superior Court Judge Marianne Espinosa Murphy, from his home county of Morris. As far as could be determined, his reservations about the judge's "judicial temperament" stemmed from her stern treatment of "deadbeat dads" in child support cases. Judge Murphy was also the wife of the Morris County prosecutor (Democrat Michael Murphy, a stepson of former Governor Hughes, who would later run in the 1997 Democratic gubernatorial primary). She was supported for tenure by Republican gubernatorial candidate Christie Whitman, Republican Senate President Donald DiFrancesco, four former state attorneys general of both parties, and all of the living governors. Nonetheless, the Republican senate caucus, in accord with the legislature's long-standing defense of the principle of senatorial courtesy, supported Dorsey, and the GOP majority on the judiciary committee refused to send the nomination to the full legislature. As expected, the state supreme court refused, in a 6–0 vote, to involve itself in the matter. In concurring opinions, three justices alluded to the separation of powers, while three others said that in principle the court could compel the full senate to act, but not on this particular case because of legal technicalities. Judge Espinosa Murphy therefore did not receive tenure and was forced to leave the bench, but she won a moral victory. In the wake of the uproar over his actions, Dorsey was defeated for reelection in his "ultra-safe" Republican district that year, and the senate changed its rules to confine senatorial courtesy to nominations of new judges, prohibiting its use in consideration of tenure for sitting judges.

Initial state supreme court nominations are the choice of the governor, and recent governors have usually chosen trusted allies. Four of the seven current justices, appointed by three different chief executives, previously served in the governor's office, cabinet departments, or both. The three exceptions—distinguished lawyers all, and also among the most recent appointments to the court—may be in part excellent examples of affirmative action. Two of Governor McGreevey's three nominees—John E. Wallace and Roberto Rivera Soto—are, respectively, the second African American and the first Hispanic to sit on the state's highest court. Helen Hoens, an appellate court judge nominated by Governor Corzine in 2006 to replace retiring Chief Justice Deborah Poritz, will ensure that women, who did not gain a place on the court until 1982, will retain the three of seven seats they have held since 2000.[33]

Until 2006, each time governors selected a new chief justice they passed over the sitting justices. Governor Driscoll chose Arthur Vanderbilt to head the reformed supreme court rather than the sitting chief justice or the chancellor of the court of errors and appeals. After Vanderbilt's death in 1957, Governor Meyner chose his counsel, Joseph Weintraub, to replace him. When Weintraub retired, Governor Cahill also named his counsel, Pierre Garven, to head the court. Garven died soon thereafter, and Republican Cahill amazed many by then nominating his gubernatorial predecessor, Democrat Richard Hughes. Hughes's retirement in 1979 led to Governor Byrne's nomination of Robert Wilentz. As described in chapter 9, Wilentz, a named partner in one of the state's most powerful law firms, had led the fight for a strict conflict of interest law for judges and resigned from the legislature when it passed.

When Chief Justice Wilentz resigned for health reasons in 1996, Governor Whitman elevated her attorney general, Deborah Poritz, to chief justice, making Poritz the first woman to occupy each of these legal pinnacles. When Poritz reached the mandatory retirement age of seventy in October 2006, Governor Corzine broke precedent by nominating as her replacement James R. Zazzali, a sitting justice. Zazzali, who was sixty-nine at the time of his appointment, was replaced a year later when he reached the mandatory retirement age.

Zazzali's successor, Stuart Rabner, a former federal prosecutor who had served as Governor Corzine's first counsel and then as attorney general, was a more conventional nominee. Widely respected throughout the political community, he was confirmed by the senate with only one negative vote, after which he received a standing ovation from both sides of the aisle. Senator Nia Gill, from Rabner's home county of Essex, who cast the negative vote and who had held up the nomination for more than a week with no explanation, had caused a brief stir when it appeared that she was using senatorial courtesy to block Rabner's appointment. Gill said later that she merely wished to arrange a personal meeting with Rabner and that her vote represented her continuing concern that the new chief justice had been a federal prosecutor, but never practiced before a New Jersey court. It was also widely reported that others saw it as a protest that the governor had not elevated a minority candidate and had not consulted with the Essex delegation before making the nomination.[34]

New Jersey's supreme court justices have less judicial experience than those in many other states and are also less likely to have attended in-state law schools. Nationally, almost half of the state supreme court justices have had prior service on the bench, and about two-thirds are graduates of in-state law schools.[35] Of New Jersey's current justices, only two had previously served on a state court, and five of the seven attended out-of-state "national" law schools.

The Tradition of Supreme Court Activism

Outside observers and the justices themselves repeatedly describe the New Jersey Supreme Court as a leader among activist state courts. Activism has many guises. One is a reliance on state grounds to find new or expanded constitutional rights. Another is limited attention to precedent. Most fundamentally, an activist court involves itself heavily in public policy.

New Jersey's high court meets all these criteria. Its justices are less likely than those of other states to say that precedent is important and are more likely to say that policy making is a proper judicial function. The New Jersey court also more often has before it issues depending on state statutes. Arthur Vanderbilt was a devotee of sociological jurisprudence, in the tradition of Oliver Wendell Holmes, Louis Brandeis, and Roscoe Pound. The court has always welcomed "Brandeis briefs," replete with social, economic and political information. It makes strong efforts to reach unanimous decisions that will have particular force.[36]

In a 1965 decision, the justices observed, "The law should be based upon current concepts of what is right and just and the judiciary should be alert to the neverending need for keeping its common law principles abreast of the times."[37] In a 1975 case, they invited a defendant to argue that the state constitution provided more stringent limits on search and seizure than does the U.S constitution, despite identical wording. The court asserted its "right to construe [the] state constitution in accordance with what we conceive to be its plain meaning."[38]

New Jersey's high court is often "unwilling to defer to the expertise or stature of the United States Supreme Court."[39] In a 1990 search and seizure decision contravening federal high court rulings on the right of police to search household trash, the 5–2 majority argued that the state constitution made privacy the "right most valued by civilized man." Therefore, "the equities so strongly favor protection of a person's privacy interest that we should apply our own standard rather than defer to the federal provision."[40] The same year, the justices offered similar language in the first decision that smokers or their survivors could sue cigarette manufacturers for damages, despite numerous federal court rulings that cigarette label warnings bar such claims.

The New Jersey Supreme Court as Policy Maker

Mary Cornelia Porter and G. Alan Tarr provide a useful list of the major categories of state supreme court policy making. First, courts may be *innovative*, by overturning or filling in gaps in state policy, and imposing a specific policy. Second, they can *set a policy agenda*, by upsetting traditional policies without specifying a new alternative. Third, their decisions may be *complementary*, by aiding legislative policy goals or "taking the heat" for the legislature. Fourth, they may be *elaborative*, by extending federal precedent. Alternatively, they can be *restrictive*, by limiting or evading U.S. Supreme Court decisions. Finally, they can seek to *advance the judicial institution* by preserving the autonomy and integrity of the courts and seeking sufficient financial support for the court system.[41] The New Jersey supreme court has involved itself in all these activities.

INNOVATION. The high court has pioneered in setting state policy through judicial decisions, particularly when defining individual rights. Abortion rights in New Jersey are among the broadest in the nation, based on the right to privacy the justices find in the state constitution. They also find a right for poor women to public funding of therapeutic abortions. In *In re Quinlan* in 1976, the court was the first to find passive euthanasia legally permissible for "brain dead" patients in a "persistent vegetative state" with no hope of recovery.[42] *Quinlan* was described as "undoubtedly one of the most activist [decisions] handed down by any court in the nation."[43] The court, in *In re Baby M*, also issued the first major decision on the rights of surrogate mothers.[44] In 2006, in a unanimous decision in *Lewis v. Harris*, the court ruled that "the unequal dispensation of rights and benefits to committed same-sex partners can no longer be tolerated under our state constitution."[45] In extending identical benefits, protections, and responsibilities to homosexual couples that heterosexual couples enjoy, New Jersey became only the fourth state to do so, joining Massachusetts, Vermont, and Connecticut, and followed shortly thereafter by New Hampshire.

The New Jersey Supreme Court is not alone in its recent tendency to use state grounds in cases involving individual civil rights.[46] Beginning in the 1970s with the advent of the Burger, Rehnquist, and Roberts-led U.S. supreme courts, which eschewed the "judicial activism" of the Warren Court, more individual rights cases turn up in state courts, in the hope of finding a more hospitable home in "the new judicial federalism."[47]

AGENDA SETTING. The most controversial policy arenas in which the court has long been heavily involved are school funding and land-use regulation. These interventions, which affect every municipality and many individuals, and challenge New Jersey's home rule tradition, have most often brought the court to public attention. (We treat its involvement in these areas later in this chapter, and again in chapters 15 and 16.) In both arenas, the court's early decisions overturned traditional policies but left it to the legislature to devise new ones. Justices often try to "combine active participation in the determination of state policy with appropriate deference to the prerogatives of elected officials," and "mandate attention to pressing problems without foreclosing the exercise of discretion and political judgment."[48]

COMPLEMENTARY DECISIONS. When state courts make complementary decisions, they support other branches of government by advancing policy goals or assist them by deflecting public criticism or buttressing controversial decisions. Many such cases involve liability law and consumer protection. In a study of the speed with which post–World War II state supreme courts adopted fourteen tort law innovations through 1975, the New Jersey high court ranked first.[49] A 1960 landmark case dealing with implied warranties is often viewed as the "effective beginning of strict liability."[50]

The long struggle to reform New Jersey's troubled car insurance system demonstrated how the court buttresses other public officials. When public furor over insurance rates reached a peak in late 1989, a coalition of activists managed to place a referendum on rate rollbacks on the ballot in all twenty-one counties. The court called the strategy unconstitutional and left auto insurance reform to the governor and legislature about to be elected. When Governor Florio took office in 1990, one of his first acts was to speed through the legislature yet another attempt to reform auto insurance. The insurance companies rebelled, and several announced they were leaving the state. Within weeks, the supreme court had upheld a superior court restraining order against one of the companies, ordering it to continue doing business in New Jersey until it came up with a plan, approved by the state insurance commissioner, for replacement coverage for its customers.

ELABORATIVE AND RESTRICTIVE DECISIONS. Elaborative and restrictive decisions involve deviations from U.S. Supreme Court decisions, most often in the field of criminal law—either to expand the rights of the accused or to limit or evade such rights. In contrast to its expansionary views in other areas, the New Jersey high court has a mixed record in this area. Despite enthusiasm for other expansionary decisions, Chief Justice Vanderbilt was a conservative on criminal law, and his successor, Joseph Weintraub, was sharply critical of the Warren U.S. Supreme Court's expansion of defendants' rights. The Weintraub court's consistent denial of motions to suppress evidence based on a claim of unreasonable search and seizure led lawyers to joke that in New Jersey, the Bill of Rights had one less amendment than in other jurisdictions.[51]

The court's most recent criminal law decisions have sought to balance the court's traditional vigilant defense of individual rights and its equally traditional support for law enforcement officials; its split decisions reveal a judicial dialogue about these equities. In 2002, state troopers were under highly publicized fire for allegedly using racial profiling when they stopped motorists to search cars for drugs and other contraband. The supreme court unanimously ruled that police could not ask motorists if they could conduct such a search "unless they had a reasonable and articulable suspicion" of criminal activity.[52] Four years later, in the view of criminal lawyers and civil rights activists, it reversed course. First, in a 5–2 decision, it asserted that a police order to stop must be obeyed even if it is unconstitutional—a determination to be made by the courts. The defendant's lawyer contended that the decision would "create crimes where there weren't any. . . . It actually rules for the first time you can be arrested for walking away from police officers even if those officers had no reason to stop you in the first place." Writing for the majority, Justice Barry Albin, retorted. "A person has no constitutional right to endanger the lives of the police or the public by fleeing or resisting a stop," even though a judge may later determine the stop "was unsupported by reasonable and articulable suspicion."[53]

A few months later, an even more divided court ruled by a 4–3 vote that police did not need a reason to ask for permission to search someone's home. An appeals court had ordered a new hearing on such a "knock and talk" investigation on the grounds that the 2002 decision about automobile searches applied to homes as well. Justice Albin, once again writing for the majority, distinguished the two cases by holding that the 2002 ruling "addressed concerns about the then intractable problem of racial profiling on our highways." An investigation by the attorney general had demonstrated that eight out of ten of those stopped on the New Jersey Turnpike were black or Hispanic, and in 70 percent of cases, no contraband was found. With no similarly discriminatory pattern shown in searches of homes, Albin held that "in the dangerous times in which we live," the state constitution "does not disallow voluntary cooperation with the police."[54]

Of recent criminal law issues however, the court's position on the death sentence has received the most public attention. After outlawing the death penalty from 1963 to 1982, the court accepted a revised capital punishment statute. Between 1982 and 2006, there were 197 capital trials and 60 convictions, of which 50 were reversed, leaving 10 men on death row. No one has been executed in New Jersey since 1963. Nor is anyone likely to be any time soon, thanks to two events in January 2006. Three days after an appeals court temporarily blocked executions until a standard method of devising lethal injections passed judicial muster, the legislature, by a wide margin in both houses, voted to suspend executions until a study commission reported on the fairness and costs of imposing the death penalty. The commission submitted its report a year later, unanimously recommending to the legislature that New Jersey replace the death penalty with a sentence of life imprisonment without possibility of parole.[55] Of the thirty-eight states that allow death sentences to be imposed, only Illinois and Maryland have similarly suspended death convictions by executive orders from the governor. New Jersey was the first state to do so by legislation. Maryland has since lifted its suspension.

INSTITUTIONAL ADVANCEMENT. Beginning with Vanderbilt's long campaign to ensure the chief justice's control over judicial administration and procedures, the state supreme court has been active in protecting and advancing its own prerogatives.

Chief Justices Weintraub and Hughes maintained the system Vanderbilt established but were less interested in judicial administration. Wilentz and Poritz, however, gave Vanderbilt-like attention to their administrative roles. In 1990, Wilentz refused to permit filming at the Essex County Courthouse of a scene in the motion picture *Bonfire of the Vanities* that depicted blacks rioting in a courtroom. The chief justice, backed by the state NAACP, said the scenes were offensive to African Americans and could undermine confidence in the justice system.

The Essex County executive and the American Civil Liberties Union sued Wilentz in federal court, accusing him of censorship. Underlying the dispute, however, was the right of the chief justice to control the use of county court buildings. A U.S. district judge ruled that Wilentz's action was "offensive to the principles of the First Amendment" and "unconstitutional," and ordered the chief justice to pay the county's legal fees. The chief justice appealed the decision to the U.S. Circuit Court of Appeals, which ruled for Wilentz on the grounds that only the film company had standing to sue. Although it declined to address them directly, the court noted that the case had serious First Amendment implications.[56]

Poritz devoted herself to implementing a major reorganization when the state took over the administration and financing of the court system in 1994. Although not the only impetus for that decision, the ever-increasing case backlog at the time was an important element, and Poritz also pursued timely decisions with zeal worthy of Vanderbilt. In her final address to the state bar association, she cited the swifter and more uniform justice brought by the restructuring as her proudest accomplishment.[57]

As with Vanderbilt, not everyone approved of all of her tactics. Attorneys felt vindicated when a unanimous three-judge appellate court found that a superior court judge had violated court rules when he granted a divorce before all the issues in the case were resolved. In a published opinion, they observed, "No one can dispute the value of a speedy disposition. . . . Premature entry of a final decision, however, may ultimately result in a significant injustice." Within a week, Poritz, with the assent of the associate justices, took the extraordinary step of "unpublishing" the opinion so that lawyers could not cite it, on the grounds that it did not establish new law or deal with the merits of the case.[58]

Under Poritz, the court also faced down the most significant legislative challenge to its administrative powers since *Winberry*. In 2002, Acting Governor DiFrancesco had signed a bill requiring the judiciary to create a special unit of at least two hundred probation officers to carry guns and have full powers to enforce the law. The Administrative Office of the Courts had long opposed arming them on the grounds that it would turn "neutral" agents of the court into law enforcement officials. The AOC immediately moved to block the unit's creation, and, after prevailing in two lower courts, won a 6–0 affirmation from the high court of its absolute right to control its own administration.[59]

New Jersey's chief justice is one of only fifteen who appoint the head of the Administrative Office of the Courts. Under Wilentz it expanded to a three-hundred-person professional bureaucracy—about six times larger than the similar office in neighboring and more populous Pennsylvania.[60] Wilentz and the AOC also created the first task forces to consider how the courts deal with gender bias, minority concerns, and linguistic minorities. Many states followed New Jersey's lead. Each year, the AOC also sponsors a state judicial conference on a major legal issue. Recent topics have included mandatory sentencing, speedy trials, dispute resolution, and municipal court reform. Although the conferences are chaired by the associate justices in rotation, the AOC staff organizes the meetings and prepares the background materials for the conference reports. In general, the chief justice depends heavily on the AOC and its executive director to administer the courts.

In manifold ways, therefore, the New Jersey high court has not hesitated to involve itself in state policy making. Its role, however, is even greater than this inventory suggests. When called upon, as it frequently is, to referee disputes between the branches of government, it also affects policy significantly. Further, although disinclined to impose remedies in agenda-setting decisions, the court has not hesitated to do so when it perceives legislative irresolution or irresponsibility.

THE NEW JERSEY SUPREME COURT AS UMPIRE AND REFEREE

State supreme courts serve as umpires and referees when they resolve conflicts about separation of powers, disputes about day to day government operations, and issues of public policy, large and small.[61] When disputes about the power of the governor versus the legislature reach the state supreme court, its rulings are almost always in the governor's favor. In 1982, the justices unanimously upheld the governor's use of the line-item veto to delete or reduce legislative appropriations, and to delete legislative language limiting executive latitude in spending appropriated funds.[62] Another unanimous decision, this one in 1984, struck down the legislature's power to delay or nullify executive branch rules and regulations. The court asserted that a legislative veto interferes "with executive attempts to enforce the law. The chief function of executive agencies is to implement statutes through the adoption of coherent regulatory schemes. The legislative veto undermines performance of that duty."[63] This decision led the legislature to propose a public referendum on a constitutional amendment to allow the practice, which passed in 1992.[64] The court has also supported the governor in resisting expansion of public employees' bargaining rights. It has repeatedly denied their right to strike and narrowly limited the issues on which public employee unions may bargain.[65] When Republican legislators went to court eight days before the start of the new budget year to complain that Governor McGreevey's borrowing to balance the FY 2005 budget was unconstitutional, the justices agreed but let the budget stand on the grounds that because the timing would cause fiscal chaos, the decision was only prospective.[66]

Even activist high courts are wary of offering specific remedies for policy problems. The extent to which the New Jersey court has become directive has depended on two factors: the ability of other branches of government to find solutions to difficult problems the court lays before them, and the disposition of the court's members at a particular time. These influences are apparent in the most conspicuous problems the high court has faced repeatedly over the last two decades: school finance and land use and zoning.

School Finance

New Jersey has always put unusual reliance on local property taxes to fund its public schools. Beginning with California's 1971 *Serrano* decision, many state courts have directed government officials to devise school-funding plans providing greater fiscal equality across school districts with unequal property tax resources. The issue first came to the New Jersey Supreme Court in 1973, in *Robinson v. Cahill*. At the time, several justices had reached or were nearing the end of their careers. Only three members of the Weintraub court, which served through the 1960s, were still sitting. By the fall of 1974, they would all be gone.

Weintraub's dealings with other officials were less stormy than those of his predecessor, Vanderbilt. Rather than direct confrontation, he preferred a three-pronged strategy. First, he thought it important to leave lawmakers wondering—and worrying—what the court would do next if they did not act. Second, he believed interim remedies should be distasteful enough to all parties to provide a strong incentive to act. Third, to encourage quick action, any remedy should also withhold government benefits from everyone affected.

Weintraub successfully employed this strategy to achieve a constitutionally acceptable legislative reapportionment plan in the late 1960s and early 1970s. By 1960, as a result of legislative deadlock, the assembly had not been reapportioned since 1941, and in the mid-1960s, U.S. Supreme Court decisions required even more politically painful redrawing of the senate as well. The state supreme court never specified detailed reapportionment plans, but rather used Weintraub's devices to compel politicians to come up with them.[67]

The strategy was clearly at work in the early *Robinson v. Cahill* rulings. The first two decisions, over which Weintraub presided, struck down the school-finance formula but offered no specific remedy. The court left every municipal government, taxpayer, and parent anxious for a solution. Shortly thereafter, however, both Governor Cahill and the chief justice departed the political scene, and the legislature was hopelessly divided. A huge Democratic majority was split between urban legislators seeking property tax relief and more state aid and suburban lawmakers whose constituents did not want to divert local funds to urban schools.

The new chief justice, former governor Richard Hughes, had the politician's bent for compromise and was willing to give the legislature more time to solve the problem. The new governor was, oddly, much less "political" than Hughes. Brendan Byrne was himself a former superior court jurist of activist bent (he had, for example, participated in declaring the death penalty unconstitutional). Byrne "viewed the legislature with contempt and the supreme court with esteem" and made an unprecedented appearance before the court to argue for "aggressive judicial action to resolve the legislative deadlock." The legislature was not happy with Hughes's tactics either. As one member observed, "This never would have happened under Vanderbilt or Weintraub. . . . Weintraub would have told us what to do and we would have done it."[68]

For two years, legislative disarray kept the case before the court. With Hughes replacing the more imperious Weintraub, the court's vaunted unanimity began to fray. A 5–2 decision in May 1975 directed that three hundred million dollars in state aid to wealthy towns be redistributed to less wealthy ones; the two dissenters saw this as improperly aggressive action that still left root problems unresolved. In the next decision, in January 1976, unity completely disintegrated. Two justices joined in a Hughes opinion, two wrote concurring opinions, one dissented, another joined except for one part of the decision, and the last joined only in that part.

In March 1976, after three years of school budgetary chaos, the assembly finally passed New Jersey's first income tax, but the senate refused to go along. In May, *Robinson v. Cahill* returned to the court for the seventh and last time. The court finally applied a Weintraub-like stratagem, ordering that no public funds be spent for education after July 1, 1976, without a constitutional funding scheme in place.

Although less draconian than shutting the schools down in September, the ruling immediately affected one hundred thousand students planning to attend summer school, as well as many handicapped students in year-round programs. On July 9, the legislature passed an income tax package and funding plan acceptable to the court, and *Robinson v. Cahill* came to an end. But it was only an apparent end, for the plan still contained constitutional defects justices had previously criticized. Only a few years later, in 1981, what might be termed the "son of *Robinson v. Cahill*" began making its way through the judicial system, reaching the state supreme court in 1985.

The new case, *Abbott v. Burke*, brought against former education commissioner Fred Burke on behalf of twenty students in Camden, East Orange, Irvington, and Jersey City, charged that the new formula still left those in poorer communities without equal protection of the law. The progress of *Abbott*, described in chapter 15, reveals the strategies of yet another set of justices and elected officials in dealing with the complexities posed by educational funding schemes. Cases directly related to the original *Robinson v. Cahill* decision were before the court for three years. In 2007 the supreme court was still considering arguments stemming from its original *Abbott* decision twenty-two years earlier.

Local Zoning: The Mount Laurel Decisions

Despite a few rhetorical threats to impeach all the justices or to amend the constitution to delete its "thorough and efficient" clause as a result of *Robinson v. Cahill*, "no one mounted an assiduous effort to take on the Court or reverse its direction." However, "If Robinson's stand had stood explicitly to benefit . . . adults trapped in poverty, a legislative counter-attack would have been more likely."[69] Public reaction to the court's next entry into the policy arena, in the cases collectively known as *Mount Laurel*, proved this prediction correct.

Mount Laurel I was decided by the Hughes court in 1975, after three years in the lower courts. The local branch of the NAACP had sued the township of Mount Laurel, saying that its large-lot zoning ordinances restricted residential choice. Historically, New Jersey courts had stayed out of local zoning matters. In 1952, they sustained the right of wealthy Bed-minster Township to zone 85 percent of its developable land in minimum five-acre lots.[70] When *Mount Laurel* came before the Hughes court, the court was in the midst of the controversial school-funding cases, and the more activist firebrands of the Weintraub court had departed.

In a unanimous decision, the court supported the NAACP's con-tention that exclusionary zoning was unconstitutional. The decision became a topic of debate for legal scholars and was frequently cited by other courts.[71] Liberals praised it as a courageous step toward equal oppor-tunity, while conservatives saw it as the worst kind of judicial social engi-neering. Its practical effect, however, was negligible. As in the early school-finance cases, the court offered no particular remedy or method of enforcing its decision. The legislature avoided the issue, and by the 1980s, *Mount Laurel I* had become a dead letter.

The plaintiffs pursued the matter, however, and in 1982 *Mount Laurel II* returned to the state supreme court. The court majority now consisted of more aggressive judges appointed by Governor Byrne and led by Chief Justice Wilentz. This time, the court unanimously imposed a sweeping remedy: it ordered municipalities to change their zoning ordinances to permit construction of a specified number of low- and moderate-income housing units.[72] If municipalities refused to comply, a "builder's remedy" came into play. Developers would be allowed to exceed the density local zoning ordinances permitted if they included a specified proportion of low- and middle-income units. It was widely believed that the court inserted this proviso to get the state's politically influential housing industry behind the push to open the suburbs. New Jersey builders were the largest single group of contributors to legislative campaigns.

As then-Governor Thomas Kean described it, "*Mount Laurel II* exploded in the state like a giant hand grenade." An avalanche of lawsuits followed the decision. Deluged with complaints from constituents, the legislature threatened a constitutional amendment to remove the court's power to intervene in local zoning matters. Kean also entered the fray, saying the decision smacked of "judicial dictatorship" and "stomped on the toes of the executive and legislative branches of government."[73]

Lawmakers took more than two years to respond, but finally, in 1985, they passed the Fair Housing Act. The act created a Council on Affordable Housing (COAH) to replace judicial oversight and also provided alternatives to the builder's remedy. Wealthier suburbs could "buy out" of half their affordable housing obligation by subsidizing such units in any other municipality that would accept them.[74] The result was a rush by wealthier suburbs to finance construction in poorer areas.

In 1986, the supreme court decided *Hills Development Co. v. Township of Bernards* (often informally called *Mount Laurel III*), a case challenging the Fair Housing Act. The court unanimously declared the Fair Housing Act constitutional, and gave control of all pending cases to COAH.[75] In a later decision, "fully developed communities" were exempted from the obligation to provide or subsidize new low and middle income units. *Mount Laurel III* seemed to reverse the court's earlier determination to "open up the suburbs." Those favoring *Mount Laurel II*'s sweeping mandate argued that transferring cases to COAH vitiated the effects of twelve years of pro bono legal work on behalf of the poor.

Although eventually backtracking from its position, the court's intrusion into actual policy making was thus greater for a time in the zoning arena than it was in school funding. The personalities on the bench at the time of each key decision, and the actions of other branches of government, seem to explain the action of the court. Significantly, however, in both instances, one of the nation's most activist state supreme courts acknowledged its policy-making limits and accepted legislative solutions difficult to reconcile fully with their reading of the constitution. *Robinson v. Cahill* thus inevitably spawned *Abbott v. Burke*; as chapter 16 of this book describes, *Mount Laurel* cases also continue.

The supreme court's ventures into the political thicket bring it criticism from both ends of the political spectrum. When it shut down the schools in

1976, it drew the ire not only of local conservatives but of syndicated columnist George Will. Will called the decision a classic example of how "progressives" and their "allies in the judiciary circumvent democratic processes."[76] Others said that an unwilling court was forced to act because the governor and legislature had "ignored" the constitution's thorough and efficient mandate since 1875 and simply "passed the buck" to local governments. In the view of these critics, the court did not go far enough and missed a golden opportunity to order a uniform statewide school tax. Similar arguments greeted the succession of zoning cases. One set of *Mount Laurel III* critics saw the decision as a sell-out and a "blueprint for delay." At the other extreme, there were arguments that COAH incorporated too much court dicta about planning and land-use regulation, which some believed should be left entirely to local and state governments.[77]

The New Jersey Courts and the Political Thicket

The New Jersey judiciary is not partisan, but it is political, in the finest sense of that word. Justices with earlier political careers are not likely to develop political amnesia, nor is the nature of the cast of characters likely to change much for some time.

Only the justices hear their own deliberations, or know their thoughts about politically potent cases. Was it mere chance that the court first chose to remand *Abbott v. Burke*—and give elected officials a lost opportunity to deal with the school-funding issue—at a time when the court was facing political attacks because of its involvement in local zoning decisions? Was it coincidental that *Mount Laurel III*, which seemed to contravene the same judges' *Mount Laurel II* decision, was decided just as Chief Justice Wilentz's tenure fate hung in the balance in the legislature? Was the timing of the first *Abbott v. Burke* decision, expected for months, unrelated to the timing of the open-seat governor's race of 1989?

When they struck down a parental notification provision in the state's abortion law signed by Governor Whitman in 2000 (who had previously vetoed an even more controversial ban on so-called partial birth abortions), did it cross their minds that the previously staunchly pro-choice governor might be courting conservative voters as she contemplated a U.S. Senate race? Two weeks before the 2006 national midterm elections and the day before Chief Justice Poritz's retirement, the court issued a "nuanced and complicated 90-page ruling" on gay couples' rights, which "left observers struggling to declare who won and who lost." Were they sensitive to the timing, or to a poll that found while a bare majority of New Jerseyans supported gay marriage, two-thirds favored civil unions?[78]

As the examples mount, it is difficult to ascribe them all to coincidence, rather than to essential qualities of today's Jersey justice. New Jersey's judges are respected for their integrity and professionalism. The state high court "has eagerly embraced opportunities to promulgate policy for the state and doctrine for the nation, confident of its own abilities and of the legitimacy of the activist posture it has adopted."[79] Today, however, as they did fifty years ago, New Jersey's courts still show many signs that they follow the election returns.

CHAPTER 12

Government and Politics in Localities

New Jerseyans must love local governments; they created
so many of them.

—Thomas M. O'Neill

It is impossible to defend the present system that
legitimizes municipalities the size of Bill Gates's living
room.

—former assembly speaker Alan J. Karcher

No Hudson officials indicted today.

—news headline, *Jersey Journal*

NEW JERSEY IS "a state governed by 566 municipalities,"
runs a famous aphorism. It has more local governments per square mile
than any state—more than Arizona, Delaware, Hawaii, Maryland, Nevada,
New Mexico, Rhode Island, and Wyoming combined. Forty-sixth in size
among the states, New Jersey ranks eleventh in total number of municipalities. Their average size is the smallest of any state; one in three is less than
two square miles in area. Governor Brendan Byrne once observed that
"home rule is a religion in New Jersey," and a journalist has called it "as
indigenous to New Jersey as the tomato, the Eastern Goldfinch and the
Pine Barrens tree frog."[1]

Curiously, given the homage to home rule, experts rank municipalities' control of their functions and personnel at about the national average,
and their control of local government structure and financial authority well
below the national average. In *Trenton v. New Jersey* in 1923, the U.S.
Supreme Court ruled that "in the absence of state constitutional provisions
safeguarding it to them, municipalities have no inherent right of self-
government beyond legislative control." In 1971, the state supreme court,

239

in *Ringlieb v. Parsippany-Troy Hills*, similarly found that "Municipalities have no powers other than those delegated to them by the Legislature and by the State Constitution."[2]

New Jersey's distinctive history accounts for the difference between de jure and de facto home rule. In the past, communities had few cultural or economic links with each other. Reliance on the local property tax to finance public services reinforced localism. Weak state government offered no counterweight. However, three trends continue to move home rule toward rhetorical principle rather than actual practice: a new state identity; a growing number of urgent problems that cross municipal boundaries; and broad-based state taxes producing increased state aid to localities, and thus more state control.[3]

The role of the counties is also changing. Traditionally, county political organizations were extremely important, while county government was extremely unimportant. Simply to transpose those adjectives now would be too strong a statement. Still, Trenton has assigned the counties growing responsibility for regional policies, from transportation planning to solid waste disposal to public higher education. This chapter looks at political change and continuity in New Jersey's localities.

MUNICIPALITIES

By 1800, every inch of New Jersey was already in an incorporated place. The first township law, in 1798, authorized but did not require support of the poor, building and maintenance of roads and animal pounds, and determination of township boundaries. The early form of local government, as in New England, was the town meeting.[4]

North Jersey municipalities became satellites of New York City as soon as there was reliable transportation across the Hudson River. Before the introduction of the steamboat in 1813, the mile-long trip by sailing ferry between Manhattan and Paulus Hook (later Jersey City) could take as long as three hours. By the mid-nineteenth century, New York's population growth brought separation of business and residential areas, and the start of commuting. Every New Jersey population center was linked to New York and Philadelphia by railroad, canal, boat, or turnpike. By 1860, a million rail passengers traveled annually between Newark and Jersey City, where ferries conveyed them across the Hudson.

The Industrial Revolution created a demand for unskilled workers, and foreign immigrants flocked to the cities. In 1850, only 38 percent of

Jersey City males were native born; an equal number were Irish immigrants. By 1860, over one-third of Newark's population was also foreign-born. It was the nation's eleventh largest city, and its most industrialized, with 74 percent of the workforce engaged in manufacturing. Industrialization also brought primitive sanitation, high accident rates, drunkenness, and crime. These problems were of little concern to urban and suburban elites and the rural leaders of the state legislature.

Newark's city fathers first hired municipal firefighters and police officers, and funded some sidewalks and lighting, in the 1850s. Descendants of Newark's founding Puritans, they saw individual effort as God's work. This attitude, combined with the growing number of immigrants, paved the way for ethnic-based urban political machines and their bosses. Jersey City elected its first Irish Catholic mayor in 1869. By the 1890s, many cities had Irish or German officials.

It was crucial to New Jersey's development, however, that the bulk of the population never lived in cities or developed empathy for them. Thirty percent of the state's residents dwelt in Newark, Jersey City, and Paterson in 1890, a high-water mark never reached before or since.[5] The wealth that cities produce created bedroom suburbs like South Orange, Montclair, and Morristown, and seaside resort towns such as Long Branch and Atlantic City.[6] By 1920, the suburban population was as large as the rural population, and about half that of the major cities.

The outlying Shore communities could ignore urban problems, but alarmed suburbs on city borders fought "to contain the trolley, the saloon and the tenement radiating out from Newark" during the "Greater Newark" movement of the 1890s.[7] Montclair required saloons to have expensive licenses and bonds. Well-to-do Republicans controlling Essex County won state legislation that mandated consent from 50 percent of all property owners along proposed trolley routes. They described such strategies with reformist catchphrases like "regional and county-wide planning."[8] European immigrants and migrating southern blacks thus remained largely confined to older cities. Jersey City's black population had grown from 39,000 in 1880 to 69,000 in 1900, when a state report expressed shock at its living conditions: "[O]ne of the most vexing urban problems of the 1960s had become manifest by the turn of the century."[9]

Constitutional language and legislative politics bred large numbers of small municipalities. The 1844 constitution allowed for unrestricted, ad hoc legislative charters of both businesses and municipalities. If legislative representation had been based on towns rather than counties—as in Connecticut for example—proliferation might not have occurred. But since it was not, "the balkanization of local government had the political merit of increasing the number of offices and jobs" without disturbing the partisan balance in Trenton.[10]

In 1800, New Jersey had about one hundred municipalities. Township fragments broke away to escape rising taxes or social problems, and Trenton granted incorporation to avoid having to provide public services itself. Municipal incorporations followed the business cycle, spiraling upward in the 1840s, 1890s, and 1920s, and essentially ending by the 1940s. So many small localities developed that while the state's population in 1967 was 26 times larger than it was in 1810, the average municipal population was only 2.5 times larger.[11]

The Rise of the Suburbs

New Jersey's cities never had a high noon, but they entered their twilight years in the mid-twentieth century. Each succeeding decade brought another blow to the cities. By the end of the 1920s, zoning and master plans protected suburbs from "infiltration" by low-income urban workers. By the late 1930s, three major highways whisked commuters out of New York City across the George Washington Bridge and into the Bergen County suburbs; three others led from the Lincoln Tunnel to the far reaches of Essex County. In the 1940s, construction began on the Garden State Parkway and the New Jersey Turnpike. In the 1950s, the federal highway program authorized three interstate highways.

The state toll roads enabled rapid travel from north to south, the interstates from east to west. Until World War II, cars were mainly feeders to the commuter railroads. When the new highways came, industry and population dispersed in new patterns: "[T]he off-ramp replaced the trolley stop and commuter station as the active node of suburbia."[12] Newark provided one-fifth of all jobs in 1909 and paid one-quarter of all wages but was reduced to less than 10 percent of both by 1939. As the economy grew, businesses moved to suburbs, which, unlike those in many other states, did not fall victim to urban annexation.

Suburbs became more than bedrooms for city workers. They grew around industrial plants (for example, Ford Motor facilities in Edison and Mahwah; Squibb Pharmaceuticals in North Brunswick), research parks (CIBA-Geigy in Summit; Colgate in Piscataway), or shopping malls (first in Bergen County; later almost everywhere). Many workers now commute from homes in one fringe suburb to jobs in another and never need enter a city. They give New Jersey its distinctive character as the nation's most suburban state.

More than half of New Jersey's 566 municipalities are genuine small towns with fewer than 10,000 residents. Only about a quarter of the population lives in communities of more than 50,000. Bergen County, home to more than one in ten New Jerseyans, epitomizes the state. Its northern half is semirural, rich, and Republican; its southern portion, bordering Hudson County, is industrial, blue-collar, and Democratic. With over 800,000 people—more than Boston or San Francisco—Bergen could qualify as one of the nation's larger cities. Instead, its residents live in seventy municipalities with an average population under 12,000. In the 1990 census, Bergen supplanted Essex (home of Newark) as the state's most populous county.

New Jersey's suburbs are thus remarkably diverse. Bergen, Monmouth, Morris, and Somerset County towns with luxurious homes and weekend retreats are among the nation's wealthiest. Other suburbs, like Toms River in Ocean County, Parsippany in Morris County, or East Brunswick in Middlesex County, consist mostly of comfortable housing developments for transient corporate middle managers attracted by their proximity to highways. Still others are company towns for blue-collar workers or offer housing for the so-called cops and firefighters market.

Although much of New Jersey's minority population remains locked in the cities, there are also suburbs with sizable or majority black populations. Some, like Irvington, border on Newark. Others, like Lawnside in Camden County, were stops on the Underground Railroad during the Civil War. Still others, like Montclair and Plainfield, house both descendants of nineteenth-century domestic servants and professional families drawn by existing minority populations and exceptionally attractive housing. There are also historically black rural communities, like the hamlets of Little Rocky Hill in Somerset County and Bivalve in Atlantic County.

Types and Forms of Municipal Government

A confusing feature of New Jersey municipal government is the frequent lack of correspondence between types of municipal incorporation and forms of government with the same names. The word "city," for example, refers to both a type and a form, but a municipality can be a chartered "city" with a different form of government. Such disjunctions between form and type produce locutions like "the Township of South Orange Village"—township referring to governmental form, village referring to the type of incorporation. *Types* of municipal incorporation include cities, towns, boroughs, townships, and villages. New Jersey is unique in that these types do not differ in their rights, powers, or duties.[13] *Forms* of government refer to organizational structure—the principal government officials, their powers and duties, and how they are selected. There are five types of municipalities and twelve forms of government in current use.

Municipal types are determined at the time of incorporation, but types did not have clear legal definitions until the end of the nineteenth century, when most municipalities were already established.[14] Even then, types and forms with the same name were only loosely related. Types remained the same while forms changed. By type (but not form), Newark is a city, and so is Corbin City (population 519). Most boroughs—the most common type of municipality—arose in the late 1800s when parts of townships split off over controversy over issues like Sunday blue laws and Prohibition, or to avoid taxes. Shrewsbury Township, founded in 1693, originally extended for a thousand square miles in Monmouth and Ocean counties. Continuously subdivided for all of the reasons just cited, it is now one-tenth of a mile in size with a population of 1,098 and is composed entirely of two federal housing projects.[15] The ease of incorporation produced "boroughs" like Tavistock, which consists of a golf club that split off from Haddonfield in 1921 when the latter banned Sunday play.

The earliest forms of government were the nineteenth-century categories with the same names as the types—city, town, township, borough, and village. All provide for partisan officials elected from wards or at-large for two- to four-year terms, and weak executives. In some, the mayor and council are elected separately; in others, the council chooses the mayor. All have been criticized for combining legislative and administrative powers. In 2005, there were 144 townships, 15 cities, 9 towns, 218 boroughs, and 1 village governed under these traditional forms.

In 1911, the Walsh Act added the commission form; in 2005, individually elected and nominally nonpartisan commissioners headed government departments in thirty-two municipalities. After 1923, municipalities could also choose a municipal manager form. In this form, nonpartisan elected council members appoint a manager who makes all other municipal appointments. The council may remove the manager for cause after three years. Unlike the commission form, this option, emphasizing non-partisanship and neutral competence, never caught on and presently has only seven adoptions.[16]

Seeking to enhance municipalities' managerial capacity, Governor Alfred Driscoll established a Commission on Municipal Government in 1948. Two years later, the commission recommended an Optional Municipal Charter Law, which the legislature passed overwhelmingly. Known as the Faulkner Act (after Montclair Mayor Bayard Faulkner, chair of the commission), its intent was to professionalize municipal government by separating executive and legislative functions and giving the executive stronger powers. The Faulkner Act offered municipalities a "veritable delicatessen" of governmental alternatives.[17] There were two basic designs: a mayor-council plan and a council manager plan. Each included many options—for the timing of elections (general elections or regular municipal elections), the size of the council (five, seven, or nine), partisan or nonpartisan elections, concurrent or staggered terms for officeholders, and wards or at-large seats (although no plan provided for wards only).

The various permutations were designated as options A through F under both basic plans. There was also a simplified version of the mayor-council system for small municipalities (now used by eighteen of them). Finally, municipalities could still petition the legislature for special charters, of which there are currently eleven. All the Faulkner plans also provided for the local initiative, referendum, and recall of elected officials.[18] In 1981, the legislature revised the Optional Municipal Charter Law, allowing municipalities to combine the various alternatives for election timing and districts, council size, and partisanship in whatever way they prefer.

Under the mayor-council plan used by sixty-seven municipalities, the mayor is chief executive, directing preparation of the municipal budget and appointing all department heads (which are limited to ten). One appointee must be a business administrator who oversees a centralized purchasing system and the personnel system and helps with budget preparation. The mayor may attend council meetings and veto ordinances, which require a two-thirds vote of the council to override. The council functions purely as a legislative body. It can reduce items in the mayoral budget by a simple majority and add items by a two-thirds vote.

The council-manager plan, with forty-two adoptions, is based on popular election of council members, who choose a mayor from among themselves. The mayor's duties are limited to presiding at council meetings.

A professional manager chosen by the council is the chief executive officer, making all municipal appointments and preparing the budget. The council may remove the manager at any time.

Municipalities can adopt a Faulkner Act form by one of two routes: voter approval of a charter study commission, placed on the ballot by ordinance or direct voter petition; or by direct voter petition to place a particular form on the ballot for immediate approval or rejection. If a study commission is established, it must make a recommendation within nine months. A public referendum must confirm the recommendation.

About one-quarter of the state's municipalities have adopted a new government form under the Faulkner Act. These include most of the larger municipalities, so about half of the state's population lives in places with Faulkner Act charters. In 2005, there were 129 such municipalities. The most frequent change has been from the commission form to the mayor-council form. More than 80 percent of municipalities still hold partisan elections, and more than half of those using nominally nonpartisan forms report that partisanship still figures in local elections.[19]

Functions of Municipal Government

Titles 40 and 40A of New Jersey's public laws delimit the functions of local governments. One large category is regulation of personal conduct—from loitering to begging to "the ringing of bells" and "the crying of goods." Municipalities may also regulate the use of private property in various ways, of which the most important is zoning. "Control over land use is the principal tool by which local governments maintain their individual character and pursue their particular goals."[20]

A 1927 constitutional amendment gave municipalities zoning powers, and for many years they had almost total discretion to decide land use. Recent court rulings on exclusionary zoning, the state Fair Housing Act, and Trenton initiatives fostering regional planning and environmental protection have eroded municipal autonomy. Despite new constraints, decisions by local zoning boards remain of great community interest. The surest—perhaps only—way to generate a crowd willing to attend public meetings through the wee hours is to bring a controversial variance request to a local zoning board.

Historically, New Jersey had few state-mandated municipal services. Robert Wood wrote in 1958, "The pattern of state-local relationships is traditionally one of the state giving limited financial aid, but abstaining from control, providing resources in a policy framework so broad as to fit any conceivable local attitude."[21] That has changed somewhat in recent years. Each locality must have a disaster control director and a local defense council, a local assistance board, and a department of health. Many communities have a recreation commission, a shade tree commission and so on, but they are not required.

Almost all municipalities have a paid police force. Many have paid firefighters, although volunteer squads, along with volunteer ambulance squads, remain a source of social life and organization in many communities. Water and sewer service, garbage removal, and street maintenance are provided by some municipalities. These services are often regionalized or individually purchased. Even in densely populated New Jersey, the well and septic system have not yet vanished.

Most municipal employees are civil servants, but the professionals that communities retain are not. All municipalities must have a full-time clerk, and most retain a municipal attorney, engineer and accountant. Commonly, those on retainer are political appointments—especially the attorney, who usually has political ties to council members and a policy-making role. Municipal attorneys are often past or present members of the state legislature or have other connections to Trenton. Many communities also retain other lawyers to work with their zoning and planning boards. With civil service and competitive bidding requirements limiting the classic forms of political patronage, lawyers are the most ubiquitous patronage beneficiaries.

To provide services, municipalities must levy taxes and prepare a budget. New Jersey's local governments depend almost entirely on the local property tax, which provides 98 percent of locally raised revenues, compared to about 73 percent nationally.[22] Property taxes are collected by municipalities, but their governing bodies receive and spend a rather small portion. Municipal governments are the collection agents for counties, whose budgets also depend heavily on property taxes. On average, 55 percent of local taxes go to finance local public schools, and this money is allocated by separate boards of education. New Jersey has even more school districts (610) than it does municipalities (566), and more (mostly elected) school board members (about 4,800) than elected local officials (about 3,400). Most municipalities have fiercely resisted proposals for regionalized schools.

Although municipalities have some discretion in choosing the services they provide, the state monitors their fiscal affairs closely. A 1917 municipal budget law (the first in the nation) began state audits of municipal accounts but did not require cash basis budgets. There were no limits on how municipalities estimated revenues, or requirements for a surplus fund. This was not a problem during the boom years after World War I, but the Great Depression brought massive difficulties.

By 1931, tax delinquencies in Camden, Newark, and Paterson approached 30 percent. Vast public works construction during the 1920s increased municipal and county debt from $400 million in 1922 to over $1 billion in 1933. The stock market crash prevented municipalities from converting bond-anticipation notes into long-term bonds. In 1934, New York City banks refused to bid on New Jersey municipal bonds not backed by cash-basis budgets, and the state government received aid petitions from 128 municipalities unable to meet local relief bills.

Faced with this crisis, Trenton finally acted. The 1936 Local Budget Law set up a Division of Local Finance (later renamed the Division of Local Government Services), located first in the Treasury Department and, after 1962, in the newly created Department of Community Affairs. Each year the division sets the important deadlines for municipal budget making and produces a manual of required budget titles, sequence of items, and the like. It also certifies the revenue estimates of all municipal budgets, and their compliance with statutory expenditures.

Municipal budgets must be certified annually by the Division of Local Government Services and enacted by ordinance no later than March 31. If municipal officials do not meet this schedule, the Division will write the budget, adjusting the past year's document. If municipalities experience financial trouble as defined in the law, the division takes control of the local budget and taxes until the problems are rectified.

Many municipalities flirt with missed deadlines—not because they are inept, but because Trenton budget battles leave them unsure of how much state aid they will receive. Most municipal budgets operate on a calendar year, while the state fiscal year begins in July. In 1989, more than two hundred municipalities gave this reason for missing the state deadline for introducing their budgets, and fifty-four were in the same position in 1990.[23] In 1991, the legislature required sixty-nine municipalities with populations over thirty-five thousand, or receiving extraordinary state aid, to move the start of their fiscal year from January to July so as to match the state fiscal year and mitigate these problems.[24]

Most municipalities now enjoy good credit ratings; the 1936 state budget law provided a prototype for the National Municipal League's model cash basis budget of 1948, and the Department of Community Affairs' professionalism and service to local governments, after a period of decline in the mid-1970s, is once again highly regarded.[25]

Another factor affecting municipal budgeting is the state's municipal cap law. The cap law was passed in 1976 in conjunction with the state income tax and was supposed to ensure that the new tax proceeds went for property tax relief rather than municipal spending sprees. For a few years, the allowable annual increase of 5 percent seemed adequate. Then hyperinflation, withdrawal of federal general revenue-sharing funds, and sharp increases in insurance costs made that figure unrealistic. By 1986, real average municipal spending increases were estimated at 11 percent.

The Department of Community Affairs now sets the cap as an annual cost of living adjustment. For calendar year 2007, the COLA was 5.5 percent. However, municipalities are permitted to increase their spending by an additional 2.5 percent or, if they pass an ordinance, by 3.5 percent. Further, thanks to creative evasion (for example, creating local authorities to take services off-budget) and amendments specifying exemptions, the typical municipal budget still contains items above the cap. In 2007, the legislature set the cap at 4 percent as part of the effort to control property taxes, but exemptions were still likely.

Municipal Politics

While Governor Kean preached the "politics of inclusion," and Governor Florio often spoke of creating "one New Jersey for all of its citizens," in many municipalities politics is still best described as tribal, with race and ethnicity playing prominent roles. Jersey City was famous for internecine warfare between Protestants and Irish Catholics, followed by conflicts between the Irish and later-arriving Italians and Poles. Now that Jersey City's white Catholics have achieved an uneasy truce, there are new feuds. Together, African Americans and Hispanics now make up more than half of the population, but they were unable to elect a mayor, African American Glenn Cunningham, until 2002. Cunningham, running as a reformer against the county Democratic organization and its leader, Robert Menendez, died suddenly in 2004, leaving an open fissure between blacks and Latinos. His successor in an eleven-candidate race, Jeremiah Healey, managed to unite the fractious Jersey City Democrats behind him, but the bitterness between Menendez and Cunningham's supporters persisted. When Menendez ascended to the U.S. Senate from the House of Representatives, Cunningham's widow and political partner did not support former assembly speaker Alberto Sires, the organization's choice to succeed Menendez in the House and announced that she would run against State Senator Joseph Doria, the mayor of Bayonne and Sires's predecessor as assembly speaker, in the June 2007 Democratic primary election. Doria chose to resign from the legislature.

Tribalism has also moved to the suburbs. In 2005 in sprawling Edison Township, a coalition of liberals and the township's Asians, who now make up over one-third of the population of about one hundred thousand, united to elect the first Korean American mayor in the continental United States. Both groups' mobilization efforts increased after a prominent radio shock jock asked on the air, "Would you really vote for someone named Jun Choi? We're forgetting the fact that we're Americans." The state chapters of Howard Dean's Democracy for America organization and MoveOn.org led an Internet-based offensive on Choi's behalf, and the dominant Asian American group, Indians, organized and turned out in unprecedented numbers.[26]

In little more than a year, however, the thirty-five-year-old mayor found himself caught between ethnic factions. Incidents between the police and Indian residents led the Edison PBA to call for his resignation. As the confrontations continued and the mayor supported police actions at a particularly ugly fracas in front of the municipal building, some of his Indian supporters turned against him. Decrying Choi's support of the police, one charged that "many longtime residents believe that 'this country belongs to them only.'" Bill Stephens, who had lost the mayoral race to Choi by fewer than three hundred votes, saw it differently, observing that "long-term white residents feared being forced from their own town. . . . [T]here's a little thought of they're taking over and I'm being pushed out of my community." The embattled mayor maintained, "My vision for Edison is to really make the American experiment work."[27]

Tribal politics does not dominate everywhere. University towns like Princeton and Highland Park (near Rutgers) have declared themselves nuclear-free zones, adopted sister cities in Nicaragua, and taken positions on the Iraq War. Many municipal contests revolve around which candidates will do better at keeping unwanted incinerators, corrections facilities, or highways out of town, or resolving conflicts between tenants and homeowners.

THE DEVELOPMENT OF COUNTIES IN NEW JERSEY

Thirteen of New Jersey's twenty-one counties were created in the colonial period, with the earliest—Bergen, Essex, Middlesex, and Monmouth—dating from 1682. Counties were formed and divided for the next 175 years, ending with the establishment of Union County in 1857. Created from a portion of Essex, "Union" was an odd name for a county whose founding stemmed from a two-hundred-year old feud between Newark and Elizabeth.

Development of counties was haphazard. The legislature usually acted for political reasons, such as majority party schemes to gain another state senate seat or, as in the case of Union, wrangles over the location of the county courthouse and its patronage jobs. Governmentally weak but politically strong county units encouraged balkanization.[28] New Jersey's counties began as popularly elected governments with some responsibilities; they were never merely state judicial or administrative units. Weaker than counties in the southern and western states, they were still of more import than in New England, where towns were dominant.[29]

Forms of County Government

Until the 1970s, elected boards of chosen freeholders governed all counties. A colonial term for "property owner," "freeholder" is a job title unique to New Jersey. State law on the composition of county freeholder boards was largely unchanged from 1798 to 1912. Until 1851, all counties elected two freeholders per township. As townships splintered into cities, towns, boroughs, and villages, the electoral system became less uniform, although the most common arrangement was one board member per municipality. By the turn of the twentieth century, boards in the larger counties had become unwieldy, with as many as forty freeholders in Essex and thirty-eight in Camden. Consequently, in 1902 and 1912 the legislature passed optional "small board" statutes, providing for three to nine members.

By 1912, twelve of the twenty-one counties, with four-fifths of the state's population, had "small boards." Most of the holdouts were in the south. In the 1950s, there were still more than twenty freeholders in Cumberland and Gloucester counties, and thirty-four in Atlantic County.

A 1965 superior court decision flowing from the U.S. Supreme Court's "one person-one vote" mandates finally produced a uniform system of three to nine freeholders (based on population) and at-large elections for staggered three-year terms.

The freeholder board resembles a commission form of government, combining administrative and legislative functions. It operates through committees, with members chairing one committee and holding membership on several others. Freeholders choose one of their number as director; he or she is a presiding officer with voice and vote but no veto. Freeholders also appoint a board clerk and a number of county officers, such as a counsel and a treasurer. Freeholder salaries in 2007 ranged from about $33,000 in Hudson to $15,000 in Cumberland.

In addition to the freeholders, voters elect three other county officials. The sheriff, who is primarily an officer of the court, oversees the service of legal papers, transport of county prisoners, and conduct of foreclosure sales. The surrogate probates wills and appoints legal guardians. The clerk keeps county records, registers deeds, and processes passport applications.

Dramatic change in county government became possible in 1972, with the passage of an Optional Charter Law that was a kind of Faulkner Act for counties. As with the Faulkner Act, the new county charter options encourage more executive responsibility.[30] They offer four alternatives to the traditional freeholder board: a county executive plan, a county manager plan, a county supervisor plan, and a board president plan. The first provides for a separately elected county executive; the second for a manager selected by the freeholders, with broad appointive and administrative powers. Both retain the freeholder board as a legislative body, and the other elected county officials. The third plan divides executive power between an elected supervisor and an appointed manager, and the fourth gives one freeholder some executive powers.[31]

As with the Faulkner Act, counties may adopt a new form by voter approval of a county charter study commission and its subsequent recommendation, or approval of a specific plan placed on the ballot by voter petition. Like the Faulkner plans, each of the basic county charters offers a "cafeteria" of options for the size of the freeholder board (five, seven, or nine members), concurrent or staggered elections, and district or at-large seats. All of the plans provide for partisan elections and the initiative, referendum, and recall.

Within three years of the law's enactment, nine counties—with two-thirds of the state's population—had held charter referenda. Not quite half initially passed. Atlantic, Hudson, Mercer, and Union approved charter changes, while Bergen, Camden, Essex, Middlesex, and Passaic rejected them. Essex reversed itself two years later, as did Bergen in 1985. Thus, six of the twenty-one counties, including most of the largest, now have reformed charters. All but Union, which adopted the county manager plan, chose the county executive option. No county has yet approved either of the other two plans.[32]

Functions of County Government

In recent years county government's functions have expanded some-what.[33] The current list of responsibilities includes operating county jails and administering elections, county library systems, mosquito control commissions, and welfare services; maintaining county roads; providing parks and recreation services; overseeing weights and measures; and establishing planning boards. This basic list is little different from that of the 1930s.[34]

However, as state government began providing more services and state aid, it delegated more tasks to the counties. Education is a prominent example. The legislature authorized establishment of county colleges in 1962. Nineteen of the twenty-one counties now have such institutions, serving 200,000 students in credit-bearing programs and 150,000 more in noncredit and workforce-training programs. By statutory formula, the state is to provide for 43 percent of their cost, but it actually contributes less than 30 percent.[35]

Since 1975, the counties have also had one of the more unpopular jobs in New Jersey government: devising solid-waste disposal plans. These plans, which must be approved by the state Department of Environmental Protection, require highly charged decisions about the siting and use of landfills, incinerators, and trash transfer stations. In 1988, the counties also became transportation planning districts. These developments are discussed further in chapter 16.

The majority of county revenues come from property tax receipts. State aid contributes most of the rest, with a small portion from fees and fines. Municipal collection of the county share of property taxes has the political virtue of making county taxes relatively invisible, but the vice of providing a weak public check on how counties spend money. County budgets undergo fiscal scrutiny by the state Department of Community Affairs, similar to the process for municipal budgets.

County Politics

For most of New Jersey's history, county politics was, in effect, state politics. County party bosses like Democrats Frank Hague of Hudson and David Wilentz of Middlesex and Republicans Arthur Vanderbilt of Essex and Enoch "Nucky" Johnson of Atlantic "made" governors, legislators, and state policy (such as it was). Court intervention, a changing population, and candidate-centered campaigning ended the dominant role of the counties in state politics, but a diminished and less visible system of organizational politics and patronage still operates in the counties. County party organizations can no longer name the governor, but they can still anoint the sheriff and, sometimes, legislators.

Some counties of strong partisan bent seem little changed from fifty years ago. Hudson may elect a Republican freeholder when there is a statewide GOP tidal wave at the top of the ticket, or Somerset a similar Democrat, but they will likely be gone in the next election. Other counties are competitive across long periods of time (like Union) or have competitive eras (like Camden).

County charter reform since 1972 has had mixed political effects. "Good government" activists hoped for more efficient and less patronage-ridden county management. The more cynical thought charter reform was just another change that could be deflected by party bosses. Some saw the county executive position as an added step on a state political ambition ladder with few rungs, while others believed the executive would be a glorified freeholder director. There is evidence for all these theories, as a few county sketches will show.

"Good government" got its severest test in Union County, where the Elizabeth newspaper led a crusade to endorse the county manager plan and end widespread patronage. "Reform" forces won in a close race, and George Albanese was named the first county manager in 1976. Albanese was a rare combination of talented administrator and gifted county pol: formerly the county's well-regarded director of criminal justice planning, he also had years of experience in Union County politics. Within a year, Albanese had achieved a triple-A bond rating for Union, the lowest per capita county budget in the state, and respect from a fractious freeholder board of six Democrats and three Republicans. The latter resulted partly from the manager's close cooperation with a longstanding bipartisan patronage ring headed by the septuagenarian director of the Department of Buildings and Grounds.

Writing about the Union County experiment in 1977, a journalist reported local concern that finding the next manager would "be far more difficult." She speculated that it was "unrealistic to expect county politicians to kick the patronage habit overnight, or ever," and that the "structural strengths" of the manager plan were its "political weaknesses."[36] After Albanese became state commissioner of human services in 1982, Union County government indeed became a continuing sea of political intrigue and litigation, with four county managers arriving and departing in the next eight years—which may explain why no other county has adopted a governing plan that only public administrators could love. George Devanney, the nephew of Union County Democratic leader Ray Lesniak, has served as county manager since 2002.

Essex County seemed at first a better example of how to make reform work in New Jersey counties. The leading local newspaper, the *Newark Star-Ledger*, led the two battles to adopt a new charter. The dominant Democratic organization was in decline because of the crumbling power of longtime boss Harry Lerner and the aspirations of Newark blacks for a larger organizational role. It nonetheless managed to raise $103,000 to fight charter reform for the second time (against the proponents' $35,000), and Lerner thundered that the change was "a scheme to break up the greatest Democratic organization in the United States since that of [Chicago] Mayor Daley."[37]

When reformers eked out a victory, Lerner retired to Florida. The Democratic organization fragmented, and nine candidates, eventually winnowed to four, entered the 1978 county executive race. Reform candidate Peter Shapiro, an assemblyman in his mid-twenties, won the Democratic nomination (tantamount to election) with 36 percent of the vote against two Italian organization candidates and a Newark African American. After running a model county government for seven years, Shapiro unsuccessfully challenged incumbent governor Tom Kean, another Essex resident, in 1985. Ensuing events seemed a parody of the old politics. When Shapiro forced incumbent sheriff Nicholas Amato off the Democratic ticket in 1986 to make room for a black candidate, Amato switched parties and ran for county executive as a Republican. He defeated Shapiro, who had postponed a big increase in county taxes until after the gubernatorial campaign.

As 1990 approached, Amato's polls showed he could not win reelection as a Republican. He thus announced he was returning to the Democratic fold, and gave an early endorsement to gubernatorial candidate Jim Florio. The Democratic organization rejected his renomination and supported the sitting Democratic sheriff, Thomas D'Alessio—the eventual winner, instead. A year later, a federal grand jury indicted D'Alessio, who was eventually convicted for accepting a bribe from a Florida garbage hauler seeking a New Jersey license.

In the wake of the D'Alessio scandal, Republican Jim Treffinger, running as a reformer, won the 1994 Essex county executive race and became the GOP county chair. After serving two terms and unsuccessfully seeking the GOP nomination for U.S. senator in 2000, Treffinger announced he would retire in 2002 to once again seek a U.S. Senate seat. He was forced to abandon this plan in April, when FBI agents raided his campaign office. In October, the erstwhile "reformer" was indicted for extortion, fraud, and obstructing the federal investigation into his actions, which included giving campaign aides no-show county jobs and trading government contracts for political contributions. Treffinger followed D'Alessio to prison. He was succeeded by the president of the Essex county freeholder board, Joseph DiVincenzo Jr., now in his second term and an apostle of zero tolerance of corruption.

In Bergen County's first executive race in 1986, there were hopes the contest would produce an energetic young reformer. Instead, the Democrats nominated a veteran state senator and Republicans chose the current sheriff. Both had been active in county politics for thirty years. Despite his nickname, "Wild Bill" McDowell, the Republican victor, ran a low-key administration that continued traditional patronage practices.[38] McDowell declined renomination, and a poll for the successful 1990 Republican candidate, Assemblyman "Pat" Schuber, revealed that only 20 percent of Bergen County voters could identify the county executive as the highest county office. Even when asked directly, only 50 percent claimed to have ever heard of it.

Schuber retired after twelve years in office, and 2002 saw the most expensive county executive race in history, with the victorious Democrats, Dennis McNerny and two freeholder candidates, spending three million dollars on the contest. McNerny came to office after two terms as a county freeholder. His Republican opponent in 2006, Todd Caliguire, served two terms as a Bergen freeholder during the 1990s and came in last in the 2005

Republican gubernatorial primary. It was widely believed he had entered that contest primarily to increase his name recognition for a planned run for the county office the following year.

As these examples demonstrate, county executive races have so far attracted more traditional county political veterans than ambitious younger officeholders. County politics and government are in flux. Most people know what county they live in but have little reason to identify with it. Counties are hampered by low public visibility, weak statutory powers, and resistance to regional policies and planning. The county executive has only partially replaced the strong party boss who used to personify the county and give it political clout, and in several cases they have become the party leaders themselves. Those who have gone to jail outnumber those who have sought higher office.

"A Culture of Corruption"

New Jersey's reputation for local political corruption may in some measure be a case of "guilty with an explanation." One exculpatory factor is the sheer number of elected local officials. With almost four thousand of them, a small percentage of bad apples can be highly visible. Amateur and poorly paid officeholders in small towns and the patronage tradition in the larger ones, and in many of the counties, also make some officials susceptible to bribery. The moralistic strain in the political culture—never dominant but always present—sends the state into periodic fits of reformism. The first decade of the twenty-first century surely represents one of the more notable of these periods.

The previous high point in the war against political corruption in New Jersey was in the early 1970s. It was led by U.S. Attorney Herbert Stern, who prosecuted "8 mayors, 2 secretaries of state, 2 state treasurers, 2 powerful political bosses, 1 U.S. congressman and 64 other public officials."[39] Although Stern oversaw the trials of 79 Garden State officeholders, his record has been eclipsed by U.S. Attorney Christopher Christie, appointed in 2002, who by 2007 had indicted or convicted about 100 of them and whose office had never lost an official corruption case.[40]

Christie's catches did not include any federal or statewide officials, but he brought down his share of county leaders, legislators, and mayors. One of his more highly publicized accomplishments was his successful prosecution of John Lynch. A former mayor of New Brunswick, senate president, and Middlesex County's Democratic chair and premier party fundraiser,

Lynch pleaded guilty to fraud and tax evasion charges in 2006 and entered a minimum security prison the following year. In 2007, Christie also announced the indictments of state senators Wayne Bryant and Sharpe James, who had been, respectively, the long-term chair and vice chair of the senate budget and appropriations committee. Bryant, whose indictment focused on the handsome salaries he received for no-show jobs at state entities to which he directed grants, was a power in Camden county politics. The indictment of James, who served as Newark's mayor for two decades from 1986 to 2006, centered on his use of city credit cards for numerous personal vacations and his arranging for a female companion to buy city land at below-market prices; she then quickly sold the properties for almost $700,000, more than fourteen times what she had paid for them.

Like Lynch, the county leaders caught in Christie's net had often headed both their governments and their parties. Two such people, already discussed, were the Essex County executive and former Verona mayor, Republican Jim Treffinger, who was frisked and handcuffed by FBI agents as he left his home for his office, and his Democratic predecessor and the former county sheriff Thomas D'Alessio. Another was Hudson County Executive Robert Janiszewksi, who pleaded guilty in 2002 to extortion and tax evasion.

Caught in an FBI sting operation when an informant tried to pass him an envelope full of cash at the League of Municipalities convention in Atlantic City in 2000, Janiszewski spent the next three years informing on Hudson politicians and contractors in hopes of receiving a reduced sentence. Paul Byrne, his political advisor and best friend since childhood, was one of those fingered. He memorably described Janiszewski's testimony as "the political equivalent of John Gotti ratting out his bookies," and proclaimed that "Judas Iscariot was his role model." Two Hudson County freeholders and a Hudson assemblyman who was the past chair of the Joint Legislative Committee on Ethical Standards were among those convicted as a result of information from the three-term county executive. Janiszewski was next heard from in 2006, when reporters discovered that he was corresponding from prison in Kentucky with an opposition researcher from the Tom Kean Jr. U.S. Senate campaign who was seeking damaging information about Kean's opponent, Robert Menendez.[41]

Big-city mayors still figure prominently among New Jersey's more celebrated crooks. From the 1950s through the early 1970s, various Atlantic

City, Camden, Jersey City, and Newark executives all spent time in federal correctional facilities. For a time, the furor they caused produced successors who were models of rectitude, or who at least stayed out of jail. A spate of white urban reformers in the 1960s (Democratic mayors Arthur Holland in Trenton, Paul Jordan in Jersey City, and Republican Lawrence "Pat" Kramer in Paterson) were succeeded by similar black leaders (Democrats Melvin "Randy" Primas in Camden, Kenneth Gibson in Newark, and Douglas Palmer in Trenton).

By the twenty-first century, however, mayoral records for probity became even more muddied. In addition to Sharpe James in Newark, in 2001 Camden mayor, Democrat Martin Milan received a seven-year sentence for fourteen counts of corruption. They included payoffs from mobsters, laundering drug money, accepting free home improvement work from city contractors, and arranging for a "burglary" at a company he owned, so as to collect insurance payments. In 2003, Republican Martin Barnes, elected as Paterson's chief executive in 1998 on a reform platform, was sentenced for collecting hundreds of thousands of dollars in bribes and kickbacks in exchange for city contracts.

It is not only urban politicians who are caught in corruption probes. Operation Bid Rig, begun in 1998 by federal investigators, had by 2006 ensnared seventeen former and current public officials in Monmouth County—ten Republicans, six Democrats, and one with no party affiliation—on charges that they had accepted bribes from developers and contractors. Monmouth ranks eighth in the United States in terms of county median family income. Some of those convicted were from the county's grittier northern municipalities such as Keyport and Long Branch, but they also included the Republican county freeholder director, known affectionately as Mr. Monmouth for his fifty years of continuous service on that body, and officeholders from wealthier suburbs filled with McMansions, like Marlboro and Middletown.

The ongoing judicial process featured vignettes more than worthy of Hudson County. One target of the investigation committed suicide outside a cemetery mausoleum; another was caught on tape while taking a payoff, bragging that he "could smell a cop a mile away." Ellen Karcher, a Marlboro councilwoman (and later state senator), had persistently opposed a redevelopment project in her town. She received threats in the mail and a pond in her backyard that was a memorial to her late father, a former speaker of the state assembly, was vandalized. Karcher contacted the local

FBI office, and agreed to wear a wire to a meeting at which a developer offered her a $150,000 bribe.[42]

Along with the remnants of its traditional political machines, a major cause of New Jersey's endemic local corruption is its many layers of government, all with public contracts to dole out and the power to approve projects. The abundance of local governments, we have noted, stems from New Jerseyans' strong attachment to home rule. In densely populated urban counties like Hudson, bribes are most often offered by contractors seeking everything from garbage-hauling assignments to psychiatric treatment of prisoners in the county jail. In those like Monmouth, where farmland has been disappearing and developers ply their trade, the local mayors appoint almost all the members of the planning board that must approve their projects. A land use lawyer describes what can then happen in small communities: "John who knows Joe says, 'I'd really like to build 50 houses on my dad's farm. You know my dad. And, by the way, why don't we go to the Caribbean and let me show you my plans?'"[43]

Nor must the seeker of government favors necessarily risk a courtroom appearance. As former governor Brendan Byrne, a former county prosecutor, superior court judge, and champion of public funding of gubernatorial campaigns has observed, "If somebody wants a permit from a local government, and he goes to the mayor and gives him $10,000 cash in an envelope, he's guilty of a crime. If he goes to that government and handles it right and has a good lawyer, makes a campaign contribution to the mayor's campaign, which is perfectly legal, it gets him exactly the same result."[44]

Home Rule: Rhetoric or Reality?

How did home rule come to have such a strong position in New Jersey, and why is it so difficult to do anything about it? Academic discussions of home rule begin with the opposing arguments in two famous nineteenth-century court cases. Dillon's Rule, promulgated by an Iowa justice, states that municipal corporations derive all powers and rights from the legislature and are creatures of the state: "As it creates, so may it destroy. If it may destroy, it may abridge and control."[45] The Cooley Doctrine of a Michigan jurist argues that American local governments, which existed before state governments, have inherent rights deriving from common law and historical tradition that cannot be abridged.[46]

In many states, and certainly in New Jersey, Dillon's Rule describes the legal case, while Cooley's Doctrine is the more accurate picture of reality.[47]

In the years between 1870 and 1920, when New Jersey municipalities pro-liferated, the legislature let them shape themselves as they pleased. An 1875 constitutional amendment prohibited the legislature from passing "private, local or special laws" that regulated "the internal affairs" of towns and counties.[48] The 1947 constitution describes legislative power over local government thusly: "The provisions of this Constitution and of any law concerning municipal corporations formed for local government, or con-cerning counties, shall be liberally construed in their favor. The powers of counties and such municipal corporations shall include not only those granted in express terms but also those of necessary or fair implication . . . not inconsistent with or prohibited by this Constitution or by law."[49] Thus, the constitution makes clear that local governments are ultimately bound by constitutional and statutory law, but it just as clearly indicates that lib-eral grants of home rule are in order. In general, the legislature and the courts have issued detailed procedural guidelines (as for local finance) but otherwise allowed municipalities and counties wide latitude (as in the "cafeteria" choices of the optional municipal and county charter laws).

This choice comports with New Jersey's history and localist culture, and with a legislature so full of former (and sometimes current) municipal and county officials. Legislative politics is an important prop to home rule. Legislative candidates base their electoral strategies on towns, because unlike county lines, town lines have generally been honored in redistrict-ing plans (Newark and Jersey City are the only municipalities split between legislative districts).

Yet, as public problems increasingly cross municipal boundaries, as state government increasingly finances municipal activities, and as citizens iden-tify as residents of the state and not just their hometowns, New Jerseyans are forced to rethink a three-hundred-year-old "theology" of home rule. Poised against distrust of state government and fears of losing community identity is recognition that municipal services are uneven, inefficient, and significant contributors to New Jersey's high local property taxes. Govern-ing a city-state of 566 municipalities that cling to a strong home rule tradi-tion is now New Jersey's central political challenge, and one that Governor Corzine has promised to confront.

CHAPTER 13

New Jersey in the Federal System

It seems proper, in treating of the vast population
occupying the cities of New York, Brooklyn, Jersey City,
Newark, and Hoboken to consider them as . . . one great
metropolitan community. . . . The villages and towns
strung along the railways for 50 miles from New York . . .
are very largely made up of persons doing business in the
city or occupied in manufactures which find there their
market.

—U.S. Census Report, 1880

New York and New Jersey will grow together or we will
perish together. The sooner both states realize that, the
better off the whole region will be.

—Governor Thomas Kean, 1988

What's more important to New York is that these jobs
remain in our regional economy. We're long past days
where New Jersey is the enemy. It's more important that
these jobs don't move to Maryland, Tampa or India.

—President, Partnership for New York City, 2006

FOR MOST OF ITS HISTORY, the interests of New Jersey's cit-
izens did not extend beyond their own borders. During the American
Revolution they saw Britain as their protector from New York. In the Civil
War era there was sympathy for the Confederacy's position on states' rights.
When the rest of the country was engaged in trust-busting, New Jersey was
called "the traitor state" for inviting corporations in on favorable terms.

Many states have sent citizens to Washington who became prominent in
American history, but few New Jerseyans are among those citizens. Garrett
Hobart of Paterson, elected vice president in 1896, might have become an
accidental president had he outlived William McKinley, but he did not.
Grover Cleveland was born and died in New Jersey but spent most of the

time in between in New York. The state's most distinguished contribution
to the nation, Woodrow Wilson, lived there less than twenty years—all of
it in Princeton which was regarded, and was pleased to regard itself, as a
place apart from the rest of New Jersey. The New Jersey congressional delegation labored in obscurity, breaking into national consciousness only
when its members were accused of corruption.[1] Strong local party machines
kept most talented politicians at home, where the real action was.[2]

Always relatively wealthy, New Jersey received little federal largesse.
Relations with other states were limited mostly to neighboring New York
and Pennsylvania and were often hostile. New Jersey financed its state
government by taxing railroad travelers between New York City and
Philadelphia. When Charles Dickens made the trip in 1842, he had this to
say about New Jersey: "The journey from New York to Philadelphia is
made by railroad, and two ferries; and usually occupies between five and six
hours."[3]

Although it still receives less federal aid than almost any other state,
today New Jersey aggressively seeks help from Washington. It takes a more
assertive posture toward New York and Pennsylvania, fares better in competition with them, and joins other states to collaborate on solving shared
problems. In the past, New Jersey reluctantly adopted innovations
pioneered in other states; now it is often the pioneer. No longer insular, it
seeks national and international markets for its goods and services. This
chapter discusses these developments.

New Jersey in the Federal System

American federalism has passed through a number of phases. The idea
of dual federalism, with different functions for national and state governments, held sway for over a century. "Layer cake" was the favored metaphor-
ical description of this system. The actual separation between the layers
was, however, less complete than the theory implied. From about 1913 to
1964, cooperative federalism, a "marble cake" of grants in aid and bargaining between levels of government, was the dominant relationship. Lyndon
Johnson's Great Society policies (1963–1968) made Washington, DC, the
dominant actor in the federal system from the mid-1960s to 1980. The
states were perceived as instruments of national purposes and direct federal
aid to local governments increased, often bypassing state capitals. Richard
Nixon, not unlike Bill Clinton, encouraged a new federalism with fewer
strings and a larger role for state governments, but provided even more

federal money. In contrast, Ronald Reagan and both Presidents Bush championed federal extrication from many programs.

All of these phases were evident in New Jersey. Dual federalism was warmly embraced. When Andrew Jackson's administration deposited excess federal funds in state banks for discretionary use, Mahlon Dickerson, U.S. senator from New Jersey, approvingly noted that the "states may be safely trusted to make the best use . . . as their interests or exigencies may require."[4] In the era of cooperative federalism, New Jersey welcomed New Deal programs that saved many communities and political machines' patronage jobs. Richard Hughes, governor during the Kennedy-Johnson administrations, was a confidante of both presidents and a strong supporter of Great Society initiatives; President Johnson chose to hold the 1964 Democratic National Convention in Atlantic City.

Thomas Kean, whose governorship spanned the Reagan years, applauded the discretion given to state governments but endorsed a "kinder, gentler" version of supply-side economics. Kean differed from many other Republicans in favoring a larger role for government in expanding economic opportunity. A study of fourteen states' responses to the sharp cuts during President's Reagan's first term put New Jersey in the group with the "most pronounced" actions to replace lost federal assistance, both fiscally and institutionally. New Jersey was among thirty-one states imposing tax hikes in 1983, increasing both its income and sales taxes.[5] New revenue flooded in as the economy recovered and budget surpluses brought expansion of social programs.

An economic slowdown hit New Jersey as Kean's second term was ending. His successor, Democrat Jim Florio, responded even more definitively than Kean had to the 1982 recession. In 1990, Florio proposed the largest tax increases in the state's history, including an increase in the sales tax and a sharply progressive income tax. Accompanying cuts in state spending were, like many of the proposed tax hikes, targeted at middle and upper-income residents. His predecessor's concern for those most affected by Washington's budget cuts was one of the few Kean policies Florio did not condemn but rather continued and expanded.

The years since have seen a slowdown in the enactment of new social programs, but no diminution of them either. Governor Whitman's rollback of much of the Florio tax increase was accompanied by massive borrowing to maintain state services, and Governor McGreevey did the same. Governor Corzine raised the sales tax.

Defense expenditures and redirection of social programs' aid to the very neediest are two important forces that shape federal spending in the states. Never a major recipient of defense contracts, and with the second highest per capita income in the nation by the start of the 1990s, New Jersey does not begin in a favorable position. Indeed, for the past twenty-five years, it has always ranked forty-ninth or fiftieth among the states in terms of return on federal taxes, getting back seventy-three cents on the dollar in 1981, sixty-two cents in 1988, and fifty-five cents in 2004. Over the same period, the state's share of the federal tax burden rose from 3.9 percent to 4.5 percent, even though its proportion of the national population declined from 3.2 percent to 2.9 percent.[6]

Although New Jersey's relative paucity of defense contracts contributes to this situation, military spending adds more to New Jersey's economy than many realize. In 2004, the state ranked seventeenth in the value of military salaries and procurement. The Lakehurst Naval Air Engineering Center and the Picatinny Arsenal do important military research and development work, and McGuire Air Force Base is the largest military air transport facility on the East Coast. However, the $5.3 billion in defense contracts and wages the state received that year amounted to less than 2 percent of all such Pentagon spending and lagged far behind California's $38 billion or Texas' $28 billion.[7]

One reason New Jersey may have fared better at receiving Pentagon funds than is commonly thought is its representatives' continued presence on the House Armed Services Committee. A 1989 bipartisan congressional base-closing commission (BRAC) recommended big cutbacks at Fort Dix, then the state's largest military installation. Two years later, recently retired Republican Representative Jim Courter, a former member of Armed Services whose district included the Picatinny Arsenal, served as chair of a second BRAC commission and deflected the recommendation of the secretary of defense to close Fort Dix entirely.

In 2005, President Bush approved the recommendations of another such base closing and realignment commission. They included closing Fort Monmouth, where over five thousand civilian and military workers pursue research on communications and electronics, by 2010. At the same time, however, the BRAC plan gave substantial new resources to other New Jersey military facilities. Most significant was the merging of McGuire Air Force Base, Fort Dix, and the Lakehurst Naval Air Station into a "superbase" that is the first tri-service installation in the continental United States; the designation will bring millions of military dollars and thousands of new employees. Several hundred new jobs proposed for the Picatinny Arsenal also confirmed its status as a center for munitions research.[8]

South Jersey Representatives Rob Andrews, Jim Sexton, and Frank LoBiondo all sat on the House Armed Services Committee during the 2005 BRAC process. Like all federal legislators, New Jersey's delegation seeks committee assignments whose jurisdiction is of special interest to the state and of benefit to their own districts. Their influence waxes and wanes with the prevailing political winds.

The 1970s and 1980s, when Democrats controlled the House of Representatives, was a period of special strength for the delegation. Jim Howard, chairman of the House Public Works and Transportation Committee from 1975 to 1987, was known as the "Colossus of Roads" and was a legendary Santa Claus. Twice in the Reagan years, Howard guided major highway and mass transit bills through the Congress. Typically, they included projects in Howard's Monmouth County district, and also that of Paterson-area Representative Robert Roe, another senior member of Public Works. Jim Florio led in federal funds for environmental programs. He was a prime mover in creating the federal Superfund in 1980, which provides money to clean up toxic waste sites, and New Jersey led the nation in initial site designations. As chair of the Judiciary Committee, Peter Rodino presided over the Nixon impeachment investigation. Other members of the delegation were also well placed. Bernard Dwyer and Dean Gallo sat on the Appropriations Committee, and Frank Guarini was on the tax-writing Ways and Means Committee. Robert Torricelli did not hurt his district's interests when he gained President Bush's gratitude for being one of the few prominent House Democrats to vote in favor of the 1991 Gulf War.

In the space of eleven days in 1987, Jim Howard died suddenly and Judiciary Committee Chairman Peter Rodino announced his retirement; in 1990 Florio departed for the governorship. The delegation seemed transformed "from a political powerhouse to a political basket case."[9] It suffered more blows in 1992. A combination of unfavorable redistricting decisions, the miasma surrounding the House of Representatives, and the Republicans' resurgence in New Jersey politics, led Representatives Dwyer, Roe, and Guarini to announce their retirements. Other Democratic incumbents faced serious general election challenges. Beginning in 1993, the members of New Jersey's House delegation, for the first time in many years, neither held nor were at the front of the line for significant committee chairmanships. The

1994 Republican takeover of the House majority did not improve matters, since most of the state's GOP members had neither seniority nor enthusiasm for issues that ignited their more conservative Republican partisans.

To some extent, New Jersey's senators, particularly Frank Lautenberg, stepped into the breach. In 1986, Lautenberg had acquired two critical chairmanships—of a new Environmental and Public Works subcommittee overseeing Superfund operations and other environmental programs, and an Appropriations subcommittee on Transportation and Related Agencies, with jurisdiction over funding for Amtrak, airports, roads, and buses. Lautenberg began producing Howard-like projects and had an especially banner year for the state in 1988, when his electoral vulnerability made the Senate Democratic caucus particularly willing to help him.

Starting in the mid-1990s, New Jersey's senators—all Democrats—began a game of musical chairs that diminished the influence gained from seniority. Bill Bradley, who had engineered changes in the tax code favorable to New Jersey from his seat on the powerful Finance Committee, chose not to seek a fourth term in 1996 and began plotting his unsuccessful run for the presidency in 2000. Frustrated by his party's minority status, Lautenberg retired in 2000, but his departure was only temporary. Robert Torricelli, Bradley's successor, was forced to withdraw from his 2002 reelection bid after allegedly accepting gifts from a wealthy donor in exchange for official favors. In a controversial move, the Democratic State Committee replaced Torricelli with Lautenberg just thirty-five days before the election. Republicans said the date for changing candidates had passed and sued, but the state supreme court unanimously ruled in the Democrats' favor.[10] Lautenberg won and returned to Washington—but without regaining his seat on Appropriations or his seniority on his other committees. Jon Corzine, who had replaced Lautenberg in 2000, served only five years before leaving to become governor.

The Democratic takeover of both the House and Senate in 2006 gave the delegation more clout, but certainly less than in the halcyon days of two and three decades earlier. Lautenberg was reappointed to the Appropriations Committee, and immediately announced, "I plan to pick up where I left off, securing federal dollars for important projects like roads, rail, hospitals and first responders throughout New Jersey."[11] Although losing the fifteen years of seniority on the panel that he had accumulated between 1985 and 2000, he will be the only senator from the tristate area on that powerful committee in the 2007–2009 congressional session, and the first from New Jersey since he left it in 2000. On the House side, Democrats will serve on the first-tier Appropriations, Energy and Commerce, and Ways and Means committees, and chair five subcommittees.

INTERSTATE COMPACTS

Just as New Jersey has stepped up its relations with the federal government in recent years, so too has it entered into more formal compacts with other states. Most are with its immediate neighbors—Delaware, Pennsylvania, and especially its historical nemesis, New York.

The most crucial of the compacts is the Port Authority of New York and New Jersey.[12] Its creation in the 1920s has been called "the most important single event in the rise of the modern compact" and the "most visible manifestation of both the gulf that separates the two states and the complex weave of economic and physical ties that bind them together.[13]

This behemoth began inauspiciously. In 1916, New Jersey interests began lobbying the U.S. Interstate Commerce Commission for lower railroad rates in the port district, and in 1920 an interstate study commission recommended establishment of a port authority. The authority district extended for a twenty-five-mile radius around the Statue of Liberty. Its purposes were to end counterproductive railroad competition and coordinate rail terminals, promote the economic well-being of the port cities, and create a comprehensive transportation plan for the region. Governor Walter Edge, who joined New York Governor Alfred E. Smith in endorsing the compact, called it "a large step toward interstate amity."[14]

The first authority enterprises were not moneymaking ventures. Three bridges linking Hudson and Middlesex counties with the New York City borough of Richmond (Staten Island), for which the authority received approval in 1925, were financial failures. Meanwhile, the Holland Tunnel between Hudson County and Manhattan—a potentially more successful venture—opened in 1927 operated by dual commissions from New York and New Jersey that did not involve the Port Authority. The authority's position improved dramatically after 1930, when it proposed issuing revenue bonds for new projects—whose toll receipts would repay the bonds and produce no burden on the states' credit. Both states accepted this idea and transferred the Holland Tunnel to the authority. The George Washington Bridge between Bergen County and northern Manhattan opened under budget and ahead of schedule in 1931. The new bridge and the Holland Tunnel generated funding for the Lincoln Tunnel, a third Hudson River crossing completed in 1937.

The Port Authority of New York, as it was named until 1972, was now launched for continuing success. Under the leadership of executive director Austin Tobin (1942–1972), it took over both states' major airports—Newark, LaGuardia, and Idlewild (later John F. Kennedy)—just as air travel began spectacular growth. The New Jersey marine freight terminals at Port Newark and Port Elizabeth were also profitable investments.

During the three decades of Tobin's rule, authority commissioners were prominent business executives, often from the banking industry. Tobin believed that businessmen would be "apolitical"; that diverse opinions would be disruptive and deflect the organization from its goals; and that elected officials, including the governors, should stay out of the authority's decision making. Governors followed Tobin's lead, appointing fellow partisans who met his criteria. By 1965, commissioners' average length of service was eleven years. The real action took place in closed committee meetings; formal ratification, usually unanimous, came about in brief "open" commission meetings.

Although at least three commissioners from each state had to approve any action and either governor could stop an action by vetoing the commission's minutes, in practice Tobin made all important decisions. Consolidated bond offerings and pooled accounting practices made it impossible to track the performance of individual facilities or projects. By the end of Tobin's tenure, these included four airports, eight marine terminals, four bridges, two tunnels, two truck terminals, two bus terminals, two heliports, the PATH rapid transit system between Manhattan and New Jersey, and nine trade development offices, including outposts in London, Tokyo, and Zurich.

Covenants in the authority's bonds, ostensibly to protect investors, permitted the commissioners to sidestep gubernatorial requests, particularly from New Jersey, that "excess money" be devoted to mass transit. PATH— a subway line between Manhattan and New Jersey—which the authority grudgingly took over in 1962 to get New Jersey's approval to build the World Trade Center in lower Manhattan, was the sole exception. The price for PATH, however, was a promise that no other mass transit projects would be proposed or approved.

By the early 1970s, New Jersey officials were increasingly frustrated by Tobin's arrogance, the Port Authority's perceived lack of cooperation with the state, and its deleterious effects on coordinated transportation planning. Resentment grew over the favoritism New Jersey believed was shown New York, starting with the authority's name. Consequently, the next several governors became much more aggressive toward the authority.

Republican William Cahill (1970–1974), who came to the governorship from the U.S. House, enlisted the Nixon White House to help kill an authority plan for a major jetport in Morris County's Great Swamp—an ecological treasure located amidst some of New Jersey's wealthiest suburbs. He was the first governor to study authority minutes carefully and regularly threaten use of his veto power. Cahill also forced the agency to change its legal name to the Port Authority of New York *and New Jersey*, and he appointed more "political" commissioners—including a former state party chair, a former state senator, a Hudson County politician, and the vice chairman of the New Jersey Turnpike Authority. Unfortunately, this message was somewhat vitiated when two of them had to resign after being indicted. However, Tobin's irritation at commissioners' "meddling" finally led to his resignation in 1972.

For the next few years, the authority was in flux as Cahill resisted appointment of an executive director close to New York Governor Nelson Rockefeller. A deal struck in 1977 between New York Governor Hugh Carey and New Jersey Governor Brendan Byrne broke the stalemate. That agreement, followed ever since, awards the commission chairmanship to New Jersey and the executive directorship to New York. Governor Byrne was the first to add some transportation expertise to the commission—nominating his own state transportation commissioner, who eventually became authority chairman.

Later governors have continued to choose chairmen from the political and policy worlds, and sometimes both. Governor Florio named Richard Leone (1988–1994), who had served as state treasurer in the Byrne administration, lost to Bill Bradley in the 1978 Democratic Senate primary, and held a Ph.D. in public affairs from Princeton University. Governor Whitman chose Lewis Eisenberg (1995–2001), an investment banker known primarily as a premier Republican fund-raiser, but also a member of the transition teams for Whitman, New York's Governor Pataki, and the first Bush-Cheney administration. Eisenberg left the authority when New York Governor Pataki selected him as the only New Jerseyan to serve on the board of the Lower Manhattan Development Corporation (charged with rebuilding that area after the September 11 attacks).

Informed observers believed that the pendulum had begun to swing too far toward political appointments to head the commission.[15] Acting Governor Donald DiFrancesco filled out Eisenberg's term with a former Republican state senator, Jack Sinagra (2001–2003). Governor McGreevey nominated Charles Kushner who, along with his relatives and business associates, had donated more than a million dollars to McGreevey's various campaigns. When Kushner was forced to withdraw because of questions about the legality of some of his contributions, McGreevey's next appointment garnered accolades that were as strong as the criticism of Kushner had been. Anthony Coscia, head of the authority commission since 2003, had led the New Jersey Economic Development Authority for ten years under two Democratic and two Republican governors. He was praised by the chair of the state GOP as "one of those rare people who can rise to the occasion and do a tremendous job for the chief executive no matter who the chief executive happens to be . . . a star appointment."[16] The *New York Times* editorialized that Coscia "drew praise from good-government groups and even from Mr. McGreevey's critics. The reason may be that he is known for intelligence and integrity, not political donations."[17]

In its ninth decade, the Port Authority has indeed become a titan, but more reliant on support from more forceful governors. The influence of New Jersey, once the clear junior partner, has grown along with the state's role in the regional economy. Newark Airport has passed LaGuardia in traffic volume; Port Newark and Port Elizabeth strongly dominate the authority's marine terminal business. Although founded in large measure as a late-Progressive era instrument of rational planning intended to end bickering and competition between New York and New Jersey, the authority remains a major venue for interstate hostility. In the boom years of the 1980s, it invested in new projects, such as an Essex County trash incinerator, industrial parks in Elizabeth, and a legal-office center in Newark (dubbed "Tort Port"). Critics asserted that it was moving away from its core transportation mission. New York interests claimed that it favored New Jersey, and New York City Mayor Rudolph Giuliani even asserted that it should be dissolved.[18] These echoes of early twentieth-century disputes came to another head in 1999, when the authority was paralyzed for seventeen months because of a bitter feud between Governor Whitman and Governor Pataki.

The immediate issue was Whitman's refusal to allow any project to move forward until Pataki agreed to subsidize a new cargo terminal at Port Elizabeth for Maersk-Sealand, the world's largest ocean cargo carrier. The company, which handled more than 20 percent of the port's cargo, had threatened to move to Baltimore in the absence of the new facility. The New York governor did not oppose the $200 million project but, pointing to about $250 million in annual operating deficits at PATH and the Port Authority bus terminal (perceived by New York as "New Jersey projects"), demanded a quid pro quo for his state. New Jersey countered that an agency study showed that between 1928 and 1998, 43 percent of all expenditures had benefited New York, 27 percent had benefited New Jersey, with the remainder of equal advantage to both states.[19]

The controversy finally ended in June 2002, with Whitman agreeing to $250 million for New York projects in exchange for the cargo terminal subsidy.[20] In recalling these events a few years later, Whitman's communications director, Peter McDonough, observed, "Over the years, we have had some difficulties with Gov. Pataki over issues involving the Port Authority. The Port Authority was never a very high priority for the New Yorkers. In New Jersey, we live and die by the Port Authority." Princeton political scientist Jameson Doig, author of the definitive study of the authority, agreed, saying, "I think it's fair to say that the governors, through most of the previous decades, seemed to be much more interested in the economic development of the region than Gov. Pataki is."[21]

An authority commission chair with professional credentials and an inclusive style, the patriotic amity produced by the September 11 disaster, and the need to focus on security and rebuilding of the World Trade Center has lowered the temperature between New York and New Jersey for now, but an eerily similar scenario was recently played out at the other end of the state by Governor Corzine and Governor Ed Rendell of Pennsylvania. As 2006 ended, the Delaware River Port Authority (DRPA), a bistate authority that runs four toll bridges and the PATCO commuter rail line as well as overseeing the port, had been immobilized for over a year. It was unable to pass a budget or move forward on any projects because of Corzine's refusal to approve a plan to deepen the river's 103-mile shipping channel from forty to forty-five feet, and Rendell's instruction to the Pennsylvania commissioners not to attend DRPA meetings until New Jersey agreed.

New Jersey argued that the dredging plan would never be cost-effective for a port that was one hundred miles upstream and could have serious environmental consequences since the river was an important source of drinking water. Pennsylvania countered that the real reason was that "traditionally New York and the port of North Jersey have never wanted South Jersey to be in competition with them."[22] Members of both states' congressional delegations joined the fray. Pennsylvania's U.S. Senator Rick Santorum, then the third-ranking member of the Republican Senate leadership, asserted, "I will do everything in my power to stop anything beneficial to New Jersey, period. . . . I will do everything I can to make sure that it gets slowed down or stopped." The three South Jersey U.S. House representatives made a similar threat to block federally funded Pennsylvania projects.[23] Finally, in May 2007, after seventeen months, New Jersey and Pennsylvania reached an agreement to end the standoff. Under its terms, financial control of the project was transferred to the Philadelphia Regional Port Authority, removing both New Jersey and the DRPA from that part of the equation. The effect was to place the entire burden of funding the project on Pennsylvania yet still require that dredging permits be obtained from the New Jersey Department of Environmental Protection, along with an environmental impact study by the Army Corps of Engineers.

New Jersey and its Neighbors

In addition to New York and Pennsylvania, New Jersey shares a border with Delaware, and at the same time that Trenton was voicing its concerns about Pennsylvania's threats to the purity of the Delaware River, the state of Delaware was protesting New Jersey's negotiations with British Petroleum to build a liquefied natural gas pier on the same waterway. Its Natural Resources and Environmental Commission blocked the plan, arguing that a 1935 U.S. Supreme Court decision placed Delaware's boundary at the low-water mark on the New Jersey side.

Claiming that an earlier state compact gave it riparian rights, New Jersey took its case to the U.S Supreme Court, which assigned it to a special master in 2006. This development did not prevent a Delaware legislative committee from voting to direct the state's National Guard to halt any construction. New Jersey's senate president retorted that in any skirmish, the guns on the retired battleship *New Jersey*, now a Camden waterfront tourist attraction, could reach Delaware. A New Jersey assemblyman added, "Peace, not war; that's my motto today. But you've got to be wary of Delaware at all times."[24] Such jovial exchanges, however, seldom mark New Jersey's disputes with New York and Pennsylvania—particularly the former.

Along with Washington Irving, who left New York's "disease and dust" to "breathe the fresh air of heaven and enjoy the clean face of nature" in Newark in 1807, New Jerseyans long viewed their largest city, along with the rest of the northern part of the state, as a dependent of New York City.[25] During the nineteenth century, as Newark became less bucolic and

more industrial, many of its goods were stamped "Made in New York."
A city newspaper editorialized, "We are only a workshop, a community of
manufactures rather than merchants."[26] Newark's Branch Brook Park,
designed by Frederick Law Olmsted, never achieved the fame of Olmsted's
Central Park in Manhattan, and the University of Newark (later absorbed
into Rutgers—The State University) was once a branch of New York
University.

New Jersey's resentment of its second-class status is seen most clearly in
its economic rivalry with New York. New Jersey had thrust upon it or
sometimes sought the least desirable moneymaking ventures. These included
shadowy enterprises like illegal gambling (an early harbinger of Atlantic
City's casinos) and legal ones like huge garbage landfills in the Meadowlands, loaded with trash from New York and Pennsylvania.

In the days when those wetlands, now regarded as a state treasure, were
simply deemed a swamp, they were the butt of humorists' allusions to New
Jersey as the landfill capital of the world. The state is now a garbage
exporter rather than importer, and out-of-state trash no longer receives a
warm welcome. During the 1980s, New Jersey also forced the closing of a
New York City ocean dumping site off Sandy Hook. The state's congressional delegation led the way in achieving a national ban on ocean dumping in 1992 and fought to end oil drilling off the entire Atlantic coast.[27]

Generation of state revenues was long predicated on taxing those who
did not live and work in the state. Well into the twentieth century, the state
budget was largely financed by levies on railroads and their interstate passengers. In 1961, fifteen years before imposing a general income tax, Trenton
began taxing only those New Jerseyans who worked in New York. The
justification was that commuters forced the state to provide otherwise
unneeded transportation facilities, and the revenue was earmarked for
transportation projects. After New Jersey passed a general income tax in
1976, it continued to tax commuters at a higher rate. By 1983, when the
state supreme court declared the commuter tax unconstitutional in a case
brought by New York, New Jersey's own tax experts estimated that over a
twenty-year period, the state collected $380 million from the commuter
tax but spent only $183 million on commuter services.[28]

Each time New Jersey alters its tax system, debate ensues about how
the changes will affect its economic competitiveness with New York and
Pennsylvania. Governor Kean called this consideration "determinative" for
his fiscal policy, asserting, "I'm a very strong supply-sider when it comes to

state government. People move because of incentives. If you can keep taxes on individuals and firms lower than your neighbors, you don't have to do anything else."[29]

When Governor Florio raised taxes in 1990, there was much unfavorable comparison of New Jersey's new rates with those in Pennsylvania, and their possible effects on the state's economy. The New Jersey Business and Industry Association's 1991 annual poll found that 71 percent of the 3,100 responding companies thought business conditions were worse in New Jersey than the rest of the nation, up from only 27 percent the previous year.

The views of the business community improved somewhat during the tax-cutting Whitman administration but became gloomy again under Democratic governors and legislatures. The nonpartisan but decidedly antitax Tax Foundation's 2007 State Business Tax Climate Index ranked New Jersey third from the bottom among the fifty states. NJBIA described the findings of its 2006 annual poll as "the most downbeat assessment since surveys conducted in the 1989–1992 recession."[30]

Sports and entertainment facilities are another source of rivalry. In the past, New Jersey sports fans rooted for professional teams in New York City and Philadelphia and had to travel there to see them, just as they did to attend most cultural events. During the late 1980s, Governor Kean greatly increased public support of the arts, and New Jersey orchestras, theaters, and ballet companies burgeoned. For the mass public, however, the Meadowlands sports and entertainment complex developed in the late 1970s was pivotal. It provided a site for rock concerts and popular entertainment such as the Ice Capades and Barnum and Bailey circus, which used to give area performances only in New York City. Its racetrack cut into revenues of older New York tracks. Most significantly, the complex attracted both of New York City's professional football franchises (the Jets and the Giants) as well as the Nets basketball team. New York tried aggressively to prevent Meadowlands development, including environmental suits and pressure on New York City banks not to buy Meadowlands development bonds.

By the turn of the twenty-first century, the Meadowlands complex was showing its age. The "New York" football teams threatened to move out of state to new stadiums with more high-profit skyboxes and other amenities. The Nets agreed to move to Brooklyn, and a new arena in Newark lured the Devils, a professional hockey franchise that was established at the Meadowlands.

New Jersey's response was to expand the Meadowlands complex with a massive theme park–cum–shopping mall. It was called Xanadu, after the "stately pleasure dome" decreed by Kublai Khan in Samuel Taylor Coleridge's famous poem. Its original plans included a NASCAR track, an indoor ski slope, a minor league baseball team, and the world's largest Ferris wheels and movie theaters. A new commuter rail station promised an end to the giant parking lot that the New Jersey Turnpike Meadowlands exit resembled at the time of major events. Complex and lengthy discussions finally led to an agreement between the state and the football teams on a new facility.

For a time, the progress of Xanadu brought to mind a different line from the Coleridge epic—"all should cry, Beware! Beware!" Its developer experienced severe financial difficulties that threatened to spell an end to the project; the owner of the proposed new minor league team sued the state for reneging on promised subsidies; and the football teams engaged in protracted negotiations about a traffic and parking situation that would, if possible, get worse during the simultaneous construction of Xanadu and their new stadium.

By late 2006, however, development was back on track, as a major investment firm took over the project and secured $1.5 billion in funding to finish it. After fourteen months of heated debate, the football teams and Xanadu came to what the head of the state Sports and Exposition Authority called "a mutual nonaggression pact" about construction issues. Visitors were promised a two-thousand seat live concert hall; a martini bar/ bowling center hybrid, and a simulated skydiving experience. NASCAR expressed renewed interest in constructing an auto-racing track if the community opposition that killed its original proposal could be assuaged. The complex and its rail link are now scheduled to open in 2009, with the new stadium to open in 2010.[31]

New Jersey's relations with surrounding states are not uniformly hostile. The Port Authority, New Jersey Transit, and New York's Metropolitan Transit Authority work together to develop joint "problem statements" for long-range improvements in the regional transportation system, such as a recently approved new Hudson River tunnel. The tristate Regional Plan Association (RPA), founded in 1929 and financed by Connecticut, New Jersey, and New York businesses, is an important example of regional cooperation. At its founding, the RPA recommended an ambitious plan for building bridges, highways, and tunnels over the next thirty years—a plan largely realized by Austin Tobin at the Port Authority and Robert Moses at New York's Triborough Bridge and Tunnel Authority. In the 1960s, a second major plan called for action on commuter railroads and the development of regional business centers like Stamford, Connecticut, New Brunswick, New Jersey, and White Plains, New York. That regional development did occur, and New Jersey and New York both took over bankrupt commuter lines. The third and current RPA plan calls for keeping the region "competitive in the global economy and livable." While earlier plans emphasized capital infrastructure, the current plan addresses social infrastructure—preserving open space and fighting high housing costs, congestion, pollution and homelessness.[32]

Although the federal government and its largest neighbors get most of its external attention, the state frequently joins in actions with others, particularly over common environmental concerns. In April 2007, the U.S. Supreme Court ruled in their favor on a case brought by New Jersey and ten other states, primarily bicoastal in location, seeking to compel the federal Environmental Protection Agency to regulate greenhouse gases from automobiles. Additionally, because the EPA rule also asserted that only the federal government had the standing to regulate such emissions, the case had broader implications for the ability of states to set their own limits on permissible levels of greenhouse gases.[33]

New Jersey, the Nation, and the World

A more confident New Jersey has expanded its influence beyond its immediate borders, and beyond the nation. A 1969 study of the diffusion of policy innovations among the American states ranked New Jersey fourth behind New York, Massachusetts, and California. The study suggested, however, that this high ranking might be due merely to proximity to New York.[34] Later research casts doubt on this. One analysis accords New Jersey the same overall ranking but shows the effects of the state's culture. Although New Jersey ranked second in its speed of adopting civil rights innovations, it was only tenth in the area of welfare policies, and twenty-second in educational policies. Another study breaks out time periods and controls for missing data, small numbers of adoptions, and universal adoption due to federal mandates. It finds that New Jersey adopted more innovations from New York before World War I, but that afterward, New York was more likely to adopt New Jersey innovations, as were its other neighbors, Delaware and Pennsylvania.[35]

Like other states, New Jersey sees an increasingly important connection between the health of its economy and the international economy. Among the states, it is in the top quarter or higher on numerous indices of participation in the global market. It ranks sixth in terms of foreign investment, seventh in the number of private industry employees working for foreign firms, and is the twelfth largest exporter.[36] In 2005, New Jersey firms exported to 216 foreign destinations, with $4.8 billion, or 23 percent, of the shipments destined for Canada. Canada was followed as a destination by the United Kingdom ($1.8 billion) and Germany ($1.3 billion). Other large markets were Japan, Mexico, Israel, France, Italy, South Korea, China, and the Netherlands. Chemical manufactures accounted for both the largest dollar total ($5.9 million) and the largest proportional export category (28 percent). Together, computers and other electronic products, transportation equipment, and primary metal manufactures accounted for a similar dollar and percentage amount.

More than 1,400 foreign subsidiaries doing business in the state take advantage of reduced or eliminated customs duties and federal excise taxes available in five foreign trade zones (FTZs), of which Port Newark/Port Elizabeth and the Mount Olive International Trade Center are the largest. Activity at the 2,900-acre Port FTZ, which also includes outposts in Jersey City and Bayonne and seven subzones at corporate locations, is consistently the highest in the nation. In FY 2004, it received almost $4 billion in foreign goods and shipped $17 billion in merchandise.[37] Aside from Rockefeller Center itself, the 667-acre Mount Olive FTZ is the largest real estate enterprise of the Rockefeller Center Development Corporation, which is a part owner of the Mount Olive International Trade Center.

Businesses from forty different countries—the most of any state—have facilities in New Jersey. Their numbers are dominated by Japan, Germany, the United Kingdom, and France, which together account for almost two-thirds of all foreign subsidiaries. Although the number of Japanese manufacturing plants in New Jersey pales in comparison to those in California, New Jersey has attracted about one-third more than either New York or Pennsylvania. Sony, Panasonic, and Sharp are among the Japanese firms with corporate headquarters in the state. Honda, Nissan, Mitsubishi, Sanyo, Toshiba, and Toyota also have a New Jersey presence. They join Britain's Rolls Royce, Jaguar, and Viking Penguin; Germany's American Hoechst and BMW; France's L'Oréal, Michelin, Peugeot, and Renault; and Italy's Olivetti.

Aggressive courtship contributes to this success. The state government and the state chamber of commerce maintain overseas offices in Brazil, Mexico, China, Japan, and Israel. Together they sponsor trade missions to larger trading partners, subsidizing the participation of smaller New Jersey companies. In 2006, Governor Corzine was one of twenty state governors who had visited China within the past year. Referring to another visitor, California's governor, Corzine said of his trip, "If we don't do this, and [Arnold] Schwarzenegger does, they win and we lose."[38] Foreign companies also profit from low interest loans from the New Jersey Economic Development Authority.

Fundamentally, however, New Jersey does well in international trade because of its geographic, economic, and demographic characteristics. It offers deepwater ports, good transportation networks, and overnight motor access to 40 percent of the nation's population. It is a leader in R and D spending, average number of patents granted, and number of high technology firms. A historically polyglot population makes newcomers feel at home. Finally, there is the ever-present proximity of New York City. In a new version of an old story, many foreign firms maintain corporate headquarters in Manhattan and locate manufacturing and distribution centers in northern New Jersey. The six northern counties of Bergen, Essex, Hudson, Middlesex, Passaic, and Union are home to 70 percent of all New Jersey–based companies engaged in foreign export.

New Jersey has also had sporadic ventures into what might be called foreign policy. Governor Kean made international news in 1983 when he and New York Governor Mario Cuomo refused to let Soviet Foreign Minister Andrei Gromyko, headed for the United Nations, land at the Port Authority's Kennedy Airport shortly after the Russians shot down a Korean Airlines plane. Although popular with the public, a State Department official called the action "preposterous," and the *New York Times* editorialized about "a hallucinatory disorder that causes local politicians to imagine themselves President or Secretary of State."[39]

In 1985, Kean was urged to withdraw two billion dollars in state pension funds invested in businesses with interests in South Africa. Both moral considerations and the South African government's then recalcitrant stance on apartheid led Kean to order total divestment.[40] Similar factors surrounding the genocide in Darfur led the state legislature in 2005 to make New Jersey the first state to order total divestment of a similar sum in from businesses operating in Sudan. It was completed ahead of schedule in

2006.[41] At roughly the same time, the state's congressional delegation led a bipartisan attack on the Bush administration's plan to allow Dubai Ports World, owned by the government of the United Arab Emirates, to manage parts of some U.S. ports, including Port Elizabeth. Both Governor Corzine and the Port Authority also filed motions in state and federal courts to block the deal. A national furor over the issue soon led the GOP-dominated U.S. Congress to quash the plan.[42]

New Jersey's new role in the federal system and in the world reflects its new economic strength and confidence. In 1964, two analysts wrote, "New Jersey is strategically located to become a major seat of economic and social power for the nation. The extent to which this happens may depend upon whether or not it can also become a major seat of political power."[43] Stronger state government has contributed significantly to New Jersey's increasing presence in the nation and in the global marketplace.

CHAPTER 14

The Politics of Taxing and Spending

The passage of a law equalizing taxation seems to be imperatively demanded by the people, and I respectfully but earnestly commend it to your early consideration and prompt and efficient action.

—Governor Daniel Haines's message to the
legislature, 1851

Our whole system of taxation, which is no system at all, needs overhauling from top to bottom.

—Governor Woodrow Wilson's inaugural
address, 1911

We're going to talk about taxes today, which Yogi Berra would say is déjà vu all over again.

—Former Governor Brendan Byrne at a conference on
state tax policy, 1987

IN 1900, NEW JERSEY state government collected and spent less than $3 million. The general public paid none of the state taxes of the time—on bank stock, insurance companies, railroads, corporate franchises, or large inheritances. Nor did the public benefit directly from Trenton's paltry services. More than half the state budget supported "charities"—aid to the blind, deaf, and mentally troubled—and "corrections"— judges and the state prison. Local governments spent four times as much, raising virtually all of it from property taxes. By 2008, however, state government collected and spent more than $33 billion. Broad-based taxes, levied at rates among the highest in the nation, produced the majority of revenues. Direct state aid to local governments accounted for the majority of spending. The "big three" state taxes—on income, sales, and corporations— together produced as much revenue as all local property taxes. Invisible and insignificant state taxing and spending at the century's beginning had become highly visible and significant at its end. What state government spends its money on, and from whom it raises it, are now important questions to everyone in New Jersey.

THE BUDGET AND BUDGET POLITICS

Before the 1947 state constitution banned them, a morass of dedicated funds made it "impossible for the state to mass its fiscal resources and direct them to the points at which they are most needed."[1] As a group of Princeton scholars further observed, "[N]o living person knows what expenditures have been authorized. . . . Only by the merest accident can the needful expenditures of a department coincide with its receipts from particular fees or taxes."[2]

Formal budget procedures today are deceptively simple. The state's fiscal year begins on July 1. By that time, the legislature must pass a balanced budget. The state constitution requires a single general appropriations bill. It also proscribes the creation of state debt exceeding 1 percent of the fiscal year's appropriations without approval in a public referendum.

The Role of the Governor in Budget Making

Generally, the legislature plays a greater role in determining how revenues will be raised than in how they will be spent. Legislators usually can do little but tinker with the governor's expenditure recommendations. A line item veto allows the governor to remove appropriations he does not favor. The governor can also prohibit or limit expenditure of any appropriation "when he determines that it is not in the best interests of the state or if revenue collections fall below the certified amount."[3] It is the governor who must "certify" the revenue predictions. Presidents must envy a New Jersey governor's ability to impound, sequester, and rescind.

To an ever greater extent, the governor's office rather than the extended executive branch develops spending recommendations. Until the 1980s, cabinet officials proposed whatever they thought they could get away with, guided by the informal mandates of an incremental budget process. The budget director, the treasurer, and the governor would then review the cabinet's recommendations. Everyone understood department requests would be cut 10 to 15 percent, and acted accordingly. With the civil servants in the budget bureau playing a larger role than the understaffed governor's office, policy aims got rather short shrift.

Governor Kean instituted a tighter and more focused process beginning in 1983. Departments file budget requests with the Office of Management and Budget (OMB) in October of the previous fiscal year. They must be predicated on specified target amounts and arrayed in "priority decision packages." The OMB director, a civil servant directed by the governor's office, "examines each request and determines the necessity or advisability of the appropriation requested."[4] The cabinet's actual role in this process was rather starkly illustrated in 1990 when Governor Florio's state treasurer, Douglas Berman, presented all FY 1991 department budgets to the legislature and cabinet officials were not permitted to testify. Although that was an extreme example of micro-management, a decade later the McGreevey administration instructed department heads not to talk to reporters without approval from the governor's office.

To some extent therefore, the annual budget is now a statement of the governor's priorities. It can also be an instrument to reward or punish departments and constituencies. Governors have far from a free hand, however. Mandated expenditures (for example, contractual salaries and benefits for state employees, Medicaid, and education expenditures required by the state supreme court) constitute about 60 percent of the budget.

Additionally, substantial amounts flowing into the state treasury are for mandated purposes. Although the constitution bans dedicated revenues, amendments have overridden that provision for most of the new revenue sources of the last three decades. Income tax monies are dedicated to property tax relief, as is the 2006 sales tax increase of 1 percent; casino revenues are dedicated to programs for the elderly and handicapped; lottery revenues are dedicated to education and state institutions; and a portion of the gasoline tax is dedicated to transportation. When added to the mandated expenditures, more than three-quarters of anticipated revenues are spoken for before the budget process even begins.

Patterns of Spending Growth

In the 1970s New Jersey's governments began increasing spending faster than most other American jurisdictions, moving the state toward the top of the state spending pack from its traditional place near the bottom. Between 1982 and 1988, the Kean administration increased spending 15 percent more than the national average, and between 1992 and 2002, including eight years of the Whitman governorship, state spending growth was 17 percent higher than the national average.[5] Table 14.1 tells the tale.

TABLE 14.1.

Average Per Capita Expenditures, State and National Governments, Selected Years

Year	N.J.	U.S.	N.J. as % of U.S. average
1962	$302	$321	94
1972	$801	$802	100
1982	$1,950	$1,868	104
1987	$2,009	$1,665	121
2004	$8,366	$7,713	119

SOURCE: *Significant Features of Fiscal Federalism*, 1962–1987; Tax Policy Center, 2006.

TABLE 14.2.

New Jersey Average Per Capita State and Local Expenditures, Selected Functions, 1977, 1987, and 2004 (as percentage of U.S. average)

Function	1977	1987	2004	1987 rank	2004 rank
Elementary/secondary education	107	115	147	5	3
Higher education	67	79	86	39	39
Highways	72	91	78	27	34
Public welfare	106	114	82	14	38
Health and hospitals	72	79	60	34	41
Police	119	131	130	6	3

SOURCE: *Significant Features of Fiscal Federalism*, 1987; Tax Policy Center, 2006.

Although New Jersey's overall state and local expenditures are now well above average, Table 14.2 depicts the considerable variation across areas of expenditure.

These data raise two intriguing questions. First, what accounts for New Jersey's sudden shift during the 1970s from a miserly state to a rather free-spending one? Second, what explains handsome spending in some areas and relative stinginess in others? The answers to these questions are not unrelated.

State government cannot spend money it does not have. As we discuss in detail later in this chapter, New Jersey imposed broad-based state taxes later than most other states. A strong home rule tradition assigned Trenton a minor role in both taxing and spending. Before 1947, the governorship, which might have represented larger state interests, was a weak office. The legislature, dominated by an upper house in which each county had one senator, favored fiscally conservative rural interests. New Jersey's urban Democrats were concentrated in a few counties. They focused their attention on the local governments that provided most fiscal and patronage resources. To have any influence in Trenton, urban Democrats had to make common cause with rural Republicans. This county-based political system was not a recipe for activist state government.

The 1947 constitution greatly strengthened the governor's office, but a quarter-century passed before governors could really exercise their new powers. The structure of the legislature was left undisturbed, and county-based politics continued. Without either political will or broad-based state taxes, the pattern of modest state budgets and activities persisted.

When federal court decisions in the late 1960s ended county-based legislative representation and weakened county parties' influence at the state level, governors could actually exercise their constitutional powers and the legislature could professionalize. Democrats could gain more seats, and with migration and population growth, they were no longer as concentrated in only a few counties. These changes made it possible to pass broad-based taxes. Once the state commanded more resources, it began spending them.

Increases in overall spending have followed the twists and turns of the state and national economies. Broad-based taxes are elastic; their revenues rise and fall along with the economy. In periods of recession state governments, most of which are constitutionally required to balance their budgets, often raise taxes to compensate for declines in revenue. When the economy improves, greater amounts of tax money flow in, and the temptation is to spend on new or expanded programs rather than to lower taxes.

As table 14.1 shows, after New Jersey raised its sales tax in 1970 to cope with economic difficulties, an improving economy brought in new revenue, which the state promptly spent and continued spending. Imposition of an income tax in 1976 did not have a big immediate effect, because the tax was at first quite low and was completely offset by decreases in local property taxes. In 1983, faced with the worst recession since the 1930s, New Jersey raised both of its broad-based taxes. The deep economic trough was followed by a strong and sustained recovery. Along with much of the Northeast, New Jersey prospered even more than the nation as a whole. With the strongest economy in its history and less federal aid, New Jersey, like its neighbors, went on an unprecedented spending spree. As recession loomed again in the early 1990s—this time hitting the Northeast the hardest—the cycle repeated, and state taxes were raised once again.

The pattern of expenditures in table 14.2 reflects historical legacies. Even before the 1970s, policies that benefited localities, and for which revenue was raised locally, enjoyed high levels of support. Wealthy suburbs had long been amenable to taxing themselves to support their public schools. Municipal employees who were the foot soldiers of local party organizations were well-paid. However, none of these parochial entities was much interested in subsidizing higher education or health facilities benefiting the whole state.

When Trenton acquired additional resources, the home rule tradition ensured that money would flow to the places it always had. If local tax dollars had always gone first and foremost to local schools, new state dollars would too. Transportation systems, colleges, and health or cultural facilities would have to wait their turn. Further, the tax system did not shift away from localities toward the state overnight; indeed, the shift is still more incomplete than in most other states. Broad-based state taxes began at modest rates and increased rather slowly. Understanding expenditure patterns requires an understanding of the evolution of the tax system.

TAXES AND TAX POLITICS

The most prominent characteristic of New Jersey's tax system is its unusual reliance on the local property tax. Taxes on property began in 1670. Three centuries later, the local property tax was still the linchpin of government finance. As late as 1962, it generated 65 percent of all own-source (state and local) tax revenues in New Jersey, compared to a 38 percent average for all the states. Even in 1989, long after New Jersey imposed broad-based sales and income taxes, property taxes still accounted for 43 percent of state and local tax dollars, compared with a national average of 30 percent.[6] Only three states—Montana, New Hampshire, and Oregon—collected a larger proportion of income from this source. By 2004, when property taxes in the Garden State represented 46 percent of own-source revenue, only New Hampshire outpaced New Jersey.[7]

Mid-Twentieth-Century State Tax Policy

By the mid-1950s, thirty-one states had a state income tax, thirty-three had a general state sales tax, and only three—including New Jersey—had neither. About two-thirds of New Jersey's state revenues came from excise taxes and fees (on public utilities, motor fuels and vehicle registrations, cigarettes and alcohol, and racing); most of the rest came from corporate taxes. In 1956, New Jersey state taxes, as a percentage of all own-source revenues, were at half the national average. On average, state and local taxes contributed about equally to states' own-source revenue in the 1950s. In New Jersey, local revenues—virtually all from the property tax—still contributed four times as much. Its county and local leaders saw broad-based taxes as the "greatest threat to the endurance of the home rule tradition."[8]

Although some states began earlier, the majority imposed broad-based taxes in reaction to the Great Depression. In 1935, as one municipality after another went bankrupt, Republican Governor Harold Hoffman proposed a 2 percent sales tax and an income tax at half the federal rate. The legislature summarily rejected an income tax. The sales tax squeaked through in June with help from Democratic boss Frank Hague rather than Hoffman's fellow Republicans, but it was repealed in October after loud public protest. Despite a stone wall against new forms of taxation, existing levies rose apace. An economist observed in 1960, "Taxes are not low in this state. Heavy property taxes and taxes adverse to business impede growth."[9]

Stung by the violent reaction to Hoffman's tax proposals, the entire New Jersey political establishment assumed "that endorsement of new taxes constitutes political suicide."[10] A state tax commission issued repeated criticisms but had an express policy of not advocating a reform program "until it is politically possible to pass it." Each year the legislature attempted "to get by without any reform of what is one of the worst tax systems of any wealthy state."[11]

One strategy to avoid new taxes, especially after World War II, was unusual reliance on public authorities. Legislative appropriations provided only $300 million of the $512 million state agencies spent in 1956. The remainder came from license fees, tuition, and, mostly, highway authority tolls. New Jersey's penchant for authorities helped shape—one might say distort—priorities. Controlled for inflation and population growth, state spending between 1946 and 1956 grew at exactly the national average—174 percent. However, the rate of increased spending on highways was more than 50 percent above average, while the rate of increase for education and public welfare was well below average.[12] The authorities responsible for the Garden State Parkway and the New Jersey Turnpike could issue bonds and spend huge sums without troubling the taxpayers; moreover, they could continue the tradition begun with railroad taxes—of extracting much of their income from out-of-state residents. Their effect on public policy, however, paled in comparison to that of massive reliance on local property taxes.

Mid-Century Tax Structure and the State-Local Finance System

Extraordinary dependence on the local property tax produced vast inequalities among counties and municipalities. Residents with low or fixed incomes suffered especially from a tax that had a limited relationship to ability to pay and no protection against housing inflation. Further, the tax system discriminated against urban areas with shrinking tax bases and increasing demands for public services. In 1951, assessment ratios (that is, the assessed valuation of a property as a proportion of its market value) were at least 50 percent above the state average in eight of the thirteen largest municipalities.[13] As cities imposed high tax rates to pay for constantly growing needs, businesses and middle-class residents fled, intensifying a vicious cycle.[14] Developers seeking cheap land and home buyers and businesses seeking low taxes produced "a premature spreading out of urban development, the creation of an automobile-dependent society, and the deterioration of established cities."[15] Thus, in mid-century, the tax system relied on local property taxes that were insensitive to economic fluctuations, had little relation to ability to pay, and covered only a small proportion of income-producing assets. It accelerated cities' decline by depressing urban property values, and was based on unstandardized and inequitable assessments.[16]

State Tax Policy and Politics: 1966–1989

By the mid-1960s, the climate finally seemed right for cautious tax reform.[17] The economy was booming. Recent migrants (especially from New York) were accustomed to higher levels of state services (and taxation). Democratic Governor Richard Hughes, who favored tax reform and more state services, began his eight-year tenure in 1962, part of the time with a Democratic legislature. Hughes managed to get assembly approval of an income tax in 1966 after a big reelection victory, but he could not persuade the senate. Much of the opposition was framed as a preference for a sales tax, and Hughes was able to enact a 3 percent sales tax—New Jersey's first permanent broad-based tax—in April 1966.[18] It was less regressive than many state excise taxes in that it exempted both food and clothing.

When Republican William Cahill succeeded Hughes in 1970, the Republican-dominated legislature grudgingly—but quickly and by a large margin—approved Cahill's request to meet pressing revenue needs by raising the sales tax from 3 to 5 percent. Although in dollar terms the increase was as large as the tax's original imposition, there was much less controversy. It reaffirmed the common wisdom that it was easier to raise an existing tax than to impose a new one. A state-run lottery—another "painless" source of revenue—was also established that year.[19]

Along with the sales tax proposal, Cahill established a Tax Policy Committee to study the entire tax system. It recommended generating state and local revenue in approximately equal proportions from income, sales, and property taxes. The proposals called for shifting much of the tax burden from localities to the state and from property to income, and for an overall increase in revenues. The plan cut local property taxes by about half the amount of an increased state tax burden of $1.5 billion, and the committee also recommended a ceiling on property tax rates. Cahill sought passage of this proposal at a special legislative session in 1972, but only nine of the thirty-nine assembly Republicans would vote for it, and prospects in the senate were even worse. Republican displeasure with the plan played a major role in Cahill's primary election defeat when he sought a second term in 1973.

In April 1973, a state supreme court decision declared New Jersey's school funding mechanism—heavily reliant on the local property tax—unconstitutional. Substantial revenues from another source were needed to meet the court's requirements. Democratic Governor Brendan Byrne, who took office in January 1974 after campaigning on a platform of no new taxes in "the foreseeable future," fared no better than Cahill in his attempts to push further tax increases and tax reform through a new heavily Democratic legislature.

After the 1975 legislative elections, there were more months of protracted bargaining and more crises—most significantly, a July 1976 court order closing all public schools until a satisfactory funding mechanism was in place. Faced with this directive, and after more than three years of chaos, the legislature finally passed a state income tax a few weeks later.[20] A constitutional amendment specified that all revenues from the income tax were to be applied only to property tax relief. Most of the "relief" was supplied by the state assuming a larger proportion (about 40 percent) of the costs of the public schools. To ensure that residents saw the connection between the income tax and property tax relief, all homeowners began receiving an annual property tax rebate check. Because it was not linked to ability to pay, the rebate program did little to remedy the basic problems with the property tax. In the first year, however, total property taxes, including the rebates, did indeed drop by 17 percent.[21]

Compared to most states, the new income tax of 2 percent on the first $20,000 of income, and 2.5 percent above that, was quite modest. During Byrne's eight years in office, corporate income taxes were also raised twice (in 1975 and 1980), and some less progressive business taxes were repealed or phased out. Finally, Byrne also oversaw the passage of a public referendum legalizing casino gambling in Atlantic City in 1977. The principal motive behind the casino policy was to revitalize the ailing resort and tourism at the Shore, but it was also yet another "painless" revenue-generating measure.[22]

Republican Tom Kean, Byrne's successor, ran on a tax-cutting platform and rejected any new taxes during his two terms, but he did significantly extend the broad-based taxes. Greeted with major cuts in federal aid and the worst economic climate since the Great Depression when he took office in January 1982, Kean went along with increases in both the sales tax and the income tax in 1983.

A sharp rebound in the economy soon produced huge budget surpluses and partisan wrangling about how to return some of the bounty to taxpayers. Kean and the Republicans suggested returning some money directly through lower taxes. In September 1985, the Democratic majority in the legislature instead passed their own proposal for a credit against income tax bills for both homeowners and tenants.[23] With the improved economy, Kean came under increasing pressure to perform major surgery on a tax system still overly reliant on the inequitable and inelastic property tax. He agreed to a bipartisan legislative proposal for yet another State and Local Expenditure and Revenue Policy Commission, known familiarly as SLERP.[24]

The commission, created in December 1984, was asked to study the effects of mandated spending, the impact of the tax system on the economic viability of the state, its long-term adequacy for funding major state services, and the equity and efficiency of the state and local tax system. Plagued by delays in selecting an executive director and the governor's appointees, SLERP did not begin work until September 1985. The commission had been directed to report in January 1986, a date conveniently

TABLE 14.3.

Revenue Sources by Percentage, New Jersey and U.S. Average, 1962–2004

Year	United States average			New Jersey		
	Federal	State	Local	Federal	State	Local
1962	14	41	46	9	28	63
1968	17	43	40	12	35	53
1972	19	42	39	16	36	48
1978	23	43	34	20	41	39
1982	20	46	34	17	49	34
1987	17	46	37	14	52	34
2004	23	60	17	16	54	30

SOURCE: *Significant Features of Fiscal Federalism*, 1962–1987; Tax Policy Center, 2004.

after the 1985 gubernatorial and legislative elections. Because of its slow start, SLERP did not finish its work until 1988. The effects of recent changes in the tax structure which SLERP was studying can be seen clearly in table 14.3.

As table 14.3 shows, since the 1960s New Jersey has lagged behind the national average in the proportion of revenue derived from the federal government. There has been a striking transformation in the proportion of revenues raised by local governments (which, relatively, dropped by close to half) and the proportion raised by state government (which rose concomitantly). The first big change is seen in 1968, two years after the imposition of the sales tax. Sales tax revenues, combined with increased intergovernmental transfers from federal Great Society programs, accounted for the 10 percent drop in the local share. The next big change, in 1978, reflects the establishment of the state income tax and still-increasing federal revenues, with a continuing decline of the local share. By 1987, the effects of the Reagan-era federal cuts are obvious. The state share of revenue continued to rise as a result of increased sales and income tax rates. Tax elasticity in a boom period permitted Trenton to replace some of the revenues no longer available from Washington, and to do so to a greater degree than most other states. The need for local governments to take up some of the slack is reflected in the slower decline of the local share after 1982, although local governments escaped the increases that occurred nationally.

TABLE 14.4.

Index of Tax Capacity

	1967	1975	1979	1981	1986	1988	2004
New Jersey	97	103	118	112	121	124	133
National rank	25	13	8	10	8	7	3

SOURCE: *Significant Features of Fiscal Federalism*, various years; Tax Policy Center, *Measuring State Fiscal Capacity* (2006).

TABLE 14.5.

Index of Tax Effort

	1965	1975	1980	1982	1986	1988	2004
New Jersey	87	94	101	100	103	101	129
National rank	40	29	18	21	16	17	3

SOURCE: *Significant Features of Fiscal Federalism*, 1965–1982; Tax Policy Center, *Measuring State Fiscal Capacity*, 1986–88 (2006).

Two other comparative measures provide further illumination. They are New Jersey's ratings in terms of tax effort and tax capacity. The tax capacity index measures the amount a state would raise, relative to all other states, if it applied a national average set of tax rates to twenty-six commonly used tax bases. Tax effort is the ratio of actual collections to tax capacity. These ratings are shown in tables 14.4 and 14.5.

Table 14.4 shows New Jersey's growing ability relative to other states to extract revenue from its citizens. From a middling position in the 1960s, New Jersey has risen much closer to the top. Table 14.5 shows the extent to which, particularly during the 1980s, political leaders were willing to do so, and the public was willing to pay.

Unlike the earlier Cahill-appointed commission, which reported before the imposition of the state income tax, SLERP concluded that new taxes were not required and that tax reform should be revenue-neutral. But like its predecessor, it advocated a massive shift of the tax burden (about $1.2 billion in current dollars) from local property taxes to broad-based state taxes. The idea was that state rather than local revenues should be used to pay for what should be state rather than local government functions.[25] SLERP recommended that Trenton assume the costs of the state court system, the local share of welfare costs, and county expenditures for psychiatric hospitals and centers for the developmentally disabled. Additionally, the state should contribute a greater proportion of the costs of the public schools and county colleges.

All this could be accomplished, the commissioners suggested, by raising marginal income tax rates to 4 percent on income between $50,000 and $100,000 and 4.5 percent on income over $100,000, and by sales tax extensions. They also proposed means-tested "circuit breakers" on property taxes, thus making the property tax rebates passed as part of the 1976 income tax package more progressive.

The State-Local Tax System, 1966–1989

The SLERP proposals would have done much to create an equitable and efficient tax system. The broad-based taxes had moved the state somewhat in that direction, but the distortions caused by the property tax had become even worse than they were in the 1960s. There were continuing disparities in assessment ratios and tax rates across the state, growing controversies about state-versus-local responsibilities, and, toward the end of the 1980s, skyrocketing local property tax increases everywhere, despite the presence of broad-based state taxes.

The issues related to assessment ratios and tax rates were many. First, although the state constitution mandated annual assessments of property at true value, in 1986, 133 of the state's 567 municipalities had not conducted revaluations for at least ten years. Cities like Newark and Trenton had not revalued for more than twenty years, causing enormous tax shocks when the revaluations were finally accomplished. The director of the state's Division of Taxation called "our utter failure, over a period of 200 years, to meet the standard of annual assessments of property for tax purposes" the "central issue of property tax administration."[26]

Growing disparities in effective tax rates between cities and suburbs were even more troublesome. In 1986, the effective tax rate in Princeton was $1.94 per $1,000 of assessed valuation, while Trenton, in the same county, had an effective rate of $4.85—against a state average of $2.38. A former state treasurer calculated that if all municipalities were taxed at the statewide average rate, Newark's rate would drop by half, and the rates in Camden and East Orange by two-thirds.[27]

Other factors also helped suburban property owners and hurt their urban counterparts. For one, businesses (cherished by local governments as "ratables") paid 30 percent of all local property taxes. Increasingly, they sought to locate in places like the Princeton area—with its low rates, open space, and prestigious address—and to leave places like Trenton. For another, tax exemptions and special rates also favored rural areas and discriminated against urban areas. Cities contained most tax-exempt property devoted to public use (10 percent of the total property in the state; almost two-thirds of Newark's twenty-four square miles) such as government buildings, public universities, parks, airports, and seaports.[28]

Conversely, rural areas contained the open land subject to the much lower rates of the Farmland Assessment Act, which covered 25 percent of all state property in 1988. Intended to maintain open space, in effect it permitted the state to "rent" such space from its owners at very high costs. For example, one 106-acre parcel in Plainsboro—a rapidly developing area between Princeton and Trenton—was taxed at $1,300 per year under the Farmland Assessment Act when the annual levy would have been $419,000 at a market value rate.[29] It was thus no wonder that SLERP recommended a graduated property tax with lower rates for urban areas and higher rates for less developed sections. The state director of taxation called this proposal "the single most important proposal in the SLERP report."[30]

Gross differences in county tax effort and tax capacity indices resulted from this overall property tax system. Tax capacity was especially high, and effort low, in wealthy counties; capacity was low and effort high in the poorer counties of the south and the urban north. Setting the state average at 100, the county tax capacity index ranged from 27 in Cumberland to 317 in Bergen, while the tax effort index ranged from 78 in Ocean to 139 in Essex and Hudson.[31]

Local officials also became increasingly irate about state mandates and state aid formulas. Mandates with price tags flooded out of Trenton, without accompanying funds to pay for them. Municipalities were directed to engage in mandatory recycling, close local landfills and transport their solid waste as far away as Texas, increase public employee salaries and pensions, and carry expensive insurance policies. Not only were there no state funds to meet these costs, but existing aid was cut. Because local governments almost never received what the statutes said they should get according to the school aid, county college, revenue sharing, and other statutory formulas, property taxes escalated sharply. Between 1982 and 1988, they rose as a percentage of true property value from 3.25 percent to 5.9 percent. Property taxes more than doubled during the 1980s, capped by a 13 percent average increase in 1989. Increases had lagged behind inflation and income growth in the late 1970s and early 1980s, but that changed as the 1980s progressed.[32]

The State-Local Tax System, 1990–2006

When Governor Jim Florio assumed office in 1990, he faced a large budget deficit and growing anger over property tax increases. Further, the state supreme court was about to render another school funding decision. The court was expected to declare again that a school funding mechanism based heavily on local property taxes was unconstitutional. Florio chose to take on both challenges—the major shortfall in the state budget and the impending school finance decision—together, and immediately. In his first months in office, Florio proposed massive tax changes embodying almost every recommendation students of the tax system had suggested over the past thirty years, and then some.

The income tax was to become sharply progressive, with the highest marginal rate rising from 3.5 to 7 percent. The new rates were projected to produce about $1.4 billion in additional revenue. Florio's plan scrapped universal property tax rebates and credits, offering larger rebates for the least wealthy and none for the most wealthy. To address the anticipated supreme court decision, Florio proposed pouring $1.4 billion more into school aid, almost half of it for the state's thirty poorest districts—mostly urban and with large numbers of minority students. "Middle-class" districts would receive the rest. About one-third of all school districts, with one-quarter of the students, were deemed wealthy enough to receive no general school aid. He emphasized that 83 percent of taxpayers would pay no more in income taxes; the wealthiest 17 percent of the population would bear the entire new income tax burden.

Another point was added to the sales tax, whose 6 percent rate would be the second highest in the nation, and it was to be extended to nonfood grocery items such as paper goods (a proposal ridiculed as the "toilet paper tax"), as well as cable television, telephone calls, and telecommunications services. There was a new tax on the gross receipts of oil companies, and increases in "sin taxes" on smoking materials and alcohol. These excise taxes were to produce about the same amount of revenue as the income tax, and close the budget gap.

The numerous elements and complicated scheduling of the Florio plan confused the public. Although already announced, neither the income tax increase nor the new property tax schedule would go into effect until July

1991, while the sales tax increase was to take effect in July 1990. A nervous Democratic legislature, though not up for reelection for more than a year, knew voters would experience short-term pain, but no short-term gain. During much of 1990 and 1991, they would pay more every time they went to the supermarket, bought a six-pack, or made a phone call. Most would also be hit with higher property taxes to cover the shortfall in state school aid. Their annual rebate checks would be nowhere in sight, and it would be another year before any benefited from the promised property tax reform.

Consequently, the legislature tinkered with the plan—advancing the start of the stiffer income taxes to January 1991 to pay for a reduced old-style rebate that fiscal year; exempting cable television and over-the-counter drugs from the sales tax; upping some more "sin taxes," and raising the significant cutting point in the income tax rates. After three attempts, the income tax increase finally received the requisite forty-one votes (one more than an absolute majority) in the assembly, as did the sales tax increase and the budget as a whole. The senate also passed all three pieces of legislation with the minimum requirement of twenty-one votes. Not a single Republican voted for any of the measures in either house.

When July 1990 came, and the price of cigarettes, beer, paper towels and gasoline all went up at once, the public erupted in anger not seen since the Hoffman tax increase of 1935. A poll found that 80 percent gave the governor negative ratings on his tax policy, and 65 percent gave him similar marks on the budget. Three-quarters could not cite anything positive Florio had done since he took office and believed the governor's economic plan would hurt "people like yourself." Despite his assertions that the plan was the greatest property tax relief measure in history, only 2 percent thought their property levies would go down, and 70 percent thought they would go up.[33]

The 1990 elections demonstrated the depth of the public's resentment. U.S. Senator Bill Bradley, who had refused to comment on the tax plan, came close to defeat. Republicans easily won a special state senate election widely seen as a referendum on taxes and deposed local Democrats all over the state. Middlesex County elected Republican freeholders for the first time in twenty years, and the GOP took control in Florio's home county of Camden. The next morning, the governor described the results as "a strong message directed at me and the policies of my administration." He acknowledged that "leadership" required not only "hard decisions," but also "bringing people to build a consensus, to build a mandate. . . . The other part of leadership in a democratic society entails doing more of what I did not do."[34]

Property taxes did decline in more than half of New Jersey municipalities in 1991. However, in April, 70 percent of residents still rated Florio's tax policy as "poor." Less than one-third gave him positive marks for anything. His approval rating sank to 17 percent, tied for historic worst with Governor Byrne's showing when the income tax was first passed in 1976. But the hostility to Florio was even deeper. At Byrne's lowest point, 34 percent had termed his performance "poor." A full 48 percent gave Florio this rating in the spring of 1991.[35]

That November, the Republicans, running on a promise to roll back the sales tax increase, gained veto-proof majorities in both houses of the legislature, and more local offices fell to the GOP. Those majorities permitted the Republicans to rewrite much of the governor's FY 1993 budget on a line item basis, and to override Florio's veto of their handiwork. The 1 percent sales tax rollback left a $600 million revenue hole. Half of it was made up by lowering property tax rebates and restricting them to households making less than $40,000. Only the disabled and the politically potent senior citizens were still able to collect as much as $500.

Amidst all the hostility and political drama, there were indications that a smaller tax package, or one introduced over a longer period of time, would have fared better with the voters. It was less what Florio did than the way he did it that enraged his constituents. First, instantly forsaking his "no new taxes" campaign pledge and his promise to conduct a thorough state audit gave the governor severe credibility problems. More than two-thirds of the state's residents believed Florio "didn't tell all he knew" about state fiscal problems during the campaign. An equal number admitted taxes had to be raised, but most felt the increases could have been much smaller.[36] Second, the heavily graduated income tax rates, along with the plan to spend much of the new revenue in a small number of urban school systems, rekindled the historic animosity between cities and suburbs. Many suburbanites had serious doubts that long mismanaged and corrupt urban school systems—now with heavy minority populations—could absorb so much new money so rapidly and use it wisely. This "class warfare," which historically had ugly religious undertones, took on more explosive racial ones when Education Commissioner John Ellis suggested that racism accounted for some of the opposition.

Many citizens also disagreed with Florio about how his plan would affect various segments of the population. A majority of those with family earnings of $70,000—the cutoff for the highest income tax rate—believed that to be a middle-class income. Despite the administration's messages and constant journalistic references to the governor as Robin Hood, two-thirds of New Jerseyans thought the plan would hurt the poor, and 71 percent thought it would "make no difference" to the rich.[37]

Shortly before the 1989 gubernatorial election, former Governor Byrne had listed four keys to the passage of the state income tax in 1976. First, a tax plan must be simple—too many things at once led to confusion and provided targets for criticism.[38] Second, tax measures had to have bipartisan support. Third, a tax plan had to emphasize "salable" issues. Finally, the public had to believe a real crisis would occur without new tax revenues. By following these rules, the governor derisively dubbed "One-Term Byrne" in 1976 had won landslide reelection in 1977 when his opponent could not convincingly explain how the state could function without an income tax.

Measured by these criteria, the Byrne and Florio tax plans stood in sharp contrast. The Byrne plan involved one simple tax—a modest and virtually flat income tax—rather than the graduated rates of the Florio scheme. It gained significant Republican support and was largely crafted in the legislature after three years of negotiation. Florio instead pushed his plan through within five months of taking office, without a single Republican vote. The 1976 plan promised property tax relief to all, which appeared almost immediately in the form of rebate checks. The 1990 plan gave increased property tax relief to about half of New Jersey's taxpayers.

Finally, the Byrne tax reform eventually passed in the midst of a genuine crisis—the state supreme court's shutdown of the public schools in July 1976—but a crisis Byrne expected, and indeed encouraged. As he recalled, "Everybody says New Jersey adopted a state income tax because there was a crisis. Actually, I created that crisis. I asked [the state supreme court] to close the schools in 1976. If I hadn't, I don't think New Jersey would have a state income tax today."[39] With another court decision looming, Florio, like Byrne, could have used the ruling to force legislative action and make some Republicans his reluctant partners. Instead, when the decision was eventually handed down, it was obvious that the Florio taxes greatly exceeded the court's requirements.

Lost in the furor—and subject to partisan or ideological interpretation— was the real shape of the New Jersey tax system after the Florio reforms.

TABLE 14.6.

Percentage of Family Income Paid in State and Local Taxes, New Jersey and U.S., Selected Years

	New Jersey 1985	New Jersey 1995	New Jersey 2002	United States average 2002
Top 1% earners	6.8	8.8	8.4	7.3
Middle quintile	9.3	10.2	9.9	9.9
Lowest quintile	13.3	15.9	12.5	11.4

SOURCE: Robert S. McIntyre et al., *Who Pays? A Distributional Analysis of the Tax System in all 50 States*, 2nd ed. (Washington, D.C.: The Institute on Taxation & Economic Policy 2003).

The data in table 14.6, from a study by the national tax study group, Citizens for Tax Justice, cast some light on this matter.[40]

At both the lowest and highest income levels, New Jerseyans were taxed more heavily than the national average—overall, more heavily than the residents of forty-one other states. High sales and property taxes made low-income residents fare poorly in absolute terms. However, the increased income tax rate for the state's wealthiest residents increased their tax burden by much the largest proportion. The "middle middle," which led the tax revolt, fared little worse than such earners do nationally. State taxes were high, but for partisans of a progressive tax system, fairer than they were.

The legacy of the tax revolt propelled Christie Whitman to a one-point victory margin when she ran against Florio in 1993 on a platform of reducing the income tax rate by 30 percent, and little else. Exit polls demonstrated the success of her strategy. Almost three-quarters of Whitman voters gave "dislike of the other candidate" as a reason for their choice, and 58 percent of all respondents still maintained that Florio had been wrong to raise taxes so much. The 2002 figures in table 14.6 reflect the impact of Whitman's tax cuts.

By the last year of her first term, the lost revenue led to a radical "gimmick" to balance the FY 1998 budget. To maintain services, pay for large increases in court-mandated educational aid to poor districts, and balance the budget without making cuts or, of course, raising taxes, Whitman proposed the largest state bond issue ($2.75 billion) in history, borrowing the money to close the future payments gap in the state employee pension funds, which was becoming an increasingly bigger piece of the balanced budget puzzle. She argued that these borrowed funds, deposited in the pension fund accounts, would earn interest income at a higher rate than the interest payments on the bonds, thus permanently solving the problem. As another short-term advantage, the state did not have to make any payments into the pension funds in the year the money was borrowed, freeing it up for other purposes in FY 1998.

Whitman supporters argued that the plan made sense, and the bond rating services implicitly agreed with them. Moody's Investors' Services calculated that the state's total debt after the bond issue stood at $1,588 per capita, up from $781 at the end of 1993, against a national median for all states of $422. However, Moody's pronounced the New Jersey debt figures "not unmanageable" and left the state's bond rating, which it had downgraded from the highest rating of Aaa in 1994, unchanged at Aa1. Opponents, including the longtime Republican chair of the Senate Appropriations Committee, maintained that the plan depended upon the uncertain fortunes of the stock market and pointed to an increase of more than 50 percent in long-term debt (from $7 billion to $13 billion) during Whitman's first term.

A stock market collapse, along with expensive new antiterrorism measures in the wake of September 11 and rising costs for health care and pensions, hit New Jersey particularly forcefully. It presented the newly elected Democratic governor, Jim McGreevey, with a projected $5 billion hole in the FY 2003 budget, which represented more than 20 percent of state expenditures—the worst shortfall for any American state. To deal with it, McGreevey instituted across-the board cuts for state agencies, froze state aid to local governments, and asked for just over a 1 percent spending increase, compared with the average 7 percent hike in each of the eight Whitman budgets.

Mindful of the years of Republican domination of the legislature after Florio's tax increases, McGreevey confined his new levies primarily to "sin taxes," a "millionaires" tax on income and estates, and closing corporate tax loopholes. Most of the shortfall was plugged by the sort of gimmicks for which he had criticized Whitman, such as borrowing more than $1 billion against the state's share of the nationwide tobacco settlement.[41] Bond raters like Moody's signaled their displeasure, lowering New Jersey's credit rating another notch to Aa2. The Republicans claimed that freezing state aid to local governments would drive up New Jersey's already stratospheric property taxes, and in this they proved correct. Property taxes rose at a 3 to 4 percent rate from 1993 to 1999, but from 5 to 7 percent between 2000 and 2005. Neither figure, however, came close to the 10 to 13 percent annual increase from 1986 to 1990.[42]

Without question, New Jersey's localities receive and spend most tax revenue, but municipal and state officials direct most of the blame at each other for New Jersey's combination of high taxes and structural budget deficits. State officials blame local governments, school boards, and powerful public employee unions for the highest per capita property taxes in the country and point to municipal and school budgets as the primary reason that ever increasing amounts of state aid have not made a dent in the local share of the tax burden. Richard Codey, senate president and former acting governor, has asked rhetorically, "Has the Legislature ever increased property taxes? I never voted to raise property taxes. I'm not a school board member. I'm not a mayor."[43]

The two largest categories of municipal employees—teachers and others serving the schools, and local police—are among the best-paid people in their professions. New Jersey police officers have the highest average salaries in the nation, and teachers' pay ranks third, behind only Connecticut and California.[44] They negotiate their salary contracts with the towns in which they work. From a financial perspective, their generous compensation is particularly troublesome because there are so many of them. Consider the example of the borough of Bogota in Bergen County. Less than a mile square and with a population of about eight thousand, it maintains two elementary schools, a grade 7–12 high school with an enrollment of about five hundred students, and employs fifteen police officers. Of the state's more than 600 school districts, the majority with their own superintendents, business administrators, and so on, 172 operate only a single school.

In part, this state of affairs stems from union advantages at the bargaining table. The fifty-seven field representatives of the New Jersey Education Association (NJEA), with long institutional memories and a network across the state, stand ready to assist their members in negotiations, as do the lawyers engaged by the police unions. PBA locals collect funds by annual solicitations of residents, who see these funds used for activities like holiday parties for local children. But as an attorney who represents municipal officials in contract negotiations describes it, "[A] good amount of what they raise goes to good causes. The rest of the money goes to hire lawyers to fight the towns."[45]

Efforts to cut expenses, and thus property taxes, by regionalizing education and public safety functions have failed dismally, and critics again point to the power of public employee unions as a major factor. Chapter 6 of this book describes the clout of the New Jersey Education Association; the New Jersey Police Benevolent Association and the Fraternal Order of Police are less visible to the public, but equally successful. Both groups play on the fear of residents that services will diminish in quality, quantity, or both if they lose their local schools or public safety personnel.

Public opinion polls would seem to show that the growing frustration over property taxes has begun to change New Jerseyans' minds. In a statewide survey conducted in 2006, 70 percent of respondents reported they favored merging fire and police departments, and 58 percent said they would be willing to merge local school districts if that brought property tax relief.[46] However, when they are faced with the reality in their own towns, the level of support often drops precipitously.

When Bergen County Executive Dennis McNerney proposed merging the eighteen police officers of Emerson (population 7,300) and the twenty-eight in Westwood (population 11,000) with the county force in 2004, the mayors of both towns supported it. PBA members from all over the region packed meetings and led emotional protests. In a referendum on the merger, the citizens of Emerson voted three to one against the proposal, launched a recall effort against the mayor, and voted his brother-in-law off the borough council. Shortly thereafter, the Westwood borough council voted unanimously to reject the mayor's plans to hold a referendum on a merger with the county. In the same year, the 6,000 residents of Blairstown in Warren County actually voted to dissolve the local department in favor of state police patrols, but new members of the township council reinstated it. By the end of 2006, no local police departments had been regionalized anywhere in the state.[47]

Similarly, since school districts were permitted to regionalize in 1931, only seventy of more than six hundred have done so, and it has been more than a decade since any school district even considered regionalization.[48] The most likely candidates might seem to be the twenty-three nonoperating school districts that spend about a million dollars a year on school board staff and supplies simply to write tuition checks to the neighboring towns that educate their students. These small towns, mostly with high property values, like their current arrangements because tuition payments are much less than the property taxes they would have to pay as part of a regionalized system. The districts receiving tuition payments incur few costs in absorbing the small numbers of students, such as the five from Mantoloking (population 450) on the Jersey Shore who attend Point Pleasant schools.

The residents of Mantoloking have heard about the financial consequences of regionalization. In regionalized districts, the school tax (the largest portion of property taxes) is set at the rate of the municipality that hosts the schools. In Beach Haven, it costs taxpayers an average of $38,000 to send each of its ninety students to Southern Regional High School in Ocean County, while the residents of Stafford Township spend less than a tenth of that sum for each of their two thousand students in the same building. In 2007, Tavistock, which consists of "eight residents and a golf course," sent one student to the Haddonfield schools and raised about $11,000 in school taxes for a tuition payment. If Tavistock regionalized with Haddonfield and became liable for the Haddonfield school tax rate, Tavistock taxpayers would have had to come up with $455,000.[49]

Issues of class and race sometimes enter the mix as well. A bitter battle with strong racial overtones in the Englewood, Englewood Cliffs and Tenafly school districts in Bergen County prevented their merger, and North Brunswick in Middlesex County withdrew from the New Brunswick school system for similar reasons. In discussing the "political realities" that are obstacles to regionalization, Alberto Sires, New Jersey's first Hispanic assembly speaker, observed in 2006, "New Jersey is a home-rule state. People are not going to go along with it. . . . You think people want to go with a Spanish kid to school in Tenafly or something?"[50]

In contrast, local officials blame the state legislature for much of their difficulty in keeping down the costs of education and public safety, which together account for the vast majority of municipal expenditures. They note that state aid for schools, which amounts to 40 percent of New Jersey's expenditures on public education, is 10 percent less than the national average and had been frozen in most districts since 2002. Of the approximately $10 billion per year that the state spent on school aid in FY 2007, 58 percent went to the thirty-one urban districts, enrolling about one-fifth of all students, which the supreme court had ordered the state to subsidize at a level equivalent to the spending in the state's wealthiest districts.

They also argue that it is the state lawmakers who raise all public employees' pensions and mandate expensive health insurance programs. Another complaint is that legislators have removed their most effective tools for containing costs. Until 2003, if negotiations on teacher salaries had reached an impasse, boards could impose a "last best offer." After an illegal teacher strike in Middletown, in 2003 the legislature overwhelmingly passed a bipartisan bill to substitute a negotiating structure instead. In the case of police officers, local officials criticize their right to seek binding arbitration when negotiations fail. Arbitrators are believed to award handsome raises, inclining towns to settle with generous contracts to avoid the substantial cost of mediation that is unlikely to produce a better deal.

Neutral observers see the legitimacy of all these arguments, ascribing the situation in which the state finds itself to a failure of political will by officeholders at every level, and to the public which sees no contradiction between its desire for more and better services and lower property taxes.

Corzine Takes on the Tax System

During his first experience with state budget preparation, Jon Corzine learned many lessons: "As a governor who has just come out of the basement after 50 days of wearing a green visor, I can tell you 75 to 85 percent of the state budget is basically state aid to municipalities, education and higher education."[51] Since only 6 percent of his FY 2007 budget was devoted to the last of these functions, roughly eight in ten dollars of all state expenditures found their way to local governments and their school systems.

By the time the legislature began considering Governor Corzine's FY 2007 budget proposal, no one could ignore the dolorous state of New Jersey's finances. Estimates of the shortfalls in the pension and health insurance funds seem to increase every week, and the state had the nation's highest per capita debt. Citizens were on the verge of another property tax rebellion. Recalling the electoral fallout after the Florio tax increases in 1991, many Democratic lawmakers, particularly in the assembly, opposed any hike in the broad-based taxes.

In what was becoming his signature style, Corzine had set forth a systematic long-term plan to put the state on a sound footing over time. It would spread the pain without fear or favor. His first attempt to start implementing it produced an impasse that "was bizarre even by Trenton's relaxed standards."[52] At the start of FY 2007, on July 1, 2006, Corzine was still locked in a battle with his fellow Democrat, Assembly Speaker Joe Roberts. Roberts commanded a majority opposed to the sales tax increase that the governor wanted to use to make the first significant payment on the pension fund debt in ten years. Without an approved budget, the governor made good on his threat to shut down state government for the first time in history. All "nonessential" state employees were furloughed. They included the casino inspectors, which caused the Atlantic City pleasure domes to shut down for the first time.

During the ensuing stalemate, a "fifty-year flood" on the Delaware River deluged the capitol building; the chair of the Assembly Budget Committee sent the sergeant of arms to find the state treasurer who, on Corzine's instructions, refused to testify; and the governor commanded the legislature to meet every day, including July 4. He also met with his campaign media consultant to script TV ads, which he was going to pay for personally, decrying legislative inaction. An assemblywoman reported, "It's like we're still in Iraq, with no way to get out."[53]

Many believed that both the governor and the speaker, each playing their official roles for the first time, were excessively rigid. Legislators claimed that Corzine, the former head of Goldman Sachs, was "treating them like junior traders," but Roberts and his allies were also "dug in."[54] It was left to senate president and former governor Richard Codey, with his acute understanding of the relationship between the executive and legislative branches, finally to persuade the antagonists to accept a compromise that dedicated half of the new sales tax revenue to property tax relief. On the early morning of July 8, Corzine signed the budget bill, and the lottery, casinos, state parks, motor vehicle offices, and the courts could all reopen.[55]

In the aftermath of the struggle, the governor called for continuing action on all of the major components of the fiscal crisis. The previous May, he had sat in the front row in the state supreme court as his then-attorney general, Zulima Farber, argued successfully for permission to freeze spending in the Abbott "special needs" districts in FY 2007 to help balance the budget, because "we simply don't have the money."[56] At about the same time, his education commissioner told the legislature that the administration wanted a new school funding formula. Corzine also warned the state employee unions that their fringe benefit packages were no longer supportable.

In a special summer session of the legislature to study property tax reform, four committees were charged with recommending policies on public school funding, government consolidation and shared services, public employee benefits, and tax reform by constitutional amendment.[57] Corzine urged lawmakers to "be bold" and to avoid the temptation of short-term fixes. From August through early December 2006, the committees worked with surprising diligence, releasing ninety-eight separate recommendations.

Although some were watered down from initial proposals, the legislature had indeed seldom been bolder, as was evident by the anguished outcries from Trenton's most powerful lobbies and even some legislators themselves. Among the proposals were a 4 percent cap on property tax increases; a 20 percent credit on property tax bills for households with less than $100,000 in income and lesser credits for incomes up to $250,000 (funded by the sales tax increase and the elimination of the rebate program); raising the retirement age for state workers; moving new employees into a 401(k) pension plan; limiting those holding more than one public job (which included a number of legislators) to one pension; establishing county school superintendents with significant authority over district budgets; and creating a state comptroller's office.

By the time Governor Corzine presented his FY 2008 budget in February 2007, the legislature had passed only the property tax cap and credit and the comptroller bills. Some of the recommendations awaited reconciling differences between the senate and assembly, but more than half had seen no action. Many of those dealt with the most politically dangerous measures restricting public employee benefits, which were shelved in December when the governor infuriated legislators by telling them that those issues should instead be addressed by the executive branch at the bargaining table. Others awaited the still-unfinished Education Department proposal for a new school-funding formula, which, along with employee benefits and the property tax measures, was essential to anything resembling real reform.

At first it appeared that the FY 2008 budget process would be much less eventful than that of the previous year. Legislators angry at the governor for undercutting their proposals on public employee benefits were both mollified and surprised when, a day before his budget address, Governor Corzine announced a tentative four-year contract agreement with the largest state employee union, the Communications Workers of America (CWA); the agreement contained a number of the lawmakers' recommendations. The existing contract did not expire until June 30, 2007, and such an early settlement was unprecedented.

For the first time, workers would contribute to the cost of their health benefits, at a rate of 1.5 percent of their salaries, as well as 5.5 percent (an additional 0.5 percent) toward their pensions. Another innovation was a cap on the total annual salary ($97,200 in 2008) on which employees could amass pension credits, doing away with some of the virtues of overtime and working multiple public jobs. Additionally, the retirement age for new hires was raised from fifty-five to sixty. Combining these measures with 13 percent wage increases over four years led the CWA political director to pronounce it "a fair contract which provides fair raises . . . while recognizing that steps have to be taken to address the rising cost of health care."[58]

Other elements of the budget proposal also made it attractive in an election year. In addition to the larger property tax credit for most homeowners, the plan also included the first increases in municipal aid and school aid since 2002. The state's officeholders looked forward to a relatively calm budget process with little of the melodrama of spring and summer 2006, and being able to put off difficult decisions until after the fall election. Foremost among these decisions was the governor's newest idea for attacking New Jersey's fiscal problems, which he called "asset monetization." In plain English, this meant selling or leasing state assets, such as the New Jersey Turnpike and the lottery, the proceeds of which could be used to pay down the state debt and fund capital projects. Pointing out that debt service annually consumed every dollar brought in by corporate taxes, Corzine estimated that asset monetization could free up as much as a billion dollars a year for other purposes. Like Washington State's pride in Mount Rainier or Mainers' affection for Mount Katahdin, New Jersey's attachment to the Turnpike as a symbol of their home state (and their concern about the prospect of increased tolls) generated much skepticism about Corzine's proposal. During March and April, however, there were events that made the previous year's budget process pale in comparison.

They began in March when presidents of two of the seven CWA locals urged their members to vote against the new contract on the grounds that state workers could have gotten a better deal if they had not settled so soon. What made their protests front page news, however, was that one of the protestors was Carla Katz, the same union leader who had become an issue in the 2005 gubernatorial campaign when it was revealed that she had previously been romantically involved with Governor Corzine, and that he had forgiven a half-million-dollar loan he made to her. The five leaders of the other CWA locals who supported the agreement questioned Katz's motives. Statehouse reporters, with little to report while legislative committees were holding initial budget hearings, seized on the story. For weeks, the governor and Ms. Katz refused to answer journalists' questions about other and even larger gifts that Katz might have received. Debates arose among the political chattering classes as to whether Katz's actions resulted from hostility to Corzine or were an attempt to demonstrate that she had not influenced what her union's political director had called a "fair deal." The possibility that she just believed she was acting in the best interests of her union's members received scant attention.

The journalists soon had a much more important story to cover. In April, a day after the CWA membership overwhelmingly approved the contract and the Corzine administration announced a similar agreement with the second largest public employees union, the governor was traveling from Atlantic City to Princeton on the Garden State Parkway in a sports utility vehicle driven by a state trooper. It went off the road and Corzine suffered severe injuries; he was taken by helicopter to Camden's Cooper University Hospital Level One Trauma Center, where he underwent repeated surgeries on a broken leg and spent several days on a ventilator, in "critical but stable condition" with twelve cracked ribs and a broken sternum and collarbone in addition to the leg injury. Once again, it fell to Senate President Richard Codey to lead the state as acting governor during the governor's recuperation.

Fortunately, the governor's recovery was uneventful and so was the rest of the budget process, which the legislature completed nine days before the June 30 deadline. In addition to its property tax assistance, it contained a 3 percent increase in school aid and a 2 percent increase in aid to municipalities—the first increases in five years—as well as a billion-dollar contribution to the state pension fund. Still unaddressed were a new school funding plan and long-term strategies for addressing the pension fund's continuing huge deficit and permanently funding the property tax credit. As he signed the $33.5 billion FY 2008 budget, Corzine also promised to battle for public acceptance of "asset monetization"; declaring, "[W]e need a solid debate on a solid program that gives us the ability to invest in our future and I'm going to fight for it." For their part, Republicans promised a statewide, single-issue campaign against "selling the Turnpike" as their rallying cry during the November 2007 legislative election campaigns. The FY 2009 budget debate had begun.[59]

CHAPTER 15

The Politics of Education

The Legislature shall provide for the maintenance and
support of a thorough and efficient system of free public
schools for the instruction of all children in the state
between the ages of five and eighteen years.

—1875 amendment to the New Jersey constitution

Whether the state acts directly or imposes the role upon
local government, the end product must be what the
constitution commands. . . . If local government fails,
the state must compel it to act, and if local government
cannot carry the burden, the state must itself meet the
continuing obligation.

—New Jersey Supreme Court in the *Robinson v. Cahill*
landmark school funding case, 1973

HOME RULE VERSUS STATE DIRECTION; cities versus sub-
urbs; local property taxes versus broad-based state taxes; how to achieve
economic development and social justice—nowhere are these debates
more prominent than in the politics of public education. The 1970s mark
a major dividing line for New Jersey education policy. Before then, coalitions
of local leaders made state policy. After the 1970s, the clarion call of "one
New Jersey" referred to nothing so much as public education and its direction
from Trenton.

EDUCATION POLICY IN HISTORIC
PERSPECTIVE

Public education in New Jersey had assumed its distinctive characteristics by World War II. It was handsomely supported; New Jersey spent at
a rate one-third above the national average by the 1920s. Teachers enjoyed
above-average salaries and state-financed pensions. As the rest of the
country saw a massive wave of consolidations, New Jersey, with its home
rule tradition, increased the number of school districts.[1]

Trenton's contribution to local education budgets through the 1940s was 3 to 6 percent. Next door, Albany already provided one-third of the funds for New York's schools.[2] More than nine out of ten New Jersey education dollars came from local property taxes. Most districts approved their budgets in annual elections and at the same time elected school board members. In urban areas, appointments to the school board and jobs in the school system were important patronage resources for local politicians.

State education commissioners came from the local educational establishment. Although controlling little money, they approved curricula, certified teachers, appointed county education superintendents, and chose the administrators and faculties of what were then the state teachers' colleges. This role in higher education was uncommon in other states. Commissioner Frederick Raubinger, appointed by Republican Governor Alfred Driscoll in 1952 and reappointed by Democrats Robert Meyner and Richard Hughes in 1957 and 1962, was often cited as an example of how state education commissioners, in symbiotic relationships with interest groups, could dominate educational policy making.[3] Raubinger "established himself as a separate entity in state government."[4] Every few months, Raubinger met at a Princeton inn with leaders of the New Jersey Education Association (NJEA), the School Boards Association, the PTA, and the superintendents' association. They discussed "tactics, general strategy . . . and intelligence on the political climate."[5] Among the participants, NJEA, with its large membership and research capacity, ranked second in influence to the commissioner. Raubinger presided over a system in which local preferences and resources produced wide regional disparities. By the late 1950s, New Jersey was second to New York in per capita expenditures for elementary and secondary education. However, in terms of state aid, it ranked thirty-seventh among the forty-eight states. Hudson and Essex counties in the north spent almost twice as much per student as did Camden and Cumberland counties in the south.

A TRANSITION PERIOD: THE HUGHES AND CAHILL YEARS

When Democrat Richard Hughes won easy reelection and control of both legislative houses in 1965, he obtained passage of the first broad-based state tax. In deciding where to spend this new revenue, he could seek more dominance over state policy. A showdown with Raubinger arose over Hughes's resolve to strengthen higher education.[6] New Jersey's public institutions for the most part had neither quality nor quantity to recommend them. Legislation establishing county colleges was not passed until 1962; the six teachers' colleges each enrolled only about two thousand students; and Rutgers—the nominal state university—had only eleven thousand students on three campuses.[7]

Other public higher education systems in the Northeast developed late because of a sizable private higher education sector, but New Jersey's private institutions were relatively few and mostly small. Almost half of high school graduates seeking higher education attended colleges elsewhere. New Jersey was known in education circles as the "Cowbird State"—after a creature that places its young in others' nests.

Hughes won creation of a cabinet-level Department of Higher Education, which struck at the heart of Raubinger's empire. The commissioner resigned in protest and orchestrated a comeback attempt. He failed, and Hughes's appointment of new commissioners of education and higher education in 1967, along with resources from the new sales tax, produced a new state role in education.

The new education commissioner, Carl Marburger, served in a time of turbulence. During his five-year term, the legislature began to develop the capacity to influence policy. The federal government demanded an end to de facto segregated schools in central and southern New Jersey. A property tax rebellion led to rejection of 170 school district budgets in 1969.[8] And just as Marburger arrived with a mandate to wrest power from the education establishment, the NJEA was being transformed from a professional organization into a union. As with many other milestones in New Jersey affairs, this change had its roots in New York City.

In December 1961, the American Federation of Teachers (AFT) won recognition as bargaining agent for New York City's teachers. A New Jersey offshoot organized some urban districts but had only sixteen hundred members in seventeen locals, as compared with the NJEA's forty-six thousand members. AFT criticism, however, led the NJEA to try to counter charges that it was not aggressive enough and to seek a "professional" bargaining law. The legislature passed the measure in 1965, but Governor Hughes vetoed it.

Concurrent efforts by all state employees to unionize and gain bargaining rights complicated matters for the NJEA. To fight AFT expansion in urban districts, the NJEA supported teacher strikes in Newark and Perth Amboy in the 1965–1966 school year while still seeking a separate bargaining law for teachers. In 1968, in a loss for Hughes as well as the NJEA, the legislature overrode a gubernatorial veto and passed the Public Employee Relations Act (PERA). PERA specified that grievance procedures, wages, and hours for all public employees, including teachers, be negotiated between employee bargaining agents and a new state Public Employee Relations Commission (PERC). None of the "professional" rights the NJEA had sought—such as its traditional voice in curricular, class-size, and teacher-transfer decisions—were included. An even less malleable Republican governor (William Cahill) and legislature took office in 1970. In response, the NJEA transformed itself from a professional association to a trade union practically overnight.

Before PERA, the NJEA sponsored professional publications, an annual conference on professional issues, selective benefits for members, and lobbying. With teachers' interest now centered on favorable contracts, the NJEA radically reoriented itself to vanquish the AFT. By the mid-1970s, the field service division, which helped with contract negotiations, made up more than half of NJEA personnel and almost as much of its budget.

Although unable to gain a "closed shop," the NJEA did win a dues checkoff and increased its membership to about 80 percent of all teachers. Declining attendance at the annual conference reflected changing interests. Although all New Jersey public schools still close for two days when the NJEA holds its annual November convention in Atlantic City, most members now regard this time as just another paid holiday.[9]

Finally, the NJEA reorganized its political operations. Its political action committee, created in 1972, became a major source of funds and campaign workers for legislative candidates. NJEA lobbyists who had operated as the "public relations" division became the mainstays of a renamed "governmental relations" office, signaling a new formalism in their relationship with the Department of Education and a shift in focus from the department to the legislature.[10]

Before coming to New Jersey, Commissioner Marburger had served President Lyndon Johnson, specializing in educational programs for the disadvantaged. Marburger shared Governor Hughes's special interest in minority education and Governor Cahill's determination to weaken NJEA influence and encourage broader participation in educational policy making. Thus began a rare period when urban reformers and fiscally conservative Republicans found common cause. The urban reformers embraced state assessment tests and merit pay for teachers as ways of holding educators responsible for students' performance. Republicans also liked the ideas of educational accountability and local control. The unusual coalition inaugurated two enduring policy changes.

First, despite NJEA opposition, the state began testing students' reading and mathematics skills. Second, the State School Incentive Equalization Law of 1970 (known as the Bateman Bill, for its chief sponsor) provided special state aid to districts with many disadvantaged students and inadequate tax bases. It guaranteed each district the average tax capacity in the state, and awarded extra funds for each student on the welfare rolls.[11] These changes generated heated debate. The NJEA, allied with legislators irate about imposed integration plans, supported the senate's refusal to reconfirm Commissioner Marburger when his term expired in 1972; it was the first such rebuff of a gubernatorial nominee in New Jersey's history.[12] The NJEA's court challenge of the state assessment tests, although eventually unsuccessful, delayed release of the results.[13] Most crucially, the new school funding law—the first state effort to aid poor and mostly urban school districts—was immediately challenged as inadequate by those it professed to assist. On February 13, 1970, a suit was filed in Hudson County Superior Court on behalf of Kenneth Robinson, a sixth-grade student in Jersey City's public schools. Almost four decades later, the issues in *Robinson v. Cahill* remain at the center of New Jersey's major political battles.

A NEW ROLE FOR THE STATE IN EDUCATION
POLICY

Robinson v. Cahill and its aftermath produced massive change in the state's role in education policy and spilled over to other areas. Education funding is central to the long-standing controversy about the entire state–local finance system. The tax system is inextricably connected to home rule—another perennial issue.

Home rule in the context of education deals with citizens' rights to determine resource commitments to their local schools by voting on school budgets. Those resources determine much about districts' curricula and other programs. New Jersey is one of only four states that allow voters a say on school spending.[14] Home rule also accounts for the presence of more than 600 separate school districts, one-third of which serve fewer than five hundred students. Texas, with twice the population and thirty-four times the land mass of New Jersey, has 188 districts. New Jersey has more school districts than Delaware, Pennsylvania, Maryland, and West Virginia combined.[15]

Home rule is also linked to the dark side of New Jersey's "tribal politics." Once a hostile rivalry between Protestant suburbs and Catholic cities, the rivalry by the 1970s was between largely white suburbs, mostly middle class or wealthy, and largely minority urban areas, mostly poorer. The *Robinson* plaintiffs argued that educational quality strongly affected social and economic mobility. The state thus had an obligation to equalize quality across communities irrespective of their resources. New Jersey's supreme court and recent governors have offered different but increasingly aggressive responses to that contention.

Education Policy in the Byrne Years

When Democrat Brendan Byrne took office in January 1974, there were already three court rulings in the matter of *Robinson v. Cahill.* The legislature's rejection of Commissioner Marburger and Republican primary voters' rejection of Governor Cahill (not unconnected events) had also left the education department leaderless for over a year.

In the first court ruling in January 1972, Superior Court Judge Theodore Botter had found the Bateman Bill violated the equal protection clauses in the federal and state constitutions. A funding formula so dependent on local property taxes discriminated against pupils in districts with low property wealth and imposed unequal burdens for "a common state purpose" on taxpayers in different localities. While acknowledging it was not the only factor, Botter wrote, "More money should make a significant difference in many poor districts . . . much can be done and doing more will cost more. Education is no exception to this fact of life."[16] Botter also accepted an *amicus* argument that the state constitution's guarantee of a "thorough and efficient" program of instruction for all pupils required the state to ensure a still–indeterminate level of educational quality. State policy thus had to address both funding strategies and the quality of education provided.

Botter's decision was immediately appealed to the state supreme court, which first ruled on *Robinson v. Cahill* in April 1973. By then, the U.S. Supreme Court had found in *Rodriguez v. San Antonio School District* that a Texas law similar to New Jersey's did not violate the federal constitution's equal protection clause. The New Jersey Supreme Court also rejected an equal protection argument grounded in the state constitution. However, it upheld Botter based on the "thorough and efficient" clause. The decision was unanimous.

The state supreme court accepted "the proposition that the quality of educational opportunity does depend in substantial measure upon the number of dollars invested" and further observed, "[W]e have been shown no other viable criterion for measuring compliance with the constitutional mandate." The court added, "The state must define in some discernible way the educational obligations and must compel the local school districts to raise the money necessary to provide that opportunity. The State has never spelled out the contents of the constitutionally mandated educational opportunity. Nor has the State required the school districts to raise money needed to achieve that unstated standard. . . . [O]ur present scheme is a patchy product reflecting provincial contests rather than a plan sensible only to the constitutional mandate."[17]

In another ruling in June 1973, the court required legislative action by December 31, 1974. To address the two decisions, Governor Byrne and the legislature had to devise an acceptable distribution scheme for state school aid, and fund it. They also had to define a "thorough and efficient" education, and how to measure and monitor it. All proved to be agonizing exercises.

The December 1974 court "deadline" was only a beginning. New court deadlines, failed tax plans, and unacceptable funding schemes came and went for two more years. Finally, the supreme court, in its seventh ruling in Robinson, closed all public schools on July 1, 1976. Eight days later and three years after the court's first "deadline," an acceptable school-funding plan was enacted. It was embodied in the Public School Education Act of 1975 (known as Chapter 212) and the income tax law of 1976.

The new funding scheme used state aid to further equalize school districts' tax capacity. Whereas the old plan favored districts with poor children, the new scheme favored districts with low property values per pupil—which, along with cities, included middle-class residential suburbs with few commercial ratables.[18] As Jersey City, Kenneth Robinson's home district, illustrates, poorer urban districts gained little additional revenue when Chapter 212 replaced the Bateman Bill, but the state picked up a larger proportion of their costs. By the 1975–1976 school year, when the Bateman Bill was fully phased in, Jersey City got 43 percent of its total school funds from Trenton and spent at a rate 94 percent of the statewide average. A year later, under Chapter 212, the state financed 58 percent of its budget, and Jersey City was spending at a rate equal to 97 percent of the average district.[19]

With tax capacity equalization accomplished, it was left to individual districts to decide how much capacity to tap. Districts could choose their own local taxing and spending levels and thus maintain or even exacerbate expenditure disparities. "Minimum state aid"—an equalization aid floor for every district regardless of wealth—was included to get suburban support for the entire package. For similar reasons, state aid was held to an average of 40 percent of education costs, as opposed to the 50 percent national average.

The new plan bespoke political pragmatism. To achieve property tax relief for urban taxpayers, it distributed considerable aid to middle-class suburbs. It respected home rule by leaving to municipalities decisions about the level of resources to commit to education. It gained support for the income tax from the NJEA (which had earlier opposed it in fear of antagonizing some legislative allies) after veiled threats to end full state payment of teacher pensions. While not a perfect plan from a "good government" point of view, it had the political virtue of leaving everyone feeling they had won something.

Similar prudence characterized the approach to defining and monitoring "thorough and efficient" education. Cahill's conflicts with the legislature made Byrne leery of state standards. The NJEA, which gave Byrne its first formal gubernatorial endorsement, was leading the charge against state testing. Still, Byrne needed some Republican votes for the income tax that was the linchpin of the funding scheme—both to pass it and to give it legitimacy. Ever suspicious of "throwing money" at social problems, the Republicans demanded "accountability" in return for new state school funds—through measurable education standards and testing.

In 1975, while still dickering over funding schemes, the legislature had passed a "T&E law" defining "a thorough and efficient education." Key phrases in the law—"reasonable levels of proficiency in the basic communication and computational skills," "program breadth to develop individual talents and abilities," "evaluation and monitoring of programs at both state and local levels," and "annual testing for achievement in basic skills areas"—were left to bureaucrats to clarify; in this case, in regulations to be developed by the Department of Education.[20]

Educational "progress" can be gauged by means of "input," "output," or "process" measures. "Inputs" are quantitative measures of facilities, staff, curricular richness, and other tangibles—all easily translatable into money. "Outputs" are also quantitative measures, such as dropout rates and test scores. "Process" measures focus on qualitative relationships between teachers, children, schools, and the community. They emphasize consensual goal setting and curricular planning. All these approaches had their partisans in New Jersey.

In *Robinson*, the state supreme court had said that inputs—defined as more money, more equally distributed—was the only "viable criterion" it had been shown for assuring a "thorough and efficient" education. The NJEA also favored input measures implying more and better-paid staff, more materials, and improved physical plants. Teachers asserted that quantitative testing did not measure different kinds of abilities or creativity and encouraged mediocrity and "teaching to the test." It also argued that failing state tests would contribute, particularly in the case of minority students, to a sense of inadequacy. Unspoken was the fear that student test scores might also be used to evaluate teachers.

Output measures were favored by the unusual alliance that had coalesced around Commissioner Marburger—Republicans, urban reformers, the school boards association, and business groups. Republicans and school board members saw test scores as a way to enforce accountability. Business groups thought them the best way to assure a trained workforce. The reformers, led by Newark's Urban Coalition and the Education Law Center (which had prepared the "thorough and efficient" *amicus* brief) believed testing could identify children needing help and make the state responsible for setting skill floors and providing the resources needed to reach them.

Developing the Byrne administration's position on how to define a thorough and efficient education fell to Fred Burke, who became education commissioner in 1975. Burke was acutely sensitive to the politics of the issue. In devising the administrative code for T&E, Burke strongly inclined toward "process" measures. He argued that "education" was too subtle to measure by either inputs or outputs and emphasized local goal setting and curricular decisions as the key elements of T&E. Process measures were less easily quantifiable and avoided the political minefields of the other choices.

Those favoring outputs won the first battles. In March 1976, Republican Assemblyman Tom Kean introduced a bill drafted by the Education Law Center mandating "minimum basic skills" tests and state standards. The bill had eighteen Republican cosponsors. Although Burke opposed it, Governor Byrne knew it was the price for Republican support of the income tax, and endorsed it. Within two weeks, it passed the assembly overwhelmingly. However, when the bill reached the senate two months later, NJEA allies managed to amend it to allow local districts to establish local "interim goals" and remediation programs. This amendment accorded with Commissioner Burke's plan for "state guidelines and local standards," and was widely seen as an NJEA victory.

The seventh draft of the administrative code, finally adopted by the state board of education in February 1978, defined T&E primarily in process terms. The state was to monitor all schools annually on over three hundred items, including financial management, curriculum planning, goal setting, and facilities planning, as well as basic skills achievement. Passing scores for the basic skills tests were set low enough that urban pass rates would not be fatally embarrassing, but high enough to require more tangible support for schools. A study of participants in local goal-setting meetings found many to be NJEA members or their relatives.[21]

Thus, all the criteria for assessing a "thorough and efficient" education as well as their supporting clienteles got some attention, but "process" measures—those least subject to easy quantification—dominated. By the time Byrne left office in January 1982, advocates of outcome measures had again made some headway. High school graduation requirements were increased, and plans were in the works for stiffer assessment tests. NJEA moved even further into a "union mentality" with a 1979 decision to admit school clerical workers, bus drivers, cafeteria workers and aides.

Education Policy in the Kean Years

When Republican Tom Kean succeeded Brendan Byrne in January 1982, the governorship passed to a leading advocate of "outcome" measures. A former teacher, doctoral candidate in education, and chair of the assembly education committee, the new governor had unusual expertise in education policy.

American schooling was becoming a national concern as Kean took office. *A Nation At Risk*, a federal study likening the effects of American educational failures to destruction by an invading enemy, was published about a year later, and the National Governors' Association made education a special focus. As "the education governor," Kean sponsored more than forty initiatives that drew national attention.[22] The Kean years had all the requirements for policy breakthroughs—a widely recognized problem, a receptive national mood, specialists with proposals at the ready, and an entrepreneur to push them.[23]

The Kean administration inaugurated a more difficult high school proficiency test all students had to pass in order to graduate. An annual school report card, sent to each student's home and printed in the state's newspapers, gave comparative information on schools' test scores, dropout rates, percentage of graduates pursuing higher education, and the like. The three hundred items on the "process" advocates' monitoring list were reduced to fifty-two. Districts passing monitoring gained certification for five years rather than one. In return for this reduced intrusiveness, failing systems had to remedy deficiencies in a reasonable time or face state takeover of their schools for at least five years. That controversial plan spawned a long legislative battle but finally passed when grievance procedures and job security for teachers and administrators were included.

In May 1988, Commissioner Cooperman moved to take over the Jersey City school system on the grounds that it was "not providing a thorough and efficient education for its children." Cooperman accused the district of fiscal mismanagement, political interference, and inadequate response to monitoring. In October 1989, after more than a year of administrative law hearings, state takeover of the district occurred—the first in American history—with Governor Kean condemning Jersey City for committing "educational child abuse."[24] In 1991, Paterson became the second district taken over by the state. Newark joined the list in 1995.

Kean pointed proudly to improved educational "outcomes" during his tenure. The proportion of students passing all sections of the high school proficiency test on their first attempt rose from 38 percent in 1986 to 68 percent in 1989. Average scores on the Scholastic Aptitude Test rose 30 points from 1981's historic low—the seventh highest increase among the twenty-two states where the SAT was the dominant test for college-bound students.[25]

Noted for his civility and reluctance to criticize, Kean became sufficiently confident of his political support and policy accomplishments to issue a savage public attack on the NJEA and step up condemnation of local school boards and administrators he believed were "ripping off the taxpayers."[26] However, the governor's opponents had not disappeared, just as Kean had bided his time while advocates of "local standards" and "process" measures held the upper hand. When appraisals of Kean's record began to appear in 1989, so did the arguments of the 1970s. Former allies of Fred Burke called his accomplishments "modest." Their contention that better test scores, particularly in urban areas, were partly a product of "teaching to the test" or statistical artifice had some confirmation.[27]

The critics reproached Kean for forcing the same standards on all students "regardless of their interests or aptitudes" and for failing to recognize that test failures "may be discouraging." Urban schools, they argued, were pouring scarce resources into teaching to the test and ignoring curricular depth and breadth. Seventy percent of Jersey City's school buildings pre-dated World War I, and Newark's Burnett School, where Abraham Lincoln gave an informal address on his way to his 1861 inauguration, was one of nine Newark schools that had been in service for at least 120 years. New Jersey was one of only two states where de facto segregation was increasing. Its schools were the fourth most segregated in the nation, making "the term urban schools . . . a euphemism for minority schools."[28]

Although spending in some urban school districts had reached or even exceeded state averages, the gulfs between them and the "lighthouse" districts in the wealthiest suburbs had grown. For example, spending per pupil in the city of Camden, which was 79 percent of that in neighboring Cherry Hill in 1975–1976, had dropped to 68 percent of the Cherry Hill level by 1989–1990.[29] In the view of the urban reformers, ever-worsening educational and social problems in the cities meant their students must have the same educational opportunity as those in the lighthouse districts. That opportunity was properly measured in "inputs"—or dollars.

These arguments did not enjoy much political currency during the 1980s, but urban advocates were counting on the New Jersey Supreme Court to make their case. Even before Kean became governor, and while Fred Burke was still education commissioner, a challenge to *Robinson v. Cahill* brought by the Education Law Center began its journey through the courts in February 1981. This new case, *Abbott v. Burke*, claimed the *Robinson* remedy did not ensure urban students a "thorough and efficient" edu-cation. It reiterated that Chapter 212 violated the state constitution's equal protection and antidiscrimination clauses. When the case reached the supreme court in 1985, the justices remanded it to an administrative law proceeding. After nine months of hearings, Administrative Law Judge Steven Lefelt rendered a 607-page decision in August 1988.

Lefelt ruled for the plaintiffs, writing that "[t]he expenditure differ-ences are in some cases greater now than before Chapter 212 was enacted. I have concluded that the funding law contains systemic defects which contribute to the continued inequity." Lefelt also addressed the controversy over "input" versus "outcome" measures, noting "a pattern where children in high wealth communities enjoy high levels of expenditures and other educational inputs and children in low-wealth communities receive low levels of school expenditures and inputs." He went on, "The Constitution does not require that the desired output be measurable on standardized tests. An opportunity for every student to achieve this outcome is all that the political system must provide."[30]

Not surprisingly, Commissioner Cooperman rejected Lefelt's reasoning in his response to the ruling on February 3, 1989: "No one has ever determined there is a minimum amount of funding necessary to provide a thorough and efficient education. Rather, the opposite is true. If a district is found to meet the criteria established by the State for T&E, then its spending is, by legal definition, adequate."[31] T&E should thus be measured by whether a district met the minimum requirements of the 1975 T&E law, which the supreme court had accepted as part of the *Robinson* remedy. "Inputs" like computers or elementary school guidance counselors might be desirable, but the constitution did not mandate them. Cooperman also called unwillingness on the part of some urban districts to meet the average district tax effort a "clear moral failure."[32]

The state board of education upheld Cooperman but also recommended that in years of funding shortfalls, minimum aid to the wealthiest districts should be eliminated before cutting equalization aid. The plaintiffs rejected these proposals and, with administrative law procedures exhausted, the supreme court reheard *Abbott* on September 25, 1989—less than two months before the November gubernatorial election. Although expected to do so some months earlier, the court did not issue its decision until June 5, 1990.

Written by Chief Justice Robert Wilentz, the decision, like the first ruling in *Robinson* by seven different justices seventeen years earlier, was unanimous. It found that Raymond Abbott, like Kenneth Robinson before him, had been denied a through and efficient education. Abbott, who was a twelve-year-old student in Camden when the suit was filed in 1981, had dropped out of school in eleventh grade. He received the news in the Camden County Jail, where he was serving time for violating parole after a previous conviction for burglary.

The justices agreed with the defendants that Chapter 212 did not violate the state constitution's equal protection clause or state antidiscrimination laws, nor was there evidence of a general failure to provide a "thorough and efficient" education. However, they saw "absolutely no question that we are failing to provide the students in the poorer urban districts with the kind of education that anyone could call thorough and efficient." Acknowledging pervasive mismanagement in some urban districts, the justices ruled that their students must receive more resources anyway:

"They are entitled to pass or fail with at least the same amount of money as their competitors." The court went on to define which students were, in terms of dollar "inputs," being denied a "thorough and efficient" education. They relied on data from the Department of Education dividing school districts into eight economic district factor groups (DFGs), labeled A (lowest socioeconomic status) through J (highest socioeconomic status). The court required that in Groups A and B, "the assured funding per pupil should be substantially equivalent to that spent in those districts providing the kind of education these students need, funding that approximates the average net current expense budgets of school districts in district factor groups I and J."

The justices also found the "minimum aid" distributed to the wealthiest districts unconstitutional. However, they rejected the plaintiffs' request to forbid any district from spending more than 5 percent above or below the state average per pupil: "The record convinces us of a failure of a thorough and efficient education only in the poorer urban districts. We have no right to extend the remedy any further . . . because of considerations of fairness unrelated to the constitutional command."

The legislature was given a year to "devise any remedy . . . as long as it achieves a thorough and efficient education as defined herein for poorer urban districts." The program could be phased in over five years. New Jersey's supreme court thus became the first to define educational equity for students in poor districts as the level of effort on behalf of students in the wealthiest districts.

In concluding their landmark opinion, the justices noted that with New Jersey's minority student population approaching one-third of all students—highly concentrated in urban districts—"it is not just that their future depends on the state, the state's future depends on them. . . . After all the analyses are completed, we are still left with these students and their lives. They are not being educated. Our constitution says they must be."[33]

In first remanding *Abbott* to the administrative law process, the court had hoped the governor and legislature could shape a constitutionally acceptable program, but that had not worked. The Cooperman-Kean proposals had tried to anticipate the likely ruling but were unacceptable to the plaintiffs. Those following the case assumed the new governor and legislature would use the *Abbott* decision, when it came, as political "cover" for whatever tax increases were needed—as they had during the 1970s with *Robinson*. This did not turn out to be the case.

The Quality Education Act: Its Genesis and Dismantling

While the state awaited the court's decision, Democrat Jim Florio easily won the governor's contest in November 1989. Neither candidate made education a campaign theme, but when asked directly about *Abbott*, the Democratic standard-bearer predicted that the court would throw out the existing school-aid formula. However, Florio said, he "would stand by his no-new-taxes pledge even if that happens and would not seek to raise taxes." He said a full-scale state audit "would root out millions of dollars in waste and inefficiency," producing the money for school aid and property tax relief.[34]

In March 1990, the governor declared urban education his highest priority. Pointing to the state's deep cleavages, Florio asserted, "We want to have one New Jersey as opposed to multiple New Jerseys. . . . We don't have one New Jersey in terms of its education system." Florio also advocated more equalized "inputs," saying uniform outcomes could not be required without uniform resources. He suspended the school-monitoring system, ordered it redesigned, and spoke critically of "teaching to the test." Acknowledging urban–suburban hostilities, the governor said, "The political task that I have is to go out and sell all the people that it is not 'us and them'—it is us."[35]

However, Governor Florio did not "sell" a plan for a "One New Jersey" educational policy, nor did he wait for an audit to find new revenues. Rather, he proposed $1.4 billion in increased income taxes, dedicated to education aid, and property tax relief as part of a $2.8 billion tax package. Before the *Abbott* decision was handed down, Florio revealed his vehicle for educational reform—the Quality Education Act (QEA). The complex QEA was pushed through the legislature in twenty-two days and passed in June 1990 with no Republican support. With the new income tax revenue, the state could provide about half of all education dollars, and lower some individuals' property taxes.

To be implemented over four years, almost half the new aid would go to thirty urban districts with low educational inputs—decaying school buildings, inexperienced teachers, outdated curricula, and inadequate equipment. The other half would go to middle-class districts, mostly in the southern half of the state where property values were lower. About one-quarter of all districts, with one-fifth of the students, would gradually lose all state equalization aid over four years. The number of districts affected and the plan's cost went far beyond the mandate of *Abbott v. Burke*.

Dissatisfaction with QEA would thus be directed not at the court but at the Democratic governor and legislature. As school boards, teachers, and citizens grasped QEA's impact on individual communities, there was a crescendo of outrage—some of it from unlikely quarters. Wealthy, middle-class, and even poor urban districts all had loud objections to the new revenue-raising and revenue-allocation schemes.

Chapter 212—the existing system—was, as we have described, a capacity-equalizing formula. Within this formula, many districts— particularly in older cities and suburbs—chose to set relatively low school taxes because of the high cost of other municipal services—a problem called "municipal overburden." Others did not tax near capacity because residents voted down school budgets, the only portion of the local property tax that could be lowered by a public referendum. Still others had low tax-collection rates. Differences in school spending thus arose based on how much of their tax capacity local districts chose to tap, or school boards and voters would approve.

In contrast, QEA was a foundation formula that guaranteed equal support of all students, regardless of local tax effort. Districts had to raise a local "fair share," based on aggregate property values and income levels; when added to state aid, the "fair share" achieved the foundation amounts. By specifying each district's "fair share," QEA virtually set school tax rates, eliminating most local discretion. "Local leeway" provisions specified how much revenue above the foundation level districts were permitted to raise.

QEA required all districts to spend at a specified foundation level within five years, unless they could demonstrate that a "thorough and efficient" education was provided for less. State aid was indexed at 1 percent above the average state increase in per capita income (PCI). To comply with *Abbott*, thirty special needs districts were granted 5 percent more foundation aid than the rest of the state. The special needs districts were also permitted to increase their own spending annually at twice the PCI increase, while the wealthiest districts were held to the PCI increase.

Pension funding and compensatory education formulas were other important elements of QEA. The state had paid the full cost of teacher retirement plans since 1955. By 1990, this amounted to $900 million, or one-quarter of all state aid. QEA specified that henceforth, individual school districts would assume these costs. Florio believed this would exert discipline on salary negotiations, since local districts could no longer negotiate with the state's pension money. Additionally, the definition of at-risk students eligible for compensatory aid was changed from those with failing test scores to those eligible for free school lunches.

Various QEA provisions were unpopular in almost every district in the state. Wealthy districts saw a triple whammy—loss of minimum aid, loss of all pension aid, and thus inevitably higher local property taxes. Superintendents in these lighthouse districts also asserted that educational leveling down would inevitably occur when residents rejected huge property tax increases: "Average education throughout the state is not wise public policy. Nor is it required by *Abbott v. Burke*."[36]

Middle-income districts discovered that much of their "increased aid" would be swallowed up by pension costs and remedial programs for students who did not qualify for free lunches. The cap on annual state aid increases at 1 percent above PCI was well below recent growth, especially for teacher salaries and pensions.[37] NJEA claimed that with the pension money removed, QEA provided only $200 million in new money at a full funding level—almost all of it to the special needs districts. It called the middle-income aid "smoke and mirrors" to subsidize thirty districts.[38]

Even many special needs districts were unhappy with QEA. Some would have to raise property taxes to meet their "fair share." Irvington calculated it would have to increase property taxes by $6.1 million to receive $5.8 million in new state aid. Trenton learned that the $3 million increase needed to reach its "fair share" would require a 13 percent property tax increase in the first year of QEA.[39]

Some urban advocates argued QEA was not enough. Marilyn Morheuser, lead attorney for the *Abbott* plaintiffs, testified to the Assembly Education Committee that forcing poor districts to raise taxes defied the court's decree that funding in poor urban districts cannot depend on the budgeting and taxing decisions of local school boards. Further, QEA did not guarantee per-pupil spending parity between the poorest and wealthiest districts.

Underlying the controversies were historic animosities of region, race, and class. In wealthy Bergen County in the north, many would see their income taxes double to pay for QEA, but seventy-one of Bergen's seventy-eight school districts would lose all equalization aid. Conversely, three-quarters of the new aid, disproportionately financed by Bergen residents, would be flowing to special needs districts and five counties in the south with low average incomes and property values.

The GOP's senate minority leader, John Dorsey of Morris (another hard-hit wealthy northern county), enraged many but said what others thought when he declared QEA and *Abbott* required "working class people in middle class communities who drive around in Fords to buy Mercedes for people in the poorest cities because they don't have cars."[40] A Monmouth County Democratic assemblyman called the cuts to his wealthy district the act of "almost a socialist state," and proclaimed, "This is New Jersey, this is not Moscow in 1950."[41]

Such comments led Education Commissioner John Ellis and some urban legislators to call the opposition racist. Race was also an unspoken issue when Ellis and Florio urged districts to consolidate for economic reasons, and it became more overt when public advocate Wilfredo Caraballo announced his office was analyzing which de facto segregated districts could be integrated by suits seeking regionalization as a remedy.[42] School-consolidation schemes in New Jersey had been as unpopular as tax increases. They often resulted in more rather than fewer districts, as residents refused to include local elementary schools in newly regionalized high school districts.[43]

Given the predictable public protest, how did QEA come about? Three major forces shaped the Florio plan. First was the governor's personal style. Whereas his predecessor, Tom Kean, was reluctant to take political risks or act decisively until the last possible moment, Florio put good policy above good politics. His fifteen-year congressional career showed a preference for comprehensive rather than incremental solutions. He developed a reputation for disdaining those who did not agree with him and being willing to lose control of issues rather than negotiate or compromise. Introducing "correct" policies gradually was anathema to Florio. Second, Florio and his advisors had embraced a political theory advocated by an unlikely coalition of Democratic and Republican political strategists and policy analysts—progressive populism. Popularized in Kevin Phillips's best-selling book, *The Politics of Rich and Poor*, it held that Reagan-era "greed" and tax cuts aimed at the wealthy had antagonized a hard-pressed middle class, which was ready to join in a rebellion against the rich. Those who could forge and lead this majority would win both political and policy battles. Education policy was a crucial test of the theory. Educational opportunity was perhaps the most universally held American value. Wealthy school districts in New Jersey spent more on their schools but taxed at a lower rate than did middle class districts. Third, political factors permitted the governor to take dramatic action. Florio's style led him to exercise his constitutional powers more fully than had his more pragmatic predecessors. A one-time high school dropout and representative of the city of Camden, he understood the resentment of city dwellers and South Jerseyans toward wealthy northern suburbanites. A landslide victory and the "honeymoon period" new executives enjoy helped him wield his powers. Finally, for the first time in a decade, urban Democrats led both houses of the legislature. Florio's fund-raising ability as governor fueled Democratic campaigns. It made legislators pause before antagonizing him. Narrow majorities in both houses also inspired more partisan coherence than larger ones would have. Thus, despite severe qualms about constituents' reactions, almost all suburban Democrats swallowed their trepidations and voted for the tax package and the QEA.

Public protest from every quarter and massive Democratic defeats in 1990's state and local elections spelled doom for the QEA before it went into effect. In January 1991, Senate President John Lynch and Majority Leader Daniel Dalton introduced legislation to divert almost 40 percent of new QEA money directly to municipalities for property tax relief. Dalton, a Florio protégé from Camden County, had been the QEA's senate sponsor. He now said he had not understood all its implications.[44] Lynch traveled the state extolling the new property tax relief and criticizing teachers' wage and benefit demands, particularly during a recession.[45]

After weeks of bicameral negotiation with the governor on the sidelines, the legislature in mid-March passed a package of major amendments known as QEA 2 by the minimum necessary vote in both houses.[46] The bills again passed with almost unanimous Democratic support, and with all Republicans opposed or abstaining. They moved $360 million of new school aid into a statewide property tax relief fund and guaranteed state funding of teacher pensions for at least two years. Of QEA's remaining $830 million, another $229 million also went to property tax reduction because of new education spending caps contained in the amendments.

Depending on districts' current spending levels, the amendments capped annual spending increases at between 7.5 and 9 percent for all but the 30 special needs districts. These urban districts could increase spending at a rate between 9.7 and 22 percent to achieve parity with the wealthiest districts within five years. In many districts, even the poorest, the caps meant the remaining new money covered little more than contractual salary increases and higher insurance costs. In Camden, often cited as the state's educational worst case, the caps and diversion of funds to property tax relief cut municipal property taxes by 60 percent but reduced new school aid from $50 million to $24.8 million.[47] The net effect, according to the director of school finance in the education department, was "an outflow of aid from the urban districts . . . to the middle and upper-wealth districts," compared with the QEA's original provisions.[48]

The plaintiffs in *Abbott* agreed, and in June 1991 they returned to the supreme court. Lead attorney Marilyn Morheuser asked the court to "assure prompt vindication of plaintiffs' constitutional rights. . . . [T]he court must set in motion a remedial process which will vindicate these rights, even if the Legislature fails to act in a constitutionally sufficient manner."[49] The justices' split decision to remand the case to a trial court in Mercer County removed the high tribunal from the education spotlight for a time, and once again gave the political process time to work its will.

In the summer of 1993, as the gubernatorial campaign was heating up, Superior Court Judge Paul G. Levy declared that QEA 2 was unconstitutional because it did not assure that funding for the special needs districts would reach the level of the wealthiest districts within five years as required, and referred the case back to the state supreme court. The following year, in its second major *Abbott* ruling, that court also rejected QEA 2 as a constitutional basis for meeting its mandate and ordered that the spending gap be closed by 1997.[50]

The Whitman and McGreevey Years: The Comprehensive Educational Improvement and Financing Act

Republican Governor Christie Whitman took office in January 1994. Like Governor Kean and his education commissioner, Saul Cooperman, she and her commissioner of education, Leo Klagholz, believed that the definition of a "thorough and efficient" education offered by the legislature in 1975 and accepted by the court as part of a remedy, was the key to achieving a constitutional settlement. Rather than funding levels, the 1975 "T&E" law emphasized skills proficiency, program breadth, evaluation and assessment, and annual testing for achievement of basic skills. The Whitman administration set out to devise a funding plan that met those criteria and used them rather than dollars as the benchmark of a "thorough and efficient" education. As Klagholz, in reference to one of the lighthouse districts, asked rhetorically, "Livingston has [A]stroturf on its football field. Is that guaranteed by the constitution?"[51]

The scheme presented by Klagholz and Whitman in November 1995 had three parts: core curriculum standards equating to a "thorough and efficient education," a funding formula to determine the cost of meeting the curriculum standards, and a district model. The curriculum standards in eight subject areas were developed by the Department of Education. The funding formula, which averaged $7,200 per student was said to be based on the estimated cost of achieving the curriculum standards. Finally, the plan included a "district model," which provided detailed accountings of how many staff members of various types a 500-student school should have to meet the standards, and what they should be paid, to achieve a thorough and efficient education with the funding per student that the state allowed. These amounts were in FY 1993–1994 dollars and were to be adjusted annually. The $7,200 average figure compared to actual district expenditures in 1994–1995 that ranged from $4,900 to $16,100 per pupil.

Each district would receive the state aid required to spend the allowable amount after taking into account the local district's contribution. The local contribution would be determined by calculations based on property tax rates, income, and the total value of property in the district. There would no longer be school elections to ratify this basic budget. If, however, a district wished to spend more than the state and local allocation needed to meet the curriculum standards, and to raise those funds locally, approval of the voters would have to be sought for that excess amount.

If voters rejected these expenditures for "extras," their decision would be final. Municipal government officials, who had traditionally determined final school budgets if a school board's budget proposal was defeated, would no longer play a role. In response to complaints that the proposal was less a funding formula than a theoretical discussion, two months later the Department of Education issued a refinement that specified skills and knowledge for each grade level in all subjects in the core curriculum. In addition, the department produced a new and more complex district model, based on a K–12 district of 3,075 students in three elementary schools, a middle school, and a high school.

As legislators contemplated this plan, a variety of constituencies voiced opposition to its provisions.[52] Many educators argued that the plan had begun with a predetermined budget and that budget had driven the program components of a "thorough and efficient education," rather than the other way around. The NJEA announced that the district model resembled only about 7 percent of real districts, and the plan would cause radical changes in the rest. The Garden State Coalition, representing the lighthouse districts, worried that they would lose what they regarded as essential programs and personnel if voters were told they were "constitutionally unnecessary." Middle-income districts with especially high property tax rates contended that the plan discriminated against them. The special needs districts argued that by equalizing state funding, the very designation "special needs" would cease to have any meaning.

Ernest Reock, an authority on New Jersey school finance, calculated that three-quarters of all of the districts in the state, including most of the special needs districts, already spent more than the plan's limits, adding to an aggregate of $869 million more statewide. It was likely that this fact alone would cause the supreme court to reject the plan. In the year of the 1990 *Abbott* decision, the special needs districts had been spending at a rate 70 percent that of the lighthouse districts, a figure that was projected to rise to 89 percent in 1996. That had not been enough for the supreme court, which had demanded parity.

To address some of these issues, the legislature and the governor restored the system of taxpayer votes on the total budget, subject to appeal to municipal authorities, but required that "excess" spending be identified and voted upon in separate ballot questions. The bill was also amended to offer up to $300,000 in extra funds to districts that spent no more than 15 percent above the state average but taxed property owners at more than 30 percent above the state equalized tax rate. The final plan also capped the amount by which districts could raise their total annual budgets at inflation plus enrollment growth but allowed them to go over those limits with approval from the state department of education.

The Comprehensive Educational Improvement and Financing Act (CEIFA) of 1996, was approved by both houses of the legislature on party-line votes. It provided for $4.9 billion in state aid to education for the 1997–1998 school year, $286 million more than had originally been included in the FY 1998 budget. Of this sum, $140 million was directed to the special needs districts, and the rest distributed to all the other districts in the state. Governor Whitman signed it on December 20.

While the state was awaiting the court's reaction to the new funding statute, voters went to the polls in April 1998 and approved 76 percent of all the budgets on the ballot, the best approval rate since 1986. In the 144 districts where residents voted on a total of 176 separate questions specifying extra funding for programs not included in the state standards, two-thirds of the questions were approved. While Governor Whitman said happily, "The sky did not fall as the doomsayers predicted. . . . [T]he process worked exactly as it was supposed to," the executive director of the New Jersey Association of School Administrators predicted that the election outcomes would be seen by the courts as evidence that the spending gap between rich and poor districts would never close, and indeed would get progressively worse.[53]

A month later, on May 14, the Supreme Court did indeed declare CEIFA unconstitutional. In a 5–1 decision, the majority found that the state curriculum standards were an acceptable definition of a "thorough and efficient education" and could, over time, offer a constitutionally acceptable definition of equity. However, the court ruled that the law's funding levels bore no relationship to the amount actually needed to meet the standards in the special needs districts. In response to the state's argument that the average spending levels in middle-income districts was a better yardstick than the average in the 120 wealthiest districts, the majority declared, "We reject the state's invitation to turn a blind eye to the most successful districts in the state." Curricular standards, while a promising strategy, did "not ensure any substantive level of achievement. Real achievement still depends on the sufficiency of educational resources."

The justices concluded, "The state has had seven years to comply with a remedy intended to address, albeit partially, a profound deprivation that has continued for at least twenty-five years. The remedy of increased funding for educational improvement should not be delayed any further." The court ordered the state to ensure that by July 1997 the special needs districts would have the resources to spend at least as much per pupil as the average expenditure in the richest districts. A superior court judge, acting as a special master was to oversee the Department of Education's research on the additional funds to be provided to the special needs districts and to assess the cost of bringing their physical facilities up to par.[54]

Opinion on the decision was again mixed. The Education Law Center, which had represented the plaintiffs in all of the major cases since 1973, also expressed its approval of curriculum standards and agreed that New Jersey should not just "throw money" into the urban schools. On the other hand, it urged the state to consult closely with those in the special needs districts and to abandon a "command and control approach."[55] Justice Marie Garibaldi, the court's lone dissenter in *Abbott IV*, delivered one of the more scathing critiques when she wrote, "There is scant evidence that the children have received the benefit of those expenditures. The experiment of parity in spending has failed. . . . For the first time, the driving force is educational standards and not the further continuance of a failed scheme."[56]

Two weeks after the decision, Whitman announced that the state would not challenge the court plan but would require that each special needs district submit a plan to the Department of Education outlining the exact uses of the additional funds. A team of state auditors would monitor their spending. The governor added, "We are not going to divert any money from any program in any district to come up with the supplementary funds to meet the Abbott decision. Let me emphasize that nothing will change for the 580-plus districts that are not part of this Abbott remedy."[57]

In January 1998, the special master, Judge Michael Patrick King, recommended a series of programs costing an additional $312 million annually, along with $2.4 billion in facilities upgrades in what had come to be known as the Abbott districts. He called for immediate adoption of full-day kindergarten classes as well as all-day preschool programs for children aged three and four. Judge King described the state's position on *Abbott v. Burke* as "likely driven by a certain measure of political pragmatism," while the Education Law Center demonstrated "optimistic, well-meaning idealism." He wrote that his decision could be "viewed in a certain sense as a compromise but the court is always aware that state constitutional rights cannot be discounted with the same currency as commercial or political utility."[58]

Four months later, the supreme court issued *Abbott v. Burke V.* Reflecting the court's historical blend of judicial activism and political realism, it was a unanimous ruling that allowed "both sides to declare victory."[59] The state pledged to continue the spending parity between the special needs and lighthouse districts finally achieved in 1997 and promised bond issues to finance a massive school construction program, as well as a variety of social service and enrichment initiatives. In return, the court agreed to accept curricular reform as the formal definition of a "thorough and efficient" education and restored responsibility for implementation to the state Department Of Education.

The chorus of support for the ruling included both the lead attorney for the plaintiffs and the state attorney general, who declared, "It's time not only to end the chapter but close the book."[60] It remains to be seen if continuing education litigation will require another book, but lengthy appendices to the volume were already in the works even before the fifth *Abbott* decision was issued.

Early in 1998, a coalition of middle-income districts filed suit in Mercer County Superior Court, arguing in *Stubaus v. Whitman* that the CEIFA formula violated the constitution's equal protection clause by penalizing areas with high incomes but few ratables and low property tax bases. The trial judge ruled against the plaintiffs and was upheld on appeal in 2001, continuing the court's resistance to equal protection claims.[61] Another case filed at about the same time, *Bacon v. Department of Education*, would have a much greater impact.

Bacon was brought to superior court on behalf of seventeen districts, mostly rural towns in South Jersey, which contended that their students suffered from the same disadvantages as those in the urban Abbott districts. For example, one of the petitioners, Woodbine, had the second lowest per capita income in the state after Camden. The districts argued that they too should be eligible for lighthouse district–level funding, full funding of school construction costs, and universal preschool. The case was remanded to an administrative law proceeding that went thorough four decisions and appeals for more than six years. In 2004, Governor McGreevey's education commissioner, William Librera, eventually agreed to add one of the districts to the Abbott list.[62] The sixteen others again appealed Librera's finding to the state board of education which, in a dramatic fifth decision on Bacon in 2006, called unanimously and urgently for a more expansive definition of T&E and a new funding scheme to replace CEIFA. While agreeing with the districts' contentions, the board did not recommend immediate additional funding for the Bacon districts. Instead, it wrote,

> We have found that our obligations under the New Jersey Constitution . . . require that we do more than decide the appeal in this case and preclude us from ignoring the fact that there are students in other school districts not involved in the litigation who are suffering similar educational inadequacies and whose communities do not have sufficient resources to address them. We have also found that to do so would be to contribute to the perpetuation of a fragmented system that does not conform to the constitutional mandate. We have concluded that it is necessary to begin the process that will ultimately result in the establishment of a unified system that ensures the provision of a constitutionally adequate education and equal educational opportunity for all students in New Jersey regardless of the district in which they live or the economic circumstances under which they were born.

The decision continued,

> In initiating this process, we recognize that the State Board by itself
> cannot effectuate the changes that are necessary to establish a unified
> system for public education that fulfills the constitutional mandate
> both with respect to the substantive education that must be provi-
> ded and the resources necessary to support such a system. Nonethe-
> less, by our decision, we take the first step toward achieving that
> goal.[63]

As if to make the board's major points, while the *Bacon* appeal was
proceeding some Democratic lawmakers in North Jersey moved to authorize and fund a new category of "Abbott rim districts." The rim districts
bordered at least three Abbott districts and had to meet at least one of five
criteria, including large class sizes and high student mobility rates. Of the
five municipalities that met the standard, three were in Hudson County
and one each in Union and Passaic counties. Two of the towns' mayors also
served in the legislature; another town was adjacent to Newark, whose
mayor, Sharpe James, was also a state senator who served on the senate
budget committee; another was in Assembly Speaker Albio Sires's district.
Together, the five received twenty million dollars in new annual aid, and the
law specified that the cost factor determining that aid should rise 10 percent
in each succeeding year.[64]

Although the rim districts' advocates maintained that they shared the
problems of the Abbott districts, their strategy was also driven by the continuing failure to fully fund CEIFA and the years of flat state aid. It was a
concern that all school districts shared, and only the most newsworthy of
annual piecemeal efforts to give some relief to municipalities beset by
higher teacher salaries, other increased costs, and irate property taxpayers.[65]
A 2005 study from the Education Law Center observed that since 1988, ad
hoc legislative amendments to CEIFA had burgeoned "to the point that
what a district should receive, and why, becomes an exercise in legislative
archaeology."[66] A year later, another of the Center's reports made the point
even more strongly: "One might say that the state has no funding 'system'
in place at all, let alone one that is thorough and efficient." This latter study
noted that the failure to calculate the actual costs of a curricular program
for a through and efficient education, instead defining it as the amounts
spent in the wealthiest suburbs, "has effectively allowed the I and J districts
to set . . . the amount of parity aid."[67]

This financial state of affairs was already untenable by the time Jim McGreevey became governor in 2001. With the lighthouse districts annually raising the bar and expensive new programs mandated by *Abbott v. Burke V* to be financed, almost 60 percent all state education aid was going to the little more than 20 percent of New Jersey students in the special needs districts. To balance the budget, in FY 2002 the governor instituted a freeze on state aid to all municipalities other than the Abbott districts, which continued through FY 2007. There were predictable reactions from the five hundred-plus non-Abbott school districts that were forced to raise property taxes or cut programs to meet their increased expenses with proportionally less money from Trenton.

GOVERNOR CORZINE AND EDUCATION POLICY

When Governor Corzine assumed office, there was much to admire about New Jersey's schools. Among all U.S. states, they had the highest high school graduation rate and the largest number of students deemed academically ready for higher education. New Jersey's students were among the top ten in the nation in the proportion of high school seniors entering college immediately after graduation, as well as on national tests of fourth graders' proficiency in math and reading. The academic achievement of minority students on these exams was consistently higher than the national average. Between 1999 and 2006, the number of African American fourth-graders scoring at a proficient level doubled.[68]

Balanced against these admirable figures, though, was the "achievement gap" between poor students and others. Although the reading proficiency of disadvantaged students compared well to such students nationally, the gap in scores between them and other New Jersey students was the second highest among the states. It was precisely the kind of finding that had led to the establishment of the Abbott districts. And within that group of special needs districts, there were major disparities. Some, like Union City, where almost every child speaks Spanish at home and qualifies for subsidized school lunches, boasted vastly improved reading test scores equal to or better than those in the suburbs. Many Newark elementary schools met all of the state's proficiency benchmarks, while others met none. Apparent spectacular improvement in the Camden schools' test scores in 2005 spurred a state investigation that revealed pervasive cheating by administrators and teachers, and the superintendent and assistant superintendent were dismissed. Outside auditors hired by the state found thirteen million dollars in "questionable" expenditures by the Camden schools, including hundreds of thousands of dollars reported as paid to employees who had been dead for years.[69]

Despite the many successes to which Abbott districts could point, widespread coverage of events like those in Camden, the creation of the Abbott rim districts, and the state board of education's decision in *Bacon* were further grist for the mill of the unhappy property taxpayers in the more than five hundred non-Abbott districts, where almost 80 percent of New Jersey students benefited from only 42 percent of state aid to education. Studies confirmed their growing concerns. Each year that state aid was frozen, the shortfall became worse, quintupling between FY 2002 and FY 2005. In terms of total dollars, the middle-income districts were the most shortchanged. Controlling for the number of students in each type of district, non-Abbott poor districts fared the worst.[70]

Another analysis found that between FY 1993–1994 and FY 2004–2005, property values in the Abbott districts had increased by 71 percent, but the total property tax levy in those municipalities went up less than 8 percent. The average tax rate per thousand dollars of assessed valuation in the Abbott districts was $1.17 in 1993–1994, against an average statewide rate of $1.14, but by 2003–2004, the comparable figures were $0.74 and $1.07. In other words, "Abbott districts as a group have gone from being among the highest school tax rate communities to among the lowest."[71] Their total tax rates (for school, municipal, and county) also fell, in some cases to below the state average. As a result in 2006, the Department of Education announced that eight Abbott districts with overall tax rates at 110 percent or less of the state average would be required to raise more money locally and see cuts in their state aid.

During the summer of 2006, the legislature convened four joint committees to address property tax reform, which issued ninety-eight final recommendations in December. Although the largest number of education recommendations came from the committee on public school funding reform, the immense cost of public education required all four committees to address these issues. The central recommendation of the school funding panel accorded with the principles enunciated in the state board of education's *Bacon* decision. It called for an end to the "Abbott district" designation and a new and greatly simplified funding formula. Such a formula would set a foundation amount of the base cost of a thorough and efficient education, and add to it weights for the numbers of special education, at-risk, and students with limited English-language proficiency, as well as a cost-of-education index that reflected differences in the cost of living throughout the state.

The local share to be raised through property taxes would be based on the most current calculations of municipal property valuation and income per capita relative to the state median. The formula would impose a revenue cap, adjusted annually for changes in inflation and enrollment. Finally, districts would receive no less than they did before a new formula went into effect, and public votes on the school budget would be eliminated for those budgets at or under the cap.

The committee studying constitutional reform also endorsed the idea of a spending cap. The committee on government consolidation and shared services, noting that administrative costs in the schools had been increasing at double the rate of teacher salary increases, proposed the creation of executive superintendent positions in each county with oversight of administrative spending in localities. It drew back from the idea of consolidating the more than six hundred school districts into twenty-one county-based districts, despite testimony that significant savings could ensue. Finally, public employee benefits reform, the charge of the fourth committee, was the central concern of active and retired teachers and administrators, who could see negative changes in their health and pension plans.

By early 2007 it was obvious that the hope of replacing CEIFA for the 2007–2008 school year would be pushed back at least a year and perhaps even longer if there were questions about its constitutionality. In his FY 2008 budget proposal, Governor Corzine called for a 3 percent increase in funding for all districts, and, adopting the recommendations in *Bacon*, he put additional money into a new category called Targeted At Risk Aid. This proposal awarded supplemental funding to all districts—estimated to be more than two hundred—in which 15 percent or more of the students were eligible for free or reduced meals.[72] The governor's plan led several Abbott districts to appeal to the Department of Education for additional money and sent the Education Law Center back to the state supreme court to demand additional funds for school construction.[73] New Jersey was about to add chapters to the book that it had thought was completed a decade earlier. The outlines of the new plot developments seemed clear, but as history had demonstrated repeatedly, the devil was in the details.

CHAPTER 16

Quality of Life Issues

Everybody wants me to pick up his garbage, but nobody
wants to let me put it down.

—New Jersey trash contractor

While we expected that planning would teach us how to
grow, we are discovering, instead, that it is growth that is
teaching us how to plan.

—Bergen County Department of Planning and
Economic Development

SOME YEARS AGO, Newark Mayor Kenneth Gibson pre-
dicted that wherever American cities were going, Newark would get there
first. His thought applies more broadly to the quality of life issues that now
preoccupy many states. As America's most densely populated state, New
Jersey may be the test of whether a desirable quality of life in urban and suburban America can be preserved. Northern New Jersey is among the
nation's most expensive housing markets. Its waterways were among the first
declared impure, and air pollution problems were evident by the 1950s.
Traffic congestion also arrived early, for New Jersey has the most roads per
square mile of any state, and two cars for every three people. However, New
Jersey has also led the way in developing remedies for environmental problems, congestion and overdevelopment.

The state's approach is shaped by the interplay of its home rule tradition
with the powers the 1947 constitution granted the governor and supreme
court. The governor is the representative and champion of the state interest. The legislature is dominated by former—and sometimes current—
local officials. When clashing state and local interests produce gridlock, the
supreme court has not hesitated to shape policy. These patterns are clearly
seen in three related policy domains: environmental policy, transportation
policy, and land use and zoning.

338

TABLE 16.1.

Public Attitudes Toward Antipollution Laws (in percentage)

Year	Maintain antipollution laws	Relax laws to create jobs	Other or don't know
1977	46	46	8
1982	56	34	10
1988	69	24	7
2003	63	31	7

SOURCE: Eagleton Poll, dates as shown.

ENVIRONMENTAL POLICY

Residents have long identified environmental degradation as one of the most important problems facing New Jersey. Industry's diminishing role in the economy has helped change public thinking about environmental issues. Since 1977, the Eagleton Poll has regularly asked whether New Jerseyans prefer maintaining antipollution laws or relaxing them to create jobs. Table 16.1 shows the results over time.

In 1977, when New Jersey's economic transformation was beginning, public opinion was evenly split. Since the end of the 1980s, when economic growth came overwhelmingly from the service sector, more than 60 percent of state residents have seen environmental protection as more important than creating jobs that could harm the environment. For a majority of New Jerseyans, a healthy environment has become linked to their own physical and economic health.

On the first Earth Day, in 1970, Governor William Cahill signed a bill establishing the state Department of Environmental Protection. Significant environmental action, however, dates back to the nation's first state air pollution law in 1954. Although initially ineffective, it contained several pioneering principles. It recognized air pollution as a public policy problem, as a menace rather than a nuisance, and as requiring regional control and enforcement.[1]

Air and Water Pollution

The environment first became a political issue in 1961 when Democratic gubernatorial candidate Richard Hughes pledged reform of the 1954

Air Pollution Control Act. A 1962 revision still did not give the statute real teeth, and during Hughes's second term lawmakers held hearings throughout the state. A stronger 1967 law required all new emission sources to have state-of-the-art pollution controls; regulated the sulfur content of fuels; and transferred rule-making authority from a weak commission to a cabinet agency.

The federal Clean Air Act later established national emissions standards, and the tough state laws enabled New Jersey to meet four of the six air standards on time. In 2002, New Jersey was also officially declared in compliance with the carbon dioxide standard, leaving only ozone as a problem area in the entire state. Still, this pollutant has been dropping rapidly. In 2004, there were only fourteen days during which monitoring stations reported unhealthy ozone levels, compared with forty-seven as recently as 1998.[2]

Progress against water pollution has been slower. In 1972, 21 percent of New Jersey waters met "swimmable, fishable" standards and 35 percent do now, with no improvement over the past decade.[3] Cleanup technologies have developed slowly, and bottom sediment endures for a long time. The ocean beaches along the Shore are the major success story. In 1988, a malfunctioning sewage treatment plant in Asbury Park forced beach closings at the Jersey Shore—decimating the tourist industry and bringing the kind of publicity state officials had labored to overcome. The unpleasant problems at the Shore set the legislature to work on a two-year effort to produce a meaningful Clean Water Enforcement Act, which the legislature passed unanimously and Governor Florio signed in May 1990. All of New Jersey's ocean beaches from Sandy Hook to Cape May became and remain "swimmable."

Toxic Waste

Strong state laws also address toxic waste hazards. New Jersey's Spill Compensation Control and Environmental Cleanup Responsibility Acts served as models for the federal Superfund law—principally authored by then-U.S. Representative Jim Florio—and for other states' legislation. Both make the polluters pay.

The Spill Compensation measure, passed in 1976, created a cleanup fund financed by a transfer tax on petroleum and hazardous substances moved from one facility to another. The state can compel violators to clean up spills. If they refuse, the state commences cleanup activities and sues to recover costs. In 1979, the law was extended to cover abandoned hazardous waste sites.

ECRA—the Environmental Responsibility Cleanup Act of 1983—
deals with potential problems before they become disasters. To be sold,
transferred, or shut down, an industrial site must be free of toxic contamination or the owners must pay for a cleanup acceptable to the state and the
purchaser. ECRA applies only to sites transferred since 1983. In 1991, however, the state supreme court ruled that companies that knowingly sold
pollution-contaminated property before 1983 may also be "forever liable"
for damages and cleanup.[4]

ECRA did spawn some concern about its effects on urban revitalization. Prohibitive cleanup costs leave land unused in old industrial cities that
could be redeveloped to produce jobs. To encourage such development,
there was a shift during the Whitman years away from the enforcement-
oriented programs of the Florio administration toward providing induce-
ments for compliance. Florio had emphasized punishment and penalties,
like stiff fines for polluters and the appointment of an environmental prosecutor. Whitman and the Republican legislators who achieved majorities
in both houses in 1991 made more efforts to achieve compromises and offer
incentives.

Two notable examples were the 1993 Industrial Sites Recovery Act
and the 1996 Environmental Opportunity Zone Act. Both made it more
attractive for developers to take on projects in environmentally stressed
areas largely, although not exclusively, in cities and older suburbs. They
contributed to the central goal of the State Development and Redevelopment Plan, which is to direct jobs and growth to urban areas and preserve
New Jersey's shrinking open space. The 1993 statute eased cleanup requirements for contaminated sites intended for industrial rather than residential
use and permitted cheaper alternatives to removing toxic wastes (such as
fences and impermeable caps to prevent seepage). Other incentives included
creation of a state fund for grants or low-interest loans to qualified municipalities and developers for use in financing cleanups.

Environmental Opportunity Zones are located in "brownfields"—sites
that are less polluted than toxic waste dumps but need more extensive
cleanups than a site with no man-made contaminants. Municipalities may
offer tax abatements of up to ten years to developers willing to reclaim such
tracts for industrial or commercial use and who follow a state-approved
work plan. Such projects benefit from an expedited approval process,
and developers do not need to post a bond at the start of the remediation
project.

Another 1996 statute gave purchasers of these sites immunity from liability from the state for past environmental problems if the sites were in qualified municipalities. Among the projects engendered by more flexible cleanup rules are new baseball stadiums housing some of the seven minor league teams that blossomed in New Jersey in the 1990s. The Newark Bears' stadium is located on a once-polluted site along the Passaic River; the Somerset Patriots home field in Bridgewater was built on the site of an old American Cyanamid chemical plant.

The state's budget woes, combined with the desire to limit suburban sprawl and direct new development to New Jersey's troubled urban areas, have led the Democratic governors who succeeded Whitman to continue her brownfields policies and to relax them even further, as long as they do not endanger water supplies.[5]

New Jersey has also been aggressive in seeking toxic waste cleanup funds from the federal Superfund program. Enacted by Congress in 1980, it required "the responsible party," if such could be found, to pay for cleanups. "Orphan" sites whose corporate owners no longer existed or could not be located were placed on a national priorities list. Their cleanups were to be paid for by a federal tax on chemical and petroleum companies, with its revenues directed to an earmarked trust fund. By 1995, the federal trust fund had swelled to four billion dollars. The new Republican Congress promptly canceled the tax and "the Bush administration ... fought any attempts to reenact it, arguing it unfairly burdens companies that played no role in the pollution."[6] The trust fund was entirely depleted in 2004, and the Superfund now has to compete with everything else in the annual federal budget process.

When the first roster of Superfund sites came out in 1982, New Jersey led the nation with ten times more than Michigan, its nearest competitor. The Lipari Landfill in Gloucester County headed the list as the worst toxic waste site in the country. Explaining these dubious distinctions, Environmental Protection Commissioner Robert Hughey observed at the time, "We aggressively tried to be number one. We wanted to be number one. We worked hard for it. . . . Other states may be worse. We're just two or three years ahead of them in identifying our sites."[7] Governor Kean also contended that the state's long-term health required some short-term embarrassment. New Jersey got so much Superfund money (about half of all allocations between 1980 and 1988) that when the program briefly lapsed in 1986, Trenton was able to lend the federal EPA funds to keep it going until it was reauthorized.[8]

At no point during the Superfund's years of operation could it be said that cleanups proceeded expeditiously. When only one site in New Jersey had been fully remediated a decade after the fund's creation, the state DEP commissioner ascribed the delays to inadequate technology, bureaucratic quagmires, shortages of engineers, and lack of uniform standards.[9] Although technological challenges remain at many of the sites, the shrinking federal funds for the cleanups became the major impediment during the George W. Bush presidency.

"Responsible parties" have also engaged in increasingly confrontational litigation over their liability for payment, causing many sites to remain on the priorities list for as long as twenty years. By 2005, New Jersey still led the nation with 113 Superfund sites awaiting action, 2 more proposed, and only 23 sites deleted from the list because of completed mitigation. Dilatory progress even led the state to pay for remediation at a site in Kearney rather than waiting for the federal EPA to come up with the money.[10]

Disposal plans for new toxic waste have also moved slowly. Although a Hazardous Waste Siting Commission was established during the 1970s, it was not until 1993 that it chose an abandoned chemical factory in Union County, across the Arthur Kill from the New York City borough of Staten Island, as the site of a hazardous waste incinerator. Local residents, joined by New York State and New York City, immediately sued to prevent construction.

As the litigation proceeded, a report found that the amount of hazardous wasted generated in New Jersey had steadily declined, to the point where the amount produced in 1997 was only 26 percent of the figure in 1990. This long-running saga concluded when the commission announced in 2001 that a new hazardous waste burner would not be needed for several years, if ever.[11]

Solid Waste

Similar problems plague more prosaic solid waste disposal—of garbage. The most densely populated state is running out of places to put it. Before 1970, each New Jersey municipality simply sent trash to the closest cheap dump. That year, the Solid Waste Management Act required landfills to register with the state Department of Environmental Protection and authorized the Board of Public Utilities to regulate trash haulers. Neither action addressed the problem of where to put the ever-growing mounds of garbage, so a County and Municipal Government Study Commission (the

Musto Commission) recommended in 1972 that county governments be given solid-waste-planning authority. Home rule advocates greeted this proposal coolly, and it took three years for the legislature to pass amendments setting up county solid-waste-planning districts. Counties submit plans to the state DEP, which can accept, reject, or modify them, and regional plans are encouraged.

In 1976, the federal Resource Conservation and Recovery Act (RCRA) required phaseout of open dumps. To comply, New Jersey shut down numerous dumps and rerouted most garbage to a dozen major landfills. As these filled up and the counties dallied in devising plans, the DEP sued eight of them and threatened as many others. The state also tried economic incentives. Statutory amendments in 1983 encouraged county incinerator construction. Dumping-fee surcharges were to subsidize burner construction and provide handsome payments to "host communities." Although this finally compelled counties to develop plans—and even produced some municipal competition for the incinerator subsidies—problems continued. After the first incinerators opened in Warren, Gloucester, and Essex counties, it became apparent that many of the planned burners were not needed. Fierce battles arose about where to locate transfer stations and dump incinerator ash.

As an "interim" solution, New Jersey became a leader among the thirty states that export garbage. After years of accepting waste from New York City and Philadelphia, in 1991 New Jersey was sending about four million tons of trash a year out of state, representing about 19 percent of the total generated. Three-quarters went to Pennsylvania, with smaller amounts traveling as far as Ohio, Indiana, Kentucky, and Michigan. In 2004, out-of-state shipments still amounted to 19 percent, but the actual tonnage had risen to 5.7 million.

Beset by high shipment costs and environmentalists' crusades against incinerator-generated pollution, New Jersey stepped up its recycling efforts. In 1987, the legislature replaced a voluntary program enacted in 1981 with the nation's first mandatory recycling act. It requires all households to recycle at least three materials—generally glass, aluminum, and paper—as well as leaves. By 1986, voluntary plans in 434 of the 567 municipalities had produced a 9 percent municipal recycling rate, the highest in the country. Within four years, the state was approaching its 25 percent goal for municipal recycling, and total recycling—including construction debris and scrap metal—reached 48 percent.

Governor Florio announced ambitious new plans—freezing twelve county incinerator projects and setting a goal of 60 percent total trash recycling by 1995. The state in fact met that goal, but from 1997 to 2003 total recycling fell by 9 percent. Environmentalists and the state DEP attributed the decline primarily to the 1998 expiration of a recycling tax, whose proceeds were returned to towns based on the total tonnage of recycled trash.[12] In the current economic climate, a bill to reinstate the tax at twice its former rate has languished in committee.

Thus, although it will take many years to erase the fallout of an industrial past and some problems still defy solution or funding, New Jersey's determined efforts to deal with environmental challenges place it in the forefront of the states.

TRANSPORTATION POLICY

As with environmental measures, transportation policies reflect the interplay of state and local forces, and the more they impinge on home rule, the more contentious their development and implementation becomes.

Highway Policy

James W. Hughes and Joseph J. Seneca have identified three major phases in the development of New Jersey's road system.[13] The Highway Department, established in 1913, pioneered the nation's first traffic circles, cloverleaf interchanges, and divided highways. It developed the state road network during the 1920s and 1930s; its fifteen elements, including Routes 1 and 9, 46, 130, and 206, are still all too familiar to commuters today.

After World War II, New Jersey began choking on increased auto traffic. That led to phase two, construction of the limited-access toll roads that came to define the state (as in, "You're from New Jersey. What exit?"). In his 1947 inaugural address, Governor Alfred Driscoll called for construction of the New Jersey Turnpike. Quiet conversations about the patronage possibilities inherent in $250 million worth of equipment contracts, construction jobs, and a small army of toll collectors helped Driscoll win legislative assent for a Turnpike Authority in 1948. The Turnpike undertaking also had the virtues of earlier transportation projects like railroads and canals. Authority bonds financed the project and left local taxpayers unscathed, and toll revenues came mostly from out-of-state travelers.

The 118-mile superhighway stretching from the Delaware to the Hudson opened in 1951.[14] It was followed by other toll roads offering access to the Shore from New York and Philadelphia—the Garden State Parkway in 1955 and the Atlantic City Expressway in 1964. Although toll roads only make up about 1 percent of route miles in the state, they carry about 19 percent of the annual traffic.[15] Seasoned travelers expect construction delays as a standard part of the trip, as toll proceeds are used to expand the roads The northern half of the Turnpike is now fourteen lanes wide, with separate roadways for cars and commercial vehicles, and more lanes are being added in the central part of the state.

The federal interstate highway system was the third and final addition to the road network. Aside from the portion of the Turnpike that was designated as I-95 (the nation's longest north–south interstate), most of the rest of New Jersey's 415-mile federal highway system—including I-78, which runs across the state from east to west, and I-287, a horseshoe-shaped beltway around New York City—was not begun until the 1980s and not completed until the 1990s.

A number of planned segments of I-95 were never built because of the logistical and political difficulties of where to put them among dense population concentrations, the same factors that delayed construction on I-78 and I-287. Once these freeways were opened, however, they set off an unprecedented commercial building boom. Eighty percent of all the rental office space ever constructed in New Jersey was built in the 1980s, "much of it in growth corridors defined by the interstate system." The 25 million square feet available to businesses in 1980 had grown to 170 million by 2000.[16]

Before the advent of the 1947 state constitution, the Highway Department was the state government's largest and best-financed operation. All proceeds from the state gasoline tax were dedicated to the department responsible for keeping interstate as well as intrastate travel moving. After the new constitution banned dedicated funds and toll roads appeared, the department still prospered because state government had few other responsibilities. In 1961, it still claimed 28 percent of the entire state budget. As Trenton took on new responsibilities, a sharp relative decline in transportation spending set in. By 1981, barely 5 percent of state funds went for transportation, and half the money generated by the gasoline tax was used for other purposes. After the Highway Department was reorganized as the Department of Transportation in 1966, it also had to support mass transit, which demanded ever increasing subsidies.

As funding for state roads declined, their traffic load increased. With rapid population growth in the 1950s and 1960s, the average household eventually contained more cars than children, and more workers commuted to suburban jobs. While traffic congestion got worse, voters rejected four transportation bond issues during the economically turbulent 1970s. A successful $475 million initiative in 1979 was only a drop in the bucket. Increasingly severe traffic problems and a healthy economy during the 1980s finally persuaded the legislature and the voters to ensure the Transportation Department a more stable and generous source of funding. In a 1984 referendum, voters approved a Transportation Trust Fund. It was supported by state bonds that were to be repaid by a dedicated portion of the revenues from car registration fees, toll receipts, and the gasoline tax.

Once the envy of other states, the fund fell victim to Trenton's penchant for budget-balancing gimmicks as officials began diverting gas tax proceeds to the general fund. As Governor Corzine took office, the federal government was warning that New Jersey would lose all of its annual $1.5 billion in federal highway matching money when the state fund was entirely depleted in June 2006. Washington accepted Trenton's proposal to produce the state's share by writing the gas tax contribution to the trust fund into the state constitution and extending the life of its bonds from twenty to thirty years. Transportation experts criticized this continuation of "borrow and spend," noting that it would leave the fund depleted again in five years. Corzine, who had already proposed adding a percentage point to the state sales tax to begin paying down the ballooning debt in the pension trust funds, was disinclined to adopt the critics' proposals for other increases in taxes and fees. He observed wryly that "five years is a pretty long time in the context of public life."[17]

Statistics illustrate the problems facing the most intensively used roads in the country. Although New Jersey has the most roadways per capita of any state, vehicle travel per lane mile is more than twice the national average. The Department of Transportation has rated half of state roads as having "undesirable ride quality," and one-third of its bridges as "obsolete or structurally deficient."[18]

Commuters experience these problems only too personally. In a 2005 survey, 64 percent of state residents called reducing traffic congestion one of New Jersey's "most critical" problems of the next five to ten years, up from 48 percent in 1987, and matched in both time periods only by the related issues of high auto insurance rates and environmental protection. In 2005, half also said traffic congestion was a "very serious" problem in their own areas, up from 37 percent in the earlier study. New Jerseyans on average have the third longest average commuting time in the country—29 minutes.[19]

Mass Transit

Road congestion would decline if some of the more than 85 percent of workers who commute by car switched to mass transit. Travelers make eight hundred thousand trips daily on eleven railroad lines, three light rail lines, and more than two hundred bus routes operated by New Jersey Transit, the nation's only statewide mass transit agency. Founded in 1979 to bail out bankrupt bus companies and railroads, it is the third largest transportation system in the nation. In the past two decades, it has expanded dramatically.

A major limitation of the privately owned commuter rail lines had always been their lack of connections to each other. Moreover, unlike the north–south lines that ran between New York and Philadelphia, the lines running east-west terminated in Hoboken, where New York City commuters had to continue into Manhattan on PATH trains. The long-awaited Kearney track connection brought direct service to New York on one major east–west commuter rail line in 1996 and to another in 2002, and intensified a real estate boom in the northwestern suburbs along their routes.[20] When the Secaucus Junction station opened in 2003, passengers on eight lines could change trains there. The Hudson County Meadowlands houses both the Kearney connection and the Secaucus station.

The most recent additions to the state's mass transit services are three light rail lines, reminiscent of the 1920s and 1930s when a web of streetcars connected many towns. The newest line, Newark Light Rail, is an extension of the preexisting Newark subway. Before the extension was completed in 2006, Newark was the only location in the state with stations serving both the north–south and east–west commuter lines, but from different terminals. With service between those terminals on the light rail line, it is finally possible to transfer between north–south and east–west lines without a bus trip or a long walk.

The Hudson-Bergen and River light rail lines are entirely new systems that began operation in 2000 and 2004 respectively. The Hudson-Bergen twenty-one-mile system connects Bayonne, Jersey City, and Hoboken with the Gold Coast of luxury apartment complexes facing the New York City skyline and provides easy transfers across the Hudson River to New York by rail and ferry. Plans call for its eventual extension to the Meadowlands sports complex. The thirty-four-mile River Line runs along the Delaware River between Camden and Trenton, including a hub station with transfers to Philadelphia.

Bus travel, which commuters see as less attractive, nonetheless commands a larger share of mass transit users than does rail. New Jersey bus commuters to New York outnumber those traveling by rail by about three to one. Although the majority of bus trips are within the state, for commuters in the densely populated northern and central parts of the state, bus travel mainly brings to mind the infamous Port Authority bus terminal in Manhattan, the busiest such facility in the country. Between 5:00 and 5:30 PM on weekdays, 182 New Jersey–bound buses leave the terminal, with long lines and long waits part of the commuting experience.

Despite the much larger number of bus riders, New Jersey Transit's capital budget for rail is ten times greater. One reason is that bus service "has across the board reached its practical, maximum load point."[21] More buses also add to the congestion on the roads, while trains diminish it. With the existing railroad tunnels under the Hudson River also at capacity, New Jersey Transit has introduced longer trains and double-decker cars. However, real relief will only come with the advent of a new trans-Hudson tunnel that will double the number of trains that can be accommodated. Construction of the tunnel is planned to begin in 2009 and to be completed in 2016.

State government, major employers, and some municipalities promote carpooling, vanpooling, and flextime in the assault against traffic jams, but New Jerseyans seem to regard private car travel as a constitutional right. Flextime's principal effect has been to extend the rush hour to much of the day, and rural dwellers in the south and west of the state have little enthusiasm for allocating tax dollars to mass transit schemes ,which mostly do not benefit them. Consequently, New Jersey Transit riders pay about 55 percent of the agency's operating costs, about 10 percent higher than the national average.

Fare hikes used to decrease the economic advantages of mass transit commuting, and each increase made more potential riders take to their cars. New Jersey Transit avoided raising fares during the 1990s by directing capital funds to its operating budget. With higher gas prices and traffic continually worsening however, mass transit ridership has continued to grow in recent years despite the return of frequent fare increases. Most commuting trips are from suburb to suburb though, and the most optimistic estimates are that mass transit users will increase from the current 10 percent to 12 to 15 percent over the next twenty-five years.[22]

LAND USE AND ZONING

How land may be used and who makes those decisions is a policy arena where state and local interests clash sharply. When New Jersey municipalities received the power to zone in 1927, land use joined education as a linchpin of home rule. It seems surprising that in a state with such a fabled affinity for local control, about 40 percent of New Jersey's land area came under the management of regional and state agencies during the 1970s. Recent governors and the state supreme court have tried to extend that control even further. Like education policy, land use has become one of the most contentious public issues New Jersey faces.

Precursors: Open Space and Farmland

Trenton's first two ventures into land use policy gave little hint of the conflict to come. Both dealt with preservation of the state's fast-disappearing open space. A 1961 Green Acres bond issue—the first in the United States for public land acquisition—passed easily, as did subsequent referenda totaling $1.4 billion over the next three decades. They helped to protect more than four hundred thousand acres of land from development.

Between 1950 and 1960, 10,000 of the 27,000 active farms in the Garden State disappeared. Agricultural land went from 37 to 30 percent of New Jersey's total acreage. In response, the legislature passed the Farmland Assessment Act in 1963, making New Jersey the second state to give farmland preferential tax status after Illinois did so in the 1930s. Qualified property must have at least five acres devoted to agriculture or horticulture or, since a 1995 amendment, the care and breeding of horses, and must generate annual sales of at least $500. About 25 percent of New Jersey's total land area falls under this program, which has drawn some criticism along with much praise.

Those who disparage the plan don't object to the benefits to genuine farmers, but rather to so-called hobby farmers who receive huge property tax breaks. For example, the family of former U.S. Treasury Secretary William Simon owns a forty-three-acre Morris County estate. The house sits on eight acres, with a 2007 residential assessment of $5 million and property taxes of $47,000. The adjoining thirty-five acres are in two parcels classified as farmland, which together are assessed at $27,000 and generate property taxes of $262.[23]

With the "real farmers" selling their land to developers, by 1980 there was one-third less agricultural land than there had been in 1960, and the decline between 1985 and 1986 was as large as the drop in the previous five years. The million farm acres of 1980 fell to about 800,000 by 1990. Despite generous tax breaks, the value of farmland and property taxes per acre are the highest in the nation.[24] This combination makes enticing offers from builders difficult to resist. However, the number of acres technically in farmland has stabilized since then, and other preserved open space has grown rapidly, thanks to major initiatives in the Whitman and McGreevey administrations.

Open space legislation in Whitman's first term was of a conventional sort. In 1994, for the second time in three years voters passed another Green Acres bond issue. A year later, the Farmland Assessment Act was expanded to include horse farms. By 1998, however, the governor was thinking of her legacy, and the public was increasingly up in arms about suburban sprawl and congestion. It was a banner year for land preservation.

The centerpiece was citizen approval of a three-billion-dollar bond issue that, along with a dedicated portion of the sales tax, was intended to protect one million acres of farmland and other open space over the next ten years.[25] Whitman had called for the initiative in her inaugural address and campaigned for it unceasingly. Voters not only approved it by two to one, but also passed a record number of local and county initiatives dedicating small local property tax increases to be used for land preservation. In the 2003 elections, thirty more towns voted to establish conservation trusts along with Hudson County, thus making New Jersey the first state in which every county had an open space program.[26]

During the McGreevey administration, the Garden State Preservation Trust—the mechanism for allocating the state bond proceeds—became politically fraught in ways that symbolized the state's deepest cleavages of class, race, and region. Northeastern cities with heavy low-income and minority populations complained that the trust's allocations, which they had expected would improve the public parks that were their only substantial greenery, were instead heavily tilted to more rural areas in the northwestern part of the state. Those recipients retorted that it was the income tax revenue that flowed out of counties like Hunterdon and Somerset that kept the whole state afloat. Complaining that they were shortchanged, South Jersey legislators held up the Trust's annual allocations for months.[27]

McGreevey was caught between the demands of his political base and his commitment to combat sprawl. Moreover, from 1998 to 2002, the per-acre price of farmland went up 54 percent, and the price of other undeveloped land rose 79 percent. That made it evident that the Trust's resources could not meet the goal of preserving a million acres, half of New Jersey's remaining undeveloped land.[28] Another approach had to be found that would not cost money, and in 2004 the governor seized on policies to protect the state's water supply. He began by issuing an executive order that broadened the regulations prohibiting new construction within three hundred feet of rivers to include tributaries, streams, and creeks; that action protected 300,000 more acres. But like Whitman, he wanted to leave a major open space legacy. It came with the passage of the Highlands Water Protection and Planning Act in 2004, discussed in detail later in this chapter. The northwestern Highlands comprise more than 850,000 acres, stretching over all or part of seven northwestern counties. Its rivers and reservoirs are the source of drinking water for more than half the state's population. McGreevey championed other open space initiatives, including restoration of urban parks and facilitating municipal purchases of farmland, but the Highlands legislation was without doubt the most important.[29]

During his fifteen months in office after McGreevey's resignation, Governor Codey signed a package of twelve open space bills providing for more than $350 million in projects across the state. When Governor Corzine succeeded him, the state land trust was almost depleted, two years earlier than anticipated. The governor and a bipartisan coalition of legislative leaders vowed to support a November 2007 referendum to replenish it.[30]

Like other Americans, New Jerseyans are sentimental about family farms, but it is the nonagricultural acres that command their attention. As with so many things in the state, their status began to change around 1970. Within ten years, use of almost half of New Jersey's land area passed out of the control of owners and local municipalities—and under the control of the New Jersey Meadowlands Commission, the state Department of Environmental Protection, and the Pinelands Development Commission. Twenty-five years later, the New Jersey Highlands joined the list of areas regulated by state government.

The New Jersey Meadowlands Commission

The first, geographically smallest, and most far-reaching assertion of state authority came in the Meadowlands. This area covers thirty-one square miles of wetlands in fourteen municipalities and two counties. Located on the Hackensack River estuary across New York Bay from Manhattan, it was potentially "some of the most valuable real estate in the country."[31]

Before the 1960s, most people called such land "swamp," and treated it accordingly. More than one-tenth of the Meadowlands was zoned as open dumps. They accepted 35 percent of the state's solid waste, from 121 municipalities, with "the additional aroma of hog farms adding to the ambience."[32] Outsiders were familiar with the area mainly through the reputation of Henry Krajewski, an eccentric Secaucus pig farmer who was a perennial third-party presidential candidate, or as the place to close car windows when traveling the New Jersey Turnpike.

Governor Richard Hughes, his commissioner of community affairs, Paul Ylvisaker, and State Senator Fairleigh Dickinson, whose Becton-Dickinson Pharmaceutical Company overlooked the Meadowlands, were among the first to grasp the potential benefits of proper development.[33] In a major legislative battle, they won establishment of the Meadowlands Development Commission (MDC) in 1968. Ironically, it was the existing dumps that helped make the victory possible. In return for the votes of their legislators, towns using the landfills were granted the right to dump in the Meadowlands "in perpetuity"—"the rest of North Jersey preserved its home rule by obliterating that of 14 other North Jersey towns."[34] Another important factor was increasing reliance on federal flood control in the low-lying Meadowlands. The U.S. Army Corps of Engineers demanded a regional land-use plan to show the benefits—"Put simply, Congress was not about to spend hundreds of millions of dollars to protect garbage dumps and junkyards from flooding."[34]

The commission's executive director and seven gubernatorial appointees have extraordinary power to plan, zone, and grant variances in the Meadowlands portions of the fourteen municipalities. Each mile of the district has an assigned use, and development projects must accord with a master plan (updated once, in 2004) to receive approval.[35] A crucial element in making the whole scheme work is that all fourteen municipalities must pool 50 percent of their tax revenues from Meadowlands ratables, which are then redistributed to them by formula. Affected towns still complain about the allocation formulas. However, protests are far more muted than they were during the battle to establish the commission, which featured posters "showing the hand of the State squeezing blood out of the crumpled body of Secaucus."[36]

Hughes's vision for the Meadowlands was carried forward by his successors. Today, the district is home to eighty thousand jobs and a nationally preeminent entertainment and sports complex. Residential development came later, but elaborate hotels and condominium complexes are gradually replacing some of the long-gone pig farms. The small areas still zoned for landfills have had to grow up rather than out. Thanks to improving technology, only the ever-present seagulls alert the Turnpike traveler who travels past the Giants and Jets football stadium, the racetrack, and the Meadowlands Hilton, that the green hills they see are man-made. Symbolic of recent history, the district's 2004 master plan envisions closing four of the operating landfills, remediating the land, and developing it as golf courses.

The Meadowlands project was conceived primarily as an economic development initiative. In contrast, three later regional land use plans across New Jersey gained passage after being promoted as environmental protection measures. They affect much larger land areas—each covering almost 20 percent of the state.

CAFRA: The Coastal Area Facilities Review Act

The Coastal Area Facilities Review Act of 1973 (CAFRA) regulates development in a 1,400-square-mile district along the shore. It includes 124 municipalities and parts of 6 counties. CAFRA designates the state Department of Environmental Protection as the district's regional planning agency and requires DEP approval of all subdivisions, building standards, and zoning ordinances. The intent is to protect the shore and regulate its development.

The DEP has not enjoyed the Meadowlands Development Commission's success in regulating growth and development in its planning area. Local municipalities do not gain the economic advantages through CAFRA that the MDC provides, and a major loophole in the law permitted about half the development in the district to escape regulation. It exempted residential projects of less than twenty-five units and strip malls with fewer than fifty parking spaces from CAFRA requirements. The predictable effect was a glut of forty-nine-space parking lots and twenty-four unit-condominium projects, connected by roads or walkways.

Later amendments, regulatory actions, and court decisions have left developers, environmentalists, and municipal officials even unhappier. In 1993 the legislature tried to assuage all of them by directing the DEP to mesh the district's land use regulations with the recently adopted state plan aimed at hindering sprawl. But at the same time it allowed municipalities to bypass the DEP approval process if they created their own regional development plans.

With sprawl increasing, in 2000 the DEP issued regulations creating more than one hundred "coastal growth zones" in seventy municipalities, which had five years to submit acceptable proposals to the state planning commission. The intent was to concentrate large-scale development in those "town centers" and preserve environmentally sensitive areas. In 2002, a state appeals court rejected an environmentalists' suit challenging the municipal permitting process, but their foes were still not happy either. Builders complained that their concerns were still being ignored. Municipalities protested that they were being cut off at the five-year deadline in 2005 because proposals were lost in the bowels of the bureaucracy, leaving large projects in limbo.[37]

The Pinelands Commission

Along with the difference in size, the other major contrasts between the Meadowlands and the coastal zone initiatives were the level of existing development and the costs and benefits to those regulated. The Meadowlands had little man-made development (except for garbage dumps and rail yards), while CAFRA affected built-up areas. Despite their initial objections, Meadowlands municipalities found that the MDC brought huge economic benefits. On the Shore, the public good of environmental protection clashed with the private good of landowners and developers and the hunger of municipalities for ratables. When Governor Byrne moved to protect the Pinelands in the 1970s, it was lightly populated but ripe for development. Given the experience with CAFRA, Byrne and the legislature sought to balance property rights and environmental protection, and the state successfully met this dual challenge.

John McPhee's sensitive 1968 book about the Pine Barrens, where fewer than 300,000 people lived in 52 municipalities in 7 counties covering almost 1,000,000 acres of South Jersey, first brought this vast, wild area to public attention.[38] Along with the stands of dwarf pines that gave it its name, the Pinelands are also home to blueberry fields, cranberry bogs, a huge, fragile aquifer of pure water, taciturn natives who call themselves "Pineys," and the legendary Jersey Devil. The Pinelands slumbered on through the 1960s, when the Port Authority began searching for a site for a fourth jetport for the New York area. Environmentalists helped defeat a scheme to build it in the Great Swamp, a much smaller area in Morris County, by buying the land and presenting it to the federal government as a wildlife refuge. Burlington County officials then proposed the

Pinelands as an alternative, accompanied by plans for a new city of 250,000 people.

In 1972, as environmentalists mobilized to fight the airport, the Pinelands Environmental Commission, dominated by local officials and developers, was created to design uses for 320,000 acres in Burlington and Ocean counties. Governor Cahill's environmental commissioner, David Bardin, characterized their 1975 plan as a "developer's dream."[39] About the same time, the U.S. Interior Department proposed making the Pinelands a national ecological reserve. This designation would have banned federal grants for projects damaging to the environment. New Jersey Senators Clifford Case and Harrison Williams introduced the appropriate legislation, and in 1978, the entire Pinelands became the first national ecological reserve.

These actions had only limited effects on development, however, and the Pinelands might well have gone the way of suburban sprawl if Governor Byrne had not counted John McPhee among his tennis partners. McPhee pressed the case to Byrne. The governor responded with an executive order imposing a building moratorium and led the fight for the Pinelands Development Act of 1979. Byrne—who as governor achieved passage of a state income tax, public financing of gubernatorial elections, legalized casino gambling in Atlantic City, and construction of the Meadowlands Sports Complex—considered saving the Pinelands his greatest accomplishment. He explained, "I'm convinced that if I hadn't done it, nobody would have done it. The Pinelands would be well on the way to extinction, as John McPhee had predicted . . . it was not a life-and-death issue with anybody. . . . [T]he legislators from Ocean County might admit that Pinelands preservation was a good idea but their campaigns were financed by developers. . . . [I]t was an economic political survival issue for them."[40]

The legislation set up a fifteen-member Pinelands Commission, composed of representatives from seven affected counties, seven gubernatorial appointees, and a member appointed by the U.S. secretary of the interior. It produced a district master plan intended to maintain large contiguous areas in a natural state, safeguard essential environmental characteristics, protect water quality, and promote compatible agricultural, recreational and development uses. The National Conference of State Legislatures called the Commission's work a model for the nation.[41]

The Pinelands master plan was implemented in 1981 and must be reviewed every three years. It requires all municipalities in the planning region to bring their zoning ordinances and local master plans into conformity with the comprehensive plan. The region is divided into a core preservation area where no development is permitted, and buffer protection areas with limited development. A state development bank buys transfer development rights or credits from landowners in the preservation areas and sells them to developers who may then build at a somewhat higher density in the buffer areas than would otherwise be permitted.[42] The executive director of the Pinelands Commissioner estimated that the region would not reach buildout until at least 2025. Although some farmers there continue to grumble, support for the Pinelands plan is wide and deep.[43]

The Highlands Region

The state's latest foray into broad-scale land use regulation is still a work in progress. The fact that it shares characteristics with both the Pinelands and CAFRA regions raises difficult issues for both politicians and regulators. Like both of the earlier initiatives, the Highlands area represents about one-fifth of all the land in the state and is prized by residents and visitors alike for its natural beauty and recreational opportunities. Like the Pinelands, protecting the state's water supply is a major concern. Like the Shore, the Highlands area was experiencing explosive and uncontrolled growth. Encompassing all or part of seven counties and eighty municipalities in the north and west of the state, it presents issues, both geographic and political, that are the most complex of all the land areas the state regulates.

New Jersey's successful efforts at regional planning in the Pinelands and the Meadowlands shared a number of characteristics. They included strong gubernatorial leadership, controlled but meaningful local participation in planning, economic sweeteners for those affected, no compromise on the authority of regional master plans, and quick start-up.[44] Most of these were absent in the less successful CAFRA planning effort at the Shore, and they have been absent in the Highlands venture as well.

Governor McGreevey rightly claims credit for courage in championing the Highlands legislation—which was much in the interest of the whole state but was sure to be condemned by home rule advocates, powerful political figures with ties to builders, and the developers themselves. But because of McGreevey's political style and the complexity of the issues, the criteria that led to success in the Meadowlands and the Pinelands did not apply to this newest regional planning effort.

The problems began after the narrow passage of the Highlands Act in the state assembly. South Jersey state senators, in league with developers and their allies, threatened to derail senate approval. To save the legislation, McGreevey offered a Smart Growth Act, a gubernatorial compromise dubbed by its opponents as "fast track." It allowed developers to pay for expedited approvals for projects in those parts of the state deemed growth areas in the 2001 State Plan. It also created a "smart growth ombudsman" to shepherd "good projects" through the permitting process and to review all new state regulations pertaining to growth. Project approval would also become automatic if state officials failed to rule on them within forty-five days. This mollified both developers and South Jersey lawmakers, and the companion bills on the Highlands and Smart Growth became law.

Environmentalists' outrage, which had been building for months, erupted. The director of the state Sierra Club chapter called Smart Growth "the worst bill on the environment I have ever seen," instancing examples of farmland and nature preserves designated as "growth zones" because they abutted interstate highways. The regional director of the federal Environmental Protection Agency, formerly a member of Governor Whitman's cabinet and a strong antisprawl advocate, supported environmentalists' claims that the Smart Growth Act would violate federal clean water standards. Governor McGreevey himself admitted that some on his own staff "thought that the so-called fast track bill was too high a price to pay for the Highlands bill."[45]

In one of his last acts before leaving office in November 2004, McGreevey issued an executive order that delayed implementation of Smart Growth until July 2005 and called for more public debate on the measure. Shortly before the expiration of the executive order, Acting Governor Codey issued one of his own. It suspended the law's implementation until the relevant regulations proposed by three cabinet agencies underwent an "interested party review" and were found to conform to federal standards. Only then could the agencies proceed to hearings and final regulatory actions. Codey's eventual successor, Jon Corzine, then still a gubernatorial candidate, praised the order, saying, "[T]he bill in its current form is wrong for New Jersey." It will be many years before new regulations can be proposed and adopted.[46]

Like uncompromising gubernatorial leadership and a quick start-up, the other factors that made for earlier regional planning successes have also been absent in the Highlands. The Meadowlands revenue-sharing plan for municipalities and the Pinelands development rights bank had blunted the disapproval of their unhappy local critics. In contrast, while the Highlands

Act promised landowners "pre-act" compensation for land that can no longer be developed, no money was set aside for that purpose. Until the state can come up with the billion dollars that the Regional Plan Association estimates will be required to pay for development rights and land acquisition between 2007 and 2014, owners can only sell their property at current market rates for preserved land, which is likely to be less than they originally paid and certainly far below what building on it would have brought.[47]

Organizing public participation to develop and implement the Highlands Plan has been torturous for all concerned, since the tract combines all of the worst possible features for systematic planning. Like the Pinelands Act, the Highlands Plan designates preservation areas where no development is permitted, and planning areas that regulate development. Like the CAFRA zone, however, the Highlands region contains a large number of municipalities—some already highly developed, some in the midst of development, and some hardly developed at all. As a result, while five towns are entirely in the preservation area and thirty-six are in the limited-growth planning area, forty-seven are split between the two designations. To make matters even more convoluted, there are "overlays" within each zone, and an agricultural zone for farmland with its own overlays. The planning area overlays dictate how many homes can be built in a particular subzone and the size of businesses there. Agricultural areas, depending on their location, can fall into either the preservation or planning labels. In some portions of the preservation area, there are small pockets, like a hamlet's center, where growth is allowed because much of the land is already covered.

The plan itself was devised by the Highlands Council, a fifteen-member bipartisan group that by statute must include at least five municipal officials and three county officials. The precise qualifications for membership, as described in the enabling legislation, are almost as complicated as the plan itself; Governor Corzine has described the process of filling of a vacancy on the council as akin to solving a Rubik's Cube puzzle.[48] After more than two years of meetings, and seven months after the law's target date, the council released a draft plan on November 30, 2006, and scheduled a series of public hearings through early 2007. The angry crowds who turned out for them made it clear that the document's most serious problem was appropriate compensation for the farmers and small developers who had seen dramatic declines in their properties' values. To produce the money, they and their frequent foes, the environmentalists, both favor a water tax on the millions of residents who get their water from Highlands sources, but legislators eliminated it from the governor's FY 2008 budget proposal.

In the midst of the hearing process, the besieged chair of the council reported that there was "no deadline" for issuing the final plan and subsequently resigned. Once it is adopted, the council envisions years of discussions with local officials to devise final zoning plans for the preservation area, and the cajoling of those in the planning area to modify their municipal zoning ordinances to conform to the Highlands Plan, which they are not required to do. Aggrieved parties and their lawyers have vowed to file lawsuits against the regulations. The Highlands Plan promises to be a work in progress for a long time.[49]

Exclusionary Zoning and Affordable Housing

Land regulation initiatives that are carried out well, as in the Pinelands and the Meadowlands, address a goal that a majority of New Jerseyans support—preserving open space even if it means ceding some local zoning powers.[50] Another major land use issue of recent years—state-mandated zoning for affordable housing—has involved far more conflict and been far less successful. Since the 1970s, the New Jersey Supreme Court's *Mount Laurel* decisions have been the force behind an effort to open the suburbs to affordable housing. Unlike regional planning, *Mount Laurel*–related developments affect home rule and land use decisions in every municipality.

Trenton first took up affordable housing in 1972, after exclusionary zoning suits were filed against a number of suburbs. Republican Senator Albert Merck of Morris County introduced legislation, supported by Governor Cahill, that allowed the state to set "fair share" affordable housing goals for municipalities and require state approval of their housing plans. It was roundly defeated, and Merck's loss of his supposedly safe seat in 1973 was widely attributed to his sponsorship of the bill.

In 1975, the state supreme court ruled unanimously for the plaintiffs in a zoning case brought against the South Jersey township of Mount Laurel by the local chapter of the NAACP. The chief justice, former governor Richard Hughes, wrote for the court, "Mount Laurel must, by its land use regulations, make realistically possible the opportunity for an appropriate variety and choice of housing for all categories of people who may desire to live there, of course including those of low and moderate income."[51]

The court directed municipalities to provide a "fair share" of affordable housing in their "region," but left the definition of those terms and the appropriate remedy unclear. Within six months of the *Mount Laurel* decision, sixty-five municipalities were in court over zoning challenges. In 1978, with the support of the League of Municipalities, Essex County Democratic Senator Martin Greenberg introduced legislation similar to the 1972 Merck Bill, and it was approved by the upper chamber. However, the League of Municipalities later withdrew its support and the bill failed in the assembly. To the court's embarrassment, *Mount Laurel* seemed unenforceable.[52]

The Mount Laurel plaintiffs resumed legal action. When *Mount Laurel II* reached the supreme court in 1983, many of those who had rendered the earlier decision had been replaced by more activist judges, led by the chief justice, Robert Wilentz. Once more writing for a unanimous court, Wilentz reiterated that zoning regulations "that do not provide the requisite opportunity for a fair share of the region's need for low and moderate income housing conflict with the general welfare and violate the state constitutional requirement of substantive due process and equal protection."[53] Noting in its decision that "[w]e may not build houses, but we do enforce the constitution," the court set up an elaborate plan for determining municipal housing obligations, to be monitored by judges in the three regions of the state (north, central, and south). A "builder's remedy" allowed developers who included affordable housing units to build at higher densities than local zoning ordinances permitted. Within two years of the decision, more than one hundred "builder's remedy" suits had been filed.

Mount Laurel II's assault on home rule produced howls of outrage from the suburbs. Governor Kean called the decision "communistic," and others described the builder's remedy as "judicial terrorism."[54] Kean asserted he would not act on the court decision until the legislature produced an appropriate statute. Within a year, Essex County Democratic Senator Wynona Lipman's Fair Housing Bill garnered the support of the League of Municipalities, the Public Advocate, and the Homebuilders Association. Released from committee in 1984, it provided for a Council on Affordable Housing in the state Department of Community Affairs to determine and adjudicate municipal housing obligations. It was blended with a bill sponsored by Middlesex County Senator John Lynch to permit municipalities to "buy out" of half their obligations by subsidizing affordable housing units in other municipalities willing to enter into such negotiations.

The Lipman-Lynch Bill was endorsed by the senate in January 1985 and passed the assembly after being further watered down. However, Governor Kean, still hostile to judicial "social engineering," conditionally vetoed it in April. Observers believed his intent was "to push down the Mount Laurel numbers as far as possible, stopping just short of flatly seeking to reverse the decision through legislative action."[55]

The Fair Housing Act that Kean finally signed later in 1985 greatly reduced the number of affordable housing units mandated by the court. It also moved many of them out of the suburbs and back into the cities; made those that were built more available to middle-income than low-income New Jerseyans; and limited the number of purchasers and renters who did not already live in a community. It did, however, produce some units that would not have otherwise been built; converted suburban fury to grudging acceptance; and returned the court to an adjudicatory rather than policy-implementing role. In a third decision, in 1986, widely if informally known as *Mount Laurel III*, the supreme court called the act the "kind of responsible remedy" it had "always wanted and sought," and transferred all its pending cases to the Council on Affordable Housing (COAH).[56]

The Fair Housing Act specified that every six years, COAH should determine the number of units municipalities must provide, based on regional growth, aggregate per capita income, and the rate of change in employment. The council did so for the first time in 1987 and again in 1993, in procedures called Round One and Round Two. Towns could meet their obligations with new or rehabilitated units or enter regional contribution agreements (RCAs), subsidizing units in other towns for up to half their quotas. Half could be restricted to current residents, and one-quarter set aside for senior citizens. Eligibility for Mount Laurel housing was open to applicants earning less than 80 percent of the area median income, and half the units were reserved for those earning less than 50 percent of that figure. If the municipal quota was over 125, one-fifth of those built had to be rental units.

Although falling far short of its numerical goals, the COAH procedures were relatively successful through their first two rounds. New Jersey produced more affordable housing per capita than any other state in that period. About 40,000 affordable housing units were constructed or rehabilitated to meet local obligations, and over 7,000 more were built or brought up to code as a result of regional contribution agreements. Municipalities were not required to submit affordable housing plans to COAH, but doing so rendered them immune from builder's remedy lawsuits for six years. Most did eventually seek certification from COAH, but by mid-2001, two years after the third round should have been completed, no new numbers had appeared, and 40 percent of towns were without plans.

There were several reasons for this state of affairs. First, an amendment to the Fair Housing Act had extended the third round guidelines from six to ten years, thus requiring many more housing units and putting even more pressure on municipalities. Next, Governor Whitman was not eager to take on the issue as she contemplated running for the U.S. Senate in 2000 or, as she eventually did, taking a cabinet post in Washington before the end of her second term. Her immediate successor, Senate President and Acting Governor Donald DiFrancesco, also preferred to keep affordable housing out of the 2001 gubernatorial campaign he then anticipated. Finally, local governments had just spent almost two decades engaged in the complex process that brought forth a new state plan for land use, while defending or fending off builders' remedy suits. They were girded for battle over the third round rules.

When affordable housing became Governor McGreevey's problem after he assumed office in January 2002, he had much experience and strong feelings about this fractious issue. For nine years prior to becoming governor, he served as mayor of Woodbridge Township in central New Jersey, which by 2001 had not produced a single one of the more than thirteen hundred affordable housing units that the COAH rules mandated. Another signal of McGreevey's attitude toward affordable housing regulations was his choice of Susan Bass Levin as commissioner of the Department of Community Affairs, home of COAH. Bass Levin came to Trenton from Cherry Hill, just outside Camden, where she had been mayor for fourteen years. By 2001, Cherry Hill, like Woodbridge, had produced none of the more than eighteen hundred affordable units which COAH had determined was its fair share. Both communities were sprawling townships with larger populations than the decaying cities in their regions, from which many of their residents had fled.

By summer 2003, almost two more years had passed without the appearance of third round rules, and COAH had in effect instituted a moratorium on the program by issuing "interim certifications;" bypassing calculation of the additional units required over the next ten years by the formula in place. While the bureaucracy dawdled, a coalition of affordable housing organizations began circulating a plan for a new, simpler formula that would produce more affordable units than the one in use. The existing method did not adequately distinguish between fully developed older suburbs and fast-growing newer ones with more vacant land, so housing advocates proposed that fair shares be calculated based on the growth of new market-rate housing and new job creation. Towns that were virtually built out would only have to provide some units for their existing low- and middle-income populations, while places like Woodbridge and Cherry Hill would bear most of the affordable housing burden.

In August 2003, some four years late, Commissioner Bass Levin finally issued third round rules and numbers devised by a new method. She claimed it reflected the "growth share" principle recommended by fair housing advocates; they claimed it was a distorted caricature of their ideas. After the public comment period, the final rules, which were to be in effect until 2014, were still closer to Bass Levin's plan than to her opponents' proposals. Compared to the affordable housing advocates' suggestions, the COAH version increased the number of new jobs and amount of new market-priced construction necessary to trigger one new affordable unit; doubled the number that could be reserved for senior citizens (to 50 percent); included new financial incentives to encourage communities to enter into RCAs rather than build in their own communities; and permitted local officials rather than the state to estimate anticipated growth.

The plan was immediately endorsed by the state League of Municipalities, gaining support from both its urban members and those from long-recalcitrant suburbs. Long waiting lists meant that the suburbs could quite conceivably meet their entire allotment by accepting only senior citizens and paying off poor cities desperate to improve their housing stock with RCA checks. The mayors of those cities welcomed the RCA funds, which over the years had already brought more than $26 million to Trenton and about half that amount to Paterson. Supporters also hailed the program's commitment to the goals of the new state plan, which sought to promote development in areas with existing infrastructure.

Fair housing advocates had quite a different perspective. They saw it as yet another ploy to keep poor people, especially those with children, out of the suburbs, and to minimize the number of units built. They also pointed to COAH's use of inaccurate statistical models to estimate growth and condemned local control of that part of the process. Retired State Supreme Court Justice Gary Stein, who had participated in the unanimous 1986 decision that turned over all *Mount Laurel* cases to COAH, called the third round rules "a recipe for obfuscation, for delay, for disaster."[57] The state's largest newspapers published negative editorials. A coalition of housing groups, joined by the state Builders Association, immediately went to court to challenge the new COAH mandates.

While officials were still trying to figure out the implications for their towns, in January 2007 a three-judge appellate panel invalidated the round three regulations. Writing for a unanimous court, Judge Mary Catherine Cuff declared, "The rules frustrate, rather than further, a realistic opportunity for the production of affordable housing." The judges found that COAH had used outdated and inappropriate data to estimate the need for affordable housing and ordered it to rework the formula within six months. They also cut back the number of permissible senior citizen units to 25 percent, saying, "We conclude the rule discriminates against low- and moderate-income households with children." During the six-month stay, municipalities with approved second round plans were permitted to continue operating according to the old rules; the fifty others with no plans and the seventy involved in builders' remedy lawsuits were held harmless during the stay.[58] Housing activists hailed the decision; the League of Municipalities predicted chaos and a flood of lawsuits stretching long into the future.

As with the allocation of the Garden State Trust funds and the "redistributive" schemes for school financing described in chapter 15, there are racial undertones to the affordable housing debate. Most regional contribution agreements are between heavily minority urban areas and heavily white suburbs. COAH has argued that if regional contribution agreements do perpetuate housing segregation, the problem is not with them, but the legislature and the courts. The 2007 superior court decision followed *Mount Laurel III* in upholding both regional contribution agreements and the entire Fair Housing Act, even as bills were being introduced in both houses of the legislature to end the use of the RCAs they had created.

New Jersey's approach to affordable housing can thus be seen as demonstrating that the state "remains hostile to the notion that the needs of poor people supersede the tradition of home rule," or, alternatively, as "a compromise between radical idealism and reactionary preservationism."[59] In any case, the influx of "poor people" many suburbs feared has not materialized, even in the relatively small number of units built. Over 80 percent of *Mount Laurel* units have been sold as condominiums, with stiff mortgage and down payment requirements and high closing costs. Their owners are mostly senior citizens, pink- and blue-collar workers, and single parents. Although more than half of the owners have children, almost all units have only one or two bedrooms, precluding large families from moving in.[60]

The State Development and Redevelopment Plan

Mount Laurel II "plucked out of bureaucratic obscurity" a little-known document called the State Development Guide Plan. Prepared by the Department of Community Affairs Division of State and Regional Planning during the 1970s to identify predicted growth zones but never officially adopted, it was used as a guide for courts hearing land use cases. The supreme court relied on it to construct its *Mount Laurel II* guidelines and ordered that it be periodically revised.[61] Governor Kean, overtly hostile to statewide planning, abolished the State and Regional Planning Division in 1983, saying *Mount Laurel II* had rendered it moot.

Based on the work of an ad hoc, broad-based committee, Democratic Senator Gerald Stockman in 1984 introduced a bill for a state plan that would meet the court's requirements. After much negotiation, Kean signed the legislature's State Planning Act in January 1986.[62] It specified a plan be drawn up in eighteen months—by July 1987. The act set the following guidelines for the plan:

- protecting the natural resources and quality of the state;
- promoting development consisting with sound planning and taking account of existing infrastructure;
- identifying areas targeted for growth, limited growth, agriculture, and open space;
- establishing state planning goals and objectives, and coordinating related activities;
- integrating concerns of the poor, minorities, and the *Mount Laurel* decisions;
- balancing development and conservation.

A compromise accepted by the governor, the legislature, the League of Municipalities, and the New Jersey Builders Association, the act established a "cross-acceptance" process unique to New Jersey. Under cross-acceptance, in eighteen months, the commission was to produce a plan; county planning boards were to gather comments from all municipalities about their role in the plan; the commission was to negotiate differences; and, finally, it was to submit a revised plan to the governor for approval.[63]

Governor Kean did not name an executive director for the State Planning Commission until September 1986—eight months after the clock had started running—and the commission was not fully staffed until the end of the year. A draft plan, "Communities of Place: The State Development and

Redevelopment Plan" was not released until December 1988, and the cross-acceptance process then began. "Communities of Place" was intended to guide population, employment and development trends through the year 2010.[64] Omitting the Meadowlands, CAFRA, and Pinelands areas, it mapped the rest of the state into square-mile quadrants, each placed in one of seven tiers, ranging from Tier I, redeveloping cities and suburbs, through stable cities and suburbs, suburban and rural towns, suburbanizing areas, future suburbanizing areas, and agricultural areas—through Tier VII, environmentally sensitive areas.

Each tier had specified development strategies, policies, and standards, such as permissible population density, with development "unconstrained" in Tier I and progressively more constrained in each succeeding tier. The basic idea was to redirect growth to already developed cities and suburbs, discourage sprawl, and restrict development in agricultural and environmentally sensitive areas. County and municipal master plans were to be brought into voluntary conformity with the state plan, which was to be reviewed every three years.

When the cross-acceptance process was finally completed in late 1990, local governments had rejected much of the "tiering" approach, and the planning commission changed "imposed" zoning requirements to "guidelines." The seven former tiers were now called planning areas and were more loosely categorized as metropolitan, suburban, fringe, rural, and environmentally sensitive. The plan also identified five types of centers—urban, town, regional, village, and hamlet, and each had its own development guidelines.

The state plan was finally approved in June 1992, five years behind schedule. Adoption of a second version, not approved until 2002, took even longer. The third cross-acceptance procedure began in 2004, with release of a preliminary plan dubbed "Building a Better New Jersey"; three years later, negotiation hearings were still being held.[65] The long-term effects of the state plan remain a question mark. Although recent governors have paid it more than lip service and populations are increasing in cities like Newark for the first time in many years, sprawl continues, and the State Planning Commission cannot compel state and local agencies to make their land use decisions conform to its own. As the Highlands experience shows, whether they will adjust regulations and resource allocations to conform with the plan over its lifetime will depend on political and economic pressures, and the will and skill of future governors.

The most complicated American state plan ever developed suggests the complexities and continuities of contemporary policy making in New Jersey. Cross-acceptance embodies an intricate balance between the culture of home rule and emerging state identity and authority. The plan is another effort to make New Jersey's cities a vibrant part of a profoundly suburban state and to balance economic growth and environmental protection. In their quest for a healthy and attractive environment, workable transportation networks, and appealing and affordable housing, state residents see themselves as New Jerseyans more than they ever have. But as this chapter once again shows, they remain also citizens of 566 municipalities.

CHAPTER 17

Epilogue

If you look at the way people live in this country, the
land of opportunity is New Jersey.

—Joel Garreau, *Edge City*, 1991

FOUR DEVELOPMENTS are significantly shaping the United
States of the twenty-first century. First, fewer Americans live in either cities
or rural areas. The United States is becoming "a suburban nation with an
urban fringe and a rural fringe."[1] There is further development of "edge
cities." An edge city is not a suburb as usually defined. It is not simply a
place where people sleep, but one where they work, create, and spend their
leisure time.[2] Peter Rowe calls such suburbs "middle landscapes" between
city and country.[3] Second, the American economy is based increasingly on
the work of brain rather than brawn, and production of services rather than
goods. An educated workforce is ever more important. Those without the
requisite skills will become increasingly marginalized. Third, politics and
government are at once more distant and more intimate. More decisions
are made in capitol buildings than in town halls. The technology-based
direct democracy of public opinion polls, referenda, and "electronic town
meetings" has claimed an important place alongside organized interest
groups and political parties. Officeholders communicate with more of
their constituents on television, Web sites, and with computer-generated
mailing lists than they do in speeches, appearances, and individual conversations. Finally, adjusting to new cultural diversity is a growing American
preoccupation. In significant measure, American political debate has always
been a dialogue about how best to assimilate newly arriving ethnic, religious, and racial groups who demand a place in the political universe.
Older groups have always harbored fears of newer ones. In the new century,
a new wave of political petitioners promises to shape American political
dialogue as dramatically as a previous wave did at the turn of the last
century.

To know what much of America will be like some decades hence, one may study New Jersey now, for all these trends are already manifest there. They have combined to shape a new suburban politics—postindustrial, posturban, and postparty. As William Schneider has written, the first century of U.S. history was dominated by the agrarian myth of the self-sufficient Jeffersonian farmer. The second century was dominated by the urban myth of the city as engine of prosperity. The third century will be the century of the suburbs.[4]

THE RISE OF SUBURBAN POLITICS

Suburban politics is distinct in style and substance from the urban politics that preceded it. Urban politics was party-centered; suburban politics is candidate-centered. Urban politics attracted adherents by providing the necessities of life; suburban politics promises quality of life. Urban politics was organized around culturally homogeneous geographic precincts accessible by shoe leather; suburban politics is organized around issue precincts accessible through targeted media. Urban politics was activist and in the forefront of people's lives. Suburban politics is less intrusive and protects private space, both physical and psychological. Political corruption was a by-product of urban politics' individualist political culture; suburban politics has a strong moralist strain.

The particular qualities of suburban politics grow from these characteristics, and they are writ large in New Jersey. A candidate rather than party-centered politics calls on officeholders to appeal to voters one by one. It is volatile and unpredictable. What appears to be strong partisan competition is often individual competition. New Jersey has often elected governors of one party and legislative majorities of the other because of the powerful appeal or affront individual candidates convey. The state's suburban voters judge political aspirants less by their policy positions than their personal characteristics. They prefer candidates who seem be like them and share their particular values.

For suburban voters, quality of life is paramount. They seek above all physical security, clean air and water, easy access to amenities, attractive and affordable housing. Economic security is important to them because it makes a desirable quality of life possible. Candidates promoting an economy that nurtures individual achievement are the ones who win their votes. New Jersey elections revolve around the issues related to quality of life as suburban residents understand it: environmental protection, steadfastness against crime, good local schools that will help their children achieve even more than they. Only in the worst economic times are New Jerseyans deflected from these quality-of-life concerns, and when they are, they see government spending as villain rather than savior. "The middle class is who lives in the suburbs. The word that best describes the middle class is 'taxpayers.'" For suburban voters, a government program "that helps the few and taxes the many is an outrage. A program that helps the many and taxes the few seems eminently fair."[5]

Old urban neighborhoods were ethnically and religiously cohesive. Suburban homeowners are linked less by these ascriptive categories and their accompanying institutions than they are by the more impersonal interests they share. Politicians reach New Jersey's suburbanites by thinking of them as motorists, environmentalists, members of professions, or senior citizens. Their campaigns depend not on armies of precinct workers but on checks from groups of developers, lawyers, auto dealers, teachers, union members, or health care professionals. "To move to the suburbs is to express a preference for the private over the public"—for backyards rather than public parks, for private cars over mass transit, for the security of the gated community rather than the potential dangers and insecurity of downtown. "Suburban voters buy 'private' government—good schools and safe streets for the people who live there."[6] New Jersey's suburban dwellers have fled the congestion, disorder, and dangers of cities for more than one hundred years. They have been both "pushed" and "pulled" to the suburbs—"pushed" by the congestion and tensions of urban life and "pulled" by the lure of homes of their own at a reasonable price, which become their most fiercely prized possessions.[7]

Urban "dangers" have always been linked to the arrival in cities of alien "others." In an earlier time, "other" was defined by religion and ethnicity. Protestant, Anglo-Saxon suburbs built walls to keep out Catholics and Jews, eastern and southern Europeans. The new arrivals were seen as bringing crime and political corruption. Suburban politicians crusaded then against alcohol, gambling, and aid to parochial schools, and sent urban mobsters and mayors to jail. Now, "other" is defined by race. "White ethnics," themselves newly middle class, emptied out of New Jersey cities after the Newark and Plainfield riots of the 1960s. Their new suburban representatives crusaded against drugs, school busing, and regionalization to achieve racial balance, and filled the jails with drug dealers. Suburban hostility is directed, as ever, less at particular groups per se than at the groups who happen to dominate the cities.

Through the 1960s, New Jersey was less a state or state of mind than a collection of antagonistic communities—urban, suburban, rural. City and country owned New Jersey state government. When their great migration began after World War II, suburbanites became numerous enough to elect the weak governor, but a coalition of urban Democrats and rural Republicans ruled the powerful, malapportioned legislature and collaborated to protect their own fiefdoms. During the 1970s, a political shock wave hit New Jersey. The U.S. Supreme Court's one-person-one vote decisions ended county-based representation in Trenton. The New Jersey Supreme Court laid siege to the locally based fiscal system when it decreed that the funding of public education could no longer rely so heavily on local property taxes. The virtually inescapable remedy for the court's decision was broad-based state taxes, which New Jersey had resisted longer than almost every other state.

New Jersey's traditional political system lay in ruins. Its suburban voters—their numbers now inflated by the flight from cities within the state and on its borders—suddenly found themselves at the center of state politics. The most suburban state in the United States was compelled to devise a politics suitable to its residents. Because so many New Jersey suburbs now melted seamlessly into one another both geographically and culturally, and their residents were so numerically dominant, it was possible to have a genuine state politics that was impossible before.

For the first two decades of New Jersey's suburban era (roughly 1970–1990), the central political symbol of the state was its governor, the only statewide elected official. Before 1970, New Jersey governors were still constrained by the traditional county politicians who dominated the legislature, the absence of fiscal resources the state could command, and the limited channels through which they could reach their constituents.

Their successors gradually surmounted these obstacles. The courts dispatched the county politicians. Commerce followed the new suburbanites to their homes. Sprawling shopping malls generated revenue for a new state sales tax. As more of the region's trained and educated work force moved to the New Jersey suburbs, more of the corporations that employed them followed them there. Media patterns were the slowest to change, but the governor was Trenton's focal point and dominated what communication channels there were.

Thus, all the changes that were occurring in New Jersey reinforced each other. Growing middle-class suburbs made a postindustrial economy possible. A postindustrial economy made a real state government possible.

State government increasingly served the political and economic interests of the new suburban majority. The old rural-urban political coalition had given little attention to the suburbs. The new suburban regime gave little attention to the cities. The governor directed Trenton's activities. Those gubernatorial aspirants who understood the psychology of suburban voters were elected and rewarded. Those who rejected or misunderstood them were punished.

The successful suburban politician's style is, first of all, moralistic, in a "good government" sense. Nothing repels New Jersey's suburban voters more rapidly than the urban politics of cronyism and petty corruption. A second component of the suburban political style is the ability to make personal contact with one's constituents. When they number in the millions, that contact is largely through television.

Gradually but inexorably, New Jersey is developing the statewide communication channels that have been the last barrier to forging a state identity. The tax revolt of the 1990s began on an almost statewide talk radio station based in Trenton that identifies itself as "New Jersey 101.5—not New York, not Philadelphia, but New Jersey!" As they had when the income tax was first passed in 1976, thousands traveled to Trenton in 1991 to take part in tax protests, but hundreds of thousands listened to New Jersey 101.5. As the national TV network audiences declined, more New Jerseyans—especially in the suburbs—turned to cable stations where legislative candidates could tailor highly targeted, reasonably priced messages to their constituents alone.

The 1991 legislative campaigns were also the first that could be seen as state-based contests for ostensibly local offices. Each individual race became a referendum on a statewide issue—the redistributive Florio tax increases of 1990. Secondary issues were founded in demographic rather than geographic constituencies. Voters were mobilized by both sides as hunters seeking loosening of the recent ban on assault weapons; as environmentalists seeking to save the Shore; as senior citizens whose property tax rebates might be threatened. These issues all spoke to "the prevailing imperative of suburban life . . . security both economic and physical."[8]

An assertive legislature and its leadership's more visible public profile have challenged if not eliminated the governor's supremacy and made the public and its representatives increasingly important players in state politics. Although the legislature will always primarily represent local interests, it is evolving into a body that, like the governor, also has a statewide perspective.

When Woodrow Wilson was elected governor of New Jersey, reporters asked him how he could win political reforms from legislators loyal to their county party organizations. He replied, "I can talk, can't I?"[9] New Jersey's political leaders must still rely on persuasive talk to win their policy priorities, but now the conversation takes place not only in the governor's office and the legislative caucus rooms but on television and in public opinion polls, and the conversants number in the millions.

New Jersey is today, as it has always been, well-endowed with people, resources, and location. Whether it can provide for all its citizens the quality of life—social, economic, and political—to which its overwhelmingly suburban voters now aspire depends more than ever on the quality of its political leadership. New Jersey is now more than the sum of its parts. The state that was once defined by the places it was near is now a place unto itself. New Jersey was once a republican state, and now is it is a democratic state. Those labels have nothing to do with its political parties, and everything to do with its politics.

NOTES

CHAPTER 1   PROLOGUE

The epigraph in this chapter is drawn from Paul Simon, "America," copyright 1968 by Paul Simon.

1. Edmund Wilson Jr., "New Jersey: The Slave of Two Cities," in *These United States: A Symposium*, ed. Ernest Gruening (New York: Boni and Liveright, 1923; repr., Freeport, NY: Books for Libraries Press, 1971), 56–57.
2. Gruening, introduction to Gruening, *These United States*, iii.
3. Wilson, "New Jersey," 61, 65.
4. Joe McGinnis, *Blind Faith* (New York: G. P. Putnam's Sons, 1989), 43.
5. Ibid., 45.
6. Michael Danielson, quoted in John J. Farmer, "Crucial Cities: Rebound is Vital to State's Future," *Newark Star-Ledger*, April 8, 1991.
7. John J. Farmer, "The *N-E-W* New Jersey: Era of a Quiet Revolution Transforms the State," *Newark Star-Ledger*, April 7, 1991.

CHAPTER 2   FOUNDATIONS: NEW JERSEY, 1600–1900

The epigraph in this chapter is drawn from Lincoln Steffens, "New Jersey: A Traitor State," in *The Struggle for Self-Government* (New York: McClure, Phillips, 1906), 212.

1. Edmund Wilson Jr., "New Jersey: The Slave of Two Cities," in *These United States,* ed. Ernest Gruening (New York: Boni and Liveright, 1923; repr., Freeport, NY: Books for Libraries Press, 1971), 56.
2. In a speech to the Newark Board of Trade, and reported by the *Newark Evening News,* January 26, 1911. Quoted in Federal Writers' Project, Works Progress Administration, *New Jersey: A Guide to its Present and its Past* (New York: Hastings House, 1939), 35.
3. See Susan Vankoski, "If At First You Don't Secede . . . ," *New Jersey Reporter,* November 1983, 16–20.
4. Carl E. Prince, "Patronage and a Party Machine: New Jersey Democratic-Republican Activists, 1801–1816," *William and Mary Quarterly*, 3rd ser., 21, no. 4 (October 1964): 571–578; Peter Levine, "State Legislative Parties in the Jacksonian Era: New Jersey 1829–1844," *Journal of American History* 62 (December 1975): 591–608.
5. Frederick Hermann notes that most other antebellum state governments played at least as active a role as their local governments in taxing and spending. Herrmann, "Stress and Structure: Political Change in Antebellum New Jersey" (Ph.D. diss., Rutgers University, 1976), 341n.

6. Quoted in Thomas Fleming, *New Jersey: A History* (New York: Norton, 1984), 65.

7. Thomas L. Purvis, "The European Origins of New Jersey's Eighteenth Century Population," *New Jersey History* 100 (Spring-Summer 1982): 15–31.

8. See Bernard Bailyn, *Voyagers to the West: A Passage in the Peopling of America on the Eve of the Revolution* (New York: Alfred A. Knopf, 1986), 246–251.

9. Quoted in Francis Bazeley Lee, *New Jersey as a Colony and as a State* (New York: Publishing Society of New Jersey, 1902), 4:28.

10. Simeon F. Moss, "The Persistence of Slavery and Involuntary Servitude in a Free State (1685–1866)," *Journal of Negro History* 35 (July 1950): 289–314. The size of the slave population was second only to New York among northern states. Although the legislature had banned the importation of slaves in 1786 and declared that anyone born after July 4, 1804, would be free, slavery was not finally abolished in the state until 1845.

11. Paul G. E. Clemens, *The Uses of Abundance: A History of New Jersey's Economy* (Trenton: New Jersey Historical Commission, 1992), 10–13; Rudolph J. Vecoli, *The People of New Jersey* (Princeton, NJ: D. Van Nostrand, 1964), 51.

12. Thomas Fleming, "Crossroads of the American Revolution," in *New Jersey in the American Revolution*, ed. Barbara J. Mitnick (New Brunswick, NJ: Rutgers University Press, 2005), 7.

13. Vecoli, *The People of New Jersey*, 60.

14. Fleming, *New Jersey*, 98.

15. Gibbons's country estate in Bottle Hill (now Madison) was later purchased by Daniel Drew, and became the site of Drew University.

16. From the charter granted by the legislature, as quoted in Wheaton J. Lane, *From Indian Trail to Iron Horse* (Princeton, NJ: Princeton University Press, 1939), 325.

17. Duane Lockard, *The New Jersey Governor: A Study in Political Power* (Princeton, NJ: D. Van Nostrand, 1964), 57.

18. Fleming, *New Jersey*, 103.

19. Floyd W. Parsons, *New Jersey: Life, Industries and Resources of a Great State* (Newark: New Jersey Chamber of Commerce, 1928), 41–44; Lockard, *The New Jersey Governor*, 61.

20. Quoted in Richard P. McCormick, "New Jersey's First Congressional Election: A Case Study in Political Skulduggery," *William and Mary Quarterly,* 3rd ser., 6, no. 2 (April 1949): 243.

21. *New Brunswick Guardian*, September 27, 1804, quoted in Richard P. McCormick, *A History of Voting in New Jersey* (New Brunswick, NJ: Rutgers University Press, 1953), 115.

22. J. R. Pole, "The Suffrage in New Jersey, 1790–1807," *Proceedings of the New Jersey Historical Society* 71 (January 1953): 39–61. Women were granted the right to vote in school board elections in 1887, "which seemed wholly in keeping with their motherly duties." John F. Reynolds, *Testing Democracy* (Chapel Hill: University of North Carolina Press, 1988), 30.

23. John Bebout, "The Making of the New Jersey Constitution," introduction to the *Proceedings of the New Jersey State Constitutional Convention of 1844* (Trenton: MacCrellish and Quigley, 1945), lxxxiv.

24. Lee, *New Jersey as a Colony and as a State*, 3:387.

25. McCormick, *History of Voting*, 124.

26. Steffens, "New Jersey," 214. See also William Edgar Sackett, *Modern Battles of Trenton* (Trenton, 1895), 1:17–18.

27. Route 1 entered New Jersey in Camden and ran through Bordentown, Princeton, New Brunswick, and Perth Amboy to Staten Island or Jersey City. Route 2

entered Salem and Cumberland Counties from Delaware, running through Woodbury, Camden, Mount Holly, and Bordentown to Princeton. It was especially favored for its large number of forested areas and friendly Quaker communities. Route 3 crossed the width rather than the length of the state, from Phillipsburg to Somerville to Elizabeth. Routes were designated with numbers, "station stops" by letters. See Giles R. Wright, *"Steal Away, Steal Away": A Guide to the Underground Railway in New Jersey* (Trenton: New Jersey Historical Commission, 2002).

28. For a fascinating picture of the life of these southern students and their political concerns as the war loomed, see Robert Manson Myers, *A Georgian at Princeton* (New York: Harcourt Brace Jovanovich, 1976).

29. John T. Cunningham, *New Jersey: America's Main Road* (Garden City, NY: Doubleday, 1966), 184. This section also draws on Elizabeth H. Salmore, "A Jersey View: An Inside Look at the Civil War, 1864–65" (Highland Park, NJ: privately printed, 1989).

30. Quoted in Cunningham, *New Jersey*, 194.

31. Mayor Orestes Cleveland, quoted in Hermann K. Platt, "Jersey City and the United Railroad Companies, 1868: A Case Study of Municipal Weakness," *New Jersey History* 91 (Winter 1973): 252.

32. Fleming, *New Jersey*, 148.

33. William Edgar Sackett, *Modern Battles of Trenton* (New York: Neal, 1914), 2:144.

34. See Herrmann, "Stress and Structure," 347.

35. Harold W. Stokes, "Economic Influences Upon the Corporate Laws of New Jersey," *Journal of Political Economy* 38 (October 1930): 568.

36. Ibid., 573.

37. Steffens, "New Jersey," 209.

38. Christopher Grandy, "New Jersey Corporate Chartermongering, 1875–1929," *Journal of Economic History* 49, no. 3 (September 1989): 677–692. Delaware began to end New Jersey's domination in 1899, when it adopted New Jersey's law verbatim, but with even lower tax rates.

39. See the discussion of New Jersey Democrats' discomfort with "Bryanism" in Reynolds, *Testing Democracy*, 80–96.

49. Jerrold G. Rusk, "The Effect of the Australian Ballot on Split-Ticket Voting, 1876–1908," *American Political Science Review* 64 (December 1970): 1221.

41. See McCormick, *History of Voting*, 156–161; quote, 161.

42. See Lockard, *New Jersey Governor*, 85–88.

43. See Walter E. Edge, *A Jerseyman's Journal* (Princeton, NJ: Princeton University Press, 1948), 60–63.

44. Ibid., 57.

45. Quoted in Steffens, "New Jersey," 281.

CHAPTER 3   "THE STATESMAN AND THE BOSS"

The comment in the first epigraph was made to Joseph Tumulty, who reports it in his *Woodrow Wilson as I Knew Him* (Garden City, NY, and Toronto: Doubleday, Page, 1921), 15. The second epigraph refers to a statement by Clinton Gilbert, quoted in Thomas Fleming, *New Jersey: A History* New York: Norton, 1977), 180.

1. The New York–area counties were Hudson, Essex, Passaic, Bergen, Union and Middlesex; the other was Camden. See Floyd W. Parsons, *New Jersey: Life, Industries and Resources of a Great State* (Newark: New Jersey Chamber of Commerce,

1928), 74–75; John T. Cunningham, *New Jersey: America's Main Road* (Garden City, NY: Doubleday, 1966), 239–240.

2. Wilson, "New Jersey: The Slave of Two Cities," in *These United States: A Symposium*, ed. Ernest Gruening (New York: Boni and Liveright; repr., Freeport, NY: Books for Libraries Press, 1971), 1923), 57.

3. Parsons, *New Jersey*, 74–75.

4. Richard J. Connors, *A Cycle of Power* (Metuchen, NJ: Scarecrow Press, 1971), 9–12. The Hudsonites who trekked to Monmouth led to its being called "Jersey City South."

5. Arthur S. Link, *Wilson: The Road to the White House* (Princeton, NJ: Princeton University Press, 1947), 135. Two overviews of the Progressive movement in New Jersey are Ransom E. Noble, *New Jersey Progressivism before Wilson* (Princeton, NJ: Princeton University Press, 1946), and John F. Reynolds, *Testing Democracy: Electoral Behavior and Progressive Reform in New Jersey, 1880–1920* (Chapel Hill: University of North Carolina Press, 1988).

6. Joseph P. Tumulty, *Woodrow Wilson as I Knew Him* (Garden City, NY, and Toronto: Doubleday, Page, 1921), 24.

7. This limited form of primary was legislated in 1903.

8. R. P. McCormick, *The History of Voting in New Jersey* (Princeton, NJ: Princeton University Press, 1953), 188–195.

9. Lincoln Steffens, "New Jersey: A Traitor State," in *The Struggle for Self-Government*, (New York: McClure, Phillips, 1906), 289–290.

10. From an article by Wilson in the *Atlantic Monthly*, November 1907; as quoted in Fleming, *New Jersey: A History* (New York: Norton, 1984), 153.

11. Link, *Wilson*, 120.

12. Ibid., 133.

13. For an account of Harvey's career, see Francis Russell, *The President Makers*, (Boston: Little, Brown, 1976), chap. 4.

14. Tumulty, *Woodrow Wilson*, 14–15.

15. Ibid., 12.

16. Woodrow Wilson to David B. Jones, June 27, 1910; reprinted in David Hirst, *Woodrow Wilson, Reform Governor*, (Princeton, NJ: Van Nostrand, 1965), 24–26. A detailed account of the dinner by an eyewitness appears in William O. Inglis, "Helping to Make a President," *Collier's Weekly* 58 (October 7, 1916): 37–39.

17. Letter to John Maynard Harlan, June 23, 1910, reprinted in Hirst, *Woodrow Wilson*, 14–15.

18. Link, *Wilson*, 156, 158.

19. Inglis, "Helping to Make a President," 12–14.

20. Tumulty, *Woodrow Wilson*, 22. Wilson's acceptance speech is reprinted in Hirst, *Reform Governor*, 53–59.

21. Wilson's answers were published in many newspapers on October 26, 1910. They are reprinted in Hirst, *Reform Governor*, 100–106.

22. Link, *Wilson*, 195.

23. Tumulty, *Woodrow Wilson*, 46.

24. *Trenton True American*, December 24, 1910; reprinted in Hirst, *Reform Governor*, 137–138.

25. Wilson to George Harvey, November 15, 1910; reprinted in Hirst, *Reform Governor*, 129–30.

26. Wilson to Mary A. Hulbert, quoted in Hirst, *Reform Governor*, 161.

27. Link, *Wilson*, 280.

28. Ibid., 281.

29. Hirst, *Reform Governor*, 242.
30. There are interesting portraits of Hague's early life in Fleming, *New Jersey*, and Connors, *A Cycle of Power*.
31. John F. Reynolds traces New Jersey party organizations' use of reform measures in *Testing Democracy* (Chapel Hill: University of North Carolina Press, 1988), especially chap. 7.
32. Connors, *Cycle of Power*, 19.
33. See ibid., 60.
34. Although five of the six governors elected between 1949 and 1985, after the 1947 constitution permitted two consecutive four-year terms, won twice, none has yet won a third nonconsecutive term. Robert Meyner, elected in 1953 and 1957, tried and failed in 1969.
35. Dayton David McKean, *The Boss: The Hague Machine in Action* (New York: Russell and Russell, 1940), 69.
36. These two arteries, the Holland Tunnel into New York and the Ben Franklin Bridge in Philadelphia, opened in 1926 and 1927 respectively.
37. *Perth Amboy Record*, quoted in George Crystal, *This Republican Hoffman: The Life Story of Harold G. Hoffman, a Modern Fighter* (Hoboken, NJ: Terminal Printing and Publishing Company, 1934), 54.
38. For Roosevelt's relations with Hague, see James A. Farley, *Behind the Ballots* (New York: Harcourt, Brace, 1938), 115, 150, 158; John Kincaid, "Frank Hague and Franklin Roosevelt: The Hudson Dictator and the Country Democrat," in *FDR: The Man, the Myth, the Era 1882–1945*, ed. Herbert D. Rosenbaum and Elizabeth Bartelme (New York: Greenwood Press, 1987), 13–38.
39. Fleming, *New Jersey*, 185.
40. McKean, *The Boss*, 127.
41. Warren E. Stickle, "Edison, Hagueism and the Split Ticket in 1940," *New Jersey History* 97 (Summer 1979): 69–80; Kincaid, "Frank Hague and Franklin Roosevelt."
42. Bennett Rich, *The Government and Administration of New Jersey* (New York: Crowell, 1957), 21.
43. See Edge's account in *A Jerseyman's Journal* (Princeton, NJ: Princeton University Press, 1948), 281–284. In other races, Roosevelt won by about 25,000 votes, and the Republican senate candidate by about 30,000. The constitutional referendum, with many fewer votes cast, went down by 126,000.
44. *Newark Evening News*, October 21, 1947, 9.
45. Connors, *Cycle of Power*, 155.
46. Edge, *Jerseyman's Journal*, 257.
47. When "reformer" John Kenny took over City Hall in 1949, he discovered 210 unfiled indictments in the county prosecutor's office, kept ready to ensure the political loyalty of those named. See John J. Farmer, "When Bossism Ruled in Jersey," *Newark Star-Ledger*, May 21, 1989.
48. Thomas F. X. Smith, *The Powerticians* (Secaucus: Lyle Stewart, 1982), 75–76.
49. The father of one of the authors of this book often told tales of working his way through medical school by recording betting transactions in a Hudson City "wire room" in the late 1920s.
50. The CIO's successful challenge of a Jersey City ordinance requiring a permit to speak on public property, which Hague refused to grant them, was one of a series of important U.S. Supreme Court cases defining the rights and limits of free speech on public property. See *Hague v. CIO*, 307 U.S. 496 (1939).

51. The definitive catalogue of Hague machine scandals, from which many of these examples are taken, is McKean, *The Boss.*

52. Incorporating women into the Hague organization after they received the vote in 1920 served to close off another possible avenue of opposition to Hague.

53. Connors, *Cycle of Power*, 76.

54. Kincaid, "Frank Hague and Franklin Roosevelt," 19.

55. Fleming, *New Jersey*, 136.

56. Farmer, "When Bossism Ruled," 1.

57. See Alvin S. Felzenberg, "The Impact of Gubernatorial Style on Policy Outcomes: An In Depth Study of Three New Jersey Governors" (Ph.D. diss., Princeton University, October 1978), chap. 2; Duane Lockard, *The New Jersey Governor: A Study in Political Power* (Princeton, NJ: D. Van Nostrand, 1964), 123–124.

58. *Newark Evening News*, January 20, 1958, as quoted in Lockard, *The New Jersey Governor*, 125.

59. Thomas J. Anton, "The Legislature, Politics and Public Policy: 1959," *Rutgers Law Review* 14 (Winter 1960): 275.

60. Interview with Byrne in Jeffrey Kanige, "Brendan Byrne on Brendan Byrne, *New Jersey Reporter*, June 1988, 8.

61. "Editorial Comment," *National Municipal Review* 39 (March 1950): 120. Eleven votes were required until 1952. The caucus reduced the number to nine partly as a result of the Meyner victory in 1949. Meyner had made caucus control a major campaign issue. See Belle Zeller, ed. *American State Legislatures* (New York: Thomas Y. Crowell, 1954), 206–207.

62. Edge, *Jerseyman's Journal*, 295.

63. Anton, "The Legislature, Politics and Public Policy," 276n.

64. Hughes's proposal for an income tax passed the assembly but was defeated in the senate when the Essex County Democratic leader withdrew his support at the last minute. With Republican support, Hughes did achieve passage of the first broad-based state levy—a sales tax. On the Hughes tax initiatives, see Richard C. Leone, "The Politics of Gubernatorial Leadership: Tax and Education Reform in New Jersey" (Ph.D. diss., Princeton University, 1969), chap. 2. On the Cahill initiatives, see Felzenberg, "Impact of Gubernatorial Style," chap. 5.

65. See Richard P. McCormick, "An Historical Overview," in *Politics in New Jersey*, rev. ed., ed. Richard Lehne and Alan Rosenthal (New Brunswick, NJ: Eagleton Institute of Politics, Rutgers University, 1979), 20; Stephen A. Salmore, "Voting, Elections and Campaigns," in *The Political State of New Jersey*, ed. Gerald M. Pomper (New Brunswick, NJ: Rutgers University Press, 1986), 76.

66. In 1984, one of the independent television stations in New York City, WOR, was required to move its license to New Jersey. However, it did not have a studio in the state until 1986, does not maintain a full-time correspondent in Trenton, and still has one of the smallest audiences among the seven VHF stations in the New York metropolitan area.

67. Stephen A. Salmore, "Public Opinion," in *Politics in New Jersey*, ed. Alan Rosenthal and John Blydenburgh (New Brunswick, NJ: Eagleton Institute of Politics, 1975), 74.

68. These decisions were successive rulings in the case of *Jackman v. Bodine* between 1964 and 1970, and *Scrimminger v. Sherwin* in 1972. See the discussion in Stanley H. Friedelbaum, "Constitutional Law and Judicial Policy Making," in Lehne and Rosenthal, *New Jersey Politics*, 212; Arthur J. Sills and Alan B. Handler, "The Imbroglio of Constitutional Revision—Another By-Product of Reapportionment," *Rutgers Law Review* 20 (1965): 1ff.

69. In the case of the Democrats, the county organizations were dealt a severe blow when they were able to engineer the nomination of former Governor Meyner in 1969 but were unable to secure his election.

70. An additional blow to the already reeling county organizations was a 1978 law that prohibited local candidates from running on the same ballot line with statewide candidates in party primary elections. This further disconnected state and local campaigns and candidates.

71. Data demonstrating the major effect of the candidates' positions on the state income tax appears in Stephen A. Salmore, "Public Opinion," 70–79.

72. The fullest account of his career is his own Thomas H. Kean, *The Politics of Inclusion* (New York: Free Press, 1988).

73. This characterization is drawn from the title of George C. Rapport, *The States-man and the Boss: A Study of American Political Leadership Exemplified by Woodrow Wilson and Frank Hague* (New York: Vantage Press, 1961).

CHAPTER 4   CONTEMPORARY POLITICAL PATTERNS

The epigraph in this chapter is drawn from Thomas H. Kean, *The Politics of Inclusion* (New York: Free Press, 1988), 144.

1. The only New Jersey organization of liberal Democratic reformers, ever, was the short-lived New Democratic Coalition. It grew out of the 1960s civil rights and antiwar movements and culminated in the 1968 presidential campaigns of Eugene McCarthy and Robert Kennedy. The New Jersey chapter self-destructed in 1969 on the shoals of disagreement between purists and pragmatists. On the liberal reformers New Jersey never had, see James Q. Wilson, *The Amateur Democrat: Club Politics in Three Cities* (Chicago: University of Chicago Press, 1962). On the short, unhappy life of the New Jersey Democratic Coalition, see Vicki Granet Semel, *At the Grass Roots in the Garden State: Reform and Regular Democrats in New Jersey* (Cranbury, NJ: Associated University Presses, 1978).

2. Demographic data in this chapter are from the *Statistical Abstract of the United States* (Washington, DC: U.S. Department of Commerce, 2005), and Audrey Singer, "The Rise of New Immigrant Gateways" (Washington, DC: Center for Urban and Metropolitan Policy, Brookings Institution, 2004).

3. Donna de la Cruz, "Immigration in Spotlight in Jersey's Senate Race," *Philadelphia Inquirer,* August 24, 2006.

4. James W. Hughes and Joseph J. Seneca, "Population Slump Saps Our Economic Strength," *New Jersey Municipalities*, March 2006, 22ff.; quote, 22.

5. Quoted in Christine Todd Whitman, "The Metropolitan Challenge: A Considered Opinion," *Brookings Review* 16 (Fall 1998): 3.

6. James W. Hughes and Joseph J. Seneca, "Anatomy of a Recovery: A New Jersey Report Card," (Rutgers Regional Report, Edward J. Bloustein School of Planning and Public Policy, Rutgers University), no. 24, July 2005, 4.

7. Hughes and Seneca, "Population Slump," 8.

8. Steve Chambers and Robert Gebeloff, "A Suburban Crossroads Becomes Boom Town," *Newark Star-Ledger*, December 31, 2003.

9. Steve Chambers and Robert Gebeloff, "Suburbs Become the Job Capital," *Newark Star-Ledger*, December 29, 2003.

10. Joel Garreau, *Edge Cities* (New York: Doubleday, 1991). New Jersey's edge cities are Fort Lee/Edgewater, Paramus/Montvale, Mahwah, and the Meadowlands in Bergen County; Whippany/Parsippany/Troy Hills in Morris County; the Bridgewater Mall area in Somerset County; the Woodbridge Mall and Metropark

areas in Middlesex County; the Route 1 corridor from New Brunswick to Princeton in Middlesex and Mercer counties; and Cherry Hill in Camden County. Emerging edge cities center on Morristown and the Hudson County waterfront.

11. Jeffrey Otteau, quoted in Richard Digener, "Public Payroll Swells, Private Sector Shrinks, Housing Prices Fall," *Atlantic City Press*, January 27, 2007.

12. Hugh R. Morley, "New Jersey Drug Makers See Future in India," *Bergen Record*, October 20, 2004; Gunjan Sinha, "Outsourcing Drug Work," *Scientific American*, August 12, 2004.

13. George Sternlieb and James W. Hughes, "The Demographic and Economic Dynamics of New Jersey," in *The Political State of New Jersey*, ed. Gerald M. Pomper (New Brunswick, NJ: Rutgers University Press), 37, 39.

14. James W. Hughes and Joseph J. Seneca, "Tri-State Affluence: Losing by Winning" (Rutgers Regional Report, Edward J. Bloustein School of Planning and Public Policy, Rutgers University), no. 22, November 2004.

15. For example, David Mayhew, *Congress: The Electoral Connection* (New Haven, CT: Yale University Press, 1974); Gary C. Jacobson and Samuel Kernell, *Strategy and Choice in Congressional Elections* (New Haven, CT: Yale University Press, 1981); Bruce Cain, John Ferejohn, and Morris P. Fiorina, *The Personal Vote* (Cambridge, MA: Harvard University Press, 1987).

16. Voters in those areas of the state where antitax sentiment was particularly strong joined in 1994's national revolt against "tax and spend" congressional Democrats. A first-term Democratic House incumbent in a Passaic County–based district lost his seat, while South Jersey elected a Republican to an open seat previously held by the Democrats. As a result, the state's House delegation swung 8–5 to the Republicans, giving it the first GOP majority since 1962. In 1996, the Democrats recaptured a House seat lost in 1994, leaving the Republicans with a 7–6 majority in the delegation. The Democrats won a GOP seat in 1998, returning the delegation to its "traditional" 7–6 Democratic margin.

17. The three retiring members were Bernard Dwyer, elected in 1980; Frank Guarini, elected in 1978; and Robert Roe, elected in a special election in 1969.

18. Maria Newman, "Harmony Reigns (Surprise!) in New Jersey Redistricting," *New York Times*, July 15, 2001.

19. The shifts described here are a conservative estimate, since more precise measures that would show even higher levels of split partisan choices (such as individual-level survey data on votes for all offices) are not available.

20. The counties represented by Republican representatives Rodney Frelinghuysen and Frank LoBiondo show by far the highest levels of ticket splitting.

21. On gubernatorial recruitment generally, see Joseph A. Schlesinger, *Ambition and Politics* (Chicago: Rand McNally, 1966); Larry J. Sabato *Goodbye to Good-Time Charlie: The American Governorship Transformed* (Washington, DC: CQ Press, 1983).

22. Recognition levels of gubernatorial candidates are discussed further in chapters 5 and 8. When some of the larger counties created the office of county executive in the 1980s, many observers thought it would be a new stepping-stone to statewide office. Through 2005, none of them (with the exception of Essex County Executive Peter Shapiro, who was the Democratic gubernatorial candidate in 1985) have figured prominently in gubernatorial primary or general elections.

23. The exception is Governor William Cahill (1969–1973), who was defeated in the 1973 Republican primary when county leaders abandoned him. Governor

Jim McGreevey was elected in 2001 and, having resigned in 2004, did not seek reelection.

24. For one such analysis, see Bob Narus, "Paradise Lost," *New Jersey Reporter*, September 1985, 8–13. Narus describes voting patterns in Middlesex County, noting that its average Democratic vote for governor between 1973 and 1981 dropped 11 percent from the average in the period from 1949 to 1969.

25. Schundler changed his mind when, to assist DiFrancesco, Republican legislators pushed through an increase that added $1.6 million to the permissible primary campaign outlays.

26. Schundler, who headed the Hudson County Republicans, was, unsurprisingly, the only defector from the DiFrancesco camp. He was joined by William Dowd of Monmouth County, home of many Garden State Parkway tollbooths, when the other nineteen leaders shifted their support to Franks.

27. Quinnipiac University Poll, May 3, 2001, and Quinnipiac University Poll, June 10, 2001.

28. The exception was Morris County, which was carried by a popular county official who came in a distant third in the overall balloting.

29. Some pundits ascribed Lonegan's decision to run as a reaction to Schundler's refusal to support conservative insurgents in several state senate primaries in 2003. See Wally Edge, "The Inside Edge," PoliticsNJ.com, June 8, 2005 (accessed June 8, 2005).

30. The relationship was also somewhat attenuated in 1981, when Governor Kean's narrow margin should have produced three more assembly seats, and the Republicans only gained one. See Stephen A. Salmore, "Sizing Up the Vote," *New Jersey Reporter* March 1986, 45–47.

31. Neal R. Peirce, "New Jersey: In the Shadows of Megalopolis," in *The Megastates of America: People, Politics and Power in the Ten Great States* (New York: W. W. Norton, 1972), 199.

CHAPTER 5   VOTERS, ELECTIONS, AND POLITICS

1. Fairleigh Dickinson University *PublicMind* Poll, January 10, 2005; Fairleigh Dickinson University *PublicMind* Poll, April 10, 2005.

2. Fairleigh Dickinson University *PublicMind Poll*, April 10, 2005.

3. David Kocieniewski, "Corzine's Mix: Bold Ambitions but Rough Edges," *New York Times*, November 2, 2005.

4. David D. Kirkpatrick, "Alito Team Says He Lacks Polish, but Grit Is a Plus," *New York Times*, January 2, 2006.

5. Judy Peet, "The Good, the Bad and the Totally Bizarre," *Newark Star-Ledger*, November 14, 2005.

6. Eagleton Poll data, reported in Steven A. Salmore, "Public Opinion," in *Politics in New Jersey*, rev. ed., ed. Richard Lehne and Alan Rosenthal (New Brunswick, NJ: Rutgers University, Eagleton Institute of Politics, 1979), 73; Zukin, "Political Culture and Public Opinion," in *The Political State of New Jersey*, ed. Gerald M. Pomper (New Brunswick, NJ: Rutgers University Press, 1986), 23; *Star-Ledger*/Eagleton Poll, April 15, 1990.

7. Quinnipiac University Poll, July 16, 2006.

8. Barbara G. Salmore and Stephen A. Salmore, *Candidates, Parties, and Campaigns*, 2nd ed. (Washington, DC: CQ Press, 1989) 71; see also 210–211.

9. Ibid., chap. 6.

10. Fairleigh Dickinson University *PublicMind* Poll, October 28, 2005.

11. During the 1940s and 1950s, when television was much less widespread, channel 13, an independent commercial station, was licensed to Newark. Channel 13 became the "New York area" Public Broadcasting System outlet in 1961 (although still technically licensed to Newark), and its programming now consists primarily of the usual PBS fare.

12. See Jeremy Gerard, "A Channel Innovates and Moves Up: WWOR Further Erodes the Barriers Between News and Entertainment," *New York Times*, September 16, 1989.

13. See the analysis in Matthew Hale, "Television Coverage of the 2005 New Jersey Election: An Analysis of the Nightly News Programs on Local, New Jersey, New York and Philadelphia Stations" (Eagleton Institute of Politics, Rutgers University, June 2006),14.

14. Ibid., and Eagleton Institute of Politics, "Do New York TV stations Short-change New Jersey Voters? Rutgers' Eagleton Institute of Politics Analyzes Garden State's 2001 Election Coverage" (press release, September 18, 2002).

15. Tammy La Gorce, "The Competition: Public TV," *New York Times*, February 25, 2007.

16. Jon Shure, quoted in Alexander Maugeri, "Voters Prefer Corzine on Issues, Survey Finds," *Daily Princetonian*, November 14, 2005.

17. Monmouth University/Gannett New Jersey Poll, October 11, 2005.

18. The Newhouse newspapers, in descending order of circulation, are the *Newark Star-Ledger*, the *Trenton Times*, the *Jersey City Journal*, the *Gloucester County Times*, the *Express-Times* (published in Easton, Pennsylvania but circulating widely across the Delaware River in Warren County), *Today's Sunbeam* (Salem County), and the *Bridgeton News* (Cumberland County).

19. See Mary Walton, "The Jersey Giant," *American Journalism Review*, October 2000.

20. The Gannett papers have been particularly prone to obliterating locational mastheads for all but the flagship *Asbury Park Press*. The following list of their other dailies notes the location of their editorial offices: *Courier-News* (Bridgewater), *Courier-Post* (Cherry Hill), *Daily Journal* (Vineland), *Daily Record* (Morristown), *Home News Tribune* (New Brunswick), *Ocean County Observer* (Toms River).

21. Mary Walton, "Energy Boost," *American Journalism Review*, October/November 2004.

22. See Mark Magyar, "The Press," *New Jersey Reporter*, January 2004, 27–36.

23. A review of the leading newspapers' coverage from September through November indicates that the *Ledger* and the *Asbury Park Press* never ran such an analysis, and the *New York Times* published only two pieces that could be considered substantive looks at the proposals. The best performance belonged to the *Bergen Record*, which ran about four such pieces.

24. Eagleton Poll, February 1995, and Eagleton Poll, June 2002.

25. S. A. Paolantonio, "Countdown: New Jersey's Independent Voters Have Proven Volatile and Potent," *Philadelphia Inquirer*, October 30, 1988.

26. Data from Eagleton Polls, 1990–2006.

27. The argument of Gary Jacobson and Samuel Kernell in *Strategy and Choice in Congressional Elections* (New Haven, CT: Yale University Press, 1982); Gary Jacobson, *The Electoral Origins of Divided Government* (Boulder, CO: Westview Press, 1990).

28. Quoted in Josh Benson, "Divided and Conquered," *New York Times*, June 12, 2005.

29. Deborah Howlett, "Forrester Risks His Right-Wing Support; Gets Nod from GOP Pro-Choice Group," *Newark Star-Ledger*, October 26, 2005.

30. An argument made by Christine Todd Whitman, *It's My Party Too: The Battle for the Heart of the GOP and the Future of America* (New York: Penguin Press, 2005), and Jacob S. Hacker and Paul Pierson, *Off Center: The Republican Revolution and the Erosion of American Democracy* (New Haven, CT: Yale University Press, 2005).

31. Tom Moran, "Kean Gets Burned in the Backfire," *Newark Star-Ledger*, November 8, 2006.

32. This includes $10.7 million spent by Republican Doug Forrester, $6.4 million spent by incumbent Democrat Robert Torricelli before he withdrew on September 30, and $3.1 million spent by Democrat Frank Lautenberg, Torricelli's replacement.

33. For a discussion of the state's experience with public financing, see Robert A. Cropf, "Public Campaign Financing in New Jersey," *Comparative State Politics* 13 (April 1992): 1–11.

34. The law was a compromise between Republican Assembly Speaker Chuck Hardwick, who saw lower primary limits and higher general election limits to his advantage, and Democratic Senate President John Russo, who saw higher primary limits and lower general election limits as advantaging him. Russo withdrew from the Democratic contest shortly thereafter; Hardwick came in third in the Republican primary.

35. See Center for Analysis of Public Issues, "Smoke and Mirrors: The Failure of Campaign Finance Reform," *New Jersey Reporter*, March–April 1994, 24–29.

36. New Jersey Election Law Enforcement Commission, *2005 Cost Index* (Trenton, NJ: December 2004); Jeffrey Gold, "Sprint to Finish for N.J. Senate Candidates Includes More Ads," Associated Press, October 31, 2006.

37. For two perspectives, see Richard L. Lau and Gerald M. Pomper, *Negative Campaigning: An Analysis of U.S. Senate Races* (Lanham, MD: Rowman & Littlefield, 2004); Shanto Iyengar and Jennifer A. McGrady, *Media Politics: A Citizen's Guide* (New York: Norton, 2006).

38. Richard M. Schlackman of the Campaign Performance Group of San Francisco, quoted in James A. Barnes, "Legislative Races Counted, Too," *National Journal*, November 11, 1989, 2760. The "leading edge" nature of New Jersey legislative tactics generated a second article; see also James A. Barnes, "Campaign Letter Bombs," *National Journal*, November 25, 1989, 2881–2887.

39. Conference on the 1991 Legislative Elections, Eagleton Institute, December 11, 1991.

40. For the development of the concept of the party in service, see John Aldrich, *Why Parties? The Origin and Transformation of Political Parties in America* (Chicago: University of Chicago Press, 1995). The following section on the impact of the *Eu* decision is based on a revised version of Stephen A. Salmore and Barbara G. Salmore, "The Transformation of State Electoral Politics," in *The State of the States*, ed. Carl Van Horn, 2nd. ed. (Washington, DC: CQ Press, 1993), 51–78.

41. As far as we can determine, legislative leadership fund-raising and campaign direction began in New Jersey after the 1973 elections, when the Republicans were reduced to fourteen members in the assembly. Assembly Minority Leader Thomas Kean raised about $70,000 purely for 1975 assembly races, and spent it on generic newspaper advertising and targeted radio ads.

42. *Eu, Secretary of State of California, et al v. San Francisco Democratic Central Committee, et al.* 489 U.S. 214 (1989).

43. In spring 1997, Democratic Party Chair Tom Byrne (son of Governor Brendan Byrne) suggested that all of that year's gubernatorial aspirants appear before a screening committee of leading Democrats, and that if a particular candidate received 65 percent of their support, all of the twenty-one Democratic county

parties would be bound to endorse him or her. All of the county chairs supported this notion; unsurprisingly, the candidates did not, nor did the press, which spoke of the "return of the bosses." The proposal died a quick death. See New Jersey Election Law Enforcement Commission (hereafter ELEC), *Repartyization: The Rebirth of County Organizations* (ELEC White Paper no. 12, Trenton, NJ, November 1997), 7.

44. Constitution and By-Laws of the New Jersey Republican State Committee (March 22, 1994).
45. Revised By-Laws of the Democratic Party of the State of New Jersey (February, 1993).
46. ELEC, *Trends in Legislative Campaign Financing, 1977–1987* (ELEC White Paper no. 2, Trenton, NJ, 1989); ELEC, *Repartyization*; ELEC, *Trends in Legislative Campaign Financing, 1987–1997* (ELEC White Paper no. 13, Trenton, NJ, 1999), vol. 2; ELEC, *Legislative Election 2003: The Rise of Party-Oriented Campaigning* (ELEC White Paper no. 17, Trenton, NJ, 2004); ELEC, *The 2005 Assembly Election: New Trends on the Horizon?* (ELEC White Paper no. 19, Trenton, NJ, 2006).
47. ELEC, *Legislative Election 2003*, 3, 5.
48. David Menefee-Libey, *The Triumph of Campaign-Centered Politics* (New York: Chatham House, 2000), 93.
49. Josh Margolin and Jeff Whelan, "'Pay to Play' Ban: A Way Around It?" *Newark Star-Ledger*, October 1, 2005. The ELEC analysis of campaign finance in the 2005 assembly election notes a shift away from PAC contributions to state and county party committees and toward the legislative campaign committees, and speculates this may have transpired in anticipation of avoiding "pay to play" restrictions. See ELEC, *The 2005 Assembly Elections*, 16.
50. Diane C. Walsh, "Reform of 'Pay to Play' Bidding Leaves Same Cast in Place," *Newark Star-Ledger*, February 6, 2006.
51. See, for example, Alan Guenther, "Boss Norcross," a three-part series on Camden County Democratic leader George Norcross, *Cherry Hill Courier-Post*, February 16–February 18, 2003; Paul D'Ambrosio, "Like Puppeteers, Bosses Pull the Strings," *Asbury Park Press*, parts 1 and 2, October 24, 2004, October 25, 2004; and the series "The Power Brokers," *New York Times*, January 1, 2006, January 7, 2006, January 9, 2006, January 16, 2006, and January 25, 2006.
52. Rick Malwitz, "Lynch Felt Frustrated by McGreevey," *Cherry Hill Courier-Post*, November 10, 2005.

CHAPTER 6   THE REPRESENTATION OF INTERESTS

The first epigraph for this chapter is drawn from Dayton David McKean, "A State Legislature and Group Pressure," *Annals*, 179 (May 1935), 127. The second epigraph is drawn from Joseph Gonzales, executive director of the New Jersey Business and Industry Association, as quoted in Dan Weissman, "Fourth Branch of Government: Lobbyists Play Pivotal Role in Legislative Action," *Newark Star Ledger*, March 22, 1987. Much of this chapter is a revised version of Stephen A. Salmore and Barbara G. Salmore, "New Jersey: From the Hacks to the Political Action Committees," in *Interest Group Politics in the Northeastern States*, ed. Ronald J. Hrebenar and Clive S. Thomas (University Park: Penn State University Press, 1993).

1. State Senator Lawrence Weiss and lobbyist Frank Capece, both quoted in Weissman, "Fourth Branch of Government."

2. McKean, "A State Legislature and Group Pressure," 129; Dayton David McKean, *Pressures on the Legislature of New Jersey* (New York: Columbia University Press, 1938), 223.

3. For a discussion of changing interest group politics in the states, see Clive S. Thomas and Ronald J. Hrebenar, "Interest Groups in the States," in *Politics and the American States: A Comparative Analysis*, ed. Virginia L. Gray and Russell L. Hanson, 8th ed. (Washington, DC: CQ Press, 2008), chap. 4.

4. McKean, *Pressures*, 52–120.

5. Wording from the questionnaire in John Wahlke et al., *The Legislative System* (New York: Wiley, 1962), appendix 6, 498–500.

6. Wahlke et al., *The Legislative System*, 315.

7. Philip H. Burch Jr., "Interest Groups," in *Politics in New Jersey*, rev. ed., ed. Richard Lehne and Alan Rosenthal (New Brunswick, NJ: Eagleton Institute of Politics, 1979), chaps. 5, 11.

8. Burch, "Interest Groups," 110, 112, 115.

9. The Gallup study's internal evidence and our conversations with Gallup lead us to speculate that the clients were probably the state's largest corporations and the state Chamber of Commerce, which they dominate. The Chamber is the only often-discussed major lobby not rated in the publicly released material. Other questions center on legislators' views of PACs and contract lobbyists. The Chamber did not establish a PAC until 1987, and these corporations have also not much utilized the burgeoning contract lobbyists, discussed below. We cannot confirm these speculations, however.

10. Anonymous quote, Gallup Organization, *The 1987 Gallup Survey of the New Jersey State Legislature* (Princeton, NJ, 1987), 5; Gerald Cardinale, quoted in Tom Moran, "In Tax Fight, the Teachers Are a Study in Clout," *Newark Star-Ledger*, August 11, 2006.

11. This finding may relate to an overrepresentation of Republicans in the Gallup sample. Although both groups give financial support to both parties, the NJBIA is usually more "bipartisan," relatively, in its giving.

12. Anonymous quote, Gallup Organization, *1987 Survey*, 6.

13. Thomas Fleming, *New Jersey: A History* (New York: Norton, 1984), 162.

14. For discussions of the political role of labor in New Jersey, see Leo Troy, *Organized Labor in New Jersey* (Princeton, NJ: D. Van Nostrand, 1964); Bob Narus, "The Marciante Mystique," *New Jersey Reporter*, April 1984, 22–27; Joel R. Jacobson, "Guilty Until Proven Innocent," *New Jersey Reporter*, March 1988; Donald Warshaw, "State AF of L Chief Urges Labor to Develop Bipartisan Political Strategy," *Newark Star-Ledger*, February 19, 1989, 42; Donald Warshaw, "IUC Pledges Major Push for Florio," *Newark Star-Ledger*, August 6, 1989, 19.

15. Cynthia Burton, "AFL Leader Ready to Pass Torch," *Newark Star-Ledger*, January 5,1997. Louis Marciante was president from 1934 to 1961, the year Charles became secretary-treasurer. The younger Marciante assumed the presidency in 1991. From 1989 to 1996 Wowkanech served as assistant to the president and after a year as secretary treasurer became president in 1997.

16. Alice Chasan Edelman, "Church and State Street," *New Jersey Reporter*, November 1985.

17. Quoted in Bill Glovin, "The Quintessential Art of Lobbying," *New Jersey Business*, July 1987, 62.

18. Nancy H. Becker, *Lobbying in New Jersey* (New Brunswick, NJ: Center for the American Woman in Politics, Eagleton Institute, Rutgers University, 1978).

19. Ibid., 53.

20. An excellent general study of lobbyists in six states, including New Jersey, is Alan Rosenthal, *The Third House* (Washington, DC: CQ Press, 1997). The source for all the data reported in this section is the New Jersey Election Law Enforcement Commission, supplemented by the annual *New Jersey Legislative Manual.*
21. Calculated by the authors from data in Gallup Organization, *1987 Survey,* 7.
22. See the report by New Jersey Citizen Action, *Political Power Lines: Running at Full Capacity,* (Hackensack, NJ: New Jersey Citizen Action, June 6, 2006).
23. For a full account of the battle, see Becker, *Lobbying in New Jersey,* and Dan Weissman, "Just One Little Word in Lobbyist Law Makes Big Difference on Disclosure," *Newark Star-Ledger,* March 24, 1987.
24. Weissman, "Just One Little Word."
25. Robert Schwaneberg, "Some Fear New Rules Make Almost Everyone a Lobbyist," *Newark Star-Ledger,* March 16, 2005.
26. In addition to a complete veto and a line item veto, New Jersey's governor may exercise a conditional veto, which permits him or her to send a bill back to the legislature with suggestions for changing in wording.
27. McKean (*Pressures,* 204) estimated that two-thirds of all bills in the 1930s were written by lobbyists.
28. Gallup Organization, *1987 Survey,* found that more than 50 percent of legislators found the provision of such information "very useful" (14). Legislators were much less likely to appreciate lobbyists' organization of constituent support or opposition (18 percent) or working with party leadership (16 percent) as "very useful" (17). Just about half said they relied on lobbyists "very" or "somewhat" frequently for information, and only 11 percent said "not frequently at all." Senior legislators were only slightly less likely to say they relied on lobbyists with some regularity.
29. In 2004, ELEC produced a study entitled "Road to the Future: Improving the Convenience and Usefulness of ELEC's Internet Site." It addressed the need for adequate funding to improve its ability to compile and analyze data including PAC information.
30. Herb Jackson and Benjamin Lesser, "Under the Influence: Money in Trenton," *Bergen Record,* August 8, 2004.
31. Gallup Organization, *1987 Survey,* 9–10.
32. Jackson and Lesser, "Under the Influence," August 8, 2004.
33. Ibid.
34. Rick Linsk, "Millions Spent on Lobbying Legislature," *Asbury Park Press,* February 24, 1991.
35. See Susan Warner, "Totally Wired," *New York Times,* January 1, 2006; Joe Donohue and Dunstan McNichol, "Cable Fight Ups Tab for Lobbying," *Newark Star-Ledger,* February 25, 2006.
36. Maine (1996) and Arizona (1998) have "clean elections" funding schemes for legislative elections. Massachusetts had a similar plan from 1998 to 2002 but repealed it in 2003 because of state budget difficulties. In 2005, Connecticut passed a law to entirely fund all legislative and statewide elections beginning in 2008. Minnesota and Wisconsin have had variant schemes involving tax return checkoffs since the 1970s.
37. Advisory referenda on nonstate issues are permitted, however. In 1982, voters endorsed a "verifiable" U.S.–Soviet nuclear weapons freeze by a margin of two to one. The Optional Municipal Charter Law of 1950, adopted by more than one hundred municipalities including all of the state's larger cities, provides for initiative and recall at the local level, as does the Commission Form of Government Law of 1916, which covers another thirty-five municipalities. Local

petition signature requirements range from 15 percent of the number of ballots cast for the state legislature in the previous election to 25 percent of the number of registered voters.

38. For a summary of New Jersey's involvement with I&R, see David Schmidt, *Citizen Lawmakers: The Ballot Initiative Revolution* (Philadelphia: Temple University Press, 1989), 5–9, 251–252, 305.

39. Kaitlin Gurney, "Try Clean Elections Again, Say Monitors," *Philadelphia Inquirer,* February 8, 2006.

40. *The 2007 New Jersey Clean and Fair Elections Pilot Project Act,* P.L. 2007, chap. 60, approved March 28, 2007. Among its other major provisions, the act provided for 50 percent funding for unopposed, independent, or minor party candidates, and a five-member committee consisting of two citizens appointed by each of the major parties, and a former governor to choose the split district if the parties' leaders could not agree on it. It appropriated a maximum of $7.675 million to fund the pilot project. This included funds to publicize the program, which had been practically invisible in 2005. Surveys taken for the clean elections commission shortly before the election found that 79 percent of likely voters statewide had heard "little or nothing" about it, and more than two-thirds of the registered and likely voters in the sixth and thirteenth districts did not know that their legislative candidates had been chosen to participate. See Peter Wooley and Tim Vercellotti, *The Well-Kept Secret of Clean Elections: Draft Report to the Citizens' Clean Election Commission,* November 21, 2005. This report is available at www.eagleton.rutgers.edu/NJProject/CleanElections (accessed April 9, 2007).

41. George Amick, "Clean Elections Bill a Sham, Critic Says," *Trenton Times,* March 19, 2007. Schluter, a Republican who served in the assembly and the senate from 1967 to 2001, resigned from the legislature to run as an independent candidate for governor.

42. Quoted in Tom Hester, "'Clean Elections' Approved," *Newark Star-Ledger,* March 16, 2007.

43. Physicians' assistants (PAs) did manage to persuade the legislature to transfer the decision to the State Board of Medical Examiners. In 1990, the board authorized PAs to practice in the state, with many restrictions, for a two-year trial period that later became permanent. Governor Corzine's suggestion in 2006 to permit self-service gas stations did not fare any better than previous proposals.

CHAPTER 7   THE CONSTITUTION

The first epigraph is drawn from a quote in Julian M. Boyd, "Introduction," in *Fundamental Laws and Constitutions of New Jersey, 1664–1964,* ed. Julian M. Boyd (Princeton: D. Van Nostrand, 1964), 8.

1. Daniel J. Elazar, "The Principles and Traditions Underlying State Constitutions," *Publius* 12 (Winter 1982): 11–25.

2. Richard N. Baisden, *Charter for New Jersey: The New Jersey Constitutional Convention of 1947* (Trenton: New Jersey State Library, 1952), 104. Principal authorship is usually attributed to Jonathan Dickinson Sergeant, a New Jersey delegate to the Continental Congress. See Charles Erdman, *The Constitution of 1776* (Princeton, NJ: Princeton University Press, 1929), 32–37.

3. Lucius Q. C. Elmer, in *The Constitution and Government of the Province and State of New Jersey* (Newark: Martin R. Dennis and Co., 1872), is the leading proponent of those who attribute chief authorship to John Witherspoon, president of the College of New Jersey at Princeton.

4. Quoted in Erdman, *The Constitution of 1776*, 39.

5. John Bebout, "The Making of the New Jersey Constitution," introduction to the reprint of *Proceedings of the New Jersey State Constitutional Convention of 1844* (1844; repr., Trenton: McCrellish and Quigley, 1945), xix.

6. William Griffith [Eumenes], *Collection of Papers Written For the Purpose of Exhibiting Some of the More Prominent Errors and Omissions of the Constitution of New Jersey and to Prove the Necessity of Calling a Convention for Revision and Amendment* (Trenton, NJ: G. Craft, 1799). The papers started appearing in the *New Jersey Gazette* in 1798, and were published as a book the following year.

7. These problems characterized many of the early state constitutions. See Albert L. Sturm, "The Development of American State Constitutions," *Publius* (Winter 1982), 62–63.

8. The legislature statutorily abolished the right to trial by jury at least fifty times between 1790 and 1800.

9. 9 New Jersey Law (IV Halsted), 1802, 427, 433. Erdman discusses the case in detail in *The Constitution of 1776*, 78–80. The earlier 1780 case, *Holmes v. Walton*, is described in Austin Scott, "*Holmes v. Walton; the New Jersey Precedent*," *American Historical Revie*, 4 (1898–1899): 463.

10. *Eumenes*, quoted in Francis Bazely Lee, *New Jersey as a Colony and as a State* (New York: Publication Society of New Jersey, 1902), 3: 267, 268.

11. There were occasions when local election officers disregarded the law, holding it to be unconstitutional and void, and permitted aliens, women and nonwhites to vote. See Elmer, *The Constitution*, 49.

12. "Publius," *Centinel of Freedom*, Newark, January 23, 1816; quoted in Bebout, *Making of the New Jersey Constitution,* xliii.

13. The opinion of Erdman, *Constitution of 1776*, 46, 47, 99.

14. For example, the major reason the legislature adjusted the representation of Hunterdon, Sussex, Cumberland, and Cape May counties in 1797 was a desire to reduce Quaker influence and ensure the defeat of a bill to abolish slavery. Lee, *New Jersey as a Colony and a State*, 272.

15. James Madison [Publius], *The Federalist Papers*, no. 47, Mentor edition, with introduction, table of contents, and index of ideas by Clinton Rossiter (New York: New American Library, 1961), 301, 305

16. Griffith [Eumenes], quoted in Bebout, *Making of the New Jersey Constitution*, xx, lvi.

17. Quoted in H. McD. Clokie, "New Jersey and the Confederation," in *New Jersey: A History*, ed. Irving S. Kull, 4 vols. (New York: American Historical Society, 1930–32), 2:563.

18. New Jersey *Minutes of the Assembly*, 1842, 18.

19. Richard J. Connors, *The Process of Constitutional Revision in New Jersey*, State Constitutional Convention Studies, no. 4. (New York: National Municipal League, 1970).

20. See Sturm, "Development of American State Constitutions," 63–64.

21. Biographies of the delegates were compiled by the New Jersey Federal Writer's Project of the WPA; the data are reported in Bebout, *Making of the New Jersey Constitution*, lxi–lxxiii.

22. The one dissenting delegate objected to the provision giving each county equal representation in the senate. This stipulation, which would have momentous consequences, was not perceived as very significant. Every county but Monmouth observed a bipartisan agreement to apportion delegates evenly, resulting in a convention of thirty Democrats and twenty-eight Whigs.

23. Bebout, *Making of the New Jersey Constitution*, lxix.

24. Ibid.

25. Although the bill of rights borrowed heavily from the federal Constitution, the local Quaker influence was evident in the strict subordination of the militia to civil authorities and the omission of a stated right to keep or bear arms.

26. "Report of the Committee of Council, on the Proposed Alteration of the Constitution," *Journal of Council*, 1844, quoted in Frederick M. Hermann, "The Constitution of 1844 and Political Change in Antebellum New Jersey," *New Jersey History* 101 (Spring and Summer 1983): 32.

27. *Trenton State Gazette*, February 26, 1844, quoted in Bebout, *Making of the New Jersey Constitution,* lxiv.

28. Boyd, "Introduction," 36.

29. Bebout, *Making of the New Jersey Constitution*, ciii.

30. Federal Writers Project, *New Jersey: A Guide to Its Present and Past* (New York: Hastings House, 1939), 56.

31. Elazar, "Principles and Traditions," 19. For an argument that the 1844 constitution took some small steps in that direction, see Frederick Herrmann, "Stress and Structure," 29–51.

32. William E. Sackett, *Modern Battles of Trenton* (New York: Neale, 1914), 2:380.

33. Connors, *Process of Constitutional Revision*, 17.

34. Quoted in Bebout, *Making of the New Jersey Constitution*, lviii.

35. For the details of these many failed efforts, see Bebout, *Making of the New Jersey Constitution*, civ–cvii; Bebout, "New Task for a Legislature," *National Municipal Review* 33 (1944): 18; notes by Bebout in *National Municipal Review* 33 (1944): 88, 200; Erdman, *The Constitution of 1776*, 31–36. The most frequent topics were court reform, longer terms for officeholders, biennial legislative sessions, single member assembly districts, and a simpler amending process. Altogether, there were seven constitutional commissions during the life of the 1844 charter, and the legislature passed amendments five other times.

36. The sectarian aspects of the 1875 election are described in Sackett, *Modern Battles of Trenton* (Trenton, NJ: J. L. Murphy, 1895), 94–97.

37. Boyd, "Introduction," 38.

38. Bebout, *Making of the New Jersey Constitution*, cvi.

39. Voorhees E. Dunn Jr., "Chief Justice Arthur T. Vanderbilt and the Judicial Revolution in New Jersey" (Ph.D. diss., Rutgers University, 1987).

40. For accounts of Edison's battles with Hague throughout his term, see John D. Venable, *Out of the Shadow: The Story of Charles Edison* (East Orange, NJ: Charles Edison Fund, 1978); Jack Alexander, "Ungovernable Governor—Charles Edison, First New Jersey Executive Since Wilson, Has Hague and His Hessians Groggy in the Second Battle of Trenton," *Saturday Evening Post*, January 23, 1943, 9ff.

41. Arthur Vanderbilt to James P. Alexander, chief justice of the Texas Supreme Court, December 20, 1943, Vanderbilt Papers, Wesleyan University, Box 147, quoted in Dunn, *Chief Justice Arthur T. Vanderbilt*, 74.

42. The report of the Commission is reprinted in *Record of the Proceedings Before the Joint Committee of the New Jersey Legislature to Ascertain the Sentiment of the People as to Change in the New Jersey Constitution*, 1942, 909–958.

43. Arthur T. Vanderbilt to Herbert Harley, July 17, 1942, Vanderbilt Papers, quoted in Dunn, "Chief Justice Arthur T. Vanderbilt," 81; Bennett M. Rich, "Convention or Commission?" *National Municipal Review* 37 (1948): 133–139.

44. *In Re Hague*, 123 N.J. Eq. 475, 150 A 323 (1930).

45. Hague had predicted that Hendrickson and Vanderbilt would use the commission "for the purpose of revising the constitution to suit themselves and the interests they represent: the railroads and other malefactors of great wealth." *Jersey Journal*, November 25, 1941, quoted in Arthur T. Vanderbilt II, *Changing Law: A Biography of Arthur T. Vanderbilt* (New Brunswick, NJ: Rutgers University Press, 1976), 125.
46. *Record of the Joint Legislative Committee*, 869.
47. Connors, *Process of Constitutional Reform*, 65.
48. *New Jersey Legislative Manual*, 1943, 632.
49. Vanderbilt, *Changing Law*, 147.
50. The only major differences from the Hendrickson product were the removal of the nine specifically named cabinet departments and dropping a proposal for limited, biennial legislative sessions—both concessions to the legislature.
51. See Connors, *Process of Constitutional Revision*, 99; Alexander, "Ungovernable Governor, 173; Venable, *Out of the Shadow*, 170–181; *Newark Evening News*, June 23, 1944, 16. The state supreme court ruled the tax debt cancellation unconstitutional in July 1943, and the court of errors and appeals, in a 10–4 ruling, upheld the supreme court in June 1944. See Dunn, : Chief Justice Arthur T. Vanderbilt," 82–83. This was a pyrrhic victory, as the Court of Errors and Appeals upheld the new tax formula in 1946. See, Baisden *Charter for New Jersey*, 88.
52. *Newark Sunday Call*, April 23, 1944, quoted in Connors, *Process of Constitutional Revision*, 90.
53. The opponents' plurality was 126,000. The constitution lost by 87,000 votes in Hudson County, and by 53,000 votes in Camden County. Connors, *Process of Constitutional Revision*, 108.
54. See the summary assessments in Connors, *Process of Constitutional Revision*, 110–112; Baisden, *Charter for New Jersey*, 1952; Dunn, "Chief Justice Arthur T. Vanderbilt," 96–99.
55. *New Jersey Legislative Manual*, 1947, 705.
56. Quoted in Vanderbilt, *Changing Law*, 150.
57. Speech to the Headquarters Committee of the Clean Government Republican Committee, April 11, 1947, Vanderbilt Papers, Box 174, quoted in Dunn, "Chief Justice Arthur T. Vanderbilt," 125, 129.
58. Baisden, *Charter for New Jersey*, 8. Connors, *Process of Constitutional Revision*, 128–129, writes that there were thirty-one legislators or ex-legislators.
59. This did not prevent interest groups from deluging the delegates with written special pleadings, mailed to them both at their homes and at the convention site. See the examples cited by Hudson County delegate Frank G. Schlosser, *Dry Revolution: Diary of a Constitutional Convention* (Newton, NJ: Onnabrite Press, 1960), 15, 32, 47.
60. Connors, *Process of Constitutional Revision*, 145.
61. In a referendum of state bar association members, there were 583 votes to retain the equity courts and 549 opposed. Of the sixteen associations that took positions, seven favored retention, three were opposed, and six so divided they could not make a recommendation (including the two largest—the state and Essex County associations). See Baisden, *Charter for New Jersey*, 47.
62. Connors, *Process of Constitutional Revision*, 156.
63. Quoted in ibid., 165.
64. Schlosser, *Dry Revolution*, 39.
65. Ibid., 176.

66. Albert Sturm called it "probably the most noteworthy accomplishment" of all constitutional action on state judiciaries in the period 1900–1950. Sturm, "Development of American State Constitutions," 71.
67. Baisden, *Charter for New Jersey*, 100; Connors, *Process of Constitutional Revision*, 181.
68. Sturm, "Development of American State Constitutions," 74. The average length is about twenty-six thousand words.
69. Connors, *Process of Constitutional Revision*, 203, 198.

CHAPTER 8   THE GOVERNOR

The first epigraph in this chapter is drawn from *Democracy in America* (New York: Vintage Books, 1954), 1:86. The second is fromThomas H. Kean, *The Politics of Inclusion* (New York: Free Press, 1988), 63. The third is from Tom Hester and Jeff Whelan, "Governor asks for Faster Action on Tax Reform and Other Top Priorities," *Newark Star-Ledger*, April 21, 2006.

1. Article 7, New Jersey Constitution of 1776.
2. Francis Bazely Lee, *New Jersey as a Colony and as a State* (New York: Publishing Society of New Jersey, 1902), 3:272.
3. Julian P. Boyd, ed., "Introduction," *Fundamental Laws and Constitutions of New Jersey, 1664–1964* (Princeton NJ: D. Van Nostrand, 1964), 29. See Duane Lockard on the "patrician governors," *The New Jersey Governor: A Study in Political Power,* (Princeton, NJ: D. Van Nostrand, 1964), 36–56; and Walter R. Fee, *The Transition from Aristocracy to Democracy in New Jersey* (Somerville, NJ: Somerset Press, 1933).
4. Speech of Delegate Peter Clark, *Proceedings of the New Jersey State Constitutional Convention of 1844*, 185. Clark's fears were well-founded. Governors of the second half of the nineteenth century were primarily business figures. See Lockard, *The New Jersey Governor*, chap. 4.
5. Article 5, Section 6, New Jersey Constitution of 1844. Coleman Ransone makes this point in *The American Governorship* (Westport, CT: Greenwood Press, 1982), 123. New Jersey's governors apparently began issuing substantive messages to the legislature as early as 1830. See Lockard, *The New Jersey Governor*, 50. Ehrenhalt believes that Wilson was the first governor to lay out a proposed legislative program. Alan Ehrenhalt, "The Unconstitutional Governor," *Governing Magazine*, May 2006.
6. The classic discussion of informal presidential power is Richard Neustadt, *Presidential Power* (New York: John Wiley, 1960). Duane Lockard applies the concept to the governorship in *The Politics of State and Local Government* (New York: Macmillan, 1963), 363–364, and specifically to New Jersey's governors in *The New Jersey Governor*, 130. See also Alan Rosenthal, *Governors and Legislators: Contending Powers,* (Washington: CQ Press, 1990), chap. 4. A survey of state senators found that in states where governors had strong formal powers, legislators saw them as most important; where governors were constitutionally weak, informal powers were seen as more important. E. Lee Bernick, "Gubernatorial Tools: Formal vs. Informal," *Journal of Politics* 41 (1979): 103–109.
7. See the comparative rankings provided by Thad Beyle at www.unc.edu/~beyle (accessed April 14, 2007).
8. New Jersey's governor may freely appoint (with the consent of the state senate) and remove all but three cabinet members. The secretary of state and the attorney

general are appointed in the same way but may not be involuntarily removed during a gubernatorial term except for cause. The agriculture secretary—an increasingly insignificant official—is selected by the self-perpetuating State Board of Agriculture and approved by the governor.

9. Quoted in Thomas H. Kean, *The Politics of Inclusion* (New York: Free Press, 1988), 63. See also Laura Mansnerus, "Call It 'Ayatollah' or 'Caesar,' It's the Imperial Governorship; When Comparing Power, New Jersey's Chief Executive, Unlike Peers in the Other States, Holds All the Cards," *New York Times*, July 30, 2000. The list of gubernatorial powers is outlined in Rosenthal, *Governors and Legislatures*, chap. 2. A final item on Rosenthal's list is the power of *experience*— their own service in the legislature, bringing friendships and understanding. Seven of New Jersey's ten postwar governors have also had this advantage.

10. Bennett Rich, *The Government and Administration of New Jersey* (New York: Thomas Y. Crowell, 1957), 100.

11. The five Catholic governors are Richard Hughes, William Cahill, Brendan Byrne, Jim Florio, and Jim McGreevey. Governor Robert Meyner, elected in the 1950s, was raised a Catholic, but later described himself as unaffiliated with a denomination. Although Florio is often called "the first Italian governor," his maternal ancestry is Irish. The first Catholic to be nominated for governor was Democrat Vincent J. Murphy of Hudson County, in 1943.

12. Anonymous quote in David Von Drehle, "In New Jersey, GOP Seeks to Reclaim Lost Ground: But Senate Race Fails to Yield Strong Contender," *Washington Post*, June 2, 2002.

13. Donald Linky, "The Governor," in *The Political State of New Jersey*, ed. Gerald M. Pomper (New Brunswick, NJ: Rutgers University Press, 1986), 93.

14. The struggling State Aquarium closed for nine months in 2004 after being sold to a private company that reopened it as the Adventure Aquarium in 2005. The facility's early troubles were attributed to the slow pace of neighboring development at its location on the Camden waterfront and its initial decision to limit exhibits to sea creatures from New Jersey waters, most of whom were a boring brown or gray in color. See Michael DeCourcy Hinds, "Camden's Aquarium Risks Ignominy: Drab Exhibits a Problem as Complex Fails to Lift Waterfront," *New York Times*, October 17, 1994; Geoff Mulvihill, "Aquarium Resurfaces With New Look: It's Back as a For-Profit Attraction With an Emphasis on Entertainment," *Bergen Record*, May 25, 2005.

15. See Sarah McCalley Morehouse, "The State Political Party and the Policy-Making Process, *American Political Science Review* 67 (March 1973): 60; Alan S. Wyner, "Gubernatorial Relations with Legislators and Administrators," *State Government* 41 (Summer 1968): 199–203; Lee Sigelman and Nelson C. Dometrious, "Governors as Chief Administrators: The Linkage Between Formal Powers and Informal Influence," *American Politics Quarterly* 16 (April 1988): 157–170.

16. Alan Karcher, quoted in Felzenberg, *Governor Tom Kean: From the New Jersey Statehouse to the 9-11 Commission* (New Brunswick, NJ: Rutgers University Press, 2006), 333.

17. Herb Jackson, "Lessons from the Whitman Years," *Bergen Record*, November 14, 2005.

18. For an analysis of gubernatorial styles, see Alvin S. Felzenberg, "The Impact of Gubernatorial Style on Policy Outcomes: An In Depth Study of Three New Jersey Governors" Ph.D. diss., Princeton University, October 1978).

19. Richard Hughes, quoted in Linky, *The Governor*, 98; Virginia D. Sederis, "Mr. Hughes Remembers," *New Jersey Reporter*, April 1985, 15; James E. McGreevey, *The Confession* (New York: HarperCollins, 2006), 165.

20. Kanige, "Brendan Byrne on Brendan Byrne," *New Jersey Reporter*, June 1988, 12.
21. Albert Burstein, quoted in ibid., 16.
22. Private communication to the authors, April 1989.
23. Brigid Harrison, quoted in Richard G. Jones and David W. Chen, "Corzine Shifts to Collegiality on the Budget," *New York Times*, June 12, 2006.
24. Jeff Whelan, Josh Margolin, and Mark Mueller, "How a Budget Dispute Became a Brawl," *Newark Star*-Ledger, July 9, 2006.
25. Joe Donohue, "Corzine Budget to Raise Pay for Judges," *Newark Star-Ledger*, February 24, 2007; Deborah Howlett and Josh Margolin, "A Hard Year, But Corzine Says He's Ready for More," *Newark Star-Ledger*, December 17, 2006.
26. See Alan Rosenthal, "The Governor and the Legislature," in *Politics in New Jersey*, rev. ed., ed. Alan Rosenthal and Richard Lehne (New Brunswick, NJ: Rutgers University, Eagleton Institute, 1979), 143–144.
27. "Three Decades in the Governor's Office: A Panel Discussion" (Trenton: New Jersey Historical Commission, 1983), 20.
28. Maureen Moakley, "New Jersey," in *The Politics of the American States*, ed. Alan Rosenthal and Maureen Moakley (New York: Praeger, 1984), 233.
29. Walter E. Edge, *A Jerseyman's Journal* (Princeton, NJ: Princeton University Press, 1948), 340.
30. Federal Writers Project, Works Public Administration, *New Jersey* (New York: Hastings House, 1939), 58.
31. "Three Decades in the Governor's Office," 19–20.
32. Kanige, "Brendan Byrne," 18; Felzenberg, "The Impact of Gubernatorial Style," 391.
33. Kean describes these experiences in his informal autobiography, *The Politics of Inclusion* (New York: The Free Press, 1988), chap. 1. They are also recounted in Felzenberg, *Governor Tom Kean*, chap. 7.
34. Kean interview, September 29, 1989.
35. For example, polling showed that one such talk and spate of weekly newspaper articles on property tax relief increased Whitman's identification with that issue by 10 percent. Robert Bostock, Whitman's senior deputy director of communications, interview with author, June 22, 2006.
36. Harvey Fisher, "The Governor: Something for Everyone," *New Jersey Reporter*, March 1984, 46.
37. Alessandra Stanley, "Governors Facing Fiscal Troubles Take Their Cases to the Airwaves," *New York Times*, July 22, 1991.
38. Thad L. Beyle, "Governors' Offices: Variations on Common Themes," *Being Governor: The View from the Office* (Durham, NC: Duke University Press, 1983), 158–173.
39. Thomas O'Neill, "Viewpoint: The Governor," *New Jersey Magazine*, January 1978, 14–15. For a description of the second-term reorganization from the point of view of Robert Mulcahey, Byrne's first chief of staff, see Don Di Maio, "The Mulcahey Formula: Loyalty and Long Hours," *New Jersey Magazine*, May 1978, 21–24.
40. Private communication to authors, May 1989.
41. See the comparative discussion in Thad L. Beyle, "The Governor as Innovator in the Federal System," *Publius* 18 (Summer 1988): 133–154.
42. Christine Walton, "On Top of Florio's Mail," *Trenton Times*, July 23, 1990; Angela delli Santi, "Governor Corzine, You've Got Mail. And Lots of It!" Associated Press, February 20, 2005.
43. Bostock interview.
44. Kean interview, September 29, 1989.

45. David W. Chen, "In Huge Merger Of 2 Utilities, 'Quiet Agency' Is in Spotlight," *New York Times*, August 20, 2006; Laura Mansnerus, "New Jersey Opposition Leads to Utility Merger's Collapse," *New York Times*, September 15, 2006.
46. Dan Weissman, "Selective Entry into the Governor's Inner Office," *Newark Star-Ledger*, May 19, 1991.
47. Private communication to authors, May 1989.
48. Joseph R. Malone, quoted in Jones and Chen, "Corzine Shifts to Collegiality on the Budget."

CHAPTER 9   THE LEGISLATURE

The first epigraph in this chapter quotes Passaic County Assemblyman Emil Olszowy, during the debate over the income tax. The second is drawn from Duane Lockard, "The Strong Governorship: Status and Problems—New Jersey," *Public Administration Review* 36 (January–February 1976): 96. The third is drawn from Alan Rosenthal, "The Legislature," in *The Political State of New Jersey*, ed. Gerald M. Pomper (New Brunswick, NJ: Rutgers University Press, 1986), 136.

1. John Wahlke, *The Legislative System: Explorations in Legislative Behavior* (New York: John Wiley, 1962), 44–62.
2. Bennett M. Rich, *The Government and Administration of New Jersey* (New York: Thomas Y. Crowell, 1957), 55.
3. Ibid., 53. The other states were Idaho, Montana, Nevada, New Mexico, and South Carolina.
4. Dayton David McKean, *Pressures on the Legislature of New Jersey* (New York: Columbia University Press, 1938), 44; Eagleton Institute of Politics, Rutgers University, *The New Jersey Legislature* (New Brunswick, NJ: November 15, 1963), 5.
5. Senators may have to run after two years as a result of the decennial census and subsequent legislative reapportionment. For example, the last several elections for the senate occurred in 1987, 1991, 1993 (as a result of reapportionment), 1997, 2001, 2003 (as a result of reapportionment), and 2007. This peculiar schedule results in alternating periods when the senate is frequently elected at the same time as the governor (for example, 1985, 1989, 1993, 1997, 2001, 2005), and periods when it is elected mostly in the gubernatorial midterm (for example, 1991, 2003, 2007). The 1980s election schedule meant the senate's Democratic majority did not have to run in the 1985 Republican landslide gubernatorial election, which saw the assembly go Republican for the first time in fourteen years.
6. Richard A. Zimmer, "Less Could Be More," *New Jersey Reporter*, June 1984, 16–17.
7. For a description of the 1980 process and the differing interests of party organizations and their incumbents, see Bob Narus, "A Rubik's Cube for Pols," *New Jersey Reporter*, May 1981, 3–15. For the 1990 process, see Peter Kerr, "New Jersey Redistricting Sets Off Debate on Shift in Minority Voters," *New York Times*, March 29, 1991; David Wald, "New Legislative Map Clears in Bitter Vote," *Newark Star-Ledger*, March 29, 1991.
8. Bartels viewed these criteria as precedents set by Stokes. "Partisan fairness" was defined as a high correlation between the percentage of votes won by a party and the resulting percentage of legislative seats; "responsiveness" entailed a mandate to encourage the creation of competitive districts; and "accountability" involved redrawing districts so as to reflect population shifts.

9. See Sam Hirsch, "Unpacking *Page v. Bartels:* A Fresh Redistricting Paradigm Emerges in New Jersey," *Election Law Journal* 1 (2002): 7–24, and Marilyn Marks, "Bartel Recalls Role in Redistricting Fight" (Princeton University Office of Communications, Princeton, NJ, July 10, 2001; James Barnes, "Let the Court Fights Begin Again," *National Journal*, May 5, 2001.
10. "Who Has The Most Women Legislators?" *State Legislatures* 31 (2000): 4.
11. New Jersey data from Rich, *Government and Administration*, 59; U.S. data from Belle Zeller, ed., *American State Legislatures* (New York: Crowell, 1954), 71.
12. Calculated from the data in the biographies on the legislature's Web page, *www.njleg.state.nj.us* (accessed March 18, 2007).
13. Survey jointly conducted by the National Conference of State Legislators, the Council of State Governments, and the State Legislative Leadership Council. The results were reported in "What Happened to the 'Citizen' in the 'Citizen Legislature'?" *State Legislatures*, July/August 2003.
14. See the data in Tom O'Neill, *The Democratic Downsides of Dual Office Holding* (Trenton: New Jersey Policy Perspective, 2006), 11.
15. However public spirited the dual office holders, it seems evident that multiple pensions upon retirement are a strong incentive. For example, Republican Senator John Bennett, who served in the legislature from Monmouth County for twenty-four years before he was defeated in 2003, was collecting a $92,000 state pension in 2006, based on his legislative service and his work as an attorney for several towns and school boards in his district. Most of the charges brought against Democratic Senator Wayne Bryant in 2007 involved his alleged use of no-show jobs that would have tripled his state pension to $81,000. George Amick, "New Jersey Leads Nation in Political Double-Dipping," *Trenton Times*, August 21, 2006; Gregory Volpe, "Bryant Told He Could Get 150 Years If Convicted," *Asbury Park Press*, April 4, 2007.
16. *Schear v. City of Elizabeth* 41 N.J. 326, 196 A.2d 774 (1964). Of the three preliminary decisions, the one that spurred lawmakers to action was *McDonough v. Roach,* N.J. 153 171 A.2d 307 (1961).
17. Eagleton Institute, *The New Jersey Legislature*, 79.
18. Governor Thomas H. Kean, interview with authors, September 29, 1989.
19. Rich, *Government and Administration*, 61.
20. For development of the legislative staff, see Alan Rosenthal, *Legislative Performance in the States* (New York: Basic Books, 1974); Alan Rosenthal, "The New Jersey Legislature: The Contemporary Shape of a Historical Institution; Not Yet Good but Better Than It Used to Be," in *The Development of the New Jersey Legislature from Colonial Times to the Present*, ed. William C Wright (Trenton: New Jersey Historical Commission, 1976), chap. 3; Alice Chasan, "The Brains Behind the Bills," *New Jersey Reporter*, April 1989, 18–25; Virginia D. Sederis, "Empty Offices, Padded Payrolls," *New Jersey Reporter*, June 1984, 6–11.
21. See the description by 1930s Assemblyman Dayton McKean. With no bill drafting office and no law degree, McKean had to go for assistance to the attorney general's office, or to lobbyists. The attorney general was so busy that a legislator was "almost compelled to use the bills handed to him by a group" (McKean, *Pressures*, 127).
22. Kean interview, September 29, 1989.
23. Data from the *Legislative Manual of New Jersey*, relevant years.
24. Albert Porroni, quoted in Chasan, "Brains," 21.
25. Peter Kerr, "Spying by Computer: Is It a Trentongate?" *New York Times*, September 25, 1990.

26. Robert Schwaneberg, "Jury Finds Aides Played Politics On State Time," *Newark Star-Ledger*, February 8, 1991. A second investigation by the state Division of Criminal Justice also "produced no evidence which warranted a continued investigation." Quoted in Robert Schwaneberg, "State Probe of Legislature Reveals No Basis for Shakedown Allegations," *Newark Star-Ledger*, July 21, 1991.

27. Data from the National Conference of State Legislators, www.ncsl.org/programs/legismgt/about/staffcount2003.htm (accessed July 5, 2007).

28. Eagleton Institute, *The New Jersey Legislature*, 22.

29. Ibid., 18

30. Neal R. Peirce, *The Megastates of America* (New York: Norton, 1972), 202; Zeller, *American State Legislatures*, 206–207.

31. Rosenthal, *Legislative Performance in the States*, 27, 37, 57. In 1971, 13 percent of all bills, and one-quarter of those dealing with the governor's legislative program, were still bypassing committees under "emergency procedures" (ibid., 113).

32. Rosenthal, "Better Than It Used To Be," 102. New Jersey's state senate was also one of five ranking "very high" in discontinuity of senate chairmanships dealing with tax and revenue. The Assembly ranked in the third quintile on a similar measure before the seventies. Rosenthal, *Legislative Performance in the States*, 178.

33. Calculated from data in McKean, *Pressures*, 45; Vincent R. Zarate, "'Recycle Fever' Quickly Gluts Legislative Hopper," *Newark Star-Ledger*, January 2, 1990; *New Jersey Legislative Manual*, 1989 and 2005.

34. Alan Rosenthal, "The Legislature," in *The Political State of New Jersey*, ed. Gerald M. Pomper (New Brunswick, NJ: Rutgers University Press, 1986), 119.

35. See Chris McGuire, "Recording Sessions," *New Jersey Reporter*, May 1988, 26–29.

36. Kean interview, September 29, 1989.

37. Chasan, *Brains*, 21. David Kehler of the Public Research Institute has suggested that the bill glut also results from the legislature's "perpetual" sessions, rather than the limited ones characterizing most other states. See Dave Neese, "Jersey Pols Pen Bill After Bill," *Trentonian*, July 19, 1991.

38. Joseph Gonzales and Jim McQueeney, quoted in Chasan, *Brains*, 25. Both of these former partisan staffers are principals in major lobbying firms, and thus well-placed to assess the changes.

39. Richard Codey and Donald DiFranceso, the two most recent senate presidents, who both served as acting governors, are examples of serious gubernatorial candidates emerging from the legislative leadership. Codey withdrew in 2005 after contemplating Jon Corzine's deep pockets; DiFrancesco was forced out of the race in 2001 as a result of personal financial scandal.

40. See, for example, Jeff Whelan and Josh Margolin, "Corzine's Clout Routs Roberts' Rebellion," *Newark Star-Ledger*, July 7, 2007.

41. Alan Rosenthal, "State Legislative Development: Observations from Three Perspectives," *Legislative Studies Quarterly* 21 (May 1996): 169–197.

42. Ibid., 185–194.

43. Citizen's Conference on State Legislatures, *The Sometimes Governments* (New York: Bantam, 1971).

44. Eighty-five percent called their constituency service activities "excellent or good," 49 percent gave this rating to their role in policy and program formulation, and only 32 percent awarded it to their role in policy and program control. The 1967–71 survey, in addition to New Jersey, included Arkansas, Connecticut, Florida, Maryland, Mississippi, and Wisconsin. See Alan Rosenthal, *Legislative Performance in the States* (New York: Free Press, 1974), 12.

45. James D. King, "Changes in Professionalism in U.S. Legislatures," *Legislative Studies Quarterly* 25 (May 2000): 331.
46. Cherie Maestas, "Professional Legislatures and Ambitious Politicians: Policy Responsiveness of State Institutions," *Legislative Studies Quarterly* 25 (November 2000): 663–690.
47. Ronald E. Weber, "Presidential Address: The Quality of State Legislative Representation: A Critical Assessment," *Journal of Politics* 69 (August 1999): 609–627.
48. See, for example, Alan Ehrenhalt, "The Ethical Conflicts That Won't Go Away," *Governing Magazine*, April 1996, and Alan Ehrenhalt, "Frankfurter's Curse," *Governing Magazine*, January 2004.
49. Alan Rosenthal, *Heavy Lifting: The Job of the American Legislature* (Washington, DC: CQ Press, 2004).
50. Quoted in Josh Gohlke, "Senate Exodus: Why So Many Are Retiring," *Bergen Record*, April 1, 2007.
51. Roberts had opposed any sales tax increase and Corzine had wanted all of his proposed increase of 1 percent to apply to the general fund. They accepted Codey's proposal to allocate half a percent to property tax relief. During the FY 2008 budget process, however, both Roberts and Codey supported a successful drive by the legislature to place a constitutional amendment referendum on the ballot in 2008, dedicating the entire proceeds of the sales tax to property tax relief.
52. Quoted in Whelan and Margolin, "Corzine's Clout."
53. Bruce Cain, John Ferejohn, and Morris Fiorina, *The Personal Vote: Constituency Service and Electoral Independence* (Cambridge, MA: Harvard University Press, 1987), 229.

CHAPTER 10　　THE STATE BUREAUCRACY

The first epigraph in this chapter is drawn from Donald Linky, "The Governor," in *The Political State of New Jersey*, ed. Gerald M. Pomper (New Brunswick, NJ: Rutgers University Press, 1986), 110. The second is from *New Jersey Reporter*, Fall 2004, 10–11.

1. Lynn R. Muchmore, "The Governor as Manager," in *Being Governor: The View from the Office*, ed. Thad L. Beyle and Lynn R. Muchmore (Durham, NC: Duke University Press, 1983), 83.
2. Constitution of the State of New Jersey, Article 5, Section 4.
3. William Edgar Sackett, *Modern Battles of Trenton* (New York: Neale, 1914), 2: 143–144.
4. National Institute of Public Administration, *Survey of the Organization and Administration of the State Government of New Jersey: A Report to the Governor and the State Audit and Finance Commission of New Jersey*, as quoted in the 1932 Inaugural Address of Governor T. Harry Moore, *New Jersey Legislative Manual, 1932*, 667–668.
5. As neutral competence had replaced the ideal of representativeness. See Herbert Kaufman, "Emerging Conflicts in the Doctrines of Public Administration," *American Political Science Review* 50 (1956): 1057.
6. The senate's rejection of Governor Cahill's reappointment of Education Commissioner Carl Marburger in 1972 was the first and last such event in modern memory.
7. For use of these resources, see Hugh Heclo, *A Government of Strangers: Executive Politics in Washington* (Washington, DC: Brookings Institution, 1977), 170–180,

and John W. Kingdon, *Agendas, Alternatives and Public Policies* (Boston: Little, Brown, 1984), 32–37.

8. On the pros and cons of rigorous monitoring vs. persuasion and incentives, see Herbert Kaufman, *The Administrative Behavior of Federal Bureau Chiefs* (Washington, DC: Brookings Institution, 1981), 190–192.

9. Data from the New Jersey Department of Personnel, January 2006.

10. A few other officials are considered members of the governor's cabinet but head entities that are not full-fledged departments. They include the secretary of the Commerce and Economic Growth Commission and the president of the Board of Public Utilities.

11. See David Osborne, *Laboratories of Democracy* (Cambridge, MA: Harvard Business School Press, 1989); Peter Eisinger, *The Rise of the Entrepreneurial State* (Madison, WI: University of Wisconsin Press, 1990); Tom Hester, "Corzine Names Three to Head State Agencies," *Philadelphia Inquirer*, February 1, 2006; Scott Goldstein, "Commerce Looks Like a Goner," *New Jersey Business*, November 27, 2006.

12. Richard P. Nathan, Fred C. Doolittle, and Associates, *Reagan and the States* (Princeton, NJ: Princeton University Press, 1987), 19; Richard W. Roper, John R. Lago, Nancy C. Beer, and Martin A. Bierbaum, *Federal Aid Cuts in New Jersey, 1981 to 1984,* Council on New Jersey Affairs working paper no. 9 (Princeton, NJ: Princeton Urban and Regional Research Center, March 1986).

13. See Joshua A. Kaufman, "The Rise and Fall of the New Jersey Department of the Public Advocate," *New Jersey History* 117 (Spring/Summer 1999); Tom Hester, "Public Advocate Office Returns to New Jersey," *Newark Star-Ledger*, July 13, 2005.

14. Public Advocate Restoration Act of 2005; PL 2005, c.155.

15. See the discussion of uses of reorganization in Harold Seidman, *Politics, Position and Power: The Dynamics of Federal Organization*, 5th ed. (New York: Oxford University Press, 1997), chap. 1.

16. The creation of the department at least temporarily settled a lawsuit by the national advocacy group, Children's Rights, Inc., first filed in 1999 during the Whitman governorship, requesting a federal takeover of New Jersey's child welfare agency. Four years later, after the decomposed body of a seven-year-old child under state supervision was found in a relative's basement in Newark, Governor McGreevey agreed to settle and enact court-supervised reforms. When the advocates went back to court in 2006 because of lack of progress, Governor Corzine negotiated a new settlement and reform plan that included the establishment of the department. See David Kocieniewski, "Corzine Makes Child Welfare a Cabinet Department," *New York Times*, July 12, 2006; Richard G. Jones, "Group Accepts Delay on Child Welfare Actions," *New York Times*, July 23, 2006.

17. See "Governor's Management Improvement Program: What We Have Accomplished With Your Help," issued by the governor's office in October 1989; Matthew Kauffman, "Tackling the Bureaucratic Machine," *New Jersey Reporter*, May 1983; Matthew Kauffman, "From the Top to the Bottom Line," *New Jersey Reporter*, April 1984, 6–11.

18. Kauffman, "From the Top to the Bottom Line," 11.

19. See Alice Chasan, "O Tempora! O Moore," *New Jersey Reporter*, June 1989, 8–15, quote, 14–15. Estimates of Moore's overspending range as high as $32 million.

20. State Senator Richard Codey, quoted in Donna Leusner, "Departing Commissioner Looks Back at Trying to Solve the Unsolvable," *Newark Star-Ledger*, August 20, 1989, 47. Codey's experiences at Marlboro State Hospital are described in

Jeffrey Kanige, "The Marlboro Man: Codey in the Cuckoo's Nest," *New Jersey Reporter*, April 1987, 15–18. Both convicts in question were deceased.

21. Susan K. Livio, "Advocates for Disabled Sue New Jersey," *Newark Star-Ledger*, September 30, 2005.

22. Dan Weissman, "Haberle Is Moving to A Staff Post in Shakeup of Florio's Inner Circle," *Newark Star-Ledger*, January 10, 1992.

23. Stephen Barr, "The Man in the White Cotton Shirt: Is Peter Verniero Tailor-made for His Job?" *New Jersey Reporter*, June 1996.

24. Transcribed remarks at the Symposium on the Transition, Princeton University, November 20, 1989.

25. James W. Hughes, dean of the Bloustein School of Public Policy at Rutgers University, quoted in Sarah Rubenstein, "A McGreevey Cabinet Takes Shape," *New York Times*, January 13, 2002.

26. Laurence E. Lynn, *Managing Public Policy* (Boston: Little, Brown, 1987), 216.

27. Private communication to authors, April 1989.

28. Jeff Whelan, "As Missteps Mount, McGreevey's Friends Seem to Be Walking; From Budget Cuts to Messy Appointments, the Governor Is Alienating His Key Allies," *Newark Star-Ledger*, April 20, 2003; Jennifer Moroz and Kaitlin Gurney, "Untouchables Group Says AG Pick Doesn't Show Corruption Fighting Commitment," *Philadelphia Inquirer*, January 12, 2006; James Ahearn, "Smart Lawyer, Dumb Move," *Bergen Record*, July 12, 2006; Laura Mansnerus and David W. Chen, "N.J. Attorney General Agrees to Resign," *New York Times*, August 15, 2006.

29. Transcribed remarks by Lewis Thurston at the Symposium on the Transition, November 20, 1989.

30. As we have noted, many observers also thought the proposal to abolish DCA was a last attempt to get rid of its defiant commissioner, who refused the governor's request that she resign.

31. Brian O'Reilly, "Power Politics," *New Jersey Magazine*, Summer 1978, 5.

32. Warren Craig, "Lights Out for Energy," *New Jersey Reporter*, April 1986, 10.

33. Alan Karcher, quoted in Craig, "Lights Out for Energy," 11.

34. Sinding, "Saving DCA: A Community Affair," *New Jersey Magazine*, June 1977, 34.

35. Kenneth J. Meier and John Bohte, *Politics and the Bureaucracy*, 5th ed. (Wadsworth Publishing, 2007), 58–61; See also Glenn Abney and Thomas P. Lauth, *The Politics of State and City Administration* (Albany: State University of New York Press, 1986), 84–105.

36. Kimberly J. Mclarin, "Deregulating Higher Education; Colleges Hail an Agency's Demise," *New York Times*, April 12, 1994; Jerry Gray, "Plan Would Replace Higher Education Dept.," *New York Times*, May 6, 1994; Joseph F. Sullivan, "New Jersey Senators Vote to Kill Education Agency," *New York Times*, June 14, 1994.

37. Michael Decourcy Hinds, "A Consumer Watchdog Is Eliminated," *New York Times*, October 9, 1994.

38. Josh Benson, "Codey Signs Law to Restore Office of Public Advocate," *New York Times*, July 13, 2005.

39. David Rebovich, quoted in Benson, "Codey Signs Law."

40. Rutgers University Center for American Women in Politics, as of September 2005; www.cawp.rutgers.edu/programs/BCWA/Boardslist.pdf.

41. Joe Malinconico, "Merged Highway Agency Adds New Jobs," *Newark Star-Ledger*, October 2, 2003.

42. Quoted in Associated Press, "Analysis: Parties in power control flow of money," *Burlington County Times*, June 2, 2003.
43. Among their bona fides: Robert DeCotiis served as Governor Florio's counsel. Michael Gluck is the son of Republican lobbyist and Kean commissioner Hazel Gluck. Michael Cole was Governor Kean's chief counsel.
44. Jeff Whelan and Joe Donohue, "In Trenton, Friends Still Repaying Their Friends," *Newark Star-Ledger*, June 1, 2003.
45. Dunstan McNichol, "Corzine Puts Clamps on Wasteful Agencies; Executive Order Calls for Reforms in Bidding and Open Operations," *Newark Star-Ledger*, September 26, 2006.
46. Quoted in Jonathan Tamari, "Corzine Reins in State's Agencies," *Asbury Park Press*, September 26, 2006.
47. Private communication to authors, April 1989.
48. Institute of Public Administration, "Review of Civil Service Reform," in "New Jersey: A Report to the New Jersey Department of Personnel" (New York: Institute of Public Administration, November 1989, photocopy), 3. Unless otherwise noted, the assessment of the act's success that follows is based on this source.
49. "New Jersey Senior Executive Service (SES)" (Trenton, NJ: Department of Personnel brochure, no date).
50. Ibid. A related initiative was the Certified Public Manager program, established in 1983. Of twenty-two similar state programs, New Jersey's is the largest. By 1989, more than 1,500 state employees, including more than half the members of the SES, had completed all six levels of courses. Another 5,000 had been nominated for some of the levels. CPM holders were seen as prime candidates for the SES.
51. See Eugene J. McCaffrey Sr., "Senior Executive Service, 1988" (New Jersey Department of Personnel, April 12, 1988), photocopy, 20 pages.
52. Vincent R. Zarate, "CWA Details Proposal for Cutting 'Fat Not Muscle' From State Budget," *Newark Star-Ledger*, December 6, 1990, 40.
53. Governor's Management Review Commission, "Operational Review of the Senior Executive Service" (Governor's Management Review Commission, Trenton, September 14, 1990). Quotes from the review, 14 and 23.
54. New Jersey Department of Personnel, "2006 Workforce Profile" (Trenton, January 6, 2006).
55. Calculated from data presented in ibid., 44.
56. Don J. DiMaio, "When It Comes to Pensions, Public Is Better than Private," *New Jersey Magazine*, August 1976, 11–13.
57. Dunstan McNichol, "The Fattest Pensions for Public Workers: Lawmakers Start Focusing on Multiple Job-Holders," *Newark Star-Ledger*, August 30, 2006.
58. Thomas H. Kean, interview with authors, September 29, 1989. The anecdote, which Kean recalled with some accuracy, is reported in Richard Neustadt, *Presidential Power* (New York: John Wiley and Sons, 1962), 9. Truman said, "[H]e'll sit here and he'll say, 'Do this! Do that! *And nothing will happen.* Poor Ike—it won't be a bit like the Army" (emphasis in original).

CHAPTER 11   THE COURTS

The first epigraph in this chapter is drawn from D. W. Brogan, *The American People, Impressions and Observations* (New York: Knopf, 1943), 108. The second is from Sheldon D. Elliott, *Improving Our Courts* (New York: Oceana, 1959). 25.

1. Robert Hendrickson, quoted in Bennett Rich, *The Government and Administration of New Jersey* (New York: Crowell, 1957), 173.

2. Arthur T. Vanderbilt to Robert Caldwell, April 7, 1951, Vanderbilt papers, Box 194, quoted in Voorhees E. Dunn Jr., "Chief Justice Arthur T. Vanderbilt and the Judicial Revolution in New Jersey" (Ph.D. diss., Rutgers University, 1987), 289.

3. Gregory Caldeira, "On the Reputation of State Supreme Courts," *Political Behavior* 5 (1983): 92.

4. Technically, there have been eight rather than seven chief justices since 1948. However, Pierre Garven died after only six weeks in office in 1973.

5. Quoted in Rich, *Government and Administration*, 173.

6. For example, in a comparison of New Jersey with five other states (California, Kentucky, Michigan, Nebraska, and Arizona), the New Jersey Supreme Court issued the fewest opinions. Susan Fino, *The Role of State Supreme Courts in the New Judicial Federalism* (Westport, CT: Greenwood Press, 1987), 66. In the year ending in August 2005, the court heard 122 cases and decided 117.

7. Data from New Jersey Judiciary, Administrative Office of the Courts, annual reports for 1988–1989 and 2004–2005.

8. New Jersey Laws of 1987, Ch. 67.

9. Another such vestige of local politics is the appointment of the part-time judges of New Jersey's 530 municipal courts, which hear traffic offenses, violations of municipal ordinances such as building codes, and the like. They are by far the primary point of contact between citizens and the court system. In 2004–2005, they reviewed 6.3 million cases. Municipal court judges must have been members of the New Jersey bar for at least five years and can maintain private law practices.

10. The tax court replaced the Treasury Department's Division of Tax Appeals, which was staffed by eight part-time judges and had a backlog of 26,000 cases in 1978.

11. Most other states did not have such an office until the 1970s. See Council of State Governments, *The Book of the States, 1986–87* (Lexington, KY: Council of State Governments, 1987), 174. The AOC collects and publishes relevant statistics, assists the chief justice in assigning judges, oversees court clerks, investigates complaints, and publishes and distributes opinions.

12. Arthur T. Vanderbilt to Hon. Milton Feller, September 1953, Vanderbilt Papers, Box 200, quoted in Dunn, "Chief Justice Arthur T. Vanderbilt," 194.

13. Quoted in Eugene Gerhart, *Arthur Vanderbilt: The Compleat Counsellor* (Albany, NY: Q Corporation, 1980), 231.

14. See the data in Arthur T. Vanderbilt, "Our New Judicial Establishment: The Record of the First Year," *Rutgers Law Review* 4 (1950): 353–365.

15. The legislature can veto judicial rule making in about half the states. See Henry R. Glick, "Supreme Courts in State Judicial Administration," in *State Supreme Courts: Policymakers in the Federal System*, ed. Mary Cornelia Porter and G. Alan Tarr (Westport CT: Greenwood Press, 1982), 114.

16. Article VI, Section 2, New Jersey Constitution of 1947.

17. Dunn, "Chief Justice Arthur T. Vanderbilt," 313.

18. Ibid., 323–324.

19. Note, "Evidence Revision: A Legislative Achievement," *New Jersey Law Journal* 83 (1960): 284.

20. Quotes from Dunn, "Chief Justice Arthur T. Vanderbilt," 221, 369.

21. Henry Robert Glick, "Supreme Courts in State Judicial Administration," in *State Supreme Courts*, ed. Porter and Tarr, 122–123. Bernard Schwartz rates Vanderbilt the "most effective judicial administrator in American history," in "The Judicial Ten: America's Greatest Judges," *Southern Illinois University Law Journal* (1979): 405, 432.

22. Caldeira, "Reputation of State Supreme Courts, 92.

23. Alan Tarr and Mary Cornelia Aldis Porter, eds., *State Supreme Courts in State and Nation* (New Haven, CT: Yale University Press, 1988), 247.

24. Council of State Governments, *The Book of the States, 1986–87*, 130–132.

25. Richard J. Connors and William J. Dunham, *The Government of New Jersey*, (Lanham, MD: University Press of America), 163.

26. Points made by Chief Justice Poritz in her request for the first judicial pay raise in five years. Tom Hester, "Chief Justice Seeks 17 Percent Raise for State's Judges," *Newark Star-Ledger*, December 20, 2005.

27. Henry Robert Glick, *Supreme Courts in State Politics* (New York: Basic Books, 1971), 62, 105, 127.

28. Quoted in Kathy Barrett Carter, "2 Judges Reprimanded for Attending Florio Ball," *Newark Star-Ledger*, January 30, 1990, 1.

29. Herb Jaffe, "Jersey Means What It Says on Disbarment," *Newark Star-Ledger*, August 28, 1990; Stacy Albin, "Trenton: Disbarments Nearly Double," *New York Times*, July 4, 2003; "Crackdown on Ethics Sweeps Up Lawyers," *Newark Star-Ledger*, November 29, 2005.

30. Quoted in Joseph F. Sullivan, "In Search of Respect for Judiciary," *New York Times*, May 23, 1990, B1.

31. See, "Senatorial Courtesy: A Public Outrage," editorial, *New Jersey Law Journal* 113 (September 22, 1983): 1.

32. Thomas H. Kean, *The Politics of Inclusion* (New York: Free Press, 1988), 196. Kean discusses the Wilentz confirmation battle in detail, 191–198.

33. Except for Justice Hoens, all of the female justices were appointed by Republican governors: Marie Garibaldi, former president of the state bar association, appointed by Governor Kean, and Deborah Poritz (former attorney general), Virginia Long, and Jaynee LaVecchia (both former banking and insurance commissioners), appointed by Governor Whitman. In 2005, a study found that of the state's 439 jurists on the state bench, 87 percent were white and 77 percent were men, figures that had declined from 93 percent and 84 percent a decade earlier. Associated Press, "Minority Judges Say State Lacks Diversity on the Bench," *Asbury Park Press*, December 12, 2005.

34. Jennifer Moroz, "Rabner Confirmed for High Court," *Philadephia Inquirer*, June 22, 2007; Richard G. Jones, "After One Objection, Senate Confirms Corzine's Choice for Chief Justice," *New York Times*, June 22, 2007; Deborah Howlett, "Gill Drops Bid to Block Rabner for Chief Justice," *Newark Star-Ledger*, June 20, 2007.

35. Fino, *The Role of State Supreme Courts*, 52–53. Other states have begun to name more politically experienced judges. See the observations by Justice John Dooley of Vermont, in *The Courts: Sharing and Separating Powers: Eagleton's 1988 Symposium on the State of the States*, ed. Lawrence Baum and David Frohnmayer (New Brunswick, NJ: Rutgers University, Eagleton Institute of Politics, 1989), 20.

36. The New Jersey Supreme Court has some of the institutional features— particularly an appointive rather than elective selection process—that have been found to promote consensual decisions in state supreme courts. See Paul Brace and Melinda Gann Hall, "Neo-Institutionalism and Dissent in State Supreme Courts," *Journal of Politics* 52 (February 1990): 54–70.

37. *Schipper v. Levitt and Sons*, 207 A.2d 314, 325 (New Jersey 1965).

38. *State v. Johnson*, 346 A.2d 66, 68n.2 (New Jersey 1975).

39. Tarr and Porter, *State Supreme Courts in State and Nation*, 209.

40. Michael Booth, "Judges Refuse to Let Cops Nose into N.J. Trash," *Trenton Times*, July 18, 1990, 1; Dennis Hevesi, "Trash Searches Illegal, Jersey Court

Finds," *New York Times*, July 19, 1990, B1. Seer also Sue Davis and Taunya Lovell Banks, "State Constitutions, Freedom of Expression and Search and Seizure: Prospects for State Court Reincarnation," *Publius* 17 (Winter 1987): 13–31.

41. Porter and Tarr, "Introduction," in *State Supreme Courts*, xvi–xviii.
42. *In re Quinlan*, 70 NJ, 355 A.2d 647 (1976). For a discussion of the privacy right and *Quinlan*, see Stanley H. Friedelbaum, "Independent State Grounds: Contemporary Invitations to Judicial Activism," in Tarr and Porter, *State Supreme Courts*, 45–46.
43. Porter, "State Supreme Courts and the Legacy of the Warren Court," in Porter and Tarr, *State Supreme Courts*, 16.
44. *In re Baby M*, 109 NJ, 537 A.2d 1227 (1988).
45. *Mark Lewis and Dennis Winslow, et al. v. Gwendolyn L. Harris, etc., et al.* (A-68–05) (2006).
46. U.S. Supreme Justice William J. Brennan, a justice of the New Jersey Supreme Court when he was elevated to the federal high court, urged this strategy on state courts. Brennan, "State Constitutions and the Protection of Individual Rights," *Harvard Law Review* 90 (1977): 489–504.
47. G. Alan Tarr and Mary Cornelia Porter, "Introduction: State Constitutionalism and State Law," *Publius* 17 (Winter 1987): 1–12.
48. Tarr and Porter, *State Supreme Courts in State and Nation*, 233.
49. Lawrence Baum and Bradley C. Canon, "State Supreme Courts as Activists: New Doctrines in the Law of Torts," in Tarr and Porter, *State Supreme Courts in State and Nation*, 98.
50. Ibid., 99. The case is *Henningsen v. Bloomfield Motors*, 161 A.2d 69 (New Jersey 1960). Another novel liability decision favoring the plaintiff is *Kelly v. Gwinnel*, 476 A.2d 1219 (New Jersey 1984), which makes "social hosts" liable for serving alcohol to guests who are intoxicated and will be driving. The legislature later limited liability in such instances.
51. Tarr and Porter, *State Supreme Courts in State and Nation*, 197–204; Dominick A. Mazzagetti, "Chief Justice Joseph Weintraub: The New Jersey Supreme Court 1957–1973," *Cornell Law Review* 59 (1974): 197–220.
52. *State v. Steven J. Carty*, 170 NJ 632, 790 A.2d 903 (2002).
53. *State v. Saleem T. Crawley*, A-52–05 (2006); Robert Schawaneberg, "Top Court: Cop's Order to Halt Must Be Obeyed; Justices Rule Even Innocent People Can't Flee," *Newark Star-Ledger*, July 25, 2006.
54. *State v. Keith R. Domicz*, A-42–05 (2006); Schwaneberg, "N.J. Court Tells Police Limits on Car Searches Don't Apply To Homes," *Newark Star-Ledger*, September 21, 2006.
55. New Jersey Death Penalty Study Commission, *Report* (Trenton, NJ: January 2, 2007). Members of the commission included two clergymen, the West Orange police chief, a former state supreme court justice, two county prosecutors, two attorneys, the sitting attorney general, the state public defender, a former senate president who was the chief sponsor of the 1982 death penalty statute, and two victims' rights activists who had lost family members to murder.
56. In 1992, directly as a result of the "Bonfire" dispute, the legislature passed a bill giving the counties control over the use of county courtrooms for non-judicial uses after business hours. Tom Johnson, "Assembly Votes to Give Counties 'Final Cut' on Courthouse Use," *Newark Star-Ledger*, June 30, 1992, 25.
57. The full text of her address appears in *New Jersey Lawyer* 15 (May 29, 2006): 7.
58. Kate Coscarelli, "Bar Group Calls State Judiciary Too Hasty," *Newark Star-Ledger*, May 3, 2006.

59. Robert Schwaneberg, "Top Court Set to Hear Debate That Will Test Judicial Authority," *Newark Star-Ledger*, January 3, 2006; Robert Schwaneberg, "Justices Overrule Legislature on Arming Probation Officers," *Newark Star-Ledger*, April 20, 2006.

60. Council of State Governments, *The Book of the States, 1986–87*, 174.

61. Tarr and Porter, *State Supreme Courts in State and Nation*, 210.

62. *In re Karcher 462 A.2d 1273, 1284–85 (N.J. 1983)*.

63. *General Assembly v. Byrne*, 448 A.2d 438 (N.J. 1982).

64. Article V, Section IV, Paragraph 6, *Constitution of the State of New Jersey*, amended effective December 3, 1992

65. *In re Karcher* 97 NJ 483, 479, A.2d 403 (1984). The line item veto case is *General Assembly of New Jersey v. Byrne*, 90 NJ 376, 448 A.2d 438 (1982). Public employee bargaining rights are confined to wages, hours and fringe benefits. Repeated efforts by teachers, in particular, to gain bargaining rights on issues such as class size and teacher transfer have been turned back by the court. See chapter 15 of this book.

66. *Hon. Leonard Lance etc. et al. v. Hon. James E. McGreevey etc. et al.*, 180 NJ 590, 853 A.2d 856.

67. See Alan Shank, *New Jersey Reapportionment Politics* (Cranbury, NJ: Associated University Presses, 1969), 168–184.

68. Richard Lehne, *The Quest for Justice* (New York: Longman, 1978), 139, 136–137.

69. Ibid., 159.

70. Russell S. Harrison, "State Court Activism in Exclusionary Zoning Cases," in Porter and Tarr, *State Supreme Courts*, 58.

71. Between 1969 and 1979, New Jersey ranked first in LEXIS citations of notable cases involving exclusionary zoning. Ibid., 64–65.

72. *South Burlington County NAACP v. Township of Mount Laurel*, 92 NJ 158, 456 A.2d 390 (1983) [*Mount Laurel II*].

73. Kean, *The Politics of Inclusion*, 194.

74. Fair Housing Act, NJSA 52:27D-301 *et seq.* (1985).

75. *Hills Development Co. v. Township of Bernards* [*Mount Laurel III*] 103 NJ 1, 510 A.2d 621 (1986).

76. Quoted in John Kolesar, "The Supreme Court Isn't Always the Last Resort," *New Jersey Magazine*, August 1976, 9–11.

77. See, respectively, Alan Mallach, "Blueprint for Delay," *New Jersey Reporter*, October 1985, 20–27; Jerome Rose, "Caving In to the Court," *New Jersey Reporter*, October 1985, 28–33.

78. Quote from David W. Chen, "New Jersey Court Backs Full Rights for Gay Couples," *New York Times*, October 26, 2006; survey results from the Rutgers-Eagleton Poll, release no. 159–3, June 23, 2006.

79. Tarr and Porter, *State Supreme Courts*, 185.

CHAPTER 12   GOVERNMENT AND POLITICS IN LOCALITIES

The first epigraph in this chapter is drawn from Thomas M. O'Neill, "LULUs, NIMBY and the Three Paradoxes of Home Rule," *New Jersey Bell Journal*, special issue, 1987, 2. The second is from Alan J. Karcher, *New Jersey's Multiple Municipal Madness* (New Brunswick, NJ: Rutgers University Press, 1998), 17. The third is quoted in David Kocieniewski and Ray Rivera, "Waterfront Project Reflects 2 Images of a Senator," *New York Times*, October 29, 2006.

1. Rick Sinding, "The Ringing of Bells, the Crying of Goods," *New Jersey Reporter*, September 1984, 6.
2. Joseph F. Zimmerman, "Measuring Local Discretionary Authority," publication M-131 (Washington, DC: Advisory Commission on Intergovernmental Relations, 1981), cited in Deil S. Wright, *Understanding Intergovernmental Relations* (Pacific Grove, CA: Brooks/Cole, 1988), 323–325; *City of Trenton v. State of New Jersey, 262 U.S. 182, 187 (1923)*; *Ringlieb v. Parsippany-Troy Hills*, 59 N.J. 348 (1971).
3. The argument in this paragraph is made by Thomas M. O'Neill, "LULUs, NIMBY and the Three Paradoxes of Home Rule," *New Jersey Bell Journal*, special issue, 1987, 6–10. See also John Trafford, "Home Rule in the '90s: Is It Alive or Dead?" www.njslom.org/homerule.html (accessed March 7, 2007).
4. New Jersey County and Municipal Government Study Commission, "Forms of Municipal Government in New Jersey," 17th report (Trenton, January 1979), 16.
5. Karcher cites seven major reasons for New Jersey cities' failure to develop, most of which are discussed earlier in this chapter: (1) no unincorporated land to annex for growth; (2) underrepresentation in the legislature; (3) tax policies favorable to the railroads; (4) riparian rights policies; (5) failure to extract benefits from the trusts; (6) restraining the growth of state banks; (7)underinvestment in urban infrastructure. By the time the state and federal governments moved to rectify some of these problems, it was too late for New Jersey cities to recover from their effects. Alan J. Karcher, *New Jersey's Multiple Municipal Madness* (New Brunswick NJ: Rutgers University Press, 1998), 133–134.
6. For an elaboration of the themes and data of this section, see John E. Bebout and Roland J. Grele, *Where Cities Meet: The Urbanization of New Jersey* (Princeton, NJ: D. Van Nostrand, 1964), 3–26; Joel Schwartz and Daniel Prosser, eds., *Cities of the Garden State: Essays in the Urban and Suburban History of New Jersey* (Dubuque, IA: Kendall/Hunt Publishing, 1977); John F. Reynolds, *Testing Democracy* (Chapel Hill: University of North Carolina Press, 1988).
7. Joel Schwartz, "Suburban Progressivism in the 1890s: The Policy of Containment in Orange, East Orange, and Montclair," in Schwartz and Prosser, *Cities of the Garden State*, 54. Karcher discusses similar developments in the "Greater Camden" movement in *New Jersey's Multiple Municipal Madness*, chap. 13.
8. Karcher, *New Jersey's Multiple Municipal Madness*, 54–67.
9. Bebout and Grele, *Where Cities Meet*, 45.
10. Ibid., 27. See also Stanley H. Friedelbaum, "Origins of New Jersey Municipal Government," in, *Governing New Jersey Municipalities*, ed. Julius J. Mastro and J. Albert Mastro (New Brunswick NJ: Rutgers University, Bureau of Government Research, 1979), 56–64.
11. Ernest C. Reock Jr., "What Are New Jersey's Local Governments?" *Proceedings of the Public Policy Forum on New Jersey Local Government* (New Brunswick, NJ: Rutgers Bureau of Government Research, September 1967), 3–4.
12. Schwartz and Prosser, "Editor's Introduction," in Schwartz and Prosser, *Cities of the Garden State*, x.
13. Michael A. Pane, "Functional Fragmentation and the Traditional Form of Municipal Government in New Jersey" (Trenton, NJ: County and Municipal Government Study Commission, November 1985).
14. A constitutional amendment in 1875 and further legislation in 1896 ended special laws permitting unique charters for single municipalities.
15. For more examples of micro-municipalities and how they came to be, see Karcher, *New Jersey's Multiple Municipal Madness*, parts 1 and 2. For the clearest explanation

of the bewildering issue of "type" and "form," see New Jersey County and Municipal Government Study Commission, "Forms of Municipal Government in New Jersey," 33–35, and New Jersey State League of Municipalities, "Types and Forms of New Jersey Municipal Government" (Trenton, NJ: New Jersey State League of Municipalities, 2003).

16. In 1950, there were sixty-one municipalities employing the commission form, including most of the largest, and only eight using the municipal manager.

17. Richard J. Connors and William J. Dunham, *The Government of New Jersey* (Lanham, MD: University Press of America, 1984), 210.

18. The Walsh and Municipal Manager acts provided for the recall, but it was never used. Indeed, the recall provision of Faulkner Act plans was not employed until 1964, when Belleville recalled two council members.

19. For extensive discussion of municipal governance and the Faulkner Act and its effects, see the New Jersey County and Municipal Government Study Commission, "Forms of Municipal Government in New Jersey," and Julius J. Mastro and J. Albert Mastro, eds., *Governing New Jersey Municipalities*, 5th ed. rev. (New Brunswick, NJ: Rutgers University Bureau of Government Research, 1984).

20. Clifford Goldman, "The Hackensack Meadowlands: The Politics of Regional Planning and Development in the Metropolis" (Ph.D. diss., Princeton University, 1975), 58.

21. Robert C. Wood, *Suburbia: Its People and Their Politics* (Boston: Houghton Mifflin, 1958), 198.

22. "Local Property Taxes as a Percentage of Local Tax Revenue," State and Local Government Finance Query System, The Urban Institute-Brookings Institution Tax Policy Center, www.taxpolicycenter.org (accessed March 7, 2007). In 1947, the legislature gave a limited number of communities along the shore the power to levy a local retail sales tax; of the eight eligible, only Atlantic City took advantage of this provision. A 1970 statute limited to Newark permitted it to impose taxes on alcoholic beverages, parking, gasoline, and employee payrolls; it adopted only some of these. Aside from state aid therefore, the reliance on the local property tax is almost total.

23. Elisabeth Ryan Sullivan, "As State Grapples with Its Budget, Local Bodies Let Their Deadlines Loom," *Philadelphia Inquirer*, March 9, 1989; Wisam Ali, "State Threatens to Set Budget If South Amboy Officials Don't," *Central New Jersey Home News*, May 11, 1990. For a brief history of the state role in municipal budgeting, see Robert M. Gordon et al., *Governing New Jersey: The Toughest Management and Policy-Making Jobs In Trenton* (New Brunswick, NJ.: Partnership for New Jersey, 1989), 22–24.

24. These local governments may retain the traditional fiscal year by adopting a resolution then approved by the Division of Local Government Services.

25. Gordon et al., "Governing New Jersey," 19; Thomas P. Murphy and John Rehfuss, *Urban Politics in the Suburban Era* (Homewood, IL: Dorsey Press, 1976), 174–175.

26. Adam Green and Matt Stoller, "Jersey Boy," *American Prospect* online edition, www.prospect.org (accessed January 9, 2006). The quote is from Craig Carton, one of the drive-time "Jersey guys" on 101.5 FM, the most listened-to radio station in the state.

27. Jonathan Miller, "Edison Works to Cope With Simmering Ethnic Tensions," *New York Times*, October 10, 2006.

28. Bebout and Grele, *Where Cities Meet*, 28.

29. Harris I. Effross, *County Governing Bodies in New Jersey* (New Brunswick, NJ: Rutgers University Press, 1975), is an exhaustive history of the governmental development of the counties. See also Stanley H. Friedelbaum, "Origins of New Jersey Municipal Government," *Proceedings of the New Jersey Historical Society* 74 (January 1955: 56–64); Matthew Kauffman, "Counting on Counties," *New Jersey Reporter*, September 1984, 25–30; and, for a social history of the counties, John T. Cunningham, *This is New Jersey*, 4th ed. (New Brunswick, NJ: Rutgers University Press, 1994).

30. Before 1972, certain counties such as Essex and Hudson had an elected county supervisor who appeared to fill an executive role. However, this was essentially a powerless office, merely providing another patronage job.

31. See New Jersey County and Municipal Government Study Commission, "The Structure of County Government: Current Status and Needs" (Trenton: New Jersey County and Municipal Government Study Commission, July 1986), 51.

32. Camden and Middlesex counties rejected the county manager plan; Passaic County rejected the board president plan.

33. Until FY 1992, counties contributed substantially to welfare costs and to county hospital budgets. That year, the state government assumed those costs as part of Governor Florio's tax reform package. The state has also taken over the costs of operating the court system which, except for judges' salaries, was also long a county function.

34. See the discussion of county government and services in Thomas H. Reed, *Twenty Years of Government in Essex County, New Jersey* (New York: D. Appleton-Century, 1938).

35. 2005 Facts at a Glance, http://www.njcc.org (accessed March 7, 2007).

36. Lucy Mackenzie, "Can Management Replace Politics?" *New Jersey Magazine*, May 1977, 41–46, quote, 46.

37. Lucy Mackenzie, "Charter Change Goes the Distance," *New Jersey Magazine*, November–December 1977, 19; see also Don Di Maio, "The Donnybrook in Essex," *New Jersey Magazine*, June 1978.

38. See Stephen Barr, "You Say You Want an Evolution," *New Jersey Reporter*, June 1989.

39. As reported by Paul Hoffman, in *Tiger in the Court* (Chicago: Playboy Press, 1973).

40. Michael Daigle, "U.S. Attorney: It's Time for 'Truth,'" *Morris Daily Record*, October 25, 2006.

41. Jeff Whelan, "Says Witness's Oldest Friend: 'Judas Iscariot Was His Role Model,'" *Newark Star-Ledger*, June 4, 2003; Joe Donohue, "Kean Jr. Unapologetic About Campaign Tactics," *Newark Star-Ledger*, October 1, 2006.

42. Ronald Smothers, "So Many Towns, So Many Temptations," *New York Times*, February 27, 2005; John P. Martin and Tom Feeney, "Monmouth Sheriff Sits Down with FBI;" *Newark Star-Ledger*, April 15, 2005; Tom Feeney and Mary Ann Spoto, "Former Dean of Freeholders Charged," *Newark Star-Ledger*, April 28, 2005; John P. Martin, "Monmouth Official Convicted of Taking Bribes," *Newark Star-Ledger*, June 9, 2006.

43. Steve Chambers and Tom Feeney, "How State's Own Laws Help Foster Corruption; Experts Say Home Rule Is Part of Problem," *Newark Star-Ledger*, April 17, 2005. Quote is from Henry Kent Smith, a Princeton attorney.

44. Tom Moran, "A State of Corruption: Four Experts Talk About How to Deal with N.J.'s Ethically Challenged Politicians," *Newark Star-Ledger*, November 10, 2002.

45. *City of Clinton v. Cedar Rapids and Missouri R.R. Co.*, 24 Iowa 455 (1868).

46. *People of Michigan ex rel LeRoy v. Hurlbut*, 24 Michigan 44 (1871).
47. An argument made by Daniel J. Elazar, "State-Local Relations: Reviving Old Theory for New Practice," in *Partnership Within the States: Local Self-Government in the Federal System*, ed. Stephanie Cole (Champaign-Urbana: University of Illinois Institute of Government and Public Affairs and the Center for the Study of Federalism, 1976), 29–42.
48. Section VII, Article 11 of the New Jersey Constitution of 1844.
49. Article IV, Section VII, paragraph 11, New Jersey State Constitution of 1947.

CHAPTER 13 NEW JERSEY IN THE FEDERAL SYSTEM

The first epigraph in this chapter is drawn from "The Social Statistics of Cities," 1880 U.S. Census Report, quoted in John E. Bebout and Roland J. Grele, *Where Cities Meet: The Urbanization of New Jersey* (Princeton, NJ: D. Van Nostrand, 1964), 91–92. the second is from Thomas H. Kean, *The Politics of Inclusion* (New York: Free Press, 1988), 111. The third is from Kathryn Wylde, quoted in Charles V. Bagli, "Quandary for Office Tenants: Downtown or Jersey City?" *New York Times*, August 11, 2006.

1. Both Senator Harrison Williams and Representative Frank Thompson were indicted and convicted in the 1980 FBI sting operation known as Abscam, and Senator Robert Torricelli was forced to abandon his reelection campaign in 2002 after an official corruption investigation.
2. A point developed by William M. Lunch in *The Nationalization of American Politics* (Berkeley and Los Angeles: University of California Press, 1987), chap. 1.
3. Charles Dickens, *American Notes* (New York: Penguin Books, 1972), 144.
4. Quoted in Daniel J. Elazar, *The American Partnership* (Chicago: University of Chicago Press, 1962), 204.
5. Richard Nathan and Fred C. Doolittle, *Reagan and the States* (Princeton, NJ: Princeton University Press, 1987), 19.
6. Data from the Tax Foundation, U.S. Internal Revenue Service, and the U.S. Census.
7. U.S. Census, Federal Consolidated Funds Summary.
8. Ledyard King, "Bush Approves BRAC Plan to Shut 22 Bases," *Asbury Park Press*, September 16, 2005; Edward Colimore, "Soon Three Will Be One: N.J. Bases Will Be Merging," *Philadelphia Inquirer*, January 18, 2006. In 2007 the Defense Department reported that because of faulty estimates, the cost of closing Fort Monmouth had doubled, and the decision came under review at the request of the New Jersey congressional delegation. See Ronald Smothers, "Officials to Take Another Look at Decision to Close New Jersey Army Bases," *New York Times*, June 27, 2007.
9. David Marziale, "Washington," *New Jersey Reporter*, March 1988, 32–33.
10. 175 NJ 178, 814 A.2d 1028.
11. Quoted in Raju Chebium, "Lautenberg Given Spot on Appropriations Panel," *Cherry Hill Courier-Post*, November 15, 2006. Lautenberg lobbied the Democratic leadership to let him replace Joe Lieberman as the ranking member and new chair of the high-profile Homeland Security Committee, but Lieberman's crucial role in caucusing with the Democrats to give them the majority led them to allow the Connecticut senator, reelected as an independent after losing the Democratic Senate primary, to retain his seniority.
12. An excellent history and analysis of the Port Authority, from which much of the following history is drawn, is Jameson W. Doig, *Empire on the*

Hudson: Entrepreurial Vision and Political Power at the Port of New York Authority (New York: Columbia University Press, 2001).

13. Richard H. Leach, "War on the Port Authority," in *Cooperation and Conflict: Readings in American Federalism*, ed. Daniel J. Elazar et al. (Itasca, IL: F. E. Peacock, 1969), 405; Jeffrey Kanige, "Bridging the Troubled Waters," *New Jersey Reporter*, February 1986, 23.

14. Walter E. Edge, *A Jerseyman's Journal* (Princeton, NJ: Princeton University Press, 1948), 96.

15. Richard Leone, "The Port Authority's Role in the World Trade Center," *New York Times*, August 6, 2002; Jameson Doig, quoted in Ronald Smothers, "Feud over How Port Authority Spends Money Creates an Impasse," *New York Times*, February 24, 2000.

16. State Senator Joseph M. Kyrillos Jr., quoted in Smothers, "At Helm of Port Authority, Behind-the-Scenes Outsider," *New York Times*, July 16, 2003.

17. "A Good Pick in New Jersey," *New York Times*, March 20, 2003. McGreevey's defense of Kushner's appointment is related in James E. McGreevey, *The Confession* (New York: HarperCollins, 2006), 224–225.

18. Doig, *Empire on the Hudson*, 399.

19. Pat R. Gilbert, "Port Authority Feud Tying Up Billions," *Bergen Record*, May 25, 2000.

20. Al Frank, "End of P.A. Feud Opens a New Door," *Newark Star-Ledger*, June 2, 2000; Doug Most, "Governors Settle Port Authority Feud," *Bergen Record*, June 2, 2000.

21. Tom Baldwin, "Codey Sees Strong Ties with New York," *Asbury Park Press*, July 28, 2005; Al Frank, "Whitman Asks Pataki for Truce on Port Authority," *Newark Star-Ledger*, February 24, 2000.

22. State Senator William Keller, quoted in Leonard N. Fleming, "Pennsylvania Baffled by N.J. Support for Dredging to the North," *Philadelphia Inquirer*, February 20, 2006.

23. Quoted in Bill Cahir, "Pa. Senator Puts Pressure on N.J. over Dredge Plan," *Gloucester County Times*, January 4, 2006; Geoff Mulvihill, "Jersey Gets Tough with a Neighbor," *Newark Star-Ledger*, October 13, 2006.

24. *New Jersey, Plaintiff, v. Delaware,* Docketed November 28, 2005, no. 220134 ORG; Rick Hepp, "Top Court to Hear New Jersey Border Fight," *Newark Star-Ledger*, November 29, 2005; Terrence Dopp, "Buzichelli Angered by Delaware's Call for National Guard," *Gloucester County Times*, January 23, 2006.

25. Quoted in Martin Bierbaum, "Living in New York's Shadow," *New Jersey Reporter*, February 1986, 32.

26. Quoted in ibid., 33.

27. A 2006 Bush administration plan to reopen some areas of the outer continental shelf for mineral exploration brought loud protests from New Jersey's federal lawmakers. One proposed site in Virginia was seventy-five miles from the southern New Jersey shore, and New Jersey's representatives feared that oil spills could wreak havoc on the state's beaches and fisheries. William H. Sokolic, "Lawmakers Criticize Oil-Drilling Plans," *Camden Courier-Post*, November 14, 2006.

28. For a discussion of the tax and the court case (*Salorio v. Glaser*, decided June 8, 1983), see Peter Buchsbaum, "The Courts," *New Jersey Reporter*, July 1983, 41; Bebout and Grele, *Where Cities Meet*, 76.

29. Kean interview with authors, June 26, 1990.

30. "State Business Tax Climate Index," Tax Foundation, Washington, DC, October 11, 2006; "Capitol Memo: NJBIA's Weekly Newsletter," December 1, 2006.

Interestingly, state taxes were named by fewer than 5 percent as a chief concern. The most important concern was the rising cost of health insurance, followed by local property taxes.

31. John Brennan, "Deals Give Troubled Xanadu new hope," *Bergen Record*, November 23, 2006.

32. *A Region at Risk: The Third Regional Plan for the New York-New Jersey-Connecticut Metropolitan Area* is available at the Regional Plan Association Web site, www.rpa.org.

33. *Massachussetts et al. v. Federal Environmental Protection Agency,* docket no. 06A473; Linda Greenhouse, "The Court and Climate Change; Justices Say E.P.A. Has Power to Act on Harmful Gases," *New York Times*, April 3, 2007.

34. Jack L. Walker, "The Diffusion of Innovations among the American States," *American Political Science Review* 63 (1969): 883, 891.

35. Virginia Gray, "Innovation in the States: A Diffusion Study," *American Political Science Review* 67 (December 1973), 1184; James M. Lutz, "Regional Leadership Patterns in the Diffusion of Public Policies," *American Political Quarterly* 15 (July 1987): 391–395. More recent studies find that New Jersey was an early and significant innovator in state right-to-die, crime victim compensation, child abuse, and campaign finance policies. See Henry R. Glick, "Judicial Innovation and Policy Re-invention: State Supreme Courts and the Right to Die," *Western Political Quarterly* 45 (March 1992): 71–92; Scott Hayes, "Influences on Reinvention During the Diffusion of Innovations," *Political Research Quarterly* 49 (September 1996): 631–650.

36. These data and those that follow, unless otherwise specified, are from the Office of Trade and Industry Information, International Trade Administration, U.S. Department of Commerce, and the New Jersey Office of Trade and Protocol.

37. U.S. Department of Commerce Foreign-Trade Zones Board, 66th Annual Report; Port of New York and New Jersey press release 34–2006, May 2, 2006. The subzones in the port FTZ are primarily chemical and pharmaceutical companies. The five smaller FTZs are located in Camden, Trenton, and Lakewood.

38. Jeff Whelan, "No Jet Lag in Corzine's Talks in China," *Newark Star-Ledger*, May 22, 2006.

39. Thomas H. Kean, *The Politics of Inclusion* (New York: Free Press, 1988), 125–126; John Kincaid, "The American Governors in International Affairs," *Publius* (Fall 1984): 94.

40. Kean, *The Politics of Inclusion*, 198–203.

41. Dunstan McNichol, "State to Wrap Up Sudan Divestment by August," *Newark Star-Ledger*, April 21, 2006.The issue became enmeshed in the 2006 Senate race when Tom Kean Jr. took credit for the legislature's action, while experts on Sudan credited the urging of Democratic U.S. Representative Donald Payne, and Kean's opponent, Senator Robert Menendez, trumpeted the passage of his amendment to provide $60 million for a U.N. peacekeeping mission in Darfur. See Donna de la Cruz, "Darfur Turns Into Political Football in New Jersey Senate Race," *Newark Star-Ledger*, May 2, 2006.

42. Carl Hulse, "Congressional Memo: Setback to Bush on Ports Deal Casts a Shadow Over His Agenda," *New York Times*, March 11, 2006.

43. Bebout and Grele, *Where Cities Meet*, 101.

CHAPTER 14   THE POLITICS OF TAXING AND SPENDING

1. Princeton University, School of Public and International Affairs, *Report on a Survey of Administration and Expenditures of the State Government of New Jersey*

(Princeton, NJ, December 1932), 11. This survey was commissioned by Governor A. Harry Moore.

2. Ibid., 10, 11.
3. New Jersey Office of Legislative Services, "Questions and Answers: A Legislator's Guide to the State Budget" (Trenton, March 1989), 12.
4. Ibid., 2.
5. Data from the Fiscal Studies Program, Nelson A. Rockefeller Institute of Government, www.rockinst.org/research/sl_finance.
6. Data from a report by the Public Affairs Research Institute, as quoted in John Froonjian, "Report: Property Tax Bad for New Jersey," *Atlantic City Press*, April 29, 1991.
7. Data from the Urban Institute-Brookings Institution Tax Policy Center, State & Local Government Finance system, www.taxpolicycenter.org.
8. Alvin S. Felzenberg, "The Impact of Gubernatorial Style on Policy Outcomes" (Ph.D. diss., Princeton University, 1978), 67.
9. Paul J. Strayer, *New Jersey's Financial Problem* (New Brunswick, NJ: Rutgers University Press, 1960), 6.
10. Morris Beck, "Government Finance in New Jersey," in Solomon J. Flink et al., eds., *The Economy of New Jersey: A Report Prepared for the Department of Conservation and Economic Development of the State of New Jersey* (New Brunswick, NJ: Rutgers University Press, 1958), 560.
11. Ibid., 3, 17. For the position of the tax commission, see, for example, Commission on State Tax Policy, "The General Property Tax in New Jersey: A Century of Inequities," 6th report of the Commission on State Tax Policy (Trenton, February 1953).
12. Beck, "Government Finance in New Jersey," 565. Beck provides a detailed comparison of New Jersey's general expenditures by function compared to all states, 566–567.
13. Commission on State Tax Policy, "The General Property Tax in New Jersey," xxvi.
14. Clifford A. Goldman, "Tax Disparities," in Council for New Jersey Affairs, *New Jersey Issues: Papers from the Council on New Jersey Affairs* (Princeton, NJ: Princeton University Urban and Regional Research Center, Woodrow Wilson School of Public and International Affairs, Program for New Jersey Affairs, March 1988).
15. Richard Lehne, "Revenue and Expenditure Policies," in *Politics in New Jersey*, ed. John Blydenburgh and Alan Rosenthal (New Brunswick, NJ: Eagleton Institute of Politics, Rutgers University, 1975), 249.
16. Beck, "Government Finance in New Jersey," 578. See also Tri-State Regional Planning Commission, "Financing Public Education: A Study of Property Taxation and Legislative Reform in New Jersey," Interim Technical Report S-887 (New York: Tri-State Planning Commission, September 1978).
17. Our summary of tax proposals from 1966 to 1976 draws on Richard Lehne, "Revenue and Expenditure Policies," in *Politics in New Jersey*, rev. ed., ed. Richard Lehne and Alan Rosenthal (New Brunswick, NJ: Eagleton Institute of Politics, Rutgers University, 1979), 229–247.
18. For analysis of the Hughes tax initiatives, see Felzenberg, "The Impact of Gubernatorial Style," chap. 4.
19. Felzenberg notes that lottery revenues, like the moral obligation bonds, state bond issues and the railroad tax before it were all "promoted as revenue devices most New Jerseyans could escape through abstinence" (Felzenberg, "The Impact of Gubernatorial Style," 62).

20. After the tax issue ended William Cahill's gubernatorial career, Byrne's strategy was to minimize political risk, paint himself as a "passive broker who sought to fulfill his legal responsibilities," and "rely on judicial pressure" to get the income tax passed (Felzenberg, "The Impact of Gubernatorial Style," 429). Although Byrne lost control of the process, and the "final product was more a legislative creation, passed under judicial pressure, than an executive one," the public saw the governor as primarily responsible for the tax (ibid., 451, 452).
21. Richard F. Keevey, "Fiscal Resources and Public Programs," in Silvio R. Laccetti, ed., *The Outlook on New Jersey* (Union City, NJ: William S. Wise, 1979), 158.
22. Casino legalization passed on its second try, after a referendum that would have permitted casinos anywhere in the state failed.
23. Known as the Ford Bill for its sponsor, Democratic Assemblywoman Marlene Lynch Ford of Ocean County, it was intended to help Ford win a tough reelection battle in 1985. She lost narrowly anyway.
24. The account of SLERP's recommendations that follows draws on Susan Lederman, ed., "The SLERP Reforms and Their Impact on New Jersey Fiscal Policy" (Princeton: Program for New Jersey Affairs, Woodrow Wilson School of Public and International Affairs, Princeton University, September 1989); Susan Lederman and Clifford Goldman, "Replenishing the Fiscal Well: Who Will Pay in the 21st Century," *New Jersey Reporter*, September 1989, 28–30; Warren Craig, "The Tax Commission: Progress or Procrastination?" *New Jersey Reporter*, June 1986, and the several commission reports.
25. Henry J. Coleman, "State Revenues and Expenditures in the 1990s," in *Meeting the Challenges of the 1990s: Proceedings from the Eighth Annual State Data Center Conference* (Trenton: New Jersey Department of Labor, Division of Planning and Research, October 19, 1987), 33–39. Coleman was executive director of the SLERP Commission.
26. John R. Baldwin, "Administrative Problems," in Council on New Jersey Affairs, *New Jersey Issues*, 39.
27. Goldman, "Tax Disparities," 42.
28. Robert Ebel, "The New Jersey Property Tax: Searching for Fiscal Balance," in Council for New Jersey Affairs, *New Jersey Issues*, 31; Joseph F. Sullivan, "In Newark, Downtown Glitter Battles Neighborhood Gloom," *New York Times*, August 13, 1991, A1.
29. Lederman, "The SLERP Reforms," 64–65.
30. John Baldwin, quoted in ibid., 64.
31. New Jersey SLERP Commission, "Revenue Capacity and Fiscal Effort: A Background Report" (Trenton, January 1987), 30. Data are for 1985. These measures are based on property tax revenue capacity and effort, and average municipal incomes. This study also examined tax capacity and effort for the 567 individual municipalities, using the same measures. It found that 14.6 percent exhibited high capacity and low effort; 39.9 percent had low capacity and low effort; 45.3 percent had low capacity and high effort; and only one (.2 percent) had high capacity and high effort.
32. New Jersey SLERP Commission, "State and Local Finances 1974 to 1984: A Background Report" (Trenton: April 1987), 11; Peter Kerr, "As Realty Taxes Go Up, Up, Dreams Die in New Jersey," *New York Times*, February 1, 1991, B1.
33. *Star-Ledger*/Eagleton Poll, July 1990.
34. Quoted in Dan Weissman, "Florio Rethinks Policy after Election Rebuke," *Newark Star-Ledger*, November 8, 1990, 1.

35. *Bergen Record* Poll, April 6–10, 1991, reported in David Blomquist, "Poll Says GOP Has New Fans," *Woodbridge News Tribune*, April 21, 1991.

36. *Bergen Record* Poll, reported in David Blomquist, "Most Don't Understand Tax Plan," *Sunday Bergen Record*, October 7, 1990, 1.

37. Ibid.; *Star-Ledger*/Eagleton Poll, July 1990.

38. This was a lesson Byrne had learned from the failure of the Cahill proposal in 1972, which involved fifty-five different bills and three constitutional amendments. "The very complexity of Cahill's proposals made them difficult to explain in public" (Felzenberg, "The Impact of Gubernatorial Style," 333).

39. Quoted in Lederman, "The SLERP Reforms," 43.

40. "Citizens for Tax Justice 1991 Study," reported in Larry McDonnell, "Split Decision on Taxes," *Asbury Park Press*, April 24, 1991, A1.

41. David Kocieniewski, "New Jersey Budget Plan Cuts Aid To Avert Worst Shortfall in U.S.," *New York Times,* March 27, 2002; Jeff Whelan, "Tireless McGreevey Stays Focused in First 100 Days," *Newark Star-Ledger*, April 21, 2002.

42. Data from Mary E. Forsberg, "If It Ain't Broke . . . New Jersey's Income Tax Makes Dollars and Sense," *New Jersey Policy Perspective Report* (Trenton: New Jersey Policy Perspective, October 2006).

43. Bob Ivry, "Can N.J. Afford the Rising Cost of Teachers and Cops?" *Bergen Record*, July 16, 2005.

44. Data from the U.S. Department of Labor, Bureau of Labor Statistics, and the National Center for Educational Statistics, U.S. Department of Education.

45. Bob Ivry, "Unions Drive a Hard Bargain," *Bergen Record*, July 17, 2006.

46. Monmouth University/Gannett New Jersey Poll, July 23, 2006.

47. Ralph Frasca, "Talk of Police Merger Sparks Anger; Westwood Cops Worried by Talks," *Bergen Record,* June 29, 2004; editorial, "Scuttling Police Merger," *Bergen Record*, August 19, 2004; Bob Ivry, "Can N.J. Afford the Rising Cost of Teachers and Cops?" *Bergen Record,* July 16, 2005; Mike Frassinelli, "Mayors Lukewarm On Regional Police Force Plan," *Newark Star-Ledger*, May 15, 2005.

48. John P. McAlpin, "Tax Panel Cites Need to Merge Services," *Bergen Record*, August 9, 2006.

49. Winnie Hu, "School Districts With Officials but No Schools? New Jersey Has Them," *New York Times*, November 15, 2006; quote from Paul Nussbaum, "State's School-less Districts Defy Push," *Philadelphia Inquirer*, February 8, 2007.

50. Jeff Whelan, "Pride and Pressure: A Speaker's Story," *Newark Star-Ledger*, January 3, 2006.

51. Tom Hester, "Corzine Prods Towns to Regionalize," *Newark Star-Ledger*, March 16, 2006.

52. David W. Chen, "Six Days that Shook New Jersey," *New York Times*, July 9, 2006.

53. Joan Quigley of Hudson County, quoted in ibid.

54. Jeff Whelan, Josh Margolin, and Mark Mueller, "How a Budget Dispute Became a Brawl," *Newark Star-Ledger*, July 9, 2006.

55. For detailed account of the week's events, see also Jeff Whelan and John P. Martin, "State Budget War Is Over," *Newark Star-Ledger*, July 7, 2006; Richard G. Jones and David W. Chen, "Corzine Ends 8-Day New Jersey Shutdown," *New York Times*, July 8, 2006.

56. Dunstan McNichol, "Justices Hear Argument for Freezing Aid to Poor Schools," *Newark Star-Ledger*, May 3, 2006; Robert Schwaneberg and Dunstan McNichol, "Top Court Orders 'Abbott Freeze,'" *Newark Star-Ledger*, May 10, 2006.

57. The final reports of the committee are available on the legislature's Web site, www.njleg.state.nj.us/PropertyTaxSession (accessed April 15, 2007).
58. Robert Master, quoted in "State Nears Deal with Unions on a Contract," *Newark Star-Ledger*, February 21, 2007.
59. David W. Chen, "Corzine Heats Up Debate Over Leasing State Assets," *New York Times*, June 29, 2007.

CHAPTER 15   THE POLITICS OF EDUCATION

1. See Federal Writers Project, Works Progress Administration, *New Jersey: A Guide to its Past and Present* (New York: Hastings House, 1939), 139; Floyd W. Parsons, *New Jersey: Life, Industries and Resources of a Great State* (Newark: New Jersey Chamber of Commerce, 1928), 93.
2. Leonard B. Irwin, *New Jersey: The State and its Government* (New York: Oxford Book, 1942), 57. Like the funds for most state programs, education aid came from a complex set of dedicated funds distributed according to different criteria—including state taxes on railroad and canal property, a small portion of the income from state riparian rights, and a state property tax collected by municipalities and counties, a minuscule portion of which was not returned to the municipalities collecting it but retained for an "equalizing fund" for districts' "special needs." See Irwin, *New Jersey*, 57–58.
3. See, for example, Stephen K. Bailey, *Schoolmen and Politics* (Syracuse, NY: Syracuse University Press, 1972); Michael D. Usdan et al., *Education and State Politics*, (New York: Teachers College Press, 1969); James Conant, *Shaping Education Policy* (New York: McGraw-Hill, 1964), 27–38.
4. Robert W. Noonan, "A Study of Factors Influencing the Establishment of the Minimum Basic Skills Tests in New Jersey" (Ed.D. diss., Rutgers University, May 1984).
5. Kenneth David Pack, "The New Jersey Department of Education: The Marburger Years" (Ph.D. diss., Rutgers University, 1974), 196.
6. See Richard Leone, "The Politics of Gubernatorial Leadership: Tax and Education Reform in New Jersey" (Ph.D. diss., Princeton University, 1969), chap. 3.
7. Rutgers, a colonial college founded by the Dutch Reformed Church, became the "state university" when it beat out Princeton for designation as New Jersey's Morrill Act land grant institution. However, it retained affiliation with the Dutch Reformed Church and an independent, self-perpetuating board of trustees, and it received only a small portion of its budget from the state. It was not officially designated "the state university" until 1945, and the state actually assumed control of the university's governing body in 1956.
8. Donald E. Langlois, "The Politics of Education in New Jersey: A Study of Legislator Behavior and Four Major Interest Groups" (Ph.D. diss., Columbia University, 1972), 8.
9. For an analysis of changes in the NJEA and other educational interest groups, see Carole Webb Holden, "The Effects of Environmental Change on New Jersey's Educational Interest Groups" (Ph.D. diss., Rutgers University, October 1980).
10. Ibid., 221–222; Albert Burstein, "Education Policy," in *The Political State of New Jersey*, ed. Gerald M. Pomper (New Brunswick, NJ: Rutgers University Press, 1986), 199–213.
11. The bill that eventually passed provided substantially less total money, and less adjustment for AFDC students, than a commission chaired by Bateman had

recommended. It was also accompanied by a controversial law providing aid for parochial schools for the first time. See Langlois, "Politics of Education," 91–119; Pack, "The New Jersey Department of Education: The Marburger Years," 124.

12. The 19–19 vote was on ideological rather than partisan lines, with almost equal numbers of Democrats and Republicans on each side (Pack, "The New Jersey Department of Education: The Marburger Years," 185).

13. The case is *Chappell v. Commissioner of Education of New Jersey*, NJ 343 A 22 811 (1975).

14. The others are Connecticut, New Hampshire, and New York.

15. John Froonjian, "Report: Property Tax Bad for New Jersey," *Atlantic City Press*, April 29, 1991,

16. *Robinson v. Cahill*, 118 N.J. Super. A.2d 187 (N.J. 1972).

17. *Robinson v. Cahill I*, 303 A.2d 273 (N.J. 1973).

18. For a discussion of these different approaches to school funding, see Kenneth K. Wong, "State Reform in Education Finance: Territorial and Social Strategies," *Publius* 21 (Summer 1991): 125–142.

19. Richard Lehne, *The Quest for Justice* (New York: Longman, 1978), 165–173.

20. The effects of such legislative discretion are described in Theodore Lowi's classic work, *The End of Liberalism* (New York: Norton, 1964).

21. Eagleton Institute of Politics, Rutgers University, *The Goal-Setting Process under T & E in New Jersey* (New Brunswick, NJ: Eagleton Institute, Rutgers University, l978).

22. Kean used this expression as the title of chapter 8 of his informal autobiography, *The Politics of Inclusion* (New York: Free Press, 1988).

23. John Kingdon, *Agendas, Alternatives and Public Policies* (Boston: Little, Brown, 1984).

24. The full state takeover of the Jersey City system was a historical first for both state and nation. Takeover laws in Kentucky and South Carolina, dating from 1984, had not been used in either state to that point. In New Jersey, the only precedent was a more modest state intervention in Trenton in 1982, which took three years to accomplish. See Robert J. Braun, "State Poised to Move In on Jersey City Schools," *Newark Star-Ledger*, October 1, 1989.

25. Thomas B. Corcoran and Herbert T. Green, "Educating New Jersey," *New Jersey Reporter*, October 1989, 32–37.

26. Jeffrey Kanige, "Showdown Over the Schools," *New Jersey Reporter*, February 1987, 24.

27. For example, the results of the state's College Basic Skills Placement Test, administered to all entering students in state colleges, showed no improvement between 1978 and 1989 despite the much higher pass rates on the HSPT. There was also evidence of very high absentee rates on test days in urban schools where scores were apparently "improving," compared with little change in those schools where attendance was high. A year after Kean left office, SAT scores once again were on the decline. Corcoran and Green, "Educating New Jersey," 34; Robert J. Braun, "'No-Shows' Skew Rise in Scores on Skills Test," *Newark Star-Ledger*, December 10, 1989.

28. From the plaintiff's brief in *Abbott v. Burke*, quoted in Kathy Barrett Carter, "Legal Brief Brands School Funding Formula Racially, Economically Biased," *Newark Star-Ledger*, June 25, 1989.

29. Jean Dykstra, "A New Path for School Funding," *New Jersey Reporter*, June-July 1990, 10.

30. Lefelt decision, quoted in Matthew Reilly, "School Funding Formula Ruled Inequitable and Unworkable," *Newark Star-Ledger*, August 26, 1988; Robert J. Braun, "Governor Leaning Toward Equalized School Spending," *Newark Star-Ledger*, March 18, 1990.

31. Quoted in Margaret E. Goertz, "Financing New Jersey's Public Schools" (paper for the Eagleton Institute of Politics Workshop on School Finance, October 17, 1989), 8–9.

32. Quoted in Joan Verdon, "Commissioner Backs School Finance Law," *Bergen Record*, February 24, 1989.

33. *Abbott v. Burke*, 119 N.J. 287, 575 A.2d 359 (N.J. 1990) (*Abbott II*).

34. Sherry Conohan and Rick Linsk, "School Funding Called Possible Without Tax Rise," *Asbury Park Press*, September 28, 1989.

35. Quotes from Florio interview with Robert J. Braun, "Governor Aims at Policy Shift on Education," *Newark Star-Ledger*, March 4, 1990, 1.

36. Robert J. Braun, "School Chiefs Say Funding Law Threatens the Best," *Newark Star-Ledger*, October 26, 1990.

37. New Jersey teachers' salaries doubled in the 1980s, averaging $38,411 in 1991, fifth highest in the country. In FY 1989–1990, New Jersey's per pupil expenditure of $8,439 was the nation's highest, according to the National Education Association. Wayne King, "Anger Increases at Teachers' Raises in New Jersey, *New York Times*, May 27, 1991.

38. Patrick Jenkins, "NJEA Seeks Cost Switch," *Newark Star-Ledger*, November 9, 1990.

39. Robert Hanley, "School Officials Vent Anger on New Jersey Financing Law," *New York Times*, November 1, 1990; Joseph Dee, "Trenton Officials Fret about Strings Tied to School Aid," *Trenton Times*, October 9, 1990.

40. Quoted in Kathy Barrett Carter, "Amorphous School Funding Decision Shouldn't Be Used As a Divisive Ploy," *Newark Star-Ledger*, August 26, 1990.

41. Daniel Jacobson, D-Monmouth, quoted in Scott Bittle, "Educators Brace as Voters Put Budget to the Test," *Atlantic City Press*, April 30, 1991.

42. Associated Press, "Breaking Racial Barriers: Public Advocate Wants to Regionalize Schools," *Trenton Times*, August 12, 1991. Caraballo's comments came in the context of a long-running court case to compel regionalization of the Englewood, Englewood Cliffs, and Tenafly school districts in Bergen County for reasons of racial balance. When an appellate panel ruled in May 1992 that the education commissioner had the power to order regionalization, Republicans legislators proposed a constitutional amendment preventing any branch of state government from forcing school systems to join regional districts.

43. When the Cahill administration gave tax breaks to municipalities forming regional school districts, for example, forty-nine new regional high school districts were formed in addition to the old districts that retained their elementary schools. There are only seventeen consolidated K–12 districts in the state. Vera Titunik, "The Great School Idea Nobody Wants to Hear," *Bergen Record*, July 21, 1991.

44. Peter Kerr, "Democrats Urge Big Shift in Florio Plan," *New York Times*, January 8, 1991, B1; Matthew Reilly, "Dems Ask 'Skimming' School Aid," *Newark Star-Ledger*, January 8, 1991.

45. The NJEA retaliated a few months later when it announced its 1991 legislative endorsements of forty-six Republicans and only three Democrats—a reverse of its customary partisan ratio (it took a neutral stance in the remaining seventy-one races).

46. For details of the revised legislation, see Matthew Reilly, "Assembly Votes QEA Revise Providing Property Tax Relief," *Newark Star-Ledger*, March 12, 1991.

47. Joseph N. DiStefano, "Insurance to Devour School Aid; Little Change Seen in Camden," *Philadelphia Inquirer*, March 26, 1991. Camden's 1991–1992 school budget of $163.3 million consisted of $132.7 million in state aid, and $17.9 million raised through the local property tax.

48. Quoted in Lisa R. Kruse, "Suburbs Gain in New Act," *Asbury Park Press*, March 17, 1991. See also Scott Bittle, "Everything You Want To Know about the QEA—So Far," *Atlantic City Press*, March 24, 1991, 1; Audrey Kelly and Raymond Fazzi, "Schools Declare QEA Plan DOA," *New Brunswick Home News*, March 24, 1991.

49. From a brief submitted to the state supreme court June 12, 1991, quoted in the *Newark Star-Ledger*, June 13, 1991.

50. *Abbott v. Burke*, 136 N.J. 444, 643 A.2d 575 (N.J. 1994) (*Abbott III*).

51. Quoted in Colleen O'Dea, "The Price of Parity," *New Jersey Reporter*, May–June 1996.

52. Colleen O'Dea, "Legislative Action: Governor Signs School Funding Bill to Address Inequity," *New Jersey Capital Report*, January 1997.

53. Caroline Hendrie, "N.J. Districts Breathe Easy After Budget Votes," *Teacher Magazine*, April 23, 1997.

54. *Abbott v. Burke*, 149 N.J. 145, 693 A.2d 417 (1997) (*Abbott IV*).

55. Abby Goodnough, "Governor Plans Supervised Aid to Poor School Districts," *New York Times*, May 28, 1997.

56. Quoted in Hendrie, "N.J. Districts Breathe Easy."

57. Goodnough, "Governor Plans Supervised Aid to Poor School Districts."

58. Report and Decision of the Remand Court, superior court docket No. A–155–97, decided January 22, 1998. The report appears as appendix 1 to *Abbott v. Burke*, 153 NJ 480, 710 A.2d 450 (N.J. 1998) (*Abbott V*).

59. Dunstan McNichol, "Court Clears Plan for Poor Schools," *Newark Star-Ledger*, May 22, 1998.

60. Peter Verniero, quoted in ibid.

61. *Stubaus v. Whitman*, 339 NJ Super. 38 (2001).

62. Larry Hanover, "State Board Seeks School Funding Overhaul," *Trenton Times*, January 5, 2006; Kristin A. Graham, "Districts Denied Abbott Status, *Philadelphia Inquirer*, January 5, 2006; John Mooney, "School Aid Case May Head to High Court," *Newark Star-Ledger*, January 5, 2006. The additional Abbott district was Salem City.

63. *Bacon v. Department of Education*, State Board of Education decision, January 4, 2006.

64. The five districts were Bayonne (in Hudson County), Clifton (in Passaic County), Hillside (in Union County), Weehawken, and West New York (both in Hudson County). Bayonne Mayor Joseph Doria was a Hudson state senator and former assembly speaker; West New York Mayor Nicholas Sacco, who devised the formula, was a Hudson state senator and also assistant superintendent of the school district. Charles Webster, "Jersey Budget Plan Fodder for Comedy Act," *Trentonian*, July 4, 2005; July 10, 2005; John P. Mcalpin and Laura Fasbach, "Political Ties Grease Way for Schools' New Funding," *Bergen Record*, July 10, 2005; Karen Ayres, "Assembly Approves Bill for Aid to Select Schools," *Trenton Times*, July 2, 2005.

65. Rutgers-Newark Institute for Education Law and Policy (hereafter IELP), *Don't Forget the Schools: Legal Considerations for Tax Reform* (Newark: Rutgers-Newark Institute for Legal and Educational Policy, June 2006), 14.

66. IELP, "Background Paper: Setting the Stage for Informed Objective Delibera-
tion on Property Tax Reform" (invitational meeting, June 3–4, 2005).

67. IELP, *Don't Forget the Schools,* 9.

68. Data from the National Assessment of Educational Progress, www.nces.ed.gov
(accessed December 12, 2006).

69. See John Mooney, "Success in the City: Test Scores Are Up," *Newark Star-
Ledger,* February 3, 2005, Mooney, "Passing Scores on N.J. School Test Inch
Higher," *Newark Star-Ledger,* December 20, 2006; New Jersey Department of
Education, "Camden City School District: Assessment Investigation and Review
of Results for 2005," August 15, 2006; Melanie Burney and Frank Kummer,
"Cheating's Roots Deep in Camden, *Philadelphia Inquirer,* December 17, 2006;
Gregory J. Volpe, "Misspent Funds Cited in Four Abbott Districts," *Asbury Park
Press,* January 31, 2007.

70. Ernest C. Reock Jr., "Estimated Financial Impact of the 'Freeze' of State Aid on
New Jersey School Districts, 2002–03 to 2005–06" (Newark: IELP, 2006).

71. IELP, *Don't Forget the* Schools, 17.

72. *Fiscal 2008 Budget in Brief,* available at www.state.nj.us/treasury/omb/publica-
tions/08bib/pdf/bib.pdf (accessed April 15, 2007).

73. Plaintiffs' brief in *Abbott v. Burke,* filed April 12, 2007, New Jersey Supreme
Court, docket no. 42,170.

CHAPTER 16   QUALITY OF LIFE ISSUES

The first epigraph in this chapter is drawn from a quote in Richard J. Sullivan, "Envi-
ronmental Policy," in *The Political State of New Jersey,* ed. Gerald M. Pomper (New
Brunswick, NJ: Rutgers University Press, 1987), 226. The second is drawn from
Bergen County Department of Planning and Economic Development, "Bergen
County's Cross-Acceptance Report to the State Planning Commission," Executive
Summary, September 1989, 2.

1. Richard J. Sullivan, "Environmental Policy," in Pomper, *The Political State of
New Jersey,* 215.

2. New Jersey Department of Environmental Protection, *New Jersey's Environment
2005: Trends* (Trenton, 2005).

3. New Jersey Department of Environmental Protection, "Water Monitoring Fact
Sheet," (Trenton, October 2003).

4. The ruling (in *T&E Industries v. Safety Light,* 123 N.J. 371, 587 A.2d 1249 [1991])
applied to Safety Light Corporation, which dumped radium-tainted waste at
an Orange industrial site from 1917 to 1926 and sold the site in 1943. When
state and federal environmental officials discovered the contamination in 1979,
the site had already been resold four times. Yet the court unanimously found
Safety Light (formerly the U.S. Radium Corp.) liable. See Kathy Barrett Carter,
"Sellers of Toxic Land Ruled 'Forever' Liable," *Newark Star-Ledger,* March 28,
1991.

5. Robert Schwaneberg, "Top State Court Upholds Rules for Clean Water at
Brownfields," *Newark Star-Ledger,* March 1, 2006.

6. Colleen Diskin, "Toxic Delays; N.J. Superfund Cleanups Drag on Due to Lack
of Funds," *Bergen Record,* March 6, 2005.

7. Robert Hanley, "Toxic Waste Rank Wanted by New Jersey," *New York Times,*
December 22, 1982.

8. Thomas H. Kean, *The Politics of Inclusion* (New York: Free Press, 1988), 103.

9. Robert Hanley, "Superfund Sites Lose New Jersey Priority," *New York Times*, November 7, 1989.

10. Colleen Diskin, "Toxic Delays"; New Jersey Department of Environmental Protection, "New Jersey Superfund Sites on the National Priority List" (Trenton, April 27, 2005).

11. Brian Donohue and Farnaz Fassihi, "Burner Not Needed for Toxins, State Says," *Newark Star-Ledger*, May 25, 2001.

12. New Jersey Department of Environmental Protection, "New Jersey Solid Waste Database Trends Analysis" (Trenton, 2005); Saba Ali, "Recycling Proposal Gets Push from DEP," *Newark Star-Ledger*, May 19, 2005; Julie Stutzbach, "Moving Backwards, NJ Recycling Declines," *NJEL* Newsletter, April–June 2006; Joseph Ax, "Residents Can Help Towns Reap More Tax Savings," *Bergen Record*, February 27, 2007.

13. James W. Hughes and Joseph J. Seneca, "A Transportation Driven World-Class Economy: New Jersey At Risk," *Rutgers Regional Report*, issue paper no. 23 (New Brunswick, NJ: Rutgers University Bloustein School of Planning, April 2005).

14. The logistics and politics of the Turnpike's construction are entertainingly described in Angus Kress Gillespie and Michael Aaron Rockland, *Looking for America on the New Jersey Turnpike* (New Brunswick, NJ: Rutgers University Press, 1989), chaps. 2 and 3. A more sober account is Arthur Warren Meixner, "The New Jersey Turnpike Authority: A Study of a Public Authority as a Technique of Government" Ph.D. diss., New York University, 1978).

15. Calculated by the authors from Department of Transportation, Federal Highway Administration, "Functional Vehicle Miles Traveled 2005," November 2006.

16. Hughes and Seneca, "A Transportation Driven World-Class Economy," 4.

17. David Kocieniewski," Corzine Offers Plan to Replenish Road Fund," *New York Times*, February 26, 2005. See also Regional Plan Association, "Putting the Trust Back in the New Jersey Trust Fund" (July 2005), and Pete McAleer, "Corzine Transit Fund Fix Buys Time," *Press of Atlantic City*, March 20, 2006.

18. New Jersey Department of Transportation, "Transportation Choices 2025" (Trenton, March 2001).

19. Survey by Public Opinion Research for the New Jersey Department of Transportation, "Transportation Choices 2030," May 11–June 13, 2005; U.S. Census Bureau, *2003 American Community Survey* (Washington, DC, 2005).

20. Kenneth E. Pringle and George Warrington, "Transit Oriented Development . . . New Jersey's Competitive Edge," *New Jersey Municipalities*, October 2006.

21. David A. Michaels, "'Maxed Out' System Challenges NJ Transit, Riders, Towns," *Bergen Record*, November 26, 2006.

22. North Jersey Transportation Authority, "Access and Mobility 2030: Regional Transportation Plan Update" (Newark, September 12, 2005, report).

23. Data from the public records of the Morris County Board of Taxation.

24. See Susan V. Lenz, "Keeping the Garden State Green" (Princeton, NJ: Woodrow Wilson School, Princeton Urban and Regional Planning Center, Program for New Jersey Affairs, October 1985); John Kolesar, "Battle for the Boondocks," *New Jersey Reporter*, May–June 1992, 25–31; Joseph F. Sullivan, "Farmland Tax Benefits May Widen," *New York Times*, March 26, 1995.

25. Of the $3 billion, $2 billion was dedicated to land purchases and $1 billion to debt service on the bonds. Sixty percent of the funds were allocated for the Green Acres open space program, and 40 percent to farmland preservation.

26. The number of towns with open space trust funds almost doubled to about one hundred and seven counties were added to the thirteen that had such funds. See Jennifer Preston, "New Jersey Legislature Puts Plan to Conserve Open Land on Ballot," *New York Times*, July 31, 1998; Kirsty Sucato, Election '98; "Lots of 'Yes' Votes for Open Space," *New York Times*, November 8, 1998. Anonymous, "Give Us Those Wide Open Spaces," *State Legislatures*, April 2004, 9.
27. Steve Chambers, "Million-Acre Promise Stalls; Squabbling Makes Open Space Goal Seem Out of Reach," *Newark Star-Ledger*, August 3, 2003.
28. Laura Mansnerus, "Trenton Eases Local Efforts to Preserve Open Space," *New York Times*, March 23, 2004.
29. See his own account in James E. McGreevey, *The Confession* (New York: HarperCollins, 2006), 274–276, 295–300.
30. Tom Hester, "Legislators and Advocates Work to Sustain Land Trust," *Newark Star-Ledger*, January 24, 2007; Angela Delli Santi, "Push Is On to Replenish Open-Space Fund," *New Brunswick Home News Tribune*, February 27, 2007.
31. Richard J. Sullivan, "Environmental Policy," 223.
32. Karen A. West, ed., *Spotlight on Government*, 6th ed. (New Brunswick, NJ: Rutgers University Press, 1988, 275.
33. See Clifford Goldman, "The Hackensack Meadowlands: the Politics of Regional Planning and Development in the Metropolis" (Ph.D, diss., Princeton University, 1975); Jon Kimmel, "The Regional Approach," *New Jersey Reporter*, September 1984, 32. South Jersey legislators thought their votes were a trade for a riparian rights referendum they wanted, but Hughes was later able to force repeal of the referendum.
34. Goldman, "The Hackensack Meadowlands," 10.
35. The 2004 master plan is available at the Commission Web site, www.meadow-lands.state.nj.us.
36. Goldman, "The Hackensack Meadowlands," 186.
37. Anthony Twyman, "Foes Look to Bury Shore Growth Limits," *Newark Star-Ledger*, August 24, 1999; Kathy Barrett Carter, "Court Affirms DEP Limits on Coastal Development," *Newark Star Ledger*, June 1, 2002; Steve Chambers, "DEP Throws Big Coastal Projects into Limbo; DEP Won't Extend Growth-Zones deal," *Newark Star-Ledger*, January 9, 2005.
38. John A. McPhee, *The Pine Barrens* (New York: Farrar, Straus and Giroux, 1968).
39. Quoted in Russell Wilkinson, "Bureaucracy Makes Plans to Save the Pinelands," *New Jersey Magazine*, September 1976, 12.
40. Jeffrey Kanige, "Brendan Byrne on Brendan Byrne," *New Jersey Reporter*, June 1988, 18.
41. West, *Spotlight on New Jersey*, 269.
42. See Kimmel, "The Regional Approach," 31–36; Michael Catania, "The Pinelands Plan at Ten," *New Jersey Reporter*, January–February, 1991, 18–21.
43. Kirk Moore, "Commission: Plenty of Room in Pinelands Left for Development," *Asbury Park Press*, December 12, 2005; Moore, "Pinelands Preservation Praised as a Strategy Worth Replicating," *Asbury Park Press*, October 1, 2006.
44. See Catania, "The Pinelands Plan," and Keith Wheelock, "New Jersey Growth Management" (Skillman, NJ: Managing Growth in New Jersey, 1989).
45. Jeff Tittel, quoted in Paul Mulshine, "Smart Growth Crowd Outsmarted," *Newark Star-Ledger*, August 1, 2004; Jane Kenney, quoted in Steve Chambers, "EPA Calls for Delay on 'Smart Growth Bill,'" *Newark Star-Ledger*, June 17, 2004; McGreevey, *The Confession*, 299.

46. Alex Nussbaum, "'Smart Growth' Rules Put on Hold; Environmentalists Happy, Builders Not," *Bergen Record*, November 6, 2004; Corzine quoted in David Chen, "Codey Calls Halt to Developers' 'Fast Track,'" *New York Times*, July 13, 2005; Kaitlin Gurney, "Fast-Track Law to Remain Stalled," *Philadelphia Inquirer*, July 13, 2006.

47. Ken Belson, "In New Jersey, a Collision Between Water, Money and Politics," *New York Times*, January 15, 2007.

48. Jan Barry, "Corzine: Highlands Plan a Must," *Bergen Record*, September 15, 2006.

49. Its progress can be followed at the council's Web site, www.highlands.state.nj.us/

50. Eagleton Poll, September 2002. Respondents chose that option by 60 percent to 31 percent.

51. *South Burlington County NAACP v. Township of Mount Laurel*, 67 N.J. 151, 336 A.2d 713 (1975) [*Mount Laurel I*].

52. See Patricia F. Fingerhood, "Viewpoint: The Courts—Mount Laurel Three Years Later," *New Jersey Magazine*, March 1978, 23–4; Alan Mallach, "Blueprint for Delay," *New Jersey Reporter*, October 1985, 21–27.

53. *South Burlington NAACP v. Township of Mount Laurel*, 92 N.J. 158, 456 A.2d 390 (1983) [*Mount Laurel II*]. "The decision echoed a dissent by Justice Frederick Hall in the 1962 case of *Vickers v. Township of Gloucester*," which upheld the town's right to zone out trailer parks: "The general welfare transcends the artificial limits of political subdivisions and cannot embrace merely local desires." Quoted in Goldman, "The Hackensack Meadowlands," 66.

54. Josh Goldfein, "The Legacy of Mount Laurel," *New Jersey Reporter*, November 1988, 20; Jerome Rose, "Caving in to the Court," *New Jersey Reporter*, October 1985, 28.

55. Mallach, "Blueprint for Delay," 25.

56. Goldfein, "Legacy of Mount Laurel," 20; *Hills Development Co. v. Township of Bernards*, 510 A.2d 621 (New Jersey 1986). This case is informally called *Mount Laurel III*.

57. Dana E. Sullivan, "Stein Keeps Bashing COAH Regs," *New Jersey Lawyer*, March 28, 2005.

58. *In the matter of the adoption of N.J.A.C. 5–94 and 5–95 by the New Jersey Council on Affordable Housing*, docket no. a2665–04, decided January 25, 2007, Superior Court of New Jersey, Appellate Division.

59. Goldfein, "Legacy of Mount Laurel," 18, 17.

60. Rick Cohen and David S. Surrey, "Development Patterns in New Jersey: Inclusion for Some and Exclusion for Others," in *The Outlook on New Jersey*, ed. Silvio Lacetti (Union City, NJ: William S. Wise, 1979), 275–276; Goldfein, "Legacy of Mount Laurel," 18–19.

61. Dan Jones, "The Sounds Of Silence," *New Jersey Reporter*, May 1983, 16–21, quote, 16.

62. Kean's counsel (and second-term attorney general) Carey Edwards, who did most of the negotiating, had led the fight in the assembly to defeat the 1972 affordable housing bill supported by his fellow Republican governor.

63. In 1987, Governor Kean vetoed a bill giving the legislature the right to review, revise, or reject the state plan. A similar bill introduced in 1992 failed to receive a majority.

64. See New Jersey State Planning Commission, "Communities of Place: The New Jersey Preliminary State Development Plan" (Trenton: State Planning Commission, 1988–89).

65. Progress on the cross-acceptance procedure can be followed at the Office of Smart Growth Web site, www.nj.gov/dca/osg/plan/crossacceptance.shtml.

Chapter 17   Epilogue

The epigraph for this chapter is drawn from Joel Garreau, *Edge City: Life on the New Frontier* (New York: Doubleday, 1991), 23.

1. William Schneider, "The Suburban Century Begins," *Atlantic*, July 1992, 33.
2. Garreau, *Edge City*.
3. Peter G. Rowe, *Making a Middle Landscape* (Cambridge, MA: The MIT Press, 1991).
4. Schneider, "The Suburban Century," 33.
5. Ibid., 38.
6. Ibid., 37.
7. Kenneth T. Jackson, *The Crabgrass Frontier* (New York: Oxford University Press, 1985).
8. Schneider, "The Suburban Century Begins," 34.
9. John Milton Cooper Jr., *The Warrior and the Priest* (Cambridge, MA: Harvard University Press, 1983), 173.

Index

Abbett, Leon, 24
Abbott, Raymond, 321
Abbott "special needs" districts, 305, 333–336
Abbott v. Burke, 234, 236–237, 320–326, 328, 330–332, 335
Abscam, 410n1
Accommodationist model, 106
activism, tradition of supreme court, 225–231
Adams, John, 152
advisory referenda, 388–389n 37
affordable housing, 360–365, 423n62
AFL. *See* American Federation of Labor
AFT. *See* American Federation of Teachers
air pollution, 339–340
Air Pollution Control Act, 340
Albanese, George, 254–255
Albania, 10
Albin, Barry, 229
Aldrich, John, 100
Alien and Sedition Acts, 14
Alito, Samuel, 82
Amato, Nicholas, 255–256
American Civil Liberties Union, 230
American Cyanamid, 342
American Diabetes Association, 118
American Federation of Labor (AFL), 43, 110, 112, 114–115, 124
American Federation of Teachers (AFT), 311
American Hoescht, 278

American Party, 17
Andrews, Rob, 70, 266
Anne, Queen, 11
Arizona, 388n36
Arthritis Foundation, 118
Asbury Park Press, 89–90, 384n20, 384n23
Ask the Governor, 163
asset monetization, 307–308
Associates of the Jersey Company, 13
Association of Freeholders, 111
Atlantic City, NJ, 2, 125, 217, 241
Atlantic County, NJ, 46, 55, 61, 75, 96, 216, 243, 251, 253, 408n22
AT&T, 197
authorities, 206–208

Bacon v. Department of Education, 333–334, 336–337
Baker v. Carr, 150
bar association, 392n61
Bardin, David, 356
bargaining rights, 406n65
Barnes, Martin, 259
Bartels, Larry, 173, 396n8
base-closing commission (BRAC), 265–266
Bateman, Raymond, 181, 416–417n11
Bateman Bill. *See* State School Incentive Equalization Law
Bayonne, NJ, 419n64
Beach Haven, NJ, 303
Becton-Dickinson Pharmaceutical Company, 353

About the Authors

Barbara G. Salmore taught American politics at Drew University, where she was professor of political science and associate dean of the College of Liberal Arts, and also served as professor of political science and dean of the Becton College of Arts and Sciences at Fairleigh Dickinson University.

Stephen A. Salmore was professor of political science at the Eagleton Institute of Politics, Rutgers University, and also served as a strategic consultant to many New Jersey political campaigns at all levels.

The Salmores co-authored a book on American political campaigns, and many articles about campaigns, elections, and state politics.

Anne Frank Tagebuch

Fassung von Otto H. Frank
und Mirjam Pressler

Aus dem Niederländischen
von Mirjam Pressler

Fischer Taschenbuch Verlag

11. Auflage: März 2007

Ergänzte Ausgabe
Veröffentlicht im Fischer Taschenbuch Verlag,
einem Unternehmen der S. Fischer Verlag GmbH,
Frankfurt am Main, Mai 2001

Die Originalausgabe mit dem Titel »De Dagboeken van Anne Frank«
erschien 1988 bei Staatsuitgeverij, 's-Gravenhage / Uitgeverij Bert Bakker, Amsterdam
Herausgeber: Rijksinstituut voor Oorlogsdocumentatie, Amsterdam
Staatsuitgeverij, 's-Gravenhage / Uitgeverij Bert Bakker, Amsterdam
© 1986 by ANNE FRANK-Fonds, Basel (Tx 1-942-854 vom 7. November 1986)
© 1986 by Rijksinstituut voor Oorlogsdocumentatie, Amsterdam
(Tx 2181757 vom 28. August 1987)
»Die Tagebücher der Anne Frank«, 1988, deutsch von Mirjam Pressler
© 1988 by S. Fischer Verlag GmbH, Frankfurt am Main
»Het Achterhuis. Dagboekbrieven 14 Juni 1942 – 1 Augustus 1944«, 1947 von Anne Frank,
Fassung: Otto H. Frank
© 1947 by Otto Frank (AF 1164, renewed 1974 578606)
© 1982 by ANNE FRANK-Fonds, Basel
»Das Tagebuch von Anne Frank« 1949, von Anne Frank, Fassung: Otto H. Frank,
deutsch von Anneliese Schütz. Lambert Schneider GmbH, Heidelberg
© 1949 by Otto Frank
© 1982 by ANNE FRANK-Fonds, Basel
»Anne Frank Tagebuch«
Einzig autorisierte und ergänzte Fassung: Otto H. Frank und Mirjam Pressler
S. Fischer Verlag GmbH, Frankfurt am Main
»Zu diesem Buch« und Nachwort des ANNE FRANK-Fonds, Basel
© 1991 by ANNE FRANK-Fonds, Basel
Alle Rechte vorbehalten
Nach den Regeln der neuen Rechtschreibung
Satz: Pinkuin Satz und Datentechnik, Berlin
Druck und Bindung: Clausen & Bosse, Leck
Printed in Germany
ISBN 978-3-596-15277-3

Zu diesem Buch

Anne Frank führte vom 12. Juni 1942 bis 1. August 1944 Tagebuch. Bis zum Frühjahr 1944 schrieb sie ihre Briefe nur für sich selbst. Dann hörte sie im Radio aus London den niederländischen Erziehungsminister im Exil, der davon sprach, dass man nach dem Krieg alles über die Leiden des niederländischen Volkes während der deutschen Besatzung sammeln und veröffentlichen müsse. Als Beispiel führte er unter anderem Tagebücher an. Unter dem Eindruck dieser Rede beschloss Anne Frank, nach Kriegsende ein Buch zu veröffentlichen. Ihr Tagebuch sollte dafür als Grundlage dienen.

Sie begann, ihr Tagebuch ab- und umzuschreiben, korrigierte, ließ Passagen weg, die sie für uninteressant hielt, und fügte anderes aus ihrer Erinnerung hinzu. Gleichzeitig führte sie ihr ursprüngliches Tagebuch weiter, das in der Kritischen Ausgabe* »Fassung a« genannt wird, im Unterschied zu »Fassung b«, dem umgearbeiteten zweiten Tagebuch. Ihr letzter Eintrag datiert vom 1. August 1944. Am 4. August wurden die acht untergetauchten Juden von der »Grünen Polizei« abgeholt.

Miep Gies und Bep Voskuijl stellten noch am Tag der Verhaftung die Aufzeichnungen Anne Franks sicher. Miep Gies bewahrte sie in ihrem Schreibtisch auf und übergab sie ungelesen Otto H. Frank, Annes Vater, als endgültig feststand, dass Anne nicht mehr lebte.

Otto Frank entschloss sich nach reiflicher Überlegung, den Wunsch seiner toten Tochter zu erfüllen und ihre Aufzeichnungen als Buch zu veröffentlichen. Dazu stellte er aus beiden Fassungen von Anne, der ursprünglichen (Fassung a) und der von ihr selbst umgearbeiteten (Fassung b), eine gekürzte dritte (Fassung c) zusammen. Der Text

---

* Die Tagebücher der Anne Frank. Rijksinstituut voor Oorlogsdocumentatie/ Niederländisches Staatliches Institut für Kriegsdokumentation (Hrsg.). Übersetzt von Mirjam Pressler. S. Fischer Verlag, Frankfurt am Main 1988.

sollte in einer Buchreihe erscheinen, deren Umfang vom niederländischen Verlag vorgegeben war.

Als das Buch 1947 in den Niederlanden erschien, war es noch nicht üblich, ungezwungen über sexuelle Themen zu schreiben, besonders nicht in Jugendbüchern. Ein anderer wichtiger Grund, ganze Passagen oder bestimmte Formulierungen nicht aufzunehmen, war, dass Otto Frank das Andenken an seine Frau und die anderen Schicksalsgenossen des Hinterhauses schützen wollte. Anne Frank schrieb im Alter von dreizehn bis fünfzehn Jahren und äußerte in ihren Aufzeichnungen ihre Abneigungen und ihren Ärger ebenso deutlich wie ihre Zuneigungen.

Otto Frank starb 1980. Die Originalaufzeichnungen seiner Tochter vermachte er testamentarisch dem Rijksinstituut voor Oorlogsdocumentatie (Niederländisches Staatliches Institut für Kriegsdokumentation) in Amsterdam. Da seit den fünfziger Jahren die Echtheit des Tagebuchs immer wieder angezweifelt wurde, ließen die Wissenschaftler des Instituts sämtliche Aufzeichnungen prüfen. Erst als die Echtheit zweifelsfrei feststand, veröffentlichten sie sämtliche Tagebuchaufzeichnungen von Anne Frank, zusammen mit den Ergebnissen ihrer Forschungen. Sie hatten dabei unter anderem die familiären Hintergründe, die Umstände der Verhaftung und Deportation, die verwendeten Schreibmaterialien und die Schrift von Anne Frank untersucht und in ihrem umfangreichen Werk auch die Verbreitung des Tagebuchs beschrieben.

Der ANNE FRANK-Fonds, Basel, der als Universalerbe von Otto Frank sämtliche Autorenrechte seiner Tochter geerbt hat, entschloss sich, von den nun vorliegenden Texten Anne Franks weitere Passagen in die neue Fassung aufzunehmen. Die von Otto Frank geleistete editorische Arbeit, die dem Tagebuch zu großer Verbreitung und politischer Bedeutung verholfen hat, wird dadurch in keiner Weise geschmälert. Mit der Redaktion wurde die Autorin und Übersetzerin Mirjam Pressler beauftragt. Dabei wurde die Fassung von Otto Frank ungeschmälert übernommen und durch weitere Passagen der Fassungen a und b des Tagebuchs ergänzt. Die von Mirjam Pressler vorgelegte, vom ANNE FRANK-Fonds autorisierte Fassung ist gut ein Viertel umfangreicher als die bisherige Veröffentlichung. Sie soll dem Leser einen tieferen Einblick in die Welt der Anne Frank ermöglichen.

Ende der neunziger Jahre tauchten fünf bisher unbekannte Manuskriptseiten auf. Mit Erlaubnis des ANNE FRANK-Fonds, Basel, wurde in die vorliegende Ausgabe eine längere Passage mit dem Datum 8. Februar 1944 aufgenommen und dem bereits existierenden Eintrag desselben Datums hinzugefügt. Die kurze Fassung des Eintrags vom 20. Juli 1942 wurde nicht berücksichtigt, weil bereits eine ausführlichere Version im Tagebuch existiert. Ferner wurde der Eintrag vom 7. November 1942 auf den 30. Oktober 1943 verschoben, wo er nach neuesten Erkenntnissen hingehört. Für weitere Informationen wird auf die revidierte und erweiterte 5. Auflage von *Dagboeken van Anne Frank*, Nederlands Instituut voor Oorlogsdocumentatie, Amsterdam, Uitgeverij Bert Bakker, 2001, hingewiesen.

Als Anne Frank ihre zweite Version (Fassung b) schrieb, legte sie fest, welche Pseudonyme sie den Personen in einem zu veröffentlichenden Buch geben wollte. Sich selbst wollte sie zuerst Anne Aulis, dann Anne Robin nennen. Otto Frank hat diese Namen nicht übernommen, sondern seinen Familiennamen beibehalten; ihre Namensvorschläge für die anderen Personen hat er hingegen berücksichtigt. Die Helfer, die heute allgemein bekannt sind, verdienen es, namentlich genannt zu werden; die Namen aller anderen Personen entsprechen der Kritischen Ausgabe: In Fällen, in denen die Personen anonym bleiben wollten, wurden die vom Rijksinstituut willkürlich gewählten Anfangsbuchstaben übernommen.

Die richtigen Namen der Versteckten waren: Familie van Pels (aus Osnabrück):

Auguste (geboren 29. 9. 1890), Hermann (geboren 31. 3. 1889), Peter (geboren 8. 11. 1926) van Pels; von Anne genannt: Petronella, Hans und Alfred van Daan; im Buch: Petronella, Hermann und Peter van Daan.

Fritz Pfeffer (geboren 1889 in Gießen); von Anne und im Buch genannt: Albert Dussel.

Anne Franks erstes Tagebuch, das sie zum 13. Geburtstag geschenkt bekommen hatte.

Anne Frank Tagebuch

Annes Liste der Namenänderungen

Anne = Anne Aulis Robin.
Margot = Betty Aulis Robin.
Pim = Frederik Aulis Robin.
Mutter = Nora Aulis Robin.
G. v. Pels = Petronella v. Daan
H. v. Pels = Hans v. Daan
P. v. Pels = Alfred v. Daan
F. Pfeffer = Albert Dussel

J. Kleiman = Simon Koophuis
V. Kugler = Harry Kraler
Bep = Elly Kuilmans
Miep = Anne v. Santen
Jan = Henk v. Santen
Gis & Co = Kolen & Cie
Opekta = Travies.

[Aus: Die Tagebücher der Anne Frank. Rijksinstituut voor Oorlogsdocumentatie/ Niederländisches Staatliches Institut für Kriegsdokumentation (Hrsg.). Übersetzt von Mirjam Pressler. S. Fischer Verlag, Frankfurt am Main 1988 (Seite 68)]

Ich werde, hoffe ich, dir alles anvertrauen können, wie ich es noch bei niemandem gekonnt habe, und ich hoffe, du wirst mir eine große Stütze sein.

28. September 1942 (Nachtrag)
Ich habe bis jetzt eine große Stütze an dir gehabt. Auch an Kitty, der ich jetzt regelmäßig schreibe. Diese Art, Tagebuch zu schreiben, finde ich viel schöner, und ich kann die Stunde fast nicht abwarten, wenn ich Zeit habe, in dich zu schreiben.
Ich bin, oh, so froh, dass ich dich mitgenommen habe!

Sonntag, 14. Juni 1942

Ich werde mit dem Augenblick beginnen, als ich dich bekommen habe, das heißt, als ich dich auf meinem Geburtstagstisch liegen gesehen habe (denn das Kaufen, bei dem ich auch dabei gewesen bin, zählt nicht).

Am Freitag, dem 12. Juni, war ich schon um sechs Uhr wach, und das ist sehr begreiflich, da ich Geburtstag hatte. Aber um sechs Uhr durfte ich noch nicht aufstehen, also musste ich meine Neugier noch bis Viertel vor sieben bezwingen. Dann ging es nicht länger. Ich lief ins Esszimmer, wo ich von Moortje, unserer Katze, mit Purzelbäumen begrüßt wurde.

Kurz nach sieben ging ich zu Papa und Mama und dann ins Wohnzimmer, um meine Geschenke auszupacken. An erster Stelle warst du es, die ich zu sehen bekam und was wahrscheinlich eines von meinen schönsten Geschenken ist. Dann ein Strauß Rosen, eine Topfpflanze und zwei Pfingstrosen. Von Papa und Mama habe ich eine blaue Bluse bekommen, ein Gesellschaftsspiel, eine Flasche Traubensaft, der ein bisschen nach Wein schmeckt (Wein wird ja aus Trauben gemacht),

Edith Frank-Holländer, Annes Mutter, Mai 1935.

Otto Frank, Annes Vater, Mai 1936.

ein Puzzle, Creme, Geld und einen Gutschein für zwei Bücher. Dann bekam ich noch ein Buch, »Camera Obscura«, aber das hat Margot schon, darum habe ich es getauscht, selbst gebackene Plätzchen (von mir gebacken, natürlich, denn im Plätzchenbacken bin ich zur Zeit stark), viele Süßigkeiten und eine Erdbeertorte von Mutter. Auch einen Brief von Omi, ganz pünktlich, aber das ist natürlich Zufall.

Dann kam Hanneli, um mich abzuholen, und wir gingen zur Schule. In der Pause bewirtete ich Lehrer und Schüler mit Butterkeksen, dann ging es wieder an die Arbeit.

Ich kam erst um fünf Uhr nach Hause, weil ich zum Turnen gegangen war (obwohl ich nie mitmachen darf, da ich mir leicht Arme und Beine ausrenke) und für meine Klassenkameraden Volleyball als Geburtstagsspiel ausgesucht habe. Sanne Ledermann war schon da. Ilse Wagner, Hanneli Goslar und Jacqueline van Maarsen habe ich mitgebracht, die sind bei mir in der Klasse. Hanneli und Sanne waren früher meine besten Freundinnen, und wer uns zusammen sah, sagte immer: »Da laufen Anne, Hanne und Sanne.« Jacqueline van Maarsen habe ich erst auf dem Jüdischen Lyzeum kennen gelernt, sie ist jetzt meine beste Freundin. Ilse ist Hannelis beste Freundin, und Sanne geht in eine andere Schule und hat dort ihre Freundinnen.

Montag, 15. Juni 1942

Sonntagnachmittag war meine Geburtstagsfeier. Rin-tin-tin* hat meinen Klassenkameraden gut gefallen. Ich habe zwei Broschen bekommen, ein Lesezeichen und zwei Bücher. Der Club hat mir ein tolles Buch geschenkt, »Niederländische Sagen und Legenden«, aber sie haben mir aus Versehen den zweiten Band gegeben. Deshalb habe ich zwei andere Bücher gegen den ersten Band getauscht. Tante Helene hat noch ein Puzzle gebracht, Tante Stephanie eine Brosche und Tante Leny ein tolles Buch, nämlich »Daisys Ferien im Gebirge«.

Heute Morgen im Bad dachte ich darüber nach, wie herrlich es wäre, wenn ich so einen Hund wie Rin-tin-tin hätte. Ich würde ihn dann auch Rin-tin-tin nennen, und er würde in der Schule immer beim Pedell oder, bei schönem Wetter, im Fahrradunterstand sein.

* Rin-tin-tin hieß der Hund in einem bekannten Kinderfilm; A. d. Ü.

Ich möchte noch einiges von meiner Klasse und der Schule erzählen und will mit ein paar Schülern anfangen.

Betty Bloemendaal sieht ein bisschen ärmlich aus, ist es, glaube ich, auch. Sie ist in der Schule sehr gescheit. Aber das liegt daran, dass sie so fleißig ist, denn nun lässt die Gescheitheit schon was zu wünschen übrig. Sie ist ein ziemlich ruhiges Mädchen.

Jacqueline van Maarsen gilt als meine beste Freundin. Aber eine wirkliche Freundin habe ich noch nie gehabt. Bei Jopie dachte ich erst, sie könnte es werden, aber es ist schief gegangen.

D. Q. ist sehr nervös, vergisst alles mögliche und bekommt Strafarbeit um Strafarbeit. Sie ist sehr gutmütig, vor allem G. Z. gegenüber.

E. S. schwätzt so entsetzlich, dass es nicht mehr schön ist. Wenn sie einen etwas fragt, fasst sie einen immer an den Haaren oder Knöpfen an. Man sagt, dass E. mich nicht ausstehen kann. Aber das ist nicht schlimm, weil ich sie auch nicht sehr sympathisch finde.

Henny Mets ist fröhlich und nett, nur spricht sie sehr laut und ist, wenn sie auf der Straße spielt, sehr kindisch. Es ist sehr schade, dass sie eine Freundin hat, Beppy, die einen schlechten Einfluss auf sie hat, weil dieses Mädchen schrecklich schmutzig und schweinisch ist.

Über J. R. könnten ganze Romane geschrieben werden. Sie ist ein angeberisches, tuschelndes, ekliges, erwachsentuendes, hinterhältiges Mädchen. Sie hat Jopie eingewickelt, und das ist schade. Sie weint beim kleinsten Anlass und ist schrecklich zimperlich. Immer muss Fräulein J. Recht haben. Sie ist sehr reich und hat einen ganzen Schrank voll mit goldigen Kleidern, in denen sie aber viel zu alt aussieht. Das Mädchen bildet sich ein, sehr schön zu sein, aber sie ist gerade das Gegenteil. J. und ich können einander nicht ausstehen.

Ilse Wagner ist ein fröhliches und nettes Mädchen, aber sie ist sehr genau und kann stundenlang jammern. Ilse mag mich ziemlich gern. Sie ist auch sehr gescheit, aber faul.

Hanneli Goslar oder Lies, wie sie in der Schule genannt wird, ist ein bisschen eigenartig. Sie ist meist schüchtern und zu Hause sehr frech. Sie tratscht alles, was man ihr erzählt, an ihre Mutter weiter. Aber sie hat eine offene Meinung, und vor allem in der letzten Zeit schätze ich sie sehr.

Nannie v. Praag-Sigaar ist ein kleines, gescheites Mädchen. Ich finde sie ganz nett. Sie ist ziemlich klug. Viel ist über sie nicht zu sagen.

15

Eefje de Jong finde ich großartig. Sie ist erst zwölf Jahre alt, aber ganz und gar eine Dame. Sie tut, als wäre ich ein Baby. Und sie ist sehr hilfsbereit, deshalb mag ich sie auch.

G. Z. ist das schönste Mädchen in der Klasse. Sie hat ein liebes Gesicht, ist aber in der Schule ziemlich dumm. Ich glaube, dass sie sitzen bleibt, aber das sage ich natürlich nicht zu ihr.

(Nachtrag)

Sie ist zu meiner großen Verwunderung doch nicht sitzen geblieben. Und am Schluss von uns zwölf Mädchen sitze ich, neben G. Z.

Über die Jungen lässt sich viel, aber auch wenig sagen.

Maurice Coster ist einer von meinen vielen Verehrern, aber er ist ein ziemlich unangenehmer Junge.

Sally Springer ist ein schrecklich schweinischer Junge, und es geht das Gerücht um, dass er gepaart hat. Trotzdem finde ich ihn toll, denn er ist sehr witzig.

Emiel Bonewit ist der Verehrer von G. Z., aber sie macht sich nicht viel daraus. Er ist ziemlich langweilig.

Rob Cohen war auch verliebt in mich, aber jetzt kann ich ihn nicht mehr ausstehen. Er ist heuchlerisch, verlogen, weinerlich, verrückt und unangenehm und bildet sich schrecklich viel ein.

Max van de Velde ist ein Bauernjunge aus Medemblik, aber ganz annehmbar, würde Margot sagen.

Herman Koopman ist auch arg schweinisch, genau wie Jopie de Beer, der ein richtiger Schürzenjäger ist.

Leo Blom ist der Busenfreund von Jopie de Beer und auch vom Schweinischsein angesteckt.

Albert de Mesquita kommt von der Montessorischule und hat eine Klasse übersprungen. Er ist sehr klug.

Leo Slager kommt von derselben Schule, ist aber nicht so klug.

Ru Stoppelmon ist ein kleiner, verrückter Junge aus Almelo, der erst später in die Klasse gekommen ist.

C. N. tut alles, was nicht erlaubt ist.

Jacques Kocernoot und Pam sitzen hinter uns, und wir lachen uns oft krank (G. und ich).

Harry Schaap ist der anständigste Junge aus unserer Klasse, er ist nett.

Werner Joseph auch, ist aber zu still und wirkt dadurch langweilig.

Edith Frank mit ihren Töchtern Anne (links) und Margot bei der Hauptwache in Frankfurt am Main, 1933.

Sam Salomon ist ein Rabauke aus der Gosse, ein Mistjunge. (Verehrer!) *admirer*

Appie Riem ist ziemlich orthodox, aber auch ein Dreckskerl. Jetzt muss ich aufhören. Beim nächsten Mal habe ich wieder so viel in dich zu schreiben, d. h. dir zu erzählen. Tschüs! Ich finde dich so toll!

Samstag, 20. Juni 1942

Es ist für jemanden wie mich ein eigenartiges Gefühl, Tagebuch zu schreiben. Nicht nur, dass ich noch nie geschrieben habe, sondern ich denke auch, dass sich später keiner, weder ich noch ein anderer, für die Herzensergüsse eines dreizehnjährigen Schulmädchens interessieren wird. Aber darauf kommt es eigentlich nicht an, ich habe Lust zu schreiben und will mir vor allem alles Mögliche gründlich von der Seele reden.

Papier ist geduldiger als Menschen. Dieses Sprichwort fiel mir ein, als ich an einem meiner leicht-melancholischen Tage gelangweilt am Tisch saß, den Kopf auf den Händen, und vor Schlaffheit nicht wusste, ob ich weggehen oder lieber zu Hause bleiben sollte, und so schließlich sitzen blieb und weitergrübelte. In der Tat, Papier ist geduldig. Und weil ich nicht die Absicht habe, dieses kartonierte Heft mit dem hochtrabenden Namen »Tagebuch« jemals jemanden lesen zu lassen, es sei denn, ich würde irgendwann in meinem Leben »den« Freund oder »die« Freundin finden, ist es auch egal.

Nun bin ich bei dem Punkt angelangt, an dem die ganze Tagebuch-Idee angefangen hat: Ich habe keine Freundin.

Um noch deutlicher zu sein, muss hier eine Erklärung folgen, denn niemand kann verstehen, dass ein Mädchen von dreizehn ganz allein auf der Welt steht. Das ist auch nicht wahr. Ich habe liebe Eltern und eine Schwester von sechzehn, ich habe, alle zusammengezählt, mindestens dreißig Bekannte oder was man so Freundinnen nennt. Ich habe einen Haufen Anbeter, die mir alles von den Augen ablesen und sogar, wenn's sein muss, in der Klasse versuchen, mit Hilfe eines zerbrochenen Taschenspiegels einen Schimmer von mir aufzufangen. Ich habe Verwandte und ein gutes Zuhause. Nein, es fehlt mir offensichtlich nichts, außer »die« Freundin. Ich kann mit keinen von meinen Bekannten etwas anderes tun als Spaß machen, ich kann nur

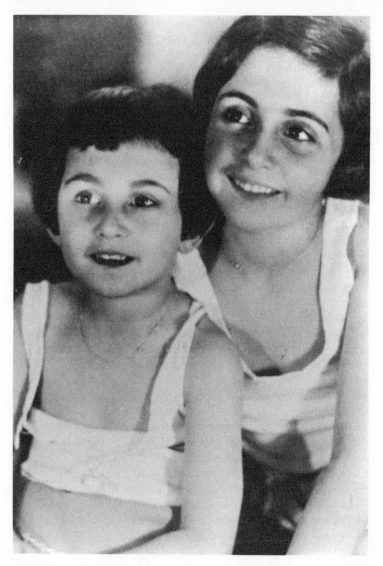

Anne (links) und Margot, 1933.

über alltägliche Dinge sprechen und werde nie intimer mit ihnen. Das ist der Haken. Vielleicht liegt dieser Mangel an Vertraulichkeit auch an mir. Jedenfalls ist es so, leider, und nicht zu ändern. Darum dieses Tagebuch.

Um nun die Vorstellung der ersehnten Freundin in meiner Phantasie noch zu steigern, will ich nicht einfach Tatsachen in mein Tagebuch schreiben wie alle andern, sondern ich will dieses Tagebuch die Freundin selbst sein lassen, und diese Freundin heißt *Kitty*.

Meine Geschichte! (Idiotisch, so etwas vergisst man nicht.)

Weil niemand das, was ich Kitty erzähle, verstehen würde, wenn ich so mit der Tür ins Haus falle, muss ich, wenn auch ungern, kurz meine Lebensgeschichte wiedergeben.

Mein Vater, der liebste Schatz von einem Vater, den ich je getroffen habe, heiratete erst mit 36 Jahren meine Mutter, die damals 25 war. Meine Schwester Margot wurde 1926 in Frankfurt am Main geboren, in Deutschland. Am 12. Juni 1929 folgte ich. Bis zu meinem vierten Lebensjahr wohnte ich in Frankfurt. Da wir Juden sind, ging dann mein Vater 1933 in die Niederlande. Er wurde Direktor der Niederländischen Opekta Gesellschaft zur Marmeladeherstellung. Meine Mutter, Edith Frank-Holländer, fuhr im September auch nach Holland, und Margot und ich gingen nach Aachen, wo unsere Großmutter wohnte. Margot ging im Dezember nach Holland und ich im Februar, wo ich als Geburtstagsgeschenk für Margot auf den Tisch gesetzt wurde.

Ich ging bald in den Kindergarten der Montessorischule. Dort blieb ich bis sechs, dann kam ich in die erste Klasse. In der 6. Klasse kam ich zu Frau Kuperus, der Direktorin. Am Ende des Schuljahres nahmen wir einen herzergreifenden Abschied voneinander und weinten beide, denn ich wurde am Jüdischen Lyzeum angenommen, in das Margot auch ging.

Unser Leben verlief nicht ohne Aufregung, da die übrige Familie in Deutschland nicht von Hitlers Judengesetzen verschont blieb. Nach den Pogromen 1938 flohen meine beiden Onkel, Brüder von Mutter, nach Amerika, und meine Großmutter kam zu uns. Sie war damals 73 Jahre alt.

Ab Mai 1940 ging es bergab mit den guten Zeiten: erst der Krieg, dann die Kapitulation, der Einmarsch der Deutschen, und das Elend für uns Juden begann. Judengesetz folgte auf Judengesetz, und unsere Freiheit wurde sehr beschränkt. Juden müssen einen Judenstern tragen; Juden müssen ihre Fahrräder abgeben; Juden dürfen nicht mit der Straßenbahn fahren; Juden dürfen nicht mit einem Auto fahren, auch nicht mit einem privaten; Juden dürfen nur von 3–5 Uhr einkaufen; Juden dürfen nur zu einem jüdischen Frisör; Juden dürfen zwischen 8 Uhr abends und 6 Uhr morgens nicht auf die Straße; Juden dürfen sich nicht in Theatern, Kinos und an anderen dem Vergnügen dienenden Plätzen aufhalten; Juden dürfen nicht ins Schwimmbad, ebenso wenig auf Tennis-, Hockey- oder andere Sportplätze; Juden dürfen nicht rudern; Juden dürfen in der Öffentlichkeit keinerlei Sport treiben; Juden dürfen nach acht Uhr abends weder in ihrem eigenen Garten noch bei Bekannten sitzen; Juden dürfen nicht zu Christen ins Haus kommen; Juden müssen auf jüdische Schulen gehen und dergleichen mehr. So ging unser Leben weiter, und wir durften dies nicht und das nicht. Jacque sagt immer zu mir: »Ich traue mich nichts mehr zu machen, ich habe Angst, dass es nicht erlaubt ist.«

Im Sommer 1941 wurde Oma sehr krank. Sie musste operiert werden, und aus meinem Geburtstag wurde nicht viel. Im Sommer 1940 auch schon nicht, da war der Krieg in den Niederlanden gerade vorbei. Oma starb im Januar 1942. Niemand weiß, wie oft ich an sie denke und sie noch immer lieb habe. Dieser Geburtstag 1942 ist dann auch gefeiert worden, um alles nachzuholen, und Omas Kerze stand daneben.

Uns vieren geht es noch immer gut, und so bin ich dann bei dem heutigen Datum angelangt, an dem die feierliche Einweihung meines Tagebuchs beginnt, dem 20. Juni 1942.

Samstag, 20. Juni 1942

Liebe Kitty!

Dann fange ich gleich an. Es ist schön ruhig, Vater und Mutter sind ausgegangen, Margot ist mit ein paar jungen Leuten zu ihrer Freundin zum Pingpongspielen. Ich spiele in der letzten Zeit auch sehr viel, sogar so viel, dass wir fünf Mädchen einen Club gegründet haben. Der Club heißt »Der kleine Bär minus 2«. Ein verrückter Name, der

Anne Frank 1934 in Aachen.

auf einem Irrtum beruht. Wir wollten einen besonderen Namen und dachten wegen unserer fünf Mitglieder sofort an die Sterne, an den Kleinen Bären. Wir meinten, er hätte fünf Sterne, aber da haben wir uns geirrt, er hat sieben, genau wie der Große Bär. Daher das »minus zwei«. Ilse Wagner hat ein Pingpongspiel, und das große Esszimmer der Wagners steht uns immer zur Verfügung. Da wir Pingpongspielerinnen vor allem im Sommer gerne Eis essen und das Spielen warm macht, endet es meistens mit einem Ausflug zum nächsten Eisgeschäft, das für Juden erlaubt ist, die Oase oder das Delphi. Nach Geld oder Portemonnaie suchen wir überhaupt nicht mehr, denn in der Oase ist es meistens so voll, dass wir immer einige großzügige Herren aus unserem weiten Bekanntenkreis oder den einen oder anderen Verehrer finden, die uns mehr Eis anbieten, als wir in einer Woche essen können.

Ich nehme an, du bist ein bisschen erstaunt über die Tatsache, dass ich, so jung ich bin, über Verehrer spreche. Leider (in einigen Fällen auch nicht leider) scheint dieses Übel auf unserer Schule unvermeidbar zu sein. Sobald mich ein Junge fragt, ob er mit mir nach Hause radeln darf, und wir ein Gespräch anfangen, kann ich in neun von zehn Fällen damit rechnen, dass der betreffende Jüngling die Gewohnheit hat, sofort in Feuer und Flamme zu geraten, und mich nicht mehr aus den Augen lässt. Nach einiger Zeit legt sich die Verliebtheit wieder, vor allem, weil ich mir aus feurigen Blicken nicht viel mache und lustig weiterradle. Wenn es mir manchmal zu bunt wird, schlenkere ich ein bisschen mit dem Rad, die Tasche fällt runter, und der junge Mann muss anstandshalber absteigen. Wenn er mir die Tasche zurückgegeben hat, habe ich längst ein anderes Gesprächsthema angefangen. Das sind aber noch die Unschuldigen. Es gibt auch einige, die mir Kusshändchen zuwerfen oder versuchen, mich am Arm zu nehmen. Aber da sind sie bei mir an der falschen Adresse! Ich steige ab und weigere mich, weiter seine Gesellschaft in Anspruch zu nehmen. Oder ich spiele die Beleidigte und sage ihm klipp und klar, er könne nach Hause gehen.

So, der Grundstein für unsere Freundschaft ist gelegt. Bis morgen!

Deine Anne

Liebe Kitty!

Unsere ganze Klasse bibbert. Der Anlass ist natürlich die anstehende Lehrerkonferenz. Die halbe Klasse schließt Wetten über Versetzungen oder Sitzenbleiben ab. G. Z., meine Nachbarin, und ich lachen uns kaputt über unsere beiden Hintermänner, C. N. und Jacques Kocernoot, die schon ihr ganzes Ferienkapital verwettet haben. »Du wirst versetzt«, »von wegen«, »doch …«, so geht es von morgens bis abends. Weder Gs flehende Blicke noch meine Wutausbrüche können die beiden zur Ruhe bringen. Meiner Meinung nach müsste ein Viertel der Klasse sitzen bleiben, solche Trottel sitzen hier drin. Aber Lehrer sind die launenhaftesten Menschen, die es gibt. Vielleicht sind sie ausnahmsweise auch mal launenhaft in der richtigen Richtung. Für meine Freundinnen und mich habe ich nicht so viel Angst, wir werden wohl durchkommen. Nur in Mathematik bin ich unsicher. Na ja, abwarten. Bis dahin sprechen wir uns gegenseitig Mut zu.

Ich komme mit allen Lehrern und Lehrerinnen ziemlich gut aus. Es sind insgesamt neun, sieben männliche und zwei weibliche. Herr Keesing, der alte Mathematiklehrer, war eine Zeit lang sehr böse auf mich, weil ich so viel schwätzte. Eine Ermahnung folgte der anderen, bis ich eine Strafarbeit bekam. Ich sollte einen Aufsatz über das Thema »Eine Schwatzliese« schreiben. Eine Schwatzliese, was kann man darüber schreiben? Aber ich machte mir erst noch keine Sorgen, steckte das Aufgabenheft in die Tasche und versuchte, mich ruhig zu verhalten.

Abends, als ich mit den anderen Aufgaben fertig war, entdeckte ich plötzlich die Eintragung für den Aufsatz. Mit dem Füllerende im Mund fing ich an, über das Thema nachzudenken. Einfach irgendetwas schreiben und die Worte so weit wie möglich auseinander ziehen, das kann jeder, aber einen schlagenden Beweis für die Notwendigkeit des Schwätzens zu finden, das war die Kunst. Ich dachte und dachte, und dann hatte ich plötzlich eine Idee. Ich schrieb die drei aufgegebenen Seiten und war zufrieden. Als Argument hatte ich angeführt, dass Reden weiblich sei, dass ich ja mein Bestes täte, mich zu bessern, aber ganz abgewöhnen könnte ich es mir wohl nie, da meine Mutter genauso viel redete wie ich, wenn nicht mehr, und dass an ererbten Eigenschaften nun mal wenig zu machen ist.

Herr Keesing musste über meine Argumente lachen. Aber als ich in der nächsten Stunde wieder schwätzte, folgte der zweite Aufsatz. Diesmal sollte es »Eine unverbesserliche Schwatzliese« sein. Auch der wurde abgeliefert, und zwei Stunden lang hatte Herr Keesing nichts zu klagen. In der dritten wurde es ihm jedoch wieder zu bunt. »Anne Frank, als Strafarbeit für Schwätzen einen Aufsatz mit dem Thema: ›Queck, queck, queck, sagte Fräulein Schnatterbeck.‹«
Die Klasse lachte schallend. Ich musste auch lachen, obwohl mein Erfindungsgeist auf dem Gebiet von Schwätzaufsätzen erschöpft war. Ich musste etwas anderes finden, etwas sehr Originelles. Meine Freundin Sanne, eine gute Dichterin, bot mir ihre Hilfe an, um den Aufsatz von vorn bis hinten in Reimen abzufassen. Ich jubelte. Keesing wollte mich mit diesem blödsinnigen Thema reinlegen, aber ich würde es ihm doppelt und dreifach heimzahlen.
Das Gedicht wurde fertig und war großartig. Es handelte von einer Mutter Ente und einem Vater Schwan mit drei kleinen Entchen, die wegen zu vielen Schnatterns von ihrem Vater totgebissen wurden. Zum Glück verstand Keesing Spaß. Er las das Gedicht samt Kommentaren in der Klasse vor, dann noch in anderen Klassen. Seitdem durfte ich schwätzen und bekam nie mehr eine Strafarbeit. Im Gegenteil, Keesing macht jetzt immer Witzchen. Deine Anne

Mittwoch, 24. Juni 1942
Liebe Kitty!
Es ist glühend heiß. Jeder schnauft und wird gebraten, und bei dieser Hitze muss ich jeden Weg zu Fuß gehen. Jetzt merke ich erst, wie angenehm eine Straßenbahn ist, vor allem eine offene. Aber dieser Genuss ist uns Juden nicht mehr beschieden, für uns sind Schusters Rappen gut genug. Gestern musste ich in der Mittagspause zum Zahnarzt in die Jan Luikenstraat. Von unserer Schule am Stadtgarten ist das ein langer Weg. Nachmittags schlief ich im Unterricht dann auch fast ein. Ein Glück, dass einem die Leute von selbst was zu trinken anbieten. Die Schwester beim Zahnarzt war wirklich eine herzliche Frau.
Das einzige Fahrzeug, das wir noch benützen dürfen, ist die Fähre. Der Fährmann an der Jozef-Israëls-Kade nahm uns sofort mit, als wir

ums Übersetzen baten. An den Holländern liegt es wirklich nicht, dass wir Juden es so schlecht haben.

Ich wünschte nur, dass ich nicht zur Schule müsste! Mein Fahrrad ist in den Osterferien gestohlen worden, und Mutters Rad hat Vater Christen zur Aufbewahrung gegeben. Aber zum Glück nähern sich die Ferien in Windeseile. Noch eine Woche, und das Leid ist vorbei.

Gestern Morgen habe ich was Nettes erlebt. Als ich am Fahrradabstellplatz vorbeikam, rief mich jemand. Ich schaute mich um und sah einen netten Jungen hinter mir stehen, den ich am vorhergehenden Abend bei Wilma getroffen hatte. Er ist ein Cousin um drei Ecken von ihr, und Wilma ist eine Bekannte. Ich fand sie erst sehr nett. Das ist sie ja auch, aber sie spricht den ganzen Tag über nichts anderes als über Jungen, und das wird langweilig. Der Junge kam ein bisschen schüchtern näher und stellte sich als Hello Silberberg vor. Ich war erstaunt und wusste nicht so recht, was er wollte. Aber das stellte sich schnell heraus. Er wollte meine Gesellschaft genießen und mich zur Schule begleiten. »Wenn du sowieso in dieselbe Richtung gehst, dann komme ich mit«, antwortete ich, und so gingen wir zusammen. Hello ist schon sechzehn und kann von allen möglichen Dingen gut erzählen.

Heute Morgen hat er wieder auf mich gewartet, und in Zukunft wird es wohl so bleiben.   Anne

Mittwoch, 1. Juli 1942

Liebe Kitty!

Bis heute hatte ich wirklich keine Zeit zum Schreiben. Donnerstag war ich den ganzen Nachmittag bei Bekannten, Freitag hatten wir Besuch, und so ging es weiter bis heute.

Hello und ich haben uns in dieser Woche gut kennen gelernt, er hat mir viel von sich erzählt. Er stammt aus Gelsenkirchen und ist hier in den Niederlanden bei seinen Großeltern. Seine Eltern sind in Belgien. Für ihn gibt es keine Möglichkeit, auch dorthin zu kommen. Hello hat ein Mädchen, Ursula. Ich kenne sie, sie ist ein Muster an Sanftmut und Langeweile. Nachdem er mich getroffen hat, hat Hello entdeckt, dass er an Ursuls Seite einschläft. Ich bin also eine Art

Wachhaltemittel! Ein Mensch weiß nie, wozu er noch einmal ge-
braucht wird.

Samstag hat Jacque bei mir geschlafen. Mittags war sie bei Hanneli,
und ich habe mich tot gelangweilt.

Hello sollte abends zu mir kommen, aber gegen sechs rief er an. Ich
war am Telefon, da sagte er: »Hier ist Helmuth Silberberg. Kann ich
bitte mit Anne sprechen?«

»Ja, Hello, hier ist Anne.«

»Tag, Anne. Wie geht es dir?«

»Gut, danke.«

»Ich muss dir zu meinem Bedauern sagen, dass ich heute Abend nicht
zu dir kommen kann, aber ich würde dich gerne kurz sprechen. Ist es
in Ordnung, wenn ich in zehn Minuten vor deiner Tür bin?«

»Ja, in Ordnung. Tschüs!«

Hörer aufgelegt. Ich habe mich rasch umgezogen und mir meine
Haare noch ein bisschen zurechtgemacht. Und dann hing ich nervös
am Fenster. Endlich kam er. Wunder über Wunder bin ich nicht sofort die Treppe hinuntergesaust, sondern habe ruhig abgewartet, bis
er geklingelt hat. Ich ging hinunter. Er fiel gleich mit der Tür ins
Haus.

»Hör mal, Anne, meine Großmutter findet dich noch zu jung, um re-
gelmäßigen Umgang mit dir zu haben. Sie meint, ich sollte zu Lö-
wenbachs gehen. Aber du weißt vielleicht, dass ich nicht mehr mit
Ursul gehe.«

»Nein, wieso? Habt ihr Streit gehabt?«

»Nein, im Gegenteil. Ich habe Ursul gesagt, dass wir doch nicht so
gut miteinander auskommen und deshalb nicht mehr zusammen gehen sollten, aber dass sie auch weiterhin bei uns sehr willkommen
wäre und ich hoffentlich bei ihnen auch. Ich dachte nämlich, dass sie
mit anderen Jungen ginge, und habe sie auch danach behandelt. Aber
das war überhaupt nicht wahr. Und nun sagte mein Onkel, ich müsste Ursul um Entschuldigung bitten. Aber das wollte ich natürlich
nicht, und darum habe ich Schluss gemacht. Doch das war nur einer
von vielen Gründen.

Meine Großmutter will nun, dass ich zu Ursul gehe und nicht zu dir.
Aber der Meinung bin ich nicht und habe es auch nicht vor. Alte Leute haben manchmal sehr altmodische Ansichten, aber danach kann

ich mich nicht richten. Ich habe meine Großeltern zwar nötig, aber sie mich auch, in gewisser Weise. Mittwochs abends habe ich immer frei, weil meine Großeltern glauben, ich gehe zum Schnitzen, aber ich gehe zum Treffen der Zionistischen Partei. Das darf ich eigentlich nicht, weil meine Großeltern sehr gegen den Zionismus sind. Ich bin zwar auch nicht fanatisch, aber ich interessiere mich dafür. In der letzten Zeit ist dort allerdings so ein Durcheinander, dass ich vorhabe auszutreten. Deshalb gehe ich nächsten Mittwoch zum letzten Mal hin. Also habe ich mittwochs abends, samstags abends und sonntags nachmittags und so weiter Zeit.«

»Aber wenn deine Großeltern das nicht wollen, solltest du es nicht hinter ihrem Rücken tun.«

»Liebe lässt sich nun mal nicht zwingen.«

Dann kamen wir an der Buchhandlung Blankevoort vorbei, und da stand Peter Schiff mit zwei anderen Jungen. Es war seit langem das erste Mal, dass er mich grüßte, und ich freute mich wirklich sehr darüber.

Montagabend war Hello bei uns zu Hause, um Vater und Mutter kennen zu lernen. Ich hatte Torte und Süßigkeiten geholt. Tee und Kekse, alles gab's. Aber weder Hello noch ich hatten Lust, ruhig nebeneinander auf den Stühlen zu sitzen. Wir sind spazieren gegangen, und er lieferte mich erst um zehn nach acht zu Hause ab. Vater war sehr böse, fand das keine Art, dass ich zu spät heimkam. Ich musste versprechen, in Zukunft schon um zehn vor acht drinnen zu sein. Am kommenden Samstag bin ich bei Hello eingeladen.

Wilma hat mir erzählt, dass Hello neulich abends bei ihr war und sie ihn fragte: »Wen findest du netter, Ursul oder Anne?« Da hat er gesagt: »Das geht dich nichts an.«

Aber als er wegging (sie hatten den ganzen Abend nicht mehr miteinander gesprochen), sagte er: »Anne! Tschüs, und niemandem sagen!« Schwupp, war er zur Tür draußen.

Man merkt, dass Hello in mich verliebt ist, und ich finde es zur Abwechslung ganz schön. Margot würde sagen, Hello ist ein annehmbarer Junge, und das finde ich auch. Sogar mehr als das. Mutter lobt ihn auch über die Maßen. »Ein hübscher, höflicher und netter Junge.« Ich bin froh, dass er der Familie so gut gefällt, nur meinen Freundinnen nicht, die findet er sehr kindlich, und da hat er Recht.

Jacque zieht mich immer mit ihm auf. Ich bin wirklich nicht verliebt, oh nein, aber ich darf doch wohl Freunde haben. Niemand findet was dabei.

Mutter will immer wissen, wen ich später heiraten möchte. Aber sie rät bestimmt nie, dass es Peter Schiff ist, weil ich es, ohne mit der Wimper zu zucken, immer ableugne. Ich habe Peter so gern, wie ich noch nie jemanden gern gehabt habe. Und ich rede mir immer ein, dass Peter, nur um seine Gefühle für mich zu verbergen, mit anderen Mädchen geht. Vielleicht denkt er jetzt auch, dass Hello und ich ineinander verliebt sind. Aber das ist nicht wahr. Er ist nur ein Freund von mir, oder, wie Mutter es ausdrückt, ein Kavalier.

Deine Anne

Sonntag, 5. Juli 1942

Beste Kitty!

Die Versetzungsfeier am Freitag ist nach Wunsch verlaufen, mein Zeugnis ist gar nicht so schlecht. Ich habe ein Ungenügend in Algebra, zwei Sechsen*, zwei Achten und sonst alles Siebenen. Zu Hause haben sie sich gefreut. Aber meine Eltern sind in Notenangelegenheiten sowieso anders als andere Eltern. Sie haben sich nie etwas aus guten oder schlechten Zeugnissen gemacht und achten nur darauf, ob ich gesund bin, nicht zu frech und Spaß habe. Wenn diese drei Dinge in Ordnung sind, kommt alles andere von selbst.

Ich bin das Gegenteil, ich möchte nicht schlecht sein. Ich bin unter Vorbehalt ins Lyzeum aufgenommen worden, ich hätte eigentlich noch die siebte Klasse in der Montessorischule bleiben sollen. Aber als alle jüdischen Kinder in jüdische Schulen mussten, hat Herr Elte mich und Lies Goslar nach einigem Hin und Her unter Vorbehalt aufgenommen. Lies ist auch versetzt worden, aber mit einer schweren Nachprüfung in Geometrie.

Arme Lies, sie kann zu Hause fast nie richtig arbeiten. In ihrem Zimmer spielt den ganzen Tag ihre kleine Schwester, ein verwöhntes Baby von fast zwei Jahren. Wenn Gabi ihren Willen nicht bekommt, schreit sie, und wenn Lies sich dann nicht mit ihr beschäf-

* Zehn ist die beste Note, fünf bedeutet knapp ungenügend; A. d. Ü.

Margot Frank, 1940.

tigt, schreit Frau Goslar. Auf so eine Art kann Lies unmöglich richtig arbeiten, da helfen auch die zahllosen Nachhilfestunden nicht, die sie immer wieder bekommt. Bei Goslars ist das aber auch ein Haushalt! Die Eltern von Frau Goslar wohnen nebenan, essen aber bei der Familie. Dann gibt es noch ein Dienstmädchen, das Baby, Herrn Goslar, der immer zerstreut und abwesend ist, und Frau Goslar, immer nervös und gereizt, die wieder guter Hoffnung ist. In dieser Lotterwirtschaft ist Lies mit ihren beiden linken Händen so gut wie verloren.

Meine Schwester Margot hat auch ihr Zeugnis bekommen, ausgezeichnet, wie immer. Wenn es in der Schule cum laude gäbe, wäre sie sicher mit Auszeichnung versetzt worden. So ein kluges Köpfchen!

Vater ist in der letzten Zeit viel zu Hause, im Geschäft hat er nichts mehr verloren. Ein unangenehmes Gefühl muss das sein, wenn man sich so überflüssig fühlt. Herr Kleiman hat Opekta übernommen und Herr Kugler »Gies und Co.«, die Firma für (Ersatz-)Kräuter, die erst 1941 gegründet worden ist. Als wir vor ein paar Tagen um unseren Platz spazierten, fing Vater an, über Untertauchen zu sprechen. Er meinte, dass es sehr schwer für uns sein wird, ganz und gar abgeschnitten von der Welt zu leben. Ich fragte, warum er jetzt schon darüber sprach.

»Du weißt«, sagte er, »dass wir schon seit mehr als einem Jahr Kleider, Lebensmittel und Möbel zu anderen Leuten bringen. Wir wollen nicht, dass unser Besitz den Deutschen in die Hände fällt. Aber noch weniger wollen wir selbst geschnappt werden. Deshalb werden wir von uns aus weggehen und nicht warten, bis wir geholt werden.«

»Wann denn, Vater?« Der Ernst, mit dem Vater sprach, machte mir Angst.

»Mach dir keine Sorgen darüber, das regeln wir schon. Genieße dein unbeschwertes Leben, solange du es noch genießen kannst.«

Das war alles. Oh, lass die Erfüllung dieser Worte noch in weiter Ferne bleiben!

Gerade klingelt es, Hello kommt, ich höre auf!   Deine Anne

Liebe Kitty! *seemed a lot of yrs had passed*

Zwischen Sonntagmorgen und jetzt scheinen Jahre zu liegen. Es ist so viel geschehen, als hätte sich plötzlich die Welt umgedreht. Aber, Kitty, du merkst, dass ich noch lebe, und das ist die Hauptsache, sagt Vater. Ja, in der Tat, ich lebe noch, aber frage nicht, wo und wie. Ich denke, dass du mich heute überhaupt nicht verstehst, deshalb werde ich einfach anfangen, dir zu erzählen, was am Sonntag geschehen ist.

Um 3 Uhr (Hello war eben weggegangen und wollte später zurückkommen) klingelte jemand an der Tür. Ich hatte es nicht gehört, da ich faul in einem Liegestuhl auf der Veranda in der Sonne lag und las. Kurz darauf erschien Margot ganz aufgeregt an der Küchentür. »Für Vater ist ein Aufruf von der SS gekommen«, flüsterte sie. »Mutter ist schon zu Herrn van Daan gegangen.« (Van Daan ist ein guter Bekannter und Teilhaber in Vaters Firma.)

Ich erschrak schrecklich. Ein Aufruf! Jeder weiß, was das bedeutet. Konzentrationslager und einsame Zellen sah ich vor mir auftauchen, und dahin sollten wir Vater ziehen lassen müssen? »Er geht natürlich nicht«, erklärte Margot, als wir im Zimmer saßen und auf Mutter warteten. »Mutter ist zu van Daan gegangen und fragt, ob wir schon morgen in unser Versteck umziehen können. Van Daans gehen mit. Wir sind dann zu siebt.«

Stille. Wir konnten nicht mehr sprechen. Der Gedanke an Vater, der, nichts Böses ahnend, einen Besuch im jüdischen Altersheim machte, das Warten auf Mutter, die Hitze, die Anspannung … das alles ließ uns schweigen.

Plötzlich klingelte es wieder. »Das ist Hello«, sagte ich. Margot hielt mich zurück. »Nicht aufmachen!«

Aber das war überflüssig. Wir hörten Mutter und Herrn van Daan unten mit Hello reden. Dann kamen sie herein und schlossen die Tür hinter sich. Bei jedem Klingeln sollten Margot oder ich nun leise hinuntergehen, um zu sehen, ob es Vater war. Andere Leute ließen wir nicht rein. Margot und ich wurden aus dem Zimmer geschickt, van Daan wollte mit Mutter allein sprechen.

Als Margot und ich in unserem Schlafzimmer saßen, erzählte sie, dass der Aufruf nicht Vater betraf, sondern sie. Ich erschrak erneut

32

und begann zu weinen. Margot ist sechzehn. So junge Mädchen wollten sie wegschicken? Aber zum Glück würde sie nicht gehen, Mutter hatte es selbst gesagt. Und vermutlich hatte auch Vater das gemeint, als er mit mir über Verstecken gesprochen hatte.

Verstecken! Wo sollten wir uns verstecken? In der Stadt? Auf dem Land? In einem Haus, in einer Hütte? Wann? Wie? Wo? Das waren Fragen, die ich nicht stellen konnte und die mich doch nicht losließen.

Margot und ich fingen an, das Nötigste in unsere Schultaschen zu packen. Das Erste, was ich hineintat, war dieses gebundene Heft, danach Lockenwickler, Taschentücher, Schulbücher, einen Kamm, alte Briefe. Ich dachte ans Untertauchen und stopfte deshalb die unsinnigsten Sachen in die Tasche. Aber es tut mir nicht Leid, ich mache mir mehr aus Erinnerungen als aus Kleidern.

Um fünf Uhr kam Vater endlich nach Hause. Wir riefen Herrn Kleiman an und fragten, ob er noch an diesem Abend kommen könnte. Van Daan ging weg und holte Miep. Sie kam, packte einige Schuhe, Kleider, Mäntel, Unterwäsche und Strümpfe in eine Tasche und versprach, abends noch einmal zu kommen. Danach war es still in unserer Wohnung. Keiner von uns vieren wollte essen. Es war noch warm, und alles war sehr sonderbar.

Das große Zimmer oben war an Herrn Goldschmidt vermietet, einen geschiedenen Mann in den Dreißigern. Anscheinend hatte er an diesem Abend nichts vor, er hing bis zehn Uhr bei uns rum und war nicht wegzukriegen.

Um elf Uhr kamen Miep und Jan Gies. Miep ist seit 1933 bei Vater im Geschäft und eine gute Freundin geworden, ebenso ihr frisch gebackener Ehemann Jan. Wieder verschwanden Schuhe, Hosen, Bücher und Unterwäsche in Mieps Beutel und Jans tiefen Taschen. Um halb zwölf waren sie wieder gegangen.

Ich war todmüde, und obwohl ich wusste, dass es die letzte Nacht in meinem eigenen Bett sein würde, schlief ich sofort ein und wurde am nächsten Morgen um halb sechs von Mutter geweckt. Glücklicherweise war es nicht mehr so heiß wie am Sonntag; den ganzen Tag fiel ein warmer Regen. Wir zogen uns alle vier so dick an, als müssten wir in einem Eisschrank übernachten, und das nur, um noch ein paar Kleidungsstücke mehr mitzunehmen. Kein Jude in unserer Lage hätte gewagt, mit einem Koffer voller Kleider aus dem Haus zu gehen. Ich hatte zwei Hemden, drei Hosen, zwei Paar Strümpfe und ein Kleid an, darüber Rock, Mantel, Sommermantel, feste Schuhe, Mütze, Schal und noch viel mehr. Ich erstickte zu Hause schon fast, aber danach fragte niemand.

Margot stopfte ihre Schultasche voll mit Schulbüchern, holte ihr Rad und fuhr hinter Miep her in eine mir unbekannte Ferne. Ich wusste nämlich noch immer nicht, wo der geheimnisvolle Ort war, zu dem wir gehen würden.

Um halb acht schlossen auch wir die Tür hinter uns. Die Einzige, von der ich Abschied nehmen musste, war Moortje, meine kleine Katze, die ein gutes Heim bei den Nachbarn bekommen sollte, wie auf einem Briefchen an Herrn Goldschmidt stand.

Die aufgedeckten Betten, das Frühstückszeug auf dem Tisch, ein Pfund Fleisch für die Katze in der Küche, das alles erweckte den Eindruck, als wären wir Hals über Kopf weggegangen. Eindrücke konnten uns egal sein. Weg wollten wir, nur weg und sicher ankommen, sonst nichts.

Morgen mehr.   Deine Anne

Donnerstag, 9. Juli 1942

Liebe Kitty!

So gingen wir dann im strömenden Regen, Vater, Mutter und ich, jeder mit einer Schul- und Einkaufstasche, bis obenhin voll gestopft mit den unterschiedlichsten Sachen. Die Arbeiter, die früh zu ihrer Arbeit gingen, schauten uns mitleidig nach. In ihren Gesichtern war deutlich das Bedauern zu lesen, dass sie uns keinerlei Fahrzeug anbieten konnten. Der auffallende gelbe Stern sprach für sich selbst.

Erst als wir auf der Straße waren, erzählten Vater und Mutter mir stückchenweise den ganzen Versteckplan. Schon monatelang hatten wir so viel Hausrat und Leibwäsche wie möglich aus dem Haus geschafft, und nun waren wir gerade so weit, dass wir am 16. Juli freiwillig untertauchen wollten. Durch diesen Aufruf war der Plan um zehn Tage vorverlegt, sodass wir uns mit weniger gut geordneten Räumen zufrieden geben mussten.

Das Versteck war in Vaters Bürogebäude. Für Außenstehende ist das

34

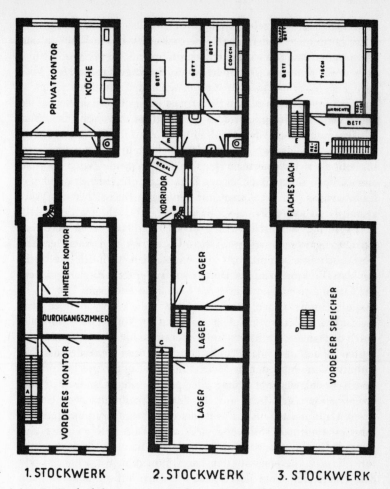

1. STOCKWERK **2. STOCKWERK** **3. STOCKWERK**

Aus: Das Tagebuch der Anne Frank (Fischer Taschenbuch Verlag, 1955, Bd. 77, S. 20).

ein bisschen schwer zu begreifen, darum werde ich es näher erklären. Vater hatte nicht viel Personal, Herrn Kugler, Herrn Kleiman und Miep, dann noch Bep Voskuijl, die 23-jährige Stenotypistin, die alle über unser Kommen informiert waren. Im Lager waren Herr Voskuijl, Beps Vater, und zwei Arbeiter, denen hatten wir nichts gesagt.

Das Gebäude sieht so aus: Im Parterre ist ein großes Magazin, das als Lager benutzt wird und wieder unterteilt ist in verschiedene Verschläge, zum Beispiel den Mahlraum, wo Zimt, Nelken und Pfeffersurrogat vermahlen werden, und den Vorratsraum. Neben der Lagertür befindet sich die normale Haustür, die durch eine Zwischentür zu einer Treppe führt. Oben an der Treppe erreicht man eine Tür mit Halbmattglas, auf der einmal mit schwarzen Buchstaben das Wort »Kontor« stand. Das ist das große vordere Büro, sehr groß, sehr hell, sehr voll. Tagsüber arbeiten da Bep, Miep und Herr Kleiman. Durch ein Durchgangszimmer mit Tresor, Garderobe und einem großen Vorratsschrank kommt man zu dem kleinen, ziemlich muffigen, dunklen Direktorenzimmer. Dort saßen früher Herr Kugler und Herr van Daan, nun nur noch Ersterer. Man kann auch vom Flur aus in Kuglers Zimmer gehen, durch eine Glastür, die zwar von innen, aber nicht ohne weiteres von außen zu öffnen ist. Von Kuglers Büro aus durch den langen, schmalen Flur, vorbei am Kohlenverschlag und vier Stufen hinauf, da ist das Prunkstück des ganzen Gebäudes, das Privatbüro. Vornehme, dunkle Möbel, Linoleum und Teppiche auf dem Boden, Radio, elegante Lampe, alles prima-prima. Daneben ist eine große, geräumige Küche mit Durchlauferhitzer und zwei Gaskochern. Dann noch ein Klo. Das ist der erste Stock. Vom unteren Flur führt eine normale Holztreppe nach oben. Dort ist ein kleiner Vorplatz, der Diele genannt wird. Rechts und links sind Türen, die linke führt zum Vorderhaus mit den Lagerräumen, dem Dachboden und dem Oberboden. Vom Vorderhaus aus führt auf der anderen Seite auch noch eine lange, übersteile, echt holländische Beinbrechtreppe zur zweiten Straßentür.

Rechts von der Diele liegt das »Hinterhaus«. Kein Mensch würde vermuten, dass hinter der einfachen, grau gestrichenen Tür so viele Zimmer versteckt sind. Vor der Tür ist eine Schwelle, und dann ist man drinnen. Direkt gegenüber der Eingangstür ist eine steile Treppe, links ein kleiner Flur und ein Raum, der Wohn- und Schlafzimmer der Familie Frank werden soll. Daneben ist noch ein kleineres Zimmer, das Schlaf- und Arbeitszimmer der beiden jungen Damen Frank. Rechts von der Treppe ist eine Kammer ohne Fenster mit einem Waschbecken und einem abgeschlossenen Klo und einer Tür in Margots und mein Zimmer. Wenn man die Treppe hinaufgeht und oben die Tür öffnet, ist man erstaunt, dass es in einem alten Grachtenhaus so einen hohen, hellen und geräumigen Raum gibt. In diesem Raum stehen ein Herd (das haben wir der Tatsache zu verdanken, dass hier früher Kuglers Laboratorium war) und ein Spülstein. Das ist also die Küche und gleichzeitig auch das Schlafzimmer des Ehepaares van Daan, allgemeines Wohnzimmer, Esszimmer und Arbeitszimmer. Ein sehr kleines Durchgangszimmerchen wird Peters Appartement werden. Dann, genau wie vorn, ein Dachboden und ein Oberboden. Siehst du, so habe ich dir unser ganzes schöne Hinterhaus vorgestellt!

Deine Anne

Freitag, 10. Juli 1942

Liebe Kitty!

Sehr wahrscheinlich habe ich dich mit meiner langatmigen Wohnungsbeschreibung ziemlich gelangweilt, aber ich finde es notwendig, dass du weißt, wo ich gelandet bin. Wie ich gelandet bin, wirst du aus den folgenden Briefen schon erfahren.

Nun die Fortsetzung meiner Geschichte, denn ich bin noch nicht fertig, das weißt du. Nachdem wir in der Prinsengracht 263 angekommen waren, führte uns Miep gleich durch den langen Flur und über die hölzerne Treppe direkt nach oben ins Hinterhaus. Sie schloss die Tür hinter uns, und wir waren allein. Margot war mit dem Rad viel schneller gewesen und hatte schon auf uns gewartet.

Unser Wohnzimmer und alle anderen Zimmer waren so voller Zeug, dass man es nicht beschreiben kann! Alle Kartons, die im Lauf der vergangenen Monate ins Büro geschickt worden waren, standen auf dem Boden und auf den Betten. Das kleine Zimmer war bis an die Decke mit Bettzeug voll gestopft. Wenn wir abends in ordentlich gemachten Betten schlafen wollten, mussten wir uns sofort dranmachen und den Kram aufräumen. Mutter und Margot waren nicht in der Lage, einen Finger zu rühren. Sie lagen auf den kahlen Betten, waren müde und schlapp und was weiß ich noch alles. Aber Vater und ich, die beiden Aufräumer der Familie, wollten sofort anfangen.

Wir räumten den ganzen Tag hindurch Schachteln aus und Schränke ein, hämmerten und werkten, bis wir abends todmüde in die sauberen Betten fielen. Den ganzen Tag haben wir kein warmes Essen bekommen, aber das störte uns nicht. Mutter und Margot waren zu müde und zu überspannt, um zu essen, Vater und ich hatten zu viel Arbeit. Dienstagmorgens fingen wir dort an, wo wir am Montag aufgehört hatten. Bep und Miep kauften mit unseren Lebensmittelmarken ein, Vater reparierte die unzureichende Verdunklung, wir schrubbten den Küchenboden und waren wieder von morgens bis abends beschäftigt. Zeit, um über die große Veränderung nachzudenken, die in mein Leben gekommen war, hatte ich bis Mittwoch kaum. Dann fand ich zum ersten Mal seit unserer Ankunft im Hinterhaus Gelegenheit, dir die Ereignisse mitzuteilen und mir gleichzeitig darüber klar zu werden, was nun eigentlich mit mir passiert war und was noch passieren würde.   Deine Anne

Samstag, 11. Juli 1942

Liebe Kitty!

Vater, Mutter und Margot können sich noch immer nicht an das Geräusch der Westerturmglocke gewöhnen, die jede Viertelstunde angibt, wie spät es ist. Ich schon, mir hat es sofort gefallen, und besonders nachts ist es so etwas Vertrautes. Es wird dich vermutlich interessieren, wie es mir als Untergetauchter gefällt. Nun, ich kann dir nur sagen, dass ich es selbst noch nicht genau weiß. Ich glaube, ich werde mich in diesem Haus nie daheim fühlen, aber damit will ich überhaupt nicht sagen, dass ich es hier unangenehm finde. Ich fühle mich eher wie in einer sehr eigenartigen Pension, in der ich Ferien mache. Eine ziemlich verrückte Auffassung von Untertauchen, aber es ist nun mal nicht anders. Das Hinterhaus ist ein ideales Versteck. Obwohl es feucht und ein bisschen schief ist, wird man wohl in ganz Amsterdam, ja vielleicht in ganz Holland, kein so bequem eingerichtetes Versteck finden.

Unser Zimmer war mit seinen nackten Wänden bis jetzt noch sehr

kahl. Dank Vater, der meine ganze Postkarten- und Filmstarsammlung schon vorher mitgenommen hatte, habe ich mit Leimtopf und
Pinsel die ganze Wand bestrichen und aus dem Zimmer ein einziges
Bild gemacht. Es sieht viel fröhlicher aus. Wenn die van Daans kommen, werden wir aus dem Holz, das auf dem Dachboden liegt, ein
paar Schränkchen und anderen netten Krimskrams machen.

Margot und Mutter haben sich wieder ein bisschen erholt. Gestern
wollte Mutter zum ersten Mal Erbsensuppe kochen, aber als sie zum
Schwätzen unten war, vergaß sie die Suppe. Die brannte so an, dass
die Erbsen kohlschwarz und nicht mehr vom Topf loszukriegen waren.

Gestern Abend sind wir alle vier hinunter ins Privatbüro gegangen
und haben den englischen Sender angestellt. Ich hatte solche Angst,
dass es jemand hören könnte, dass ich Vater buchstäblich anflehte,
wieder mit nach oben zu gehen. Mutter verstand meine Angst und
ging mit. Auch sonst haben wir große Angst, dass die Nachbarn uns
hören oder sehen könnten. Gleich am ersten Tag haben wir Vorhänge
genäht. Eigentlich darf man nicht von Vorhängen sprechen, denn es
sind nur Lappen, vollkommen unterschiedlich in Form, Qualität und
Muster, die Vater und ich sehr unfachmännisch schief aneinander genäht haben. Mit Reißnägeln wurden diese Prunkstücke vor den Fen-
stern befestigt, um vor Ablauf unserer Untertauchzeit nie mehr herunterzukommen.

Rechts neben uns ist das Haus einer Firma aus Zaandam, links eine
Möbeltischlerei. Diese Leute sind also nach der Arbeitszeit nicht in
den Gebäuden, aber trotzdem könnten Geräusche durchdringen. Wir
haben Margot deshalb auch verboten, nachts zu husten, obwohl sie
eine schwere Erkältung erwischt hat, und geben ihr große Mengen
Codein zu schlucken.

Ich freue mich sehr auf die Ankunft der van Daans, die auf Dienstag
festgelegt ist. Es wird viel gemütlicher und auch weniger still sein.
Diese Stille ist es nämlich, die mich abends und nachts so nervös
macht, und ich würde viel darum geben, wenn jemand von unseren
Beschützern hier schlafen würde.

Sonst ist es hier überhaupt nicht so schlimm, denn wir können selbst
kochen und unten in Papis Büro Radio hören. Herr Kleiman, Miep
und Bep haben uns sehr geholfen. Wir haben sogar schon Rhabarber,

Anne (rechts) und Spielkameradin Sanne am Merwedeplein, Amsterdam.

Erdbeeren und Kirschen gehabt, und ich glaube nicht, dass wir uns hier vorläufig langweilen werden. Zu lesen haben wir auch, und wir kaufen noch einen Haufen Spiele. Aus dem Fenster schauen oder hinausgehen dürfen wir natürlich nie. Tagsüber müssen wir auch immer sehr leise gehen und leise sprechen, denn im Lager dürfen sie uns nicht hören.

Gestern hatten wir viel Arbeit, wir mussten für das Büro zwei Körbe Kirschen entkernen, Herr Kugler wollte sie einmachen. Aus den Kirschenkisten machen wir Bücherregale.

Gerade werde ich gerufen!

Deine Anne

28. September 1942 (Nachtrag)
Es beklemmt mich doch mehr, als ich sagen kann, dass wir niemals hinaus dürfen, und ich habe große Angst, dass wir entdeckt und dann erschossen werden. Das ist natürlich eine weniger angenehme Aussicht.

Sonntag, 12. Juli 1942

Heute vor einem Monat waren sie alle so nett zu mir, weil ich Geburtstag hatte, aber nun fühle ich jeden Tag mehr, wie ich mich von Mutter und Margot entfremde. Ich habe heute hart gearbeitet, und alle haben mich ungeheuer gelobt, doch fünf Minuten später schimpften sie schon wieder mit mir.

Man kann deutlich den Unterschied sehen, wie sie mit Margot umgehen und mit mir. Margot hat zum Beispiel den Staubsauger kaputtgemacht, und deshalb hatten wir den ganzen Tag kein Licht. Mutter sagte: »Aber Margot, man sieht, dass du keine Arbeit gewöhnt bist, sonst hättest du gewusst, dass man einen Staubsauger nicht an der Schnur herauszieht.« Margot sagte irgendwas, und damit war die Geschichte erledigt.

Aber heute Mittag wollte ich etwas von Mutters Einkaufsliste abschreiben, weil ihre Schrift so undeutlich ist. Sie wollte das nicht und hielt mir sofort wieder eine gepfefferte Standpauke, in die sich die ganze Familie einmischte.

Ich passe nicht zu ihnen, das merke ich vor allem in der letzten Zeit sehr deutlich. Sie sind so gefühlvoll miteinander, und das will ich lieber sein, wenn ich allein bin. Sie sagen, wie gemütlich wir vier es doch haben und dass wir so harmonisch zusammenpassen. Dass ich es ganz anders empfinde, daran denken sie keinen Augenblick.

Nur Papa versteht mich manchmal, ist aber meistens auf der Seite von Mutter und Margot. Ich kann es auch nicht ausstehen, wenn sie vor Fremden erzählen, dass ich geheult habe oder wie vernünftig ich bin, oder dass sie von Moortje anfangen. Das kann ich überhaupt nicht ertragen. Moortje ist mein weicher und schwacher Punkt. Ich vermisse sie jede Minute, und niemand weiß, wie oft ich an sie denke. Ich bekomme dann immer Tränen in die Augen. Moortje ist so lieb, und ich habe sie so gern, und ich mache schon Traumpläne, dass sie wieder zurückkommt.

Ich träume hier so schön. Aber die Wirklichkeit ist, dass wir hier sitzen müssen, bis der Krieg vorbei ist. Wir dürfen nie hinausgehen, und Besuch können wir nur von Miep, ihrem Mann Jan, Bep, Herrn Kugler und Herrn und Frau Kleiman bekommen, aber diese kommt nicht, sie findet es zu gefährlich.

28. September 1942 (Nachtrag)

Papi ist immer so lieb. Er versteht mich vollkommen, und ich würde gern mal vertraulich mit ihm reden, ohne dass ich sofort in Tränen ausbreche. Aber das scheint an meinem Alter zu liegen. Ich würde am liebsten immerfort schreiben, aber das wird viel zu langweilig.

Bis jetzt habe ich fast ausschließlich Gedanken in mein Buch geschrieben, aber zu hübschen Geschichten, die ich später mal vorlesen kann, ist es nie gekommen. Aber ich werde in Zukunft nicht oder weniger sentimental sein und mich mehr an die Wirklichkeit halten.

Freitag, 14. August 1942

Beste Kitty!

Einen Monat lang habe ich dich im Stich gelassen, aber es passiert auch wirklich nicht so viel, um dir jeden Tag etwas Schönes zu erzählen. Van Daans sind am 13. Juli angekommen. Wir dachten, sie kämen erst am 14., aber weil die Deutschen immer mehr Aufrufe verschickten, fanden sie es sicherer, lieber einen Tag zu früh als einen Tag zu spät umzuziehen.

Morgens um halb zehn (wir saßen noch beim Frühstück) kam Peter van Daan, ein ziemlich langweiliger und schüchterner Lulatsch, noch nicht sechzehn, von dessen Gesellschaft nicht viel zu erwarten ist. Frau und Herr van Daan kamen eine halbe Stunde später.

Frau van Daan hatte zu unserem großen Vergnügen einen Nachttopf in ihrer Hutschachtel. »Ohne Nachttopf fühle ich mich nirgends daheim«, erklärte sie, und der Topf bekam auch gleich seinen festen Platz unter der Bettcouch. Herr van Daan brachte keinen Topf mit, sondern hatte einen zusammenklappbaren Teetisch unter dem Arm.

Wir aßen am ersten Tag unseres Zusammenseins gemütlich miteinander, und nach drei Tagen hatten wir alle sieben das Gefühl, dass wir eine große Familie geworden waren. Selbstverständlich wussten die van Daans noch viel zu erzählen, sie hatten eine Woche länger in der Welt draußen verbracht. Unter anderem interessierte uns sehr, was mit unserer Wohnung und mit Herrn Goldschmidt passiert war.

Herr van Daan erzählte: »Montagmorgen um neun Uhr rief Goldschmidt an und fragte, ob ich mal schnell vorbeikommen könnte. Ich ging sofort hin und fand ihn in großer Aufregung vor. Er gab mir den Zettel zu lesen, den Sie zurückgelassen hatten, und wollte die Katze laut Anweisung zu den Nachbarn bringen, was ich sehr gut fand. Er hatte Angst vor einer Hausdurchsuchung, deshalb gingen wir durch alle Zimmer, deckten den Tisch ab und räumten ein bisschen auf. Plötzlich entdeckte ich auf Frau Franks Schreibtisch einen Zettel, auf dem eine Adresse in Maastricht stand. Obwohl ich wusste, dass Frau Frank ihn absichtlich hingelegt hatte, tat ich sehr erstaunt und erschrocken und bat Herrn Goldschmidt dringend, dieses Unglückspapierchen zu verbrennen. Die ganze Zeit blieb ich dabei, dass ich nichts von Ihrem Verschwinden wüsste. Aber nachdem ich den Zettel gesehen hatte, bekam ich eine gute Idee. ›Herr Goldschmidt‹, sagte ich, ›jetzt fällt mir auf einmal ein, was diese Adresse bedeuten kann. Ich erinnere mich genau, dass vor ungefähr einem halben Jahr ein hoher Offizier im Büro war, der sich als ein Jugendfreund von Herrn Frank erwies und versprach, ihm zu helfen, wenn es nötig sein würde, und der tatsächlich in Maastricht stationiert war. Ich nehme an, er hat Wort gehalten und die Franks auf irgendeine Art nach Belgien und von dort in die Schweiz gebracht. Erzählen Sie das auch den Bekannten, die vielleicht nach den Franks fragen. Maastricht brauchen Sie dann natürlich nicht zu erwähnen.‹ Und damit ging ich weg. Die meisten Bekannten wissen es jetzt schon, denn ich habe meinerseits schon von verschiedenen Seiten diese Erklärung gehört.«

Wir fanden die Geschichte sehr witzig, lachten aber noch mehr über die Einbildungskraft der Leute. So hatte eine Familie vom Merwedeplein uns alle vier morgens auf dem Fahrrad vorbeikommen sehen, und eine andere Frau wusste sicher, dass wir mitten in der Nacht auf ein Militärauto geladen worden waren.   Deine Anne

Freitag, 21. August 1942

Beste Kitty!

Unser Versteck ist nun erst ein richtiges Versteck geworden. Herr Kugler fand es nämlich besser, vor unsere Zugangstür einen Schrank zu stellen (weil viele Hausdurchsuchungen gemacht werden, um versteckte Fahrräder zu finden), aber natürlich einen Schrank, der drehbar ist und wie eine Tür aufgeht. Herr Voskuijl hat das Ding geschreinert. (Wir haben ihn inzwischen über die sieben Untergetauchten informiert, und er ist die Hilfsbereitschaft selbst.)

Wenn wir nach unten gehen wollen, müssen wir uns jetzt immer erst bücken und dann einen Sprung machen. Nach drei Tagen liefen wir alle mit Beulen an der Stirn herum, weil jeder sich an der niedrigen Tür stieß. Peter hat dann ein Tuch mit Holzwolle davor genagelt. Mal sehen, ob es hilft!

Lernen tue ich nicht viel, bis September mache ich Ferien. Danach will Vater mir Unterricht geben, doch erst müssen wir die neuen Schulbücher kaufen.

Viel Veränderung kommt in unser Leben hier nicht. Heute sind Peters Haare gewaschen worden, aber das ist nicht so etwas Besonderes. Herr van Daan und ich sind dauernd zerstritten. Mama tut immer, als ob ich ein Baby wäre, und das kann ich nicht ausstehen. Peter finde ich noch immer nicht netter. Er ist ein langweiliger Junge, faulenzt den ganzen Tag auf seinem Bett, tischlert mal ein bisschen und geht dann wieder dösen. Was für ein Dummkopf!

Mama hat mir heute Morgen wieder eine elende Predigt gehalten.

Peter van Pels.

Wir sind immer genau gegenteiliger Meinung. Papa ist ein Schatz, auch wenn er mal fünf Minuten böse auf mich ist.

Draußen ist schönes, warmes Wetter, und trotz allem nutzen wir das so weit wie möglich aus, indem wir uns auf dem Dachboden auf das Harmonikabett legen.

Deine Anne

21. September 1942 (Nachtrag)

Herr van Daan ist in der letzten Zeit katzenfreundlich zu mir, ich lasse es mir ruhig gefallen.

Mittwoch, 2. September 1942

Liebe Kitty!

Herr und Frau van Daan haben heftigen Streit gehabt. So etwas habe ich noch nie erlebt, da Vater und Mutter nicht daran denken würden, einander derartig anzuschreien. Der Anlass war so geringfügig, dass es nicht mal der Mühe wert war, ein einziges Wort darüber zu verlieren. Na ja, jeder nach seinem Geschmack.

Für Peter ist es natürlich unangenehm, er steht doch dazwischen. Aber er wird von niemand mehr ernst genommen, weil er schrecklich zimperlich und faul ist. Gestern war er ganz beunruhigt, weil er statt einer roten eine blaue Zunge bekommen hatte. Diese seltsame Erscheinung verschwand aber genauso schnell, wie sie gekommen war. Heute läuft er mit einem dicken Schal um den Hals herum, weil der steif ist. Ferner klagt der Herr über Hexenschuss. Schmerzen zwischen Herz, Niere und Lunge sind ihm auch nicht fremd. Er ist ein echter Hypochonder! (So heißt das doch, oder?)

Mutter und Frau van Daan vertragen sich nicht sehr gut. Anlässe für Unannehmlichkeiten gibt's genug. Als kleines Beispiel will ich dir erzählen, dass Frau van Daan jetzt aus dem gemeinsamen Wäscheschrank ihre Laken bis auf drei herausgeholt hat. Sie nimmt natürlich an, dass Mutters Wäsche für die ganze Familie verwendet werden kann. Sie wird schwer enttäuscht sein, wenn sie merkt, dass Mutter ihrem guten Beispiel gefolgt ist.

Außerdem hat sie eine Stinkwut, dass nicht unser Tischgeschirr im Gebrauch ist, sondern das ihre. Immer versucht sie herauszubekommen, wo wir unsere Teller hingetan haben. Sie sind näher als sie denkt, sie stehen in Kartons auf dem Dachboden hinter einem ganzen Haufen Reklamematerial von Opekta. Solange wir uns verstecken, sind die Teller unerreichbar, und das ist auch gut so! Mir passieren dauernd Missgeschicke. Gestern habe ich einen Suppenteller von Frau van Daans Geschirr kaputtgeschmissen.

»Oh«, rief sie wütend, »sei doch ein bisschen vorsichtiger! Das ist das Einzige, was ich noch habe.«

(Bitte berücksichtige, Kitty, dass die beiden Damen hier ein fürchterliches Niederländisch sprechen. Über die Herren wage ich nichts zu sagen, sie wären sehr beleidigt. Wenn du diese Haspelei hören könntest, würdest du laut lachen. Wir beachten es gar nicht mehr, verbessern nützt doch nichts. Ich werde aber, wenn ich über Mutter oder Frau van Daan schreibe, nicht ihre Originalsprache wiedergeben, sondern ordentliches Niederländisch.)

Letzte Woche hatten wir eine kleine Unterbrechung in unserem so eintönigen Leben, und das lag an einem Buch über Frauen und an Peter. Du musst nämlich wissen, dass Margot und Peter fast alle Bücher lesen dürfen, die Herr Kleiman für uns leiht. Aber dieses besondere Buch über ein Frauenthema wollten die Erwachsenen lieber nicht aus den Händen geben. Das stachelte Peters Neugier an. Was für verbotene Dinge würden wohl in dem Buch stehen? Heimlich nahm er es seiner Mutter weg, als sie unten am Reden war, und lief mit seiner Beute zum Oberboden. Zwei Tage ging das gut. Frau van Daan wusste längst, was er tat, verriet aber nichts, bis Herr van Daan dahinter kam. Er wurde böse, nahm Peter das Buch weg und dachte, dass die Sache damit erledigt wäre. Er hatte aber nicht mit der Neugier seines Sohnes gerechnet, der durch das energische Auftreten seines Vaters keineswegs aus der Fassung gebracht war. Er sann auf Möglichkeiten, dieses mehr als interessante Buch doch zu Ende zu lesen.

Frau van Daan hatte inzwischen Mutter gefragt, was sie von dieser Sache halte. Mutter fand das Buch nicht gut für Margot, aber in den meisten anderen sah sie nichts Schlimmes.

»Zwischen Margot und Peter ist ein großer Unterschied«, sagte Mutter. »Erstens ist Margot ein Mädchen, und Mädchen sind immer reifer als Jungen, zweitens hat Margot schon mehr ernste Bücher gelesen und sucht nicht nach Dingen, die für sie nicht mehr verboten sind, und drittens ist sie viel weiter entwickelt und verständiger, was auch ihre vier Jahre Oberschule mit sich bringen.«

Frau van Daan stimmte dem zu, fand es aber doch prinzipiell falsch, Jugendliche Erwachsenenbücher lesen zu lassen.

Inzwischen hatte Peter den richtigen Zeitpunkt gefunden, an dem niemand auf das Buch oder auf ihn achtete. Abends um halb acht, als die ganze Familie unten im Privatbüro Radio hörte, nahm er seinen Schatz mit hinauf zum Oberboden. Um halb neun hätte er wieder unten sein müssen, aber weil das Buch so spannend war, vergaß er die Zeit und kam gerade die Dachbodentreppe herunter, als sein Vater ins Zimmer kam. Was folgte, ist klar. Ein Klaps, ein Schlag, ein Ruck, das Buch lag auf dem Tisch, und Peter war auf dem Oberboden.

So standen die Dinge, als die Familie zum Essen kam. Peter blieb oben, niemand kümmerte sich um ihn, er sollte ohne Essen ins Bett. Wir setzten unsere Mahlzeit fort und plauderten fröhlich, als auf einmal ein durchdringendes Pfeifen zu uns drang. Wir legten die Gabeln hin und schauten uns mit bleichen und erschrockenen Gesichtern an. Dann hörten wir Peters Stimme, die durch das Ofenrohr rief: »Ich komme doch nicht hinunter!«

Herr van Daan sprang auf, seine Serviette fiel zu Boden, und mit einem feuerroten Kopf schrie er: »Jetzt ist es aber genug.«

Vater nahm ihn am Arm, da er Schlimmes befürchtete, und zusammen gingen die beiden Herren zum Dachboden. Nach viel Sträuben und Trampeln landete Peter in seinem Zimmer. Die Tür ging zu, und wir aßen weiter.

Frau van Daan wollte ein Butterbrot für ihr Sohnemännchen übrig lassen, aber Herr van Daan war unerbittlich. »Wenn er nicht sofort um Entschuldigung bittet, muss er auf dem Dachboden schlafen.«

Wir protestierten und fanden, ohne Essen zu bleiben sei schon Strafe genug. Und wenn er sich erkälten würde, könnte noch nicht mal ein Doktor vorbeikommen.

Peter bat nicht um Entschuldigung, er war schon wieder auf dem Oberboden. Herr van Daan kümmerte sich nicht mehr darum, bemerkte aber morgens, dass Peters Bett doch benutzt worden war. Um sieben Uhr war Peter schon wieder auf dem Dachboden, wurde aber durch Vaters freundschaftliche Worte dazu gebracht, herunterzukommen.

Drei Tage mürrische Gesichter, hartnäckiges Schweigen, und alles lief wieder in gewohnten Gleisen. Deine Anne

Montag, 21. September 1942

Liebe Kitty!

Heute werde ich dir kurz die allgemeinen Neuigkeiten vom Hinterhaus erzählen. Über meiner Bettcouch ist ein Licht angebracht worden, damit ich nur an der Schnur zu ziehen brauche, wenn nachts geschossen wird. Im Augenblick geht das aber nicht, da unser Fenster Tag und Nacht spaltbreit geöffnet ist.

Die männlichen van Daans haben einen komfortablen, gebeizten Vorratsschrank geschreinert, mit richtigem Fliegengitter. Dieses glorreiche Ding stand bis jetzt in Peters Zimmer, ist nun aber wegen der größeren Frische auf den Dachboden gestellt worden. Jetzt gibt es stattdessen ein Brett. Ich habe Peter geraten, den Tisch dort hinzustellen, mit einer hübschen Decke, und das eine Schränkchen an die Wand zu hängen, wo jetzt der Tisch ist. Dann könnte es noch ein gemütliches Kämmerchen werden, auch wenn ich nicht gern da schlafen wollte.

Frau van Daan ist unausstehlich. Ständig bekomme ich von oben Standpauken, weil ich zu viel schwätze. Ich mache mir aus ihren Worten aber nichts! Mit Madame ist immer was anderes. Jetzt will sie die Töpfe nicht abwaschen. Wenn noch ein Restchen drin ist, tut sie das nicht in eine Glasschale, sondern lässt es lieber im Topf verderben. Und wenn Margot dann mittags beim Spülen viele Töpfe hat, sagt Madame auch noch: »Och, Margotchen, Margotchen, du hast aber viel zu tun!«

Herr Kleiman bringt jede zweite Woche ein paar Mädchenbücher für mich mit. Ich bin begeistert von der Joop-ter-Heul-Serie. Cissy van Marxfeldt gefällt mir im Allgemeinen besonders gut. »Eine Sommertorheit« habe ich schon viermal gelesen und muss noch immer über die komischen Situationen lachen.

Mit Vater bin ich jetzt damit beschäftigt, einen Stammbaum seiner Familie zu machen, und dabei erzählt er etwas von jedem.

Das Lernen hat angefangen. Ich mache viel für Französisch und pauke jeden Tag fünf unregelmäßige Verben. Aber ich habe bitter viel von dem, was ich in der Schule gelernt habe, vergessen. Peter hat seufzend seine Englischaufgaben wieder aufgenommen. Gerade sind einige Schulbücher angekommen. Einen umfangreichen Vorrat an Heften, Bleistiften, Radiergummis, Etiketten usw. habe ich von zu Hause mitgebracht. Pam (das ist Vaters Kosename) erhebt Anspruch auf Unterricht in Niederländisch. Ich finde das prima, sozusagen als Gegenleistung für seine Hilfe in Französisch und anderen Fächern. Aber die Schnitzer, die er macht, sind unglaublich!
Ich höre manchmal den Sender Oranje. Kürzlich sprach Prinz Bernhard. Ungefähr im Januar wird wieder ein Kind bei ihnen geboren werden, sagte er. Ich finde das schön. Hier verstehen sie nicht, dass ich so oranje-treu gesinnt bin.

Vor einigen Tagen sprachen wir darüber, dass ich noch viel lernen müsste, mit der Folge, dass ich mich am nächsten Tag gleich hart an die Arbeit gemacht habe. Ich habe wirklich keine Lust, mit vierzehn oder fünfzehn Jahren noch in der ersten Klasse* zu sitzen. Es kam auch zur Sprache, dass ich fast nichts lesen darf. Mutter liest gerade »Heeren, Vrouwen en Knechten«, das darf ich natürlich noch nicht lesen (Margot schon!), ich muss erst noch etwas weiter entwickelt sein, so wie meine begabte Schwester. Wir sprachen auch darüber, dass ich über Philosophie, Psychologie und Physiologie (diese Wörter habe ich erst mal nachgeschlagen) tatsächlich nichts weiß. Vielleicht bin ich im nächsten Jahr klüger!
Ich bin zu der erschreckenden Erkenntnis gekommen, dass ich nur ein Kleid mit langen Ärmeln und drei Strickjacken für den Winter habe. Vater hat erlaubt, dass ich mir einen Pullover aus weißer Schafwolle stricke. Die Wolle ist nicht sehr schön, die Wärme wird den Mangel wettmachen müssen. Wir haben noch einige Kleider bei anderen Leuten, aber die kann man erst nach dem Krieg zurückholen, falls sie dann noch da sind. Als ich neulich etwas über Frau van Daan an dich schrieb, kam sie gerade ins Zimmer. Klapp, Buch zu.

* Gemeint ist die erste Klasse einer weiterführenden Schule nach sechs Klassen Grundschule; A. d. Ü.

Annes Klasse an der Montessori-Schule.

»Na, Anne, darf ich nicht mal schauen?«

»Nein, Frau van Daan.«

»Nur die letzte Seite?«

»Nein, auch die nicht, Frau van Daan.«

Ich bekam einen Mordsschreck, denn gerade auf dieser Seite war sie schlecht weggekommen.

So passiert jeden Tag was, aber ich bin zu faul und zu müde, um alles aufzuschreiben.   Deine Anne

Freitag, 25. September 1942

Liebe Kitty!

Vater hat einen alten Bekannten, einen Herrn Dreher, einen Mann von siebzig, sehr schwerhörig, krank und arm. An seiner Seite als lästiges Anhängsel eine Frau, die siebenundzwanzig Jahre jünger ist, auch arm, aber vollgehängt mit echten und unechten Armbändern und Ringen, die noch aus früheren goldenen Zeiten übrig sind. Dieser Herr Dreher hat Vater schon ziemlich viel Mühe bereitet, und ich bewunderte Vater immer wegen der Engelsgeduld, mit der er dem bedauernswerten alten Herrchen am Telefon Rede und Antwort stand. Als wir noch zu Hause waren, hat Mutter oft vorgeschlagen, Vater sollte doch ein Grammophon vor das Telefon stellen, das alle drei Minuten »Ja, Herr Dreher« und »Nein, Herr Dreher« sagt, denn der alte Mann verstand sowieso nichts von Vaters ausführlichen Antworten.

Heute rief nun Herr Dreher im Büro an und fragte Herrn Kugler, ob er nicht kurz vorbeikommen könnte. Herr Kugler hatte keine Lust und wollte Miep schicken. Miep sagte telefonisch ab. Frau Dreher rief danach dreimal an. Und weil Miep angeblich ja den ganzen Nachmittag nicht da war, musste sie am Telefon Beps Stimme nachmachen. Unten im Büro und auch hier oben haben alle schrecklich gelacht. Jedes Mal, wenn jetzt das Telefon klingelt, sagt Bep: »Das ist Frau Dreher!« Woraufhin Miep sofort anfängt zu lachen und unhöflich kichernd den Leuten Auskunft gibt.

Wirklich, so eine verrückte Firma gibt es nicht noch einmal! Die Direktoren machen zusammen mit den Büromädchen den größten Spaß!

Ich gehe manchmal abends zu den van Daans, um mich ein bisschen zu unterhalten. Dann essen wir Mottenkekse mit Sirup (die Keksdose stand in einem Kleiderschrank, der eingemottet ist) und amüsieren uns. Neulich ging das Gespräch um Peter. Ich habe erzählt, dass Peter mir so oft über die Wange streichelt und ich das nicht mag. Auf echte Elternart fragten sie, ob ich Peter nicht ein bisschen gern haben könnte, er hätte mich bestimmt sehr gern. Ich dachte »Oje!«, und sagte »Oh nee!« Stell dir das vor! Dann sagte ich, dass Peter sich ein bisschen linkisch anstellt. Ich nehme an, er ist schüchtern. Das ist mit allen Jungen so, die noch nicht oft Umgang mit Mädchen gehabt haben.

Ich muss wirklich sagen, dass die Versteckkommission Hinterhaus (Abteilung Herren) sehr erfinderisch ist. Hör nur, was sie sich jetzt wieder ausgedacht haben! Sie wollen Herrn Broks, Vertreter der Opekta-Gesellschaft und illegaler Sachen-Verstecker, eine Nachricht von uns zukommen lassen! Sie tippen an einen Opekta-Kunden in Zeeuws-Vlaanderen einen Brief mit einer Anfrage, und zwar so, dass der Mann einen Zettel ausfüllen und mit dem beigelegten Umschlag zurückschicken muss. Die Adresse auf dem Umschlag schreibt Vater mit der Hand. Wenn dieser Umschlag zurückkommt, wird der Brief des Kunden herausgeholt und ein handgeschriebenes Lebenszeichen von Vater hineingesteckt. So wird Broks den Brief lesen, ohne misstrauisch zu werden. Sie haben ausgerechnet Zeeland gewählt, weil es dicht an der belgischen Grenze liegt und der Brief also einfach über die Grenze geschmuggelt worden sein kann. Außerdem darf dort niemand ohne besondere Genehmigung hin, und ein gewöhnlicher Vertreter wie Broks wird diese Genehmigung nicht bekommen.

Vater hat gestern Abend wieder einmal ein Theater aufgeführt. Ihm war schlecht vor Müdigkeit, und er torkelte ins Bett. Dort hatte er kalte Füße, und ich habe ihm meine Bettschuhe angezogen. Fünf Minuten später lagen sie doch wieder neben seinem Bett. Dann wollte er kein Licht haben und hat sich mit dem Kopf unter die Decke gelegt. Als das Licht ausgemacht wurde, kam er sehr vorsichtig zum Vorschein. Es war zu komisch. Dann sprachen wir darüber, dass Peter Margot »eine Tante« nennt, und auf einmal kam Papas Stimme aus der Tiefe: »Eine Kaffeetante.«

Mouschi, die Katze, wird immer lieber zu mir, aber ich habe immer noch ein bisschen Angst.

Deine Anne

Liebe Kitty!

Heute habe ich wieder eine so genannte »Diskussion« mit Mutter gehabt. Das Schlimme ist, ich breche immer sofort in Tränen aus, ich kann es nicht ändern. Papa ist immer lieb zu mir, und er versteht mich auch viel besser. Ach, ich kann Mutter in solchen Momenten nicht ausstehen, und ich bin für sie auch eine Fremde. Das sieht man gleich, sie weiß noch nicht mal, wie ich über die normalsten Dinge denke.

Wir sprachen über Dienstmädchen, dass man sie Haushaltshilfe nennen sollte und dass das nach dem Krieg sicher verlangt werden wird. Ich sah das nicht sofort ein. Und da sagte sie, dass ich so oft über »später« spreche und mich dann als große Dame aufspiele. Aber das ist überhaupt nicht wahr. Ich darf mir doch wirklich mal kleine Luftschlösser bauen, das ist doch nicht schlimm, das braucht man doch nicht so ernst zu nehmen. Papi verteidigt mich wenigstens, ohne ihn würde ich es hier bestimmt nicht aushalten.

Auch mit Margot verstehe ich mich nicht sehr gut. Obwohl es in unserer Familie nie so einen Ausbruch wie oben gibt, ist es doch längst nicht immer gemütlich. Ich habe eine ganz andere Natur als Margot und Mutter, sie sind so fremd für mich. Ich verstehe mich mit meinen Freundinnen besser als mit meiner eigenen Mutter. Das ist schade, gell!

Frau van Daan ist wieder eine Laus über die Leber gekrochen. Sie ist sehr launisch und schließt immer mehr von ihren Privatsachen weg. Schade, dass Mutter nicht jeden Van-Daan-Schwund mit einem Frank-Schwund beantwortet.

Manche Leute scheinen ein besonderes Vergnügen daran zu finden, nicht nur ihre eigenen Kinder zu erziehen, sondern auch die ihrer Bekannten, so sind auch die van Daans. An Margot ist nicht viel zu erziehen, sie ist von Natur aus die Gut-, Lieb- und Klugheit selbst. Aber ich trage ihren Anteil an Untugenden ausreichend mit. Mehr als einmal fliegen beim Essen ermahnende Worte und freche Antworten hin und her. Vater und Mutter verteidigen mich immer heftig, ohne sie könnte ich den Kampf nicht so ohne weiteres aufnehmen. Zwar ermahnen sie mich immer, weniger zu reden, mich in nichts einzumischen und bescheidener zu sein, aber das schaffe ich selten.

Wäre Vater nicht immer wieder so geduldig, hätte ich die Hoffnung schon längst aufgegeben, die Forderungen meiner Eltern zu erfüllen, dabei sind sie wirklich nicht zu hoch.

Wenn ich von einem Gemüse, das ich überhaupt nicht mag, wenig nehme und stattdessen Kartoffeln esse, kann vor allem Frau van Daan diese Verwöhntheit nicht ertragen. »Nimm noch etwas Gemüse, Anne, komm«, sagt sie dann gleich.

»Nein, danke«, antworte ich. »Mir reichen die Kartoffeln.«

»Gemüse ist sehr gesund, das sagt deine Mutter auch. Nimm noch was«, drängt sie dann, bis Vater eingreift und mir Recht gibt.

Dann fängt Frau van Daan an zu wettern und sagt: »Da hätten Sie mal bei uns zu Hause sein müssen, da wurden die Kinder wenigstens erzogen! Das ist doch keine Erziehung! Anne ist schrecklich verwöhnt, ich würde das nie zulassen. Wenn Anne meine Tochter wäre …«

Damit beginnt und endet immer der ganze Wortschwall. »Wenn Anne meine Tochter wäre …« Zum Glück bin ich das nicht.

Aber um auf das Erziehungsthema zurückzukommen: Gestern trat nach Frau van Daans letzten viel sagenden Worten eine Stille ein, und dann sagte Vater: »Ich finde, dass Anne sehr gut erzogen ist. Sie hat wenigstens schon so viel gelernt, dass sie auf Ihre langen Predigten keine Antwort mehr gibt. Und was das Gemüse betrifft, kann ich nichts anderes sagen als vice versa.«

Madame war geschlagen, und zwar gründlich. Das bezog sich natürlich auf sie, weil sie abends keine Bohnen und überhaupt keine Kohlsorten vertragen kann, denn dann lässt sie »Winde«. Das könnte ich auch sagen. Sie ist doch idiotisch, nicht wahr? Soll sie wenigstens über mich den Mund halten.

Es ist komisch zu sehen, wie schnell Frau van Daan rot wird. Ich nicht, bätsch! Und darüber ärgert sie sich insgeheim schrecklich.

Deine Anne

Montag, 28. September 1942

Liebe Kitty!

Mein Brief von gestern war noch lange nicht fertig, als ich mit dem Schreiben aufhören musste. Ich kann die Lust nicht unterdrücken, dir von einer anderen Unstimmigkeit zu erzählen. Doch bevor ich damit anfange, noch dies: Ich finde es sehr seltsam, dass erwachsene Menschen so schnell, so viel und über alle möglichen Kleinigkeiten Streit anfangen. Bisher dachte ich immer, dass nur Kinder sich so zanken und dass sich das später legen würde. Natürlich gibt es schon mal Anlass für einen »richtigen« Streit, aber diese Wortgefechte hier sind nichts anderes als Zankereien. Sie gehören zur Tagesordnung, und ich müsste eigentlich schon daran gewöhnt sein. Das ist jedoch nicht der Fall und wird auch nicht der Fall sein, solange ich bei fast jeder Diskussion (dieses Wort wird hier statt Streit verwendet, ganz falsch natürlich, aber das wissen Deutsche eben nicht besser!) zur Sprache komme.

Nichts, aber auch gar nichts lassen sie an mir gelten. Mein Auftreten, mein Charakter, meine Manieren werden Stück für Stück von vorn bis hinten und von hinten bis vorn bequatscht und betratscht, und etwas, an das ich überhaupt nicht gewöhnt war, nämlich harte Worte und Geschrei an meine Adresse, soll ich jetzt laut befugter Seite wohlgemut schlucken. Das kann ich nicht! Ich denke nicht daran, diese Beleidigungen auf mir sitzen zu lassen. Ich werde ihnen schon zeigen, dass Anne Frank nicht von gestern ist! Sie werden sich noch wundern und ihre große Klappe halten, wenn ich ihnen klarmache, dass sie nicht mit meiner, sondern erst mal mit ihrer eigenen Erziehung beginnen müssen. Das ist eine Art aufzutreten! Einfach barbarisch! Ich bin jedes Mal wieder verblüfft von so viel Ungezogenheit und vor allem Dummheit (Frau van Daan). Aber sobald ich mich daran gewöhnt haben werde, und das wird schon bald sein, werde ich ihnen ihre Wörter ungesalzen zurückgeben, da werden sie anders reden! Bin ich denn wirklich so ungezogen, eigenwillig, störrisch, unbescheiden, dumm, faul usw., wie sie es oben behaupten? Na ja, ich weiß schon, dass ich viele Fehler und Mängel habe, aber sie übertreiben wirklich maßlos. Wenn du nur wüsstest, Kitty, wie ich manchmal bei diesen Schimpfkanonaden koche! Es wird wirklich nicht mehr lange dauern, bis meine angestaute Wut zum Ausbruch kommt.

Aber nun genug hierüber, ich habe dich lange genug mit meinen Streitereien gelangweilt. Doch ich kann es nicht lassen, eine hochinteressante Tischdiskussion muss ich dir noch erzählen.

Irgendwie kamen wir auf Pims weitgehende Bescheidenheit. Die ist eine so feststehende Tatsache, dass selbst von den idiotischsten Leuten nicht daran gezweifelt werden kann. Plötzlich sagte Frau van Daan, die jedes Gespräch auf sich beziehen muss: »Ich bin auch sehr bescheiden, viel bescheidener als mein Mann!«

Hast du je im Leben so was gehört? Dieser Satz zeigt doch schon sehr deutlich ihre Bescheidenheit!

Herr van Daan fand es nötig, das »als mein Mann« näher zu erklären, und sagte ganz ruhig: »Ich will auch nicht bescheiden sein. Ich habe immer festgestellt, dass unbescheidene Leute es viel weiter bringen als bescheidene.« Und dann wandte er sich an mich: »Sei nur nicht bescheiden, Anne, damit kommt man wirklich nicht weiter.«

Mutter stimmte dieser Ansicht vollkommen bei. Aber wie gewöhnlich musste Frau van Daan zu diesem Erziehungsthema ihren Senf dazugeben. Diesmal wandte sie sich jedoch nicht an mich, sondern an mein Elternpaar, und sagte: »Sie haben eine seltsame Lebensanschauung, so etwas zu Anne zu sagen. In meiner Jugend war das ganz anders. Aber ich bin sicher, dass es jetzt auch noch anders ist, außer eben in Ihrer modernen Familie.«

Damit war Mutters mehrmals verteidigte moderne Erziehungsmethode gemeint. Frau van Daan war feuerrot vor Aufregung. Jemand, der rot wird, regt sich durch die Erhitzung immer mehr auf und hat das Spiel bald verloren.

Mutter, die nicht rot geworden war, wollte die Geschichte so schnell wie möglich vom Tisch haben und überlegte kurz, bevor sie antwortete: »Frau van Daan, auch ich finde tatsächlich, dass es im Leben viel besser ist, etwas weniger bescheiden zu sein. Mein Mann, Margot und Peter sind außergewöhnlich bescheiden. Ihr Mann, Anne, Sie und ich sind nicht unbescheiden, aber wir lassen uns auch nicht bei jeder Gelegenheit einfach zur Seite schieben.«

Frau van Daan: »Aber Frau Frank, ich verstehe Sie nicht! Ich bin wirklich außergewöhnlich bescheiden. Wie kommen Sie dazu, mich unbescheiden zu nennen?«

Mutter: »Sie sind sicher nicht unbescheiden, aber niemand würde Sie besonders bescheiden finden.«

Frau van Daan: »Ich würde gerne wissen wollen, worin ich unbescheiden bin! Wenn ich hier nicht für mich selbst sorgen würde, müsste ich verhungern, ein anderer täte es bestimmt nicht. Aber deshalb bin ich wirklich genauso bescheiden wie Ihr Mann.«

Mutter konnte bei dieser albernen Selbstverteidigung nur lachen. Das irritierte Frau van Daan, die ihre Ausführungen noch mit einer langen Reihe prächtiger deutsch-niederländischer und niederländisch-deutscher Worte fortsetzte, bis die geborene Rednerin sich so in ihren eigenen Worten verheddert, dass sie sich schließlich vom Stuhl erhob und aus dem Zimmer gehen wollte. Ihr Blick fiel auf mich. Das hättest du sehen müssen! Unglücklicherweise hatte ich in dem Moment, als sie uns den Rücken zeigte, mitleidig und ironisch mit dem Kopf geschüttelt, nicht mit Absicht, sondern ganz unwillkürlich, so intensiv hatte ich den Wortschwall verfolgt. Frau van Daan kehrte um und fing an zu keifen, laut, deutsch, gemein und unhöflich, genau wie ein dickes, rotes Fischweib. Es war ein Vergnügen, sie anzuschauen. Wenn ich zeichnen könnte, hätte ich sie am liebsten in dieser Haltung gezeichnet, so komisch war dieses kleine, verrückte, dumme Weib! Aber eines weiß ich jetzt: Man lernt die Menschen erst gut kennen, wenn man einmal richtigen Streit mit ihnen gehabt hat. Erst dann kann man ihren Charakter beurteilen!

Deine Anne

Dienstag, 29. September 1942

Liebe Kitty!

Versteckte erleben seltsame Sachen! Weil wir keine Badewanne haben, waschen wir uns in einem Waschzuber, und weil nur das Büro (damit meine ich immer das gesamte untere Stockwerk) warmes Wasser hat, nutzen wir alle sieben der Reihe nach diesen Vorteil aus. Weil wir nun aber auch so verschieden sind und einige sich mehr genieren als andere, hat sich jedes Familienmitglied einen anderen Badeplatz ausgesucht. Peter badet in der Küche, obwohl die Küche eine Glastür hat. Wenn er vorhat, ein Bad zu nehmen, teilt er jedem einzeln mit, dass wir in der nächsten halben Stunde nicht an der Küche vorbeigehen dürfen. Diese Maßnahme scheint ihm ausreichend. Herr van Daan badet ganz oben. Für ihn macht die Sicherheit des eigenen Zimmers die Unbequemlichkeit wett, das heiße Wasser die ganzen Treppen hochzutragen. Frau van Daan badet vorläufig überhaupt nicht, sie wartet ab, welcher Platz der beste ist. Vater badet im Privatbüro, Mutter in der Küche hinter einem Ofenschirm, und Margot und ich haben das vordere Büro als Planschplatz gewählt. Samstagnachmittags sind dort die Vorhänge zugezogen. Dann reinigen wir uns im Dunkeln, und diejenige, die gerade nicht an der Reihe ist, schaut durch einen Spalt zwischen den Vorhängen aus dem Fenster und beobachtet die komischen Leute draußen.

Seit letzter Woche gefällt mir dieses Bad nicht mehr, und ich habe mich auf die Suche nach einem bequemeren Platz gemacht. Peter hat mich auf die Idee gebracht, meine Schüssel in die geräumige Bürotoilette zu stellen. Dort kann ich mich hinsetzen, Licht machen, die Tür abschließen, das Wasser ohne fremde Hilfe weggießen und bin sicher vor indiskreten Blicken. Am Sonntag habe ich mein schönes Badezimmer erstmals benutzt, und so verrückt es klingt, ich finde es besser als jeden anderen Platz.

Am Mittwoch war der Installateur im Haus, um unten die Rohre der Wasserleitung von der Bürotoilette auf den Flur zu verlegen. Diese Veränderung ist in Hinblick auf einen eventuellen kalten Winter gemacht worden, damit die Rohre nicht einfrieren. Der Installateurbesuch war für uns alles andere als angenehm. Nicht nur, dass wir tagsüber kein Wasser laufen lassen durften, wir durften natürlich auch nicht aufs Klo.

Es ist wohl sehr unfein, wenn ich dir erzähle, was wir getan haben, um dem Übel abzuhelfen. Aber ich bin nicht so prüde, über solche Dinge nicht zu sprechen. Vater und ich haben uns zu Beginn unseres Untertauchens einen improvisierten Nachttopf angeschafft, das bedeutet, wir haben aus Mangel an einem Topf ein Weckglas geopfert. Diese Weckgläser haben wir während des Installateurbesuchs ins Zimmer gestellt und unsere Bedürfnisse tagsüber aufbewahrt. Das fand ich lange nicht so eklig wie die Tatsache, dass ich den ganzen Tag stillsitzen musste und auch nicht reden durfte. Du kannst dir gar nicht vorstellen, wie schwer das dem Fräulein Quak-quak-quak gefallen ist. An normalen Tagen dürfen wir ja auch nur flüstern, aber überhaupt nicht zu sprechen und sich nicht zu bewegen, das ist noch zehnmal schlimmer. Mein Hintern war nach drei Tagen Sitzen plattgedrückt und ganz steif und tat weh. Abendgymnastik hat geholfen.

Deine Anne

Beste Kitty!

Gestern bin ich schrecklich erschrocken. Um acht Uhr klingelte es plötzlich ganz laut. Ich dachte natürlich, da käme jemand … Wer, kannst du dir wohl denken. Als aber alle behaupteten, es wären sicher Straßenjungen oder die Post gewesen, beruhigte ich mich.

Die Tage werden hier sehr still. Levinsohn, ein kleiner jüdischer Apotheker und Chemiker, arbeitet für Kugler in der Küche. Er kennt das ganze Haus sehr gut, und darum haben wir ständig Angst, dass es ihm einfallen könnte, auch mal das frühere Labor zu besichtigen. Wir sind so still wie Babymäuschen. Wer hätte vor drei Monaten angenommen, dass die Quecksilber-Anne stundenlang ruhig sitzen müsste und auch kann?

Am 29. September hatte Frau van Daan Geburtstag. Obwohl nicht groß gefeiert wurde, bekam sie doch Blumen und kleine Geschenke, und es gab gutes Essen. Rote Nelken von dem Herrn Gemahl scheinen bei der Familie Tradition zu sein.

Um noch kurz bei Frau van Daan zu bleiben: Eine Quelle ständigen Ärgers sind für mich ihre Flirtversuche mit Vater. Sie streicht ihm über Wange und Haare, zieht ihr Röckchen sehr hoch hinauf, sagt Dinge, die sie für witzig hält, und versucht so, Pims Aufmerksamkeit auf sich zu ziehen. Glücklicherweise findet Pim sie nicht schön und auch nicht nett und geht daher auf die Flirtereien nicht ein. Aber ich bin ziemlich eifersüchtig ausgefallen, wie du weißt, also kann ich das nicht haben. Mutter tut das doch auch nicht bei Herrn van Daan. Das habe ich ihr auch ins Gesicht gesagt.

Peter kann ab und zu recht witzig sein. Eine Vorliebe, die alle zum Lachen bringt, hat er jedenfalls mit mir gemeinsam, und zwar Verkleiden. Er in einem sehr engen Kleid seiner Mutter, ich in seinem Anzug, so erschienen wir, mit Hut und Mütze geschmückt. Die Erwachsenen bogen sich vor Lachen, und wir hatten nicht weniger Spaß.

Bep hat im Warenhaus neue Röcke für Margot und mich gekauft. Der Stoff ist schlecht, wie Jute, aus der Kartoffelsäcke gemacht werden. So ein Ding, das die Läden früher nicht zu verkaufen gewagt hätten, kostet jetzt 7,75 respektive 24 Gulden.

Noch etwas Schönes haben wir in Aussicht: Bep hat für Margot, Peter und mich schriftlichen Steno-Unterricht bestellt. Du wirst schon sehen, was für perfekte Stenographen wir nächstes Jahr sein werden. Ich finde es jedenfalls sehr wichtig, so eine Geheimschrift zu lernen.

Ich habe schreckliche Schmerzen in meinem Zeigefinger (von der linken Hand) und kann deshalb nicht bügeln, was für ein Glück!

Herr van Daan wollte lieber, dass ich mich neben ihn an den Tisch setze, denn Margot isst nicht mehr genug, meint er. Nun, ich finde so eine Veränderung auch ganz schön. Im Garten läuft immer ein kleines, schwarzes Kätzchen herum. Das erinnert mich so an mein Moortje, oh, dieser Schatz! Mama hat ständig was auszusetzen, vor allem bei Tisch, auch deshalb ist die Veränderung ganz schön. Jetzt hat Margot den Ärger damit, oder besser gesagt, keinen Ärger damit, denn über sie macht Mama nicht solche stacheligen Bemerkungen, über das vorbildliche Kind! Mit dem vorbildlichen Kind piesacke ich sie jetzt immer, das kann sie nicht ausstehen. Vielleicht gewöhnt sie es sich ab, es wird auch höchste Zeit.

Zum Schluss dieser Kuddelmuddelmitteilungen noch einen besonders komischen Witz, der von Herrn van Daan stammt:

Was macht 999 mal klick und einmal klack?

Ein Tausendfüßler mit einem Klumpfuß!   Tschüs, deine Anne

Samstag, 3. Oktober 1942

Beste Kitty!

Gestern haben sie mich geneckt, weil ich mit Herrn van Daan zusammen auf dem Bett gelegen habe. »So früh schon, ein Skandal!«, und lauter solche Ausdrücke. Blöd natürlich. Ich würde nie mit Herrn van Daan schlafen wollen, in der allgemeinen Bedeutung natürlich.

Gestern gab es wieder einen Zusammenstoß, und Mutter hat sich schrecklich aufgespielt. Sie hat Papa alle meine Sünden erzählt und heftig angefangen zu weinen. Ich natürlich auch, und ich hatte sowieso schon schreckliche Kopfschmerzen. Ich habe Papi endlich gesagt, dass ich »ihn« viel lieber habe als Mutter. Daraufhin hat er gesagt, dass das schon wieder vorbeigehen würde, aber das glaube ich nicht. Mutter kann ich nun mal nicht ausstehen, und ich muss mich mit Gewalt zwingen, sie nicht immer anzuschnauzen und ruhig zu bleiben. Ich könnte ihr glatt ins Gesicht schlagen. Ich weiß nicht, wie es kommt, dass ich eine so schreckliche Abneigung gegen sie habe. Papa hat gesagt, ich müsste ihr mal von selbst anbieten, ihr zu helfen, wenn sie sich nicht wohl fühlt oder Kopfschmerzen hat. Aber das tue ich nicht, weil ich sie nicht liebe, und dann fühle ich das nicht. Ich kann mir auch gut vorstellen, dass Mutter mal stirbt. Aber dass Papa mal stirbt, das könnte ich, glaube ich, nicht aushalten. Das ist sehr gemein von mir, aber so fühle ich es. Ich hoffe, dass Mutter dieses und alles andere niemals lesen wird.

In letzter Zeit darf ich etwas mehr Erwachsenenbücher lesen. Ich lese gerade »Evas Jugend« von Nico van Suchtelen. Den Unterschied zwischen Mädchenbüchern und diesem finde ich nicht so arg groß. Eva denkt, dass Kinder wie Äpfel an einem Baum wachsen und der Storch sie dort abpflückt, wenn sie reif sind, und sie den Müttern bringt. Aber die Katze ihrer Freundin hatte Junge bekommen, die kamen aus der Katze. Nun dachte Eva, dass die Katze, genau wie ein Huhn, Eier legt und sie ausbrütet. Auch Mütter, die ein Kind bekommen, würden ein paar Tage zuvor ins Schlafzimmer gehen und ein Ei legen, um es dann auszubrüten. Wenn das Kind dann da ist, sind die Mütter noch etwas schwach vom langen Hocken. Eva wollte nun auch ein Kind haben. Sie nahm einen Wollschal und legte ihn auf den Boden, da hinein sollte das Ei fallen. Dann kauerte sie sich hin, drückte und fing an zu gackern, aber es kam kein Ei. Endlich, nach sehr langem Sitzen, kam etwas heraus, aber kein Ei, sondern eine Wurst. Eva schämte sich sehr. Sie dachte, dass sie krank wäre. Witzig, nicht wahr? In »Evas Jugend« steht auch was darüber, dass Frauen ihre Körper auf der Straße verkaufen und dafür einen Haufen Geld verlangen. Ich würde mich totschämen vor so einem Mann. Außerdem steht drin, dass Eva ihre Periode bekommen hat. Danach sehne ich mich so sehr, dann bin ich wenigstens erwachsen. Papa mault schon wieder und droht, dass er mir mein Tagebuch wegnehmen wird. Oh, was für ein Schreck! Ich werde es in Zukunft verstecken!   Anne Frank

Ich stelle mir jetzt vor, dass …

ich in die Schweiz gehe. Papa und ich schlafen in einem Zimmer, während das Zimmer der Jungen* mein Zimmer wird, wo ich sitze und meine Gäste empfange. Dort haben sie mir als Überraschung neue Möbel gekauft, Teetisch, Schreibtisch, Sessel und Diwan, einfach großartig. Nach ein paar Tagen gibt Papa mir 150 Gulden, umgerechnet natürlich, aber ich bleibe einfach bei Gulden, und sagt, dass ich mir dafür alles kaufen kann, nur für mich selbst, was ich für nötig halte. (Später soll ich dann jede Woche einen Gulden bekommen, dafür kann ich mir auch kaufen, was ich will.) Ich gehe mit Bernd los und kaufe:

    3 Sommerhemden à 0,50 = 1,50
    3 Sommerhosen à 0,50 = 1,50
    3 Winterhemden à 0,75 = 2,25
    3 Winterhosen à 0,75 = 2,25
    2 Unterkleider à 0,50 = 1,00
    2 Büstenhalter (kleinste Größe) à 0,50 = 1,00
    5 Pyjamas à 1,00 = 5,00
    1 Sommermorgenrock à 2,50 = 2,50
    1 Wintermorgenrock à 3,00 = 3,00
    2 Bettjäckchen à 0,75 = 1,50
    1 kleines Kissen à 1,00 = 1,00
    1 Paar Sommerpantoffeln à 1,00 = 1,00
    1 Paar Winterpantoffeln à 1,50 = 1,50
    1 Paar Sommerschuhe (Schule) à 1,50 = 1,50
    1 Paar Sommerschuhe (gut) à 2,00 = 2,00
    1 Paar Winterschuhe (Schule) à 2,50 = 2,50
    1 Paar Winterschuhe (gut) à 3,00 = 3,00
    2 Schürzen à 0,50 = 1,00
   25 Taschentücher à 0,05 = 1,25
    4 Paar Seidenstrümpfe à 0,75 = 3,00
    4 Paar Kniestrümpfe à 0,50 = 2,00
    4 Paar Socken à 0,25 = 1,00

* Gemeint sind ihre Cousins Bernhard und Stephan; A. d. Ü.

2 Paar dicke Socken à 1,00 = 2,00
3 Knäuel weiße Wolle (Hosen, Mütze) = 1,50
3 Knäuel blaue Wolle (Pullover, Rock) = 1,50
3 Knäuel farbige Wolle (Mütze, Schal) = 1,50
Schals, Gürtel, Krägen, Knöpfe = 1,25

Dann noch 2 Schulkleider (Sommer), 2 Schulkleider (Winter), 2 gute Kleider (Sommer), 2 gute Kleider (Winter), 1 Sommerrock, 1 guter Winterrock, 1 Schulwinterrock, 1 Regenmantel, 1 Sommermantel, 1 Wintermantel, 2 Hüte, 2 Mützen.

Das sind zusammen 108 Gulden.

2 Taschen, 1 Eiskostüm, 1 Paar Schlittschuhe mit Schuhen, 1 Schachtel (mit Puder, Fettcreme, Pudercreme, Abschminkcreme, Sonnenöl, Watte, Verbandsschachtel, Rouge, Lippenstift, Augenbrauenstift, Badesalz, Körperpuder, Eau de Cologne, Seife, Quaste).

Dann noch 4 Pullover à 1,50, 4 Blusen à 1,00, diverse Dinge à 10,00 und Bücher, Geschenke à 4,50.

Freitag, 9. Oktober 1942

Liebe Kitty!
Nichts als traurige und deprimierende Nachrichten habe ich heute. Unsere jüdischen Bekannten werden gleich gruppenweise festgenommen. Die Gestapo geht nicht im geringsten zart mit diesen Menschen um. Sie werden in Viehwagen nach Westerbork gebracht, dem großen Judenlager in Drente. Miep hat von jemandem erzählt, der aus Westerbork geflohen ist. Es muss dort schrecklich sein. Die Menschen bekommen fast nichts zu essen, geschweige denn zu trinken. Sie haben nur eine Stunde pro Tag Wasser und ein Klo und ein Waschbecken für ein paar tausend Menschen. Schlafen tun sie alle durcheinander, Männer und Frauen, und die letzteren und Kinder bekommen oft die Haare abgeschoren. Fliehen ist fast unmöglich. Die Menschen sind gebrandmarkt durch ihre kahl geschorenen Köpfe und viele auch durch ihr jüdisches Aussehen.

Wenn es in Holland schon so schlimm ist, wie muss es dann erst in Polen sein? Wir nehmen an, dass die meisten Menschen ermordet werden. Der englische Sender spricht von Vergasungen, vielleicht ist das noch die schnellste Methode zu sterben.

Ich bin völlig durcheinander. Miep erzählt all diese Gräuelgeschichten so ergreifend und ist selbst ganz aufgeregt dabei. Erst neulich saß zum Beispiel eine alte, lahme jüdische Frau vor ihrer Tür und musste auf die Gestapo warten, die weggegangen war, um ein Auto zu holen, um sie abzutransportieren. Die arme Alte hatte solche Angst vor der Schießerei auf die englischen Flugzeuge und auch vor den grellen, flitzenden Scheinwerfern. Trotzdem wagte Miep nicht, sie ins Haus zu holen, das würde niemand tun. Die Herren Deutschen sind nicht zimperlich mit ihren Strafen.

Auch Bep ist still. Ihr Freund muss nach Deutschland. Sie hat jedes Mal Angst, wenn die Flugzeuge über unsere Häuser fliegen, dass sie ihre Bombenlast von oft einer Million Kilo auf Bertus' Kopf fallen lassen. Witze wie: »Eine Million wird er wohl nicht bekommen« und »Eine einzige Bombe ist schon genug« finde ich nicht gerade angebracht. Bertus ist nicht der Einzige, der gehen muss, jeden Tag fahren Züge voll mit jungen Leuten weg. Manchen gelingt es, heimlich auszusteigen, wenn sie auf einem kleinen Bahnhof halten, und dann unterzutauchen. Einem kleinen Prozentsatz gelingt das vielleicht.

Ich bin noch nicht fertig mit meinem Trauergesang. Hast du schon mal was von Geiseln gehört? Das führen sie nun als neueste Strafmethode für Sabotage ein. Etwas Schrecklicheres kann man sich nicht vorstellen. Angesehene, unschuldige Bürger werden verhaftet und warten auf ihre Ermordung. Wird irgendwo sabotiert und der Täter nicht gefunden, stellt die Gestapo seelenruhig so fünf Geiseln an die Wand. Oft stehen die Todesmeldungen in der Zeitung. Ein »schicksalhaftes Unglück« wird dieses Verbrechen dann genannt.

Ein schönes Volk, die Deutschen, und da gehöre ich eigentlich auch noch dazu! Aber nein, Hitler hat uns längst staatenlos gemacht. Und im Übrigen gibt es keine größere Feindschaft auf dieser Welt als zwischen Deutschen und Juden.   Deine Anne

Mittwoch, 14. Oktober 1942

Beste Kitty!

Ich habe schrecklich viel zu tun. Gestern habe ich ein Kapitel von »La belle Nivernaise« übersetzt und die Wörter aufgeschrieben. Dann eine Mistrechenaufgabe gemacht und noch drei Seiten französische

Sprachlehre übersetzt. Heute französische Sprachlehre und Geschichte. Ich denke nicht daran, jeden Tag solche Mistrechenaufgaben zu machen. Papa findet sie auch schrecklich, ich kann sie fast noch besser als er, aber in Wirklichkeit können wir sie alle beide nicht, sodass wir immer Margot holen müssen. Ich bin auch eifrig beim Stenographieren, das finde ich toll, ich bin am weitesten von uns dreien. Ich habe »De stormers« gelesen. Es war ganz nett, aber lange nicht so gut wie »Joop ter Heul«. Übrigens, in beiden Büchern kommen dieselben Wörter vor, klar, bei derselben Autorin. Cissy van Marxveldt schreibt wirklich toll. Bestimmt werde ich ihre Bücher meinen Kindern auch zu lesen geben.

Außerdem habe ich eine Menge Theaterstücke von Körner gelesen. Ich finde, dass der Mann schön schreibt. Zum Beispiel »Hedwig«, »Der Vetter aus Bremen«, »Die Gouvernante«, »Der grüne Domino« usw.

Mutter, Margot und ich sind wieder die besten Freundinnen, und das ist eigentlich viel angenehmer. Gestern Abend lagen Margot und ich zusammen in meinem Bett. Es war sehr eng, aber gerade deshalb witzig. Sie fragte, ob sie mal mein Tagebuch lesen dürfte. »Manche Stücke schon«, sagte ich und fragte nach ihrem. Das dürfte ich dann auch lesen.

So kamen wir auf die Zukunft, und ich fragte sie, was sie werden wollte. Aber das wollte sie nicht sagen, sie machte ein großes Geheimnis daraus. Ich habe mal so etwas aufgeschnappt wie Unterricht. Ich weiß natürlich nicht, ob das stimmt, aber ich vermute, dass es in diese Richtung geht. Eigentlich darf ich nicht so neugierig sein.

Heute Morgen lag ich auf Peters Bett, nachdem ich ihn erst verjagt hatte. Er war wütend auf mich, aber das kann mir herzlich wenig ausmachen. Er könnte ruhig mal etwas freundlicher zu mir sein, denn gestern Abend habe ich ihm noch einen Apfel geschenkt.

Ich habe Margot mal gefragt, ob sie mich sehr hässlich fände. Sie sagte, ich sähe witzig aus und hätte hübsche Augen. Ziemlich vage, findest du nicht auch?

Bis zum nächsten Mal!

Anne Frank

P. S. heute Morgen sind wir wieder alle auf der Waage gewesen. Margot wiegt nun 120 Pfund, Mutter 124, Vater 141, Anne 87, Peter 134,

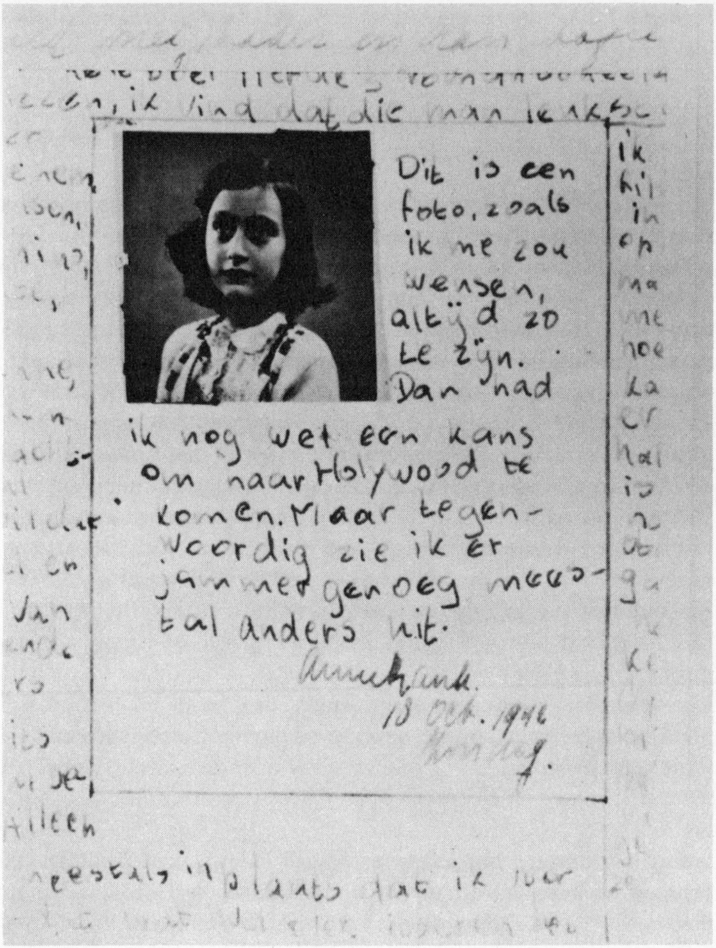

Eine Seite aus dem Tagebuch, 18. Oktober 1942.

Frau van Daan 106, Herr van Daan 150. Ich habe in den drei Monaten, die ich hier bin, 17 Pfund zugenommen, enorm, gell?

pound

Dienstag, 20. Oktober 1942

Liebe Kitty!

shaky

Meine Hand zittert noch, obwohl der Schreck, den wir hatten, schon zwei Stunden her ist. Du musst wissen, dass wir fünf Minimax-Feuerlöscher im Haus haben. Weil sie unten so gescheit sind, haben sie uns nicht gewarnt, dass der Zimmermann, oder wie der Bursche sonst heißt, die Geräte auffüllte. Deshalb waren wir überhaupt nicht leise, bis ich plötzlich draußen auf dem Treppenabsatz (gegenüber unserer Schranktür) Hammerschläge hörte. Ich dachte sofort an den Zimmermann und warnte Bep, die gerade beim Essen war, dass sie nicht nach unten gehen konnte. Vater und ich bezogen Posten hinter der Tür, um zu hören, wann der Mann weggehen würde. Nachdem er eine Viertelstunde gearbeitet hatte, legte er seinen Hammer und andere Werkzeuge auf unseren Schrank (so meinten wir!) und klopfte an unsere Tür. Wir wurden ganz weiß! Sollte er doch etwas gehört haben und nun dieses geheimnisvolle Ungetüm untersuchen wollen? Es schien so, denn das Klopfen, Ziehen, Schieben und Reißen hörte nicht auf.

Ich wurde fast ohnmächtig vor Angst, dass es dem wildfremden Mann doch gelingen könnte, unseren schönen Schlupfwinkel zu enttarnen. Ich dachte gerade, ich hätte die längste Zeit gelebt, da hörten wir die Stimme von Herrn Kleiman sagen: »Macht doch mal auf, ich bin es.«

Sofort machten wir auf. Was war passiert? Der Haken, mit dem der Schrank an der Tür festsitzt, hatte geklemmt, deshalb konnte uns niemand vor dem Zimmermann warnen. Der Mann war inzwischen nach unten gegangen, und Kleiman wollte Bep abholen, bekam aber den Drehschrank wieder nicht auf. Ich kann dir kaum sagen, wie erleichtert ich war. Der Mann, von dem ich meinte, dass er zu uns herein wollte, hatte in meiner Einbildung immer größere Formen angenommen. Zuletzt sah er aus wie ein Riese und war so ein Faschist, wie es keinen schlimmeren gibt. Gell, zum Glück ist es diesmal gut abgelaufen!

Am Montag hatten wir hier viel Spaß. Miep und Jan haben bei uns übernachtet. Margot und ich haben für die eine Nacht bei Vater und Mutter geschlafen, sodass das Ehepaar Gies unsere Plätze einnehmen konnte. Das Ehrenmenü schmeckte herrlich. Eine kleine Unterbrechung war, dass Vaters Lampe einen Kurzschluss verursachte und wir mit einem Schlag im Dunkeln saßen. Was tun? Neue Sicherungen waren zwar da, mussten aber ganz hinten im dunklen Lager eingeschraubt werden, und abends war das keine besonders hübsche Aufgabe. Trotzdem wagten es die Herren, und nach zehn Minuten konnten wir unsere Kerzenbeleuchtung wieder wegräumen.

Morgens war ich schon früh auf. Jan war schon angezogen. Er musste um halb neun weg, also saß er schon um acht Uhr oben und frühstückte. Miep zog sich gerade an und stand im Hemd da, als ich hereinkam. Sie hat genau solche wollenen Unterhosen wie ich fürs Fahrrad. Margot und ich zogen uns nun an und waren viel früher oben als gewöhnlich. Nach einem gemütlichen Frühstück ging Miep nach unten. Es goss, und sie war froh, dass sie heute nicht mit dem Fahrrad ins Büro zu fahren brauchte. Ich machte mit Papi die Betten, dann lernte ich fünf unregelmäßige Verben. Fleißig, nicht wahr?

Margot und Peter saßen in unserem Zimmer und lasen, und Mouschi saß bei Margot auf der Couch. Ich setzte mich nach meinen französischen Unregelmäßigkeiten auch dazu und las »Und ewig singen die Wälder«. Es ist ein sehr schönes, aber seltsames Buch, ich habe es fast ausgelesen.

Bep kommt nächste Woche auch mal auf Nachtbesuch!

Deine Anne

Donnerstag, 29. Oktober 1942

Liebste Kitty!

Ich bin ziemlich beunruhigt, Vater ist krank. Er hat hohes Fieber und roten Ausschlag, es scheinen die Masern zu sein. Stell dir vor, wir können nicht mal einen Doktor holen! Mutter lässt ihn kräftig schwitzen, vielleicht geht das Fieber davon runter.

Heute Morgen erzählte Miep, dass die Wohnung der van Daans nun von den Deutschen entmöbelt worden ist. Wir haben es Frau van Daan noch nicht gesagt, sie ist ohnehin schon so »nervenmäßig« in der letzten Zeit, und wir haben keine Lust, uns das Gejammer über ihr schönes Service und die feinen Sesselchen anzuhören, die zu Hause geblieben sind. Wir haben doch auch fast alles, was schön war, im Stich lassen müssen, was hilft nun das Geklage?

Vater will nun, dass ich Bücher von bekannten deutschen Schriftstellern lese. Das Deutschlesen geht schon relativ flott. Nur flüstere ich meistens, statt dass ich für mich lese. Aber das wird wohl vorbeigehen. Vater hat Goethes und Schillers Dramen aus dem großen Bücherschrank geholt, er will mir nun jeden Abend etwas vorlesen. Mit »Don Carlos« haben wir schon angefangen.

Um Vaters gutem Vorbild zu folgen, hat Mutter mir ihr Gebetbuch in die Hand gedrückt. Anstandshalber habe ich ein paar Gebete in Deutsch gelesen. Ich finde es schon schön, aber es sagt mir nicht viel. Warum zwingt sie mich, so fromm-religiös zu tun?

Morgen wird der Ofen zum ersten Mal angemacht. Wir werden wohl ziemlich im Rauch sitzen, der Schornstein ist schon lange Zeit nicht gefegt worden. Hoffen wir, dass das Ding zieht!

Deine Anne

Montag, 2. November 1942

Beste Kitty!

Freitagabend war Bep bei uns. Es war ziemlich gemütlich, aber sie hat nicht gut geschlafen, weil sie Wein getrunken hatte. Sonst gibt es nichts Besonderes. Gestern hatte ich schlimme Kopfschmerzen und bin früh ins Bett gegangen. Margot ist wieder mal garstig.

Heute Morgen habe ich angefangen, für das Büro einen Karteikasten zu sortieren. Der war umgefallen und ganz durcheinander. Ich wurde schon bald wahnsinnig davon und fragte Margot und Peter, ob sie mir helfen wollten, aber die beiden waren zu faul. Da habe ich die Sachen auch weggeräumt. Ich bin doch nicht verrückt und mache das alleine!

Anne Frank

P. S. Ich habe noch vergessen, dir die wichtige Neuigkeit zu erzählen, dass ich wahrscheinlich bald meine Periode bekomme. Das merke ich an dem klebrigen Zeug in meiner Hose, und Mutter hat es mir vorausgesagt. Ich kann es kaum erwarten. Es scheint mir so wichtig! Nur schade, dass ich nun keine Damenbinden tragen kann, die bekommt man nicht mehr. Und die Stäbchen von Mama können nur Frauen tragen, die schon mal ein Kind gehabt haben.

22. Januar 1944 (Nachtrag)
Ich würde so etwas nun nicht mehr schreiben können.
Wenn ich jetzt, eineinhalb Jahre später, wieder in mein Tagebuch schaue, staune ich sehr, dass ich jemals ein so unverdorbener Backfisch gewesen bin. Unwillkürlich weiß ich, dass ich, wie sehr ich es auch wollte, nie mehr so sein kann. Die Launen und die Äußerungen über Margot, Mutter und Vater verstehe ich noch genauso gut, als ob ich sie gestern geschrieben hätte. Aber dass ich so ungeniert über andere Dinge geschrieben habe, kann ich mir nicht mehr vorstellen. Ich schäme mich wirklich, wenn ich die Seiten lese, die von Themen handeln, die ich mir gerne schöner vorstelle. Ich habe es so unfein hingeschrieben. Aber nun genug davon.
Was ich sehr gut verstehe, sind das Heimweh und die Sehnsucht nach Moortje. Oft bewusst, aber noch viel öfter unbewusst, hatte ich die ganze Zeit, die ich hier war und bin, ein Verlangen nach Vertrauen, Liebe und Zärtlichkeit. Dieses Verlangen ist manchmal stärker und manchmal schwächer, aber es ist immer da.

Donnerstag, 5. November 1942
Beste Kitty!
Die Engländer haben nun endlich in Afrika ein paar Erfolge, also sind die Herren sehr fröhlich, und wir haben heute Morgen Kaffee und Tee getrunken. Sonst nichts Besonderes.
Ich habe in dieser Woche sehr viel gelesen und wenig gearbeitet. So muss man es tun, so wird man sicher weiterkommen!
Mutter und ich kommen in der letzten Zeit wieder besser miteinander aus, aber vertraulich sind wir <u>nie</u>. Und Vater hat was, was er nicht sagen will. Aber er ist ein Schatz, wie immer.
Seit ein paar Tagen ist der Ofen an, und das ganze Zimmer ist voller

Rauch. Ich halte doch mehr von Zentralheizung, und ich werde wohl nicht die Einzige sein. Margot kann ich nur als Miststück bezeichnen, das mich Tag und Nacht schrecklich reizt.　　Anne Frank

Montag, 9. November 1942

Liebe Kitty!

Gestern hatte Peter Geburtstag, er ist sechzehn geworden. Um acht bin ich schon nach oben gegangen und habe mit Peter die Geschenke betrachtet. Er hat unter anderem das Börsenspiel bekommen, einen Rasierapparat und ein Feuerzeug. Nicht dass er so viel raucht, überhaupt nicht, nur für die Eleganz.

Die größte Überraschung brachte Herr van Daan um ein Uhr mit der Nachricht, dass die Engländer in Tunis, Casablanca, Algier und Oran gelandet wären.

»Das ist der Anfang vom Ende«, sagten alle.

Aber Churchill, der englische Premierminister, der wahrscheinlich in England auch diesen Ausspruch gehört hatte, sagte: »Diese Landung ist ein wichtiger Schritt, doch darf man nicht glauben, dass dies der Anfang vom Ende sei. Ich sage eher, dass es das Ende vom Anfang bedeutet.«

Merkst du den Unterschied? Grund für Optimismus gibt es aber doch. Stalingrad, die russische Stadt, wird nun auch schon seit drei Monaten verteidigt und ist immer noch nicht den Deutschen in die Hände gefallen.

Ich werde dir doch auch mal was von unserer Lebensmittelversorgung erzählen müssen. (Du musst wissen, dass die oben richtige Leckermäuler sind!)

Unser Brot liefert ein sehr netter Bäcker, ein Bekannter von Kleiman. Wir bekommen natürlich nicht so viel, wie wir zu Hause hatten, aber es ist ausreichend. Lebensmittelkarten werden illegal eingekauft. Der Preis dafür steigt ständig, erst 27 Gulden, jetzt schon 33. Und das nur für ein Blatt bedrucktes Papier!

Um außer unseren hundert Konservenbüchsen noch etwas Haltbares im Haus zu haben, haben wir 270 Pfund Hülsenfrüchte gekauft. Nicht nur für uns allein, auch das Büro wurde einberechnet. Die Säcke mit den Hülsenfrüchten hingen an Haken in unserem kleinen Flur hinter der Verstecktür. Durch das schwere Gewicht sind ein paar Nähte an den Säcken aufgegangen. Wir beschlossen dann doch, den Wintervorrat lieber auf den Dachboden zu bringen, und vertrauten Peter das Hochschleppen an. Fünf von sechs Säcken waren schon heil oben angekommen, und Peter war gerade dabei, Nummer sechs hochzuschleppen, als die untere Naht des Sackes riss und ein Regen – nein, ein Hagel! – von braunen Bohnen durch die Luft und die Treppe hinunterflog. In dem Sack waren ungefähr 50 Pfund, es war dann auch ein Höllenlärm! Unten dachten sie schon, dass sie das alte Haus samt Inhalt auf den Kopf bekämen. Peter erschrak, dann musste er aber schrecklich lachen, als er mich unten an der Treppe stehen sah, wie eine Insel in Bohnenwellen, so war ich umringt von den braunen Dingern, die mir bis zum Knöchel reichten. Schnell machten wir uns ans Aufsammeln. Aber Bohnen sind so glatt und klein, dass sie in alle möglichen und unmöglichen Ecken und Löcher rollen. Jedes Mal, wenn jetzt jemand die Treppe hinaufgeht, bückt er sich und liefert dann eine Hand voll Bohnen bei Frau van Daan ab.

Fast hätte ich vergessen zu vermelden, dass Vaters Krankheit wieder ganz vorbei ist.   Deine Anne

P. S. Gerade kommt die Nachricht durch das Radio, dass Algier gefallen ist. Marokko, Casablanca und Oran sind schon in englischen Händen. Jetzt wird noch auf Tunis gewartet.

Dienstag, 10. November 1942

Liebe Kitty!

Großartige Neuigkeiten, wir wollen einen achten Untertaucher aufnehmen!

Ja, wirklich, wir sind immer der Meinung gewesen, dass es hier noch genug Platz und Essen für eine achte Person gibt. Wir hatten nur Angst, Kugler und Kleiman noch mehr zu belasten. Als nun die Gräuelberichte wegen der Juden immer schlimmer wurden, hat Vater mal bei den beiden entscheidenden Personen vorgefühlt, und sie fanden die Idee ausgezeichnet. »Die Gefahr ist für sieben genauso groß wie für acht«, sagten sie völlig zu Recht. Als dieser Punkt ge-

73

regel war, sind wir in Gedanken unseren Bekanntenkreis durchgegangen, um einen allein stehenden Menschen zu finden, der gut zu unserer Versteckfamilie passen würde. Es war nicht schwer, so jemanden zu finden. Nachdem Vater alle Verwandten der van Daans abgelehnt hatte, fiel unsere Wahl auf einen Zahnarzt namens Albert Dussel. Er lebt mit einer viel jüngeren und netten Christin zusammen, mit der er wahrscheinlich nicht verheiratet ist, aber das ist nebensächlich. Er gilt als ruhig und höflich, und nach der flüchtigen Bekanntschaft zu urteilen, schien er sowohl uns als auch den van Daans sympathisch. Miep kennt ihn auch, sodass sie alles regeln kann. Wenn er kommt, muss er in meinem Zimmer schlafen. Margot bekommt dann das Harmonikabett* als Lagerstatt.

Wir werden ihn fragen, ob er etwas mitbringen kann, um hohle Backenzähne zu füllen.
                                                                    Deine Anne

                                              Donnerstag, 12. November 1942
Liebe Kitty!
Miep hat uns erzählt, dass sie bei Dr. Dussel gewesen ist. Dussel fragte Miep gleich, als sie ins Zimmer kam, ob sie nicht einen Versteckplatz für ihn wüsste. Er war sehr froh, als sie ihm sagte, dass sie etwas für ihn hätte und dass er so schnell wie möglich hingehen müsste, am besten schon am Samstag. Er hatte Bedenken, er müsste seine Kartei noch in Ordnung bringen, zwei Patienten behandeln und die Kasse machen. Mit diesem Bericht kam Miep heute zu uns. Wir fanden es nicht gut, noch so lange zu warten. Diese Vorbereitungen erfordern Erklärungen an etliche Leute, die wir lieber raushalten würden. Miep sollte fragen, ob er nicht doch am Samstag kommen würde. Er sagte Nein und wird nun am Montag kommen.

Ich finde es verrückt, dass er nicht sofort auf jeden Vorschlag eingeht. Wenn er auf der Straße mitgenommen wird, kann er weder der Kartei noch den Patienten nützen. Warum dann der Aufschub? Ich persönlich finde es dumm von Vater, dass er nachgegeben hat.

Sonst nichts Neues.
                                                                    Deine Anne

---

* Margot zog nach Dussels Ankunft ins Zimmer der Eltern; A. d. Ü.

Liebe Kitty!

Dussel ist angekommen. Es hat alles gut geklappt. Miep hatte zu ihm gesagt, er müsse um elf Uhr an einer bestimmten Stelle vor dem Postamt sein, dort würde ihn ein Herr abholen. Dussel stand an dem verabredeten Platz, pünktlich, Herr Kleiman ging auf ihn zu und sagte, dass der genannte Herr noch nicht kommen könne und ob er so lange zu Miep ins Büro kommen wolle. Kleiman stieg in die Straßenbahn und fuhr zurück ins Büro, und Dussel ging denselben Weg zu Fuß.

Um zehn Minuten vor halb zwölf klopfte Dussel an die Bürotür. Miep ließ ihn seinen Mantel ausziehen, sodass der Stern nicht zu sehen war, und brachte ihn ins Privatbüro. Dort kümmerte sich Kleiman um ihn, bis die Putzfrau weg war. Unter dem Vorwand, dass das Privatbüro nicht länger frei sei, ging Miep mit Dussel nach oben, öffnete den Drehschrank und stieg vor den Augen des verblüfften Mannes hinein.

Wir sieben saßen oben um den Tisch und erwarteten mit Kaffee und Kognak unseren Mitverstecker. Miep führte ihn erst in unser Wohnzimmer. Er erkannte sofort unsere Möbel, dachte aber nicht im Entferntesten daran, dass wir uns über seinem Kopf befänden. Als Miep ihm das erzählte, fiel er fast in Ohnmacht vor Staunen. Aber zum Glück ließ Miep ihm nicht lange Zeit und brachte ihn nach oben. Dussel ließ sich auf einen Stuhl fallen und starrte uns alle eine Weile sprachlos an, als wollte er die genaue Wahrheit von unseren Gesichtern ablesen. Dann stotterte er: »Aber... nein ... aber sind Sie denn nicht in Belgien? Ist der Offizier nicht gekommen? Das Auto? Die Flucht ... ist sie nicht geglückt?«

Wir erklärten ihm die ganze Sache, dass wir das Märchen von dem Militär und dem Auto extra ausgestreut hatten, um die Leute und die Deutschen, die vielleicht nach uns suchen würden, auf die falsche Spur zu locken. Dussel war sprachlos über so viel Erfindungsgeist und konnte sich nur immer wieder erstaunt umschauen, als er unser hyperpraktisches und schönes Hinterhäuschen näher beschnüffelte. Wir aßen zusammen, dann schlief er ein bisschen, trank dann Tee mit uns, ordnete sein bisschen Zeug, das Miep bereits vorher gebracht hatte, und fühlte sich schon ziemlich heimisch. Vor allem, als er die folgende getippte Hinterhausordnung (Fabrikat van Daan) in die Hände bekam.

PROSPEKT UND LEITFADEN VOM HINTERHAUS
Spezielle Einrichtung für die vorübergehende Unterkunft von Juden und ihresgleichen.
Während des ganzen Jahres geöffnet.
Schöne, ruhige, waldfreie Umgebung im Herzen von Amsterdam. Keine privaten Nachbarn. Zu erreichen mit den Straßenbahnlinien 13 und 17, ferner auch mit Auto oder Fahrrad. In bestimmten Fällen, in denen die Deutschen die Benutzung dieser Transportmittel nicht erlauben, auch zu Fuß. Möblierte und unmöblierte Wohnungen und Zimmer ständig verfügbar, mit oder ohne Pension.
Miete: gratis.
Diätküche, fettfrei.
Fließendes Wasser im Badezimmer (leider keine Wanne) und an diversen Innen- und Außenwänden. Herrliche Feuerstellen.
Geräumige Lagerplätze für Güter aller Art. Zwei große, moderne Panzerschränke.
Eigene Radiozentrale mit direkter Verbindung nach London, New York, Tel-Aviv und vielen anderen Stationen. Dieser Apparat steht allen Bewohnern ab sechs Uhr abends zur Verfügung, wobei es <u>keine</u> verbotenen Sender gibt, unter einer Bedingung, dass nur ausnahmsweise deutsche Sender gehört werden dürfen, z. B. klassische Musik u. Ä. Es ist strengstens verboten, deutsche Nachrichten zu hören (egal, woher sie gesendet werden) und sie zu verbreiten.
Ruhezeiten: 10 Uhr abends bis 7.30 Uhr morgens, sonntags 10.15 Uhr. Unter besonderen Umständen werden auch tagsüber Ruhestunden abgehalten, je nach Anweisung der Direktion. Ruhestunden müssen im Interesse der allgemeinen Sicherheit unbedingt eingehalten werden!!!
Freizeit: Fällt bis auf weiteres aus (sofern außer Haus).
Gebrauch der Sprache: Es wird zu allen Zeiten gefordert, leise zu sprechen. Erlaubt sind alle Kultursprachen, also kein Deutsch.
Lektüre und Entspannung: Es dürfen keine deutschen Bücher gelesen werden, ausgenommen wissenschaftliche und klassische, alle anderen sind frei.

Gymnastik: Täglich.
Gesang: Ausschließlich leise und nach 6 Uhr abends.
Film: nach Abmachung.
Unterricht: In Stenographie jede Woche eine schriftliche Lektion. In Englisch, Französisch, Mathematik und Geschichte jederzeit. Bezahlung durch Gegenunterricht, z. B. Niederländisch.
Spezielle Abteilung für kleine Haustiere mit guter Versorgung. (Ausgenommen Ungeziefer, für das eine besondere Genehmigung erforderlich ist ...)
Mahlzeiten:
Frühstück: täglich morgens um 9 Uhr, Sonn- und Feiertage ca. 11.30 Uhr.
Mittagessen: zum Teil ausgedehnt. 1.15 Uhr bis 1.45 Uhr.
Abendessen: kalt und/oder warm, keine feste Zeit, abhängig vom Nachrichtendienst.
Verpflichtungen gegenüber der Versorgungskolonne: Bereitschaft, jederzeit bei Büroarbeiten zu helfen.
Baden: Sonntags ab 9 Uhr steht der Zuber allen Hausgenossen zur Verfügung. Gebadet wird in der Toilette, in der Küche, im Privatbüro oder im vorderen Büro, ganz nach Wunsch.
Starke Getränke: nur gegen ärztliches Attest.
Ende.   Deine Anne

Donnerstag, 19. Nov. 1942
Liebe Kitty!
Wie wir alle annahmen, ist Dussel ein sehr netter Mann. Er war natürlich einverstanden, das Zimmer mit mir zu teilen. Ich bin, ehrlich gesagt, nicht so erfreut darüber, dass ein Fremder meine Sachen benutzt, aber für die gute Sache muss man was übrig haben, und ich bringe dieses kleine Opfer dann auch gern. »Wenn wir jemanden retten können, ist alles andere Nebensache«, sagte Vater, und damit hat er vollkommen Recht.
Dussel hat mich am ersten Tag, als er hier war, gleich über alles ausgefragt, so z. B., wann die Putzfrau kommt, wann die Badezimmerzeiten sind, wann man auf die Toilette gehen darf. Du wirst lachen, aber das alles ist in einem Versteck gar nicht so einfach. Wir dürfen

tagsüber nicht so viele Umstände machen, dass sie uns unten hören, und wenn eine Extraperson unten ist, z. B. die Putzfrau, müssen wir extra vorsichtig sein. Ich erklärte Dussel alles sehr genau, aber etwas erstaunt mich dabei sehr, dass er so schwer von Begriff ist. Alles fragt er doppelt und behält es auch dann noch nicht. Vielleicht geht das vorbei, und er ist nur wegen der Überraschung so durcheinander. Ansonsten geht es prima.

Dussel hat uns viel von der Außenwelt erzählt, die wir nun schon so lange vermissen. Es ist traurig, was er alles gewusst hat. Zahllose Freunde und Bekannte sind weg, zu einem schrecklichen Ziel. Abend für Abend fahren die grünen oder grauen Militärfahrzeuge vorbei, und an jeder Tür wird geklingelt und gefragt, ob da auch Juden wohnen. Wenn ja, muss die ganze Familie sofort mit, wenn nicht, gehen sie weiter. Niemand kann seinem Schicksal entkommen, wenn er sich nicht versteckt. Sie gehen auch oft mit Listen herum und klingeln nur dort, wo sie wissen, dass sie eine reiche Beute finden. Kopfgeld wird oft bezahlt, pro Kopf soundsoviel. Es ist wirklich wie bei den Sklavenjagden, die es früher gab. Aber es ist kein Witz, dafür ist es viel zu dramatisch. Ich sehe abends oft die Reihen guter, unschuldiger Menschen vor mir, mit weinenden Kindern! Immer nur laufen müssen, kommandiert von ein paar Kerlen, geschlagen und gepeinigt, bis sie fast zusammenbrechen. Niemand wird geschont. Alte, Kinder, Babys, schwangere Frauen, Kranke … alles, alles geht mit in dem Zug zum Tod.

Wie gut haben wir es hier, wie gut und ruhig. Wir brauchten uns aus dem ganzen Elend nichts zu machen, wenn wir nicht so viel Angst um all jene hätten, die uns teuer sind und denen wir nicht helfen können. Ich fühle mich schlecht, weil ich in einem warmen Bett liege, während meine liebsten Freundinnen irgendwo draußen niedergeworfen werden oder zusammenbrechen.

Ich bekomme selbst Angst, wenn ich an alle denke, mit denen ich mich draußen immer so eng verbunden fühlte und die nun den Händen der brutalsten Henker ausgeliefert sind, die es jemals gegeben hat.

Und das alles, weil sie Juden sind.   Deine Anne

Liebe Kitty!

Wir wissen nicht, wie wir uns verhalten sollen. Bis jetzt ist von den Berichten über die Juden nie viel zu uns durchgedrungen, und wir haben es vorgezogen, so heiter wie möglich zu bleiben. Wenn Miep ab und zu mal etwas über das schreckliche Los eines Bekannten erzählte, fingen Mutter oder Frau van Daan immer an zu weinen, sodass Miep lieber gar nichts mehr sagte. Aber Dussel wurde sofort mit Fragen bestürmt, und die Geschichten, die er erzählte, waren so grauenhaft und barbarisch, dass es nicht zu einem Ohr rein und zum anderen wieder rausgeht. Trotzdem werden wir, wenn die Berichte ein bisschen gesackt sind, wohl wieder Witze machen und uns necken. Es hilft uns und denen da draußen nicht, wenn wir so bedrückt bleiben, wie wir es im Augenblick sind, und was hat es für einen Sinn, aus dem Hinterhaus ein melancholisches Hinterhaus zu machen?

Bei allem, was ich tue, muss ich an die anderen denken, die weg sind. Und wenn ich wegen etwas lachen muss, höre ich erschrocken wieder auf und denke mir, dass es eine Schande ist, so fröhlich zu sein. Aber muss ich denn den ganzen Tag weinen? Nein, das kann ich nicht, und sie wird wohl auch wieder vorbeigehen, diese Niedergeschlagenheit.

Zu all diesem Traurigen kommt noch etwas anderes, das persönlicher Art ist und neben dem eben erzählten Elend ins Nichts verschwindet. Trotzdem muss ich dir erzählen, dass ich mich in der letzten Zeit immer verlassener fühle. Um mich herum ist eine große Leere. Früher dachte ich darüber nie nach, Vergnügungen und Freundinnen erfüllten mein Denken. Nun denke ich oft über unglückliche Dinge oder mich selbst nach. Und ich bin schließlich zu der Überzeugung gekommen, dass Vater, wie lieb er auch ist, mir doch nicht meine frühere Welt ersetzen kann. Mutter und Margot zählen in meinen Gefühlen schon lange nicht mehr mit.

Aber warum falle ich dir mit solchen dummen Dingen zur Last? Ich bin so schrecklich undankbar, Kitty, ich weiß es ja. Aber mir wird oft schwindlig, wenn ich zu viel abbekomme und dann noch an all das andere Schlimme denken muss!

Deine Anne

Anne (rechts) und Freundin Sanne am Merwedeplein, Amsterdam.

Liebe Kitty!

Wir haben zu viel Licht verbraucht und unsere Elektrizitätsration überschritten. Die Folge: übertriebene Sparsamkeit und eine drohende Abschaltung. Vierzehn Tage kein Licht, hübsch, gell? Aber wer weiß, vielleicht geht es ja gut! Ab vier oder halb fünf Uhr ist es zu dunkel, um zu lesen. Wir verkürzen uns die Zeit mit allerlei verrückten Sachen. Rätsel aufgeben, Gymnastik im Dunkeln machen, Englisch oder Französisch sprechen, Bücher kritisieren – das alles langweilt auf die Dauer. Gestern Abend habe ich etwas Neues entdeckt, und zwar: mit einem scharfen Fernglas in die erleuchteten Zimmer der hinteren Nachbarn zu spähen. Tagsüber dürfen die Vorhänge niemals einen einzigen Zentimeter zur Seite geschoben werden, aber wenn es dunkel ist, kann das nicht schaden.

Ich wusste früher nie, dass Nachbarn so interessante Menschen sein können, jedenfalls unsere. Einige habe ich bei der Mahlzeit angetroffen, bei einer Familie wurde ein Film vorgeführt, und der Zahnarzt gegenüber hatte eine alte, ängstliche Dame in Behandlung.

Herr Dussel, der Mann, von dem immer gesagt wurde, dass er hervorragend mit Kindern zurechtkäme und sie auch gern hätte, entpuppt sich als der altmodischste Erzieher und Prediger von ellenlangen Manierenreihen. Da ich das seltene Glück (!) habe, mit dem hochedelwohlerzogenen Herrn mein leider sehr enges Zimmer teilen zu dürfen, und da ich allgemein als die am schlechtesten Erzogene der drei Jugendlichen gelte, habe ich ziemlich zu tun, um den allzu häufig wiederholten Standpauken und Ermahnungen zu entgehen und mich taub zu stellen. Das alles würde noch gehen, wenn der Herr nicht auch noch ein großer Petzer wäre und sich ausgerechnet Mutter als Beschwerdestelle ausgesucht hätte. Wenn ich von ihm gerade den Wind von vorn abbekommen habe, setzt Mutter noch eins drauf, und ich kriege also den Wind von hinten, und wenn ich dann noch besonders großes Glück habe, ruft Frau van Daan mich fünf Minuten später zur Verantwortung, und der Wind bläst von oben!

Wirklich, glaube ja nicht, dass es einfach ist, der unerzogene Mittelpunkt einer Versteckerfamilie zu sein, bei der sich jeder ständig in alles einmischt. Abends im Bett, wenn ich über meine vielen Sünden und angedichteten Mängel nachdenke, komme ich so durcheinander durch die große Zahl der Dinge, die betrachtet werden müssen, dass ich entweder lache oder weine, je nach meiner inneren Verfassung. Und dann schlafe ich mit dem verrückten Gefühl ein, anders sein zu wollen als zu sein oder anders zu sein als zu wollen oder vielleicht auch anders zu tun als zu wollen oder zu sein.

Lieber Himmel, jetzt bringe ich auch dich noch durcheinander. Verzeih mir, aber durchstreichen mag ich nicht, und Papier wegwerfen ist in Zeiten großer Papierknappheit verboten. Also kann ich dir nur raten, den vorhergehenden Satz nicht noch einmal durchzulesen und dich vor allem nicht hineinzuvertiefen, denn du kommst da doch nicht raus!   Deine Anne

Montag, 7. Dezember 1942

Liebe Kitty!

Chanukka und Nikolaus fielen dieses Jahr fast zusammen, der Unterschied war nur ein Tag. Für Chanukka haben wir nicht viele Umstände gemacht, ein paar hübsche Sächelchen hin und her und dann die Kerzen. Da ein Mangel an Kerzen herrscht, wurden sie nur zehn Minuten angezündet, aber wenn das Lied nicht fehlt, ist das auch ganz gut. Herr van Daan hatte einen Leuchter aus Holz gemacht, sodass das auch geregelt ist.

Der Nikolausabend am Samstag war viel schöner. Bep und Miep hatten uns sehr neugierig gemacht und schon die ganze Zeit immer mit Vater geflüstert, sodass wir irgendwelche Vorbereitungen wohl vermutet hatten. Und wirklich, um acht Uhr gingen wir alle die Treppe hinunter, durch den stockdunklen Flur (mir schauderte, und ich wünschte mich schon wieder heil und sicher oben!) zu dem Durchgangszimmer. Dort konnten wir Licht anmachen, weil dieser Raum keine Fenster hat. Vater machte den großen Schrank auf.

»Oh, wie hübsch!«, riefen wir alle.

In der Ecke stand ein großer Korb, mit Nikolauspapier geschmückt, und ganz oben war eine Maske vom Schwarzen Piet befestigt.

Schnell nahmen wir den Korb mit nach oben. Es war für jeden ein schönes Geschenk mit einem passenden Vers drin. Nikolausverse wirst du wohl kennen, darum werde ich sie dir auch nicht schreiben.

Ich bekam eine Puppe aus Brotteig, Vater Buchstützen und so weiter. Es war jedenfalls alles schön ausgedacht, und da wir alle acht noch nie in unserem Leben Nikolaus gefeiert haben, war diese Premiere gut gelungen.   Deine Anne

P. S. Für unsere Freunde unten hatten wir natürlich auch was, alles noch aus den früheren guten Zeiten, und bei Miep und Bep ist Geld außerdem immer passend.
Heute haben wir gehört, dass Herr Voskuijl den Aschenbecher für Herrn van Daan, den Bilderrahmen für Dussel und die Buchstützen für Vater selbst gemacht hat. Wie jemand so kunstvolle Sachen mit der Hand machen kann, ist mir ein Rätsel!

                                        Donnerstag, 10. Dezember 1942
Liebe Kitty!
Herr van Daan kommt aus dem Wurst-, Fleisch- und Gewürzhandel. In der Firma wurde er wegen seiner Gewürzkenntnisse angestellt, doch nun zeigt er sich von der wurstigen Seite, was uns keineswegs unangenehm ist.
Wir hatten viel Fleisch bestellt (illegal natürlich!) und wollten es einmachen, falls wir noch schwere Zeiten durchmachen müssten. Er wollte Bratwurst, Geldersche Wurst und Mettwurst machen. Es war ein schöner Anblick, wie erst die Fleischstücke durch den Wolf gedreht wurden, zwei- oder dreimal, dann alle Zutaten in die Fleischmasse gemengt und die schließlich mit Hilfe einer Tülle in Därme gefüllt wurde. Die Bratwurst aßen wir mittags sofort zum Sauerkraut auf, aber die Geldersche Wurst, die zum Aufheben bestimmt war, musste erst gut trocknen, und dafür wurde sie an eine Stange gehängt, die mit zwei Schnüren an der Decke hing. Jeder, der in das Zimmer kam und die aufgehängten Würste erblickte, fing an zu lachen. Es war ein äußerst drolliger Anblick.
Im Zimmer herrschte ein heilloses Durcheinander. Herr van Daan hatte eine Schürze seiner Frau umgebunden und war in seiner ganzen Dicke (er sah viel dicker aus, als er ist) mit dem Fleisch beschäftigt. Mit seinen blutigen Händen, dem roten Kopf und der bekleckerten Schürze sah er aus wie ein richtiger Metzger. Frau van Daan tat

alles gleichzeitig: Niederländisch aus einem Buch lernen, die Suppe rühren, nach dem Fleisch schauen und über ihre gebrochene obere Rippe seufzen und klagen. Das kommt davon, wenn ältere (!) Damen solche äußerst idiotischen Gymnastikübungen machen, um ihren dicken Hintern wieder loszuwerden!

Dussel hat ein entzündetes Auge und betupfte es am Herd mit Kamillentee. Pim saß auf einem Stuhl in dem Sonnenstrahl, der durch das Fenster kam, und wurde von der einen Seite zur anderen geschoben. Dabei hatte er sicher wieder Rheumaschmerzen, denn er saß ziemlich krumm und mit einem verstörten Gesicht da und schaute Herrn van Daan auf die Finger. Er sah aus wie ein alter Invalide aus einem Diakonissenheim. Peter tobte mit der Katze Mouschi im Zimmer herum, Mutter, Margot und ich pellten Kartoffeln. Aber schließlich arbeiteten wir alle nicht besonders gut, weil wir van Daan zuschauten.

Dussel hat seine Zahnarztpraxis eröffnet. Ich werde dir zum Spaß erzählen, wie die erste Behandlung abgelaufen ist.

Mutter bügelte, und Frau van Daan, die Erste, die dran glauben musste, setzte sich mitten im Zimmer auf einen Stuhl. Dussel fing wichtigtuerisch an, seine Instrumente auszupacken, bat um Eau de Cologne als Desinfektionsmittel und um Vaseline als Wachsersatz. Dann schaute er Frau van Daan in den Mund, berührte einen Schneidezahn und einen Backenzahn, wobei Frau van Daan sich jedes Mal krümmte, als ob sie vor Schmerzen verginge, und unzusammenhängende Töne ausstieß. Nach einer langen Untersuchung (für Frau van Daan wenigstens, denn es dauerte nicht länger als zwei Minuten) fing Dussel an, ein Loch auszukratzen. Aber daran war nicht zu denken! Frau van Daan schlug wild mit Armen und Beinen um sich, sodass Dussel irgendwann den Kratzer losließ und … dieser in Frau van Daans Zahn stecken blieb. Da war erst recht der Teufel los! Frau van Daan schlug um sich, weinte (soweit das möglich ist mit so einem Instrument im Mund), versuchte den Kratzer aus dem Mund zu bekommen und stieß ihn bei alledem noch fester hinein. Herr Dussel betrachtete das Schauspiel völlig ungerührt, die Hände in die Seiten gestemmt. Der Rest der Zuschauer lachte unbändig. Das war natürlich gemein, denn ich bin sicher, dass ich noch viel lauter geschrien hätte. Nach vielem Drehen,

Treten, Schreien und Rufen hatte Frau van Daan den Kratzer endlich heraus, und Herr Dussel setzte seine Arbeit fort, als wäre nichts passiert. Er tat dies so rasch, dass Frau van Daan keine Zeit hatte, noch einmal anzufangen. Aber er hatte auch so viel Hilfe wie noch nie in seinem Leben. Herr van Daan und ich assistierten gut. Das Ganze sah aus wie auf einem Bild aus dem Mittelalter mit dem Titel »Quacksalber bei der Arbeit«. Die Patientin hatte jedoch nicht so viel Geduld, sie musste auf »ihre« Suppe und »ihr« Essen aufpassen!

Eines ist sicher, Frau van Daan lässt sich so schnell nicht mehr behandeln!   Deine Anne

Sonntag, 13. Dezember 1942

Liebe Kitty!

Ich sitze sehr gemütlich im vorderen Büro und schaue durch einen Spalt zwischen den schweren Vorhängen hinaus. Hier ist es dämmrig, aber noch hell genug, um dir zu schreiben.

Es ist ein sehr seltsamer Anblick, wenn ich mir die Leute draußen betrachte. Es sieht aus, als hätten sie es alle schrecklich eilig und würden fast über ihre eigenen Füße stolpern. Die Radfahrer – dieses Tempo ist kaum mitzuhalten! Ich kann nicht mal sehen, was für ein Individuum auf dem Vehikel sitzt. Die Menschen hier in der Nachbarschaft sehen nicht sehr anziehend aus, und vor allem die Kinder sind so schmutzig, dass man sie nicht mal mit der Zange anfassen möchte, richtige Gossenkinder mit Rotznasen, und ihren Dialekt kann ich kaum verstehen.

Gestern Nachmittag haben Margot und ich hier gebadet, und da sagte ich: »Wenn wir nun mal die Kinder, die hier vorbeilaufen, Stück für Stück mit einer Angel heraufholen würden, sie ins Bad stopfen, ihre Wäsche waschen und flicken und sie dann wieder laufen ließen, dann ...«

»Würden sie morgen wieder genauso schmutzig und zerrissen aussehen wie vorher«, antwortete Margot.

Aber was fasele ich hier herum, es gibt noch andere Dinge zu sehen, Autos, Schiffe und den Regen. Ich höre die Straßenbahn und die Kinder und amüsiere mich.

Unsere Gedanken haben genauso wenig Abwechslung wie wir selbst. Wie bei einem Karussell dreht sich alles von den Juden zum Essen, vom Essen zur Politik. Apropos Juden, gestern habe ich, als wäre es ein Weltwunder, durch den Vorhang zwei Juden gesehen. Das war ein seltsames Gefühl, als hätte ich die Menschen verraten und würde nun heimlich ihr Unglück betrachten.

Direkt gegenüber liegt ein Hausboot, auf dem ein Schiffer mit Frau und Kindern lebt. Der Mann hat einen kleinen Kläffer, den wir nur vom Bellen kennen und von seinem Schwanz, den man sieht, wenn er am Bootsrand entlangläuft.

Bah, jetzt hat es angefangen zu regnen, und die meisten Leute haben sich unter ihren Schirmen versteckt. Ich sehe nur noch Regenmäntel und manchmal einen bemützten Hinterkopf. Eigentlich brauche ich auch nicht mehr zu sehen. So allmählich kenne ich die Frauen auswendig, aufgeschwemmt von zu viel Kartoffeln, mit einem roten oder grünen Mantel und abgetretenen Absätzen, einer Tasche am Arm und mit einem grimmigen oder gutmütigen Gesicht, je nach der Laune ihres Mannes.

Deine Anne

Dienstag, 22. Dezember 1942

Liebe Kitty!

Das Hinterhaus hat mit Freude vernommen, dass jeder zu Weihnachten ein viertel Pfund Butter extra bekommt. In der Zeitung steht zwar ein halbes Pfund, aber das gilt nur für die glücklichen Sterblichen, die ihre Lebensmittelkarten vom Staat bekommen, nicht für untergetauchte Juden, die, weil der Preis so hoch ist, nur vier statt acht Karten illegal kaufen können. Wir wollen alle etwas backen mit dieser Butter. Ich habe heute Morgen Plätzchen und zwei Torten gemacht. Oben gibt es viel Arbeit, und Mutter hat verboten, dass ich lerne oder lese, bevor die ganze Hausarbeit erledigt ist.

Frau van Daan liegt mit ihrer gequetschten Rippe im Bett, klagt den ganzen Tag, lässt sich ständig neue Verbände anlegen und ist mit nichts zufrieden. Ich werde froh sein, wenn sie wieder auf ihren beiden Beinen steht und ihren Kram selbst macht. Denn das muss man sagen, sie ist außergewöhnlich fleißig und ordentlich, und solange sie sich körperlich und geistig in einem guten Zustand befindet, auch fröhlich.

Als ob ich tagsüber nicht schon genug »pst, pst« zu hören bekomme, weil ich immer zu viel Lärm mache, ist mein Herr Zimmergenosse nun auf die Idee gekommen, mir auch nachts wiederholt »pst, pst« zuzurufen. Ich dürfte mich, wenn es nach ihm ginge, noch nicht mal umdrehen. Ich denke nicht daran, das zu beachten, und das nächste Mal rufe ich einfach auch »pst«.

Er wird von Tag zu Tag unangenehmer und egoistischer. Von den freigiebig versprochenen Plätzchen habe ich nach der ersten Woche kein Stück mehr gesehen. Vor allem sonntags macht er mich wütend, wenn er so früh das Licht anmacht und mit seinen zehn Minuten Gymnastik anfängt.

Mir armen Geplagten kommt es wie Stunden vor, denn die Stühle, mit denen mein Bett verlängert ist, schieben sich ständig unter meinem schläfrigen Kopf hin und her. Nachdem er mit ein paar heftigen Armschwüngen seine Gelenkigkeitsübungen beendet hat, beginnt der Herr mit seiner Toilette. Die Unterhose hängt am Haken, also erst dorthin, dann wieder zurück. Die Krawatte liegt auf dem Tisch, also wieder schiebend und stoßend an meinen Stühlen vorbei und auf die gleiche Art zurück.

Aber ich will dich nicht mit Gejammer über alte, unangenehme Herren aufhalten, es wird doch nicht besser davon. Und alle meine Rachepläne (Birnen ausschrauben, Tür abschließen, Kleider verstecken) muss ich um des lieben Friedens willen leider unterlassen.

Ach, ich werde ja so vernünftig! Alles muss hier mit Vernunft geschehen, lernen, zuhören, Mund halten, helfen, lieb sein, nachgeben und was weiß ich noch alles! Ich habe Angst, dass ich meinen Vorrat an Vernunft, der ohnehin nicht besonders groß ist, viel zu schnell verbrauche und für die Nachkriegszeit nichts mehr übrig behalte.

Deine Anne

Mittwoch, 13. Januar 1943

Liebe Kitty!

Heute Morgen war ich wieder ganz verstört und konnte nicht ordentlich arbeiten.

Wir haben eine neue Beschäftigung, nämlich Päckchen mit Bratensoße (in Pulverform) abfüllen. Diese Bratensoße ist ein Fabrikat der Firma Gies & Co. Herr Kugler kann keine Abfüller finden, und wenn wir es machen, ist es auch viel billiger. Es ist eine Arbeit, wie sie von Leuten im Gefängnis gemacht werden muss. Sie ist seltsam langweilig, und man wird ganz schwindlig und albern davon.

Draußen ist es schrecklich. Tag und Nacht werden die armen Menschen weggeschleppt, sie haben nichts anderes bei sich als einen Rucksack und etwas Geld. Diese Besitztümer werden ihnen unterwegs auch noch abgenommen. Die Familien werden auseinander gerissen, Männer, Frauen und Kinder werden getrennt. Kinder, die von der Schule nach Hause kommen, finden ihre Eltern nicht mehr. Frauen, die Einkäufe machen, finden bei ihrer Heimkehr die Wohnung versiegelt, ihre Familie verschwunden. Die niederländischen Christen haben auch schon Angst, ihre Söhne werden nach Deutschland geschickt. Jeder fürchtet sich. Und jede Nacht fliegen Hunderte von Flugzeugen über die Niederlande zu deutschen Städten und pflügen dort die Erde mit ihren Bomben, und jede Stunde fallen in Russland und Afrika Hunderte, sogar Tausende Menschen. Niemand kann sich raushalten, der ganze Erdball führt Krieg, und obwohl es mit den Alliierten besser geht, ist ein Ende noch nicht abzusehen.

Und wir, wir haben es gut, besser als Millionen anderer Menschen. Wir sitzen sicher und ruhig und essen sozusagen unser Geld auf. Wir sind so egoistisch, dass wir über »nach dem Krieg« sprechen, uns über neue Kleider und Schuhe freuen, während wir eigentlich jeden Cent sparen müssten, um nach dem Krieg anderen Menschen zu helfen, zu retten, was noch zu retten ist.

Die Kinder hier laufen in dünnen Blusen und mit Holzschuhen an den Füßen herum, kein Mantel, keine Mütze, keine Strümpfe und niemand, der ihnen hilft. Sie haben nichts im Bauch, sondern kauen an einer Mohrrübe herum. Sie gehen aus ihrer kalten Wohnung auf die kalte Straße und kommen in der Schule in eine noch kältere Klasse. Ja, es ist sogar so weit mit Holland gekommen, dass viele Kinder auf der Straße die Vorübergehenden anhalten und um ein Stück Brot bitten.

Stundenlang könnte ich dir über das Elend, das der Krieg mit sich bringt, erzählen, aber das macht mich nur noch bedrückter. Es bleibt uns nichts anderes übrig, als so ruhig wie nur möglich das Ende dieser Misere abzuwarten. Die Juden warten, die Christen warten, der ganze Erdball wartet, und viele warten auf ihren Tod.

Deine Anne

Samstag, 30. Januar 1943

Liebe Kitty!

Ich dampfe vor Wut und darf es nicht zeigen. Ich würde am liebsten mit den Füßen aufstampfen, schreien, Mutter gründlich durchschütteln, weinen und was weiß ich noch alles wegen der bösen Worte, der spöttischen Blicke, der Beschuldigungen, die mich jeden Tag aufs Neue treffen wie Pfeile von einem straff gespannten Bogen und die so schwer aus meinem Körper zu ziehen sind. Ich möchte Mutter, Margot, van Daan, Dussel und auch Vater anschreien: »Lasst mich in Ruhe! Lasst mich endlich mal eine Nacht schlafen, ohne dass mein Kissen nass von Tränen ist, meine Augen brennen und Schmerzen in meinem Kopf hämmern! Lasst mich weg, weg von allem, am liebsten weg von der Welt!« Aber ich kann es nicht. Ich kann ihnen meine Verzweiflung nicht zeigen. Ich kann sie keinen Blick auf die Wunden werfen lassen, die sie mir zufügen. Ich würde das Mitleid und den gutmütigen Spott nicht aushalten, auch dann noch würde ich schreien müssen!

Jeder findet mich übertrieben, wenn ich was sage, lächerlich, wenn ich schweige, frech, wenn ich eine Antwort gebe, gerissen, wenn ich eine gute Idee habe, faul, wenn ich müde bin, egoistisch, wenn ich einen Bissen zu viel esse, dumm, feige, berechnend usw. usw. Den ganzen Tag höre ich nichts anderes, als dass ich ein unausstehlicher Fratz bin. Und obwohl ich darüber lache und tue, als wäre es mir egal, macht es mir sehr wohl etwas aus, würde ich Gott bitten wollen, mir eine andere Natur zu geben, die nicht alle Leute gegen mich in Harnisch bringt.

Aber das geht nicht, meine Natur ist mir gegeben, und ich kann nicht schlecht sein, ich fühle es. Ich gebe mir mehr Mühe, es allen recht zu machen, als sie auch nur im Entferntesten vermuten. Wenn ich oben bin, versuche ich zu lachen, weil ich ihnen meinen Kummer nicht zeigen will.

Mehr als einmal habe ich Mutter nach einer Reihe ungerechter Verweise an den Kopf geworfen: »Es ist mir egal, was du sagst. Ziehe deine Hände ruhig ganz von mir ab, ich bin doch ein hoffnungsloser Fall.« Dann bekam ich natürlich zu hören, ich sei frech, wurde zwei Tage ein bisschen ignoriert, und dann war auf einmal wieder alles vergessen, und ich wurde behandelt wie jeder andere.

Mir ist es aber unmöglich, den einen Tag katzenfreundlich zu sein und ihnen am folgenden Tag meinen Hass ins Gesicht zu schleudern. Ich wähle lieber den goldenen Mittelweg, der gar nicht vergoldet ist, und halte meinen Mund über das, was ich denke, und versuche, ihnen gegenüber einmal genauso verächtlich zu werden, wie sie zu mir sind. Ach, wenn ich das nur könnte! Deine Anne

Freitag, 5. Februar 1943

Liebe Kitty!

Obwohl ich dir lange nichts mehr von den Streitereien geschrieben habe, hat sich daran doch nichts geändert. Herr Dussel nahm anfangs die schnell vergessenen Auseinandersetzungen noch sehr ernst, aber nun gewöhnt er sich daran und versucht nicht mehr, zu vermitteln.

Margot und Peter sind überhaupt nicht das, was man »jung« nennt, beide sind so langweilig und still. Ich steche schrecklich dagegen ab und bekomme immer wieder zu hören: »Margot und Peter tun das auch nicht. Schau mal, deine liebe Schwester!« Grässlich finde ich das.

Ich gebe auch gerne zu, dass ich ganz und gar nicht wie Margot werden will. Sie ist mir viel zu lasch und gleichgültig, lässt sich von jedem überreden und gibt in allem nach. Ich will einen kräftigeren Geist! Aber solche Theorien behalte ich für mich, sie würden mich schrecklich auslachen, wenn ich mit dieser Verteidigung ankäme.

Bei Tisch ist die Stimmung meistens gespannt. Zum Glück werden manche Ausbrüche wegen der Suppen-Esser zurückgehalten. Die Suppen-Esser sind alle, die von unten kommen, um einen Teller Suppe zu kriegen.

Heute Mittag sprach Herr van Daan wieder darüber, dass Margot zu wenig isst. »Sicher wegen der schlanken Linie«, sagte er spöttisch.

Mutter, die immer für Margot eintritt, sagte laut: »Ich kann Ihr dummes Geschwätz nicht mehr hören.«

Frau van Daan wurde feuerrot, er schaute vor sich hin und schwieg. Oft lachen wir auch über irgendetwas. Erst kürzlich kramte Frau van Daan so herrlichen Blödsinn hervor. Sie erzählte von früher, wie gut sie mit ihrem Vater zurechtkam und wie viel sie geflirtet hat. »Und wissen Sie«, fuhr sie fort, »wenn ein Herr ein bisschen handgreiflich wird, hat mein Vater gesagt, dann musst du zu ihm sagen: ›Mein Herr, ich bin eine Dame!‹ Dann weiß er schon, was du meinst.« Wir brachen in Lachen aus wie über einen guten Witz.

Auch Peter, so still er meistens ist, gibt uns manchmal Grund zu Fröhlichkeit. Er hat das Pech, versessen auf Fremdwörter zu sein, deren Bedeutung er aber oft nicht kennt. An einem Nachmittag durften wir nicht auf die Toilette gehen, weil im Büro Besuch war. Peter musste aber sehr dringend, zog die Spülung jedoch nicht. Um uns nun vor dem wenig angenehmen Geruch zu warnen, befestigte er einen Zettel an der Tür: »S. V. P. Gas.« Er hatte natürlich gemeint »Vorsicht, Gas«, fand aber S. V. P. * vornehmer. Dass es »bitte« bedeutet, davon hatte er keine blasse Ahnung.   Deine Anne

Samstag, 27. Februar 1943

Liebe Kitty!

Pim erwartet jeden Tag die Invasion. Churchill hat eine Lungenentzündung gehabt, aber es geht ihm langsam besser. Gandhi, der indische Freiheitskämpfer, hält seinen soundsovielten Hungerstreik.

Frau van Daan behauptet, sie sei eine Fatalistin. Aber wer hat am meisten Angst, wenn geschossen wird? Niemand anderes als Petronella!

Jan hat den Hirtenbrief der Bischöfe an die Menschen in der Kirche für uns mitgebracht. Er war sehr schön und ermutigend geschrieben. »Bleibt nicht ruhig, Niederländer! Jeder kämpfe mit seinen eigenen Waffen für die Freiheit von Land, Volk und Religion! Helft, gebt, zögert nicht!« Das verkünden sie einfach von der Kanzel! Ob es hilft? Unseren Glaubensbrüdern bestimmt nicht.

---

* S'il vous plait; A. d. Ü.

Stell dir vor, was uns nun wieder passiert ist! Der Besitzer dieses Gebäudes hat, ohne Kugler und Kleiman zu informieren, das Haus verkauft. Eines Morgens kam der neue Hausbesitzer mit einem Architekten, um das Haus zu besichtigen. Zum Glück war Herr Kleiman da, der den Herren alles gezeigt hat, bis auf unser Hinterhäuschen. Er hatte angeblich den Schlüssel von der Zwischentür zu Hause vergessen. Der neue Hausbesitzer fragte nicht weiter.

Wenn er nur nicht zurückkommt und doch das Hinterhaus sehen will, dann sieht es schlecht für uns aus!

Vater hat für Margot und mich einen Karteikasten leer gemacht und Kärtchen hineingetan, die auf einer Seite noch unbeschrieben sind. Das wird unsere Bücherkartei. Wir schreiben nämlich beide auf, welche Bücher wir gelesen haben, von wem sie geschrieben wurden und das Datum. Ich habe gerade wieder was gelernt, »Bordell« und »Kokotte«. Dafür habe ich mir ein besonderes Heft angelegt.

Neue Butter- oder Margarineverteilung! Jeder bekommt sein Stückchen Aufstrich auf den Teller. Aber die Verteilung läuft sehr ungerecht. Van Daans, die immer das Frühstück machen, geben sich selbst anderthalbmal so viel wie uns. Meine Eltern haben viel zu viel Angst vor Streit, um was dazu zu sagen. Schade, ich finde, dass man es solchen Leuten immer mit gleicher Münze zurückzahlen muss.

Deine Anne

Donnerstag, 4. März 1943

Liebe Kitty!

Frau van Daan hat einen neuen Namen, wir nennen sie Mrs. Beaverbrook. Was das bedeutet, verstehst du natürlich nicht, ich werde es dir erzählen: Im englischen Sender spricht nämlich oft ein Mr. Beaverbrook über die viel zu laschen Bombardierungen auf Deutschland. Frau van Daan widerspricht sonst jedem, sogar Churchill und dem Nachrichtendienst, aber mit Herrn Beaverbrook ist sie geradezu rührend einig. Wir hielten es darum für das Beste, dass sie Herrn Beaverbrook heiratet. Und weil sie sich deshalb geschmeichelt fühlte, heißt sie fortan Mrs. Beaverbrook.

Wir bekommen einen neuen Lagerarbeiter, der alte muss nach Deutschland. Das ist schlimm, aber für uns ganz gut, weil ein neuer das Haus nicht kennt. Wir haben vor den Lagerarbeitern noch immer Angst.

Gandhi isst wieder.

Der Schwarzhandel funktioniert hervorragend. Wir könnten uns rund und fett essen, wenn wir Geld hätten, um die unmöglichen Preise zu bezahlen. Unser Gemüsehändler kauft Kartoffeln bei der deutschen Wehrmacht und bringt sie in Säcken ins Privatbüro. Er weiß, dass wir uns hier verstecken, und kommt deshalb auch immer in der Mittagspause, wenn die Lagerarbeiter weg sind.

Wir können nicht atmen, ohne zu niesen und zu husten, so viel Pfeffer wird durch die Mühlen gedreht. Jeder, der heraufkommt, begrüßt uns mit »hatschi«. Frau van Daan behauptet, dass sie nicht hinuntergehen kann, sie würde krank, wenn sie noch mehr Pfeffer riecht.

Ich finde Vaters Firma überhaupt nicht schön. Nichts als Geliermittel oder scharfer Pfeffer. Wenn man schon mit Lebensmitteln handelt, dann sollte es doch auch was zum Naschen geben!

Heute Morgen habe ich wieder ein donnerndes Gewitter von Worten über mich ergehen lassen müssen. Es blitzte nur so von unfreundlichen Ausdrücken, dass meine Ohren gellten von den vielen »Anne-schlecht« und »Van-Daan-gut«. Zum Donnerwetter!

Deine Anne

Mittwoch, 10. März 1943

Liebe Kitty!

Gestern Abend hatten wir Kurzschluss, und außerdem ballerten sie unaufhörlich. Ich habe meine Angst vor Schießereien und Flugzeugen noch nicht abgelegt und liege fast jede Nacht bei Vater im Bett, um Trost zu suchen. Das ist vielleicht sehr kindisch, aber du müsstest das mal mitmachen! Man kann sein eigenes Wort nicht mehr verstehen, so donnern die Kanonen. Mrs. Beaverbrook, die Fatalistin, fing fast an zu weinen und sprach mit einem sehr beklommenen Stimmchen: »Oh, es ist so unangenehm! Oh, sie schießen so laut!« Das heißt doch nur: Ich habe solche Angst!

Bei Kerzenlicht kam es mir nicht so schlimm vor wie in der Dunkelheit. Ich zitterte, als ob ich Fieber hätte, und flehte Vater an, die Kerze wieder anzumachen. Er war unerbittlich, das Licht blieb aus. Plötzlich schossen Maschinengewehre, das ist noch zehnmal schlimmer als Kanonen. Mutter sprang aus dem Bett und steckte zu Pims großem Ärger die Kerze an. Ihre resolute Antwort auf sein Murren war: »Anne ist doch kein alter Soldat!« Damit basta!

Habe ich dir schon von Frau van Daans anderen Ängsten erzählt? Ich glaube nicht. Damit du über alle Hinterhausabenteuer informiert bist, musst du auch das wissen. Frau van Daan hörte eines Nachts Diebe auf dem Dachboden. Sie vernahm richtige laute Schritte und hatte solche Angst, dass sie ihren Mann weckte. Genau in diesem Augenblick verschwanden die Diebe und der Lärm, und Herr van Daan hörte nur noch das Klopfen des ängstlichen Herzens der Fatalistin.

»Ach, Putti (Herrn van Daans Kosename), sie haben sicher die Würste und alle Hülsenfrüchte mitgenommen. Und Peter! Oh, ob Peter wohl noch in seinem Bett liegt?«

»Peter haben sie bestimmt nicht gestohlen. Hab keine Angst und lass mich schlafen!«

Doch daraus wurde nichts. Frau van Daan schlief vor lauter Angst nicht mehr ein.

Ein paar Nächte später wurde die ganze obere Familie wieder von dem gespenstischen Lärm geweckt. Peter ging mit einer Taschenlampe auf den Dachboden, und rrrrt, was lief da weg? Ein Haufen großer Ratten! Als wir wussten, wer die Diebe waren, haben wir Mouschi auf dem Dachboden schlafen lassen, und die ungebetenen Gäste sind nicht mehr zurückgekommen – wenigstens nicht nachts.

Vor einigen Tagen ging Peter abends zum Oberboden (es war erst halb acht und noch hell), um ein paar alte Zeitungen zu holen. Um die Treppe hinunterzuklettern, musste er sich gut an der Luke festhalten. Ohne hinzuschauen, legte er seine Hand hin … und fiel fast vor Schreck und Schmerz die Treppe hinunter. Er hatte seine Hand auf eine Ratte gelegt, die ihn fest in den Arm biss. Das Blut lief durch seinen Pyjama, und er war so weiß wie ein Handtuch, als er mit weichen Knien zu uns kam. Kein Wunder, eine große Ratte zu streicheln ist nicht sehr angenehm, und dann noch obendrein ein Biss, das ist schrecklich.

Deine Anne

Liebe Kitty!

Darf ich dir vorstellen: Mama Frank, Vorkämpferin der Kinder! Extra Butter für die Jugendlichen, moderne Jugendprobleme, in allem setzt sich Mutter für die Jugend ein und bekommt nach einer Portion Streit fast immer ihren Willen.

Ein Glas eingemachte Zunge ist verdorben. Eine Galamahlzeit für Mouschi und Moffi.

Moffi kennst du noch nicht, aber sie ist schon in der Firma gewesen, bevor wir uns hier versteckten. Sie ist die Lager- und Bürokatze und hält die Ratten vom Lager fern. Auch ihr politischer Name* ist leicht zu erklären. Eine Zeit lang hatte die Firma zwei Katzen, eine für das Lager und eine für den Dachboden. Manchmal trafen sich die beiden, was immer zu heftigen Kämpfen führte. Die Lagerkatze war immer diejenige, die angriff, während das Dachbodentier am Ende doch den Sieg errang. Genau wie in der Politik. Also wurde die Lagerkatze die Deutsche oder Moffi genannt, und die Dachbodenkatze der Engländer oder Tommy. Tommy ist später abgeschafft worden, und Moffi dient uns allen zur Unterhaltung, wenn wir hinuntergehen.

Wir haben so viele braune und weiße Bohnen gegessen, dass ich sie nicht mehr sehen kann. Wenn ich nur daran denke, wird mir schlecht.

Die abendliche Brotverteilung ist ganz eingestellt worden.

Papi hat gerade gesagt, dass er schlechte Laune hat. Er hat wieder so traurige Augen, der Ärmste!

Ich bin einfach süchtig nach dem Buch »De klop op de deur« von Ina Boudier-Bakker. Dieser Familienroman ist außerordentlich gut geschrieben. Nur was drumherum ist über Krieg, Schriftsteller oder Emanzipation der Frau, ist nicht so gut. Ehrlich gesagt, es interessiert mich nicht so sehr.

Schreckliche Bombenangriffe auf Deutschland.

Herr van Daan ist schlecht gelaunt. Der Anlass: Zigarettenknappheit. Die Diskussion über die Frage, ob die Dosen aufgegessen werden oder nicht, ist zu unseren Gunsten ausgegangen.

---

* Mof. pl. Moffen: Name für Deutsche; A. d. Ü.

Ich kann keine Schuhe mehr anziehen, außer hohen Skischuhen, die im Haus sehr unpraktisch sind. Ein paar Strohsandalen für 6,50 Gulden konnte ich nur eine Woche tragen, dann versagten sie den Dienst. Vielleicht treibt Miep im Schwarzhandel was auf.

Ich muss jetzt noch Vaters Haare schneiden. Pim behauptet, dass er nach dem Krieg nie mehr einen anderen Frisör nimmt, so gut erledige ich meine Arbeit. Wenn ich nur nicht so oft sein Ohr mitschneiden würde!

Deine Anne

Donnerstag, 18. März 1943

Liebste Kitty!

Die Türkei ist im Krieg. Große Aufregung. Warten mit Spannung auf die Nachrichten im Radio.

Freitag, 19. März 1943

Liebe Kitty!

Die Enttäuschung ist der Freude schon nach einer Stunde gefolgt und hat letztere überholt. Die Türkei ist doch nicht im Krieg, der dortige Minister sprach lediglich von einer baldigen Aufhebung der Neutralität. Ein Zeitungsverkäufer auf dem Dam schrie: »Türkei auf der Seite Englands!« Auf diese Art wurden ihm die Zeitungen aus der Hand gerissen, und das erfreuliche Gerücht hat auch uns erreicht.

Die Tausendguldenscheine werden für ungültig erklärt. Das ist ein großer Schlag für alle Schwarzhändler und dergleichen Leute, aber noch mehr für andere Besitzer von schwarzem Geld oder für Untergetauchte. Man muss, wenn man einen Tausendguldenschein wechseln will, genau nachweisen, wie man ihn bekommen hat. Steuern dürfen allerdings noch damit bezahlt werden, doch auch das läuft nächste Woche ab. Gleichzeitig verfallen die Fünfhundertguldenscheine. Gies & Co. hatte noch schwarzes Geld in Tausendguldenscheinen, sie haben für eine ganze Zeit die Steuern im Voraus bezahlt, auf diese Art war alles legal.

Dussel hat eine Tretbohrmaschine bekommen, und ich werde wohl bald einer ernsthaften Kontrolle unterzogen.

Dussel gehorcht den Versteckregeln überhaupt nicht. Er schreibt nicht nur Briefe an seine Frau, sondern führt auch eine rege Korrespondenz mit diversen anderen Leuten und lässt Margot, die Hinterhauslehrerin für Niederländisch, die Briefe korrigieren. Vater hat ihm streng verboten, damit weiterzumachen. Margots Korrigieren hat aufgehört, aber ich persönlich glaube, dass er das Schreiben wohl bald wieder aufnehmen wird.

Der Führer aller Germanen hat vor verwundeten Soldaten gesprochen. Es war traurig anzuhören. Die Fragen und Antworten waren ungefähr so:

»Heinrich Scheppel ist mein Name.«

»Wo verwundet?«

»Bei Stalingrad.«

»Was verwundet?«

»Zwei abgefrorene Füße und ein Gelenkbruch am linken Arm.«

Genau so gab das Radio dieses schreckliche Marionettentheater an uns weiter. Die Verwundeten schienen noch stolz auf ihre Verwundung zu sein, je mehr, umso besser! Einer brachte vor Rührung, weil er seinem Führer die Hand reichen durfte (falls er diese noch hatte), fast kein Wort heraus.

Ich habe Dussels Duftseife auf den Boden fallen lassen und bin draufgetreten, und jetzt ist ein ganzes Stück rausgebrochen. Ich habe Vater um einen Schadensersatz für ihn gebeten, weil Dussel nur ein Stück Seife im Monat bekommt.
Deine Anne

Donnerstag, 25. März 1943

Liebe Kitty!

Mutter, Vater, Margot und ich saßen gestern Abend sehr gemütlich zusammen. Auf einmal kam Peter herein und flüsterte Vater etwas ins Ohr. Ich hörte was von »eine Tonne umgefallen im Lager« und »jemand an der Tür rütteln«.

Margot hatte es auch verstanden, versuchte aber, mich ein bisschen zu beruhigen, denn ich war natürlich gleich kreideweiß und nervös. Wir drei warteten, Vater war inzwischen mit Peter hinuntergegangen. Keine zwei Minuten später kam Frau van Daan vom Radiohören herauf und sagte, Pim hätte sie gebeten, das Radio auszumachen und leise hinaufzugehen. Aber wie es so ist, wenn man besonders leise sein will, dann krachen die Stufen einer alten Treppe doppelt so laut. Wieder fünf Minuten danach kamen Peter und Pim, weiß bis an die Nasenspitzen, und erzählten uns ihre Widrigkeiten.

Sie hatten sich unten an die Treppe gesetzt und gewartet, ohne Resultat. Aber plötzlich hörten sie auf einmal zwei harte Schläge, als würden hier im Haus zwei Türen zugeschlagen. Pim war mit einem Satz oben, Peter warnte erst noch Dussel, der umständlich und geräuschvoll endlich auch oben landete. Nun ging es auf Strümpfen eine Etage höher, zur Familie van Daan. Herr van Daan war sehr erkältet und lag schon im Bett, deshalb scharten wir uns um sein Lager und tauschten flüsternd unsere Vermutungen aus. Immer wieder, wenn Herr van Daan laut hustete, bekamen seine Frau und ich fast Krämpfe vor Angst. Das ging so lange, bis einer von uns die glänzende Idee hatte, ihm Codein zu geben. Der Husten ließ dann sofort nach.

Wieder warteten und warteten wir, aber nichts war zu hören. Nun nahmen wir eigentlich alle an, dass die Diebe weggelaufen waren, als sie Schritte in dem sonst so stillen Haus gehört hatten. Das Unglück wollte, dass unten am Radio noch der englische Sender eingestellt war und unsere Stühle auch noch ordentlich drumherum standen. Falls die Tür aufgebrochen wäre und der Luftschutzwart das sehen und der Polizei Bescheid sagen würde, könnte das sehr unangenehme Folgen für uns haben. Also stand Herr van Daan auf, zog Hose und Jacke an, setzte einen Hut auf und ging sehr vorsichtig hinter Vater die Treppe hinunter, gefolgt von Peter, der zur Sicherheit mit einem schweren Hammer bewaffnet war. Die Damen oben (mich und Margot eingeschlossen) warteten mit Spannung, bis fünf Minuten später die Herren wieder oben erschienen und sagten, dass im Haus alles ruhig sei. Wir machten aus, dass wir kein Wasser laufen lassen und im Klo nicht die Spülung ziehen würden. Aber da die Aufregung fast allen Hausgenossen auf den Magen geschlagen war, kannst du dir vorstellen, was für ein Gestank dort herrschte, nachdem wir einer nach dem anderen unser Geschäft erledigt hatten.

Wenn so etwas passiert, kommt immer alles Mögliche zusammen. So auch jetzt. Erstens spielte die Westerturmglocke nicht mehr, die mir immer so ein beruhigendes Gefühl gab, und dann war Herr Voskuijl am Abend vorher früher weggegangen, und wir wussten nicht genau, ob Bep den Schlüssel noch bekommen und vielleicht vergessen hatte, die Tür abzuschließen.

Aber jetzt kam es darauf nicht an, es war noch immer Abend, und wir waren noch sehr unsicher, obwohl wir uns inzwischen doch etwas beruhigt hatten, weil wir von Viertel nach acht, als der Dieb unser Haus unsicher gemacht hatte, bis halb elf nichts mehr gehört hatten. Bei genauerer Überlegung kam es uns dann auch sehr unwahrscheinlich vor, dass ein Dieb so früh am Abend, wenn noch Leute auf der Straße sein können, eine Tür aufgebrochen hätte. Außerdem kam einer von uns auf den Gedanken, dass der Lagermeister von den Nachbarn, der Firma Keg, vielleicht noch an der Arbeit gewesen war, denn in der Aufregung und bei unseren dünnen Wänden konnte man sich leicht bei den Geräuschen irren, und in solchen heiklen Augenblicken spielt auch die Aufregung eine große Rolle.

Wir gingen also ins Bett, aber der Schlaf wollte nicht bei allen kommen. Vater, Mutter und Herr Dussel wachten oft auf, und auch ich kann (mit ein bisschen Übertreibung) ruhig sagen, dass ich kein Auge zugemacht habe. Heute Morgen sind die Herren hinuntergegangen und haben an der Haustür gezogen, ob sie noch abgeschlossen wäre. Alles war in Ordnung!

Die Ereignisse, die alles andere als angenehm waren, wurden natürlich lang und breit dem gesamten Büro erzählt, denn hinterher kann man leicht lachen, und nur Bep hat uns ernst genommen.

Deine Anne

P. S. Das Klo war heute Morgen verstopft, und Vater hat alle Erdbeerrezepte (unser gegenwärtiges Klopapier) samt einigen Kilo Kot mit einem langen, hölzernen Stock aus der Toilette stochern müssen. Der Stock wurde später verbrannt.

Samstag, 27. März 1943

Liebe Kitty!

Der Stenokurs ist zu Ende, wir fangen nun an, Geschwindigkeit zu üben. Was werden wir klug! Ich will dir noch etwas von meinen

»Tagtotschlagefächern« erzählen (ich nenne sie so, weil wir nichts anderes tun, als die Tage so schnell wie möglich vorbeigehen zu lassen, damit das Ende der Untertauchzeit schnell näher kommt): Ich bin versessen auf Mythologie, am meisten auf griechische und römische Götter. Hier glauben alle, dass es nur eine vorübergehende Neigung ist, sie haben noch nie von einem Backfisch gehört, der Götter hoch schätzt. Nun, dann bin ich der Erste!

Herr van Daan ist erkältet, oder besser gesagt: er hat ein bisschen Halskratzen. Er macht ein gewaltiges Getöse darum. Gurgeln mit Kamillentee, Gaumen pinseln mit Myrrhentinktur, Balsam auf Brust, Nase, Zähne und Zunge, und dann auch noch schlechte Laune!

Rauter, irgendein hoher Deutscher, hat eine Rede gehalten. »Alle Juden müssen bis zum 1. Juli die germanischen Länder verlassen haben. Vom 1. April bis 1. Mai wird die Provinz Utrecht gesäubert (als wären es Kakerlaken!), vom 1. Mai bis 1. Juni die Provinzen Nord- und Südholland.« Wie eine Herde armes, krankes und verwahrlostes Vieh werden die armen Menschen zu ihren schmutzigen Schlachtplätzen geführt. Aber lass mich lieber schweigen, ich bekomme nur Albträume von meinen eigenen Gedanken.

Noch eine tolle Neuigkeit ist, dass die deutsche Abteilung des Arbeitsamts durch Sabotage in Brand gesteckt worden ist. Einige Tage danach folgte das Standesamt. Männer in deutschen Polizeiuniformen haben die Wachtposten geknebelt und dafür gesorgt, dass somit wichtige Unterlagen futsch sind.   Deine Anne

                                            Donnerstag, 1. April 1943

Liebe Kitty!

Ich bin wirklich nicht in Scherzstimmung (siehe Datum), ganz im Gegenteil. Heute kann ich ruhig das Sprichwort anführen: Ein Unglück kommt selten allein.

Erstens hat unser Aufheiterer, Herr Kleiman, gestern eine starke Magenblutung bekommen und muss mindestens drei Wochen das Bett hüten. Du musst wissen, dass er oft an Magenblutungen leidet, gegen die kein Kraut gewachsen zu sein scheint. Zweitens: Bep hat Grippe. Drittens geht Herr Voskuijl nächste Woche ins Krankenhaus. Er hat wahrscheinlich ein Magengeschwür und muss operiert werden. Und viertens kamen die Direktoren der Pomesinwerke aus Frankfurt, um die neuen Opekta-Lieferungen zu besprechen. Alle Punkte zu dieser Besprechung hatte Vater mit Kleiman diskutiert, und Kugler konnte in der Eile nicht mehr so gut informiert werden.

Die Frankfurter Herren kamen, und Vater zitterte schon im Voraus wegen des Ablaufs der Besprechung. »Wenn ich doch nur dabei sein könnte«, rief er. »Wäre ich doch bloß unten!«

»Dann leg dein Ohr auf den Fußboden! Die Herren kommen doch ins Privatbüro, da kannst du alles hören.«

Vaters Gesicht hellte sich auf, und gestern um halb elf nahmen Pim und Margot (zwei Paar Ohren hören mehr als eines) ihre Stellung auf dem Fußboden ein. Die Besprechung war am Vormittag noch nicht beendet, aber nachmittags war Vater nicht mehr in der Lage, die Lauschaktion fortzusetzen. Er war wie gerädert durch die ungewohnte und unbequeme Haltung. Ich nahm seinen Platz ein, als wir um halb drei Stimmen im Flur hörten. Margot leistete mir Gesellschaft. Das Gespräch war teilweise so weitschweifig und langweilig, dass ich plötzlich auf dem harten, kalten Linoleumboden eingeschlafen war. Margot wagte nicht, mich anzufassen, aus Angst, sie könnten uns unten hören. Und rufen ging erst recht nicht. Ich schlief eine gute halbe Stunde, wachte dann erschrocken auf und hatte alles von der wichtigen Besprechung vergessen. Zum Glück hatte Margot besser aufgepasst.

Freitag, 2. April 1943

Liebe Kitty!

Ach, ich habe wieder etwas Schreckliches in meinem Sündenregister stehen. Gestern Abend lag ich im Bett und wartete, dass Vater zum Beten und Gutenachtsagen kommen würde, als Mutter ins Zimmer kam, sich auf mein Bett setzte und sehr bescheiden sagte: »Anne, Papi kommt noch nicht. Sollen wir nicht mal zusammen beten?«

»Nein, Mansa«, antwortete ich.

Mutter stand auf, blieb neben meinem Bett stehen, ging dann langsam zur Tür. Plötzlich drehte sie sich um und sagte mit einem verzerrten Gesicht: »Ich will nicht böse auf dich sein. Liebe lässt sich nicht erzwingen.« Ein paar Tränen liefen über ihr Gesicht, als sie zur Tür hinausging.

Ich blieb still liegen und fand es sofort gemein von mir, dass ich sie so rüde von mir gestoßen hatte. Aber ich wusste auch, dass ich nichts anderes antworten konnte. Ich konnte nicht so heucheln und gegen meinen Willen mit ihr beten. Es ging einfach nicht. Ich hatte Mitleid mit ihr, sehr viel Mitleid. Zum ersten Mal in meinem Leben habe ich gemerkt, dass meine kühle Haltung sie nicht gleichgültig lässt. Ich habe den Kummer auf ihrem Gesicht gesehen, als sie sagte, dass Liebe sich nicht zwingen lässt. Es ist hart, die Wahrheit zu sagen, und doch ist es die Wahrheit, dass sie mich selbst von sich gestoßen hat, dass sie mich selbst durch ihre taktlosen Bemerkungen für jede Liebe von ihrer Seite abgestumpft hat, durch ihre rohen Scherze über Dinge, die ich nicht witzig finde. So wie sich in mir jedes Mal alles zusammenkrampft, wenn sie mir harte Worte sagt, so krampfte sich ihr Herz zusammen, als sie merkte, dass die Liebe zwischen uns wirklich verschwunden ist.

Sie hat die halbe Nacht geweint und die ganze Nacht nicht gut geschlafen. Vater schaut mich nicht an, und wenn er es doch tut, lese ich in seinen Augen die Worte: »Wie konntest du so gemein sein, wie wagst du es, Mutter solchen Kummer zu bereiten!«

Alle erwarten, dass ich mich entschuldige. Aber das ist eine Sache, für die ich mich nicht entschuldigen kann, weil ich etwas gesagt habe, was wahr ist und was Mutter früher oder später doch wissen muss. Ich scheine und bin gleichgültig gegenüber Mutters Tränen und Vaters Blicken, weil sie beide zum ersten Mal fühlen, was ich unaufhörlich merke. Ich kann nur Mitleid haben mit Mutter, die selbst ihre Haltung wieder finden muss. Ich für meinen Teil schweige und bin kühl und werde auch weiterhin vor der Wahrheit nicht zurückschrecken, weil sie umso schwerer zu ertragen ist, je länger sie verschoben wird.   Deine Anne

                                                    Dienstag, 27. April 1943

Liebe Kitty!

Das ganze Haus dröhnt vor Streit. Mutter und ich, van Daan und Papa, Mutter und Frau van Daan, jeder ist böse auf jeden. Eine nette

Anne (zweite von links) mit Freundinnen an ihrem 10. Geburtstag, 1939.

Atmosphäre, gell? Annes übliches Sündenregister kam in seinem vollen Umfang neu aufs Tapet.

Vergangenen Samstag kamen die ausländischen Herren wieder zu Besuch. Sie sind bis sechs Uhr geblieben, und wir saßen alle oben und wagten nicht, uns zu rühren. Wenn sonst niemand im Haus ist oder in der Nachbarschaft niemand arbeitet, hört man im Privatbüro jeden Schritt von oben. Ich hatte wieder das Sitzfieber. So lange mucksmäuschenstill zu sitzen, ist wirklich nicht erfreulich.

Herr Voskuijl liegt schon im Krankenhaus, Herr Kleiman ist wieder im Büro, die Magenblutungen waren schneller gestillt als sonst. Er hat erzählt, dass das Standesamt bei dem Brand neulich noch mal zusätzlich von den Feuerwehrleuten zugerichtet worden ist, die, statt das Feuer zu löschen, den ganzen Kram unter Wasser gesetzt haben. Macht mir Spaß!

Das Carlton-Hotel ist kaputt, zwei englische Flugzeuge mit einer großen Ladung Brandbomben an Bord sind genau auf dieses »Offiziersheim« gefallen. Die ganze Ecke Vijzelstraat-Singel ist abgebrannt.

Die Luftangriffe auf deutsche Städte werden von Tag zu Tag stärker. Wir haben keine Nacht mehr Ruhe. Ich habe schwarze Ringe unter den Augen durch den Mangel an Schlaf.

Unser Essen ist miserabel. Frühstück mit trockenem Brot und Kaffee-Ersatz. Mittagessen schon seit vierzehn Tagen: Spinat oder Salat. Zwanzig Zentimeter lange Kartoffeln schmecken süß und faul. Wer abmagern will, logiere im Hinterhaus! Oben klagen sie Stein und Bein, wir finden es nicht so tragisch.

Alle Männer, die 1940 gekämpft haben oder mobilisiert waren, sind aufgerufen worden, um in Kriegsgefangenenlagern für den Führer zu arbeiten. Sicher eine Vorsichtsmaßnahme für den Fall der Invasion.

Deine Anne

Samstag, 1. Mai 1943

Liebe Kitty!

Dussel hatte Geburtstag. Zuvor hat er getan, als ob er nichts davon wissen wollte, aber als Miep mit einer großen Einkaufstasche kam, die vor Päckchen überquoll, war er so aufgeregt wie ein kleines Kind.

Seine Charlotte hat ihm Eier, Butter, Kekse, Limonade, Brot, Kognak, Kräuterkuchen, Blumen, Orangen, Schokolade, Bücher und Briefpapier geschickt. Er baute einen Geburtstagstisch auf und stellte ihn nicht weniger als drei Tage zur Schau, dieser alte Blödian!

Du musst nicht glauben, dass er Hunger leidet. Wir haben in seinem Schrank Brot, Käse, Marmelade und Eier gefunden. Es ist mehr als ein Skandal, dass er, den wir hier so liebevoll aufgenommen haben, nur um ihn vor dem Untergang zu retten, sich hinter unserem Rücken den Bauch voll stopft und uns nichts abgibt. Wir haben doch auch alles mit ihm geteilt! Noch schlimmer finden wir aber, dass er auch gegenüber Kleiman, Voskuijl und Bep so kleinlich ist, sie bekommen nichts von ihm. Die Orangen, die Kleiman so nötig für seinen kranken Magen braucht, findet Dussel für seinen eigenen Magen noch gesünder.

Heute Nacht habe ich viermal alle meine Besitztümer einpacken müssen, so laut haben sie draußen geballert. Heute habe ich ein Köfferchen gepackt und die notwendigsten Fluchtgegenstände hineingestopft. Aber Mutter sagte ganz richtig: »Wohin willst du denn flüchten?«

Ganz Holland wird gestraft, weil so viele Arbeiter streiken. Deshalb ist der Ausnahmezustand ausgerufen worden, und jeder bekommt eine Buttermarke weniger. So straft man ungezogene Kinder!

Heute Abend habe ich Mutter die Haare gewaschen. Das ist in diesen Zeiten gar nicht so einfach. Wir müssen uns mit klebriger grüner Seife behelfen, weil es kein Schampoo gibt, und außerdem kann Mans ihre Haare nicht richtig auskämmen, denn unser Familienkamm hat nicht mehr als zehn Zähne.   Deine Anne

Sonntag, 2. Mai 1943

Wenn ich manchmal darüber nachdenke, wie wir hier leben, komme ich meistens zu dem Schluss, dass wir es hier im Vergleich zu den anderen Juden, die sich nicht verstecken, wie im Paradies haben. Aber später, wenn wieder alles normal ist, werde ich mich doch wundern, wie wir, die wir es zu Hause sehr ordentlich hatten, so, ja, man kann wohl sagen, heruntergekommen sind. Heruntergekommen, was die Manieren betrifft. Wir haben zum Beispiel schon seit unserer Ankunft eine Wachstuchdecke auf dem Tisch, die durch den häufigen Gebrauch nicht mehr zu den saubersten gehört. Ich versuche zwar oft, sie noch etwas herzurichten, aber mit einem Abwaschlappen, der mehr Loch ist als Lappen und ebenfalls vor dem Verstecken – vor langer Zeit also – mal neu war, kann man auch mit noch so viel Schrubben mit dem Tisch keinen Staat mehr machen. Van Daans schlafen schon den ganzen Winter auf einem Flanelltuch, das man hier nicht waschen kann, weil das Seifenpulver, das man auf Marken bekommt, viel zu knapp und außerdem viel zu schlecht ist. Vater läuft mit einer ausgefransten Hose herum, und auch seine Krawatte zeigt Verschleiß. Mamas Korsett ist heute aus Altersschwäche zusammengebrochen und nicht mehr zu reparieren, während Margot mit einem um zwei Nummern zu kleinen Büstenhalter herumläuft. Mutter und Margot sind den ganzen Winter mit zusammen drei Hemden ausgekommen, und die meinen sind so klein, dass sie mir noch nicht mal bis zum Bauch reichen. Das sind zwar alles Dinge, über die man hinwegsehen kann, aber trotzdem überlege ich manchmal mit Schrecken: Wie können wir, die wir von meiner Unterhose bis zu Vaters Rasierpinsel nur verschlissenes Zeug haben, später wieder zu unserem Vorkriegsstand zurückkommen?

Sonntag, 2. Mai 1943

Die Hinterhausansichten über den Krieg

Herr van Daan: Der ehrenwerte Herr hat nach unser aller Meinung viel Durchblick in der Politik. Aber er sagt uns doch voraus, dass wir uns noch bis Ende 43 hier aufhalten müssen. Das ist zwar sehr lange, wird aber trotzdem auszuhalten sein. Doch wer gibt uns die Zusicherung, dass dieser Krieg, der jedem nur Leid und Kummer bereitet, dann vorbei sein wird? Und wer kann uns versprechen, dass bis dahin weder mit uns noch mit unseren Helfern nicht längst was passiert ist? Doch niemand! Und darum leben wir auch jeden Tag in Anspannung. Einer Anspannung von Erwartung und Hoffnung, aber auch von Angst, wenn man im Haus oder draußen Geräusche hört, wenn geschossen wird oder wenn neue »Bekanntmachungen« in der Zeitung stehen. Es könnte auch jeden Tag passieren, dass einige von unseren Helfern sich selbst hier verstecken müssen. Untertauchen ist ein ganz normales Wort geworden. Wie viele Menschen werden sich wohl verstecken? Im Verhältnis natürlich nicht viel, aber trotzdem werden wir später bestimmt staunen, wie viele gute Menschen es in den Niederlanden gegeben hat, die Juden oder auch geflohene Christen mit oder ohne Geld zu sich genommen haben. Es ist auch unglaublich, von wie vielen Leuten man hört, die einen falschen Personalausweis haben.

Frau van Daan: Als diese schöne Dame (nur ihrer eigenen Meinung nach) hörte, dass es nicht mehr so schwierig ist wie früher, an einen falschen Personalausweis zu kommen, schlug sie sofort vor, für uns alle welche machen zu lassen. Als ob das nichts wäre und das Geld bei Vater und Herrn van Daan auf dem Rücken wächst!

Während Frau van Daan immer größeren Unsinn behauptet, geht Putti oft in die Luft. Das kann er auch leicht, denn den einen Tag sagt seine Kerli: »Ich lasse mich später taufen!« Und am nächsten Tag heißt es: »Ich wollte schon immer nach Jerusalem, denn ich fühle mich nur unter Juden heimisch.«

Pim ist ein großer Optimist, aber er kann immer einen Grund dafür angeben.

Herr Dussel denkt ins Blaue hinein, und wenn jemand seiner Hoheit widerspricht, dann kommt er schlecht weg. Ich glaube, bei Herrn Albert Dussel zu Hause ist alles, was er sagt, Gesetz. Aber Anne Frank paßt solches ganz und gar nicht!

Was die anderen Mitglieder des Hinterhauses über den Krieg denken, ist nicht interessant. Nur diese vier zählen in der Politik, eigentlich nur zwei, aber Madame van Daan und Herr Dussel zählen sich auch dazu.

Dienstag, 18. Mai 1943

Liebe Kit!

Ich war Zuschauerin bei einem schweren Luftgefecht zwischen deutschen und englischen Fliegern. Ein paar Alliierte mussten leider Gottes aus ihren brennenden Maschinen springen. Unser Milchmann, der in Halfweg wohnt, hat am Straßenrand vier Kanadier sitzen sehen, von denen einer fließend Holländisch sprach. Er bat den Milchmann um Feuer für eine Zigarette und erzählte, dass die Besatzung der Maschine aus sechs Personen bestanden hätte. Der Pilot war verbrannt, und der fünfte Mann hatte sich irgendwo versteckt. Die grüne Polizei hat die vier kerngesunden Männer später abholen lassen. Wie ist es möglich, dass man nach einem so gewaltigen Fallschirmabsprung noch so bei Sinnen ist!

Obwohl es so warm ist, müssen wir jeden zweiten Tag unsere Öfen anmachen, um Gemüseabfälle und Schmutz zu verbrennen. In den Mülleimer können wir nichts werfen, weil wir immer mit den Lagerarbeitern rechnen müssen. Wie leicht verrät man sich durch eine kleine Unvorsichtigkeit!

Alle Studenten sollen auf einer Liste unterschreiben, dass sie »mit allen Deutschen sympathisieren und der neuen Ordnung gut gesonnen« sind. Achtzig Prozent haben ihr Gewissen und ihre Überzeugung nicht verleugnet, doch die Folgen sind nicht ausgeblieben. Alle Studenten, die nicht unterzeichnet haben, müssen nach Deutschland in ein Arbeitslager. Was bleibt von der niederländischen Jugend noch übrig, wenn alle in Deutschland hart arbeiten müssen?

Wegen der lauten Schießerei hat Mutter heute Nacht das Fenster geschlossen. Ich war in Pims Bett. Plötzlich sprang über unserem Kopf Frau van Daan aus ihrem Bett, wie von Mouschi gebissen, und gleich darauf hörten wir einen lauten Schlag. Es klang, als sei eine Brandbombe direkt neben meinem Bett eingeschlagen. Ich schrie: »Licht! Licht!«

Pim knipste die Lampe an, und ich erwartete, das Zimmer würde in wenigen Minuten lichterloh brennen. Nichts geschah. Wir rannten hinauf, um zu sehen, was dort los war. Herr und Frau van Daan hatten durch das offene Fenster eine rötliche Glut gesehen. Herr van Daan glaubte, dass es in der Nachbarschaft brannte, und Frau van Daan dachte, dass unser Haus bereits Feuer gefangen hätte. Bei dem Schlag, der folgte, stand die Dame schon auf ihren zitternden Beinen. Dussel blieb oben und rauchte eine Zigarette, wir legten uns wieder in unsere Betten. Es war noch keine Viertelstunde vergangen, da begann die Schießerei erneut. Frau van Daan stand sofort auf und ging die Treppe hinunter in Dussels Zimmer, um dort den Schutz zu finden, der ihr bei ihrem Ehegatten offenbar nicht beschert war. Dussel empfing sie mit den Worten: »Komm in mein Bett, mein Kind!«

Das Haus in der Prinsengracht 263.

Was uns in schallendes Gelächter ausbrechen ließ! Das Kanonenfeuer konnte uns nichts mehr anhaben, unsere Angst war wie weggefegt.

Deine Anne

Sonntag, 13. Juni 1943

Liebe Kitty!

Mein Geburtstagsvers von Vater ist zu schön, als dass ich dir dieses Gedicht vorenthalten kann.

Da Pim in Deutsch dichtete, musste Margot sich ans Übersetzen machen. Urteile selbst, ob sie ihre freiwillige Aufgabe prima erledigt hat. Nach der üblichen kurzen Zusammenfassung der Jahresereignisse folgt:

Als Jüngste von allen und doch nicht mehr klein
Hast du es nicht leicht; ein jeder will sein
Ein bisschen dein Lehrer, dir oft zur Pein!
»Wir haben Erfahrung! – Nimm's von mir an.«
»Wir haben so was schon öfter getan
Und wissen besser, was einer kann oder mag.«
Ja, ja, so geht es seit Jahr und Tag.
Die eignen Fehler wiegen nicht schwer,
Doch die der anderen umso mehr.
Oft wirst du ermahnt, musst vieles hören,
Gar manches wird dich sicher stören.
Doch können nicht immer dir Recht wir geben.
Nachgiebig muss man sein im Leben.
Und um des lieben Friedens willen
Schluckt manches man wie bittre Pillen.
Das Lebensjahr, das nun beendet,
Hast du sehr nützlich angewendet,
Durch Lernen, Arbeit und viel Lesen
Ist's doch nie »langweilig« gewesen.
Und nun zur Kleidung: Ich höre dich fragen:
Was kann ich eigentlich noch tragen?
Mein Kleid, mein Rock, alles zu kurz,
Mein Hemd nur noch ein Lendenschurz.

Und dann die Schuhe, es ist nicht zu sagen,
Wie viele Schmerzen mich da plagen.
Ja, wächst man auch zehn Zentimeter,
Passt nichts mehr, das versteht ein jeder!

Bei dem Stück zum Thema Essen ist Margot keine Übersetzung mit
Reimen gelungen, deshalb lasse ich es hier ganz weg. Findest du meinen Vers nicht schön?
Ich bin sehr verwöhnt worden und habe sehr schöne Sachen bekommen. U. a. ein dickes Buch über mein Lieblingsthema, die Mythologie von Hellas und Rom. Auch über einen Mangel an Süßigkeiten kann ich nicht klagen, alle haben ihre letzten Vorräte angegriffen. Als Benjamin der Untertauchfamilie bin ich wirklich mit viel mehr beschenkt worden, als mir zusteht.   Deine Anne

Dienstag, 15. Juni 1943
Liebe Kitty!
Es ist eine Menge passiert, aber ich denke oft, dass all mein uninteressantes Geschwätz dich langweilt und du froh bist, wenn du nicht so viele Briefe bekommst. Darum werde ich dir auch nur kurz berichten.
Herr Voskuijl ist nicht an seinem Magengeschwür operiert worden. Als sie ihn auf dem Operationstisch hatten und sein Magen offen war, sahen die Ärzte, dass er Krebs hat, der schon so weit gewachsen war, dass es nichts mehr zu operieren gab. Sie haben die Wunde also nur wieder geschlossen, ihn drei Wochen lang im Bett behalten, ihm gut zu essen gegeben und ihn dann nach Hause geschickt. Aber sie haben eine unverzeihliche Dummheit begangen, nämlich dem armen Mann genau gesagt, wie es um ihn steht. Er kann nicht mehr arbeiten, sitzt zu Hause, umringt von seinen acht Kindern, und grübelt über seinen nahen Tod nach. Er tut mir schrecklich Leid, und ich finde es schlimm, dass wir nicht hinaus können, sonst würde ich ihn bestimmt oft besuchen, um ihn abzulenken. Für uns ist es ein Unglück, dass der gute Voskuijl uns nicht mehr über alles auf dem Laufenden hält, was im Lager passiert und was man so hört. Er war unsere beste Hilfe, was die Vorsicht betrifft, wir vermissen ihn sehr.

Nächsten Monat sind wir an der Reihe, wir müssen unser Radio abliefern. Kleiman hat zu Hause ein illegales Baby-Gerät, das wir als Ersatz für unseren großen Philips bekommen sollen. Es ist ja schade, dass der schöne Apparat abgeliefert werden muss. Aber ein Haus, in dem Leute untergetaucht sind, darf sich auf keinen Fall die Regierung mutwillig auf den Hals laden. Das kleine Radio stellen wir dann natürlich bei uns oben hin. Zu illegalen Juden und illegalem Geld passt auch ein illegales Radio ganz gut. Alle Leute versuchen, einen alten Apparat statt ihrer »Bleib-tapfer-Quelle« abzuliefern. Es ist wirklich wahr, wenn die Berichte von draußen immer schlimmer werden, hilft das Radio mit seiner Wunderstimme, dass wir den Mut nicht verlieren und jedes Mal wieder sagen: »Kopf hoch! Tapfer bleiben! Es kommen auch wieder bessere Zeiten!«

Deine Anne

Sonntag, 11. Juli 1943

Liebe Kitty!

Um zum soundsovielten Mal auf das Erziehungsthema zurückzukommen, muss ich dir sagen, dass ich mir sehr viel Mühe gebe, hilfsbereit, freundlich und lieb zu sein und alles so zu machen, dass aus dem Beanstandungsregen ein Nieselregen wird. Es ist verflixt schwer, sich Menschen gegenüber, die man nicht ausstehen kann, vorbildlich zu benehmen, während man doch nichts davon so meint. Aber ich sehe wirklich, dass ich weiter komme, wenn ich ein bisschen heuchle, statt meine alte Gewohnheit beizubehalten und jedem geradeheraus meine Meinung zu sagen (obwohl nie jemand nach meiner Meinung fragt oder Wert darauf legt). Natürlich falle ich sehr oft aus der Rolle und kann mir bei Ungerechtigkeiten die Wut nicht verbeißen, sodass wieder vier Wochen lang über das frechste Mädchen der Welt hergezogen wird. Findest du nicht auch, dass ich manchmal zu bedauern bin? Es ist nur gut, dass ich nicht nörglerisch bin, sonst würde ich versauern und meine gute Laune verlieren. Meistens nehme ich die Standpauken von der humorvollen Seite, aber das kann ich besser, wenn jemand anderes sein Fell vollbekommt, als wenn ich selbst die Gelackmeierte bin.

Außerdem habe ich beschlossen (es hat langes Nachdenken gekostet),

Steno erst mal sausen zu lassen. Erstens, um meinen anderen Fächern noch mehr Zeit widmen zu können, und zweitens wegen meiner Augen. Eine elende Misere: Ich bin sehr kurzsichtig geworden und müsste längst eine Brille haben. (Buh, wie eulenhaft werde ich aussehen!) Aber du weißt ja, Versteckte ...

Gestern sprach das ganze Haus von nichts anderem als von Annes Augen, weil Mutter vorgeschlagen hatte, Frau Kleiman mit mir zum Augenarzt zu schicken. Bei dieser Mitteilung wurde mir einen Moment ganz schwindlig, denn das ist auch keine Kleinigkeit. Auf die Straße! Stell dir vor, auf die Straße! Zuerst bekam ich eine Todesangst, später war ich froh. Aber so einfach ging das nicht, denn nicht alle Instanzen, die über einen solchen Schritt zu beschließen haben, waren so schnell damit einverstanden. Alle Schwierigkeiten und Risiken mussten erwogen werden, obwohl sich Miep direkt mit mir auf den Weg machen wollte. Ich holte schon meinen grauen Mantel aus dem Schrank, aber der war so klein, dass er aussah, als gehörte er einer jüngeren Schwester von mir. Der Saum war aufgegangen, und zuknöpfen ließ er sich auch nicht mehr. Ich bin wirklich neugierig, was passiert. Aber ich glaube nicht, dass der Plan ausgeführt werden wird, denn inzwischen sind die Engländer auf Sizilien gelandet, und Vater ist wieder auf ein »baldiges Ende« eingestellt.

Bep gibt Margot und mir viel Büroarbeit, das finden wir beide wichtig, und ihr hilft es. Korrespondenz ablegen und Verkaufsbuch führen kann jeder, aber wir tun es besonders sorgfältig.

Miep schleppt sich ab wie ein Packesel. Fast jeden Tag treibt sie irgendwo Gemüse auf und bringt es in großen Einkaufstaschen auf dem Fahrrad mit. Sie ist es auch, die jeden Samstag fünf Bücher aus der Bibliothek bringt. Sehnsüchtig warten wir immer auf den Samstag, weil dann die Bücher kommen, wie kleine Kinder auf ein Geschenk. Normale Leute können nicht wissen, was Bücher für einen Eingeschlossenen bedeuten. Lesen, Lernen und Radio hören sind unsere einzige Ablenkung.

Deine Anne

Das beste Tischchen

Gestern Nachmittag hatte ich mit Vaters Erlaubnis Dussel gefragt, ob er bitte damit einverstanden sein wolle (doch sehr höflich), dass ich zweimal in der Woche unseren Tisch nachmittags von vier bis halb sechs benutzen dürfe. Von halb drei bis vier Uhr sitze ich jeden Tag dort, während Dussel schläft, und sonst sind das Zimmer und der Tisch verbotenes Gebiet. Drinnen, in unserem allgemeinen Zimmer, ist nachmittags viel zu viel los, da kann man nicht arbeiten. Im Übrigen sitzt Vater nachmittags auch gern am Schreibtisch und arbeitet.

Der Grund war berechtigt und die Frage nur reine Höflichkeit. Was glaubst du nun, was der hochgelehrte Herr Dussel antwortete? »Nein.« Glattweg und nur »Nein«!

Ich war empört und ließ mich nicht einfach so abweisen, fragte ihn also nach den Gründen seines Neins. Aber da habe ich Pech gehabt. Er legte sofort los: »Ich muss auch arbeiten. Wenn ich nachmittags nicht arbeiten kann, bleibt mir überhaupt keine Zeit mehr übrig. Ich muss mein Pensum erledigen, sonst habe ich ganz umsonst damit angefangen. Du arbeitest doch nicht ernsthaft. Die Mythologie, was ist das schon für eine Arbeit! Stricken und Lesen ist auch keine Arbeit! Ich bin und bleibe an dem Tisch.«

Meine Antwort war: »Herr Dussel, ich arbeite sehr wohl ernsthaft. Ich kann drinnen nachmittags nicht arbeiten und bitte Sie freundlich, noch mal über meine Bitte nachzudenken.«

Mit diesen Worten drehte sich die beleidigte Anne um und tat, als wäre der hochgelehrte Doktor Luft. Ich kochte vor Wut, fand Dussel schrecklich unhöflich (und das war er auch!) und mich sehr freundlich.

Abends, als ich Pim erwischte, erzählte ich ihm, wie die Sache abgelaufen war, und besprach mit ihm, was ich nun weiter tun sollte. Denn aufgeben wollte ich nicht, und ich wollte die Angelegenheit lieber allein erledigen. Pim erklärte mir so ungefähr, wie ich die Sache anpacken sollte, ermahnte mich aber, lieber bis zum nächsten Tag zu warten, weil ich so aufgeregt war.

Diesen letzten Rat schlug ich in den Wind und wartete Dussel abends nach dem Spülen ab. Pim saß im Zimmer neben uns, und das gab mir große Ruhe.

»Herr Dussel«, fing ich an, »ich glaube, dass Sie es nicht der Mühe wert fanden, die Sache genauer zu betrachten, und ersuche Sie, es doch zu tun.«

Mit seinem freundlichsten Lächeln bemerkte Dussel daraufhin: »Ich bin immer und jederzeit bereit, über diese inzwischen erledigte Sache zu sprechen.«

Ich fuhr mit dem Gespräch fort, wobei Dussel mich ständig unterbrach: »Wir haben am Anfang, als Sie hierher kamen, abgemacht, dass dieses Zimmer uns beiden gemeinsam gehören soll. Wenn die Aufteilung gerecht wäre, müssten Sie den Vormittag und ich den ganzen Nachmittag bekommen. Aber das verlange ich noch nicht mal, und mir scheint, dann sind zwei Nachmittage in der Woche doch wohl berechtigt.«

Bei diesen Worten sprang Dussel hoch, als hätte ihn jemand mit der Nadel gestochen. »Über Recht hast du hier überhaupt nicht zu sprechen. Wo soll ich denn bleiben? Ich werde Herrn van Daan fragen, ob er auf dem Dachboden einen Verschlag für mich baut, dort kann ich dann sitzen. Ich kann ja auch nirgends mal ruhig arbeiten. Mit dir hat ein Mensch auch immer nur Streit. Wenn deine Schwester Margot, die doch mehr Grund dazu hat, mit dieser Bitte zu mir käme, würde es mir nicht einfallen, sie ihr abzuschlagen, aber du …«

Und dann folgte wieder das von der Mythologie und dem Stricken, und Anne war wiederum beleidigt. Ich zeigte es jedoch nicht und ließ Dussel aussprechen. »Aber mit dir kann man ja nicht reden, du bist eine schändliche Egoistin. Wenn du nur deinen Willen durchsetzen kannst, dann können alle anderen sehen, wo sie bleiben. So ein Kind habe ich noch nie erlebt! Aber letzten Endes werde ich doch genötigt sein, dir deinen Willen zu lassen, denn sonst bekomme ich später zu hören, Anne Frank ist durch das Examen gefallen, weil Herr Dussel ihr den Tisch nicht überlassen wollte.«

So ging es weiter und immer weiter. Zuletzt wurde eine solche Flut daraus, dass ich fast nicht mehr mitkam. Den einen Augenblick dachte ich: Ich schlage ihm direkt aufs Maul, dass er mit seinen Lügen gegen die Wand fliegt! Und im nächsten Augenblick sagte ich mir: Bleib ruhig, dieser Kerl ist es nicht wert, dass du dich so über ihn aufregst.

Endlich hatte sich Herr Dussel ausgetobt und ging mit einem Gesicht, auf dem sowohl Wut als auch Triumph zu lesen waren, und mit seinem Mantel voller Esswaren aus dem Zimmer.

Ich rannte zu Vater und erzählte ihm die ganze Geschichte, soweit er sie nicht mitbekommen hatte. Pim beschloss, noch am selben Abend mit Dussel zu sprechen, und so geschah es. Sie redeten mehr als eine halbe Stunde miteinander. Erst ging es darum, ob Anne an dem Tisch sitzen solle oder nicht. Vater erinnerte Dussel daran, dass sie schon einmal über dieses Thema gesprochen hätten und dass er damals Dussel Recht gegeben hätte, um den Älteren der Jüngeren gegenüber nicht ins Unrecht zu setzen, aber berechtigt habe er es damals schon nicht gefunden. Dussel meinte, dass ich nicht sprechen dürfe, als wäre er ein Eindringling und nähme alles in Beschlag. Aber dem widersprach Vater entschieden, denn er hatte selbst gehört, dass ich darüber kein Wort gesagt hatte. So ging es hin und her, Vater verteidigte meinen angeblichen Egoismus und meine Pfuscharbeit, und Dussel maulte.

Endlich musste Dussel dann doch nachgeben, und ich bekam an zwei Nachmittagen in der Woche die Gelegenheit, ungestört zu arbeiten. Dussel sah sehr betreten aus, sprach zwei Tage nicht mit mir und musste sich dann von fünf bis halb sechs doch noch an den Tisch setzen. Kindisch, natürlich.

Jemand, der schon 54 Jahre alt ist und noch so pedantisch und kleinlich, ist von der Natur so gemacht und gewöhnt sich das auch nie mehr ab.

Freitag, 16. Juli 1943

Liebe Kitty!

Schon wieder ein Einbruch, aber diesmal ein echter! Heute Morgen ging Peter wie gewöhnlich um sieben Uhr zum Lager und sah sofort, dass sowohl die Lager- als auch die Straßentür offen standen. Er berichtete das sofort Pim, der im Privatbüro das Radio auf den deutschen Sender zurückdrehte und die Tür schloss. Zusammen gingen sie dann nach oben. Das normale Kommando in solchen Fällen »Nicht waschen, still sein, um acht Uhr fix und fertig dasitzen, nicht zum Klo gehen!«, wurde wie gewöhnlich genau befolgt. Wir waren alle acht froh, dass wir nachts so gut geschlafen und nichts gehört hatten. Ein wenig waren wir empört, als sich den ganzen Morgen niemand um uns kümmerte und Herr Kleiman uns bis halb zwölf warten ließ. Er erzählte, dass die Einbrecher die Außentür mit einem Stemmeisen eingestoßen und die Lagertür aufgebrochen hatten. Im Lager gab es jedoch nicht viel zu stehlen, und deshalb versuchten die Diebe ihr Glück eben eine Etage höher. Sie haben zwei Geldkassetten mit vierzig Gulden und Scheckbücher gestohlen und, was am schlimmsten ist, unsere ganzen Marken für die Zuckerzuteilung von 150 kg. Es wird nicht leicht sein, neue Marken zu besorgen.

Herr Kugler denkt, dass dieser Einbrecher zur selben Gilde gehört wie derjenige, der vor sechs Wochen hier war und an allen drei Türen (1 Lagertür, 2 Haustüren) versucht hat, hereinzukommen, dem es damals aber nicht gelungen war.

Der Fall hat wieder etwas Aufregung verursacht, aber ohne das scheint das Hinterhaus nicht auszukommen. Wir waren natürlich froh, dass die Schreibmaschinen und die Kasse sicher in unserem Kleiderschrank verwahrt waren.   Deine Anne

P. S. Landung auf Sizilien. Wieder ein Schritt näher zum …

                                        Montag, 19. Juli 1943
Liebe Kitty!
Am Sonntag ist Amsterdam-Nord sehr schwer bombardiert worden. Die Verwüstung muss entsetzlich sein, ganze Straßen liegen in Schutt, und es wird noch lange dauern, bis alle Verschütteten ausgegraben sind. Bis jetzt gibt es 200 Tote und unzählige Verwundete, die Krankenhäuser sind übervoll. Man hört von Kindern, die verloren in den schwelenden Ruinen nach ihren toten Eltern suchen. Es überläuft mich immer noch kalt, wenn ich an das dumpfe, dröhnende Grollen in der Ferne denke, das für uns das Zeichen der nahenden Vernichtung war.

Freitag, 23. Juli 1943

Bep kann im Moment wieder Hefte bekommen, vor allem Journale und Hauptbücher, nützlich für Margot, meine buchhaltende Schwester. Andere Hefte gibt es auch zu kaufen, aber frage nicht, was für welche und für wie lange noch. Hefte haben zur Zeit die Aufschrift »Markenfrei erhältlich«. Genau wie alles andere, was noch »markenfrei« ist, sind sie unter aller Kritik. So ein Heft besteht aus zwölf Seiten grauem, schief- und engliniertem Papier. Margot überlegt, ob sie einen Fernkurs in Schönschreiben belegen soll. Ich habe ihr zugeraten. Mutter will aber auf keinen Fall, dass ich auch mitmache, wegen meiner Augen. Ich finde das dumm. Ob ich nun das mache oder etwas anderes, das bleibt sich doch gleich.

Da du noch nie einen Krieg mitgemacht hast, Kitty, und du trotz all meiner Briefe doch wenig vom Verstecken weißt, will ich dir zum Spaß mal erzählen, was der erste Wunsch von uns acht ist, wenn wir wieder mal hinauskommen.

Margot und Herr van Daan wünschen sich am meisten ein heißes Bad, bis zum Rand gefüllt, und wollen darin mehr als eine halbe Stunde bleiben. Frau van Daan will am liebsten sofort Torten essen. Dussel kennt nichts als seine Charlotte, und Mutter ihre Tasse Kaffee. Vater geht zu Voskuijls, Peter in die Stadt und ins Kino, und ich würde vor lauter Seligkeit nicht wissen, wo anfangen.

Am meisten sehne ich mich nach unserer eigenen Wohnung, nach freier Bewegung und endlich wieder nach Hilfe bei der Arbeit, also nach der Schule!

Bep hat uns Obst angeboten, aber es kostet ein kleines Vermögen. Trauben 5 Gulden pro Kilo, Stachelbeeren 1,40 Gulden, ein Pfirsich 40 Cent, ein Kilo Melonen 1,50 Gulden. Und dann steht jeden Tag mit Riesenbuchstaben in der Zeitung: »Preistreiberei ist Wucher!«

Montag, 26. Juli 1943

Beste Kitty!

Gestern war ein stürmischer Tag, und wir sind noch immer aufgeregt. Eigentlich kannst du fragen, welcher Tag bei uns ohne Aufregung vorbeigeht.

Morgens beim Frühstück gab es zum ersten Mal Voralarm, aber das

Das drehbare Bücherregal, das den Zugang zum Hinterhaus verbarg.

stört uns nicht, weil es bedeutet, dass die Flugzeuge an der Küste sind. Nach dem Frühstück habe ich mich eine Stunde hingelegt, denn ich hatte starke Kopfschmerzen, und dann ging ich hinunter ins Büro. Es war ungefähr zwei Uhr. Um halb drei war Margot mit ihrer Büroarbeit fertig. Sie hatte ihren Kram noch nicht wieder weggeräumt, als die Sirenen heulten, daher ging ich mit ihr hinauf. Es war höchste Zeit, denn fünf Minuten später fing die Schießerei an, so laut, dass wir uns in den Flur stellten. Das Haus dröhnte, und die Bomben fielen. Ich drückte meine Fluchttasche an mich, mehr, um mich an etwas festzuhalten, als um zu flüchten, denn wir können ja doch nicht weg. Im Notfall ist für uns die Straße genauso lebensgefährlich wie eine Bombardierung. Nach einer halben Stunde kamen weniger Flugzeuge, aber die Geschäftigkeit im Haus nahm zu. Peter kam von seinem Beobachtungsposten auf dem vorderen Dachboden herunter, Dussel war im vorderen Büro, Frau van Daan fühlte sich im Privatbüro sicher, Herr van Daan hatte vom Oberboden aus zugeschaut, und wir in der Diele zerstreuten uns auch, um die Rauchsäulen zu sehen, die über dem IJ* aufstiegen. Bald roch es überall nach Brand, und draußen sah es aus, als ob ein dicker Nebel über der Stadt hinge.

Ein so großer Brand ist kein schöner Anblick, aber wir waren froh, dass wir es mal wieder glücklich hinter uns hatten, und begaben uns an unsere jeweiligen Tätigkeiten.

Abends beim Essen: Luftalarm! Wir hatten ein leckeres Essen, aber der Appetit verging mir schon allein bei dem Geräusch. Es passierte jedoch nichts, und eine Dreiviertelstunde später war die Gefahr vorbei. Als der Abwasch an die Reihe kam: Luftalarm, Schießen, fürchterlich viele Flugzeuge. Oje, zweimal an einem Tag, das ist sehr viel, dachten wir. Aber es half nichts, wieder regnete es Bomben, diesmal auf der anderen Seite, auf Schiphol, laut Bericht der Engländer. Die Flugzeuge tauchten, stiegen, es sauste in der Luft, und es war sehr unheimlich. Jeden Augenblick dachte ich, jetzt stürzt er ab, das war's dann.

Ich versichere dir, dass ich meine Beine noch nicht gerade halten konnte, als ich um neun Uhr ins Bett ging. Punkt zwölf wurde ich wach: Flugzeuge! Dussel zog sich gerade aus. Ich kümmerte mich

* Hafen von Amsterdam; A. d. Ü.

nicht darum, ich sprang beim ersten Schuss hellwach aus dem Bett. Bis ein Uhr war ich drüben, um halb zwei im Bett, um zwei wieder bei Vater, und sie flogen immer und immer noch. Dann wurde kein Schuss mehr abgegeben, und ich konnte zurück. Um halb drei bin ich eingeschlafen.

Sieben Uhr. Mit einem Schlag saß ich aufrecht im Bett. Van Daan war bei Vater. Einbrecher, war mein erster Gedanke. »Alles«, hörte ich van Daan sagen und dachte, dass alles gestohlen worden sei. Aber nein, es war ein herrlicher Bericht, so schön, wie wir ihn seit Monaten, vielleicht noch nie in all den Kriegsjahren, gehört haben. Mussolini ist abgetreten, der Kaiserkönig von Italien hat die Regierung übernommen.

Wir jubelten. Nach all dem Schrecklichen von gestern endlich wieder was Gutes, und … Hoffnung! Hoffnung auf das Ende! Hoffnung auf den Frieden!

Kugler ist eben vorbeigekommen und hat erzählt, dass Fokker schwer heimgesucht worden ist. Auch heute Morgen hatten wir wieder Luftalarm, mit Flugzeugen, die über uns hinwegflogen, und noch einmal Voralarm. Ich ersticke in Alarmen, bin nicht ausgeschlafen und habe keine Lust zu arbeiten. Aber jetzt hält uns die Spannung um Italien wach, und die Hoffnung auf das Ende des Jahres … Deine Anne

Donnerstag, 29. Juli 1943

Liebe Kitty!

Frau van Daan, Dussel und ich waren mit dem Abwasch beschäftigt, und ich war, was selten vorkommt und ihnen auffallen musste, außergewöhnlich still. Um Fragen vorzubeugen, suchte ich also schnell nach einem ziemlich neutralen Thema und hielt das Buch »Henri van de Overkant« für geeignet. Aber ich hatte mich verrechnet. Wenn ich von Frau van Daan nichts aufs Dach kriege, dann ist es Herr Dussel. Es lief auf Folgendes hinaus: Herr Dussel hatte uns dieses Buch als etwas ganz Besonderes empfohlen, Margot und ich fanden es jedoch alles andere als hervorragend. Der Junge war zwar gut beschrieben, aber der Rest … Darüber schweige ich lieber. Etwas Derartiges brachte ich beim Abwaschen aufs Tapet, und dann bekam ich es ab, aber dick!

»Wie kannst du die Psyche eines Mannes begreifen? Die von einem Kind, das ist nicht so schwierig(!). Du bist viel zu jung für ein solches Buch. Ein Zwanzigjähriger könnte es kaum erfassen.« (Warum hat er mir und Margot dieses Buch dann so empfohlen?)

Nun fuhren Dussel und Frau van Daan gemeinsam fort: »Du weißt viel zu viel von Dingen, die für dich nicht geeignet sind, du bist völlig falsch erzogen. Später, wenn du älter bist, hast du an nichts mehr Vergnügen, dann sagst du: Das habe ich vor zwanzig Jahren schon in Büchern gelesen. Du musst dich schon beeilen, wenn du noch einen Mann bekommen oder dich verlieben willst, du bist bestimmt von allem enttäuscht. In der Theorie weißt du alles, nur die Praxis fehlt dir noch!«

Wer könnte sich meine Situation nicht vorstellen? Ich wunderte mich, dass ich ruhig antworten konnte. »Sie denken vielleicht, dass ich falsch erzogen bin, aber diese Meinung teilt nicht jeder!«

Sicher ist es gute Erziehung, wenn sie mich gegen meine Eltern aufhetzen! Denn das tun sie oft. Und einem Mädchen in meinem Alter nichts über bestimmte Dinge zu erzählen, ist wohl auch hervorragend. Die Ergebnisse einer solchen Erziehung sieht man nur allzu deutlich.

Ich hätte den beiden, die mich so lächerlich machten, in diesem Moment ins Gesicht schlagen können. Ich war außer mir vor Wut und würde die Tage zählen (wenn ich wüsste, wo aufhören), bis ich diese Menschen los bin.

Sie ist schon ein Exemplar, diese Frau van Daan! An ihr sollte man sich ein Beispiel nehmen ... aber ein schlechtes Beispiel! Frau van Daan ist bekannt als unbescheiden, egoistisch, schlau, berechnend und mit nichts zufrieden. Eitelkeit und Koketterie kommen noch dazu. Sie ist, daran ist nichts zu rütteln, eine ausgesprochen unangenehme Person. Ganze Bände könnte ich über sie füllen, und wer weiß, vielleicht komme ich noch dazu. Einen schönen Firnis auf der Oberfläche kann sich jeder zulegen. Frau van Daan ist freundlich zu Fremden, vor allem zu Männern, und deshalb täuscht man sich, wenn man sie erst kurz kennt.

Mutter findet sie zu dumm, um ein Wort darüber zu verlieren, Margot zu unwichtig, Pim zu hässlich (buchstäblich und im übertragenen Sinn), und ich bin nach langer Beobachtung, denn ich bin nie voreingenommen, zu dem Schluss gekommen, dass sie dies alles ist – und noch viel mehr. Sie hat so viele schlechte Eigenschaften, warum sollte ich dann mit einer davon anfangen? Deine Anne

P. S. Die Leser mögen zur Kenntnis nehmen, dass, als diese Geschichte geschrieben wurde, die Wut der Schreiberin noch nicht abgekühlt war.

Dienstag, 3. August 1943

Liebe Kitty!

Mit der Politik geht es ausgezeichnet. In Italien ist die faschistische Partei verboten worden. An vielen Stellen kämpft das Volk gegen die Faschisten, auch Soldaten nehmen an dem Kampf teil. Wie kann so ein Land noch weiter Krieg mit England führen?

Unser schönes Radio ist letzte Woche weggebracht worden. Dussel war sehr böse, dass Kugler es zum festgelegten Datum abgeliefert hat. Dussel sinkt in meiner Achtung immer tiefer, er ist schon unter Null. Was er auch sagt über Politik, Geschichte, Erdkunde oder andere Themen, es ist so ein Unsinn, dass ich es fast nicht zu wiederholen wage. Hitler verschwindet in der Geschichte. Der Hafen von Rotterdam ist größer als der von Hamburg. Die Engländer sind Idioten, weil sie im Augenblick Italien nicht kurz und klein bombardieren usw. usw.

Eine dritte Bombardierung hat stattgefunden, und ich habe die Zähne aufeinander gebissen und mich in Mut geübt.

Frau van Daan, die immer sagt »Lass sie nur kommen« oder »Besser ein Ende mit Schrecken als gar kein Ende« ist nun die Feigste von uns allen. Heute Morgen hat sie gebebt wie ein Rohrstängel und brach sogar in Tränen aus. Ihr Mann, mit dem sie nach einer Woche Streit gerade wieder Frieden geschlossen hatte, tröstete sie. Ich wurde fast sentimental bei diesem Anblick.

Dass Katzenhaltung nicht nur Vorteile bringt, hat Mouschi uns eindeutig bewiesen. Das ganze Haus ist voller Flöhe, und die Plage nimmt mit jedem Tag zu. Herr Kleiman hat gelben Puder in alle Ecken gestreut, den Flöhen macht das aber nichts aus. Wir werden schon ganz nervös. Immer meint man, etwas auf Armen, Beinen oder anderen Körperteilen herumkrabbeln zu fühlen, und dauernd verrenkt sich jemand, um etwas auf Bein oder Hals zu entdecken. Nun rächt sich die geringe körperliche Bewegung: Wir sind viel zu steif geworden, um den Nacken richtig zu drehen. Wirkliche Gymnastik haben wir schon längst aufgegeben.   Deine Anne

Mittwoch, 4. August 1943

Liebe Kitty!

Du weißt nun, nachdem wir seit gut einem Jahr Hinterhäusler sind, schon einiges über unser Leben, aber vollständig kann ich dich doch nicht informieren. Es ist alles so anders als in normalen Zeiten und bei normalen Leuten. Um dir einen genaueren Einblick in unser Leben zu ermöglichen, werde ich jetzt ab und zu einen Teil unseres normalen Tagesablaufs beschreiben. Heute fange ich mit dem Abend und der Nacht an.

<u>Abends um neun</u> Uhr fängt im Hinterhaus der Rummel mit dem Ins-Bett-Gehen an, und es ist tatsächlich immer ein Rummel. Stühle werden geschoben, Betten herausgeholt, Decken aufgefaltet, und nichts bleibt, wo es tagsüber zu sein hat. Ich schlafe auf der kleinen Couch, die noch nicht mal 1,50 Meter lang ist. Also müssen Stühle als Verlängerung dienen. Plumeau, Laken, Kissen, Decken – alles wird aus Dussels Bett geholt, wo es tagsüber untergebracht ist.

Von drüben hört man ein schreckliches Knarren von Margots Bett à la Harmonika. Wieder Couchdecken und Kissen, um die hölzernen Latten ein bisschen bequemer zu machen. Oben scheint es zu gewittern, es ist aber nur das Bett von Frau van Daan. Das wird nämlich ans Fenster geschoben, damit Ihre Hoheit im rosa Bettjäckchen etwas frische Luft in die kleinen Nasenlöcher bekommt.

<u>Neun Uhr:</u> Nach Peter betrete ich das Badezimmer, wo dann eine gründliche Wäsche folgt. Nicht selten passiert es (nur in den heißen Monaten, Wochen oder Tagen), dass ein kleiner Floh im Waschwasser treibt. Dann Zähne putzen, Haare locken, Nägel pflegen, der Wattebausch mit Wasserstoff (um schwarze Schnurrbarthaare zu bleichen), und das alles in einer knappen halben Stunde.

<u>Halb zehn:</u> Schnell den Bademantel angezogen. Die Seife in der einen Hand, Nachttopf, Haarnadeln, Hose, Lockenwickler und Watte in der

anderen, eile ich aus dem Badezimmer, meistens noch zurückgerufen wegen der Haare, die in zierlichen, aber für den nachfolgenden Wäscher nicht angenehmen Bögen das Waschbecken verunzieren.

<u>Zehn Uhr:</u> Verdunklung vor, gute Nacht! Eine gute Viertelstunde lang noch das Knarren von Betten und das Seufzen von kaputten Federn, dann ist alles still. Wenigstens dann, wenn die oben keinen Streit im Bett haben.

<u>Halb zwölf:</u> Die Zimmertür quietscht. Ein dünner Lichtstreifen fällt ins Zimmer. Das Knarren von Schuhen, ein großer Mantel, noch größer als der Mann, der in ihm steckt ... Dussel kommt von seiner nächtlichen Arbeit in Kuglers Büro zurück. Zehn Minuten lang Schlurfen auf dem Boden, das Rascheln von Papier (von den Esswaren, die er versteckt), ein Bett wird gemacht. Dann verschwindet die Gestalt wieder, und man hört nur von Zeit zu Zeit aus der Toilette ein verdächtiges Geräusch.

<u>Ungefähr drei Uhr:</u> Ich muss aufstehen, um ein kleines Geschäft in die Blechdose unter meinem Bett zu verrichten, unter die vorsichtshalber noch eine Gummimatte gelegt worden ist, falls das Ding leckt. Wenn das nötig ist, halte ich immer die Luft an, denn es plätschert in die Dose wie ein Bach von einem Berg. Dann kommt die Dose wieder an ihren Platz, und die Gestalt in dem weißen Nachthemd, das Margot jeden Abend den Ausruf entlockt »Oh, dieses unsittliche Nachthemd«, steigt wieder ins Bett. Eine knappe Viertelstunde liegt dann die gewisse Person und horcht auf die nächtlichen Geräusche. Zuerst, ob unten vielleicht ein Dieb sein könnte, dann auf die Geräusche von den diversen Betten, oben, nebenan und im Zimmer, denen man meistens entnehmen kann, ob die verschiedenen Hausgenossen schlafen oder halb wach die Nacht verbringen. Letzteres ist nicht angenehm, vor allem, wenn es um ein Familienmitglied namens Dr. D. geht. Erst höre ich ein Geräusch, als ob ein Fisch nach Luft schnappt. Das wiederholt sich ungefähr zehnmal, dann werden umständlich die Lippen befeuchtet oder man hört kleine Schmatzgeräusche, gefolgt von einem langdauernden Hin- und Herdrehen im Bett und dem Verschieben von Kissen. Fünf Minuten herrscht vollkommene Ruhe, dann wiederholt sich der Ablauf der Ereignisse mindestens noch dreimal, bis sich der Doktor wieder für eine Weile in den Schlaf gelullt hat.

Es kann auch vorkommen, dass irgendwann nachts zwischen eins und vier geschossen wird. Ich bin mir dessen kaum bewusst, da stehe ich aus Gewohnheit neben meinem Bett. Manchmal bin ich auch so in Träume versunken, dass ich an französische unregelmäßige Verben oder einen kleinen Streit oben denke und erst dann merke, dass geschossen wird und ich ruhig im Zimmer geblieben bin. Aber meistens passiert, was ich oben gesagt habe. Schnell ein Kissen und ein Taschentuch geschnappt, Bademantel und Pantoffeln angezogen und zu Vater gerannt, genau so, wie Margot es in dem Geburtstagsgedicht beschrieben hat:

»Des Nachts, beim allerersten Krach

Steht gleich danach in unsrem Gemach

Ein kleines Mädchen, lieb und nett

Mit flehendem Blick an Vaters Bett.«

Im großen Bett angelangt, ist der ärgste Schreck schon vorbei, außer wenn das Schießen sehr laut ist.

<u>Viertel vor sieben:</u> Rrrrr … Der Wecker, der zu jeder Stunde des Tages, ob man es braucht oder nicht, loslegen kann. Knack … peng, Frau van Daan hat ihn ausgemacht. Krach … Herr van Daan ist aufgestanden. Wasser aufstellen, dann flugs ins Badezimmer.

<u>Viertel nach sieben:</u> Die Tür knarrt wieder. Dussel kann ins Badezimmer gehen. Endlich allein, entferne ich die Verdunklung, und der neue Tag im Hinterhaus hat begonnen.   Deine Anne

Donnerstag, 5. August 1943

Heute nehmen wir mal die Mittagspause dran.

<u>Es ist halb eins.</u> Der ganze Haufen atmet auf. Nun sind van Maaren, der Mann mit der dunklen Vergangenheit, und de Kok nach Hause gegangen. Oben hört man das Stampfen des Staubsaugers auf dem schönen und einzigen Teppich von Frau van Daan. Margot nimmt ein paar Bücher unter den Arm und geht zum Unterricht für »lernbehinderte Kinder«, denn so wirkt Dussel. Pim setzt sich mit seinem ewigen Dickens in eine ruhige Ecke. Mutter eilt eine Etage höher, um der eifrigen Hausfrau zu helfen, und ich gehe ins Badezimmer, um dieses – gleichzeitig mit mir selbst – etwas zu verschönern.

<u>Viertel vor eins:</u> Nach und nach tröpfeln alle ein. Erst Herr Gies, dann Kleiman oder Kugler, Bep und manchmal für kurze Zeit auch Miep.

<u>Ein Uhr:</u> Alle sitzen um das kleine Radio und lauschen gespannt dem BBC, und das sind die einzigen Minuten, in denen sich die Mitglieder des Hinterhauses nicht gegenseitig ins Wort fallen, denn da spricht jemand, dem sogar Herr van Daan nicht widersprechen kann.

<u>Viertel nach eins:</u> Das große Austeilen. Jeder von unten bekommt eine Tasse Suppe, und wenn es mal Nachtisch gibt, auch davon etwas. Zufrieden setzt sich Herr Gies auf die Couch oder lehnt sich an den Schreibtisch, die Zeitung und die Tasse und meistens auch die Katze neben sich. Wenn eines von den dreien fehlt, hört er nicht auf zu protestieren. Kleiman erzählt die letzten Neuigkeiten aus der Stadt, dafür ist er tatsächlich eine hervorragende Quelle. Kugler kommt holterdiepolter die Treppe herauf. Ein kurzes und kräftiges Klopfen an der Tür, und er kommt händereibend herein, je nach Stimmung gut gelaunt und geschäftig oder schlecht gelaunt und still.

<u>Viertel vor zwei:</u> Die Esser erheben sich, und jeder geht wieder seiner Beschäftigung nach. Margot und Mutter machen den Abwasch, Herr und Frau van Daan legen sich auf die Couch, Peter geht auf den Dachboden, Vater auf die Couch, Dussel auch, und Anne macht sich an die Arbeit.

Nun folgt die ruhigste Stunde. Wenn alle schlafen, wird niemand gestört. Dussel träumt von leckerem Essen, das sieht man seinem Gesicht an. Aber ich betrachte es nicht lange, denn die Zeit rennt, und um vier Uhr steht der pedantische Doktor schon mit der Uhr in der Hand da, weil ich eine Minute zu spät den Tisch für ihn räume.

Deine Anne

Samstag, 7. August 1943

Liebe Kitty!

Ich habe vor ein paar Wochen angefangen, eine Geschichte zu schreiben, etwas, das ganz ausgedacht ist, und es macht mir so viel Freude, dass sich meine Federkinder schon stapeln.   Deine Anne

Liebe Kitty!

Diesmal die Fortsetzung des Tagesablaufs im Hinterhaus. Nach der Mittagspause ist der Mittagstisch an der Reihe.

<u>Herr van Daan:</u> Er eröffnet den Reigen. Er wird als Erster bedient, nimmt beträchtlich viel von allem, wenn es ihm schmeckt. Er redet meistens mit, gibt immer seine Meinung zum Besten, und wenn er das getan hat, gibt es nichts mehr daran zu rütteln. Wenn jemand das wagt, dann hat er es in sich. Ach, er kann einen anfauchen wie eine Katze! Ich möchte das lieber nicht erleben. Wer es einmal mitgemacht hat, hütet sich vor dem zweiten Mal. Er hat die einzig richtige Meinung, er weiß über alles das meiste. Na gut, er hat einen gescheiten Kopf, aber die Selbstgefälligkeit dieses Herrn hat ein hohes Maß erreicht.

<u>Die gnädige Frau:</u> Eigentlich sollte ich besser schweigen. An manchen Tagen, vor allem, wenn sie schlecht gelaunt ist, schaut man ihr Gesicht besser nicht an. Genau genommen ist sie an allen Diskussionen schuld. Nicht das Objekt! Oh nein, jeder hütet sich davor, sie anzugreifen, aber man könnte sie die Anstifterin nennen. Hetzen, das ist ihre liebste Beschäftigung. Hetzen gegen Frau Frank und Anne. Gegen Margot und Herrn Frank geht Hetzen nicht so leicht.

Aber nun zu Tisch. Frau van Daan kommt nicht zu kurz, auch wenn sie das manchmal denkt. Die kleinsten Kartoffeln, die leckersten Häppchen, das Zarteste von allem heraussuchen, das ist Madames Parole. Die anderen kommen schon noch an die Reihe, wenn ich erst das Beste habe. (Genau das, was sie von Anne Frank denkt.) Das andere ist Reden. Hauptsache, es hört jemand zu, ob es denjenigen interessiert oder nicht, darauf kommt es offenbar nicht an. Sie denkt sicher, was Frau van Daan interessiert, interessiert jeden. Kokett lächeln, tun, als wüsste man von allem etwas, jedem einen guten Rat geben und jeden bemuttern, das <u>muss</u> doch einen guten Eindruck machen. Aber schaut man genauer hin, geht der Lack ab. Fleißig, *eins,* fröhlich, *zwei,* kokett, *drei,* und manchmal ein hübsches Lärvchen. Das ist Petronella van Daan.

<u>Der dritte Tischgenosse:</u> Man hört nicht viel von ihm. Der junge Herr van Daan ist meistens still und unauffällig. Was den Appetit betrifft: ein Danaidenfass, es wird niemals voll, und nach der kräftigsten

Mahlzeit behauptet er seelenruhig, dass er bestimmt noch mal das Doppelte essen könnte.

Nummer 4 ist Margot!: Isst wie ein Mäuschen, redet überhaupt nicht. Das Einzige, was bei ihr reingeht, ist Gemüse oder Obst. »Verwöhnt« ist das Urteil von Herrn und Frau van Daan. »Zu wenig frische Luft und Sport« ist unsere Meinung.

Daneben Mama: Appetit gut, redet eifrig. Niemand kommt bei ihr, wie bei Frau van Daan, auf den Gedanken: Das ist die Hausfrau. Worin der Unterschied liegt? Nun, Frau van Daan kocht, und Mutter spült und putzt.

Nummer 6 und 7: Über Vater und mich werde ich nicht viel sagen. Ersterer ist der Bescheidenste am Tisch. Er schaut immer erst, ob die anderen schon haben. Er braucht nichts, die besten Sachen sind für die Kinder. Er ist ein Vorbild an Güte, und neben ihm sitzt das Nervenbündel vom Hinterhaus!

Dussel: Nimmt, schaut nicht, isst, redet nicht. Und wenn schon geredet werden muss, dann um Himmels willen nur über Essen, das führt nicht zu Streit, nur zu Aufschneiderei. Enorme Portionen passen in ihn, und »nein« sagt er nie, nicht bei den guten Sachen und auch nicht oft bei schlechten.

Die Hose bis zur Brust hochgezogen, eine rote Jacke, schwarze Lackpantoffeln und eine Hornbrille. So kann man ihn am Arbeitstisch sehen, ewig arbeitend, ohne Fortschritte, nur unterbrochen vom Mittagsschläfchen, dem Essen und (seinem Lieblingsort) dem Klo. Drei-, vier-, fünfmal am Tag steht jemand ungeduldig vor der Klotür und verkneift es sich, hüpft von einem Bein aufs andere und kann es kaum mehr halten. Stört er sich daran? Nicht doch! Von Viertel nach sieben bis halb acht, von halb eins bis eins, von zwei bis Viertel nach zwei, von vier bis Viertel nach vier, von sechs bis Viertel nach sechs und von halb zwölf bis zwölf Uhr nachts, danach kann man sich richten, das sind seine festen »Sitzungen«. Davon wird nicht abgewichen, und er lässt sich auch nicht durch die flehende Stimme vor der Tür stören, die vor einem schnell nahenden Unheil warnt.

Nummer 9 ist kein Hinterhaus-Familienmitglied, aber doch Haus- und Tischgenossin. Bep hat einen gesunden Appetit. Sie lässt nichts stehen, ist nicht wählerisch. Mit allem kann man sie erfreuen, und

das gerade erfreut uns. Fröhlich und gut gelaunt, willig und gutmütig, das sind ihre Kennzeichen.

Liebe Kitty!

Eine neue Idee! Ich rede bei Tisch mehr mit mir selbst als mit den
anderen. Das ist in zweierlei Hinsicht günstig. Erstens sind alle froh,
wenn ich nicht ununterbrochen quatsche, und zweitens brauche ich
mich über die Meinung anderer Leute nicht zu ärgern. Meine eigene
Meinung finde ich nicht blöd, die anderen tun das aber, also kann ich
sie genauso gut für mich behalten. Ebenso mache ich es, wenn ich etwas essen muss, was ich überhaupt nicht ausstehen kann. Ich stelle
den Teller vor mich und bilde mir ein, es sei etwas sehr Leckeres,
schaue möglichst wenig hin, und ehe ich mich versehe, ist es aufgegessen. Morgens beim Aufstehen – auch etwas, was nicht angenehm
ist – springe ich aus dem Bett, denke mir »du legst dich gleich wieder
gemütlich rein«, laufe zum Fenster, mache die Verdunklung weg,
schnüffle so lange an dem Spalt, bis ich ein bisschen frische Luft spü-
re, und bin hellwach. Das Bett wird so schnell wie möglich auseinander gelegt, dann ist die Verführung weg. Weißt du, wie Mutter so etwas nennt? Eine Lebenskünstlerin. Findest du das Wort nicht auch
witzig?

Seit einer Woche sind wir alle ein bisschen durcheinander mit der
Zeit, weil anscheinend unsere liebe und teure Westerturmglocke
weggeholt worden ist, für irgendeine Fabrik, und wir wissen seither
weder bei Tag noch bei Nacht genau, wie spät es ist. Ich hoffe, man
wird etwas finden, was der Nachbarschaft die Glocke wenigstens ein
bisschen ersetzt, ein zinnernes, kupfernes oder was weiß ich für ein
Ding.

Wo ich auch bin, unten oder oben oder wo auch immer, jeder schaut
mir bewundernd auf die Füße, an denen ein paar außergewöhnlich
schöne Schuhe (für diese Zeit!) prangen. Miep hat sie für 27,50 Gulden ergattert. Weinrot, Peau de Suède und mit einem ziemlich hohen
Blockabsatz. Ich gehe wie auf Stelzen und sehe noch größer aus, als
ich ohnehin schon bin.

Gestern hatte ich einen Unglückstag. Ich stach mich mit dem hinteren Ende einer dicken Nadel in den rechten Daumen. Die Folge war, dass Margot an meiner Stelle die Kartoffeln schälen musste (das Gute beim Schlechten) und ich krakelig schrieb. Dann rannte ich mit dem Kopf gegen die Schranktür, fiel fast rückwärts um, bekam einen Rüffel wegen des Lärms, den ich wieder gemacht hatte, durfte den Wasserhahn nicht aufdrehen, um meine Stirn zu betupfen, und laufe nun mit einer Riesenbeule über dem rechten Auge herum. Zu allem Unglück blieb ich mit meinem rechten kleinen Zeh im Stift vom Staubsauger hängen. Es blutete und tat weh, aber ich hatte so viel mit meinen anderen Leiden zu tun, dass dieses Wehwehchen dagegen ins Nichts versank. Dumm genug, denn nun laufe ich mit einem infizierten Zeh und Zugsalbe, Verbandmull und Heftpflaster herum und kann meine großartigen Schuhe nicht anziehen.

Dussel hat uns zum soundsovielten Mal in Lebensgefahr gebracht. Miep brachte wahrhaftig ein verbotenes Buch für ihn mit, eine Schmähschrift über Mussolini. Unterwegs wurde sie von einem SS-Motorrad angefahren. Sie verlor die Nerven, schrie »Elende Schufte!«, und fuhr weiter. Ich will lieber nicht daran denken, was passiert wäre, wenn sie mit zum Büro gemusst hätte!

Deine Anne

Die Pflicht des Tages in der Gemeinschaft: Kartoffelschälen!
Der eine holt das Zeitungspapier, der zweite die Messer (und behält natürlich das beste für sich selbst), der dritte die Kartoffeln, der vierte das Wasser.

Herr Dussel fängt an. Er schält nicht immer gut, dafür aber ohne Pause, schaut kurz nach links und rechts, ob jeder es auch ja auf die gleiche Art tut wie er. Nein!

»Anne, schau mal, ich nehme das Messer so in die Hand, schäle von oben nach unten! Nein, so nicht, sondern so!«

»Ich finde es anders bequemer, Herr Dussel«, bemerke ich schüchtern.

»Aber das ist doch die beste Art, du kannst es mir glauben. Mir kann es natürlich egal sein, du musst es selbst wissen.«

Wir schälen wieder weiter. Ich schaue verstohlen zu meinem Nachbarn hinüber. Der schüttelt gedankenverloren den Kopf (sicher über mich), schweigt aber.

Ich schäle weiter, schaue dann kurz zur anderen Seite, wo Vater sitzt. Für Vater ist Kartoffelschälen nicht einfach eine Tätigkeit, sondern eine Präzisionsarbeit. Wenn er liest, hat er eine tiefe Falte am Hinterkopf, wenn er aber hilft, Kartoffeln, Bohnen oder anderes Gemüse vorzubereiten, dann scheint überhaupt gar nichts zu ihm durchzudringen, dann hat er sein Kartoffelgesicht. Und nie wird er eine weniger gut geschälte Kartoffel abliefern, das gibt es einfach nicht, wenn er so ein Gesicht macht.

Ich arbeite weiter, schaue kurz auf und weiß genug. Frau van Daan versucht, ob sie Dussels Aufmerksamkeit auf sich ziehen kann. Erst schaut sie zu ihm hin, und Dussel tut, als ob er nichts merkt. Dann zwinkert sie ihm zu, Dussel arbeitet weiter. Dann lacht sie, Dussel schaut nicht hoch. Jetzt lacht Mutter auch, Dussel macht sich nichts daraus. Frau van Daan hat nichts erreicht, nun muss sie es also anders anfangen. Kurze Stille, dann kommt: »Putti, nimm doch eine Schürze vor! Morgen muss ich auch wieder die Flecken an deinem Anzug sauber machen.«

»Ich mache mich nicht schmutzig.«

Wieder einen Moment Stille, dann: »Putti, warum setzt du dich nicht hin?«

»Ich stehe gut so, ich stehe lieber.« Pause.

»Putti, schau, du spritzt schon.«

»Ja, Mami, ich passe schon auf.«

Frau van Daan sucht ein anderes Thema. »Sag, Putti, warum bombardieren die Engländer jetzt nicht?«

»Weil das Wetter zu schlecht ist, Kerli.«

»Aber gestern war das Wetter doch schön, und sie sind auch nicht geflogen.«

»Reden wir nicht darüber.«

»Warum? Darüber kann man doch reden und seine Meinung sagen.«

»Nein!«

»Warum denn nicht?«

»Sei jetzt mal still, Mamichen.«

»Herr Frank gibt seiner Frau doch auch immer Antwort.«

Herr van Daan kämpft, das ist seine empfindliche Stelle, das kann er nicht aushalten, und Frau van Daan fängt wieder an: »Die Invasion kommt doch nie!«

Herr van Daan wird weiß. Als Frau van Daan das merkt, wird sie rot, fährt aber trotzdem fort: »Die Engländer leisten nichts!«

Die Bombe platzt. »Jetzt halt mal deinen Mund, zum Donnerwetter noch mal!«

Mutter kann sich das Lachen kaum verbeißen, ich schaue stur vor mich hin.

So etwas wiederholt sich fast jeden Tag, wenn sie nicht gerade einen schlimmen Streit gehabt haben. Dann halten sowohl Herr van Daan als auch seine Frau den Mund.

Ich muss noch ein paar Kartoffeln holen und gehe zum Dachboden. Dort ist Peter damit beschäftigt, die Katze zu entflöhen. Er schaut hoch, die Katze merkt es, wupp ... weg ist sie, durch das offene Fenster in die Dachrinne.

Peter flucht, ich lache und verschwinde.

Die Freiheit im Hinterhaus

Halb sechs: Bep kommt herauf, um uns die Abendfreiheit zu schenken. Jetzt kommt sofort Schwung in den Betrieb. Ich gehe erst mit Bep nach oben, wo sie meistens unseren Nachtisch vom Abendessen im Voraus bekommt.

Bep sitzt noch nicht richtig, da fängt Frau van Daan schon an, ihre Wünsche aufzuzählen. »Ach, Bep, ich habe noch einen Wunsch ...«

Bep zwinkert mir zu. Frau van Daan lässt keine Gelegenheit aus, um jedem, der nach oben kommt, ihre Wünsche mitzuteilen. Das ist sicher einer der Gründe, dass sie alle nicht gern hinaufgehen.

Viertel vor sechs: Bep geht. Ich gehe zwei Stockwerke tiefer. Erst in die Küche, dann ins Privatbüro, dann in den Kohlenverschlag, um für Mouschi das Mäusetürchen aufzumachen.

Nachdem ich mich überall umgeschaut habe, lande ich in Kuglers Zimmer. Dort sucht van Daan in allen Schubladen und Mappen nach der Tagespost. Peter holt die Lagerschlüssel und Moffi, Pim schleppt die Schreibmaschinen nach oben, Margot sucht sich einen ruhigen Platz für ihre Büroarbeit, Frau van Daan setzt einen Kessel Wasser auf den Gasherd, und Mutter kommt mit einem Topf Kartoffeln die Treppe herunter. Jeder weiß, welche Arbeit er zu tun hat.

Schon bald kommt Peter vom Lager zurück. Die erste Frage gilt dem Brot: Es ist vergessen worden. Er macht sich so klein wie möglich, kriecht auf allen vieren durch das vordere Büro zum Stahlschrank, nimmt das Brot und verschwindet. Das heißt, er will verschwinden, denn bevor er kapiert, was geschieht, ist Mouschi über ihn hinweggesprungen und hat sich unter dem Schreibtisch verkrochen.

Peter sucht in allen Ecken. Hach, dort ist die Katze! Wieder kriecht er in das Büro hinein und zieht das Tier am Schwanz. Mouschi faucht. Peter seufzt. Was hat er erreicht? Mouschi sitzt nun direkt am Fenster und leckt sich, sehr zufrieden damit, dass sie Peter entkommen ist. Jetzt hält er als letztes Lockmittel der Katze ein Stück Brot hin. Jawohl, sie folgt ihm, und die Tür schließt sich.

Ich habe alles durch den Türspalt beobachtet.

Herr van Daan ist böse, schmeißt mit der Tür. Margot und ich schauen uns an und denken das Gleiche: Er hat sich bestimmt wieder über irgendeine Dummheit von Kugler aufgeregt und denkt jetzt nicht an unsere Nachbarn.

Da hört man wieder Schritte im Flur. Dussel kommt herein, geht in Besitzerhaltung zum Fenster, atmet tief – und hustet, niest, keucht! Er hat Pech gehabt, das war Pfeffer. Nun setzt er seinen Weg zum vorderen Büro fort. Die Vorhänge sind offen, das bedeutet, dass er sich kein Briefpapier holen kann. Mit mürrischem Gesicht verschwindet er.

Margot und ich werfen uns einen Blick zu. »Morgen bekommt seine Liebste ein Blatt weniger«, sagt sie. Ich nicke zustimmend.

Auf der Treppe hört man noch Elefantengetrampel. Das ist Dussel, der auf seinem geliebten Ort Trost sucht.

Wir arbeiten weiter. Tik, tik, tik … Dreimal klopfen, Essenszeit!

Wenn die Uhr halb neune schlägt …

Margot und Mutter sind nervös. »Pst, Vater! Still, Otto! Pst, Pim! Es ist halb neun. Komm jetzt her, du kannst kein Wasser mehr laufen lassen. Geh leise!« Das sind die diversen Ausrufe für Vater im Badezimmer. Schlag halb neun muss er im Zimmer sein. Kein Tröpfchen Wasser, kein Klo, nicht herumlaufen, alles still! Wenn im Büro noch niemand ist, kann man im Lager alles hören.

Oben wird um zehn vor halb neun die Tür geöffnet und kurz danach dreimal auf den Fußboden geklopft. Der Brei für Anne. Ich steige hinauf und hole das Hundeschüsselchen.

Unten angekommen, geht alles schnell-schnell. Haare kämmen, Plätscherdose ausgießen, Bett auf seinen Platz. Still! Die Uhr schlägt. Frau van Daan wechselt die Schuhe und schlurft auf Badeschlappen durch das Zimmer, Herr Charlie Chaplin auch auf Schlappen, und alles ist ruhig.

Nun ist die ideale Familienszenerie vollkommen. Ich möchte lesen oder lernen, Margot auch, ebenso Vater und Mutter. Vater sitzt (natürlich mit Dickens und Wörterbuch) auf dem Rand seines ausgeleierten Quietschbettes, auf dem noch nicht mal anständige Matratzen liegen. Zwei aufeinander gelegte Keilkissen tun's auch. »Muss ich nicht haben, es geht auch ohne.«

Einmal am Lesen, schaut er nicht auf oder um, lacht ab und zu, gibt sich schreckliche Mühe, Mutter eine Geschichte aufzudrängen.

»Ich habe jetzt keine Zeit.«

Einen Moment sieht er enttäuscht aus, dann liest er weiter. Kurz darauf, wenn wieder etwas Schönes und Typisches kommt, versucht er es wieder: »Das musst du lesen, Mutter!«

Mutter sitzt auf dem Klappbett, liest, näht, strickt oder lernt, was eben an der Reihe ist. Auf einmal fällt ihr etwas ein. Schnell sagt sie: »Anne, du weißt doch …«, oder: »Margot, schreib mal eben auf …«

Nach einer Weile ist wieder Ruhe eingekehrt. Plötzlich schlägt Margot mit einem Knall ihr Buch zu. Vater zieht die Augenbrauen zu einem witzigen Bogen, seine Lesefalte bildet sich aufs Neue, und er ist wieder vertieft. Mutter fängt an, mit Margot zu schwätzen, ich werde neugierig, höre auch zu. Pim wird in das Gespräch hineingezogen …

Neun Uhr! Frühstück!

Freitag, 10. September 1943

Liebe Kitty!

Jedes Mal, wenn ich an dich schreibe, ist wieder etwas Besonderes passiert, aber meistens sind es mehr unangenehme als angenehme Dinge. Jetzt jedoch ist es etwas Schönes.

Am Mittwochabend, dem 8. September, saßen wir um sieben Uhr am Radio, und das Erste, was wir hörten, war folgendes: »Here follows the best news of the whole war: Italy has capitulated.« Italien hat bedingungslos kapituliert! Um Viertel nach acht fing der Sender Oranje an:

»Hörer, vor eineinviertel Stunden, gerade als ich mit der Chronik des Tages fertig war, traf die herrliche Nachricht von der Kapitulation Italiens hier ein. Ich kann Ihnen sagen, dass ich noch nie meine Papiere mit so viel Befriedigung in den Papierkorb geworfen habe wie heute!«

God save the King, die amerikanische Hymne und die russische Internationale wurden gespielt. Wie immer war der Sender Oranje herzerfrischend und doch nicht zu optimistisch.

Die Engländer sind in Neapel gelandet. Norditalien ist von den Deutschen besetzt. Am Freitag, dem 3. September, war der Waffenstillstand schon unterzeichnet, genau an dem Tag, als die Engländer in Italien gelandet sind. Die Deutschen fluchen und wettern in allen Zeitungen über den Verrat Badoglios und des italienischen Königs.

Aber wir haben auch Sorgen, es geht um Herrn Kleiman. Du weißt, wir haben ihn alle sehr gern. Obwohl er immer krank ist, viele Schmerzen hat und nicht viel essen und herumgehen darf, ist er immer fröhlich und bewundernswert tapfer. »Wenn Herr Kleiman hereinkommt, geht die Sonne auf«, sagte Mutter gerade neulich, und damit hat sie Recht.

Nun muss er für eine unangenehme Darmoperation ins Krankenhaus, für mindestens vier Wochen. Du hättest sehen sollen, wie er von uns Abschied genommen hat. Als würde er einkaufen gehen, so normal.

Deine Anne

Donnerstag, 16. September 1943

Liebe Kitty!

Hier wird das Verhältnis untereinander immer schlechter, je länger es dauert. Bei Tisch wagt niemand, den Mund aufzumachen (außer, um einen Bissen hineinzuschieben), denn was man sagt, wird entweder übel genommen oder verkehrt verstanden. Herr Voskuijl kommt manchmal zu Besuch. Leider geht es ihm sehr schlecht. Er macht es seiner Familie auch nicht einfacher, weil er immer mit der Vorstellung herumläuft: Was kann es mir noch ausmachen, ich sterbe sowieso bald! Ich kann mir die Stimmung bei Voskuijls zu Hause gut vorstellen, wenn ich mir überlege, wie gereizt hier schon alle sind.

Ich schlucke jeden Tag Baldriantabletten, gegen Angst und Depression, aber das verhütet doch nicht, dass meine Stimmung am Tag darauf noch miserabler ist. Einmal richtig und laut zu lachen, das würde mehr helfen als zehn Baldriantabletten. Aber das Lachen haben wir fast verlernt. Manchmal habe ich Angst, dass ich vor lauter Ernst ein starres Gesicht und Falten um den Mund bekommen werde. Mit den anderen ist es auch nicht besser, alle erwarten mit bangen Gefühlen den großen Brocken, der vor uns liegt, den Winter.

Noch etwas trägt nicht zu unserer Erheiterung bei, der Lagerarbeiter van Maaren ist misstrauisch geworden, was das Hintergebäude betrifft. Es muss jemandem, der ein bisschen Gehirn hat, wohl auffallen, dass Miep sagt, sie geht ins Laboratorium, Bep ins Archiv, Kleiman zum Opekta-Vorrat. Und Kugler behauptet, das Hinterhaus gehöre nicht zu dem Gebäude, sondern zum Nachbarhaus.

Es könnte uns egal sein, was Herr van Maaren von der Sache hält, wenn er nicht als unzuverlässig bekannt und sehr neugierig wäre, sodass er sich nicht mit ein paar leeren Worten abspeisen lässt.

Eines Tages wollte Kugler mal besonders vorsichtig sein, zog zehn Minuten vor halb eins seinen Mantel an und ging zur Drogerie um die Ecke. Keine fünf Minuten später war er wieder zurück, schlich wie ein Dieb über die Treppe und kam zu uns. Um Viertel nach eins wollte er wieder gehen, traf aber auf dem Treppenabsatz Bep, die ihn warnte, dass van Maaren im Büro säße. Kugler machte rechtsum kehrt und saß bis halb zwei bei uns. Dann nahm er seine Schuhe in die Hand und ging auf Strümpfen (trotz seiner Erkältung) zur Tür des vorderen Dachbodens, balancierte Stufe um Stufe die Treppe hinunter, um jedes Knarren zu vermeiden, und kam nach einer Viertelstunde von der Straßenseite ins Büro.

Bep, die van Maaren inzwischen losgeworden war, kam, um Herrn Kugler bei uns abzuholen, aber der war schon längst weg, der war inzwischen noch in Strümpfen auf der Treppe. Was werden die Leute auf der Straße wohl gedacht haben, als der Direktor seine Schuhe draußen wieder anzog? Hach, der Direktor in Socken!

Deine Anne

Mittwoch, 29. September 1943

Liebe Kitty!

Frau van Daan hat Geburtstag. Wir haben ihr außer einer Käse-, Fleisch- und Brotmarke nur noch ein Glas Marmelade geschenkt. Von ihrem Mann, Dussel und vom Büro hat sie auch ausschließlich Blumen oder Esswaren bekommen. So sind die Zeiten nun einmal!

Bep hat in dieser Woche einen halben Nervenzusammenbruch bekommen, so oft wurde sie geschickt. Zehnmal am Tag bekam sie Aufträge, immer wurde darauf gedrängt, dass sie etwas schnell holen müsse, dass sie noch einmal gehen müsse oder dass sie es falsch gemacht habe. Wenn man dann bedenkt, dass sie auch unten im Büro ihre Arbeit erledigen muss, Kleiman krank ist, Miep zu Hause ist mit einer Erkältung und sie selbst sich den Knöchel verstaucht hat, Liebeskummer und zu Hause einen murrenden Vater hat, dann kann man sich vorstellen, dass sie weder aus noch ein weiß. Wir haben sie getröstet und gesagt, sie müsse nur ein paar Mal energisch sagen, dass sie keine Zeit hätte, dann würde die Einkaufsliste bestimmt von alleine kleiner werden.

Am Samstag spielte sich hier ein Drama ab, das in seiner Heftigkeit noch nicht seinesgleichen hatte. Es begann mit van Maaren und endete mit einem allgemeinen Streit und Geschluchze. Dussel hat sich bei Mutter darüber beklagt, dass er wie ein Ausgestoßener behandelt würde, dass niemand von uns freundlich zu ihm sei und dass er uns doch gar nichts getan habe und noch eine Reihe süßlicher Schmeicheleien, auf die Mutter diesmal zum Glück nicht reinfiel. Sie sagte ihm, dass er alle sehr enttäuscht und uns mehr als einmal Anlass zu Ärger gegeben hätte. Dussel versprach das Blaue vom Himmel herunter, aber wie immer ist bisher nichts dabei herausgekommen.

Mit van Daans geht es schief, ich sehe es kommen! Vater ist wütend, weil sie uns betrügen, sie unterschlagen Fleisch und Ähnliches. Oh, welch ein Ausbruch schwebt wieder über unseren Köpfen? Wenn ich nur nicht in all diese Scharmützel verwickelt wäre, wenn ich nur weg gehen könnte! Sie machen uns noch verrückt!   Deine Anne

Liebe Kitty!

Kleiman ist wieder zurück, was für ein Glück! Er sieht noch ein bisschen blass aus, aber geht doch wohlgemut los, um für van Daan Kleidungsstücke zu verkaufen.

Es ist sehr unangenehm, dass das Geld der van Daans radikal zu Ende ist. Seine letzten hundert Gulden hat er im Lager verloren, was uns auch Schwierigkeiten gemacht hat. Wie können an einem Montagmorgen hundert Gulden ins Lager geraten sein? Alles Anlässe für Argwohn. Inzwischen sind die hundert Gulden gestohlen worden. Wer ist der Dieb?

Aber ich sprach über Geldmangel. Frau van Daan will von ihrem Stoß Mäntel, Kleider und Schuhen nichts missen, der Anzug von Herrn van Daan lässt sich schwer verkaufen, und Peters Fahrrad ist von der Besichtigung zurück, niemand wollte es haben. Das Ende vom Lied ist nicht in Sicht. Frau van Daan wird wohl doch ihren Pelzmantel hergeben müssen. Ihr Standpunkt, dass die Firma für unseren Unterhalt aufkommen muss, stimmt wohl nicht. Oben haben sie deswegen wieder einen Mordskrach hinter sich und sind in die Versöhnungsphase mit »Ach, lieber Putti« und »Süße Kerli« eingetreten.

Mir ist ganz schwindlig von all den Schimpfworten, die im letzten Monat durch dieses ehrbare Haus geflogen sind. Vater geht mit zusammengepressten Lippen herum, und wenn jemand ihn anspricht, schaut er so erschrocken hoch, als hätte er Angst, wieder eine schwierige Aufgabe lösen zu müssen. Mutter hat vor Aufregung rote Flecken auf den Backen, Margot klagt über Kopfschmerzen, Dussel kann nicht schlafen, Frau van Daan jammert den ganzen Tag, und ich selbst bin ganz aus der Fassung. Ehrlich gesagt, ich vergesse ab und zu, mit wem wir Streit haben und mit wem die Versöhnung bereits stattgefunden hat.

Das Einzige, was mich ablenkt, ist Lernen, und das tue ich viel.

Deine Anne

Freitag, 29. Oktober 1943

Liebste Kitty!

Herr Kleiman ist wieder nicht da, sein Magen lässt ihm keine Ruhe. Er weiß selbst noch nicht, ob die Blutung schon aufgehört hat. Er war zum ersten Mal wirklich down, als er uns erzählt hat, dass er sich nicht gut fühle, und nach Hause ging.

Hier gab es wieder laute Streitereien zwischen Herrn van Daan und seiner Frau. Das kam so: Ihr Geld ist alle. Sie wollten einen Wintermantel und einen Anzug von Herrn van Daan verkaufen, aber dafür war niemand zu finden. Er wollte einen viel zu hohen Preis dafür haben.

Eines Tages, es ist schon eine Weile her, sprach Kleiman über einen befreundeten Kürschner. Dadurch kam Herr van Daan auf die Idee, den Pelzmantel seiner Frau zu verkaufen. Es ist ein Pelzmantel aus Kaninchenfell und siebzehn Jahre getragen. Frau van Daan bekam 325 Gulden dafür, das ist enorm viel. Frau van Daan wollte das Geld behalten, um dafür nach dem Krieg neue Kleider zu kaufen. Es war eine ganz schön harte Nuss, bis Herr van Daan ihr klargemacht hatte, dass das Geld dringend für den Haushalt benötigt wurde.

Das Gekreische, Geweine, Gestampfe und Geschimpfe kannst du dir unmöglich vorstellen. Es war beängstigend. Meine Familie stand mit angehaltenem Atem unten an der Treppe, bereit, die Kämpfenden notfalls auseinander zu halten. All das Keifen, das Weinen und die Nervosität sind so aufregend und anstrengend, dass ich abends weinend ins Bett falle und dem Himmel danke, dass ich mal eine halbe Stunde für mich allein habe.

Mir selbst geht es ganz gut, außer dass ich überhaupt keinen Appetit habe. Immer wieder höre ich: »Was siehst du aber schlecht aus!« Ich muss sagen, dass sie sich große Mühe geben, mich ein bisschen bei Kräften zu halten. Traubenzucker, Lebertran, Hefetabletten und Kalk sollen helfen. Meine Nerven gehen oft mit mir durch, vor allem sonntags fühle ich mich elend. Dann ist die Stimmung im Haus drückend, schläfrig und bleiern. Draußen hört man keinen Vogel singen, eine tödliche und bedrückende Stille liegt über allem. Diese Schwere hängt sich an mir fest, als würde sie mich in die Tiefe ziehen. Vater, Mutter und Margot lassen mich dann oft gleichgültig. Ich irre von einem Zimmer zum anderen, die Treppe hinunter und wieder hinauf, und habe ein Gefühl wie ein Singvogel, dem die Flügel mit harter Hand ausgerissen worden sind und der in vollkommener Dunkelheit gegen die Stäbe seines engen Käfigs fliegt. »Nach draußen, Luft und Lachen!«, schreit es in mir. Ich antworte nicht mal mehr, lege mich auf die Couch und schlafe, um die Zeit, die Stille und auch die schreckliche Angst abzukürzen, denn abzutöten sind sie nicht.

Deine Anne

Samstag, 30. Oktober 1943

Liebe Kitty!

Mutter ist schrecklich nervös, und das ist für mich immer sehr gefährlich. Sollte es Zufall sein, dass Vater und Mutter Margot nie ausschimpfen und ich immer alles abbekomme? Gestern Abend zum Beispiel: Margot las ein Buch, in dem prächtige Zeichnungen waren. Sie stand auf und legte das Buch zur Seite, um es später weiterzulesen. Ich hatte gerade nichts zu tun, nahm das Buch und betrachtete die Bilder. Margot kam zurück, sah »ihr« Buch in meiner Hand, bekam eine Falte in die Stirn und verlangte es böse zurück. Ich wollte es nur noch kurz weiterbetrachten. Margot wurde immer böser. Mutter mischte sich mit den Worten ein: »Das Buch liest Margot, gib es ihr also.«

Vater kam ins Zimmer, wusste nicht mal, um was es ging, sah, dass Margot etwas angetan wurde, und fuhr mich an: »Ich würde dich mal sehen wollen, wenn Margot in deinem Buch herumblättern würde!«

Ich gab sofort nach, legte das Buch hin und ging, ihrer Meinung nach beleidigt, aus dem Zimmer. Doch ich war weder beleidigt noch böse, wohl aber traurig.

Es war nicht richtig von Vater, dass er geurteilt hat, ohne die Streitfrage zu kennen. Ich hätte das Buch Margot von selbst zurückgegeben, und dazu noch viel schneller, wenn Vater und Mutter sich nicht eingemischt und Margot in Schutz genommen hätten, als würde ihr das größte Unrecht geschehen.

Dass Mutter sich für Margot einsetzt, versteht sich von selbst, die beiden setzen sich immer füreinander ein. Ich bin daran so gewöhnt, dass ich völlig gleichgültig gegen Mutters Standpauken und

Margots gereizte Launen geworden bin. Ich liebe sie nur deshalb, weil sie nun einmal Mutter und Margot sind, als Menschen können sie mir gestohlen bleiben. Bei Vater ist das was anderes. Wenn er Margot vorzieht, alle ihre Taten gutheißt, sie lobt und mit ihr zärtlich ist, dann nagt etwas in mir. Denn Vater ist mein Alles, er ist mein großes Vorbild, und ich liebe niemanden auf der Welt außer Vater. Er ist sich nicht bewusst, dass er mit Margot anders umgeht als mit mir. Margot ist nun mal die Klügste, die Liebste, die Schönste und die Beste. Aber ein bisschen Recht habe ich doch auch darauf, ernst genommen zu werden. Ich war immer der Clown und der Taugenichts der Familie, musste immer für alle Taten doppelt büßen, einmal durch die Standpauken und einmal durch meine eigene Verzweiflung. Die oberflächlichen Zärtlichkeiten befriedigen mich nicht mehr, ebenso wenig die so genannten ernsthaften Gespräche. Ich verlange etwas von Vater, was er mir nicht geben kann. Ich bin nicht neidisch auf Margot, war es nie. Ich begehre weder ihre Klugheit noch ihre Schönheit. Ich würde nur so gerne Vaters echte Liebe fühlen, nicht nur als sein Kind, sondern als Anne-als-sie-selbst.

Ich klammere mich an Vater, weil ich jeden Tag verächtlicher auf Mutter hinunterschaue und er der Einzige ist, der in mir noch ein Restchen Familiengefühl aufrechterhält. Vater versteht nicht, dass ich mich manchmal über Mutter aussprechen muss. Er will nicht über sie reden, vermeidet alles, was sich auf Mutters Fehler bezieht.

Und doch liegt mir Mutter mit all ihren Mängeln am schwersten auf dem Herzen. Ich weiß nicht, wie ich mich beherrschen soll. Ich kann ihr nicht ihre Schlampigkeit, ihren Sarkasmus und ihre Härte unter die Nase reiben, kann jedoch auch nicht immer die Schuld bei mir finden.

Ich bin das genaue Gegenteil von ihr, und deshalb prallen wir natürlich aufeinander. Ich urteile nicht über Mutters Charakter, denn darüber kann ich nicht urteilen, ich betrachte sie nur als Mutter. Für mich ist sie eben keine Mutter. Ich selbst muss meine Mutter sein. Ich habe mich von ihnen abgesondert, laviere mich alleine durch und werde später schon sehen, wo ich lande. Es liegt alles daran, dass ich eine genaue Vorstellung in mir habe, wie eine Mutter und eine Frau sein soll, und nichts davon finde ich in ihr, der ich den Namen Mutter geben muss.

Ich nehme mir immer vor, nicht mehr auf Mutters falsche Beispiele zu achten, ich will nur ihre guten Seiten sehen, und was ich bei ihr nicht finde, bei mir selbst suchen. Aber das gelingt mir nicht. Besonders schlimm ist es, dass weder Vater noch Mutter erkennen, dass sie mir gegenüber ihren Verpflichtungen nicht nachkommen und dass ich sie dafür verurteile. Kann eigentlich jemand seine Kinder voll und ganz zufrieden stellen?

Manchmal glaube ich, dass Gott mich auf die Probe stellen will, jetzt und auch später. Muss ich ein guter Mensch werden, ohne Vorbilder und ohne Reden, damit ich später besonders stark werde?

Wer außer mir wird später alle diese Briefe lesen? Wer außer mir wird mich trösten? Ich habe so oft Trost nötig. Ich bin so häufig nicht stark genug und versage öfter, als dass ich den Anforderungen genüge. Ich weiß es und versuche immer wieder, jeden Tag aufs Neue, mich zu bessern.

Ich werde unterschiedlich behandelt. Den einen Tag ist Anne so vernünftig und darf alles wissen, am nächsten höre ich wieder, dass Anne noch ein kleines, dummes Schaf ist, das nichts weiß und nur glaubt, Wunder was aus Büchern gelernt zu haben! Ich bin nicht mehr das Baby und das Hätschelkind, das immer ausgelacht werden darf. Ich habe meine eigenen Ideale, Vorstellungen und Pläne, aber ich kann sie noch nicht in Worte fassen.

Ach, mir kommt so viel hoch, wenn ich abends allein bin, auch tagsüber, wenn ich die Leute aushalten muss, die mir zum Hals heraushängen oder meine Absichten immer verkehrt auffassen. Letztlich komme ich deshalb immer wieder auf mein Tagebuch zurück, das ist mein Anfang und mein Ende, denn Kitty ist immer geduldig. Ich verspreche ihr, dass ich trotz allem durchhalten werde, mir meinen eigenen Weg suche und meine Tränen hinunterschlucke. Ich würde nur so gern auch mal einen Erfolg sehen und ein einziges Mal von jemandem ermutigt werden, der mich lieb hat.

Verurteile mich nicht, sondern betrachte mich als jemanden, dem es auch mal zu viel wird!   Deine Anne

Mittwoch, 3. November 1943

Liebe Kitty!

Um uns etwas Abwechslung und Fortbildung zu verschaffen, hat Vater den Prospekt des Leidener Lehrinstituts angefordert. Margot hat das dicke Buch schon dreimal durchgeschaut, ohne dass sie etwas nach ihrem Geschmack oder ihrer Geldbörse fand. Vater entschied sich schneller, er wollte eine Probelektion »Grundkurs Latein« bestellen. Gesagt, getan. Die Lektion kam, Margot machte sich begeistert an die Arbeit, und der Kurs, egal wie teuer, wurde genommen. Für mich ist er viel zu schwer, obwohl ich sehr gerne Latein lernen würde.

Damit ich auch etwas Neues anfangen kann, bat Vater Kleiman um eine Kinderbibel, damit ich endlich auch etwas vom Neuen Testament erfahre.

»Willst du Anne zu Chanukka etwa eine Bibel schenken?«, fragte Margot etwas entsetzt.

»Ja … eh, ich denke, dass Nikolaus eine passendere Gelegenheit ist«, antwortete Vater.

Jesus zu Chanukka, das passt nun mal nicht.

Weil der Staubsauger kaputt ist, muss ich jeden Abend den Teppich mit einer alten Bürste ausbürsten. Fenster zu, Licht an, Ofen auch, und dann los, mit einem Handbesen über den Fußboden. Das kann nicht gut gehen, dachte ich mir schon beim ersten Mal, das muss zu Klagen führen. Und jawohl, Mutter bekam Kopfschmerzen von den dicken Staubwolken, die im Zimmer herumwirbelten, Margots neues lateinisches Wörterbuch war vom Schmutz bedeckt, und Pim murrte, dass sich der Boden überhaupt nicht verändert hätte. Gestank als Dank, nennt man das.

Die neue Hinterhaus-Regelung ist, dass der Ofen sonntags um halb acht angemacht wird statt um halb sechs Uhr morgens. Ich finde das gefährlich. Was werden wohl die Nachbarn über unseren rauchenden Schornstein denken?

Dasselbe ist mit den Vorhängen. Von Anfang unserer Versteckzeit an sind sie festgesteckt. Manchmal bekommt aber einer der Herren oder Damen eine Anwandlung und muss mal schnell hinausschauen. Ein Sturm von Vorwürfen ist die Folge. Die Antwort: »Das sieht man doch nicht.« Damit beginnt und endet jede Unvorsichtigkeit. Das sieht man nicht, das hört man nicht, darauf achtet niemand. Das ist leicht gesagt, aber ob es der Wahrheit entspricht?

Die Streitereien haben sich zur Zeit etwas gelegt, nur Dussel hat noch Krach mit van Daans. Wenn er über Frau van Daan spricht, sagt er nur »die dumme Kuh« oder »das alte Kalb«, und sie wiederum betitelt den unfehlbaren studierten Herrn als »alte Jungfer« oder »alten Junggesellen, der sich ewig auf den Schlips getreten fühlt« und so weiter.

Der Topf wirft dem Kessel vor, dass er schwarz aussieht!

Deine Anne

Montagabend, 8. November 1943

Liebe Kitty!

Wenn du meinen Stapel Briefe hintereinander durchlesen könntest, würde dir sicher auffallen, in was für unterschiedlichen Stimmungen sie geschrieben sind. Ich finde es selbst schlimm, dass ich hier im Hinterhaus so sehr von Stimmungen abhängig bin. Übrigens nicht ich alleine, wir sind es alle. Wenn ich ein Buch lese, das mich beeindruckt, muss ich erst in mir selbst gründlich Ordnung machen, bevor ich mich wieder unter die Leute begebe, sonst würden die anderen denken, ich wäre ein bisschen komisch im Kopf. Im Augenblick habe ich wieder eine Periode, in der ich niedergeschlagen bin, wie du wohl merken wirst. Ich kann dir wirklich nicht sagen, warum, aber ich glaube, dass es meine Feigheit ist, gegen die ich immer wieder stoße.

Heute Abend, als Bep noch hier war, klingelte es lang, laut und durchdringend. Ich wurde sofort weiß, bekam Bauchweh und Herzklopfen, und das alles vor Angst!

Abends im Bett sehe ich mich allein in einem Kerker, ohne Vater und Mutter. Manchmal irre ich auf der Straße herum, oder unser Hinterhaus steht in Brand, oder sie kommen uns nachts holen, und ich lege mich vor Verzweiflung unters Bett. Ich sehe alles so, als würde ich es am eigenen Leib erleben. Und dann noch das Gefühl, das alles könnte sofort passieren!

Miep sagt oft, dass sie uns beneidet, weil wir hier Ruhe haben. Das kann schon stimmen, aber an unsere Angst denkt sie sicher nicht.

Ich kann mir überhaupt nicht vorstellen, dass die Welt für uns je wieder normal wird. Ich spreche zwar über »nach dem Krieg«, aber dann ist es, als spräche ich über ein Luftschloss, etwas, das niemals Wirklichkeit werden kann.

Ich sehe uns acht im Hinterhaus, als wären wir ein Stück blauer Himmel, umringt von schwarzen, schwarzen Regenwolken. Das runde Fleckchen, auf dem wir stehen, ist noch sicher, aber die Wolken rücken immer näher, und der Ring, der uns von der nahenden Gefahr trennt, wird immer enger. Jetzt sind wir schon so dicht von Gefahr und Dunkelheit umgeben, dass wir in der verzweifelten Suche nach Rettung aneinander stoßen. Wir schauen alle nach unten, wo die Menschen gegeneinander kämpfen, wir schauen nach oben, wo es ruhig und schön ist, und wir sind abgeschnitten durch die düstere Masse, die uns nicht nach unten und nicht nach oben gehen lässt, sondern vor uns steht wie eine undurchdringliche Mauer, die uns zerschmettern will, aber noch nicht kann. Ich kann nichts anderes tun, als zu rufen und zu flehen: »O Ring, Ring, werde weiter und öffne dich für uns!«   Deine Anne

                                                   Donnerstag, 11. November 1943

Liebe Kitty!

Ich habe einen passenden Titel für dieses Kapitel:
Ode an meinen Füllhalter
»In memoriam«

Mein Füllhalter war mir immer ein kostbarer Besitz. Ich schätzte ihn sehr, vor allem wegen seiner dicken Feder, denn ich kann nur mit dicken Federn wirklich schön schreiben. Er hat ein sehr langes und interessantes Füllerleben geführt, von dem ich hier kurz erzählen möchte.

Als ich neun Jahre alt war, kam mein Füller in einem Päckchen (in Watte gewickelt) als »Muster ohne Wert« den ganzen Weg von Aachen, dem Wohnort meiner Großmutter, der gütigen Geberin. Ich lag mit Grippe im Bett, und der Februarwind heulte ums Haus. Der glorreiche Füller lag in einem roten Lederetui und wurde gleich am ersten Tag allen Freundinnen gezeigt. Ich, Anne Frank, die stolze Besitzerin eines Füllhalters!

Schulfoto der elfjährigen Anne.

Als ich zehn Jahre alt war, durfte der Füller mit in die Schule, und die Lehrerin erlaubte wahrhaftig, dass ich damit schrieb. Als ich elf war, musste mein Schatz jedoch wieder weggepackt werden, da die Lehrerin der sechsten Klasse nur Schulfedern und Tintenfass erlaubte. Als ich mit zwölf ins Jüdische Lyzeum ging, bekam mein Füller ein neues Etui, in das auch noch ein Bleistift passte und das außerdem viel echter aussah, weil es einen Reißverschluss hatte. Mit dreizehn ging der Füller mit mir ins Hinterhaus und begleitete mich durch zahllose Tagebücher und Hefte. Als ich vierzehn Jahre alt war, endete auch das letzte Jahr, das mein Füller mit mir verbrachte ...

Es war am Freitagnachmittag nach fünf Uhr, dass ich aus meinem Zimmer kam und mich an den Tisch setzen wollte, um zu schreiben, als ich grob zur Seite geschoben wurde und für Margot und Vater Platz machen musste, die Latein übten. Der Füller blieb unbenutzt auf dem Tisch liegen, seine Besitzerin nahm seufzend mit einer kleinen Tischecke vorlieb und fing an, Bohnen zu reiben. »Bohnen reiben« bedeutet hier, verschimmelte braune Bohnen wieder sauber zu machen. Um Viertel vor sechs fegte ich den Boden und warf den Schmutz zusammen mit den schlechten Bohnen auf einer Zeitung in den Ofen. Eine gewaltige Flamme schlug heraus, und ich fand es großartig, dass sich das Feuer auf diese Art wieder erholt hatte.

Ruhe war wieder eingekehrt, die Lateiner abgezogen, und ich setzte mich an den Tisch, um meine geplante Schreibarbeit aufzunehmen. Aber wo ich auch suchte, mein Füller war nirgends zu entdecken. Ich suchte noch einmal, Margot suchte, Mutter suchte, Vater suchte, Dussel suchte, aber das Ding war spurlos verschwunden.

»Vielleicht ist er in den Ofen gefallen, zusammen mit den Bohnen!«, meinte Margot.

»Aber nein!«, antwortete ich.

Als jedoch mein Füllhalter auch abends noch nicht zum Vorschein kommen wollte, nahmen wir alle an, dass er verbrannt war, umso mehr, da Zelluloid so gut brennt. Und wirklich, diese traurige Annahme bestätigte sich, als Vater am nächsten Morgen beim Ofen-Saubermachen den Klip, mit dem man den Füller feststeckt, mitten in einem Aschehaufen fand. Von der goldenen Feder war nichts mehr zu entdecken. »Sicher festgebacken an irgendeinem Stein«, meinte Vater.

Ein Trost ist mir geblieben, wenn auch ein magerer. Mein Füllhalter ist eingeäschert worden, genau, was ich später auch will.

Deine Anne

Mittwoch, 17. November 1943

Liebe Kitty!

Hauserschütternde Ereignisse sind im Gang. Bei Bep daheim herrscht Diphtherie, deshalb darf sie sechs Wochen lang nicht mit uns in Berührung kommen. Das ist sehr unangenehm, sowohl wegen des Essens als auch wegen der Einkäufe, ganz zu schweigen von der mangelnden Geselligkeit. Kleiman liegt noch immer und hat schon drei Wochen lang nichts anderes als Milch und dünnen Brei gegessen. Kugler hat unheimlich viel zu tun.

Margots lateinische Übungen werden eingeschickt und von einem Lehrer korrigiert zurückgeschickt. Margot schreibt unter Beps Namen. Der Lehrer ist sehr nett und obendrein witzig. Sicher ist er froh, dass er eine so gescheite Schülerin bekommen hat.

Dussel ist ganz durcheinander. Keiner von uns weiß, warum. Es hat damit angefangen, dass er oben den Mund zusammenkniff und weder mit Herrn van Daan noch mit Frau van Daan ein Wort sprach. Das fiel jedem auf, und als es ein paar Tage anhielt, nutzte Mutter eine Gelegenheit und warnte ihn vor Frau van Daan, die ihm tatsächlich viele Unannehmlichkeiten bereiten könnte. Dussel sagte, Herr van Daan habe mit dem Schweigen angefangen, deshalb habe er auch nicht vor, das seine zu brechen. Nun musst du wissen, dass gestern der 16. November war, der Tag, an dem er ein Jahr im Hinterhaus ist. Mutter bekam aus diesem Anlass einen Blumentopf geschenkt, aber Frau van Daan, die schon Wochen zuvor mehrmals auf dieses Datum angespielt und gemeint hatte, dass Dussel etwas spendieren müsste, bekam nichts. Statt seine Dankbarkeit für die uneigennützige Aufnahme zu äußern, sprach er überhaupt nicht. Und als ich ihn am Morgen des Sechzehnten fragte, ob ich ihm gratulieren oder kondolieren solle, antwortete er, dass ihm alles recht sei. Mutter, die in der schönen Rolle als Friedensstifterin fungieren wollte, kam auch keinen Schritt weiter mit ihm, und der Zustand änderte sich nicht.

Es ist keine Übertreibung, wenn ich sage, dass in Dussels Gehirn ein Bindeglied fehlt. Wir machen uns oft insgeheim lustig, dass er kein Gedächtnis hat, keine Meinung und kein Urteil, und so manches Mal lachen wir darüber, wenn er Berichte, die er eben gehört hat, völlig verkehrt weitererzählt und alles durcheinander stottert.

Für jeden Vorwurf und für jede Beschuldigung hat er viele schöne Versprechungen, von denen aber nicht eine ausgeführt wird.

> »Der Mann hat einen großen Geist
> und ist so klein von Taten!«
> Deine Anne

Samstag, 27. November 1943

Liebe Kitty!

Gestern vor dem Einschlafen stand mir plötzlich Hanneli vor den Augen.

Ich sah sie vor mir, in Lumpen gekleidet, mit einem eingefallenen und abgemagerten Gesicht. Ihre Augen waren sehr groß, und sie sah mich so traurig und vorwurfsvoll an, dass ich in ihren Augen lesen konnte: »O Anne, warum hast du mich verlassen? Hilf, o hilf mir, rette mich aus dieser Hölle!«

Und ich kann ihr nicht helfen. Ich kann nur zuschauen, wie andere Menschen leiden und sterben. Ich muss untätig dasitzen und kann Gott nur bitten, sie zu uns zurückzuführen. Ausgerechnet Hanneli sah ich, niemand anderen, und ich verstand es. Ich habe sie falsch beurteilt, war noch zu sehr Kind, um ihre Schwierigkeiten zu begreifen. Sie hing an ihrer Freundin, und für sie sah es aus, als wollte ich sie ihr wegnehmen. Wie muss sich die Ärmste gefühlt haben! Ich weiß es, ich kenne dieses Gefühl selbst so gut!

Manchmal, wie ein Blitz, erkannte ich etwas von ihrem Leben und ging dann, egoistisch, sofort wieder in meinen eigenen Vergnügungen und Schwierigkeiten auf.

Es war gemein, wie ich mit ihr umgegangen bin, und jetzt schaute sie mich mit ihrem blassen Gesicht und ihren flehenden Augen so hilflos an. Könnte ich ihr bloß helfen! O Gott, dass ich hier alles habe, was ich mir wünschen kann, und dass sie vom Schicksal so hart angefasst worden ist! Sie war mindestens so fromm wie ich, sie wollte auch das Gute. Warum wurde ich dann auserwählt, um zu leben, und sie musste womöglich sterben? Welcher Unterschied war zwischen uns? Warum sind wir jetzt so weit voneinander entfernt?

Ehrlich gesagt, ich habe sie monatelang, ja ein Jahr, fast vergessen. Nicht ganz, aber doch nicht so, dass ich sie in all ihrem Elend vor mir sah.

Ach, Hanneli, ich hoffe, dass ich dich bei uns aufnehmen kann, wenn du das Ende des Krieges erlebst, um etwas von dem Unrecht an dir gutzumachen, das ich dir angetan habe.

Aber wenn ich wieder im Stande bin, ihr zu helfen, hat sie meine Hilfe nicht mehr so nötig wie jetzt. Ob sie manchmal an mich denkt? Und was sie dann wohl fühlt?

Lieber Gott, hilf ihr, dass sie wenigstens nicht allein ist. Wenn du ihr nur sagen könntest, dass ich mit Liebe und Mitleid an sie denke, es würde sie vielleicht in ihrem Durchhaltevermögen stärken.

Ich darf nicht weiter denken, denn ich komme nicht davon los. Ich sehe immer wieder ihre großen Augen, die mich nicht loslassen. Hat Hanneli wirklich den Glauben in sich selbst? Hat sie ihn nicht von außen aufgedrängt bekommen? Ich weiß es nicht, nie habe ich mir die Mühe gemacht, sie danach zu fragen.

Hanneli, Hanneli, könnte ich dich bloß wegholen von dem Ort, an dem du jetzt bist, könnte ich dich an allem teilhaben lassen, was ich genieße! Es ist zu spät, ich kann nicht mehr helfen und nicht mehr gutmachen, was ich falsch gemacht habe. Aber ich werde sie niemals vergessen und immer für sie beten!   Deine Anne

                                        Montag, 6. Dezember 1943
Liebe Kitty!

Als Nikolaus näher kam, dachten wir alle unwillkürlich an den schön hergerichteten Korb vom vergangenen Jahr. Vor allem mir kam es langweilig vor, Nikolaus dieses Jahr zu übergehen. Ich dachte lange nach, bis ich etwas gefunden hatte, etwas zum Lachen. Pim wurde zu Rate gezogen, und vor einer Woche gingen wir an die Arbeit, um für alle acht ein Gedicht zu machen.

Sonntagabend um Viertel nach acht erschienen wir oben mit dem großen Wäschekorb zwischen uns, der mit Figuren und Bändern aus rosa und blauem Durchschlagpapier geschmückt war. Über dem Korb lag ein großes Stück braunes Packpapier, auf dem ein Zettel befestigt war. Alle waren ziemlich erstaunt.

Ich nahm den Zettel von dem Packpapier und las:

> Prolog:
> Nikolaus ist auch dieses Jahr gekommen,
> Sogar das Hinterhaus hat es vernommen.
> Leider können wir's nicht so schön begehen,
> wie es vergangenes Jahr geschehen.
> Damals, so denken wir heute zurück,
> glaubten wir alle an unser Glück.
> Und dachten, dass in diesem Jahr frei
> Sankt Nikolaus zu feiern sei.
> Doch wollen wir des Tags gedenken.
> Weil's aber nichts mehr gibt zum Schenken,
> so müssen wir was andres tun:
> Ein jeder schaue in seinen Schuh'n.

Ein schallendes Gelächter folgte, als jeder Eigentümer seinen Schuh aus dem Korb holte. In dem Schuh befand sich ein kleines Päckchen, in Packpapier gewickelt, mit dem Namen des Besitzers und einem Vers.

Mittwoch, 22. Dezember 1943

Liebe Kitty!

Eine hartnäckige Grippe hat mich gehindert, dir eher als heute zu schreiben. Es ist ein Elend, wenn man hier krank ist. Wenn ich husten musste, kroch ich eins-zwei-drei unter die Decke und versuchte, so geräuschlos wie möglich meine Kehle zu beruhigen, was meistens zur Folge hatte, dass das Kribbeln gar nicht mehr wegging und Milch mit Honig, Zucker oder Pastillen notwendig war. Wenn ich an die Kuren denke, die sie mich haben machen lassen, wird mir schwindlig. Schwitzen, Umschläge, feuchte Brustwickel, trockene Brustwickel, heiße Getränke, Gurgeln, Pinseln, Stilliegen, Heizkissen, Wärmflaschen, Zitronenwasser und dabei alle zwei Stunden das Thermometer. Kann man auf so eine Art eigentlich gesund werden?

Am schlimmsten fand ich aber, als Herr Dussel angefangen hat, den Doktor zu spielen, und seinen Pomadenkopf auf meine nackte Brust legte, um die Geräusche da drinnen abzuhören. Nicht nur, dass mich seine Haare schrecklich gekitzelt haben, ich genierte mich auch, obwohl er vor dreißig Jahren studiert und den Doktortitel hat. Was hat sich dieser Kerl an mein Herz zu legen? Er ist doch nicht mein Geliebter! Übrigens, was da drin gesund oder nicht gesund ist, hört er ohnehin nicht. Seine Ohren müssten erst ausgespült werden, er scheint nämlich beängstigend schwerhörig zu werden. Aber genug mit der Krankheit. Ich fühle mich wieder pudelwohl, bin einen Zentimeter gewachsen, habe zwei Pfund zugenommen und bin blass und lernlustig.

Ausnahmsweise ist das Einvernehmen hier gut, niemand hat Streit. Aber es wird wohl nicht lange dauern, wir haben einen solchen Hausfrieden bestimmt ein halbes Jahr nicht gehabt.

Bep ist noch immer von uns getrennt, aber bald wird ihre kleine Schwester wohl bazillenfrei sein.

Zu Weihnachten gibt es extra Öl, Süßigkeiten und Sirup. Zu Chanukka hat Herr Dussel Frau van Daan und Mutter eine Torte geschenkt. Miep hat sie auf Dussels Ersuchen gebacken. Bei all der Arbeit musste sie auch das noch tun. Margot und ich haben eine Brosche bekommen, aus einem Centstück gemacht und schön glänzend. Es lässt sich kaum beschreiben, wie prächtig!

Für Miep und Bep habe ich auch etwas zu Weihnachten. Ich habe seit ungefähr einem Monat den Zucker zum Brei gespart und Kleiman hat zu Weihnachten Fondant davon machen lassen.

Das Wetter ist trüb, der Ofen stinkt, das Essen drückt schwer auf aller Magen, was von allen Seiten donnernde Geräusche verursacht. Kriegsstillstand, Miststimmung.   Deine Anne

Freitag, 24. Dezember 1943

Beste Kitty!

Ich habe dir schon öfter geschrieben, dass wir hier alle so unter Stimmungen leiden, und ich glaube, dass das vor allem in der letzten Zeit bei mir stark zunimmt.

»Himmelhoch jauchzend, zu Tode betrübt« ist da bestimmt zutreffend. »Himmelhoch jauchzend« bin ich, wenn ich daran denke, wie gut wir es hier noch haben im Vergleich zu all den anderen jüdischen Kindern. Und »zu Tode betrübt« überfällt mich zum Beispiel, wenn Frau Kleiman hier gewesen ist und von Jopies Hockeyclub, von Kanufahrten, Theateraufführungen und Teetrinken mit Freunden erzählt hat.

Ich glaube nicht, dass ich eifersüchtig auf Jopie bin. Aber ich bekomme dann so eine heftige Sehnsucht, auch mal wieder Spaß zu machen und zu lachen, bis ich Bauchweh habe. Vor allem jetzt im Winter, mit den freien Weihnachts- und Neujahrstagen, da sitzen wir hier wie Ausgestoßene. Und doch dürfte ich diese Worte nicht aufschreiben, weil ich dann undankbar erscheine. Aber ich kann nicht alles für mich behalten und führe noch einmal meine Anfangsworte an: »Papier ist geduldig.«

Wenn jemand gerade von draußen hereinkommt, mit dem Wind in den Kleidern und der Kälte im Gesicht, dann würde ich am liebsten meinen Kopf unter die Decke stecken, um nicht zu denken: »Wann ist es uns wieder mal vergönnt, Luft zu riechen?« Und obwohl ich meinen Kopf nicht unter der Decke verstecken darf, mich im Gegenteil aufrecht und stark halten muss, kommen die Gedanken doch, nicht nur einmal, sondern viele Male, unzählige Male.

Glaub mir, wenn man eineinhalb Jahre eingeschlossen sitzt, kann es einem an manchen Tagen mal zu viel werden, ob es nun berechtigt oder undankbar ist. Gefühle lassen sich nicht zur Seite schieben. Radfahren, tanzen, pfeifen, die Welt sehen, mich jung fühlen, wissen, dass ich frei bin – danach sehne ich mich. Und doch darf ich es nicht zeigen. Denn stell dir vor, wenn wir alle acht anfingen, uns zu beklagen oder unzufriedene Gesichter zu machen, wohin sollte das führen?

Manchmal überlege ich mir: »Kann mich wohl irgendjemand verstehen, über die Undankbarkeit hinwegsehen, hinwegsehen über Jude oder nicht Jude, und nur den Backfisch in mir sehen, der so ein großes Bedürfnis nach ausgelassenem Vergnügen hat?« Ich weiß es nicht, und ich könnte auch nie, mit niemandem, darüber sprechen, denn ich würde bestimmt sofort anfangen zu weinen. Weinen kann so eine Erleichterung bringen, wenn man nur einen Menschen hat, bei dem man weinen kann. Trotz allem, trotz aller Theorien und Bemühungen, vermisse ich jeden Tag und jede Stunde die Mutter, die mich versteht. Und deshalb denke ich bei allem, was ich tue und was ich schreibe, dass ich später für meine Kinder die Mutter sein will, wie ich sie mir vorstelle. Die Mams, die nicht alles so ernst nimmt, was dahingesagt wird, und doch ernst nimmt, was von mir kommt. Ich merke, ich kann es nicht beschreiben, aber das Wort »Mams« sagt schon alles. Weißt du, was ich für einen Ausweg gefunden habe, um doch so etwas wie Mams zu meiner Mutter zu sagen? Ich nenne sie oft Mansa, und davon kommt Mans. Es ist sozusagen die unvollkommene Mams, die ich so gerne noch mit einem Strich am »n« ehren möchte. Zum Glück begreift Mans das nicht, denn sie wäre sehr unglücklich darüber.

Nun ist es genug, mein »zu Tode betrübt« ist beim Schreiben ein bisschen vorbeigegangen!   Deine Anne

In diesen Tagen, an Weihnachten, muss ich immer wieder an Pim denken und an das, was er mir vergangenes Jahr erzählt hat. Vergangenes Jahr, als ich die Bedeutung seiner Worte nicht so verstand, wie ich sie jetzt verstehe. Wenn er doch noch einmal sprechen würde, vielleicht würde ich ihm dann zeigen können, dass ich ihn verstehe.

Ich glaube, dass Pim darüber gesprochen hat, weil er, der so viele »Herzensgeheimnisse« von anderen weiß, sich auch mal aussprechen musste. Denn Pim sagt sonst nie etwas über sich selbst, und ich glaube nicht, dass Margot vermutet, was Pim hat durchmachen müssen. Der arme Pim! Er kann mir nicht weismachen, dass er sie vergessen hat. Nie wird er das vergessen. Er ist nachgiebig geworden, denn auch er sieht Mutters Fehler. Ich hoffe, dass ich ihm ein bisschen ähnlich werde, ohne dass ich das auch durchmachen muss!   Anne

Montag, 27. Dezember 1943

Freitagabend habe ich zum ersten Mal in meinem Leben etwas zu Weihnachten bekommen. Die Mädchen, Kleiman und Kugler hatten wieder eine herrliche Überraschung vorbereitet. Miep hat einen wunderbaren Weihnachtskuchen gebacken, auf dem »Friede 1944« stand. Bep hat ein Pfund Butterkekse in Vorkriegsqualität besorgt. Für Peter, Margot und mich gab es eine Flasche Joghurt und für die Erwachsenen je eine Flasche Bier. Alles war wieder so hübsch eingepackt, mit Bildchen auf den verschiedenen Paketen. Ansonsten sind die Weihnachtstage schnell vorbeigegangen. Anne

Mittwoch, 29. Dezember 1943

Gestern Abend war ich wieder sehr traurig. Oma und Hanneli kamen mir vor Augen. Oma – die liebe Oma, wie wenig haben wir verstanden, was sie gelitten hat. Wie lieb war sie immer wieder zu uns, wie viel Interesse brachte sie allem entgegen, was uns betraf. Und dabei bewahrte sie stets sorgfältig das schreckliche Geheimnis, das sie mit sich trug.*

Wie treu und gut war Oma immer, nie hätte sie einen von uns im Stich gelassen. Was auch war, wie ungezogen ich auch war, Oma entschuldigte mich immer. Oma, hast du mich geliebt oder hast du mich auch nicht verstanden? Ich weiß es nicht. Wie einsam muss Oma gewesen sein, wie einsam, obwohl wir da waren. Ein Mensch kann einsam sein, trotz der Liebe von vielen, denn für niemanden ist er der »Liebste«.

Und Hanneli? Lebt sie noch? Was tut sie? O Gott, beschütze sie und bringe sie zu uns zurück. Hanneli, an dir sehe ich immer, wie mein Schicksal auch hätte sein können, immer sehe ich mich an deiner Stelle.

Warum bin ich denn so oft traurig wegen dem, was hier passiert? Müsste ich nicht immer froh, zufrieden und glücklich sein, außer wenn ich an sie und ihre Schicksalsgenossen denke? Ich bin selbstsüchtig und feige. Warum träume und denke ich immer die schlimmsten Dinge und würde vor Angst am liebsten schreien? Weil ich doch noch, trotz allem, Gott nicht genügend vertraue. Er hat mir so viel gegeben, was ich sicher noch nicht verdient habe, und doch tue ich jeden Tag so viel Falsches!

Man könnte weinen, wenn man an seinen Nächsten denkt, man könnte eigentlich den ganzen Tag weinen. Aber man kann nur beten, dass Gott ein Wunder geschehen lässt und einige von ihnen verschont. Ich hoffe, dass ich das ausreichend tue! Anne

---

* Die Großmutter war schwer krank; A. d. Ü.

Donnerstag, 30. Dezember 1943

Liebe Kitty!

Hier ist nach den letzten heftigen Streitereien alles wieder gut geworden, sowohl zwischen uns, Dussel und oben, als auch zwischen Herrn und Frau van Daan. Aber jetzt brauen sich wieder dicke Unwetterwolken zusammen, und zwar wegen Essen. Frau van Daan kam auf die unselige Idee, morgens weniger Bratkartoffeln zu machen und sie lieber aufzuheben. Mutter und Dussel und wir auch waren damit nicht einverstanden. Nun haben wir auch die Kartoffeln aufgeteilt. Aber jetzt geht es mit dem Fett ungerecht zu, und Mutter muss wieder einen Riegel vorschieben. Wenn das alles ein einigermaßen interessantes Ende nimmt, werde ich dir darüber bestimmt noch schreiben. Im Lauf der letzten Zeit haben wir nun geteilt: das Fleisch (sie fett, wir ohne Fett); sie Suppe, wir keine Suppe; die Kartoffeln (sie geschält, wir gepellt). Getrennt einkaufen, und jetzt auch noch die Bratkartoffeln.

Wären wir nur schon wieder ganz geteilt! Deine Anne

P. S. Bep hat für mich eine Ansichtskarte von der ganzen Königlichen Familie abziehen lassen. Juliane sieht darauf sehr jung aus, ebenso die Königin. Die drei Mädchen sind goldig. Ich fand das riesig nett von Bep, du nicht?

Sonntag, 2. Januar 1944

Liebe Kitty!

Als ich heute Morgen nichts zu tun hatte, blätterte ich mal in meinem Tagebuch und stieß mehrmals auf Briefe, die das Thema »Mutter« in so heftigen Worten behandelten, dass ich darüber erschrak und mich fragte: »Anne, bist du das, die über Hass gesprochen hat? O Anne, wie konntest du das?«

Ich blieb mit dem offenen Buch in der Hand sitzen und dachte darüber nach, wie es kam, dass ich so randvoll mit Wut und wirklich so voller Hass war, dass ich dir das alles anvertrauen musste. Ich habe versucht, die Anne von vor einem Jahr zu verstehen und zu entschuldigen, denn mein Gewissen ist nicht rein, solange ich dich mit diesen Beschuldigungen sitzen lasse, ohne dir nun hinterher zu erklären, wie ich so wurde. Ich litt (und leide) an Stimmungen, die mich (bildlich) mit dem Kopf unter Wasser hielten und mich die Dinge nur subjektiv sehen ließen. Ich habe nicht versucht, ruhig über die Worte der Gegenpartei nachzudenken und bei meinen Handlungen an den zu denken, den ich mit meinem aufbrausenden Temperament beleidigt oder traurig gemacht habe.

Ich habe mich in mir selbst versteckt, nur mich selbst betrachtet und alle meine Freude, meinen Spott und meine Traurigkeit ungestört in mein Tagebuch geschrieben. Dieses Tagebuch hat für mich bereits einen Wert, weil es oft ein Memoirenbuch geworden ist. Aber über viele Seiten könnte ich schon das Wort »Vorbei« setzen.

Ich war wütend auf Mutter (bin es noch oft). Sie verstand mich nicht, das ist wahr, aber ich verstand sie auch nicht. Da sie mich liebte, war sie zärtlich. Aber sie ist durch mich auch in viele unangenehme Situationen gebracht worden und wurde dadurch und durch viele andere traurige Umstände nervös und gereizt. Es ist gut zu verstehen, dass sie mich anschnauzte.

Ich nahm das viel zu ernst, war beleidigt, frech und unangenehm zu ihr, was sie ihrerseits wieder bekümmerte. Es war also eigentlich ein Hin und Her von Unannehmlichkeiten und Verdruss. Angenehm war es für uns beide sicher nicht, aber es geht vorbei. Dass ich dies nicht einsehen wollte und viel Mitleid mit mir selbst hatte, ist ebenfalls verständlich.

Diese zu heftigen Sätze sind lauter Äußerungen von Wut, die ich im normalen Leben mit ein paar Mal Aufstampfen in meinem Zimmer, hinter verschlossener Tür, oder mit Schimpfen hinter Mutters Rücken ausgelebt hätte.

Die Zeit, in der ich Mutter unter Tränen verurteilt habe, ist vorbei. Ich bin klüger geworden, und Mutters Nerven haben sich etwas beruhigt. Ich halte meistens den Mund, wenn ich mich ärgere, und sie tut das auch. Deshalb geht es uns augenscheinlich viel besser. Denn Mutter so richtig lieben, mit der anhänglichen Liebe eines Kindes, das kann ich nicht.

Ich beruhige mein Gewissen jetzt einfach mit dem Gedanken, dass Schimpfworte besser auf dem Papier stehen, als dass Mutter sie in ihrem Herzen tragen muss.   Deine Anne

Donnerstag, 6. Januar 1944

Liebe Kitty!

Heute muss ich dir zwei Dinge bekennen, die ziemlich viel Zeit in Anspruch nehmen werden, die ich aber unbedingt irgendjemandem erzählen muss. Das tue ich natürlich am besten bei dir, denn ich bin sicher, dass du immer und unter allen Umständen schweigen wirst.

Das Erste geht um Mutter. Du weißt, dass ich oft über sie geklagt habe und mir dann doch immer wieder Mühe gab, nett zu ihr zu sein. Plötzlich ist mir klar geworden, was ihr fehlt. Mutter hat uns selbst gesagt, dass sie uns mehr als Freundinnen denn als Töchter betrachtet. Das ist natürlich ganz schön, aber trotzdem kann eine Freundin nicht die Mutter ersetzen. Ich habe das Bedürfnis, mir meine Mutter als Vorbild zu nehmen und sie zu achten. Meistens ist sie auch ein Beispiel für mich, aber eben umgekehrt, wie ich es nicht machen soll. Ich habe das Gefühl, dass Margot über das alles ganz anders denkt und es nie begreifen würde. Und Vater weicht allen Gesprächen aus, bei denen es um Mutter gehen könnte.

Eine Mutter stelle ich mir als eine Frau vor, die vor allem viel Takt an den Tag legt, besonders für Kinder in unserem Alter. Nicht wie Mansa, die mich laut auslacht, wenn ich wegen etwas weine, nicht wegen Schmerzen, sondern wegen anderer Dinge.

Eine Sache, sie mag vielleicht unbedeutend erscheinen, habe ich ihr nie vergeben. Es war an einem Tag, als ich zum Zahnarzt musste. Mutter und Margot gingen mit und waren einverstanden, dass ich mein Fahrrad mitnahm. Als wir beim Zahnarzt fertig waren und wieder vor der Tür standen, sagten Margot und Mutter ganz fröhlich, sie gingen nun in die Stadt, um etwas anzuschauen oder zu kaufen, ich weiß es nicht mehr so genau. Ich wollte natürlich mit, aber das durfte ich nicht, weil ich mein Fahrrad dabeihatte. Vor Wut sprangen mir Tränen in die Augen, und Margot und Mutter fingen laut an zu lachen. Da wurde ich so wütend, dass ich ihnen auf der Straße die Zunge rausstreckte, als zufällig gerade ein kleines Frauchen vorbeikam und mich ganz erschrocken anschaute. Ich fuhr mit dem Fahrrad nach Hause und habe noch lange geweint. Seltsam, dass bei den unzähligen Wunden, die Mutter mir zugefügt hat, ausgerechnet diese immer noch anfängt zu brennen, wenn ich daran denke, wie wütend ich damals war.

Das Zweite fällt mir sehr schwer, dir zu erzählen, denn es geht um mich selbst. Ich bin nicht prüde, Kitty, aber wenn die anderen so oft im Detail darüber sprechen, was sie auf der Toilette erledigen, habe ich doch das Gefühl, dass ich mich mit meinem ganzen Körper dagegen wehre.

Gestern habe ich nun einen Artikel von Sis Heyster gelesen, über das Erröten. Sie spricht darin so, als meinte sie mich persönlich. Obwohl ich nicht so schnell rot werde, passen aber die anderen Dinge genau. Sie sagt so ungefähr, dass ein Mädchen in der Zeit der Pubertät still wird und anfängt, über die Wunder nachzudenken, die in ihrem Körper passieren. Auch ich habe das, und deshalb fange ich in der letzten Zeit an, mich zu genieren. Vor Margot, Mutter und Vater. Margot hingegen, die sonst viel schüchterner ist als ich, geniert sich überhaupt nicht.

Ich finde es so sonderbar, was da mit mir passiert, und nicht nur das, was äußerlich an meinem Körper zu sehen ist, sondern das, was sich innen vollzieht. Gerade weil ich über mich und vor allem über so etwas nie mit anderen spreche, spreche ich mit mir selbst darüber. Immer, wenn ich meine Periode habe (das war erst dreimal), habe ich das Gefühl, dass ich trotz der Schmerzen, des Unangenehmen und Ekligen ein süßes Geheimnis in mir trage. Deshalb, auch wenn es mir nur Schwierigkeiten macht, freue ich mich in gewisser Hinsicht immer wieder auf diese Zeit, in der ich es wieder fühle.

Sis Heyster schreibt auch noch, dass junge Mädchen in diesen Jahren nicht sehr selbstsicher sind und erst entdecken, dass sie selbst ein Mensch mit Ideen, Gedanken und Gewohnheiten sind. Ich habe, da ich schon mit kaum dreizehn Jahren hierher gekommen bin, früher damit angefangen, über mich nachzudenken, und früher gewusst, dass ich ein eigenständiger Mensch bin. Manchmal bekomme ich abends im Bett das heftige Bedürfnis, meine Brüste zu betasten und zu hören, wie ruhig und sicher mein Herz schlägt.

Unbewusst habe ich solche Gefühle schon gehabt, bevor ich hierher kam. Ich weiß, dass ich einmal, als ich abends bei Jacque schlief, mich nicht mehr halten konnte, so neugierig war ich auf ihren Körper, den sie immer vor mir versteckt gehalten und den ich nie gesehen hatte. Ich fragte sie, ob wir als Beweis unserer Freundschaft uns gegenseitig die Brüste befühlen sollten. Jacque lehnte das ab. Ich hatte auch ein schreckliches Bedürfnis, sie zu küssen, und habe das auch getan. Ich gerate jedes Mal in Ekstase, wenn ich eine nackte Frauengestalt sehe, zum Beispiel in dem Buch über Kunstgeschichte eine Venus. Manchmal finde ich das so wunderbar und schön, dass ich an mich halten muss, dass ich die Tränen nicht laufen lasse.

Hätte ich nur eine Freundin!

Donnerstag, 6. Januar 1944

Liebe Kitty!

Mein Verlangen, mit jemandem zu sprechen, wurde so groß, dass es mir irgendwie in den Kopf kam, Peter dafür auszuwählen. Wenn ich manchmal in Peters Zimmerchen kam, bei Licht, fand ich es dort immer sehr gemütlich, aber weil er so bescheiden ist und nie jemanden, der lästig wird, vor die Tür setzt, traute ich mich nie, länger zu bleiben. Ich hatte Angst, dass er mich schrecklich langweilig finden könnte. Ich suchte nach einer Gelegenheit, unauffällig in seinem Zimmer zu bleiben und ihn am Reden zu halten, und diese Gelegenheit ergab sich gestern. Peter hat nämlich plötzlich eine Manie für Kreuzworträtsel entwickelt und tut nichts anderes mehr, als den ganzen Tag zu raten. Ich half ihm dabei, und schon bald saßen wir uns an seinem Tisch gegenüber, er auf dem Stuhl, ich auf der Couch.

Mir wurde ganz seltsam zumute, als ich in seine dunkelblauen Augen schaute und sah, wie verlegen er bei dem ungewohnten Besuch war. Ich konnte an allem sein Inneres ablesen, ich sah in seinem Gesicht noch die Hilflosigkeit und die Unsicherheit, wie er sich verhalten sollte, und gleichzeitig einen Hauch vom Bewusstsein seiner Männlichkeit. Ich sah seine Verlegenheit und wurde ganz weich von innen. Ich hätte ihn gerne gebeten: Erzähl mir was von dir. Schau doch über die verhängnisvolle Schwatzhaftigkeit hinweg! Ich merkte jedoch, dass solche Fragen leichter vorzubereiten als auszuführen sind.

Der Abend ging vorbei, und nichts passierte, außer dass ich ihm von dem Erröten erzählte. Natürlich nicht das, was ich hier aufgeschrieben habe, sondern dass er mit den Jahren bestimmt sicherer werden würde.

Abends im Bett musste ich weinen, weinen, und doch durfte es niemand hören. Ich fand die Vorstellung, dass ich um Peters Gunst flehen sollte, einfach abstoßend. Man tut eine Menge, um seine Wünsche zu befriedigen, das siehst du an mir. Denn ich nahm mir vor, mich öfter zu Peter zu setzen und ihn auf irgendeine Art zum Sprechen zu bringen.

Du musst nicht meinen, dass ich in Peter verliebt bin, davon ist keine Rede. Wenn die van Daans statt eines Sohnes eine Tochter hier gehabt hätten, würde ich auch versucht haben, mit ihr Freundschaft zu schließen.

Heute Morgen wurde ich fünf vor sieben wach und wusste gleich ganz genau, was ich geträumt hatte. Ich saß auf einem Stuhl, und mir gegenüber saß Peter ... Schiff. Wir blätterten in einem Buch mit Illustrationen von Mary Bos. So deutlich war mein Traum, dass ich mich teilweise noch an die Zeichnungen erinnere. Aber das war nicht alles, der Traum ging weiter. Auf einmal trafen Peters Augen die meinen, und lange schaute ich in diese schönen, samtbraunen Augen. Dann sagte Peter sehr leise: »Wenn ich das gewusst hätte, wäre ich schon längst zu dir gekommen.« Brüsk drehte ich mich um, denn die Rührung wurde mir zu stark. Und dann fühlte ich eine weiche, o so kühle und wohl tuende Wange an meiner, und alles war so gut, so gut ...

An dieser Stelle wachte ich auf, während ich noch seine Wange an meiner fühlte und seine braunen Augen tief in mein Herz schauten, so tief, dass er darin gelesen hatte, wie sehr ich ihn geliebt habe und ihn noch liebe. Wieder sprangen mir die Tränen in die Augen, und ich war so traurig, weil ich ihn wieder verloren hatte, aber gleichzeitig doch froh, weil ich wusste, dass Peter noch immer mein Auserwählter ist.

Seltsam, dass ich hier oft so deutliche Traumbilder habe. Erst sah ich Omi* eines Nachts so klar, dass mir ihre Haut wie aus dickem, weichem Faltensamt vorkam. Dann erschien mir Oma als Schutzengel, danach Hanneli, die für mich das Symbol des Elends meiner Freunde und aller Juden ist. Wenn ich also für sie bete, bete ich für alle Juden und alle armen Menschen.

* Omi ist die Großmutter mütterlicherseits, Oma die Mutter des Vaters; A. d. Ü.

Und nun Peter, mein lieber Peter. Noch nie habe ich ihn so deutlich gesehen. Ich brauche kein Foto von ihm, ich sehe ihn so gut, so gut.

Liebe Kitty!

Dummkopf, der ich bin! Ich habe überhaupt nicht daran gedacht, dass ich dir die Geschichte meiner großen Liebe nie erzählt habe.

Als ich noch sehr klein war, noch im Kindergarten, war meine Sympathie auf Sally Kimmel gefallen. Er hatte keinen Vater mehr und wohnte mit seiner Mutter bei einer Tante. Ein Vetter von Sally, Appy, war ein hübscher, schlanker, dunkler Junge, der später aussah wie ein Filmstar und der immer mehr Bewunderung erweckte als der kleine humorvolle Moppel Sally. Eine Zeit lang waren wir viel zusammen, aber ansonsten blieb meine Liebe unerwidert, bis mir Peter über den Weg lief und ich von einer heftigen Kinderverliebtheit gepackt wurde. Er mochte mich ebenso gerne, und einen Sommer lang waren wir unzertrennlich. Ich sehe uns noch in Gedanken Hand in Hand auf der Straße gehen, er in einem weißen Baumwollanzug, ich in einem kurzen Sommerkleid. Am Ende der großen Ferien kam er in die erste Klasse der Oberschule, ich in die sechste Klasse der Primarschule. Er holte mich von der Schule ab, und umgekehrt holte ich ihn ab.

Peter war ein Bild von einem Jungen, groß, hübsch, schlank, mit einem ernsten, ruhigen und intelligenten Gesicht. Er hatte dunkle Haare und wunderschöne braune Augen, rotbraune Backen und eine spitze Nase. Besonders verrückt war ich nach seinem Lachen, dann sah er so lausbubenhaft und frech aus.

In den großen Ferien war ich nicht da, und als ich zurückkam, fand ich Peter nicht mehr an seiner alten Adresse. Er war inzwischen umgezogen und wohnte mit einem viel älteren Jungen zusammen. Der machte ihn anscheinend darauf aufmerksam, dass ich noch ein kindischer Knirps war, und Peter verließ mich. Ich liebte ihn so sehr, dass ich die Wahrheit nicht sehen wollte, bis mir schließlich bewusst wurde, dass ich als mannstoll verschrien würde, wenn ich ihm noch länger nachliefe.

Die Jahre gingen vorbei, Peter verkehrte mit Mädchen seines eigenen Alters und dachte nicht mehr daran, mich zu grüßen. Ich kam ins Jüdische Lyzeum, und viele Jungen aus unserer Klasse verliebten sich in mich. Ich fand das schön, fühlte mich geschmeichelt, aber es berührte mich nicht weiter. Noch später war Hello verrückt nach mir, aber wie gesagt, ich habe mich nie mehr verliebt.

Es gibt ein Sprichwort: »Die Zeit heilt alle Wunden.« So ging es auch bei mir. Ich bildete mir ein, dass ich Peter vergessen hätte und ihn überhaupt nicht mehr nett fände. Die Erinnerung an ihn lebte jedoch so stark fort, dass ich mir manchmal eingestand, dass ich eifersüchtig auf die anderen Mädchen war und ihn deshalb nicht mehr nett fand. Heute Morgen habe ich gemerkt, dass sich nichts geändert hat. Im Gegenteil, während ich älter und reifer wurde, wuchs meine Liebe in mir mit. Jetzt kann ich verstehen, dass Peter mich damals zu kindlich fand, und doch tat es mir weh, dass er mich so schnell vergessen hatte. Ich habe sein Gesicht so deutlich vor mir gesehen und weiß jetzt, dass niemand anders so fest in mir verhaftet bleiben kann.

Heute bin ich dann auch völlig verwirrt. Als Vater mir heute Morgen einen Kuss gab, hätte ich am liebsten geschrien: »Oh, wärest du bloß Peter!« Bei allem denke ich an ihn und wiederhole den ganzen Tag heimlich für mich: »O Petel, lieber, lieber Petel …«

Was kann mir helfen? Ich muss einfach weiterleben und Gott bitten, dass er mir, wenn ich hier rauskomme, Peter über den Weg führt und der in meinen Augen meine Gefühle liest und sagt: »O Anne, wenn ich das gewusst hätte, wäre ich schon längst zu dir gekommen.«

Vater sagte einmal zu mir, als wir über Sexualität sprachen, dass ich dieses Verlangen noch nicht verstehen könnte. Ich wusste aber immer, dass ich es verstand, und nun verstehe ich es ganz. Nichts ist mir so teuer wie er, mein Petel.

Ich habe im Spiegel mein Gesicht gesehen, und das sieht so anders aus als sonst. Meine Augen sind so klar und tief, meine Wangen sind, was seit Wochen nicht der Fall war, rosig gefärbt, mein Mund ist viel weicher. Ich sehe aus, als wäre ich glücklich, und doch ist so etwas Trauriges in meinem Ausdruck, das Lächeln verschwindet sofort wieder von meinen Lippen. Ich bin nicht glücklich, denn ich kann mir denken, dass Petels Gedanken nicht bei mir sind. Und doch, ich fühle immer wieder seine Augen auf mich gerichtet und seine kühle, weiche Wange an meiner …

O Petel, Petel, wie komme ich wieder von deinem Bild los? Ist jeder andere an deiner Stelle nicht ein armseliger Ersatz? Ich liebe dich so sehr, dass die Liebe nicht länger in meinem Herzen wachsen konnte, sondern zum Vorschein kommen musste und sich mir plötzlich in so gewaltigem Umfang offenbarte.

Vor einer Woche, noch vor einem Tag, würde ich, wenn du mich gefragt hättest: Welchen von deinen Bekannten findest du am besten geeignet, um ihn zu heiraten?, geantwortet haben: »Sally, denn bei ihm ist es gut, ruhig und sicher.« Jetzt würde ich schreien: »Petel, denn ihn liebe ich mit meinem ganzen Herzen, mit meiner ganzen Seele in vollkommener Hingabe!« Außer einem – er darf mich nur im Gesicht berühren, weiter nicht.

In Gedanken saß ich heute Morgen mit Petel auf dem vorderen Dachboden, auf dem Holz vor dem Fenster, und nach einem kurzen Gespräch fingen wir beide an zu weinen. Und später fühlte ich seinen Mund und seine herrliche Wange! O Petel, komm zu mir, denke an mich, mein lieber Petel!

Mittwoch, 12. Januar 1944

Liebe Kitty!

Seit vierzehn Tagen ist Bep nun wieder bei uns, obwohl ihre Schwester erst nächste Woche wieder zur Schule darf. Sie selbst lag zwei Tage mit einer heftigen Erkältung im Bett. Auch Miep und Jan konnten zwei Tage nicht kommen, sie hatten sich den Magen verdorben.

Ich habe im Augenblick Tanz- und Ballettanwandlungen und übe jeden Abend fleißig. Aus einem helllila Spitzenunterrock von Mansa habe ich mir ein hypermodernes Tanzkleid hergestellt. Oben ist ein Band durchgezogen, das über der Brust schließt, und ein Band aus rosa gerippter Seide vollendet das Ganze. Allerdings habe ich vergeblich versucht, aus meinen Turnschuhen Ballettschuhe zu machen.

Meine steifen Gliedmaßen sind auf dem besten Weg, wieder so geschmeidig zu werden wie früher. Eine tolle Übung finde ich: auf dem Boden sitzen, mit jeder Hand eine Ferse halten und dann die Beine in die Höhe heben. Ich muss jedoch ein Kissen als Unterlage verwenden, sonst wird mein armes Steißbein zu sehr misshandelt.

Hier lesen sie ein Buch mit dem Titel »Wolkenloser Morgen«. Mutter fand es außerordentlich gut, weil viele Probleme Jugendlicher darin beschrieben werden. Ein bisschen ironisch dachte ich mir: »Kümmere du dich erst mal um deine eigenen Jugendlichen.«

Ich glaube, Mutter denkt, dass Margot und ich das beste Verhältnis zu unseren Eltern haben, das es nur gibt, und dass niemand sich mehr mit dem Leben seiner Kinder beschäftigt als sie. Dabei hat sie bestimmt nur Margot im Auge, denn ich glaube, dass die solche Probleme und Gedanken wie ich nie hat. Ich will Mutter gar nicht auf die Idee bringen, dass es in einem ihrer Sprösslinge ganz anders aussieht, als sie sich das vorstellt. Sie wäre völlig verblüfft und wüsste doch nicht, wie sie die Sache anders anpacken sollte. Den Kummer, der für sie daraus folgen würde, will ich ihr ersparen, vor allem, weil ich weiß, dass es für mich doch dasselbe bleiben würde. Mutter fühlt wohl, dass Margot sie viel lieber hat als ich, aber sie denkt, dass das nur vorübergehend ist.

Margot ist so lieb geworden, sie scheint mir ganz anders zu sein als früher. Sie ist längst nicht mehr so schnippisch und wird nun eine wirkliche Freundin. Sie sieht nicht mehr den kleinen Knirps in mir, mit dem man nicht zu rechnen braucht.

Es ist ein seltsames Phänomen, dass ich mich manchmal wie mit den Augen eines anderen sehe. Ich betrachte mir die Angelegenheit einer gewissen Anne Frank und blättere seelenruhig in meinem eigenen Lebensbuch, als wäre es das einer Fremden.

Früher, zu Hause, als ich noch nicht so viel nachdachte, hatte ich zuweilen das Gefühl, dass ich nicht zu Mansa, Pim und Margot gehörte und immer eine Außenseiterin bleiben würde. Manchmal spielte ich dann vielleicht ein halbes Jahr lang die Rolle eines Waisenkindes, bis ich mir selbst vorwarf, dass ich nur durch meine eigene Schuld die Leidende spielte, wo ich es doch immer so gut hatte. Dann folgte eine Periode, in der ich mich zwang, freundlich zu sein. Jeden Morgen, wenn jemand die Treppe herabkam, hoffte ich, dass es Mutter sein würde, die käme, um mir guten Morgen zu sagen. Ich begrüßte sie sehr lieb, weil ich mich wirklich darüber freute, dass sie mich so lieb anschaute. Dann schnauzte sie mich wegen irgendeiner Bemerkung

Anne auf dem Dach des Hauses im Merwedeplein, 1940.

an, und ich ging ganz entmutigt zur Schule. Auf dem Heimweg entschuldigte ich sie dann, dachte, dass sie Sorgen hatte, kam fröhlich nach Hause und redete drauflos, bis sich das Gleiche wie morgens wiederholte und ich mit einem nachdenklichen Gesicht wieder ging. Manchmal nahm ich mir auch vor, böse zu bleiben. Aber aus der Schule heimgekommen, hatte ich so viele Neuigkeiten, dass ich mein Vorhaben schon längst vergessen hatte und Mutter unter allen Umständen ein offenes Ohr für meine Erlebnisse haben musste. Bis wieder die Zeit kam, wo ich morgens nicht mehr auf die Schritte von der Treppe horchte, mich einsam fühlte und abends mein Kissen mit Tränen übergoss.

Hier ist alles viel schlimmer geworden, du weißt es ja. Aber jetzt hat Gott mir eine Hilfe geschickt: Peter. Ich fasse schnell an meinen Anhänger, drücke einen Kuss darauf und denke: »Was kann mir der ganze Kram ausmachen! Petel gehört zu mir, und niemand weiß davon!« Auf diese Art kann ich jedes Anschnauzen überwinden.

Wer hier wohl ahnt, was alles in einer Backfischseele vorgeht?

Samstag, 15. Januar 1944

Liebste Kitty!

Es hat keinen Zweck, dass ich dir immer wieder bis in die kleinsten Einzelheiten unsere Streitereien und Auseinandersetzungen beschreibe. Es genügt, wenn ich dir erzähle, dass wir jetzt viele Dinge wie Fett und Fleisch getrennt haben und unsere eigenen Bratkartoffeln machen. Seit einiger Zeit essen wir etwas Roggenbrot extra, weil wir um vier Uhr schon sehnsüchtig auf das Essen warten und unsere knurrenden Mägen es fast nicht aushalten.

Mutters Geburtstag nähert sich. Sie hat von Kugler zusätzlich Zucker bekommen, ein Anlass für Eifersucht, weil zu Frau van Daans Geburtstag die Bewirtung ausgefallen war. Aber wozu könnte es gut sein, dich weiter mit harten Worten, Heulausbrüchen und giftigen Gesprächen zu langweilen. Wenn du nur weißt, dass sie uns noch mehr langweilen!

Mutter hat den vorläufig unerfüllbaren Wunsch geäußert, Herrn van Daans Gesicht mal vierzehn Tage nicht sehen zu müssen.

Ich frage mich, ob man mit allen Menschen, mit denen man so lange zusammenwohnt, auf die Dauer Streit bekommt. Oder haben wir vielleicht nur großes Pech gehabt? Wenn Dussel am Tisch von einer halben Schüssel Soße ein Viertel wegnimmt und alle anderen seelenruhig ihr Essen ohne Soße essen lässt, dann ist mir der Appetit vergangen. Dann würde ich am liebsten aufspringen und ihn vom Stuhl und aus der Tür hinaus stoßen.

Ist die Mehrheit der Menschen so egoistisch und knauserig? Ich finde es ganz gut, dass ich hier ein bisschen Menschenkenntnis bekommen habe, aber nun reicht's. Peter sagt das auch.

Der Krieg stört sich nicht an unseren Streitereien, an unserer Sehnsucht nach Freiheit und Luft, und darum müssen wir versuchen, das Beste aus unserem Aufenthalt hier zu machen.

Ich predige, aber ich glaube, wenn wir noch lange hier bleiben, werde ich eine ausgetrocknete Bohnenstange. Und ich würde so gerne noch ein richtiger Backfisch sein!

Deine Anne

Mittwochabend, 19. Januar 1944

Liebe Kitty!

Ich (schon wieder dieser Fehler!) weiß nicht, was es ist, aber ich merke immer wieder, dass ich nach meinem Traum verändert bin. Nebenbei bemerkt, heute Nacht träumte ich wieder von Peter und sah seine durchdringenden Augen, aber dieser Traum war nicht so schön und auch nicht so klar wie der vorige.

Du weißt, dass ich früher, was Vater betraf, immer eifersüchtig auf Margot war. Davon ist nichts mehr zu merken. Es tut mir zwar noch weh, wenn Vater nervös ist und mich ungerecht behandelt, aber ich denke: »Ich kann es euch eigentlich nicht übel nehmen, dass ihr so seid. Ihr redet viel über die Gedanken von Kindern und Jugendlichen, aber ihr habt ja keine Ahnung.« Ich sehne mich nach mehr als Vaters Küssen, nach mehr als seinen Liebkosungen. Bin ich nicht schrecklich, dass ich mich immer mit mir selbst beschäftige? Muss ich, die ich gut und lieb sein will, ihnen nicht erst mal verzeihen? Ich vergebe Mutter ja, aber ich kann mich fast nicht beherrschen, wenn sie so sarkastisch ist und mich immer wieder auslacht.

Ich weiß, ich bin noch lange nicht so, wie ich sein muss. Werde ich jemals so werden?

Anne Frank

P. S. Vater fragte, ob ich dir von der Torte erzählt habe. Mutter hat nämlich an ihrem Geburtstag eine richtige Vorkriegstorte vom Büro bekommen, mit Mokka. Sie war wirklich toll. Aber ich habe im Augenblick so wenig Platz in meinen Gedanken für solche Sachen.

Samstag, 22. Januar 1944

Liebe Kitty!

Kannst du mir vielleicht erzählen, wie es kommt, dass alle Menschen ihr Inneres so ängstlich verbergen? Wie kommt es, dass ich mich in Gesellschaft immer ganz anders verhalte, als ich mich verhalten sollte? Warum vertraut der eine dem anderen so wenig? Ich weiß, es wird einen Grund dafür geben, aber manchmal finde ich es sehr schlimm, dass man nirgends, selbst bei den Menschen, die einem am nächsten stehen, ein wenig Vertraulichkeit findet.

Es kommt mir vor, als wäre ich seit meinem Traum älter geworden, eine eigenständigere Person. Du wirst auch erstaunt sein, wenn ich dir sage, dass sogar van Daans jetzt eine andere Position bei mir einnehmen. Ich betrachte auf einmal all die Diskussionen und so weiter nicht mehr von unserem voreingenommenen Standpunkt aus. Warum bin ich so verändert? Ja, siehst du, ich dachte plötzlich daran, dass unsere Beziehung ganz anders gewesen wäre, wenn Mutter anders wäre, eine richtige Mams. Es stimmt natürlich, dass Frau van Daan alles andere als ein feiner Mensch ist. Trotzdem denke ich, dass die Hälfte aller Streitereien hätte vermieden werden können, wenn Mutter im Umgang und bei jedem scharfen Gespräch nicht so unmöglich wäre. Frau van Daan hat nämlich eine Sonnenseite, und die ist, dass man mit ihr reden kann. Trotz allem Egoismus, aller Raffgier und Rückständigkeit kann man sie leicht zum Nachgeben bewegen, wenn man sie nicht reizt und widerborstig macht. Bis zum nächsten Anlass funktioniert dieses Mittel nicht, aber wenn man geduldig ist, kann man immer wieder versuchen, wie weit man damit kommt.

All die Fragen über unsere Erziehung, die Verwöhnerei, das Essen, alles, alles, alles hätte einen anderen Verlauf genommen, wenn man offen und freundschaftlich geblieben wäre und nicht immer nur die schlechten Seiten gesehen hätte.

Ich weiß genau, was du jetzt sagen würdest, Kitty: »Aber Anne, kommen diese Worte wirklich von dir? Von dir, die so viele harte Worte von oben hören musste? Von dir, die all das Unrecht kennt, das geschehen ist?«

Ja, sie kommen von mir. Ich möchte alles neu erforschen und dabei nicht nach dem Sprichwort vorgehen: »Wie die Alten sungen, so zwitschern auch die Jungen.« Ich will die van Daans beobachten und sehen, was wahr und was übertrieben ist. Wenn ich dann eine Enttäuschung erlebe, kann ich ja wieder mit Vater und Mutter am selben Strick ziehen. Und wenn nicht, nun, dann werde ich versuchen, sie von ihren falschen Vorstellungen abzubringen. Auch wenn mir das nicht gelingt, halte ich an meiner eigenen Meinung und meinem Urteil fest. Ich werde jetzt jede Gelegenheit ergreifen, um offen mit Frau van Daan über viele Streitpunkte zu sprechen, und keine Angst haben, neutral meine Meinung zu sagen, auch wenn sie mich für einen Naseweis hält.

Was gegen meine eigene Familie verstößt, das muss ich wohl verschweigen, aber ab heute gehört Tratschen, was mich betrifft, der Vergangenheit an, obwohl das nicht bedeutet, dass ich nachlasse, sie zu verteidigen, gegen wen auch immer.

Bisher glaubte ich felsenfest, dass alle Schuld an den Streitereien bei den van Daans liegt, aber ein großer Teil lag sicher auch an uns. Wir hatten schon Recht, was die Themen anging, aber von vernünftigen Menschen (zu denen wir uns rechnen!) kann man doch etwas mehr Einsicht beim Umgang mit Menschen erwarten.

Ich hoffe, dass ich ein Tüpfelchen von jener Einsicht bekommen habe und die Gelegenheit finden werde, sie gut anzuwenden.

Deine Anne

Montag, 24. Januar 1944

Liebe Kitty!

Mir ist etwas passiert (oder eigentlich kann ich von passieren nicht sprechen), was ich selbst ganz verrückt finde.

Früher wurde zu Hause und in der Schule über Geschlechtsfragen entweder geheimnisvoll oder Ekel erregend gesprochen. Worte, die sich darauf bezogen, wurden geflüstert, und wenn jemand etwas nicht wusste, wurde er ausgelacht. Ich fand das seltsam und dachte oft: »Warum spricht man über diese Dinge immer so geheimnisvoll oder hässlich?« Aber weil doch nichts daran zu ändern war, hielt ich so weit wie möglich den Mund oder bat meine Freundinnen um Auskunft.

Als ich über vieles Bescheid wusste, sagte Mutter einmal: »Anne, ich gebe dir einen guten Rat, sprich über dieses Thema nie mit Jungen und gib keine Antwort, wenn sie damit anfangen.«

Ich weiß meine Antwort noch ganz genau, ich sagte: »Nein, natürlich nicht, was stellst du dir vor!« Und dabei ist es geblieben.

In der ersten Zeit im Versteck sprach Vater häufig von Dingen, die ich lieber von Mutter gehört hätte, und den Rest erfuhr ich aus Büchern oder Gesprächen.

Peter van Daan war in dieser Hinsicht nie so unangenehm wie die Jungen in der Schule, am Anfang vielleicht schon mal, aber niemals, um mich herauszufordern. Frau van Daan hat mal gesagt, dass sie nie mit Peter über diese Dinge gesprochen hat, ihr Mann auch nicht. Offensichtlich wusste sie nicht einmal, wie und über was Peter informiert war.

Gestern nun, als Margot, Peter und ich beim Kartoffelschälen waren, kam das Gespräch auf Moffi, die Katze. »Wir wissen noch immer nicht, welches Geschlecht Moffi hat, gell?«, fragte ich.

»Doch, schon«, antwortete Peter. »Es ist ein Kater.«

Ich fing an zu lachen. »Ein schöner Kater, der in anderen Umständen ist.«

Peter und Margot lachten mit. Vor zwei Monaten hatte Peter nämlich gesagt, es würde nicht mehr lange dauern und Moffi bekäme Kinder, ihr Bauch wurde so erstaunlich dick. Der dicke Bauch kam aber, wie sich herausstellte, von den vielen gestohlenen Leckerbissen, denn die Kinderchen wuchsen nicht, geschweige denn, dass sie geboren wurden.

Peter musste sich nun doch verteidigen. »Du kannst selbst mitkommen und ihn betrachten. Als ich mal mit ihm gebalgt habe, habe ich ganz genau gesehen, dass er ein Kater ist.«

Ich konnte meine Neugier nicht zurückhalten und ging mit ins Lager. Moffi hatte jedoch keine Sprechstunde und war nirgends zu entdecken. Wir warteten eine Weile, fingen an zu frieren und stiegen die Treppe wieder hinauf.

Später am Nachmittag hörte ich, dass Peter wieder hinunterging. Ich nahm meinen ganzen Mut zusammen und ging allein durch das stille Haus hinunter ins Lager. Peter spielte mit Moffi auf dem Packtisch und wollte Moffi gerade auf die Waage setzen, um sein Gewicht zu kontrollieren.

»Hallo, willst du mal sehen?« Er machte keine langen Vorbereitungen, hob das Tier hoch, drehte es auf den Rücken, hielt sehr geschickt Kopf und Pfoten fest, und der Unterricht begann. »Das ist das männliche Geschlechtsteil, das sind ein paar lose Härchen, und das ist der Hintern.«

Die Katze machte nochmals eine halbe Umdrehung und stand wieder auf ihren weißen Socken.

Jeden anderen Jungen, der mir so »das männliche Geschlechtsteil« gezeigt hätte, hätte ich nicht mehr angeschaut. Aber Peter sprach ganz seelenruhig über das sonst so peinliche Thema und hatte überhaupt keine Hintergedanken, sodass ich mich schließlich beruhigte und auch normal wurde. Wir spielten mit Moffi, amüsierten uns gut, tratschten miteinander und schlenderten schließlich durch das Lager zur Tür.

»Bist du dabei gewesen, als Mouschi kastriert wurde?«, fragte ich.

»Ja, sicher, das geht sehr schnell. Das Tier wird natürlich betäubt.«

»Holen sie da was raus?«

»Nein, der Doktor knipst einfach den Samenleiter durch. Man kann von außen nichts sehen.«

Ich sammelte Mut, denn so einfach ging es bei mir doch nicht. »Peter, Geschlechtsteile haben doch bei Männchen und Weibchen verschiedene Namen.«

»Das weiß ich.«

»Bei Weibchen heißt es Vagina, soviel ich weiß, bei Männchen weiß ich es nicht mehr.«

»Ja.«

»Ach ja«, sagte ich wieder. »Wie soll man diese Worte auch wissen, meist trifft man sie durch Zufall.«

»Warum? Ich frage sie oben. Meine Eltern wissen das besser als ich und haben auch mehr Erfahrung.«

Wir standen schon auf der Treppe, und ich hielt den Mund.

Ja, wirklich, so einfach hätte ich nie mit einem Mädchen darüber gesprochen. Ich bin auch sicher, dass Mutter nicht dieses gemeint hat, als sie mich vor den Jungen warnte.

Trotzdem war ich den ganzen Tag ein bisschen durcheinander, wenn ich an unser Gespräch zurückdachte, es kam mir doch seltsam vor. Aber in einem Punkt bin ich wenigstens klüger geworden: Es gibt auch junge Menschen, sogar vom anderen Geschlecht, die ungezwungen und ohne Witze darüber sprechen können.

Ob Peter wirklich seine Eltern fragt? Ist er wirklich so, wie er sich gestern gezeigt hat?

Ach, was weiß ich davon?!!! Deine Anne

Freitag, 28. Januar 1944

Liebe Kitty!

In der letzten Zeit habe ich eine starke Vorliebe für Stammbäume und genealogische Tabellen von königlichen Häusern. Wenn man einmal mit Suchen anfängt, muss man immer weiter in der Vergangenheit graben und kommt zu immer interessanteren Entdeckungen. Obwohl ich außerordentlich eifrig bin, was meine Lehrfächer angeht, schon ziemlich gut dem Home-Service vom englischen Sender folgen kann, widme ich doch viele Sonntage dem Aussuchen und Sortieren meiner großen Filmstarsammlung, die einen respektablen Umfang angenommen hat. Herr Kugler macht mir jeden Montag eine Freude, wenn er mir die »Cinema & Theater« mitbringt. Obwohl das von den unmondänen Hausgenossen oft als Geldverschwendung bezeichnet wird, sind sie dann jedes Mal wieder erstaunt über die Genauigkeit, mit der ich nach einem Jahr noch präzise die Mitwirkenden eines bestimmten Films angeben kann. Bep, die oft ihre freien Tage mit ihrem Freund im Kino verbringt, teilt mir den Titel des geplanten Films samstags mit, und ich rassle ihr sowohl die Hauptdarsteller als auch die Kritik herunter. Es ist noch nicht lange her, da sagte Mans, dass ich später nicht ins Kino zu gehen bräuchte, weil ich Inhalt, Besetzung und Kritiken bereits im Kopf hätte.

Wenn ich mal mit einer neuen Frisur angesegelt komme, schauen mich alle mit missbilligenden Gesichtern an, und bestimmt fragt einer, welche Filmschauspielerin denn diese Frisur auf ihrem Kopf prangen hat. Wenn ich antworte, dass sie eine eigene Erfindung ist, glauben sie mir immer nur halb. Was die Frisur betrifft, die hält nicht länger als eine halbe Stunde, dann bin ich die abweisenden Urteile so leid, dass ich ins Badezimmer renne und schnell meine normale Lockenfrisur wieder herstelle.

Deine Anne

Freitag, 28. Januar 1944

Liebe Kitty!

Heute Morgen habe ich mich gefragt, ob du dir nicht vorkommst wie eine Kuh, die alle alten Neuigkeiten immer wiederkäuen muss und, von der einseitigen Ernährung gelangweilt, schließlich laut gähnt und sich im Stillen wünscht, dass Anne mal was Neues auftreibt.

Leider, ich weiß, das Alte ist langweilig für dich, aber stell dir mal vor, wie gelangweilt ich von den alten, immer wieder aufgewärmten Geschichten werde. Wenn es bei einem Tischgespräch nicht um Politik oder herrliche Mahlzeiten geht, nun, dann rücken Mutter oder Frau van Daan bloß wieder mit längst schon erzählten Geschichten aus ihrer Jugendzeit heraus. Oder Dussel schwafelt über den reichhaltigen Kleiderschrank seiner Frau, über schöne Rennpferde, lecke Ruderboote, von Jungen, die mit vier Jahren schwimmen können, von Muskelkater und von ängstlichen Patienten. Wenn einer von den acht seinen Mund aufmacht, können die anderen sieben seine angefangene Geschichte fertig machen. Die Pointe eines jeden Witzes wissen wir schon im Voraus, und der Erzähler lacht alleine darüber. Die diversen Milchmänner, Lebensmittelhändler und Metzger der Exhausfrauen sehen wir in unserer Einbildung schon mit einem Bart, so oft sind sie bei Tisch in den Himmel gehoben oder fertig gemacht worden. Es ist unmöglich, dass etwas noch jung und frisch ist, wenn es im Hinterhaus zur Sprache kommt.

Das wäre ja noch zu ertragen, wenn die Erwachsenen nicht die Angewohnheit hätten, Geschichten, die Kleiman, Jan oder Miep zum Besten geben, zehnmal nachzuerzählen und sie jedes Mal mit eigenen Erfindungen auszuschmücken, sodass ich mich oft unterm Tisch in den Arm kneifen muss, damit ich dem begeisterten Erzähler nicht den richtigen Weg zeige. Kleine Kinder wie Anne dürfen Erwachsene unter keinen Umständen verbessern, egal, welche Schnitzer sie auch machen oder welche Unwahrheiten oder Erfindungen sie sich aus den Fingern saugen.

Ein Thema, über das Kleiman und Jan oft reden, ist Verstecken oder Untertauchen. Sie wissen, dass wir ebenso mitleiden, wenn Versteckte gefangen werden, wie wir uns mitfreuen, wenn Gefangene befreit werden.

Untertauchen und Verstecken sind jetzt so normale Begriffe wie früher Papas Pantoffeln, die vor dem Ofen stehen mussten. Es gibt viele Organisationen wie »Freie Niederlande«. Sie fälschen Personalausweise, geben Untergetauchten Geld, treiben Verstecke auf, beschaffen untergetauchten christlichen jungen Männern Arbeit, und es ist erstaunlich, wie oft, wie nobel und wie uneigennützig diese Arbeit verrichtet wird und wie die Leute unter Einsatz ihres Lebens anderen helfen und andere retten.

Das beste Beispiel dafür sind doch wohl unsere Helfer, die uns bis jetzt durchgebracht haben und uns hoffentlich noch ans sichere Ufer bringen. Sonst müssten sie das Schicksal all derer teilen, die gesucht werden. Nie haben wir von ihnen ein Wort gehört, das auf die Last hinweist, die wir doch sicher für sie sind. Niemals klagt einer, dass wir ihnen zu viel Mühe machen. Jeden Tag kommen sie herauf, sprechen mit den Herren über Geschäft und Politik, mit den Damen über Essen und die Beschwerden der Kriegszeit, mit den Kindern über Bücher und Zeitungen. Sie machen, soweit es geht, ein fröhliches Gesicht, bringen Blumen und Geschenke zu Geburts- und Festtagen, stehen immer und überall für uns bereit. Das ist etwas, was wir nie vergessen dürfen. Andere zeigen Heldenmut im Krieg oder gegenüber den Deutschen, aber unsere Helfer beweisen ihren Heldenmut in ihrer Fröhlichkeit und Liebe.

Die verrücktesten Geschichten machen die Runde, und die meisten sind wirklich passiert. Kleiman erzählte zum Beispiel diese Woche, dass in Gelderland zwei Fußballmannschaften gegeneinander gespielt haben. Die eine bestand ausschließlich aus Untergetauchten, die zweite aus Feldjägern. In Hilversum werden neue Stammkarten ausgeteilt. Damit die vielen Versteckten auch welche bekommen (Lebensmittelkarten sind ausschließlich auf Stammkarten oder für 60

Gulden je Stück erhältlich), haben Beamte der Zuteilungsstelle alle Untergetauchten aus der Umgebung zu einer bestimmten Zeit bestellt, um ihre Ausweise abzuholen.

Man muss aber sehr vorsichtig sein, dass solche Kunststückchen den Moffen nicht zu Ohren kommen. Deine Anne

Sonntag, 30. Januar 1944

Liebste Kit!

Wir sind wieder an einem Sonntag angelangt. Ich finde Sonntage zwar nicht mehr so schlimm wie früher, aber immer noch langweilig genug.

Im Lager bin ich noch nicht gewesen, vielleicht klappt es später. Gestern bin ich ganz allein im Dunkeln hinuntergegangen. Ich stand oben an der Treppe, deutsche Flugzeuge flogen hin und her, und ich wusste, dass ich ein Mensch-für-sich-selbst bin, der nicht mit der Hilfe anderer rechnen darf. Meine Angst war verschwunden. Ich sah hinauf zum Himmel und vertraute auf Gott.

Ich habe ein schreckliches Bedürfnis, allein zu sein. Vater merkt, dass ich anders bin als sonst, aber ich kann ihm auch nichts erzählen. Am liebsten würde ich immer nur sagen: »Lass mich in Ruhe, lass mich allein!«

Wer weiß, vielleicht werde ich noch einmal mehr allein gelassen, als mir lieb ist! Anne Frank

Donnerstag, 3. Februar 1944

Liebe Kitty!

Die Invasionsstimmung im Land steigt mit jedem Tag. Wenn du hier wärest, wärest du sicher genauso beeindruckt wie ich von all diesen Vorbereitungen, aber andererseits würdest du uns auch auslachen, weil wir uns so aufregen, und vielleicht umsonst!

Alle Zeitungen sind voll von der Invasion. Sie machen die Leute ganz verrückt, weil sie schreiben: »Falls die Engländer in den Niederlanden landen, werden die deutschen Machthaber alle Mittel einsetzen, das Land zu verteidigen, es notfalls auch unter Wasser setzen.« Dazu sind Karten veröffentlicht worden, in denen die Teile der Niederlande, die unter Wasser gesetzt werden können, schraffiert sind. Da große Teile von Amsterdam dazugehören, war die erste Frage, was zu tun ist, wenn das Wasser einen Meter hoch in den Straßen steht. Auf diese schwierige Frage kamen von allen Seiten die verschiedensten Antworten.

»Weil Radfahren oder zu Fuß gehen ausgeschlossen sind, werden wir eben durch das Wasser waten müssen, wenn es zum Stillstand gekommen ist.«

»Nicht doch, man muss versuchen zu schwimmen. Wir ziehen uns alle eine Bademütze und einen Badeanzug an und schwimmen soviel wie möglich unter Wasser, dann sieht niemand, dass wir Juden sind.«

»Was für ein Geschwätz! Ich sehe die Damen schon schwimmen, wenn die Ratten sie in die Beine beißen!« (Das war natürlich ein Mann! Mal sehen, wer am lautesten schreit!)

»Wir werden nicht aus dem Haus können. Das Lager ist so wacklig, das fällt bestimmt gleich zusammen, wenn das Wasser strömt.«

»Hört mal, Leute, Spaß beiseite. Wir müssen versuchen, ein kleines Boot zu bekommen.«

»Wozu ist das nötig? Ich weiß etwas viel Besseres. Wir nehmen jeder eine Milchzuckerkiste vom vorderen Dachboden und rudern mit einem Kochlöffel.«

»Ich gehe auf Stelzen, das konnte ich in meiner Jugend primissima.«

»Jan Gies hat das nicht nötig. Der nimmt seine Frau auf den Rücken, dann hat Miep Stelzen.«

Nun weißt du es schon so ungefähr, nicht wahr, Kitty? Dieses Gerede ist ja ganz witzig, aber die Wahrheit wird anders aussehen.

Die zweite Invasionsfrage konnte nicht ausbleiben. Was tun, wenn die Deutschen Amsterdam evakuieren?

»Mitgehen, uns so gut wie möglich vermummen.«

»Auf keinen Fall auf die Straße! Das Einzige ist hier bleiben. Die Deutschen sind im Stande, die ganze Bevölkerung immer weiterzutreiben, bis sie in Deutschland sterben.«

»Ja, natürlich, wir bleiben hier. Hier ist es am sichersten. Wir werden versuchen, Kleiman zu überreden, dass er mit seiner Familie herkommt und hier wohnt. Wir werden uns einen Sack Holzwolle besorgen, dann können wir auf dem Boden schlafen. Miep und Kleiman sollen jetzt schon Decken herbringen. Wir werden zu unseren 60 Pfund noch Korn dazubestellen. Jan soll versuchen, Hülsenfrüchte zu bekommen. Wir haben jetzt ungefähr 60 Pfund Bohnen und 10 Pfund Erbsen im Haus. Und vergesst die 50 Dosen Gemüse nicht.«

»Mutter, zähl mal die anderen Dosen.«

»10 Dosen Fisch, 40 Dosen Milch, 10 Kilo Milchpulver, 3 Flaschen Öl, 4 Weckgläser Butter, 4 Weckgläser Fleisch, 2 Korbflaschen Erdbeeren, 2 Flaschen Himbeeren-Johannisbeeren, 20 Flaschen Tomaten, 10 Pfund Haferflocken, 8 Pfund Reis. Das ist alles.«

Unser Vorrat ist recht erfreulich. Aber wenn man bedenkt, dass wir dann zusätzlich Besuch füttern müssen und jede Woche etwas davon verbraucht wird, dann scheint er größer, als er ist. Kohlen und Brennholz sind genug im Haus, auch Kerzen.

»Wir wollen uns Brustsäckchen nähen, um, wenn nötig, all unser Geld mitzunehmen.«

»Wir werden Listen erstellen, was bei einer Flucht mitgenommen werden muss, und jetzt schon Rucksäcke packen.«

»Wenn es soweit ist, stellen wir zwei Wachtposten auf, einen auf den vorderen und einen auf den hinteren Oberboden.«

»Sagt, was fangen wir mit so viel Esswaren an, wenn wir kein Wasser, kein Gas und keinen Strom kriegen?«

»Dann müssen wir auf dem Ofen kochen. Wasser filtern und abkochen. Wir werden große Korbflaschen sauber machen und Wasser darin aufheben. Ferner haben wir als Wasserreservoir noch drei Weckkessel und eine Waschschüssel.«

»Wir haben außerdem noch eineinhalb Zentner Winterkartoffeln im Gewürzraum stehen.«

Dieses Gerede höre ich den ganzen Tag. Invasion vorne, Invasion hinten. Dispute über Hungern, Sterben, Bomben, Feuerspritzen, Schlafsäcke, Judenausweise, Giftgase und so weiter. Alles nicht erheiternd.

Ein Beispiel für diese unzweideutigen Warnungen unserer Herren ist das folgende Gespräch mit Jan:

Hinterhaus: »Wir haben Angst, dass die Deutschen bei einem Rückzug die ganze Bevölkerung mitnehmen.«

Jan: »Das ist doch nicht möglich. Dafür haben sie keine Züge.«

Hinterhaus: »Züge? Denken Sie, dass sie die Zivilisten auch noch in

Züge setzen? Keine Rede! Schusters Rappen können sie benützen.«
(Per pedes apostolorum, sagt Dussel immer.)

Jan: »Das glaube ich nicht. Sie sehen alles durch eine viel zu schwarze Brille. Was sollten sie für ein Interesse daran haben, alle Zivilisten wegzutreiben?«

Hinterhaus: »Wissen Sie nicht, dass Goebbels gesagt hat: Wenn wir abtreten müssen, schlagen wir in allen besetzten Gebieten hinter uns die Tür zu.«

Jan: »Sie haben schon so viel gesagt.«

Hinterhaus: »Glauben Sie, dass die Deutschen für so eine Tat zu edel oder zu menschenfreundlich sind? Die denken: Wenn wir untergehen müssen, dann sollen alle Menschen innerhalb unseres Machtbereichs auch untergehen.«

Jan: »Sie können mir viel erzählen, ich glaube kein Wort davon!«

Hinterhaus: »Es ist immer dasselbe Lied. Niemand will die Gefahr sehen, bevor er sie nicht am eigenen Leib spürt.«

Jan: »Sie wissen es doch auch nicht mit Sicherheit. Sie nehmen es auch nur an.«

Hinterhaus: »Wir haben das alles doch selbst mitgemacht, erst in Deutschland und dann hier. Und was passiert in Russland?«

Jan: »Die Juden müssen Sie mal außer Betracht lassen. Ich glaube, dass niemand weiß, was in Russland los ist. Die Engländer und die Russen werden aus Propagandagründen übertreiben, genau wie die Deutschen.«

Hinterhaus: »Davon kann nicht die Rede sein. Der englische Sender hat immer die Wahrheit gesagt. Und angenommen, dass die Berichte zehn Prozent übertrieben sind, dann sind die Tatsachen noch schlimm genug. Sie können nicht leugnen, dass in Polen viele Millionen Menschen mir nichts, dir nichts hingemordet und vergast werden.«

Die weiteren Gespräche werde ich dir ersparen. Ich bin ganz ruhig und mache mir nichts aus der ganzen Aufregung. Ich bin jetzt so weit, dass es mir nicht mehr viel ausmachen kann, ob ich sterbe oder am Leben bleibe. Die Welt wird sich auch ohne mich weiterdrehen, und ich kann mich gegen die Ereignisse doch nicht wehren. Ich lasse es darauf ankommen und tue nichts als lernen und auf ein gutes Ende hoffen.
Deine Anne

Beste Kitty!

Wie ich mich fühle, könnte ich dir nicht sagen. Den einen Augenblick sehne ich mich nach Ruhe, den anderen wieder nach etwas Fröhlichkeit. Lachen sind wir hier nicht mehr gewöhnt, so richtig lachen, bis man nicht mehr kann.

Heute Morgen hatte ich einen »Lachanfall«, du weißt schon, wie man ihn manchmal in der Schule hat. Margot und ich kicherten wie richtige Backfische.

Gestern Abend hatte ich wieder was mit Mutter. Margot rollte sich in ihre Wolldecke, sprang aber plötzlich wieder aus dem Bett und untersuchte die Decke gründlich. Eine Stecknadel war drin. Mutter hatte einen Flicken in die Decke gesetzt. Vater schüttelte den Kopf und sprach über Mutters Schlampigkeit. Schon bald kam Mutter aus dem Badezimmer, und ich sagte zum Spaß: »Du bist eine echte Rabenmutter!«

Sie fragte natürlich, warum, und wir erzählten ihr von der Stecknadel.

Sie machte sofort ein hochmütiges Gesicht und sagte zu mir: »Ausgerechnet du musst etwas über Schlamperei sagen! Wenn du nähst, ist der ganze Boden mit Stecknadeln übersät. Und hier, schau mal, hier liegt wieder das Nageletui. Das räumst du auch nie auf.«

Ich sagte, ich hätte es nicht benutzt, und Margot sprang ein, denn sie war die Schuldige.

Mutter redete noch eine Weile über Schlampigkeit zu mir, bis ich wieder randvoll war und ziemlich kurz angebunden sagte: »Ich habe doch gar nichts über Schlampigkeit gesagt! Immer bekomme ich es ab, wenn ein anderer was tut.«

Mutter schwieg. Und ich war gezwungen, ihr keine Minute später den Gutenachtkuss zu geben. Der Vorfall ist vielleicht unwichtig, aber mich ärgert alles.

Da ich im Augenblick eine Zeit des Nachdenkens zu haben scheine und alle Gebiete abgrase, wo es etwas zum Nachdenken gibt, kamen meine Gedanken wie von selbst auf Vaters und Mutters Ehe. Mir war diese immer als Vorbild einer idealen Ehe hingestellt worden. Nie Krach, keine bösen Gesichter, vollkommene Harmonie usw. usw.

Von Vaters Vergangenheit weiß ich einiges und was ich nicht weiß, habe ich dazu phantasiert. Ich meine zu wissen, dass Vater Mutter geheiratet hat, weil er Mutter für geeignet hielt, den Platz als seine Frau einzunehmen. Ich muss sagen, dass ich Mutter bewundere, wie sie diesen Platz eingenommen hat und dass sie, soweit ich weiß, nie gemurrt hat und auch nie eifersüchtig war. Es kann für eine Frau, die liebt, nicht einfach sein zu wissen, dass sie im Herzen ihres Mannes nie den ersten Platz einnehmen wird, und Mutter wusste das. Vater hat Mutter dafür bestimmt bewundert und fand ihren Charakter hervorragend. Warum sollte er eine andere heiraten? Seine Ideale waren verflogen und seine Jugend war vorbei. Was ist aus ihrer Ehe geworden? Kein Streit und keine Meinungsverschiedenheiten – nein, aber eine Ideal-Ehe ist es doch auch nicht. Vater schätzt Mutter und hat sie gern, aber nicht mit der Liebe einer Ehe, die ich mir vorstelle. Vater nimmt Mutter so, wie sie ist. Er ärgert sich oft, aber sagt so wenig wie möglich, weil er weiß, welche Opfer Mutter bringen hat müssen. Über das Geschäft, über andere Dinge, über Menschen, über alles. Vater fragt sie längst nicht immer nach ihrem Urteil, erzählt nicht alles, denn er weiß, dass sie viel zu übertrieben, viel zu kritisch und oft viel zu voreingenommen ist. Vater ist nicht verliebt, er gibt ihr einen Kuss, wie er uns küsst, er stellt sie nie zum Vorbild, weil er das nicht tun kann. Er schaut sie neckend und spottend an, aber nie liebevoll. Es mag sein, dass Mutter durch das große Opfer hart und unangenehm für ihre Umgebung geworden ist, aber auf diese Art wird sie immer weiter vom Weg der Liebe abtreiben und immer weniger Bewunderung wecken. Bestimmt wird Vater einmal wissen, dass sie zwar niemals nach außen hin Anspruch auf seine volle Liebe gestellt hat, aber dadurch von innen langsam, aber sicher, abgebröckelt ist. Sie liebt ihn wie keinen anderen, und es ist hart, diese Art Liebe immer unbeantwortet zu sehen.

Muss ich folglich nicht sehr viel Mitleid mit Mutter haben, muss ihr helfen? Und Vater? – Ich kann nicht, ich sehe immer eine andere Mutter vor mir, ich kann es nicht. – Wie sollte ich auch? Sie hat mir nichts von sich erzählt, ich habe sie nie danach gefragt. Was wissen wir von unseren gegenseitigen Gedanken? Ich kann nicht mit ihr sprechen, ich kann nicht liebevoll in diese kalten Augen schauen, ich

Margot (links) und Anne am Strand in Zandvoort, 1940.

kann nicht, nie! – Wenn sie nur ein bisschen was von einer verständnisvollen Mutter hätte, entweder Weichheit oder Freundlichkeit oder Geduld oder etwas anderes; ich würde mich ihr immer wieder zu nähern versuchen. Aber diese gefühllose Natur zu lieben, dieses spöttische Wesen, ist mir mit jedem Tag unmöglicher!

Deine Anne

Samstag, 12. Februar 1944

Liebe Kitty!

Die Sonne scheint, der Himmel ist tiefblau, es weht ein herrlicher Wind, und ich sehne mich so, sehne mich so nach allem ... Nach Reden, nach Freiheit, nach Freunden, nach Alleinsein. Ich sehne mich so ... nach Weinen! Ich habe ein Gefühl, als ob ich zerspringe, und ich weiß, dass es mit Weinen besser würde. Ich kann es nicht. Ich bin unruhig, laufe von einem Zimmer ins andere, atme durch die Ritze eines geschlossenen Fensters, fühle mein Herz klopfen, als ob es sagt: »Erfülle doch endlich meine Sehnsucht.«

Ich glaube, dass ich den Frühling in mir fühle. Ich fühle das Frühlingserwachen, fühle es in meinem Körper und in meiner Seele. Ich muss mich mit Gewalt zusammennehmen, um mich normal zu verhalten. Ich bin völlig durcheinander, weiß nicht, was zu lesen, was zu schreiben, was zu tun ist, weiß nur, dass ich mich sehne ...

Deine Anne

Montag, 14. Februar 1944

Liebe Kitty!

Für mich hat sich viel geändert. Das kam so: Ich sehnte mich (und ich sehne mich noch), aber ... ein ganz kleines bisschen ist mir schon geholfen.

Am Sonntagmorgen merkte ich schon (ehrlich gesagt, zu meiner großen Freude), dass Peter mich immerfort anschaute. So ganz anders als gewöhnlich. Ich weiß nicht wie, ich kann es nicht erklären, aber ich hatte auf einmal das Gefühl, dass er doch nicht so verliebt in Margot ist, wie ich gedacht habe. Den ganzen Tag schaute ich ihn absichtlich nicht oft an, denn wenn ich das tat, schaute er auch immer.

Und dann – ja dann, dann bekam ich ein so schönes Gefühl, das ich besser nicht zu oft bekommen sollte.

Sonntagabend saßen sie alle am Radio, außer Pim und mir, und lauschten der »unsterblichen Musik deutscher Meister«. Dussel drehte andauernd an dem Gerät, Peter ärgerte sich darüber, die anderen auch. Nach einer halben Stunde unterdrückter Nervosität bat ihn Peter einigermaßen gereizt, das Gedrehe einzustellen. Dussel antwortete in seinem hochmütigsten Ton: »Ich mache das schon richtig.« Peter wurde böse, wurde frech, Herr van Daan stimmte ihm zu, und Dussel musste nachgeben. Das war alles.

Der Anlass war an sich nicht außergewöhnlich wichtig, aber Peter hat sich die Sache anscheinend sehr zu Herzen genommen. Jedenfalls kam er heute Morgen, als ich in der Bücherkiste auf dem Dachboden herumwühlte, und erzählte mir die Geschichte. Ich wusste noch nichts davon. Peter merkte, dass er eine aufmerksame Zuhörerin gefunden hatte, und kam in Schwung.

»Ja, und siehst du«, sagte er, »ich sage nicht schnell was, denn ich weiß schon im Voraus, dass ich nichts richtig rauskriege. Ich fange an zu stottern, werde rot und verdrehe die Worte, die ich sagen wollte, so lange, bis ich abbrechen muss, weil ich die Worte nicht mehr finde.

Gestern ging es mir auch so. Ich wollte etwas ganz anderes sagen, aber als ich mal angefangen hatte, habe ich den Kopf verloren, und das ist schrecklich. Früher hatte ich eine schlechte Gewohnheit, die ich am liebsten jetzt noch anwenden würde: Wenn ich böse auf jemanden war, dann habe ich ihn lieber mit meinen Fäusten bearbeitet, als dass ich mit Worten mit ihm gestritten hätte. Aber ich weiß, dass ich mit dieser Methode nicht weiterkomme. Deshalb bewundere ich dich auch so. Du kannst dich wenigstens richtig ausdrücken, sagst den Leuten, was du zu sagen hast, und bist nicht im Mindesten schüchtern.«

»Da irrst du dich sehr«, antwortete ich. »Ich sage in den meisten Fällen was ganz anderes, als ich mir vorgenommen hatte. Und dann rede ich viel zu viel und zu lange, das ist ein ebenso schlimmer Fehler.«

»Kann sein. Aber du hast den Vorteil, dass man dir nie ansieht, dass du verlegen bist. Du bleibst in Farbe und Form gleich.«

Insgeheim musste ich über diesen letzten Satz lachen. Ich wollte ihn jedoch ruhig weiter von sich selbst sprechen lassen, ließ mir meine Fröhlichkeit nicht anmerken, setzte mich auf den Boden auf ein Kissen, schlug die Arme um die angezogenen Beine und schaute ihn aufmerksam an.

Ich bin riesig froh, dass noch jemand im Haus ist, der genau solche Wutanfälle wie ich kriegen kann. Peter tat es sichtbar gut, dass er Dussel mit den schlimmsten Ausdrücken kritisieren durfte, ohne dass er Angst vor Petzen haben musste. Und ich, ich fand es auch schön, weil ich ein starkes Gefühl von Gemeinschaft empfand, wie ich es früher nur mit meinen Freundinnen hatte. Deine Anne

Dienstag, 15. Februar 1944

Diese kleine Angelegenheit mit Dussel hatte noch ein langes Nachspiel, und zwar nur durch seine eigene Schuld. Am Montagabend kam Dussel triumphierend zu Mutter, erzählte, dass Peter ihn am Morgen gefragt habe, ob er die Nacht gut verbracht hatte. Er habe noch hinzugefügt, dass ihm die Angelegenheit vom Sonntag Leid tue und er seinen Ausbruch nicht böse gemeint habe. Daraufhin beruhigte ihn Dussel mit der Versicherung, er habe es auch nicht böse aufgefasst. Alles war also in bester Ordnung.

Mutter erzählte mir diese Geschichte, und ich war insgeheim erstaunt, dass Peter sich trotz seiner Versicherungen so erniedrigt hatte.

Ich konnte es dann auch nicht lassen, erkundigte mich bei Peter und erfuhr sogleich, dass Dussel gelogen hatte. Du hättest Peters Gesicht sehen müssen, es hätte sich gelohnt, es zu fotografieren. Empörung wegen der Lüge, Wut, Überlegung, was er tun könnte, Unruhe und noch viel mehr erschienen mit kleinen Zwischenpausen auf seinem Gesicht.

Abends hielten Herr van Daan und Peter Dussel eine gepfefferte Standpauke. Aber so schlimm kann es nicht gewesen sein, da Peter heute in zahnärztlicher Behandlung war.

Eigentlich wollten sie nicht mehr miteinander sprechen.

Mittwoch, 16. Februar 1944

Den ganzen Tag sprachen wir nicht miteinander, wir wechselten nur ein paar belanglose Worte. Es war zu kalt, um auf den Dachboden zu gehen, und außerdem hatte Margot Geburtstag. Um halb eins kam er, um die Geschenke anzuschauen, und blieb viel länger, als nötig gewesen wäre und als er es sonst je getan hätte. Aber nachmittags kam die Chance. Da ich Margot einmal im Jahr besonders verwöhnen wollte, ging ich den Kaffee holen, danach die Kartoffeln. Ich kam in Peters Zimmer, und er räumte sofort seine Papiere von der Treppe. Ich fragte, ob ich die Luke vom Dachboden schließen solle.

»Ja«, antwortete er, »mach das. Wenn du zurückkommst, klopfst du einfach, dann mache ich sie dir wieder auf.«

Ich dankte ihm, ging hinauf und suchte ungefähr zehn Minuten lang die kleinsten Kartoffeln aus der großen Tonne. Dann bekam ich Rückenschmerzen, und mir wurde kalt. Ich klopfte natürlich nicht, sondern machte selbst die Luke auf, aber er kam mir doch sehr diensteifrig entgegen und nahm mir den Topf ab.

»Ich habe lange gesucht, aber kleinere konnte ich nicht finden.«

»Hast du in der großen Tonne nachgeschaut?«

»Ja, ich habe alles mit den Händen umgewühlt.«

Inzwischen stand ich unten an der Treppe, er schaute prüfend in den Topf, den er noch in den Händen hielt. »Aber die sind doch prima«, sagte er und als ich ihm den Topf abnahm, fügte er hinzu: »Mein Kompliment!«

Dabei sah er mich mit einem so warmen, weichen Blick an, dass mir auch ganz warm und weich von innen wurde. Ich konnte richtig merken, dass er mir eine Freude machen wollte, und weil er keine großen Lobreden halten konnte, legte er seine Gedanken in seinen Blick. Ich verstand ihn gut und war ihm schrecklich dankbar. Noch jetzt werde ich froh, wenn ich an seine Worte und den Blick denke!

Als ich runterkam, sagte Mutter, dass noch mehr Kartoffeln geholt werden müssten, jetzt für das Abendessen. Ich bot sehr bereitwillig an, noch einmal nach oben zu gehen. Als ich zu Peter kam, entschuldigte ich mich, dass ich noch einmal stören müsste. Er stand auf, stellte sich zwischen die Treppe und die Wand, nahm meinen Arm, als ich schon auf der Treppe stand, und wollte mich mit Gewalt zurückhalten.

»Ich gehe schon«, sagte er, »ich muss sowieso hinauf.«

Aber ich antwortete, das sei wirklich nicht nötig, und diesmal brauche ich keine kleinen Kartoffeln zu holen. Da war er überzeugt und ließ meinen Arm los. Als ich zurückkam, öffnete er die Luke und nahm mir wieder den Topf ab. An der Tür fragte ich noch: »Was machst du gerade?«

»Französisch«, war die Antwort.

Ich fragte, ob ich mir die Aufgaben mal anschauen dürfe, wusch meine Hände und setzte mich ihm gegenüber auf die Couch.

Nachdem ich ihm einiges in Französisch erklärt hatte, fingen wir bald an, uns zu unterhalten. Er erzählte mir, dass er später nach Niederländisch-Indien gehen und dort auf einer Plantage leben wolle. Er sprach über sein Leben zu Hause, über den Schwarzhandel und dass er so ein Nichtsnutz wäre. Ich sagte, dass er sehr starke Minderwertigkeitsgefühle hätte. Er sprach über den Krieg, dass die Russen und die Engländer sicher auch wieder Krieg miteinander bekommen würden, und er sprach über die Juden. Er hätte es bequemer gefunden, wenn er Christ wäre oder wenn er es nach dem Krieg sein könnte. Ich fragte, ob er sich taufen lassen würde, aber das war auch nicht der Fall. Er könnte doch nicht fühlen wie die Christen, sagte er, aber nach dem Krieg würde niemand wissen, ob er Christ oder Jude sei. Dabei ging mir ein Stich durchs Herz. Ich finde es so schade, dass er immer noch einen Rest Unehrlichkeit in sich hat.

Er sagte noch: »Die Juden sind immer das auserwählte Volk gewesen und werden es wohl immer bleiben!«

Ich antwortete: »Ich hoffe nur, dass sie einmal zum Guten auserwählt sind.«

Aber sonst sprachen wir ganz gemütlich über Vater und über Menschenkenntnis und über alle möglichen Dinge, ich weiß selbst nicht mehr, über was.

Um Viertel nach fünf ging ich erst weg, weil Bep kam.

Abends sagte er noch etwas Schönes. Wir sprachen über Filmschauspieler, deren Bilder er mal von mir bekommen hat. Sie hängen nun schon anderthalb Jahre in seinem Zimmer. Er fand sie so schön, und ich bot ihm an, ihm mal ein paar andere Bilder zu geben.

»Nein«, antwortete er, »ich lasse es lieber so, diese hier, die schaue ich jeden Tag an, das sind meine Freunde geworden.«

Warum er Mouschi immer so an sich drückt, verstehe ich jetzt auch viel besser. Er hat natürlich auch ein Bedürfnis nach Zärtlichkeit. Noch etwas habe ich vergessen, worüber er sprach. Er sagte: »Nein, Angst kenne ich nicht, nur wenn mir selbst etwas fehlt. Aber das gewöhne ich mir auch noch ab.«

Peters Minderwertigkeitskomplex ist sehr schlimm. So denkt er zum Beispiel immer, dass er so blöd wäre und wir so klug. Wenn ich ihm bei Französisch helfe, bedankt er sich tausendmal. Irgendwann werde ich bestimmt mal sagen: »Hör auf mit diesen Sprüchen. Du kannst dafür Englisch und Geographie viel besser!« Anne Frank

Donnerstag, 17. Februar 1944

Beste Kitty!

Heute Morgen war ich oben, ich hatte Frau van Daan versprochen, mal ein paar Geschichten vorzulesen. Ich fing mit Evas Traum an, das fand sie sehr schön. Dann las ich noch ein paar Sachen aus dem Hinterhaus, über die sie schallend lachten. Peter hörte auch teilweise zu (ich meine nur bei dem letzten) und fragte, ob ich mal zu ihm käme, um noch mehr vorzulesen. Ich dachte, dass ich nun mein Glück probieren könnte, holte mein Tagebuch und ließ ihn das Stück von Cady und Hans über Gott lesen. Ich kann überhaupt nicht sagen, was das für einen Eindruck auf ihn gemacht hat. Er sagte etwas, was ich nicht mehr weiß, nicht, ob es gut war, sondern etwas über den Gedanken selbst. Ich sagte, dass ich nur mal hatte zeigen wollen, dass ich nicht nur witzige Sachen aufschrieb. Er nickte mit dem Kopf, und ich ging aus dem Zimmer. Mal sehen, ob ich noch was davon höre!

Deine Anne M. Frank

Freitag, 18. Februar 1944

Liebste Kitty!

Wann immer ich auch nach oben gehe, hat das zum Ziel, »ihn« zu sehen. Mein Leben hier ist also viel besser geworden, weil es nun wieder einen Sinn hat und ich mich auf etwas freuen kann.

Der Gegenstand meiner Freundschaft ist wenigstens immer im Haus, und ich brauche (außer vor Margot) keine Angst vor Rivalen zu haben. Du brauchst wirklich nicht zu denken, dass ich verliebt bin, das ist nicht wahr. Aber ich habe ständig das Gefühl, dass zwischen Peter und mir noch einmal etwas sehr Schönes wachsen wird, das Freundschaft und Vertrauen gibt. Wann immer es möglich ist, gehe ich zu ihm, und es ist nicht mehr so wie früher, dass er nicht genau weiß, was er mit mir anfangen soll. Im Gegenteil, er redet noch, wenn ich schon fast zur Tür hinaus bin.

Mutter sieht es nicht gern, dass ich nach oben gehe. Sie sagt immer, dass ich Peter lästig falle und ihn in Ruhe lassen soll. Versteht sie denn nicht, dass ich genug Intuition habe? Immer wenn ich hinaufgehe, schaut sie mich so seltsam an. Wenn ich von oben herunterkomme, fragt sie, wo ich gewesen bin. Das finde ich schlimm, und langsam kann ich sie nicht ausstehen!   Deine Anne M. Frank

Samstag, 19. Februar 1944

Liebe Kitty!

Es ist wieder Samstag, und das sagt eigentlich schon genug. Der Morgen war ruhig. Ich war fast eine Stunde oben, aber »ihn« habe ich nur flüchtig gesprochen.

Als alle um halb drei entweder lasen oder schliefen, zog ich mit Decken und allem hinunter, um mich an den Schreibtisch zu setzen und zu lesen oder zu schreiben. Es dauerte nicht lange, da wurde es mir zu viel, mein Kopf fiel auf meinen Arm, und ich brach in Schluchzen aus. Die Tränen strömten, und ich fühlte mich tief unglücklich. Wäre »er« nur gekommen, um mich zu trösten.

Es war schon vier Uhr, als ich wieder hinaufging. Um fünf holte ich Kartoffeln, wieder mit einer neuen Hoffnung im Herzen, ihn zu treffen. Aber als ich noch im Badezimmer war und meine Haare zurechtmachte, ging er zu Moffi ins Lager.

Ich wollte Frau van Daan helfen und setzte mich mit meinem Buch oben hin. Aber auf einmal fühlte ich wieder die Tränen aufsteigen und rannte hinunter zur Toilette, nicht ohne unterwegs schnell noch den Handspiegel mitzunehmen. Da saß ich dann, auch nachdem ich schon längst fertig war, völlig angezogen auf dem Klo, meine Tränen machten dunkle Flecken auf das Rot meiner Schürze, und ich war sehr traurig.

Ich dachte ungefähr Folgendes: »So erreiche ich Peter nie. Wer weiß, vielleicht findet er mich überhaupt nicht nett und hat gar kein Bedürfnis nach Vertrauen. Vielleicht denkt er nur oberflächlich an mich? Ich muss wieder allein weiter, ohne Vertrauen und ohne Peter. Womöglich bald wieder ohne Hoffnung, Trost und Erwartung. Ach, könnte ich jetzt nur meinen Kopf an seine Schulter legen, damit ich mich nicht so hoffnungslos allein und verlassen fühle. Wer weiß, vielleicht macht er sich überhaupt nichts aus mir und schaut die anderen auch so freundlich an. Vielleicht habe ich mir nur eingebildet, dass es mir gilt. O Peter, könntest du mich nur hören oder sehen! Aber die Wahrheit, die vielleicht enttäuschend ist, könnte ich nicht ertragen.«

Später war ich doch wieder hoffnungsvoll und voller Erwartung, während innerlich meine Tränen noch flossen. Deine Anne

Sonntag, 20. Februar 1944

Was bei anderen Leuten in der Woche passiert, passiert im Hinterhaus sonntags. Wenn andere Leute schöne Kleider anhaben und in der Sonne spazieren gehen, sind wir hier am Schrubben, Fegen und Waschen.

<u>Acht Uhr:</u> Ungeachtet aller Langschläfer steht Dussel schon um acht Uhr auf, geht zum Badezimmer, anschließend nach unten, wieder nach oben, dann folgt im Badezimmer eine gründliche Wäsche, die eine volle Stunde dauert.

<u>Halb zehn:</u> Ofen werden angemacht, es wird entdunkelt, und van Daan geht ins Badezimmer. Eine der sonntäglichen Heimsuchungen ist, dass ich von meinem Bett aus Dussel genau auf den Rücken schauen muss, wenn er betet. Jeder wird sich wundern, wenn ich sage, dass ein betender Dussel ein schrecklicher Anblick ist. Nicht dass er weint und übermäßig gefühlvoll tut, o nein, aber er hat die Angewohnheit, eine Viertelstunde lang, wohlgemerkt, eine Viertelstunde, von den Fersen auf die Zehen zu wippen. Hin und her, hin und her, endlos dauert das, und wenn ich meine Augen nicht zukneife, wird mir fast schwindlig.

<u>Viertel nach zehn:</u> Die van Daans pfeifen, das Badezimmer ist leer. Bei uns erheben sich die ersten verschlafenen Gesichter aus den Kissen. Dann geht alles schnell, schnell, schnell. Der Reihe nach gehen Margot und ich mit hinunter zum Waschen. Da es dort ordentlich kalt ist, sind lange Hosen und ein Kopftuch angebracht. Inzwischen ist Vater im Badezimmer. Um elf Uhr gehen Margot oder ich, dann ist jeder wieder sauber.

<u>Halb zwölf:</u> Frühstücken. Hierüber werde ich mich nicht weiter auslassen, denn über das Essen wird auch ohne mich schon genug gesprochen.

<u>Viertel nach zwölf:</u> Alle Personen gehen ihrer Wege. Vater liegt im Overall bald auf den Knien und bürstet den Teppich so fest, dass das Zimmer in eine dicke Staubwolke gehüllt ist. Herr Dussel macht die Betten (natürlich verkehrt) und pfeift dabei immer dasselbe Violinkonzert von Beethoven. Mutter hört man auf dem Dachboden schlurfen, während sie Wäsche aufhängt. Herr van Daan setzt seinen Hut auf und verschwindet in die unteren Regionen, meist gefolgt von Peter und Mouschi. Frau van Daan zieht eine lange Schürze, eine schwarze Wollweste und Überschuhe an, bindet sich einen dicken roten Wollschal um den Kopf, nimmt ein Bündel schmutzige Wäsche unter den Arm und geht, nach einem gut einstudierten Waschfrauenknicks, zum Waschen. Margot und ich spülen und räumen das Zimmer auf.

Mittwoch, 23. Februar 1944

Liebste Kitty!

Seit gestern ist draußen herrliches Wetter, und ich bin vollkommen aufgekratzt. Meine Schreibarbeit, das Schönste, was ich habe, geht gut voran. Ich gehe fast jeden Morgen zum Dachboden, um mir die dumpfe Stubenluft aus den Lungen wehen zu lassen. Heute Morgen, als ich wieder zum Dachboden ging, war Peter am Aufräumen. Bald war er fertig, und während ich mich auf meinen Lieblingsplatz auf den Boden setzte, kam er auch. Wir betrachteten den blauen Himmel, den kahlen Kastanienbaum, an dessen Zweigen kleine Tropfen glitzerten, die Möwen und die anderen Vögel, die im Tiefflug wie aus Silber aussahen. Das alles rührte und packte uns beide so, dass wir nicht mehr sprechen konnten. Er stand mit dem Kopf an einen dikken Balken gelehnt, ich saß. Wir atmeten die Luft ein, schauten hinaus und fühlten, dass dies nicht mit Worten unterbrochen werden durfte. Wir schauten sehr lange hinaus, und als er anfangen musste, Holz zu hacken, wusste ich, dass er ein feiner Kerl ist. Er kletterte die Treppe zum Oberboden hinauf, und ich folgte ihm. Während der Viertelstunde, die er Holz hackte, sprachen wir wieder kein Wort. Ich schaute ihm von meinem Stehplatz aus zu, wie er sichtlich sein Bestes tat, gut zu hacken und mir seine Kraft zu zeigen. Aber ich schaute auch aus dem offenen Fenster über ein großes Stück Amsterdam, über alle Dächer, bis an den Horizont, der so hellblau war, dass man ihn kaum mehr sehen konnte.

»Solange es das noch gibt«, dachte ich, »und ich es erleben darf, diesen Sonnenschein, diesen Himmel, an dem keine Wolke ist, so lange kann ich nicht traurig sein.«

Für jeden, der Angst hat, einsam oder unglücklich ist, ist es bestimmt das beste Mittel, hinauszugehen, irgendwohin, wo er ganz allein ist, allein mit dem Himmel, der Natur und Gott. Dann erst, nur dann, fühlt man, dass alles so ist, wie es sein soll, und dass Gott die Menschen in der einfachen und schönen Natur glücklich sehen will.

Solange es das noch gibt, und das wird es wohl immer, weiß ich, dass es unter allen Umständen auch einen Trost für jeden Kummer gibt. Und ich glaube fest, dass die Natur viel Schlimmes vertreiben kann.

Wer weiß, vielleicht dauert es nicht mehr lange, bis ich dieses überwältigende Glücksgefühl mit jemandem teilen kann, der es genauso empfindet wie ich.

Deine Anne

P. S. Gedanken: An Peter.

Wir vermissen hier viel, sehr viel, und auch schon lange. Ich vermisse es auch, genau wie du. Du musst nicht denken, dass ich von äußerlichen Dingen spreche, damit sind wir hier hervorragend versorgt. Nein, ich meine die inneren Dinge. Ich sehne mich, genauso wie du, nach Freiheit und Luft, aber ich glaube, dass wir für diese Entbehrungen reichlich Entschädigung bekommen haben. Ich meine innere Entschädigung. Als ich heute Morgen vor dem Fenster saß und Gott und die Natur genau und gut betrachtete, war ich glücklich, nichts anderes als glücklich. Und, Peter, solange es dieses innere Glück gibt, das Glück über Natur, Gesundheit und noch sehr viel mehr, solange man das in sich trägt, wird man immer wieder glücklich werden.

Reichtum, Ansehen, alles kann man verlieren, aber das Glück im eigenen Herzen kann nur verschleiert werden und wird dich, solange du lebst, immer wieder glücklich machen.

Wenn du allein und unglücklich bist, dann versuche mal, bei schönem Wetter vom Oberboden aus in den Himmel zu schauen. Solange du furchtlos den Himmel anschauen kannst, so lange weißt du, dass du innerlich rein bist und dass du wieder glücklich werden wirst.

Sonntag, 27. Februar 1944

Liebste Kitty!

Von morgens früh bis abends spät denke ich eigentlich an nichts anderes als an Peter. Ich schlafe mit seinem Bild vor Augen ein, träume von ihm und werde wieder wach, wenn er mich anschaut.

Ich glaube, dass Peter und ich gar nicht so verschieden sind, wie das von außen wirkt, und ich erkläre dir auch warum: Peter und ich vermissen beide eine Mutter. Seine ist zu oberflächlich, flirtet gern und kümmert sich nicht viel um Peters Gedanken. Meine bemüht sich zwar um mich, hat aber keinen Takt, kein Feingefühl, kein mütterliches Verständnis.

Peter und ich kämpfen beide in unserem Inneren. Wir sind beide noch unsicher und eigentlich zu zerbrechlich und innerlich zu zart, um so hart angepackt zu werden. Dann will ich raus oder will mein Inneres verbergen. Ich werfe mit Töpfen und Wasser und bin laut und lärmend, sodass jeder sich wünscht, ich wäre weit weg. Er zieht sich dann zurück, spricht fast nicht, ist still und träumt und verbirgt sich ängstlich.

Aber wie und wann werden wir uns endlich finden?

Ich weiß nicht, wie lange ich dieses Verlangen noch mit meinem Verstand beherrschen kann.   Deine Anne M. Frank

Liebste Kitty!

Es wird ein Nacht- und Tagalbtraum. Ich sehe ihn fast jede Stunde und kann nicht zu ihm. Ich darf nichts zeigen, niemandem, muss fröhlich sein, während in mir alles verzweifelt ist.

Peter Schiff und Peter van Daan sind zusammengeflossen zu einem Peter, der gut und lieb ist und nach dem ich mich schrecklich sehne. Mutter ist furchtbar, Vater lieb und dadurch noch lästiger. Margot ist am lästigsten, denn sie erhebt Anspruch auf ein freundliches Gesicht, und ich will meine Ruhe haben.

Peter kam nicht zu mir auf den Dachboden, er ging zum Oberboden und schreinerte dort etwas. Mit jedem Krachen und jedem Schlag bröckelte ein Stück von meinem Mut ab, und ich wurde noch trauriger. Und in der Ferne spielte eine Uhr: »Aufrecht der Körper, aufrecht die Seele!«

Ich bin sentimental, ich weiß es. Ich bin verzweifelt und unvernünftig, das weiß ich auch.

O hilf mir!   Deine Anne M. Frank

Liebe Kitty!

Meine eigenen Angelegenheiten sind in den Hintergrund gedrängt worden, und zwar durch … einen Einbruch. Ich werde langweilig mit meinen Einbrüchen, aber was kann ich dafür, dass die Einbrecher so ein Vergnügen daran haben, Kolen & Co. die Ehre eines Besuchs anzutun? Dieser Einbruch ist viel komplizierter als der vorige vom Juli 43.

Als Herr van Daan gestern Abend wie gewöhnlich um halb acht in Kuglers Büro ging, sah er die gläserne Zwischentür und die Bürotür offen stehen. Das wunderte ihn. Er ging weiter und staunte immer mehr, als die Kabinettstüren ebenfalls geöffnet waren und im vorderen Büro ein schreckliches Durcheinander herrschte. Hier war ein Dieb, schoss es ihm durch den Kopf. Um sich sofort Gewissheit zu verschaffen, ging er die Treppe hinunter, kontrollierte die Vordertür und das Sicherheitsschloss, alles war zu. »Dann werden Bep und Peter heute sehr schlampig gewesen sein«, nahm er an. Er blieb eine

Weile in Kuglers Zimmer sitzen, drehte dann die Lampe aus, ging nach oben und machte sich weder über die offenen Türen noch über das unordentliche Büro viele Gedanken.

Heute Morgen klopfte Peter schon früh an unsere Zimmertür und kam mit der wenig hübschen Neuigkeit, dass die Vordertür weit offen stand und das Projektionsgerät und Kuglers neue Aktentasche aus dem Wandschrank verschwunden waren. Peter bekam den Auftrag, die Tür zu schließen, van Daan erzählte seine Beobachtungen vom vergangenen Abend, und wir waren ziemlich unruhig.

Die ganze Sache ist nicht anders zu erklären, als dass der Dieb einen Nachschlüssel von der Tür hat, denn die war nicht aufgebrochen worden. Er muss schon sehr früh am Abend hereingeschlüpft sein, schloss die Tür hinter sich, wurde von van Daan gestört, versteckte sich, bis dieser weggegangen war, flüchtete dann mit seiner Beute und ließ in der Eile die Tür offen stehen.

Wer kann unseren Schlüssel haben? Warum ist der Dieb nicht ins Lager gegangen? War vielleicht einer unserer eigenen Lagerarbeiter der Täter? Würde er uns nun nicht verraten, da er van Daan gehört und vielleicht sogar gesehen hatte?

Es ist sehr unheimlich, weil wir nicht wissen, ob es dem betreffenden Einbrecher nicht noch mal einfällt, unsere Tür zu öffnen. Oder war er selbst erschrocken über den Mann, der da herumlief?

Deine Anne

P. S. Wenn du vielleicht einen guten Detektiv für uns auftreiben könntest, wäre uns das sehr angenehm. Erste Forderung ist natürlich Zuverlässigkeit in Sachen Verstecken.

Donnerstag, 2. März 1944

Liebe Kitty!

Margot und ich waren heute zusammen auf dem Dachboden. Aber mit ihr kann ich es nicht so genießen, wie ich es mir mit Peter vorstelle (oder mit einem anderen), obwohl ich weiß, dass sie die meisten Dinge genauso empfindet wie ich!

Beim Abwaschen fing Bep an, mit Mutter und Frau van Daan über ihre Niedergeschlagenheit zu sprechen. Was helfen ihr die beiden?

Vor allem unsere taktlose Mutter verhilft einem Menschen nur noch tiefer in die Pfütze. Weißt du, was sie Bep für einen Rat gab? Sie sollte mal an all die Menschen denken, die in dieser Welt zugrunde gehen! Wem hilft der Gedanke an Elend, wenn er sich selbst schon elend fühlt? Das sagte ich auch. Die Antwort war natürlich, dass ich bei solchen Dingen nicht mitreden kann!

Was sind die Erwachsenen doch idiotisch und blöd! Als ob Peter, Margot, Bep und ich nicht alle dasselbe fühlten! Und dagegen hilft nur Mutterliebe oder die Liebe von sehr, sehr guten Freunden. Aber die beiden Mütter hier verstehen nicht das geringste bisschen von uns! Frau van Daan vielleicht noch mehr als Mutter. Oh, ich hätte der armen Bep gern was gesagt, etwas, von dem ich aus Erfahrung weiß, dass es hilft. Aber Vater kam dazwischen und schob mich sehr grob beiseite. Wie blöd sind sie doch alle!

Ich habe auch noch mit Margot über Vater und Mutter gesprochen. Wie nett könnten wir es hier haben, wenn die nicht so schrecklich langweilig wären. Wir könnten Abende organisieren, an denen jeder der Reihe nach über ein Thema spricht. Aber da sind wir schon beim springenden Punkt. Ich kann hier nicht sprechen. Herr van Daan greift immer an, Mutter wird scharf und kann über gar <u>nichts</u> normal reden, Vater hat keine Lust zu so etwas, ebenso wenig wie Herr Dussel, und Frau van Daan wird immer angegriffen, sodass sie mit rotem Kopf dasitzt und sich kaum mehr wehren kann. Und wir? Wir dürfen kein Urteil haben! Ja, sie sind so schrecklich modern! Kein Urteil haben! Man kann jemandem sagen, er soll den Mund halten. Aber kein Urteil haben, das gibt es nicht. Niemand kann einem anderen sein Urteil verbieten, auch wenn der andere noch so jung ist! Bep, Margot, Peter und mir hilft nur eine große, hingebungsvolle Liebe, die wir hier nicht bekommen. Und niemand hier kann uns verstehen, vor allem diese idiotischen Besserwisser nicht. Denn wir sind empfindsamer und viel weiter in unseren Gedanken, als einer von ihnen es wohl auch nur im Entferntesten vermuten würde.

<u>Liebe, was ist Liebe? Ich glaube, dass Liebe etwas ist, was sich eigentlich nicht in Worte fassen lässt. Liebe ist, jemanden zu verstehen, ihn gern zu haben. Glück und Unglück mit ihm zu teilen. Und dazu gehört auf die Dauer auch die körperliche Liebe. Du hast etwas geteilt, etwas hergegeben und etwas empfangen. Und ob du dann verheiratet</u>

oder unverheiratet bist, ob du ein Kind kriegst oder nicht, ob die Ehre weg ist, auf das alles kommt es nicht an, wenn du nur weißt, dass für dein ganzes weiteres Leben jemand neben dir steht, der dich versteht und den du mit niemandem zu teilen brauchst!

Zur Zeit mault Mutter wieder. Sie ist sichtbar eifersüchtig, weil ich mehr mit Frau van Daan rede als mit ihr. Das ist mir egal!

Heute Nachmittag habe ich Peter erwischt, wir haben uns mindestens eine dreiviertel Stunde lang unterhalten. Es fiel ihm schwer, etwas von sich zu sagen, aber es kam dann doch ganz langsam. Ich wusste wirklich nicht, ob ich besser daran täte, hinunterzugehen oder oben zu bleiben. Aber ich wollte ihm so gern helfen. Ich erzählte ihm von Bep und dass die beiden Mütter so taktlos sind. Er erzählte, dass seine Eltern immer streiten, über Politik und Zigaretten und alles Mögliche. Wie schon gesagt, Peter war sehr schüchtern, aber dann ließ er doch heraus, dass er seine Eltern gerne mal zwei Jahre lang nicht sehen möchte. »Mein Vater ist wirklich nicht so toll, wie er aussieht«, sagte er, »und in der Zigarettenfrage hat Mutter absolut Recht!«

Ich erzählte ihm auch von meiner Mutter. Doch Vater verteidigte er, er findet ihn einen »Mordskerl«.

Heute Abend, als ich nach dem Spülen meine Schürze aufhängte, rief er mich und bat mich, unten nichts davon zu sagen, dass sie wieder Streit hatten und nicht miteinander reden. Ich versprach es ihm, obwohl ich es Margot schon erzählt hatte. Aber ich bin überzeugt, dass sie ihren Mund hält.

»Nein, Peter«, sagte ich, »du brauchst vor mir keine Angst zu haben. Ich habe es mir abgewöhnt, alles weiterzusagen. Ich sage nie etwas, was du mir erzählst.«

Das fand er toll. Ich erzählte ihm auch von den schrecklichen Tratschereien bei uns und sagte: »Da hat Margot natürlich sehr Recht, wenn sie meint, dass ich nicht ehrlich bin. Denn obwohl ich nicht mehr tratschen will, über Herrn Dussel tue ich es noch viel zu gern.«

»Das ist schön von dir«, sagte er. Er war rot geworden, und ich wurde bei diesem aufrichtigen Kompliment auch fast verlegen.

Dann sprachen wir noch über die oben und uns. Peter war wirklich ein bisschen erstaunt, dass wir seine Eltern noch immer nicht mögen.

»Peter«, sagte ich, »du weißt, dass ich ehrlich bin. Warum sollte ich es dir nicht sagen? Wir kennen ihre Fehler doch auch.«

Ich sagte auch noch: »Peter, ich würde dir so gern helfen, geht das nicht? Du stehst hier so dazwischen, und ich weiß, auch wenn du es nicht sagst, dass dir das was ausmacht.«

»Ich werde deine Hilfe immer gern annehmen.«

»Vielleicht gehst du lieber zu Vater. Der sagt auch nie etwas weiter, dem kannst du ruhig alles erzählen.«

»Ja, er ist ein echter Kamerad.«

»Du hast ihn sehr gern, nicht wahr?«

Peter nickte, und ich fuhr fort: »Nun, er dich auch!«

Er wurde rot. Es war wirklich rührend, wie froh er über diese paar Worte war. »Glaubst du?«, fragte er.

»Ja«, sagte ich, »das merkt man doch an dem, was er ab und zu von sich gibt.«

Dann kam Herr van Daan zum Diktieren. Peter ist sicher auch ein »Mordskerl«, genau wie Vater.   Deine Anne M. Frank

Freitag, 3. März 1944

Liebste Kitty!

Als heute Abend die Kerzen angezündet wurden, wurde ich wieder froh und ruhig. Oma ist für mich in dieser Kerze, und Oma ist es auch, die mich behütet und beschützt und mich wieder froh macht. Aber ... ein anderer beeinflusst meine Stimmung, und das ist Peter. Als ich heute die Kartoffeln holte und noch mit dem vollen Topf auf der Treppe stand, fragte er schon: »Was hast du über Mittag gemacht?«

Ich setzte mich auf die Treppe, und wir fingen an zu reden. Um Viertel nach fünf (eine Stunde, nachdem ich sie geholt hatte) kamen die Kartoffeln erst im Zimmer an. Peter sprach mit keinem Wort mehr über seine Eltern, wir redeten nur über Bücher und über früher. Was hat dieser Junge für einen warmen Blick! Es fehlt, glaube ich, nicht mehr viel, und ich verliebe mich in ihn.

Darüber sprach er heute Abend. Ich kam zu ihm, nach dem Kartoffelschälen, und sagte, dass mir so heiß wäre. »An Margot und mir kann man sofort die Temperatur sehen. Wenn es kalt ist, sind wir weiß, und wenn es warm ist, rot«, sagte ich.

»Verliebt?«, fragte er.

»Warum sollte ich verliebt sein?« Meine Antwort (oder besser gesagt Frage) war ziemlich albern.

»Warum nicht!«, sagte er, und dann mussten wir zum Essen.

Ob er mit dieser Frage etwas beabsichtigt hat? Ich bin heute endlich dazu gekommen, ihn zu fragen, ob er mein Gerede nicht lästig fände. Er sagte nur: »Mir gefällt's gut!« Inwieweit diese Antwort nur Schüchternheit war, kann ich nicht beurteilen.

Kitty, ich bin wie eine Verliebte, die von nichts anderem erzählen kann als von ihrem Schatz. Peter ist aber auch wirklich ein Schatz. Wann werde ich ihm das mal sagen können? Natürlich nur, wenn er mich auch für einen Schatz hält. Aber ich bin kein Kätzchen, das man ohne Handschuhe anpackt, das weiß ich wirklich. Und er liebt seine Ruhe, also habe ich keine Ahnung, inwieweit er mich nett findet. Jedenfalls lernen wir uns ein bisschen besser kennen. Ich wünschte nur, dass wir uns mit viel mehr Dingen heraustrauen würden. Aber wer weiß, vielleicht kommt diese Zeit schneller, als ich denke. Ein paar Mal am Tag fange ich einen Blick des Einvernehmens von ihm auf, ich zwinkere zurück, und wir sind beide froh. Ich bin verrückt, wenn ich auch von <u>seiner</u> Freude spreche, aber ich habe das unumstößliche Gefühl, dass er genauso denkt wie ich.

Deine Anne M. Frank

Samstag, 4. März 1944

Beste Kitty!

Dieser Samstag ist seit Monaten und Monaten mal nicht so langweilig, traurig und öde wie alle vorherigen. Kein anderer als Peter ist die Ursache. Heute Morgen ging ich zum Dachboden, um meine Schürze aufzuhängen, als Vater fragte, ob ich nicht bleiben wolle, um ein bisschen Französisch zu reden. Ich fand das prima. Wir sprachen zuerst Französisch, ich erklärte etwas, dann machten wir Englisch. Vater las aus Dickens vor, und ich war selig, denn ich saß auf Vaters Stuhl, dicht neben Peter.

Um Viertel vor elf ging ich nach unten. Als ich um halb zwölf wieder hinaufkam, stand er schon auf der Treppe und wartete auf mich. Wir redeten bis Viertel vor eins. Wenn es nur eben möglich ist, zum Beispiel nach dem Essen, wenn niemand es hört, sagt er: »Tschüs, Anne, bis später!«

Ach, ich bin so froh! Fängt er jetzt doch an, mich zu mögen? Jedenfalls ist er ein netter Kerl, und wer weiß, wie toll ich noch mit ihm reden kann.

Frau van Daan findet es gut, wenn wir zusammen sind, aber heute fragte sie neckend: »Kann ich euch beiden da oben denn trauen?«

»Natürlich« sagte ich protestierend. »Sie beleidigen mich!«

Ich freue mich von morgens bis abends, dass ich Peter sehen werde.

Deine Anne M. Frank

P. S. Dass ich es nicht vergesse: Heute Nacht ist ein Haufen Schnee gefallen. Jetzt ist schon fast nichts mehr zu sehen, alles ist weggetaut.

Montag, 6. März 1944

Liebe Kitty!

Findest du es nicht verrückt, dass ich mich für Peter, nachdem er mir das von seinen Eltern erzählt hat, ein bisschen verantwortlich fühle? Es kommt mir vor, als gingen mich die Streitereien ebenso viel an wie ihn. Doch ich wage nicht mehr, mit ihm darüber zu sprechen, ich habe Angst, dass er das nicht mag. Um nichts in der Welt möchte ich nun unsensibel sein.

Ich sehe Peters Gesicht an, dass er genauso viel nachdenkt wie ich, und gestern Abend habe ich mich dann auch sehr geärgert, als Frau van Daan spöttisch sagte: »Der Denker!« Peter wurde rot und verlegen, und ich bin fast geplatzt.

Die Leute sollen doch ihren Mund halten! Es ist schlimm, untätig mit anzusehen, wie einsam er ist. Ich kann mir so gut, als würde ich es selbst mitmachen, vorstellen, wie verzweifelt er sich manchmal bei Streitereien fühlen muss. Armer Peter, wie sehr hat er Liebe nötig!

Wie hart klang es in meinen Ohren, als er davon sprach, dass er keine Freunde nötig hätte. Wie er sich irrt! Ich glaube auch, dass er diese Worte nicht ernst gemeint hat. Er klammert sich an seine Männlichkeit, seine Einsamkeit und seine gespielte Gleichgültigkeit, nur um nicht aus der Rolle zu fallen, um nie, nie zu zeigen, wie er sich fühlt.

Armer Peter, wie lange kann er diese Rolle spielen? Wird dieser übermenschlichen Anstrengung kein schrecklicher Ausbruch folgen? O Peter, könnte und dürfte ich dir nur helfen! Wir zusammen würden unser beider Einsamkeit schon vertreiben!

Ich denke viel, aber ich sage nicht viel. Ich bin froh, wenn ich ihn sehe, und wenn dann auch noch die Sonne scheint. Gestern war ich beim Haarewaschen sehr ausgelassen und wusste die ganze Zeit, dass er im Zimmer nebenan war. Ich konnte es nicht ändern. Je stiller und ernster ich von innen bin, desto lärmender bin ich von außen. Wer wird der Erste sein, der diesen Panzer entdeckt und ihn durchbricht?
Es ist doch gut, dass van Daans kein Mädchen haben. Nie wäre die Eroberung so schwierig, so schön und so toll, wenn nicht gerade das andere Geschlecht so anziehen würde!   Deine Anne M. Frank

P. S. Du weißt, dass ich dir alles ehrlich schreibe. Darum muss ich dir auch sagen, dass ich eigentlich von einem Treffen zum anderen lebe. Immer hoffe ich zu entdecken, dass er auch so auf mich wartet, und ich bin innerlich ganz entzückt, wenn ich seine kleinen, schüchternen Versuche merke. Er würde sich, meiner Meinung nach, gern genauso ausdrücken wie ich, und er weiß nicht, dass gerade seine Unbeholfenheit mich so anrührt.

Dienstag, 7. März 1944

Liebe Kitty!
Wenn ich so über mein Leben von 1942 nachdenke, kommt es mir so unwirklich vor. Dieses Götterleben erlebte eine ganz andere Anne Frank als die, die hier jetzt vernünftig geworden ist. Ein Götterleben, das war es. An jedem Finger fünf Verehrer, ungefähr zwanzig Freundinnen und Bekannte, der Liebling der meisten Lehrer, verwöhnt von Vater und Mutter, viele Süßigkeiten, genug Geld – was will man mehr?
Du wirst mich natürlich fragen, wie ich denn all die Leute so um den Finger gewickelt habe. Peter sagt »Anziehungskraft«, aber das stimmt nicht ganz. Die Lehrer fanden meine schlauen Antworten, mein lachendes Gesicht und meinen kritischen Blick nett, amüsant

und witzig. Mehr war ich auch nicht, nur kokett und amüsant. Ein paar Vorteile hatte ich, durch die ich ziemlich in der Gunst blieb, nämlich Fleiß, Ehrlichkeit und Großzügigkeit. Nie hätte ich mich geweigert, jemanden, egal wen, abschauen zu lassen, Süßigkeiten verteilte ich mit offenen Händen, und ich war nicht eingebildet.

Ob ich bei all der Bewunderung nicht übermütig geworden wäre? Es ist ein Glück, dass ich mittendrin, auf dem Höhepunkt des Festes sozusagen, plötzlich in der Wirklichkeit landete, und es hat gut ein Jahr gedauert, bevor ich mich daran gewöhnt hatte, dass von keiner Seite mehr Bewunderung kam.

Wie sahen sie mich in der Schule? Die Anführerin von Späßen und Späßchen, immer vorne dran und niemals schlecht gelaunt oder weinerlich. War es ein Wunder, dass jeder gern mit mir mitradelte oder mir eine Aufmerksamkeit erwies?

Ich betrachte diese Anne Frank jetzt als ein nettes, witziges, aber oberflächliches Mädchen, das nichts mehr mit mir zu tun hat. Was sagte Peter über mich? »Wenn ich dich sah, warst du immer umringt von zwei oder mehr Jungen und einem Haufen Mädchen. Immer hast du gelacht und warst der Mittelpunkt!« Er hatte Recht.

Was ist von dieser Anne Frank übrig geblieben? O sicher, ich habe mein Lachen und meine Antworten nicht verlernt, ich kann noch genauso gut oder besser die Menschen kritisieren, ich kann noch genauso flirten und amüsant sein, wenn ich will …

Das ist der Punkt. Ich möchte gerne noch mal für einen Abend, für ein paar Tage, für eine Woche so leben, scheinbar unbekümmert und fröhlich. Am Ende der Woche wäre ich dann todmüde und würde bestimmt dem Erstbesten, der vernünftig mit mir redet, sehr dankbar sein. Ich will keine Anbeter, sondern Freunde, keine Bewunderung für ein schmeichelndes Lächeln, sondern für mein Auftreten und meinen Charakter. Ich weiß sehr gut, dass dann der Kreis um mich viel kleiner würde. Aber was macht das, wenn ich nur ein paar Menschen, aufrechte Menschen übrig behalte.

Trotz allem war ich 1942 auch nicht ungeteilt glücklich. Ich fühlte mich oft verlassen, aber weil ich von morgens bis abends beschäftigt war, dachte ich nicht nach und machte Spaß. Bewusst oder unbewusst versuchte ich, die Leere mit Witzchen zu vertreiben.

Nun betrachte ich mein Leben und merke, dass eine Zeitspanne schon unwiderruflich abgeschlossen ist. Die sorglose, unbekümmerte Schulzeit kommt niemals zurück. Ich sehne mich noch nicht mal danach, ich bin darüber hinausgewachsen. Ich kann nicht mehr nur Unsinn machen, ein Teil von mir bewahrt immer seinen Ernst.

Ich betrachte mein Leben bis Neujahr 1944 wie unter einer scharfen Lupe. Daheim das Leben mit viel Sonne, dann 1942 hierher, der plötzliche Übergang, die Streitereien, die Anschuldigungen. Ich konnte es nicht fassen, ich war überrumpelt und habe meine Haltung nur durch Frechheit bewahren können.

Dann die erste Hälfte von 1943: Meine Heulanfälle, die Einsamkeit, das langsame Einsehen der Fehler und Mängel, die groß sind und doppelt so groß schienen. Ich redete tagsüber über alles hinweg und versuchte Pim auf meine Seite zu ziehen. Das gelang mir nicht. Ich stand allein vor der schwierigen Aufgabe, mich so zu verändern, dass ich keine Tadel mehr hören musste, denn die drückten mich nieder bis zur schrecklichen Mutlosigkeit.

In der zweiten Hälfte des Jahres wurde es etwas besser. Ich wurde ein Backfisch, galt als erwachsener. Ich fing an nachzudenken, Geschichten zu schreiben, und kam zu dem Schluss, dass die anderen nichts mehr mit mir zu tun hatten. Sie hatten kein Recht, mich hin und her zu zerren. Ich wollte mich selbst umformen, nach meinem eigenen Willen. Ich verstand, dass ich auf Mutter verzichten kann, ganz und vollständig. Das tat weh. Aber eines traf mich noch mehr, nämlich die Einsicht, dass Vater nie mein Vertrauter werden würde. Ich vertraute niemandem mehr, nur noch mir selbst.

Nach Neujahr dann die zweite große Veränderung, mein Traum ... Durch ihn entdeckte ich meine Sehnsucht nach einem Jungen. Nicht nach einer Mädchenfreundschaft, sondern nach einem Jungenfreund. Entdeckte auch das Glück in mir selbst und meinen Panzer aus Oberflächlichkeit und Fröhlichkeit. Aber dann und wann wurde ich ruhig. Nun lebe ich nur noch von Peter, denn von ihm wird sehr viel davon abhängen, was weiter mit mir passieren wird.

Abends, wenn ich im Bett liege und mein Gebet mit den Worten beende: »Ich danke dir für all das Gute und Liebe und Schöne«, dann jubelt es in mir. Dann denke ich an »das Gute«: das Verstecken, meine Gesundheit, mein ganzes Selbst. »Das Liebe« von Peter, das, was noch klein und empfindlich ist und das wir beide noch nicht zu benennen wagen, die Liebe, die Zukunft, das Glück. »Das Schöne«, das die Welt meint, die Welt, die Natur und die weite Schönheit von allem, allem Schönen zusammen.

Dann denke ich nicht an das Elend, sondern an das Schöne, das noch immer übrig bleibt. Hier liegt zu einem großen Teil der Unterschied zwischen Mutter und mir. Ihr Rat bei Schwermut ist: »Denke an all das Elend in der Welt und sei froh, dass du das nicht erlebst.« Mein Rat ist: »Geh hinaus in die Felder, die Natur und die Sonne. Geh hinaus und versuche, das Glück in dir selbst zurückzufinden. Denke an all das Schöne, das noch in dir und um dich ist, und sei glücklich!«

Meiner Meinung nach kann Mutters Satz nicht stimmen, denn was tust du dann, wenn du das Elend doch erlebst? Dann bist du verloren. Ich hingegen finde, dass noch bei jedem Kummer etwas Schönes übrig bleibt. Wenn man das betrachtet, entdeckt man immer mehr Freude, und man wird wieder ausgeglichen. Und wer glücklich ist, wird auch andere glücklich machen. Wer Mut und Vertrauen hat, wird im Unglück nicht untergehen!   Deine Anne M. Frank

Mittwoch, 8. März 1944

Margot und ich haben uns Briefchen geschrieben, nur zum Spaß, natürlich.

Anne: Verrückt, nicht wahr, mir fallen nächtliche Begebenheiten immer erst viel später ein. Jetzt weiß ich plötzlich, dass Herr Dussel heute Nacht sehr laut geschnarcht hat (jetzt ist es mittwochnachmittags, Viertel vor drei, und Herr Dussel schnarcht wieder, deshalb ist es mir natürlich eingefallen). Ich habe, als ich auf den Topf musste, absichtlich etwas mehr Lärm gemacht, damit das Schnarchen aufhört.

Margot: Was ist besser, das Geschnappe nach Luft oder das Schnarchen?

Anne: Schnarchen, denn wenn ich Krach mache, hört es auf, ohne dass die betreffende Person wach wird.

Etwas habe ich Margot nicht geschrieben, aber dir will ich es bekennen, Kitty, nämlich dass ich sehr viel von Peter träume. Vorgestern

Nacht war ich im Traum hier, in unserem Wohnzimmer, auf dem Eis. Mit mir war der kleine Junge von der Kunsteisbahn, der mit seinem Schwesterchen in dem ewigen blauen Kleid und den Storchenbeinen hier lief. Ich stellte mich ihm geziert vor und fragte nach seinem Namen. Er hieß Peter. Schon im Traum fragte ich mich, wie viele Peters ich nun kenne.

Dann träumte ich, dass wir in Peters Zimmer standen, einander gegenüber. Ich sagte etwas zu ihm, er gab mir einen Kuss. Aber er sagte, dass er mich doch nicht so gern hätte und ich nicht flirten sollte. Mit einer verzweifelten und flehenden Stimme sagte ich: »Ich flirte nicht, Peter!«

Als ich wach wurde, war ich froh, dass Peter das nicht gesagt hatte. Heute Nacht küssten wir uns auch. Aber Peters Wangen waren sehr enttäuschend. Sie waren nicht so weich, wie sie aussehen, sondern wie Vaters Wangen, also die eines Mannes, der sich schon rasiert.

Freitag, 10. März 1944

Liebste Kitty!

Heute passt das Sprichwort »Ein Unglück kommt selten allein«. Peter sagte es gerade. Ich werde dir erzählen, was wir für Unannehmlichkeiten haben und was uns vielleicht noch bevorsteht.

Erstens ist Miep krank. Sie war bei einer Trauung in der Westernkirche und hat sich erkältet. Zweitens ist Kleiman noch immer nicht zurück von seiner letzten Magenblutung, und Bep ist also allein im Büro. Drittens ist ein Mann, dessen Namen ich nicht nennen will, verhaftet worden. Das ist nicht nur für den Betreffenden sehr schlimm, sondern auch für uns, da wir auf Kartoffeln, Butter und Marmelade warten. Herr M., nennen wir ihn mal so, hat fünf Kinder unter 13 Jahren, und eins ist unterwegs.

Gestern Abend haben wir mal wieder einen kleinen Schreck erlebt, weil plötzlich neben uns an die Wand geklopft wurde. Wir waren gerade beim Essen. Der weitere Abend verlief bedrückt und nervös.

Ich habe in der letzten Zeit überhaupt keine Lust, die Ereignisse hier aufzuschreiben, meine eigenen Angelegenheiten gehen mir mehr zu Herzen. Versteh das nicht falsch, ich finde das Schicksal des armen

Herrn M. schrecklich, aber in meinem Tagebuch ist doch nicht viel Platz für ihn.

Dienstag, Mittwoch und Donnerstag war ich von halb fünf bis Viertel nach fünf bei Peter. Wir haben Französisch gemacht und über alles und noch was getratscht. Ich freue mich wirklich auf dieses kleine Stündchen nachmittags, und am schönsten ist, dass Peter, glaube ich, mein Kommen auch schön findet.   Deine Anne M. Frank

Samstag, 11. März 1944

Liebe Kitty!

In der letzten Zeit habe ich kein Sitzfleisch mehr. Ich gehe von oben nach unten und von unten wieder nach oben. Ich finde es schön, mit Peter zu reden, habe aber immer Angst, dass ich ihm lästig falle. Er hat mir einiges von früher erzählt, von seinen Eltern und sich selbst, aber ich finde es viel zu wenig und frage mich doch alle fünf Minuten, wie ich dazu komme, mehr zu verlangen. Er fand mich früher unausstehlich, ich ihn auch. Jetzt habe ich meine Meinung geändert, muss er seine auch geändert haben? Ich glaube ja, doch das bedeutet noch nicht, dass wir dicke Freunde werden müssen, obwohl ich meinerseits das ganze Verstecken dann leichter ertragen könnte. Aber ich will mich nicht verrückt machen, ich beschäftige mich genug mit ihm und muss dich nicht auch noch langweilen, weil ich so lahm bin!

Sonntag, 12. März 1944

Liebe Kitty!

Alles wird immer verrückter, je länger es dauert. Seit gestern schaut Peter mich nicht an, als wäre er böse auf mich. Ich gebe mir dann auch Mühe, ihm nicht nachzulaufen und so wenig wie möglich mit ihm zu reden, aber es fällt mir schwer. Was ist es denn, das ihn oft von mir abhält und oft zu mir hindrängt? Vielleicht bilde ich mir auch nur ein, dass es schlimm ist. Vielleicht hat er auch Launen, vielleicht ist morgen alles wieder gut.

Am schwersten ist es, dass ich nach außen hin normal sein muss, auch wenn ich so traurig bin. Ich muss helfen, mit anderen reden und zusammensitzen und vor allem fröhlich sein! Ganz besonders vermisse ich die Natur und einen Platz, wo ich allein sein kann, solange ich will. Ich glaube, ich bringe alles durcheinander, aber ich bin auch völlig verwirrt. Auf der einen Seite bin ich verrückt vor Sehnsucht nach ihm, kann kaum im Zimmer sein, ohne zu ihm hinzuschauen, und auf der anderen Seite frage ich mich, warum es mir eigentlich so viel ausmacht, warum ich nicht wieder ruhig werden kann!

Tag und Nacht, immer wenn ich wach bin, tue ich nichts anderes, als mich zu fragen: »Hast du ihn nicht genug in Ruhe gelassen? Bist du zu oft oben? Redest du zu oft über ernste Dinge, über die er noch nicht sprechen kann? Findet er dich vielleicht überhaupt nicht sympathisch? War der ganze Rummel vielleicht nur Einbildung? Aber warum hat er dir dann so viel über sich selbst erzählt? Tut ihm das vielleicht Leid?« Und noch viel mehr.

Gestern Nachmittag war ich nach einer Reihe trauriger Neuigkeiten von draußen so durchgedreht, dass ich mich auf meine Couch legte. Ich wollte nichts als schlafen, um nicht nachzudenken. Ich schlief bis vier Uhr, dann musste ich hinüber. Es fiel mir schwer, Mutters Fragen zu beantworten und mir für Vater eine Ausrede auszudenken, die mein Schlafen erklärte. Ich schob Kopfschmerzen vor, was nicht gelogen war, da ich auch Kopfschmerzen hatte … von innen!

Normale Menschen, normale Mädchen, Backfische wie ich, werden mich wohl für übergeschnappt halten mit meinem Selbstmitleid. Aber es ist ja so, dass ich dir alles sage, was mir auf dem Herzen liegt, den übrigen Tag bin ich so frech, fröhlich und selbstbewusst wie möglich, um alle Fragen zu vermeiden, und ärgere mich innerlich über mich selbst.

Margot ist sehr lieb und möchte gern meine Vertraute sein, aber ich kann ihr doch nicht alles sagen. Ihr fehlt es an Ungezwungenheit. Sie nimmt mich ernst, viel zu ernst, und denkt lange über ihre verrückte Schwester nach. Sie schaut mich bei allem, was ich sage, prüfend an und denkt: Ist das jetzt Komödie, oder meint sie es wirklich?

Wir sind eben dauernd zusammen, und ich könnte meine Vertraute nicht immer um mich haben.

Wann komme ich wieder heraus aus diesem Wirrwarr von Gedanken? Wann wird wieder Ruhe und Frieden in mir sein?

Deine Anne

Dienstag, 14. März 1944

Liebe Kitty!

Für dich ist es vielleicht vergnüglich (für mich weniger) zu hören, was wir heute essen werden. Da die Putzfrau unten ist, sitze ich im Augenblick bei van Daans am Wachstuchtisch und habe ein Taschentuch, das mit wohlriechendem Parfüm aus der Vorversteckzeit durchzogen ist, gegen Mund und Nase gedrückt. Das wirst du so natürlich nicht verstehen, also »mit dem Anfang beginnen«.

Da unsere Markenlieferanten festgenommen worden sind, haben wir außer unseren fünf schwarzen Lebensmittelkarten keine Marken und kein Fett. Und weil Miep und Kleiman wieder krank sind, kann Bep auch nichts besorgen. Und weil die ganze Stimmung trübselig ist, ist es das Essen auch. Ab morgen haben wir kein Stückchen Fett, Butter oder Margarine mehr. Zum Frühstück gibt es nun nicht mehr Bratkartoffeln (aus Brotersparnis), sondern Brei, und da Frau van Daan glaubt, dass wir verhungern, haben wir dafür extra Vollmilch gekauft. Unser Mittagessen heute ist Grünkohleintopf aus dem Fass. Daher auch die Vorsichtsmaßnahme mit dem Taschentuch. Unglaublich, wie Grünkohl, der wahrscheinlich ein paar Jahre alt ist, stinken kann! Es riecht hier im Zimmer nach einer Mischung aus verdorbenen Pflaumen, Konservierungsmittel und faulen Eiern. Bah, mir wird schon übel allein bei dem Gedanken, dass ich dieses Zeug essen muss!

Dazu kommt noch, dass sich unsere Kartoffeln sonderbare Krankheiten zugezogen haben und von zwei Eimern »pommes de terre« einer im Herd landet. Wir machen uns einen Spaß daraus, die verschiedenen Krankheiten herauszufinden, und sind zu dem Schluss gekommen, dass Krebs, Pocken und Masern einander abwechseln. O ja, es ist kein Vergnügen, im vierten Kriegsjahr versteckt zu leben. Wäre der ganze Mist nur schon vorbei!

Ehrlich gesagt, mir würde das Essen nicht so viel ausmachen, wenn es sonst etwas vergnüglicher hier wäre. Der Haken ist, dass dieses langweilige Leben anfängt, uns unleidlich zu machen. Hier folgen die Meinungen von fünf erwachsenen Untertauchern über den gegenwärtigen Zustand (Kinder dürfen keine Meinung haben, ich habe mich für diesmal daran gehalten).

Frau van Daan:

»Die Arbeit als Küchenfee gefällt mir schon lange nicht mehr, aber dazusitzen und nichts zu tun zu haben ist langweilig. Also koche ich doch wieder und beklage mich: ›Kochen ohne Fett ist unmöglich. Mir wird übel von all den ekelhaften Gerüchen. Nichts als Undankbarkeit und Geschrei ist der Lohn für meine Mühe. Ich bin immer das schwarze Schaf, an allem bekomme ich die Schuld.‹ Ferner bin ich der Meinung, dass der Krieg nicht viel Fortschritte macht, die Deutschen werden am Schluss doch noch gewinnen. Ich habe schreckliche Angst, dass wir verhungern, und schimpfe jeden aus, wenn ich schlechte Laune habe.«

Herr van Daan:

»Ich muss rauchen, rauchen, rauchen, dann sind Essen, Politik und Kerlis Launen nicht so schlimm, und Kerli ist eine liebe Frau. Wenn ich nichts zu rauchen bekomme, dann werde ich krank, dann brauche ich Fleisch. Dann leben wir zu schlecht, ist nichts gut genug, es folgt bestimmt ein heftiger Streit, und meine Kerli ist eine schrecklich dumme Frau.«

Frau Frank:

»Das Essen ist nicht so wichtig, aber gerade jetzt hätte ich gerne eine Scheibe Roggenbrot, denn ich habe schrecklichen Hunger. Wenn ich Frau van Daan wäre, hätte ich dem ewigen Rauchen meines Mannes schon längst einen Riegel vorgeschoben. Aber jetzt brauche ich dringend eine Zigarette, ich habe schon einen ganz blöden Kopf. Die van Daans sind schreckliche Leute, die Engländer machen viele Fehler, aber der Krieg geht voran. Ich muss reden und froh sein, dass ich nicht in Polen bin.«

Herr Frank:

»Alles in Ordnung, ich brauche nichts. Immer mit der Ruhe, wir haben Zeit. Gib mir meine Kartoffeln, dann halte ich den Mund. Schnell noch was von meiner Ration zur Seite legen, für Bep. Politisch geht es voran, ich bin optimistisch.«

Herr Dussel:

»Ich muss mein Pensum schaffen, alles rechtzeitig fertig machen. Mit der Politik geht es ausgezeichnet, dass wir geschnappt werden, ist unmöglich. Ich, ich, ich …!«   Deine Anne

Liebe Kitty!

Puh, ein Weilchen von den düsteren Szenen befreit! Heute habe ich nichts anderes gehört als: »Wenn dies oder das passiert, dann bekommen wir Schwierigkeiten, wenn der noch krank wird, stehen wir allein auf der Welt ..., wenn dann ...«

Nun ja, den Rest weißt du schon. Ich vermute wenigstens, dass du die Hinterhäusler inzwischen gut genug kennst, um ihre Gespräche zu erraten.

Der Anlass für dieses »wenn, wenn« ist, dass Kugler zu sechs Tagen Arbeitsdienst aufgerufen worden ist, Bep mehr als nur einen Stockschnupfen hat und wahrscheinlich morgen zu Hause bleiben muss, Miep von ihrer Grippe noch nicht genesen ist und Kleiman eine Magenblutung mit Bewusstlosigkeit gehabt hat. Eine wahre Trauerliste für uns.

Kugler muss unserer Meinung nach zu einem zuverlässigen Arzt gehen, sich ein Attest schreiben lassen und es auf dem Rathaus in Hilversum vorlegen. Für morgen haben die Arbeiter vom Lager einen Tag frei bekommen, Bep ist dann allein im Büro. Wenn (schon wieder ein Wenn) sie zu Hause bleibt, dann bleibt die Tür verschlossen und wir müssen mäuschenstill sein, dass die Leute im Nachbarhaus nichts hören. Jan will um ein Uhr kommen und die Verlassenen für eine halbe Stunde besuchen, er spielt dann sozusagen die Rolle eines Zoowärters.

Jan hat heute Mittag zum ersten Mal seit langer Zeit wieder mal was von der großen Welt erzählt. Du hättest sehen müssen, wie wir acht um ihn herum saßen, genau wie auf einem Bild »Wenn Großmutter erzählt«.

Er kam vom Hundertsten ins Tausendste vor seinem dankbaren Publikum und sprach in erster Linie natürlich vom Essen. Eine Bekannte von Miep kocht für ihn. Vorgestern bekam er Karotten mit grünen Erbsen, gestern musste er Reste essen, heute kocht sie Ackererbsen, und morgen gibt's aus den übrig gebliebenen Karotten Eintopf.

Wir erkundigten uns nach Mieps Doktor.

»Doktor?«, fragte Jan. »Was wollen Sie vom Doktor? Ich rief heute Morgen bei ihm an, bekam so ein Assistentchen ans Telefon, bat um ein Rezept gegen Grippe und erhielt die Antwort, dass ich es zwischen acht und neun abholen könnte. Wenn man eine sehr schwere Grippe hat, kommt der Doktor selbst kurz an den Apparat und sagt: ›Strecken Sie mal Ihre Zunge raus! Sagen Sie aah! Ich höre schon, Sie haben einen roten Hals. Ich schreibe ein Rezept für Sie, damit können Sie zur Apotheke gehen. Guten Tag, mein Herr.‹ Und damit basta. Bequeme Praxis ist das, ausschließlich Bedienung durchs Telefon. Aber ich sollte den Ärzten nichts vorwerfen, schließlich hat jeder Mensch nur zwei Hände, und heute gibt es einen Überfluss an Patienten und nur eine minimale Zahl an Ärzten.«

Trotzdem mussten wir lachen, als Jan das Telefongespräch wiedergab. Ich kann mir wirklich vorstellen, wie ein Wartezimmer gegenwärtig aussieht. Man schaut nicht mehr auf Kassenpatienten hinab, sondern auf Leute, denen nichts Schlimmes fehlt, und denkt sich: Mensch, was hast du hier zu suchen? Hinten anstellen, wirklich Kranke haben Vorrang!   Deine Anne M. Frank

Donnerstag, 16. März 1944

Liebe Kitty!

Das Wetter ist herrlich, unbeschreiblich schön. Ich gehe sicher bald zum Dachboden.

Ich weiß jetzt, warum ich so viel unruhiger bin als Peter. Er hat ein eigenes Zimmer, in dem er arbeitet, träumt, denkt und schläft. Ich werde von einer Ecke in die andere geschoben. Allein bin ich in meinem geteilten Zimmer nie, und doch sehne ich mich so sehr danach. Das ist auch der Grund, weshalb ich zum Dachboden flüchte. Dort und bei dir kann ich mal kurz, ganz kurz, ich selbst sein. Doch ich will nicht über meine Sehnsüchte jammern, im Gegenteil, ich will mutig sein!

Glücklicherweise merkt niemand etwas von meinen Gefühlen, außer dass ich mit jedem Tag kühler und verächtlicher gegen Mutter bin, mit Vater weniger schmuse und auch Margot gegenüber nichts mehr rauslasse, ich bin völlig zugeknöpft. Ich muss vor allem meine äußere Sicherheit bewahren, niemand darf wissen, dass in mir noch immer Krieg herrscht. Krieg zwischen meinem Verlangen und meinem Verstand. Bis jetzt hat letzterer den Sieg errungen, aber wird das Gefühl nicht doch stärker sein? Manchmal fürchte ich es, und oft ersehne ich es.

Es ist so schwierig, Peter gegenüber nichts zu zeigen, aber ich weiß, dass er anfangen muss. Es fällt mir schwer, all die Gespräche und Handlungen, die ich in meinen Träumen mit ihm erlebt habe, tagsüber wieder als nicht geschehen zu betrachten. Ja, Kitty, Anne ist verrückt, aber ich lebe auch in einer verrückten Zeit und unter noch verrückteren Umständen.

Am besten gefällt mir noch, dass ich das, was ich denke und fühle, wenigstens aufschreiben kann, sonst würde ich komplett ersticken.

Was denkt Peter wohl über all das? Immer wieder glaube ich, dass ich eines Tages mit ihm darüber sprechen kann. Es muss doch etwas geben an mir, das er erraten hat, denn die äußere Anne, die er bis jetzt kennt, kann er doch nicht gern haben! Wie kann er, der Ruhe und Frieden so sehr liebt, Sympathie für mein lärmendes und lebhaftes Benehmen fühlen? Ist er vielleicht der Erste und Einzige, der hinter meine Betonmaske geschaut hat? Wird er vielleicht bald dahintersteigen? Gibt es nicht einen alten Spruch, dass auf Mitleid oft Liebe folgt oder dass beides oft Hand in Hand geht? Ist das nicht auch bei mir der Fall? Ich habe genauso viel Mitleid mit ihm, wie ich es oft mit mir selbst habe!

Ich weiß wirklich nicht, wie ich die ersten Worte finden sollte. Wie könnte er es dann, der noch viel mehr Schwierigkeiten hat zu sprechen? Könnte ich ihm nur schreiben! Dann wüsste ich wenigstens, dass er weiß, was ich sagen wollte, mit Worten ist es so entsetzlich schwer. Deine Anne M. Frank

Freitag, 17. März 1944

Allerliebster Schatz!

Es ist noch mal gut gegangen, Beps Erkältung ist keine Grippe geworden, sondern nur Heiserkeit, und Herr Kugler ist vom Arbeitsdienst durch das Attest eines Arztes befreit worden. Durch das Hinterhaus weht ein Wind der Erleichterung. Alles ist in Ordnung, außer dass Margot und ich unsere Eltern ein bisschen satt haben.

Du darfst das nicht falsch verstehen, ich liebe Vater, und Margot liebt Vater und Mutter, aber wenn man so alt ist wie wir, will man auch ein bisschen für sich selbst entscheiden, will man mal von der Elternhand los. Wenn ich nach oben gehe, wird gefragt, was ich tun will. Bei Tisch darf ich kein Salz nehmen, jeden Abend um Viertel nach acht fragt Mutter, ob ich mich noch nicht ausziehen sollte, jedes Buch, das ich lese, muss geprüft werden. Ehrlich gesagt, diese Prüfung ist überhaupt nicht streng, und ich darf fast alles lesen, aber all diese Be- und Anmerkungen plus die Fragerei den ganzen Tag finden wir lästig.

Noch etwas passt ihnen nicht, ich will nicht mehr den ganzen Tag Küsschen hier und Küsschen da geben. All die süßen, ausgedachten Kosenamen finde ich geziert. Und Vaters Vorliebe, über Winde lassen und die Toilette zu sprechen, finde ich scheußlich. Kurz, ich möchte sie gern mal für eine Weile loshaben, und das verstehen sie nicht. Nicht dass wir ihnen etwas davon erzählt haben, nein, wozu auch, sie würden es nicht kapieren.

Margot hat gestern Abend gesagt: »Ich finde es wirklich blöd. Wenn man kurz den Kopf auf die Hände legt und zweimal seufzt, fragen sie gleich, ob man Kopfweh hat oder sich nicht gut fühlt.«

Es ist für Margot und mich ein richtiger Schlag, dass wir nun plötzlich sehen, wie wenig von dem vertrauten und harmonischen Zuhause übrig ist. Und das liegt zu einem großen Teil daran, dass unser Verhältnis zueinander so schief ist. Ich meine, dass wir wie kleine Kinder behandelt werden, was die äußerlichen Dinge betrifft, und wir innerlich viel älter sind als Mädchen unseres Alters. Auch wenn ich erst vierzehn bin, weiß ich doch sehr gut, was ich will, ich weiß, wer Recht und Unrecht hat, ich habe meine Meinung, meine Auffassungen und Prinzipien. Vielleicht klingt das verrückt für einen Backfisch, aber ich fühle mich viel mehr Mensch als Kind, ich fühle mich unabhängig, von wem auch immer. Ich weiß, dass ich besser debattieren und diskutieren kann als Mutter, ich weiß, dass ich einen objektiveren Blick habe und nicht so übertreibe, ordentlicher und geschickter bin, und dadurch fühle ich mich (du kannst darüber lachen) ihr in vielen Dingen überlegen. Wenn ich jemanden lieben soll, muss ich in erster Linie Bewunderung für ihn fühlen, Bewunderung und Respekt, und diese beiden Punkte vermisse ich bei Mutter vollkommen.

Alles wäre gut, wenn ich nur Peter hätte, denn ihn bewundere ich in vielem. Nicht wahr, er ist so ein feiner und hübscher Junge!

Deine Anne M. Frank

Anne, 1941.

Liebe Kitty!

Niemandem auf der Welt habe ich mehr über mich selbst und meine Gefühle erzählt als dir, warum sollte ich dir dann nicht auch etwas über sexuelle Dinge erzählen?

Eltern und Menschen im Allgemeinen verhalten sich bei diesem Thema sehr eigenartig. Statt dass sie sowohl ihren Mädchen als auch ihren Jungen von zwölf Jahren alles erzählen, werden Kinder bei solchen Gesprächen aus dem Zimmer geschickt und dürfen selbst sehen, wo sie ihre Weisheit herbekommen. Wenn die Eltern dann später entdecken, dass ihre Kinder doch etwas erfahren haben, nehmen sie an, dass die Kinder mehr oder weniger wissen, als tatsächlich wahr ist. Warum versuchen sie dann nicht noch, das Versäumte nachzuholen, und fragen, wie es damit steht?

Ein wichtiges Hindernis gibt es für die Erwachsenen, doch ich finde es sehr klein. Sie denken nämlich, dass Kinder sich die Ehe dann nicht mehr heilig und unversehrt vorstellen, wenn sie wissen, dass diese Unversehrtheit in den meisten Fällen bloß Unsinn ist. Ich persönlich finde es für einen Mann überhaupt nicht schlimm, wenn er ein bisschen Erfahrung mit in die Ehe bringt. Damit hat die Ehe doch nichts zu tun.

Als ich gerade elf geworden war, klärten sie mich über die Periode auf. Woher sie kam oder was sie für eine Bedeutung hat, wusste ich aber noch lange nicht. Mit zwölfeinhalb Jahren erfuhr ich mehr, weil Jopie nicht so blöd war wie ich. Wie Mann und Frau zusammenleben, hat mir mein Gefühl selbst gesagt. Am Anfang fand ich diese Vorstellung verrückt, aber als Jacque es mir bestätigte, war ich schon ein bisschen stolz auf meine Intuition.

Dass Kinder nicht aus dem Bauch geboren werden, habe ich auch von Jacque, die sagte einfach: »Wo es hineingeht, kommt es fertig wieder heraus.« Über Jungfernhäutchen und andere Einzelheiten wussten Jacque und ich aus einem Buch über sexuelle Aufklärung. Dass man Kinderkriegen verhindern kann, wusste ich auch, aber wie das alles innerlich geht, war mir ein Geheimnis. Als ich hierher kam, erzählte Vater mir von Prostituierten und so weiter, aber alles in allem bleiben genug Fragen übrig.

Wenn eine Mutter ihren Kindern nicht alles erzählt, erfahren sie es stückchenweise, und das ist sicher verkehrt.

Obwohl Samstag ist, bin ich nicht gelangweilt. Das liegt daran, dass ich mit Peter auf dem Dachboden war. Mit geschlossenen Augen habe ich dagesessen und geträumt, es war herrlich.

Deine Anne M. Frank

Sonntag, 19. März 1944

Liebe Kitty!

Gestern war ein sehr wichtiger Tag für mich. Nach dem Mittagessen verlief alles ganz normal. Um fünf Uhr setzte ich Kartoffeln auf, und Mutter gab mir etwas von der Blutwurst, um sie Peter zu bringen. Ich wollte erst nicht, ging dann aber doch. Er wollte die Wurst nicht annehmen, und ich hatte das elende Gefühl, dass es noch immer wegen des Streites über das Misstrauen war. Auf einmal konnte ich nicht mehr, die Tränen schossen mir in die Augen. Ich brachte die Untertasse wieder zu Mutter und ging aufs Klo, zum Ausweinen. Dann beschloss ich, die Sache mit Peter durchzusprechen. Vor dem Essen saßen wir zu viert bei ihm an einem Kreuzworträtsel, da konnte ich also nichts sagen. Aber als wir zu Tisch gingen, flüsterte ich ihm zu: »Machst du heute Abend Steno?«

»Nein«, antwortete er.

»Dann möchte ich dich später kurz sprechen.« Er war einverstanden. Nach dem Abwasch ging ich also zu ihm und fragte, ob er die Blutwurst wegen des letzten Streits nicht angenommen hätte. Das war es zum Glück nicht, er fand es aber nur nicht richtig, so schnell nachzugeben. Es war sehr warm im Zimmer gewesen, und mein Gesicht war rot wie ein Krebs. Deshalb ging ich, nachdem ich Margot das Wasser hinuntergebracht hatte, noch mal nach oben, um etwas Luft zu schnappen. Anstandshalber stellte ich mich erst bei van Daans ans Fenster, ging aber schon bald zu Peter. Er stand an der linken Seite des offenen Fensters, ich stellte mich an die rechte. Es war viel leichter, am offenen Fenster und im Dunkeln zu sprechen, als bei Licht. Ich glaube, Peter fand das auch. Wir haben uns so viel erzählt, so schrecklich viel, das kann ich gar nicht alles wiederholen. Aber es war toll, der schönste Abend, den ich im Hinterhaus je hatte. Einige Themen kann ich dir doch kurz wiedergeben.

Erst sprachen wir über die Streitereien, dass ich denen nun ganz anders gegenüberstehe, dann über die Entfremdung zwischen uns und unseren Eltern. Ich erzählte Peter von Mutter und Vater, von Margot und mir selbst. Irgendwann fragte er: »Ihr sagt euch doch bestimmt immer Gutenacht mit einem Kuss?«

»Mit einem? Mit einem ganzen Haufen. Du nicht, oder?«

»Nein, ich habe fast nie jemandem einen Kuss gegeben.«

»Auch nicht an deinem Geburtstag?«

»Doch, dann schon.«

Wir sprachen auch darüber, dass wir beide unseren Eltern nicht so viel Vertrauen schenken. Dass seine Eltern ihn zwar sehr lieben und wohl auch gern sein Vertrauen haben wollten, aber dass er es nicht wollte. Dass ich meinen Kummer im Bett ausweine und er auf den Oberboden geht und flucht. Dass Margot und ich uns auch erst seit kurzem richtig kennen und dass wir uns doch nicht so viel erzählen, weil wir immer beieinander sind. Wir sprachen über alles Mögliche, über Vertrauen, Gefühl und uns selbst. Er war genauso, wie ich ihn mir vorgestellt hatte.

Dann kamen wir auf das Jahr 1942, wie anders wir damals waren. Wir erkennen uns beide nicht mehr wieder. Wie wir uns am Anfang nicht ausstehen konnten. Er fand mich lebhaft und lästig, und ich fand schon bald an dem ganzen Jungen nichts. Ich verstand nicht, dass er nicht flirtete, aber jetzt bin ich froh. Er sprach auch noch darüber, dass er sich so oft abgesondert hat, und ich sagte, dass zwischen meinem Lärm und Übermut und seiner Stille nicht so viel Unterschied sei und ich auch die Ruhe liebe, aber nirgends für mich allein wäre, außer mit meinem Tagebuch. Und dass mich jeder lieber gehen als kommen sieht, vor allem Herr Dussel, und im Zimmer der Eltern will ich nicht immer sein. Er ist froh, dass meine Eltern Kinder haben, und ich bin froh, dass er hier ist. Ich sagte ihm, dass ich ihn in seiner Zurückgezogenheit und seinem Verhalten seinen Eltern gegenüber verstehe und ihm gerne helfen würde bei den Streitereien.

»Du hilfst mir doch immer!«, sagte er.

»Womit denn?«, fragte ich sehr erstaunt.

»Mit deiner Fröhlichkeit.«

Das war wohl das Schönste, was er mir gesagt hat. Er sagte auch noch, dass er es überhaupt nicht mehr lästig fände, wenn ich zu ihm komme, sondern toll. Und ich erzählte ihm, dass mir all die Kosenamen von Vater und Mutter leer vorkommen und ein Küsschen hier und ein Küsschen da noch kein Vertrauen schafft. Wir sprachen über unseren eigenen Willen, das Tagebuch und die Einsamkeit, den Unterschied zwischen einem Innen- und einem Außenmenschen, den jeder hat, meine Maske und so weiter.

Es war herrlich. Er muss angefangen haben, mich als Kameraden gern zu haben, und das ist vorläufig genug. Ich habe keine Worte dafür, so dankbar und froh bin ich. Und ich muss mich schon bei dir entschuldigen, Kitty, dass mein Stil heute unter dem sonstigen Niveau liegt. Ich habe einfach aufgeschrieben, was mir eingefallen ist.

Ich habe das Gefühl, als teilten Peter und ich ein Geheimnis. Wenn er mich anschaut, mit diesen Augen, diesem Lachen und diesem Zwinkern, ist es, als gehe in meinem Inneren ein Licht an. Ich hoffe, dass es so bleibt, dass wir noch viele, viele schöne Stunden zusammen verbringen. <u>Deine dankbare und frohe Anne</u>

<u>Montag, 20. März 1944</u>

Liebe Kitty!

Heute Morgen fragte Peter, ob ich abends mal öfter käme. Ich würde ihn wirklich nicht stören, und in seinem Zimmer wäre genauso gut auch Platz für zwei. Ich sagte, dass ich nicht jeden Abend kommen könnte, weil sie das unten nicht richtig fänden, aber er meinte, dass ich mich daran nicht stören sollte. Ich sagte, dass ich am Samstagabend gerne käme, und bat ihn, mir vor allem Bescheid zu sagen, wenn man den Mond sehen könnte.

»Dann gehen wir hinunter«, sagte er, »und schauen uns von dort den Mond an.« Ich war einverstanden, und so große Angst vor Dieben habe ich auch wirklich nicht.

Inzwischen ist ein Schatten auf mein Glück gefallen. Ich dachte schon längst, dass Margot Peter mehr als nett findet. Ob sie ihn liebt, weiß ich nicht, aber ich finde es sehr schlimm. Jedes Mal, wenn ich Peter nun treffe, muss ich ihr wehtun, und es ist schön, dass sie sich fast nichts anmerken lässt. Ich wäre verzweifelt vor Eifersucht, aber Margot sagt nur, dass ich kein Mitleid mit ihr haben müsste.

»Ich finde es so schlimm, dass du als Dritte dabeistehst«, sagte ich.
»Das bin ich gewöhnt«, sagte sie ziemlich bitter.

Das wage ich Peter nicht zu erzählen. Vielleicht später mal. Wir müssen uns erst noch richtig aussprechen.

Mutter hat mir gestern einen kleinen Schlag verpasst, den ich wirklich verdient habe. Ich darf mich in meiner Gleichgültigkeit und Verachtung ihr gegenüber nicht so gehen lassen. Also wieder mal versuchen, trotz allem freundlich zu sein und meine Bemerkungen zu unterlassen.

Auch Pim ist nicht mehr so herzlich. Er versucht sich das Kindische ein bisschen abzugewöhnen und ist nun viel zu kühl. Mal sehen, was daraus wird. Er hat mir gedroht, dass ich später bestimmt keine Nachhilfestunden bekomme, wenn ich kein Algebra mache. Obwohl ich das abwarten könnte, will ich doch wieder damit anfangen, vorausgesetzt, ich bekomme ein neues Buch.

Vorläufig kann ich nichts anderes tun, als Peter anzuschauen, und ich bin randvoll!

Deine Anne M. Frank

Ein Beweis von Margots Güte. Dies erhielt ich heute, am 20. März 1944:

»Anne, als ich gestern sagte, dass ich nicht eifersüchtig auf dich wäre, war das nur zu 50% ehrlich. Es ist nämlich so, dass ich weder auf dich noch auf Peter eifersüchtig bin. Ich finde es nur für mich selbst ein bisschen schade, dass ich noch niemanden gefunden habe und vorläufig sicher nicht finden werde, mit dem ich über meine Gedanken und Gefühle sprechen könnte. Aber deshalb gönne ich es euch beiden doch von Herzen, wenn ihr euch etwas Vertrauen schenken könntet. Du vermisst hier schon genug von dem, was für viele andere so selbstverständlich ist. Andererseits weiß ich genau, dass ich mit Peter doch nie so weit gekommen wäre, weil ich das Gefühl habe, dass ich mit demjenigen, mit dem ich viel besprechen möchte, auf ziemlich intimem Fuß stehen müsste. Ich würde das Gefühl brauchen, dass er mich, auch ohne dass ich viel sage, durch und durch versteht. Deshalb müsste es jemand sein, bei dem ich das Gefühl habe, dass er mir geistig überlegen ist, und das ist bei Peter nicht der Fall. Bei dir und Peter könnte ich es mir aber gut vorstellen.

Du brauchst dir also überhaupt keine Vorwürfe zu machen, dass ich zu kurz komme und du etwas tust, was mir zukäme. Nichts ist weniger wahr. Du und Peter werdet nur gewinnen können durch den Umgang miteinander.«

Meine Antwort:
Liebe Margot!
Deinen Brief fand ich außerordentlich lieb, aber ich bin doch nicht völlig beruhigt und werde es wohl auch nicht werden.
Von Vertrauen ist in dem Maße, das du meinst, zwischen Peter und mir vorläufig noch keine Rede, aber an einem offenen und dunklen Fenster sagt man einander mehr als im hellen Sonnenschein. Auch kann man seine Gefühle leichter flüsternd sagen, als wenn man sie ausposaunen muss. Ich glaube, dass du für Peter eine Art schwesterlicher Zuneigung fühlst und ihm gern helfen willst, mindestens so gern wie ich. Vielleicht wirst du das auch noch mal tun können, obwohl das kein Vertrauen in unserem Sinn ist. Ich finde, dass Vertrauen von zwei Seiten kommen muss. Ich glaube, das ist auch der Grund, dass es zwischen Vater und mir nie so weit gekommen ist. Hören wir jetzt damit auf und reden auch nicht mehr darüber. Wenn du noch etwas willst, mache es bitte schriftlich, denn so kann ich viel besser ausdrücken, was ich meine, als mündlich. Du weißt nicht, wie sehr ich dich bewundere, und ich hoffe nur, dass ich noch mal etwas von Vaters und deiner Güte bekomme, denn darin sehe ich zwischen euch nicht mehr viel Unterschied. Deine Anne

Mittwoch, 22. März 1944

Liebe Kitty!
Dies bekam ich gestern Abend von Margot:
»Beste Anne!
Nach deinem Brief von gestern habe ich das unangenehme Gefühl, dass du Gewissensbisse hast, wenn du zu Peter gehst, um zu arbeiten oder zu reden. Dazu gibt es jedoch wirklich keinen Grund. In meinem Inneren hat jemand Recht auf gegenseitiges Vertrauen, und ich würde Peter noch nicht auf dieser Stelle dulden können. Es ist jedoch so, wie du geschrieben hast, dass ich das Gefühl habe, Peter

ist eine Art Bruder, aber ... ein jüngerer Bruder. Unsere Gefühle strecken Fühler aus, um uns vielleicht später, vielleicht auch nie, in geschwisterlicher Zuneigung zu berühren. So weit ist es jedoch noch lange nicht. Du brauchst also wirklich kein Mitleid mit mir zu haben. Genieße so oft wie möglich die Gesellschaft, die du nun gefunden hast.«

Es wird hier immer schöner. Ich glaube, Kitty, dass wir hier im Hinterhaus vielleicht noch eine echte große Liebe erleben. All das Gewitzel über eine Heirat mit Peter, wenn wir noch lange hier bleiben, war also doch nicht so verrückt. Ich denke wirklich nicht darüber nach, ihn zu heiraten. Ich weiß nicht, wie er mal sein wird, wenn er erwachsen ist. Ich weiß auch nicht, ob wir uns einmal so lieb haben, dass wir gerne heiraten würden.

Ich bin inzwischen sicher, dass Peter mich auch gern hat. Auf welche Art er mich mag, weiß ich nicht. Ob er nur eine gute Kameradin wünscht oder ob er mich als Mädchen anziehe oder aber als Schwester, dahinter bin ich noch nicht gekommen. Als er sagte, dass ich ihm bei den Streitereien zwischen seinen Eltern immer helfe, war ich enorm froh und schon einen Schritt weiter auf dem Weg, an seine Freundschaft zu glauben. Gestern fragte ich ihn, was er tun würde, wenn es hier ein Dutzend Annes gäbe und alle immer zu ihm kommen würden. Seine Antwort war: »Wenn sie alle so wären wie du, wäre das wirklich nicht so schlimm!«

Er ist sehr gastfreundlich zu mir, und ich glaube schon, dass er mich wirklich gern kommen sieht. Französisch lernt er inzwischen sehr eifrig, sogar abends im Bett bis Viertel nach zehn.

Ach, wenn ich an Samstagabend denke, an unsere Worte, unsere Stimmen, dann bin ich zum ersten Mal mit mir selbst zufrieden. Dann meine ich, dass ich nun dasselbe sagen würde und nicht alles ganz anders, was sonst meistens der Fall ist. Er ist so hübsch, sowohl wenn er lacht, als auch wenn er still vor sich hin schaut. Er ist lieb und gut und hübsch. Meiner Meinung nach war er am meisten überrumpelt, als er merkte, dass ich überhaupt nicht das oberflächlichste Mädchen der Welt bin, sondern genauso verträumt wie er, mit ebenso vielen Schwierigkeiten, wie er sie selbst hat.

Gestern Abend nach dem Spülen wartete ich darauf, dass er mich bitten würde, oben zu bleiben. Aber nichts passierte. Ich ging weg, und er kam herunter, um Dussel zum Radio zu rufen. Er trödelte im Badezimmer herum, aber als Dussel zu lange brauchte, ging er nach oben. Er lief in seinem Zimmer auf und ab und ging sehr früh ins Bett.

Ich war so unruhig den ganzen Abend, dass ich immer wieder ins Badezimmer ging, mir das Gesicht kalt abwusch, las, wieder träumte, auf die Uhr schaute und wartete, wartete, wartete und horchte, ob er käme. Ich lag früh im Bett und war todmüde.

Heute Abend ist Baden dran, und morgen?

Das ist noch so lange! Deine Anne M. Frank

Meine Antwort:

»Liebe Margot!

Am besten würde ich finden, dass wir nun einfach abwarten, was daraus wird. Es kann nicht mehr sehr lange dauern, dass die Entscheidung zwischen Peter und mir fällt, entweder wieder normal oder anders. Wie das gehen soll, weiß ich nicht, aber ich denke, was das betrifft, nicht weiter, als meine Nase lang ist.

Aber eines tue ich bestimmt. Wenn Peter und ich Freundschaft schließen, dann erzähle ich ihm, dass du ihn auch sehr gern hast und für ihn da bist, falls es nötig ist. Letzteres wirst du sicher nicht wollen, aber das macht mir jetzt nichts aus. Was Peter über dich denkt, weiß ich nicht, aber ich werde ihn dann schon fragen. Bestimmt nichts Schlechtes, im Gegenteil! Komm ruhig auf den Dachboden oder wo auch immer wir sind, du störst uns wirklich nicht, da wir, glaube ich, stillschweigend abgemacht haben, dass, wenn wir sprechen wollen, wir das abends im Dunkeln tun.

Halte dich tapfer! Ich tue es auch, obwohl es nicht immer einfach ist. Deine Zeit kommt vielleicht schneller, als du denkst.«

Deine Anne

Liebe Kitty! Donnerstag, 23. März 1944

Hier läuft alles wieder ein bisschen. Unsere Markenmänner sind zum Glück aus dem Gefängnis entlassen worden.

Miep ist seit gestern wieder hier, heute hat sich ihr Ehemann in die

Falle gelegt. Frösteln und Fieber, die bekannten Grippesymptome. Bep ist gesund, obwohl ihr Husten anhält. Nur Kleiman wird noch lange zu Hause bleiben müssen.

Gestern ist hier ein Flugzeug abgestürzt. Die Insassen sind noch rechtzeitig mit dem Fallschirm abgesprungen. Die Maschine stürzte auf eine Schule, in der keine Kinder waren. Es gab einen kleinen Brand und ein paar Tote. Die Deutschen haben auf die sinkenden Flieger geschossen. Die zuschauenden Amsterdamer schäumten vor Wut über eine so feige Tat. Wir, das heißt die Damen, erschraken auch zu Tode. Brrr, ich finde Schießen äußerst übel!

Jetzt über mich selbst.

Als ich gestern bei Peter war, kamen wir, ich weiß wirklich nicht mehr wie, auf das Thema Sexualität. Ich hatte mir längst vorgenommen, ihn einiges zu fragen. Er weiß alles. Als ich ihm sagte, dass Margot und ich überhaupt nicht richtig aufgeklärt wurden, war er ganz erstaunt. Ich erzählte ihm viel von Margot und mir und Mutter und Vater, und dass ich mich in der letzten Zeit nicht mehr traue zu fragen. Er bot dann an, mich aufzuklären, und ich machte davon dankbar Gebrauch. Er hat mir erklärt, wie Verhütungsmittel funktionieren, und ich fragte ihn tollkühn, woran Jungen merken, dass sie erwachsen sind. Darüber musste er erst mal nachdenken, er wollte es mir abends sagen. Unter anderem erzählte ich ihm die Geschichte von Jacque und mir und dass Mädchen starken Jungen gegenüber wehrlos sind. »Vor mir brauchst du keine Angst zu haben«, sagte er.

Abends, als ich wieder zu ihm kam, erzählte er mir dann von den Jungen. Ein bisschen genierlich war es schon, aber doch auch toll, mit ihm darüber zu sprechen. Er und ich konnten uns beide nicht vorstellen, dass wir noch mal mit einem Mädchen beziehungsweise mit einem Jungen so offen über die intimsten Angelegenheiten reden würden. Ich glaube, ich weiß jetzt alles. Er hat mir viel von Präsentivmitteln* erzählt.

Abends im Badezimmer haben Margot und ich lange über zwei frühere Bekannte geredet.

Heute Morgen erwartete mich etwas sehr Unangenehmes. Nach dem Frühstück winkte mir Peter, mit ihm nach oben zu gehen. »Du hast

* Deutsch im Original; A. d. Ü.

224

mich ganz schön reingelegt«, sagte er. »Ich habe gehört, was Margot und du gestern im Badezimmer besprochen habt. Ich glaube, du wolltest mal sehen, was Peter davon weiß, und dir dann einen Spaß damit machen!«

Mir verschlug es die Sprache. Ich habe es ihm ausgeredet, so gut ich konnte. Ich kann so gut verstehen, wie ihm zumute gewesen sein muss, und dabei war es nicht mal wahr!

»O nein, Peter«, sagte ich, »so gemein würde ich nie sein. Ich habe versprochen, den Mund zu halten, und das tue ich auch. Dir etwas vorzumachen und dann so gemein zu handeln, nein, Peter, das wäre nicht mehr witzig, das wäre unfair. Ich habe nichts erzählt, ehrlich, glaubst du mir?«

Er sagte mir, dass er mir glaubte, aber ich muss noch mal mit ihm darüber sprechen. Den ganzen Tag grüble ich schon darüber nach. Ein Glück, dass er gleich gesagt hat, was er dachte. Stell dir vor, er wäre mit einem so gemeinen Verdacht rumgelaufen. Der liebe Peter!

Nun werde und muss ich ihm alles erzählen!   Deine Anne

Freitagmorgen, 24. März 1944

Beste Kitty!

Ich gehe zur Zeit oft abends hinauf, um bei Peter im Zimmer etwas frische Atemluft zu schnappen. In einem dunklen Zimmer kommt man viel schneller zu richtigen Gesprächen, als wenn einen die Sonne im Gesicht kitzelt. Ich finde es gemütlich, neben ihm auf einem Stuhl zu sitzen und hinauszuschauen. Van Daan und Dussel stellen sich sehr blöd an, wenn ich in Peters Zimmer verschwinde. »Annes zweite Heimat«, heißt es dann. Oder: »Schickt es sich für Herren, abends im Dunkeln noch junge Mädchen zu Besuch zu haben?«

Peter ist erstaunlich gelassen bei solchen angeblich witzigen Bemerkungen. Meine Mutter ist übrigens auch nicht wenig neugierig und würde mich sicher nach den Themen unserer Gespräche fragen, wenn sie nicht insgeheim Angst vor einer abweisenden Antwort hätte. Peter sagt, dass die Erwachsenen neidisch seien, weil wir jung sind und uns aus ihren Gehässigkeiten nicht viel machen.

Manchmal holt Peter mich unten ab. Aber das ist auch peinlich, denn er bekommt trotz allem ein feuerrotes Gesicht und kriegt fast kein Wort raus. Ich bin nur froh, dass ich nie rot werde, das muss wirklich sehr unangenehm sein.

Außerdem ist es mir nicht recht, dass Margot alleine unten sitzt, während ich oben gute Gesellschaft habe. Aber was soll ich machen? Ich fände es prima, wenn sie mit hinaufginge, aber dann ist sie wieder das fünfte Rad am Wagen.

Ich muss mir von allen ganz schön was über die plötzliche Freundschaft anhören und weiß wirklich nicht, wie viele Tischgespräche nicht schon vom Heiraten im Hinterhaus handelten, falls der Krieg noch fünf Jahre dauern würde. Was gehen uns eigentlich diese Elternsprüche an? Nicht viel jedenfalls, sie sind alle so blöd. Haben meine Eltern vergessen, dass sie mal jung waren? Es scheint so. Wenigstens nehmen sie uns immer ernst, wenn wir einen Witz machen, und lachen über uns, wenn wir es ernst meinen.

Wie das nun weitergeht, weiß ich wirklich nicht, ebenso wenig, ob wir immer was zu reden haben. Aber wenn es weitergeht zwischen uns, werden wir wohl auch zusammen sein, ohne dass wir reden. Wenn sich die Alten da oben nur nicht so blöd anstellen würden. Bestimmt sehen sie mich nicht so gern. Dabei sagen Peter und ich doch niemandem, worüber wir sprechen. Stell dir vor, sie wüssten, dass wir über so intime Themen sprechen.

Ich würde Peter gern fragen, ob er weiß, wie ein Mädchen eigentlich aussieht. Ein Junge ist von unten, glaube ich, nicht so kompliziert gestaltet wie ein Mädchen. Auf Fotos und Abbildungen von nackten Männern kann man doch sehr gut sehen, wie die aussehen, aber bei Frauen nicht. Da sind die Geschlechtsteile oder wie das heißt mehr zwischen den Beinen. Er hat doch vermutlich noch nie ein Mädchen von so nahe gesehen, ehrlich gesagt, ich auch nicht. Tatsächlich ist es bei Jungen viel einfacher. Wie sollte ich die Installation um Himmels willen erklären? Denn dass er es nicht genau weiß, habe ich aus seinen Worten schließen können. Er sprach vom »Muttermund«, aber der sitzt innen, den kann man nicht sehen. Es ist bei uns doch sehr gut eingeteilt. Bevor ich elf oder zwölf Jahre alt war, wusste ich nicht mal, dass es auch noch die inneren Schamlippen gab, die waren überhaupt nicht zu sehen. Und das Schönste war, dass ich dachte, der Urin käme aus dem Kitzler. Als ich Mutter einmal fragte, was dieser Stumpen bedeutet, sagte sie, dass sie das nicht wüsste. Die stellen sich immer so dumm!

Aber zurück zum Thema. Wie soll man ohne Beispiele erklären, wie das alles zusammenhängt? Soll ich es hier gleich mal probieren? Also los!

Von vorn siehst du, wenn du stehst, nur Haare. Zwischen den Beinen sind eine Art Kissen, weiche Dinger, auch mit Haaren, die beim Stehen aneinander liegen. Man kann das, was drinnen ist, dann nicht sehen. Wenn du dich setzt, spalten sie sich auseinander, und innen sieht es sehr rot und hässlich fleischig aus. Am oberen Teil, zwischen den großen Schamlippen, ist eine Hautfalte, die bei näherer Betrachtung eigentlich eine Art Bläschen ist. Das ist der Kitzler. Dann kommen die kleinen Schamlippen, die sind auch aneinander gedrückt, wie eine Falte. Wenn die aufgeht, ist darin ein fleischiger Stummel, nicht größer als die Oberkante meines Daumens. Der obere Teil davon ist porös, da sind verschiedene Löcher drin, aus denen kommt der Urin. Der untere Teil scheint nur Haut zu sein, aber dort ist doch die Scheide. Sie ist ganz von Hautfalten bedeckt und fast nicht zu entdecken. So entsetzlich klein ist das Loch darunter, dass ich mir fast nicht vorstellen kann, wie dort ein Mann hinein soll, geschweige denn ein ganzes Kind heraus. In dieses Loch kannst du noch nicht mal so leicht mit deinem Zeigefinger! Das ist alles, und das spielt doch so eine große Rolle.   Deine Anne M. Frank

Samstag, 25. März 1944

Liebe Kitty!

Wenn man sich selbst verändert, merkt man das erst, wenn man verändert ist. Ich bin verändert, und zwar gründlich, ganz und gar. Meine Meinungen und Auffassungen, mein kritischer Blick, mein Äußeres und mein Inneres, alles ist verändert, und zwar zum Guten.

Ich habe dir schon mal erzählt, wie schwierig es für mich war, als ich hierher kam, aus dem Leben einer angebeteten Person in die kalte Wirklichkeit von Standpauken und Erwachsenen. Aber Vater und Mutter sind zu einem großen Teil mit schuld, dass ich so viel ausstehen musste, sie hätten mich nicht noch zusätzlich aufhetzen und mir bei allen Streitereien nur »ihre« Seite zeigen dürfen. Bevor ich dahinter kam, dass sie bei ihren Streitereien fifty-fifty stehen, dauerte es eine ganze Zeit. Aber jetzt weiß ich, wie viele Fehler von allen begangen worden sind. Der größte Fehler von Vater und Mutter gegenüber den van Daans ist, dass sie nie offenherzig und freundschaftlich sprechen (auch wenn die Freundschaft ein bisschen geheuchelt sein sollte).

Ich möchte vor allem Frieden bewahren und weder streiten noch klatschen. Bei Vater und Margot ist das nicht schwierig, bei Mutter schon. Deshalb ist es sehr gut, dass sie mir manchmal auf die Finger klopft. Herrn van Daan kann man auch gewinnen, wenn man ihm Recht gibt, ihm ruhig zuhört, nicht viel sagt und vor allem auf seine Scherze und blöden Witze mit einem anderen Scherz eingeht. Frau van Daan gewinnt man durch offenherziges Reden und Alles-Zugeben. Sie selbst gibt ihre Fehler, die sehr zahlreich sind, auch offen zu. Ich weiß nur zu gut, dass sie nicht mehr so schlecht über mich denkt wie am Anfang. Das kommt nur, weil ich ehrlich bin und den Menschen auch weniger schmeichelhafte Dinge einfach ins Gesicht sage. Ich will ehrlich sein und finde, dass man damit viel weiter kommt. Hinzu kommt, dass man sich selbst viel besser fühlt.

Gestern sprach Frau van Daan mit mir über den Reis, den wir Kleiman gegeben haben. »Wir haben gegeben, gegeben und noch mal gegeben«, sagte sie. »Aber dann kam ich an einen Punkt, dass ich sagte: Jetzt ist es genug. Herr Kleiman kann selbst an Reis kommen, wenn er sich Mühe gibt. Warum müssen wir denn alles aus unserem Vorrat weggeben? Wir haben es genauso nötig.«

»Nein, Frau van Daan« antwortete ich, »ich bin nicht Ihrer Meinung. Herr Kleiman kann vielleicht an Reis kommen, aber er findet es unangenehm, sich darum zu kümmern. Es ist nicht unsere Aufgabe, die Leute, die uns helfen, zu kritisieren. Wir müssen ihnen geben, was wir nur eben entbehren können und was sie brauchen. Ein Teller Reis in der Woche bringt uns auch nichts, wir können genauso gut Hülsenfrüchte essen.«

Frau van Daan fand das nicht, aber sie sagte auch, dass sie, obwohl sie nicht damit einverstanden war, gerne nachgeben wolle, das wäre eine andere Frage.

Na gut, höre ich auf, manchmal weiß ich, wo mein Platz ist, aber manchmal zweifle ich noch. Aber ich werde es schaffen! O ja! Vor allem, da ich nun Hilfe habe. Denn Peter hilft mir bei manch harter Nuss und manch saurem Apfel!

Ich weiß wirklich nicht, wie sehr er mich mag und ob wir je zu einem Kuss kommen, ich will es jedenfalls nicht erzwingen! Vater habe ich gesagt, dass ich viel zu Peter gehe und ob er es in Ordnung fände. Natürlich fand er es in Ordnung.

Peter erzähle ich auch viel lockere Dinge, die ich sonst nie rauslasse. So habe ich ihm gesagt, dass ich später schreiben will. Wenn ich schon keine Schriftstellerin werde, dann will ich doch neben meinem Beruf oder anderen Aufgaben das Schreiben nie vernachlässigen.

Ich bin nicht reich, ich bin nicht hübsch, nicht intelligent, nicht klug, aber ich bin und werde glücklich sein! Ich habe eine glückliche Natur, ich liebe die Menschen, bin nicht misstrauisch und will alle mit mir zusammen glücklich sehen.

Deine ergebene Anne M. Frank

Wieder hat der Tag mir nichts gebracht
Er war gleich einer dunklen Nacht.
(Das ist schon ein paar Wochen her und zählt nicht mehr. Da meine Verse aber so selten sind, habe ich diese einfach aufgeschrieben.)

Montag, 27. März 1944

Liebe Kitty!

Ein sehr großes Kapitel in unserer Versteckgeschichte auf Papier müsste eigentlich die Politik einnehmen, aber da dieses Thema mich persönlich nicht so sehr beschäftigt, habe ich es zu sehr links liegen gelassen. Darum werde ich heute mal einen ganzen Brief der Politik widmen.

Dass es sehr viele verschiedene Auffassungen zu diesem Thema gibt, ist selbstverständlich, dass in schlimmen Kriegszeiten auch viel darüber gesprochen wird, ist noch logischer, aber dass so viel deswegen gestritten wird, ist einfach dumm! Sollen sie wetten, lachen, schimpfen, nörgeln, sollen sie in ihrem eigenen Fett schmoren, wenn sie nur nicht streiten. Das hat meistens böse Folgen. Die Leute, die von draußen kommen, bringen viele unwahre Nachrichten mit, unser Radio hat bis jetzt noch nie gelogen. Jan, Miep, Kleiman, Bep und Kugler sind in ihren politischen Stimmungen up und down, Jan allerdings am wenigsten.

Hier im Hinterhaus ist die Stimmung, was Politik betrifft, immer gleich. Bei den zahllosen Debatten über Invasion, Luftangriffe, Reden und so weiter hört man auch zahllose Bemerkungen wie: »Unmöglich!« »Um Gottes willen, wenn sie jetzt erst anfangen wollen, was soll dann werden?« »Es geht ausgezeichnet, prima, bestens!«

Optimisten, Pessimisten und, nicht zu vergessen, die Realisten geben mit unermüdlicher Energie ihre Meinung zum Besten, und wie das immer so ist: jeder denkt, dass er allein Recht hat. Eine gewisse Dame ärgert sich über das beispiellose Vertrauen, das ihr Herr Gemahl in die Engländer setzt. Ein gewisser Herr greift seine Dame immer an wegen ihrer spöttischen und geringschätzigen Bemerkungen hinsichtlich seiner geliebten Nation! Von morgens früh bis abends spät, und das Schönste ist, dass es ihnen nie langweilig wird!

Ich habe etwas herausgefunden, und die Wirkung ist enorm. Es ist, als ob du jemanden mit einer Nadel stichst und er aufspringt. Genauso funktioniert mein Mittel. Fange mit der Politik an, eine Frage, ein Wort, ein Satz, und sofort sind alle mittendrin!

Als ob nun die deutschen Wehrmachtsberichte und der englische BBC noch nicht genug wären, ist vor kurzem noch eine »Luftlagemeldung« eingerichtet worden, großartig, aber andererseits oft enttäuschend. Die Engländer machen aus ihren Luftwaffen einen Dauerbetrieb, nur mehr zu vergleichen mit den deutschen Lügen.

Das Radio ist schon morgens um acht Uhr an, wenn nicht früher, und wird bis abends um neun, zehn, manchmal auch elf jede Stunde gehört. Das ist doch der beste Beweis, dass die Erwachsenen Geduld und nur schwer zu erreichende Gehirne haben (manche natürlich, ich will niemanden beleidigen). Wir hätten nach einer, höchstens zwei Sendungen schon genug für den ganzen Tag. Aber die alten Gänse, na ja, ich sagte es schon! Arbeiterprogramm, Oranje, Frank Philips oder Ihre Majestät Wilhelmina, alles kommt an die Reihe und bekommt ein williges Ohr. Und sind sie nicht am Essen oder Schlafen, dann sitzen sie am Radio und reden über Essen, Schlafen und Politik. Uff, es wird langweilig und ein richtiges Kunststück, dabei nicht selbst ein langweiliges altes Mütterchen zu werden! Den alten Herrschaften kann Letzteres nicht mehr viel schaden!

Ein ideales Beispiel ist die Rede des von uns allen geschätzten Winston Churchill.

Neun Uhr, Sonntagabend. Der Tee steht unter der Haube auf dem Tisch, die Gäste kommen herein. Dussel setzt sich links neben das Radio, Herr van Daan davor, Peter daneben. Mutter neben Herrn van Daan, Frau van Daan dahinter. Margot und ich ganz hinten, Pim an den Tisch. Ich merke, dass das nicht ganz klar ist, aber unsere Plätze tun letztlich nicht viel zur Sache. Die Herren paffen, Peters Augen fallen von dem anstrengenden Zuhören zu. Mama, in einem langen, dunklen Morgenrock, und Frau van Daan bibbern wegen der Flieger, die sich aus der Rede nichts machen und lustig nach Essen fliegen. Vater schlürft Tee, Margot und ich sind schwesterlich vereint durch die schlafende Mouschi, die zwei verschiedene Knie in Beschlag nimmt. Margot hat Lockenwickler in den Haaren, ich bin in ein viel zu kleines, zu enges und zu kurzes Nachtgewand gekleidet. Es scheint intim, gemütlich, friedlich, ist es für diesmal auch. Aber ich warte mit Schrecken auf die Folgen der Rede. Sie können es ja fast nicht abwarten, zappeln vor Ungeduld, ob nicht wieder ein Streit entsteht! Kst, kst, wie eine Katze, die eine Maus aus ihrem Loch lockt, stacheln sie sich gegenseitig zu Streit und Uneinigkeit auf.

Deine Anne

Dienstag, 28. März 1944

Liebste Kitty!

Ich könnte über Politik noch viel mehr schreiben, aber ich habe heute wieder eine Menge anderes zu berichten. Erstens hat Mutter mir eigentlich verboten, so oft nach oben zu gehen, da ihrer Meinung nach Frau van Daan eifersüchtig ist. Zweitens hat Peter Margot eingeladen, mit nach oben zu kommen, ob aus Höflichkeit oder weil er es ernst meint, weiß ich nicht. Drittens habe ich Vater gefragt, ob er meinte, dass ich mich an der Eifersucht stören müsse. Er meint das nicht.

Was nun? Mutter ist böse, will mich nicht nach oben lassen, will mich wieder drinnen bei Dussel arbeiten lassen, ist vielleicht auch ein bisschen eifersüchtig. Vater gönnt Peter und mir die Stunden und findet es prima, dass wir so gut miteinander auskommen. Margot hat Peter auch gern, fühlt aber, dass man zu dritt nicht das besprechen kann, was man zu zweit kann.

Außerdem denkt Mutter, dass Peter in mich verliebt ist. Ich wünsche mir, ehrlich gestanden, dass es wahr wäre. Dann wären wir quitt und könnten uns viel leichter näher kommen. Sie sagt auch, dass er mich so oft anschaut. Es stimmt, dass wir uns mehr als einmal zuzwinkern. Und dass er nach meinen Wangengrübchen schaut, dafür kann ich doch nichts! Stimmt's?

Ich bin in einer sehr schwierigen Lage. Mutter ist gegen mich, und ich bin gegen sie. Vater schließt die Augen vor dem stillen Kampf zwischen uns beiden. Mutter ist traurig, weil sie mich noch lieb hat, ich bin überhaupt nicht traurig, weil sie für mich erledigt ist.

Und Peter … Peter will ich nicht aufgeben. Er ist so lieb, und ich bewundere ihn. Es könnte so schön zwischen uns werden, warum stecken die Alten ihre Nasen hinein? Zum Glück bin ich daran gewöhnt, mein Inneres zu verbergen. Es gelingt mir ausgezeichnet, nicht zu zeigen, wie versessen ich auf ihn bin. Wird er je etwas sagen? Werde ich je seine Wange fühlen, wie ich Petels Wange im Traum gefühlt habe? Peter und Petel, ihr seid eins! Sie begreifen uns nicht, würden nie verstehen, dass wir schon zufrieden sind, wenn wir nur zusammensitzen, ohne zu reden. Sie begreifen nicht, was uns zueinander zieht. Wann würden alle Schwierigkeiten überwunden sein? Und doch ist es gut, sie zu überwinden, dann ist das Ende umso schöner. Wenn er mit dem Kopf auf den Armen daliegt, die Augen geschlossen, dann ist er noch ein Kind. Wenn er mit Mouschi spielt oder über sie spricht, dann ist er liebevoll. Wenn er Kartoffeln oder andere schwere Sachen trägt, dann ist er stark. Wenn er bei einer Schießerei oder im Dunkeln nachschaut, ob Diebe da sind, dann ist er mutig. Und wenn er so unbeholfen und ungeschickt tut, dann ist er eben lieb. Ich finde es viel schöner, wenn er mir was erklärt, als wenn ich ihm was beibringen muss. Ich hätte es so gerne, dass er mir in fast allem überlegen wäre.

Die Mütter können mir egal sein. Wenn er nur sprechen würde!

Vater sagt immer, dass ich eine Zierpuppe bin, aber das ist nicht wahr. Ich bin nur eitel. Bis jetzt haben mir noch nicht viele Leute gesagt, dass sie mich hübsch finden, außer ein Junge aus der Schule, der sagte, dass ich so nett aussehe, wenn ich lache. Gestern bekam ich ein richtiges Kompliment von Peter, und ich will dir zum Spaß unser Gespräch so ungefähr wiedergeben.

Peter sagte so oft: »Lach mal!«

Das fiel mir auf, und ich fragte gestern: »Warum soll ich immer lachen?«

»Weil das hübsch ist. Du bekommst dann Grübchen in die Wangen. Wie kommt das eigentlich?«

»Damit bin ich geboren, im Kinn habe ich ja auch eins. Das ist auch das einzig Schöne, das ich habe.«

»Aber nein, das ist nicht wahr!«

»Doch. Ich weiß, dass ich kein hübsches Mädchen bin. Das bin ich nie gewesen und werde es auch nie sein!«

»Das finde ich überhaupt nicht. Ich finde dich hübsch.«

»Das ist nicht wahr.«

»Wenn ich das sage, kannst du es mir glauben.«

Ich sagte dann natürlich dasselbe von ihm.   Deine Anne M. Frank

Mittwoch, 29. März 1944

Liebe Kitty!

Gestern Abend sprach Minister Bolkestein im Sender Oranje darüber, dass nach dem Krieg eine Sammlung von Tagebüchern und Briefen aus dieser Zeit herauskommen soll. Natürlich stürmten alle gleich auf mein Tagebuch los. Stell dir vor, wie interessant es wäre, wenn ich einen Roman vom Hinterhaus herausgeben würde. Nach dem Titel allein würden die Leute denken, dass es ein Detektivroman wäre.

Aber im Ernst, es muss ungefähr zehn Jahre nach dem Krieg schon seltsam erscheinen, wenn erzählt wird, wie wir Juden hier gelebt, gegessen und gesprochen haben. Auch wenn ich dir viel von uns erzähle, weißt du trotzdem nur ein kleines bisschen von unserem Leben. Wie viel Angst die Damen haben, wenn bombardiert wird, wie zum Beispiel am Sonntag, als 350 englische Maschinen eine halbe

Million Kilo Bomben auf Ijmuiden abgeworfen haben, wie die Häuser dann zittern wie Grashalme im Wind, wie viele Epidemien hier herrschen …

Von all diesen Dingen weißt du nichts, und ich müsste den ganzen Tag schreiben, wenn ich dir alles bis in die Einzelheiten erzählen sollte. Die Leute stehen Schlange für Gemüse und alle möglichen anderen Dinge. Die Ärzte kommen nicht zu ihren Kranken, weil ihnen alle naselang ihr Fahrzeug gestohlen wird. Einbrüche und Diebstähle gibt es jede Menge, sodass man anfängt, sich zu fragen, ob etwas in die Niederländer gefahren ist, weil sie plötzlich so diebisch geworden sind. Kleine Kinder von acht bis elf Jahren schlagen die Scheiben von Wohnungen ein und stehlen, was nicht niet- und nagelfest ist. Niemand wagt, seine Wohnung auch nur für fünf Minuten zu verlassen, denn kaum ist man weg, ist der Kram auch weg. Jeden Tag stehen Anzeigen in der Zeitung, die eine Belohnung für das Wiederbringen von gestohlenen Schreibmaschinen, Perserteppichen, elektrischen Uhren, Stoffen usw. versprechen. Elektrische Straßenuhren werden abmontiert, die Telefone in den Zellen bis auf den letzten Draht auseinander genommen. Die Stimmung unter der Bevölkerung kann nicht gut sein, jeder hat Hunger. Mit der Wochenration kann man keine zwei Tage auskommen (außer mit dem Ersatzkaffee). Die Invasion lässt auf sich warten, die Männer müssen nach Deutschland. Die Kinder sind unterernährt und werden krank, und alle haben schlechte Kleidung und schlechte Schuhe. Eine Sohle kostet »schwarz« 7.50 Gulden. Dabei nehmen die meisten Schuhmacher keine Kunden mehr an, oder man muss vier Monate auf die Schuhe warten, die dann inzwischen oft verschwunden sind.

Ein Gutes hat die Sache, dass die Sabotage gegen die Obrigkeit immer stärker wird, je schlechter die Ernährung ist und je strenger die Maßnahmen gegen das Volk werden. Die Leute von der Lebensmittelzuteilung, die Polizei, die Beamten, alle beteiligen sich entweder dabei, ihren Mitbürgern zu helfen, oder sie verraten sie und bringen sie dadurch ins Gefängnis. Zum Glück steht nur ein kleiner Prozentsatz der Niederländer auf der falschen Seite.

Deine Anne

Liebe Kitty!

Es ist noch ziemlich kalt, aber die meisten Leute sind schon ungefähr einen Monat ohne Kohlen. Schlimm, nicht? Die Stimmung ist im Allgemeinen wieder optimistisch für die russische Front, denn da ist es großartig! Ich schreibe zwar nicht viel über Politik, aber wo sie jetzt stehen, muss ich dir doch kurz mitteilen, nämlich dicht vor dem Generalgouvernement und bei Rumänien am Pruth. Ganz dicht bei Odessa stehen sie, und Tarnopol haben sie eingekesselt. Hier erwarten sie jeden Abend ein Sonderkommuniqué von Stalin.

In Moskau wird so viel Salut geschossen, dass die Stadt jeden Tag förmlich dröhnen muss. Ob sie es schön finden, so zu tun, als wäre der Krieg in der Nähe, oder ob sie ihre Freude nicht anders äußern können, ich weiß es nicht!

Ungarn ist von deutschen Truppen besetzt. Dort gibt es noch eine Million Juden, die werden nun wohl auch draufgehen.

Hier gibt es nichts Besonderes. Heute hat Herr van Daan Geburtstag. Er hat zwei Päckchen Tabak bekommen, Kaffee für eine Tasse (den hatte seine Frau noch aufgespart), Zitronenpunsch von Kugler, Sardinen von Miep, Eau de Cologne von uns, Flieder und Tulpen. Nicht zu vergessen eine Torte, mit Himbeeren gefüllt und ein bisschen pappig durch das schlechte Mehl und die Abwesenheit von Butter, aber doch lecker.

Das Gerede über Peter und mich hat sich ein bisschen beruhigt. Er wird mich heute Abend abholen. Nett von ihm, findest du nicht, wo es ihm doch so unangenehm ist. Wir sind sehr gute Freunde, sind viel zusammen und unterhalten uns über alles Mögliche. Es ist toll, dass ich mich, wenn wir auf heikles Gebiet kommen, nie zurückhalten muss, wie es bei anderen Jungen der Fall wäre. So sprachen wir zum Beispiel über Blut und kamen auf Menstruation. Er findet uns Frauen sehr zäh, dass wir den Blutverlust so aushalten. Auch mich findet er zäh. Ra-ra warum?

Mein Leben hier ist besser geworden, viel besser. Gott hat mich nicht allein gelassen und wird mich nicht allein lassen.

Deine Anne M. Frank

Liebste Kitty!

Und doch ist alles noch so schwierig. Du weißt sicher, was ich meine, gell? Ich sehne mich so sehr nach einem Kuss von ihm, dem Kuss, der so lange ausbleibt. Ob er mich immer noch als Kameradin betrachtet? Bin ich denn nicht mehr?

Du weißt und ich weiß, dass ich stark bin, dass ich die meisten Belastungen allein tragen kann. Ich bin es nie gewöhnt gewesen, sie mit jemandem zu teilen, und an einer Mutter habe ich mich nie festgeklammert. Aber jetzt würde ich so gern mal meinen Kopf an seine Schulter legen und nur ganz ruhig sein.

Ich kann nicht, nie, den Traum von Peters Wange vergessen, als alles nur gut war! Ob er sich nicht danach sehnt? Ist er nur zu schüchtern, um seine Liebe zu bekennen? Warum will er mich so oft bei sich haben? Oh, warum spricht er nicht?

Ich will aufhören, ruhig sein. Ich werde mich wieder tapfer halten, und mit etwas Geduld wird das andere wohl auch kommen. Aber, und das ist das Schlimme, es sieht so sehr danach aus, als ob ich ihm nachlaufe. Immer muss ich hinauf, er kommt nicht zu mir. Aber das liegt an der Zimmeraufteilung, und er versteht meine Bedenken. O ja, er wird wohl mehr verstehen.   Deine Anne M. Frank

Liebste Kitty!

Ganz gegen meine Gewohnheit werde ich dir doch mal ausführlich über das Essen schreiben, denn es ist nicht nur hier im Hinterhaus, sondern auch in ganz Holland, in ganz Europa und überall ein sehr wichtiger und schwieriger Faktor geworden.

Wir haben in den einundzwanzig Monaten, die wir nun hier sind, schon etliche Essens-Perioden mitgemacht. Was das bedeutet, wirst du gleich hören. Unter Essens-Periode verstehe ich eine Periode, in der man nichts anderes zu essen bekommt als ein bestimmtes Gericht oder ein bestimmtes Gemüse. Eine Zeit lang gab es jeden Tag Endivie, mit Sand, ohne Sand, Eintopf und in der feuerfesten Form. Dann war es Spinat, danach folgten Kohlrabi, Schwarzwurzeln, Gurken, Tomaten, Sauerkraut und so weiter.

Es ist wirklich nicht schön, jeden Mittag und Abend zum Beispiel Sauerkraut zu essen, aber man tut viel, wenn man Hunger hat. Nun haben wir jedoch die schönste Periode, wir bekommen überhaupt kein Gemüse.

Unser Wochenmenü besteht mittags aus braunen Bohnen, Erbsensuppe, Kartoffeln mit Mehlklößen, Kartoffelauflauf, mit Gottes Hilfe auch mal Steckrüben oder angefaulte Karotten, dann wieder nur braune Bohnen. Kartoffeln essen wir zu jeder Mahlzeit, beginnend (aus Brotmangel) mit dem Frühstück, aber da werden sie wenigstens noch ein bisschen gebacken. Für die Suppe nehmen wir braune und weiße Bohnen, Kartoffeln und Päckchensuppen (Julienne-, Königin-, Bohnensuppe). In allem sind braune Bohnen, nicht zuletzt im Brot. Abends essen wir immer Kartoffeln mit künstlicher Soße und, das haben wir zum Glück noch, Rote-Bete-Salat. Über die Mehlklöße muss ich auch noch was sagen: Die machen wir aus »Regierungsmehl« mit Wasser und Hefe. Sie sind so pappig und zäh, dass sie einem wie ein Stein im Magen liegen, aber was soll's.

Unsere größte Attraktion ist die Scheibe Leberwurst jede Woche und die Marmelade auf trockenem Brot. Aber wir leben noch, und es schmeckt uns sogar oft gut.   Deine Anne M. Frank

Mittwoch, 5. April 1944

Liebste Kitty!

Eine Zeit lang wusste ich überhaupt nicht mehr, wofür ich noch arbeite. Das Ende des Krieges ist so entsetzlich weit, so unwirklich, märchenhaft und schön. Wenn der Krieg im September nicht vorbei ist, dann gehe ich nicht mehr zur Schule, denn zwei Jahre will ich nicht zurückfallen.

Die Tage bestanden aus Peter, nichts als Peter. Nur Träume und Gedanken, bis ich am Samstagabend ganz schlaff wurde, fürchterlich. Ich kämpfte bei Peter gegen meine Tränen, lachte später schrecklich viel mit van Daan beim Zitronenpunsch, war fröhlich und aufgekratzt. Aber kaum war ich allein, wusste ich, dass ich mich ausweinen musste. Im Nachthemd ließ ich mich auf den Boden gleiten und betete sehr intensiv und lange, dann weinte ich mit dem Kopf auf den Armen, die Knie angezogen, zusammengekauert auf dem kahlen Fußboden. Bei einem lauten Schluchzer kam ich wieder zu mir und bekämpfte meine Tränen, weil sie drüben nichts hören durften. Dann begann ich, mir Mut zuzusprechen. Ich sagte nur immer: »Ich muss, ich muss, ich muss …« Ganz steif von der ungewohnten Haltung fiel ich gegen die Bettkante und kämpfte weiter, bis ich kurz vor halb elf wieder ins Bett stieg. Es war vorbei!

Und jetzt ist es völlig vorbei. Ich muss arbeiten, um nicht dumm zu bleiben, um weiterzukommen, um Journalistin zu werden, das will ich! Ich weiß, dass ich schreiben <u>kann</u>. Ein paar Geschichten sind gut, meine Hinterhausbeschreibungen humorvoll, vieles in meinem Tagebuch ist lebendig, aber ob ich wirklich Talent habe, das steht noch dahin.

Evas Traum war mein bestes Märchen, und das Seltsame dabei ist, dass ich wirklich nicht weiß, wo es herkommt. Viel aus Cadys Leben ist auch gut, aber insgesamt ist es nichts. Ich bin selbst meine schärfste und beste Kritikerin hier, ich weiß genau, was gut und was nicht gut geschrieben ist. Keiner, der nicht selbst schreibt, weiß, wie toll Schreiben ist. Früher habe ich immer bedauert, dass ich überhaupt nicht zeichnen kann, aber jetzt bin ich überglücklich, dass ich wenigstens schreiben kann.

Und wenn ich nicht genug Talent habe, um Zeitungsartikel oder Bücher zu schreiben, nun, dann kann ich noch immer für mich selbst schreiben. Aber ich will weiterkommen. Ich kann mir nicht vorstellen, dass ich so leben muss wie Mutter, Frau van Daan und all die anderen Frauen, die ihre Arbeit machen und später vergessen sind. Ich muss neben Mann und Kindern etwas haben, dem ich mich ganz widmen kann! O ja, ich will nicht umsonst gelebt haben wie die meisten Menschen. Ich will den Menschen, die um mich herum leben und mich doch nicht kennen, Freude und Nutzen bringen. Ich will fortleben, auch nach meinem Tod. Und darum bin ich Gott so dankbar, dass er mir bei meiner Geburt schon eine Möglichkeit mitgegeben hat, mich zu entwickeln und zu schreiben, also alles auszudrücken, was in mir ist.

Mit Schreiben werde ich alles los. Mein Kummer verschwindet, mein Mut lebt wieder auf. Aber, und das ist die große Frage, werde ich jemals etwas Großes schreiben können, werde ich jemals Journalistin und Schriftstellerin werden?

Anne und ihre Mutter in der Ganghoferstraße, Frankfurt am Main, 1931.

Ich hoffe es, ich hoffe es so sehr! Mit Schreiben kann ich alles ausdrücken, meine Gedanken, meine Ideale und meine Phantasien.

An Cadys Leben habe ich lange nichts mehr getan. In meinen Gedanken weiß ich genau, wie es weitergehen soll, aber es ist nicht so richtig geflossen. Vielleicht wird es nie fertig, vielleicht landet es im Papierkorb oder im Ofen. Das ist keine angenehme Vorstellung. Aber dann denke ich wieder: »Mit vierzehn Jahren und so wenig Erfahrung kann man auch noch nichts Philosophisches schreiben.«

Also weiter, mit neuem Mut. Es wird schon gelingen, denn schreiben will ich!
Deine Anne M. Frank

Donnerstag, 6. April 1944

Liebe Kitty!

Du hast mich gefragt, was meine Hobbys und Interessen sind, und darauf will ich dir antworten. Aber ich warne dich, erschrick nicht, denn es sind eine ganze Menge.

An erster Stelle: Schreiben. Aber das zählt eigentlich nicht als Hobby.

Zweitens: Stammbäume. In Zeitungen, Büchern u. Ä. suche ich nach den Stammbäumen der deutschen, spanischen, englischen, österreichischen, russischen, skandinavischen und niederländischen Fürstenfamilien. Mit vielen bin ich schon sehr weit gekommen, vor allem, weil ich mir immer Aufzeichnungen mache, wenn ich Biographien oder Geschichtsbücher lese. Ich schreibe sogar ganze Abschnitte aus der Geschichte ab.

Mein drittes Hobby ist dann auch Geschichte. Vater hat schon viele Bücher für mich gekauft. Ich kann den Tag fast nicht erwarten, an dem ich in den öffentlichen Bibliotheken alles nachschlagen kann.

Nummer vier ist die Mythologie Griechenlands und Roms. Auch darüber habe ich verschiedene Bücher. Die neun Musen oder sieben Geliebten von Zeus kann ich dir einfach so aufsagen. Die Frauen von Herakles usw. kenne ich aus dem Effeff.

Weitere Liebhabereien sind Filmstars und Familienfotos. Außerdem bin ich versessen auf Lesen und Bücher, interessiere mich für Kunstgeschichte und für Schriftsteller, Dichter und Maler. Musiker kommen vielleicht später noch. Eine gewisse Antipathie habe ich gegen Algebra, Geometrie und Rechnen. Alle übrigen Schulfächer mache ich mit Vergnügen, aber vor allem Geschichte!

Deine Anne M. Frank

Dienstag, 11. April 1944

Liebste Kitty!

Ich weiß nicht, wo mir der Kopf steht, ich weiß wirklich nicht, womit ich anfangen soll. Der Donnerstag (als ich dir das letzte Mal schrieb) verlief normal. Freitag (Karfreitag) spielten wir nachmittags Gesellschaftsspiele, ebenso am Samstag. Die Tage vergingen sehr schnell. Am Samstag gegen zwei fing eine Schießerei an. Schnellfeuerkanonen, haben die Herren gesagt. Sonst war alles ruhig.

Am Sonntagnachmittag kam Peter auf meine Einladung um halb fünf zu mir, etwas später gingen wir zum vorderen Dachboden, wo wir bis sechs Uhr blieben. Von sechs bis Viertel nach sieben gab es im Radio ein schönes Mozartkonzert, vor allem die »Kleine Nachtmusik« hat mir gut gefallen. Ich kann nicht gut zuhören, wenn die anderen dabei sind, weil mich schöne Musik sehr bewegt.

Am Sonntagabend gingen Peter und ich nicht baden, weil der Zuber unten in der Küche stand und mit Wäsche gefüllt war. Um acht gingen wir zusammen zum vorderen Dachboden, und um weich zu sitzen, nahm ich das einzige Sofakissen mit, das in unserem Zimmer zu finden war. Wir nahmen auf einer Kiste Platz. Kiste als auch Kissen waren sehr schmal. Wir saßen dicht nebeneinander und lehnten uns an andere Kisten. Mouschi leistete uns Gesellschaft, also waren wir nicht unbeobachtet. Plötzlich, um Viertel vor neun, pfiff Herr van Daan und fragte, ob wir ein Kissen von Herrn Dussel hätten. Beide sprangen wir auf und gingen mit Kissen, Katze und van Daan nach unten. Dieses Kissen hat zu einer ganzen Tragödie geführt. Dussel war böse, weil ich sein Nachtkissen mitgenommen hatte, und fürchtete, es wären Flöhe darin. Alle hat er wegen diesem Kissen in Aufregung versetzt! Peter und ich steckten ihm aus Rache für seine Ekelhaftigkeit zwei harte Bürsten ins Bett, aber später kamen sie wieder raus. Wir haben schrecklich gelacht über dieses Intermezzo.

Aber unser Vergnügen sollte nicht lange dauern. Um halb zehn klopfte Peter leise an die Tür und fragte Vater, ob er ihm mal schnell bei einem schwierigen englischen Satz helfen würde.

»Da ist was nicht geheuer«, sagte ich zu Margot. »Die Ausrede ist zu dick. Die Herren reden in einem Ton, als wäre eingebrochen worden.«

Meine Vermutung stimmte, im Lager wurde gerade eingebrochen. Innerhalb kürzester Zeit waren Vater, van Daan und Peter unten. Margot, Mutter, Frau van Daan und ich warteten. Vier Frauen, die Angst haben, müssen reden. So auch wir, bis wir unten einen Schlag hörten. Danach war alles still, die Uhr schlug Viertel vor zehn. Aus unseren Gesichtern war die Farbe gewichen, aber noch waren wir ruhig, wenn auch ängstlich. Wo waren die Herren geblieben? Was war das für ein Schlag? Kämpften sie vielleicht mit den Einbrechern? Weiter dachten wir nicht, wir warteten.

Zehn Uhr: Schritte auf der Treppe. Vater, blass und nervös, kam herein, gefolgt von Herrn van Daan. »Licht aus, leise nach oben, wir erwarten Polizei im Haus!«

Es blieb keine Zeit für Angst. Die Lichter gingen aus, ich nahm noch schnell eine Jacke, und wir waren oben.

»Was ist passiert? Schnell, erzählt!«

Es war niemand da zum Erzählen, die Herren waren wieder unten. Erst um zehn nach zehn kamen sie alle vier herauf, zwei hielten Wache an Peters offenem Fenster. Die Tür zum Treppenabsatz war abgeschlossen, der Drehschrank zu. Über das Nachtlämpchen hängten wir einen Pullover, dann erzählten sie:

Peter hörte auf dem Treppenabsatz zwei harte Schläge, lief nach unten und sah, dass an der linken Seite der Lagertür ein großes Brett fehlte. Er rannte nach oben, verständigte den wehrhaften Teil der Familie, und zu viert zogen sie hinunter. Die Einbrecher waren noch am Stehlen, als sie ins Lager kamen. Ohne zu überlegen, schrie van Daan: »Polizei!« Schnelle Schritte nach draußen, die Einbrecher waren geflohen. Um zu verhindern, dass die Polizei das Loch bemerkte, wurde das Brett wieder eingesetzt, aber ein kräftiger Tritt von draußen beförderte es noch mal auf den Boden. Die Herren waren perplex über so viel Frechheit. Van Daan und Peter fühlten Mordgelüste in sich aufsteigen. Van Daan schlug mit dem Beil kräftig auf den Boden, und alles war wieder still. Erneut kam das Brett vor das Loch, erneut eine Störung. Ein Ehepaar leuchtete von draußen mit einer grellen Taschenlampe das ganze Lager ab. »Verflixt«, murmelte einer der Herren, und nun änderten sich ihre Rollen, sie wurden von Polizisten zu Einbrechern. Alle vier rannten sie nach oben, Peter öffnete die Türen und Fenster von Küche und Privatbüro, warf das Telefon auf den Boden, und schließlich landeten sie alle, samt Waschzuber, im Versteck. (Ende des ersten Teils.)

Aller Wahrscheinlichkeit nach hatte das Ehepaar mit der Taschenlampe die Polizei benachrichtigt. Es war Sonntagabend, der Abend des ersten Ostertages. Am zweiten Feiertag kam niemand ins Büro, wir konnten uns also vor Dienstagmorgen nicht rühren. Stell dir vor, zwei Nächte und einen Tag in dieser Angst zu verbringen! Wir stellten uns nichts vor, wir saßen nur im Stockdunkeln, weil Frau van Daan aus Angst die Lampe ganz ausgedreht hatte, wir flüsterten, und bei jedem Knarren klang es: »Pst! Pst!«
Es wurde halb elf, elf Uhr, kein Geräusch. Abwechselnd kamen Vater und van Daan zu uns. Dann, um Viertel nach elf, ein Geräusch von unten. Bei uns konnte man das Atmen der ganzen Familie hören, ansonsten rührten wir uns nicht. Schritte im Haus, im Privatbüro, in der Küche, dann … auf unserer Treppe. Keine Atemzüge waren mehr zu hören, acht Herzen hämmerten. Schritte auf unserer Treppe, dann Gerüttel am Drehschrank. Dieser Moment ist unbeschreiblich.
»Jetzt sind wir verloren«, sagte ich und sah uns schon alle fünfzehn noch in derselben Nacht von der Gestapo mitgenommen.
Wieder Gerüttel am Drehschrank, zweimal, dann fiel etwas herunter, die Schritte entfernten sich. Für den Moment waren wir gerettet. Ein Zittern durchlief uns alle, ich hörte Zähneklappern, aber niemand sagte ein Wort. So saßen wir bis halb zwölf.
Im Haus war nichts zu hören, aber auf dem Treppenabsatz direkt vor dem Schrank brannte Licht. War es deshalb, weil unser Schrank so geheimnisvoll war? Hatte die Polizei vielleicht das Licht vergessen? Kam noch jemand, um es auszumachen? Die Zungen lösten sich, im Haus war niemand mehr. Vielleicht noch ein Bewacher vor der Tür.
Drei Dinge taten wir nun, Vermutungen äußern, zittern vor Angst

und zum Klo gehen. Die Eimer waren auf dem Dachboden, so musste Peters Blechpapierkorb herhalten. Van Daan machte den Anfang, danach Vater. Mutter schämte sich zu sehr. Vater brachte das Blechgefäß ins Zimmer, wo Margot, Frau van Daan und ich es gern benutzten. Endlich entschied sich auch Mutter dazu. Die Nachfrage nach Papier war groß, ich hatte zum Glück welches in der Tasche. Das Gefäß stank, alle flüsterten, und wir waren müde, es war zwölf Uhr.

»Legt euch doch auf den Boden und schlaft!«

Margot und ich bekamen jede ein Kissen und eine Decke. Margot lag in der Nähe vom Vorratsschrank, ich zwischen den Tischbeinen. Auf dem Boden stank es nicht so schlimm, aber Frau van Daan holte doch leise ein bisschen Chlor und legte ein altes Tuch über den Topf.

Gerede, Geflüster, Angst, Gestank, Winde – und dauernd jemand auf dem Topf! Dabei soll einer schlafen! Um halb drei wurde ich jedoch zu müde, und bis halb vier hörte ich nichts. Ich wurde wach, als Frau van Daan ihren Kopf auf meine Füße legte.

»Geben Sie mir bitte was zum Anziehen!«, bat ich. Ich bekam auch was, aber frag nicht, was! Eine wollene Hose über meinen Pyjama, den roten Pullover und den schwarzen Rock, weiße Socken und darüber kaputte Kniestrümpfe.

Frau van Daan nahm dann wieder auf dem Stuhl Platz, und Herr van Daan legte sich auf meine Füße. Ich fing an nachzudenken. Ich zitterte immer noch so, dass van Daan nicht schlafen konnte. In Gedanken bereitete ich mich darauf vor, dass die Polizei zurückkommen würde. Dann müssen wir sagen, dass wir Untertaucher sind. Entweder sind es gute Niederländer, dann ist alles in Ordnung, oder es sind Nazis, dann muss man sie bestechen.

»Tu doch das Radio weg!«, seufzte Frau van Daan.

»Ja, in den Herd«, antwortete Herr van Daan. »Wenn sie uns finden, dürfen sie auch das Radio finden.«

»Dann finden sie auch Annes Tagebuch«, mischte sich Vater ein.

»Verbrennt es doch!«, schlug die Ängstlichste von uns vor.

Das und der Moment, als die Polizei an der Schranktür rüttelte, waren meine angstvollsten Augenblicke. Mein Tagebuch nicht! Mein Tagebuch nur zusammen mit mir! Aber Vater antwortete zum Glück nicht.

Es hat überhaupt keinen Zweck, die Gespräche zu wiederholen, an die ich mich erinnere. Es wurde so viel geredet. Ich tröstete Frau van Daan in ihrer Angst. Wir sprachen über Flucht, Verhöre bei der Gestapo, über Telefonieren und über Mut.

»Nun müssen wir uns eben wie Soldaten verhalten, Frau van Daan. Wenn wir draufgehen, na gut, dann eben für Königin und Vaterland, für Freiheit, Wahrheit und Recht, genau was im Sender Oranje immer wieder gesagt wird. Das Schlimme ist nur, dass wir die anderen dann mit ins Unglück ziehen.«

Herr van Daan wechselte nach einer Stunde wieder den Platz mit seiner Frau. Vater kam zu mir. Die Herren rauchten ununterbrochen. Ab und zu war ein tiefer Seufzer zu hören, dann wieder Pinkeln, und dann fing alles wieder von vorn an.

Vier Uhr, fünf Uhr, halb sechs. Nun setzte ich mich zu Peter. Dicht aneinander gedrückt, so dicht, dass wir die Schauer im Körper des anderen fühlten, saßen wir da, sprachen ab und zu ein Wort und lauschten angestrengt. Im Zimmer zogen sie die Verdunklung hoch und schrieben die Punkte auf, die sie Kleiman am Telefon sagen wollten.

Um sieben Uhr wollten sie ihn nämlich anrufen, damit jemand kam. Das Risiko, dass ein möglicher Bewacher vor der Tür oder im Lager das Telefonieren hörte, war groß. Aber noch größer, dass die Polizei wieder zurückkam. Obwohl ich den Erinnerungszettel hier beilege, zur größeren Deutlichkeit noch die Abschrift der Punkte:

Eingebrochen. Polizei war im Haus, bis zum Drehschrank, weiter nicht.

Einbrecher sind offenbar gestört worden, haben Lager aufgebrochen und sind durch den Garten geflüchtet.

Haupteingang verriegelt. Kugler muss durch die zweite Tür weggegangen sein.

Schreibmaschine und Rechenmaschine sind sicher in der schwarzen Kiste im Privatbüro.

Wäsche von Miep oder Bep liegt in der Waschwanne in der Küche.

Schlüssel für zweite Tür haben nur Bep oder Kugler, möglicherweise Schloss kaputt.

Versuchen, Jan zu benachrichtigen, Schlüssel holen und zum Büro gehen, um nachzuschauen. Katze muss gefüttert werden.

Alles verlief nach Wunsch. Kleiman wurde angerufen, die Schreibmaschine in die Kiste gebracht. Danach saßen wir wieder am Tisch und warteten auf Jan oder die Polizei.

Peter war eingeschlafen, Herr van Daan und ich lagen auf dem Boden, als wir unten laute Schritte hörten. Leise stand ich auf. »Das ist Jan!«

»Nein, nein, das ist die Polizei!«, sagten alle anderen.

Es wurde geklopft, Miep pfiff. Frau van Daan wurde es zu viel. Leichenblass und schlaff hing sie in ihrem Stuhl, und wenn die Spannung noch eine Minute länger gedauert hätte, wäre sie ohnmächtig geworden.

Als Jan und Miep hereinkamen, bot unser Zimmer einen herrlichen Anblick. Der Tisch alleine wäre schon ein Foto wert gewesen: Ein »Cinema & Theater« aufgeschlagen, die Seite mit Tänzerinnen voll mit Marmelade und einem Mittel gegen Durchfall, zwei Marmeladengläser, ein halbes und ein viertel Brötchen, Pektin, Spiegel, Kamm, Streichhölzer, Asche, Zigaretten, Tabak, Aschenbecher, Bücher, eine Unterhose, eine Taschenlampe, Toilettenpapier usw. usw.

Jan und Miep wurden natürlich mit Jauchzen und Tränen begrüßt. Jan zimmerte das Loch mit Holz zu und ging schon bald mit Miep wieder weg, um der Polizei den Einbruch zu melden. Miep hatte unter der Lagertür einen Zettel von Nachtwächter Slagter gefunden, der das Loch entdeckt und der Polizei Bescheid gesagt hatte. Bei ihm wollte Jan auch vorbeigehen.

Eine halbe Stunde hatten wir also, um uns zurechtzumachen, und noch nie habe ich gesehen, wie sich innerhalb von einer halben Stunde so viel verändert hat. Margot und ich legten unten die Betten aus, gingen zur Toilette, putzten die Zähne, wuschen die Hände und kämmten die Haare. Danach räumte ich das Zimmer noch ein bisschen auf und ging wieder nach oben. Dort war der Tisch schon abgeräumt. Wir holten Wasser, machten Kaffee und Tee, kochten Milch und deckten für die Kaffeestunde. Vater und Peter reinigten die Pinkeltöpfe mit warmem Wasser und Chlorkalk. Der größte war bis oben voll und so schwer, dass er kaum zu heben war. Außerdem leckte das Ding, sodass es in einem Eimer weggetragen werden musste.

Um elf Uhr saßen wir mit Jan, der zurückgekommen war, am Tisch, und es wurde allmählich schon wieder gemütlich. Jan erzählte Folgendes:

Bei Slagters erzählte seine Frau (Slagter selbst schlief noch), dass er bei seiner Runde das Loch bei uns entdeckt hatte und mit einem herbeigeholten Polizisten durch das Gebäude gelaufen war. Herr Slagter ist privater Nachtwächter und radelt jeden Abend mit seinen zwei Hunden die Grachten entlang. Am Dienstag will er zu Kugler kommen und die Sache besprechen. Auf dem Polizeibüro hatten sie noch nichts von dem Einbruch gewusst, es aber sofort notiert. Sie wollen ebenfalls am Dienstag kommen und mal nachschauen.

Auf dem Rückweg ging Jan zufällig bei unserem Kartoffellieferanten vorbei und erzählte ihm, dass eingebrochen worden war.

»Das weiß ich«, sagte der seelenruhig. »Ich kam gestern Abend mit meiner Frau an dem Gebäude vorbei und sah ein Loch in der Tür. Meine Frau wollte schon weitergehen, aber ich schaute mit der Taschenlampe nach, und da sind die Diebe bestimmt weggelaufen. Sicherheitshalber habe ich die Polizei nicht angerufen, ich wollte das bei Ihnen nicht. Ich weiß zwar nichts, aber ich vermute viel.« Jan bedankte sich und ging. Bestimmt nimmt der Mann an, dass wir hier sind, denn er bringt die Kartoffeln immer in der Mittagspause, zwischen halb eins und halb zwei. Ein prima Mann!

Nachdem Jan weggegangen war und wir abgewaschen hatten, war es ein Uhr. Alle acht gingen wir schlafen. Um Viertel vor drei wurde ich wach und sah, dass Herr Dussel schon verschwunden war. Ganz zufällig begegnete ich Peter mit meinem verschlafenen Gesicht im Badezimmer. Wir verabredeten uns für unten. Ich machte mich zurecht und ging hinunter.

Traust du dich noch, auf den vorderen Dachboden zu gehen?«, fragte er. Ich war einverstanden, holte mein Kopfkissen, wickelte es in ein Tuch, und wir gingen hinauf. Das Wetter war großartig, und schon bald heulten dann auch die Sirenen. Wir blieben, wo wir waren. Peter legte seinen Arm um meine Schulter, ich legte meinen Arm um seine Schulter, und so blieben wir und warteten ruhig, bis Margot uns um vier Uhr zum Kaffee holte.

Wir aßen Brot, tranken Limonade und machten schon wieder Witze, auch sonst lief alles normal. Abends dankte ich Peter, weil er der Mutigste von allen war.

Keiner von uns hat sich je in solch einer Gefahr befunden wie in dieser Nacht. Gott hat uns beschützt. Stell dir vor, die Polizei an unserem Versteckschrank, das Licht davor an, und wir bleiben doch unbemerkt! Wenn die Invasion mit Bombardierungen kommt, ist jeder für sich selbst verantwortlich. Aber hier gab es auch die Angst um unsere unschuldigen und guten Helfer.
»Wir sind gerettet, rette uns weiterhin!« Das ist das Einzige, was wir sagen können.
Diese Geschichte hat viele Veränderungen mit sich gebracht. Dussel sitzt fortan abends im Badezimmer. Peter geht um halb neun und um halb zehn durch das Haus, um alles zu kontrollieren. Sein Fenster darf nachts nicht mehr offen bleiben, weil ein Arbeiter der Nachbarfirma es gesehen hat. Nach halb zehn abends darf das Wasser auf dem Klo nicht mehr gezogen werden. Herr Slagter ist als Nachtwächter engagiert worden. Heute Abend kommt ein Zimmermann und zimmert aus unseren weißen Frankfurter Betten eine Verbarrikadierung. Im Hinterhaus gibt es hier jetzt Debatten vorn und Debatten hinten. Kugler hat uns Unvorsichtigkeit vorgeworfen. Auch Jan sagte, wir dürften nie nach unten. Man muss jetzt der Sache auf den Grund gehen, ob Slagter zuverlässig ist, ob die Hunde anschlagen, wenn sie jemanden hinter der Tür hören, wie das mit der Verbarrikadierung klappt, alles Mögliche.
Wir sind sehr stark daran erinnert worden, dass wir gefesselte Juden sind, gefesselt an einen Fleck, ohne Rechte, aber mit Tausenden von Pflichten. Wir Juden dürfen nicht unseren Gefühlen folgen, müssen mutig und stark sein, müssen alle Beschwerlichkeiten auf uns nehmen und nicht murren, müssen tun, was in unserer Macht liegt, und auf Gott vertrauen. Einmal wird dieser schreckliche Krieg doch vorbeigehen, einmal werden wir doch wieder Menschen und nicht nur Juden sein!
Wer hat uns das auferlegt? Wer hat uns Juden zu einer Ausnahme unter allen Völkern gemacht? Wer hat uns bis jetzt so leiden lassen? Es ist Gott, der uns so gemacht hat, aber es wird auch Gott sein, der uns aufrichtet. Wenn wir all dieses Leid ertragen und noch

immer Juden übrig bleiben, werden sie einmal von Verdammten zu Vorbildern werden. Wer weiß, vielleicht wird es noch unser Glaube sein, der die Welt und damit alle Völker das Gute lehrt, und dafür, dafür allein müssen wir auch leiden. Wir können niemals nur Niederländer oder nur Engländer oder was auch immer werden, wir müssen daneben immer Juden bleiben. Aber wir wollen es auch bleiben.

Seid mutig! Wir wollen uns unserer Aufgabe bewusst bleiben und nicht murren, es wird einen Ausweg geben. Gott hat unser Volk nie im Stich gelassen, durch alle Jahrhunderte hin sind Juden am Leben geblieben, durch alle Jahrhunderte hindurch mussten Juden leiden. Aber durch alle Jahrhunderte hindurch sind sie auch stark geworden. Die Schwachen fallen, aber die Starken bleiben übrig und werden nicht untergehen!

In dieser Nacht dachte ich eigentlich, dass ich sterben müsste. Ich wartete auf die Polizei, ich war bereit, bereit wie ein Soldat auf dem Schlachtfeld. Ich wollte mich gern opfern für das Vaterland. Aber nun, da ich gerettet bin, ist es mein erster Wunsch für nach dem Krieg, dass ich Niederländerin werde. Ich liebe die Niederländer, ich liebe unser Land, ich liebe die Sprache und will hier arbeiten. Und wenn ich an die Königin selbst schreiben muss, ich werde nicht aufgeben, bevor mein Ziel erreicht ist.

Ich werde immer unabhängiger von meinen Eltern. So jung ich bin, habe ich mehr Lebensmut, ein sichereres Rechtsgefühl als Mutter. Ich weiß, was ich will, habe ein Ziel, habe eine eigene Meinung, habe einen Glauben und eine Liebe. Lasst mich ich selbst sein, dann bin ich zufrieden! Ich weiß, dass ich eine Frau bin, eine Frau mit innerer Stärke und viel Mut!

Wenn Gott mich am Leben lässt, werde ich mehr erreichen, als Mutter je erreicht hat. Ich werde nicht unbedeutend bleiben, ich werde in der Welt und für die Menschen arbeiten.

Und nun weiß ich, dass Mut und Fröhlichkeit das Wichtigste sind!

Deine Anne M. Frank

Beste Kitty!

Die Stimmung hier ist noch sehr gespannt. Pim ist auf dem Siedepunkt, Frau van Daan liegt mit Erkältung im Bett und schimpft, Herr van Daan ist ohne Glimmstängel und blass, Dussel, der viel von seiner Bequemlichkeit geopfert hat, hat alle möglichen Beanstandungen usw. usw. Wir haben im Augenblick kein Glück. Das Klo ist undicht, der Hahn überdreht. Dank der vielen Beziehungen wird sowohl das eine als auch das andere schnell repariert sein.

Manchmal bin ich sentimental, das weiß ich, aber manchmal ist Sentimentalität auch angebracht. Wenn Peter und ich irgendwo zwischen Gerümpel und Staub auf einer harten Holzkiste sitzen, einer dem anderen den Arm um die Schultern gelegt hat, er mit einer Locke von mir in der Hand, und wenn draußen die Vögel trillern, wenn die Bäume grün werden, wenn die Sonne hinauslockt, wenn der Himmel so blau ist, oh, dann will ich so viel!
Nichts als unzufriedene und mürrische Gesichter sieht man hier, nichts als Seufzen und unterdrückte Klagen sind zu hören, und es scheint, als wäre plötzlich alles schrecklich geworden. In Wirklichkeit ist es hier so schlecht, wie man es sich selbst macht. Hier im Hinterhaus geht niemand mit gutem Beispiel voran, hier muss jeder selbst sehen, wie er mit seinen Launen klarkommt.
»Wäre es nur schon vorbei!« Das hört man jeden Tag.

Meine Würde, meine Hoffnung, meine Liebe, mein Mut,
das alles hält mich aufrecht und macht mich gut!

Kitty, ich glaube, ich spinne heute ein bisschen, und ich weiß nicht, warum. Alles steht durcheinander, man merkt keinen Zusammenhang, und ich bezweifle manchmal ernsthaft, ob sich später mal jemand für mein Geschwätz interessieren wird. »Die Bekenntnisse eines hässlichen jungen Entleins« wird der ganze Unsinn dann heißen. Herr Bolkestein* und Herr Gerbrandy* werden von <u>meinen</u> Tagebüchern wirklich nicht viel haben.   Deine Anne

---

* Mitglieder der niederländischen Exilregierung in London; A. d. Ü.

Samstag, 15. April 1944

Liebe Kitty!

»Ein Schreck folgt dem anderen. Wann wird das zu Ende sein?« So können wir wirklich sagen. Stell dir vor, was nun schon wieder passiert ist: Peter hat vergessen, den Riegel vor der Tür aufzumachen. Die Folge war, dass Kugler mit den Arbeitern nicht ins Haus kam. Er ist zur Nachbarfirma gegangen und hat von da aus das Küchenfenster eingeschlagen. Unsere Fenster standen offen, und die Nachbarn haben es gesehen. Was sie sich wohl denken? Und van Maaren? Kugler ist wütend. Er bekommt die Vorwürfe, dass er nichts an den Türen verändern lässt, und wir machen so eine Dummheit! Peter ist vollkommen außer Fassung, das kann ich dir sagen. Als Mutter bei Tisch sagte, Peter tue ihr Leid, fing er fast an zu weinen. Es ist ebenso unsere Schuld, denn wir und auch van Daan fragen sonst fast jeden Tag, ob der Riegel weg ist. Vielleicht kann ich ihn nachher ein bisschen trösten. Ich würde ihm so gerne helfen.

Hier folgen noch einige vertrauliche Hinterhausmeldungen von den letzten Wochen:

Vor einer Woche wurde Moffi plötzlich krank, er war sehr still und sabberte. Miep nahm ihn, rollte ihn in ein Tuch, steckte ihn in die Einkaufstasche und brachte ihn zur Tierklinik. Der Doktor gab ihm eine Medizin, weil er es an den Eingeweiden hatte. Peter gab ihm ein paar Mal von der Arznei, aber schon bald ließ Moffi sich nicht mehr sehen und war Tag und Nacht unterwegs, sicher bei seiner Liebsten. Aber jetzt ist seine Nase geschwollen, und er fiept, wenn man ihn anfasst. Wahrscheinlich hat er irgendwo, wo er was klauen wollte, einen Klaps bekommen. Mouschi hatte ein paar Tage lang eine Art Stimmbruch. Gerade als wir sie auch zum Doktor schicken wollten, war sie schon wieder fast gesund.

Unser Dachbodenfenster bleibt nun auch nachts etwas offen. Peter und ich sitzen jetzt oft abends noch oben.

Dank Gummilösung und Ölfarbe kann unser Klo wieder gerichtet werden. Auch der überdrehte Hahn ist durch einen anderen ersetzt worden.

Herrn Kleiman geht es zum Glück wieder besser. Bald wird er zu einem Spezialisten gehen. Wir wollen nur hoffen, dass er nicht am Magen operiert werden muss.

Diesen Monat haben wir acht Lebensmittelkarten bekommen. Unglücklicherweise hat es in den ersten vierzehn Tagen statt Haferflocken oder Graupen nur Hülsenfrüchte auf die Marken gegeben. Unser neuester Leckerbissen ist Piccalilly. Wenn man Pech hat, sind in einem Glas nur ein paar Gurken und etwas Senfsoße. Gemüse gibt es gar nicht. Vorher Salat und nachher Salat. Unsere Mahlzeiten bestehen nur noch aus Kartoffeln und künstlicher Soße.

Die Russen haben jetzt mehr als die Hälfte der Krim erobert. Bei Cassino kommen die Engländer nicht vorwärts. Rechnen wir eben mit dem Westwall. Bombardierungen gibt es oft, noch dazu unvorstellbar schwere. In Den Haag wurde das Rathaus von einer Bombe getroffen, und viele Dokumente wurden zerstört. Alle Niederländer bekommen neue Stammkarten.

Genug für heute!   Deine Anne M. Frank

                                             Sonntag, 16. April 1944

Liebste Kitty!

Behalte den gestrigen Tag, er ist sehr wichtig für mein ganzes Leben. Ist es nicht für jedes Mädchen wichtig, wenn sie den ersten Kuss bekommt? Nun, bei mir ist es auch so. Der Kuss von Bram auf meine rechte Backe zählt nicht, auch nicht der Handkuss von Woudstra. Wie ich so plötzlich zu diesem Kuss gekommen bin? Nun, das werde ich dir erzählen.

Gestern Abend um acht saß ich mit Peter auf seiner Couch. Schon bald legte er einen Arm um mich. (Weil Samstag war, hatte er keinen Overall an.) »Rücken wir ein bisschen weiter«, sagte ich, »damit ich mit dem Kopf nicht an das Schränkchen stoße.«

Er rückte fast bis zur Ecke, ich legte meinen Arm unter seinem Arm hindurch auf seinen Rücken, und er begrub mich fast, weil sein Arm um meine Schulter hing. Wir hatten schon öfter so gesessen, aber nie so dicht nebeneinander wie gestern Abend. Er drückte mich fest an sich, meine Brust lag an seiner, mein Herz klopfte. Aber das war noch nicht alles. Er ruhte nicht eher, bis mein Kopf auf seiner Schulter lag und der seine darauf. Als ich mich nach ungefähr fünf Minuten etwas aufrichtete, nahm er meinen Kopf in die Hände und zog ihn wieder an sich. Oh, es war so herrlich! Ich konnte nicht sprechen, der Genuss war zu groß. Er streichelte ein bisschen ungeschickt meine Wange und meinen Arm, fummelte an meinen Locken, und unsere Köpfe lagen fast die ganze Zeit aneinander.

Das Gefühl, das mich dabei durchströmte, kann ich dir nicht beschreiben, Kitty. Ich war überglücklich, und ich glaube, er auch.

Um halb neun standen wir auf. Peter zog seine Turnschuhe an, um bei einer zweiten Runde durch das Haus auch leise zu gehen, und ich stand dabei. Wie ich plötzlich die richtige Bewegung fand, weiß ich nicht, aber bevor wir nach unten gingen, gab er mir einen Kuss auf die Haare, halb auf meine linke Wange und halb auf mein Ohr. Ohne mich umzuschauen rannte ich hinunter und warte mit großer Sehnsucht auf heute.

<u>Sonntagmorgen, kurz vor 11 Uhr.</u>   Deine Anne M. Frank

                                      Montag, 17. April 1944

Liebe Kitty!

Glaubst du, dass Vater und Mutter es gutheißen würden, dass ich auf einer Couch sitze und einen Jungen küsse? Ein Junge von siebzehneinhalb und ein Mädchen von fast fünfzehn? Ich glaube es eigentlich nicht, aber ich muss mich bei dieser Sache auf mich selbst verlassen. Es ist so ruhig und sicher, in seinen Armen zu liegen und zu träumen, es ist so aufregend, seine Wange an meiner zu fühlen, es ist so herrlich zu wissen, dass jemand auf mich wartet. Aber – und ein Aber gibt es tatsächlich – wird Peter es dabei belassen wollen? Ich habe sein Versprechen nicht vergessen, aber … er ist ein Junge!

Ich weiß schon, dass ich sehr früh dran bin. Noch keine fünfzehn und schon so selbstständig, das ist für andere wohl unbegreiflich. Ich bin mir fast sicher, dass Margot niemals einem Jungen einen Kuss geben würde, ohne dass auch von Verloben oder Heiraten die Rede ist. Solche Pläne haben weder Peter noch ich. Auch Mutter hat vor Vater sicher keinen Mann berührt. Was würden meine Freundinnen dazu sagen, wenn sie wüssten, dass ich in Peters Armen lag, mit meinem Herzen auf seiner Brust, mit meinem Kopf auf seiner Schulter, mit seinem Kopf und Gesicht auf dem meinen!

O Anne, wie skandalös! Ich finde es aber wirklich nicht skandalös. Wir sind hier eingesperrt, abgeschlossen von der Welt, immer in Angst und Sorge, ganz besonders in der letzten Zeit. Warum sollten wir, die einander lieben, uns dann voneinander fern halten? Warum sollten wir uns in diesen Zeiten keinen Kuss geben? Warum sollten wir warten, bis wir das passende Alter haben? Warum sollten wir viel fragen?

Ich habe es auf mich genommen, selbst auf mich aufzupassen. Er würde mir nie Kummer oder Schmerz zufügen wollen. Warum sollte ich dann nicht tun, was mir das Herz eingibt, und uns beide glücklich machen?

Doch ich glaube, Kitty, dass du ein bisschen von meinen Zweifeln merkst. Ich denke, dass es meine Ehrlichkeit ist, die sich gegen Heimlichkeiten auflehnt. Findest du, dass es meine Pflicht wäre, Vater zu erzählen, was ich tue? Findest du, dass unser Geheimnis einem Dritten zu Ohren kommen soll? Von dem, was schön ist, würde viel verloren gehen. Und würde ich dadurch innerlich ruhiger werden? Ich werde mit <u>ihm</u> darüber sprechen.

O ja, ich will über so viel mit ihm sprechen, denn nur miteinander schmusen, darin sehe ich keinen Sinn. Es gehört viel Vertrauen dazu, einander die Gedanken zu erzählen, aber sicher werden wir beide stärker im Bewusstsein dieses Vertrauens.

Deine Anne M. Frank

P. S. Gestern Morgen waren wir schon wieder um sechs Uhr auf den Beinen, da die ganze Familie Einbruchgeräusche gehört hatte. Vielleicht ist diesmal ein Nachbar das Opfer geworden. Bei der Kontrolle um sieben Uhr waren unsere Türen fest verschlossen, zum Glück.

Dienstag, 18. April 1944

Liebe Kitty!

Hier ist alles gut. Gestern Abend war der Zimmermann wieder da und hat angefangen, eiserne Platten vor die Türfüllungen zu schrauben.

Vater hat gerade gesagt, dass er vor dem 20. Mai noch ganz groß angelegte Operationen erwartet, sowohl in Russland als auch in Italien und im Westen. Ich kann mir die Befreiung aus unserer Lage immer weniger vorstellen, je länger es dauert.

Gestern sind Peter und ich dann endlich zu unserem Gespräch gekommen, das mindestens schon zehn Tage verschoben worden ist. Ich habe ihm alles von den Mädchen erklärt und mich nicht gescheut, die intimsten Dinge zu besprechen. Ich fand es allerdings witzig, dass er dachte, dass sie den Eingang bei Frauen auf Bildern einfach weglie-ßen. Er konnte sich also nicht vorstellen, dass das wirklich zwischen den Beinen liegt.

Der Abend endete mit einem Kuss, ein bisschen neben dem Mund. Es ist wirklich ein tolles Gefühl!

Vielleicht nehme ich mein Schöne-Sätze-Buch doch mal mit hinauf, um endlich etwas tiefer auf die Dinge einzugehen. Ich finde keine Befriedigung darin, sich Tag um Tag immer nur in den Armen zu liegen, und wünsche mir, dass es ihm auch so geht.

Wir haben nach unserem unbeständigen Winter wieder ein prachtvolles Frühjahr. Der April ist tatsächlich wunderbar, nicht zu warm und nicht zu kalt und ab und zu ein kleiner Regenschauer. Unsere Kastanie ist schon ziemlich grün, und hier und da sieht man sogar schon kleine Kerzen.

Bep hat uns am Samstag Blumen gebracht, drei Sträuße Narzissen, und für mich Traubenhyazinthen. Und Herr Kugler versorgt uns immer besser mit Zeitungen.

Ich muss Algebra machen, Kitty, auf Wiedersehen!

Deine Anne M. Frank

Mittwoch, 19. April

Lieber Schatz!

(Das ist der Titel eines Films mit Dorit Kreysler, Ida Wüst und Harald Paulsen.)

Was gibt es Schöneres auf der Welt, als aus einem offenen Fenster hinaus in die Natur zu schauen, die Vögel pfeifen zu hören, die Sonne auf den Wangen zu fühlen und einen lieben Jungen in den Armen zu haben? Es ist so ruhig und sicher, seinen Arm um mich zu fühlen, ihn nahe zu wissen und doch zu schweigen. Es kann nicht schlecht sein, denn diese Ruhe ist gut. Oh, wenn sie doch nie gestört würde, noch nicht einmal von Mouschi!

Deine Anne M. Frank

Freitag, 21. April 1944

Liebste Kitty!

Gestern Nachmittag lag ich mit Halsweh im Bett, aber weil ich mich schon am ersten Tag langweilte und kein Fieber hatte, bin ich heute wieder aufgestanden. Das Halsweh ist auch fast verschwunden.

Gestern wurde, wie du vermutlich gemerkt hast, unser »Führer« 55 Jahre alt. Heute ist der achtzehnte Geburtstag Ihrer Königlichen Hoheit, der Kronprinzessin Elisabeth von York. Im BBC wurde durchgegeben, dass sie noch nicht für volljährig erklärt worden ist, wie es bei Prinzessinnen sonst der Fall ist. Wir haben uns schon gefragt, mit welchem Prinzen diese Schönheit mal verheiratet wird, konnten jedoch keinen geeigneten finden. Vielleicht kann ihre Schwester, Prinzessin Margaret Rose, den Kronprinzen Baudouin von Belgien bekommen.

Hier geraten wir von einer Misere in die andere. Kaum haben wir nun die Außentüren gut verrammelt, tritt van Maaren, der Lagerarbeiter, wieder in Erscheinung. Aller Wahrscheinlichkeit nach hat er Kartoffelmehl gestohlen und will jetzt Bep die Schuld in die Schuhe schieben. Das Hinterhaus ist begreiflicherweise in Aufruhr. Bep ist außer sich vor Wut. Vielleicht lässt Kugler dieses heruntergekommene Subjekt jetzt beschatten.

Heute Morgen war ein Schätzer aus der Beethovenstraat hier. Er will für unsere Truhe 400 Gulden geben. Auch seine anderen Angebote sind unserer Meinung nach zu niedrig.

Ich will bei der Zeitung anfragen, ob sie ein Märchen von mir nehmen wollen, natürlich unter einem Pseudonym. Aber weil meine Märchen noch zu lang sind, glaube ich nicht, dass ich viel Aussicht auf Erfolg habe.

Bis zum nächsten Mal, Darling!   Deine Anne M. Frank

Herr Pfeffer.

Liebe Kitty!

Seit ungefähr zehn Tagen spricht Dussel wieder nicht mit van Daan, und das nur, weil wir nach dem Einbruch eine ganze Menge neuer Sicherheitsvorkehrungen getroffen haben. Eine davon ist, dass er abends nicht mehr hinunter darf. Peter macht jeden Abend um halb zehn mit Herrn van Daan die letzte Runde, und dann darf niemand mehr hinunter. Von abends acht Uhr an darf auch die Klospülung nicht mehr gezogen werden, auch morgens um acht nicht. Die Fenster gehen erst auf, wenn in Kuglers Büro das Licht brennt, und abends dürfen keine Stöckchen mehr dazwischengesteckt werden. Letzteres ist der Anlass zu Dussels Schmollen gewesen. Er behauptet, dass van Daan ihn angeschnauzt habe, aber daran ist er selbst schuld. Er sagte auch, dass er eher ohne Essen als ohne Luft leben könne und eine Methode gefunden werden müsse, die Fenster zu öffnen.

»Ich werde mit Herrn Kugler darüber sprechen«, sagte er zu mir. Ich antwortete, dass solche Dinge nie von Herrn Kugler beschlossen werden, sondern in der Gemeinschaft.

»Alles passiert hier hinter meinem Rücken, dann werde ich wohl mit deinem Vater darüber sprechen.«

Er darf sich samstags nachmittags und sonntags auch nicht mehr in Kuglers Büro setzen, weil der Chef der Nachbarfirma ihn da hören könnte, falls er käme. Prompt setzte sich Dussel doch rein. Van Daan war rasend, und Vater ging hinunter, um mit ihm zu reden. Natürlich hatte er wieder eine Ausrede, aber diesmal kam er sogar bei Vater nicht damit durch. Vater spricht nun auch so wenig wie möglich mit ihm, weil Dussel ihn beleidigt hat. Wie, weiß ich nicht, wir wissen es alle nicht, aber es muss schlimm sein.

Und nächste Woche hat der Unglückswurm auch noch Geburtstag. Geburtstag haben, nicht den Mund aufmachen, schmollen und Geschenke bekommen, wie passt das zusammen?

Mit Herrn Vossen geht es schnell bergab, er hat seit über zehn Tagen fast vierzig Fieber. Der Doktor hält seinen Zustand für hoffnungslos, es wird angenommen, dass der Krebs auf die Lunge übergegriffen hat. Der arme Mann, man würde ihm so gern helfen, aber niemand als Gott kann hier helfen.

Ich habe eine schöne Geschichte geschrieben. Sie heißt »Blurry, der Weltentdecker« und hat meinen drei Zuhörern sehr gefallen.

Ich bin noch immer erkältet und habe sowohl Margot als auch Mutter und Vater angesteckt. Wenn Peter es nur nicht bekommt! Er musste unbedingt einen Kuss haben und nannte mich sein Eldorado. Es geht doch nicht, du verrückter Junge! Aber lieb ist er doch!

Deine Anne M. Frank

Donnerstag, 27. April 1944

Liebe Kitty!

Heute Morgen hatte Frau van Daan schlechte Laune, nichts als Klagen, zuerst über die Erkältung, dass sie keine Hustenbonbons bekam, dass das viele Schnäuzen nicht auszuhalten ist. Dann, dass die Sonne nicht scheint, dass die Invasion nicht kommt, dass wir nicht aus dem Fenster schauen können usw. usw. Wir mussten schrecklich über sie lachen. Es war dann doch nicht so schlimm, und sie lachte mit.

Das Rezept für unseren Kartoffelauflauf, wegen Mangels an Zwiebeln geändert:

Man nehme geschälte Kartoffeln, drehe sie durch eine Mühle, füge etwas trockenes Regierungsmehl und Salz hinzu. Man schmiere die Backform oder die feuerfeste Schüssel mit Paraffin oder Stearin ein, backe den Rührteig zweieinhalb Stunden und esse ihn dann mit angefaultem Erdbeerkompott. (Zwiebeln nicht vorhanden, auch kein Fett, weder für Schüssel noch für Teig.)

Im Augenblick lese ich »Kaiser Karl V.«, von einem Göttinger Universitätsprofessor geschrieben. Er hat vierzig Jahre an diesem Buch gearbeitet. In fünf Tagen habe ich fünfzig Seiten gelesen, mehr ist nicht möglich. Das Buch hat 598 Seiten, da kannst du dir ausrechnen, wie lange ich dazu brauchen werde. Und dann noch der zweite Band! Aber sehr interessant!

Was ein Schulmädchen an einem Tag nicht alles macht! Nimm mich mal! Erst habe ich ein Stück von Nelsons letzter Schlacht aus dem Niederländischen ins Englische übersetzt. Dann nahm ich die Fortsetzung des nordischen Krieges (1700–1721) durch. Peter der Große, Karl XII., August der Starke, Stanislaus Leczinsky, Mazeppa, Brandenburg, Vorder-Pommern, Hinter-Pommern und Dänemark, samt den dazugehörigen Jahreszahlen. Anschließend landete ich in Brasilien, las vom Bahia-Tabak, dem Überfluss an Kaffee, den anderthalb Millionen Einwohnern von Rio de Janeiro, von Pernambuco und São Paulo, den Amazonasfluss nicht zu vergessen. Von Negern, Mulatten, Mestizen, Weißen, mehr als 50% Analphabeten und der Malaria. Da mir noch etwas Zeit blieb, nahm ich noch schnell einen Stammbaum durch: Jan der Alte, Wilhelm Ludwig, Ernst Casimir I., Heinrich Casimir I. bis zu der kleinen Margriet Franciska (geboren 1944 in Ottawa).

Zwölf Uhr: Auf dem Dachboden setzte ich meine Lernzeit fort mit Dekanen, Pfarrern, Pastoren, Päpsten und … Puh, bis ein Uhr.

Nach zwei Uhr saß das arme Kind schon wieder an der Arbeit, Schmal- und Breitnasenaffen waren dran. Kitty, sag schnell, wie viel Zehen ein Nilpferd hat!

Dann folgte die Bibel, die Arche Noah, Sem, Ham und Japhet, danach Karl V. Dann mit Peter Englisch, »Der Oberst« von Thackeray. Französische Vokabeln abhören und dann den Mississippi mit dem Missouri vergleichen!

Genug für heute, adieu!   Deine Anne M. Frank

                                                  Freitag, 28. April 1944

Liebe Kitty!

Meinen Traum von Peter Schiff habe ich nie vergessen. Ich fühle, wenn ich daran denke, heute noch seine Wange an meiner, mit jenem herrlichen Gefühl, das alles gut machte. Mit Peter hier hatte ich das Gefühl auch manchmal, aber nie so stark, bis wir gestern Abend zusammensaßen, wie gewöhnlich auf der Couch und einer in den Armen des anderen. Da glitt die normale Anne plötzlich weg, und dafür kam die zweite Anne, die nicht übermütig und witzig ist, sondern nur lieb haben will und weich sein.

Ich lehnte mich fest an ihn und fühlte die Rührung in mir aufsteigen. Tränen sprangen mir in die Augen, die linke fiel auf seinen Overall, die rechte rann an meiner Nase vorbei und fiel auch auf seinen Overall. Ob er es gemerkt hat? Keine Bewegung verriet es. Ob er genauso fühlt wie ich? Er sprach auch fast kein Wort. Ob er weiß, dass er zwei Annes vor sich hat? Das alles sind unbeantwortete Fragen.

Wand in Annes Zimmer mit einem Teil ihrer Filmstar- und Ansichtskartensamm-
lung.

Um halb neun stand ich auf und ging zum Fenster. Dort nehmen wir immer Abschied voneinander. Ich zitterte noch, ich war noch Anne Nummer zwei. Er kam auf mich zu, ich legte meine Arme um seinen Hals und drückte einen Kuss auf seine linke Wange. Gerade wollte ich auch zur rechten, als mein Mund den seinen traf. Taumelnd drückten wir uns aneinander, noch einmal und noch einmal, um nie mehr aufzuhören!

Peter hat so viel Bedürfnis nach Zärtlichkeit. Er hat zum ersten Mal in seinem Leben ein Mädchen entdeckt, hat zum ersten Mal gesehen, dass die lästigsten Mädchen auch ein Inneres und ein Herz haben und sich verändern, sobald sie mit einem allein sind. Er hat zum ersten Mal in seinem Leben seine Freundschaft und sich selbst gegeben, er hat noch nie zuvor einen Freund oder eine Freundin gehabt. Nun haben wir uns gefunden. Ich kannte ihn auch nicht, hatte auch nie einen Vertrauten, und nun ist es doch so weit gekommen.
Wieder die Frage, die mich nicht loslässt: »Ist es richtig?« Ist es richtig, dass ich so schnell nachgebe, dass ich so heftig bin, genauso heftig und verlangend wie Peter? Darf ich, ein Mädchen, mich so gehen lassen?
Es gibt nur eine Antwort darauf: »Ich sehne mich so ... schon so lange. Ich bin so einsam und habe nun einen Trost gefunden.«
Morgens sind wir normal, nachmittags auch noch ziemlich, aber abends kommt die Sehnsucht des ganzen Tages hoch, das Glück und die Wonne von all den vorherigen Malen, und wir denken nur aneinander. Jeden Abend, nach dem letzten Kuss, möchte ich am liebsten wegrennen, ihm nicht mehr in die Augen sehen, nur weg, weg in die Dunkelheit und allein sein.
Aber was erwartet mich, wenn ich die vierzehn Stufen hinuntergegangen bin? Volles Licht, Fragen hier und Lachen dort. Ich muss reagieren und darf mir nichts anmerken lassen.
Mein Herz ist noch zu weich, um so einen Schock wie gestern Abend einfach zur Seite zu schieben. Die weiche Anne kommt zu selten und lässt sich darum auch nicht sofort wieder zur Tür hinausjagen. Peter hat mich berührt, tiefer, als ich je in meinem Leben berührt wurde, außer in meinem Traum! Peter hat mich angefasst, hat mein Inneres nach außen gekehrt. Ist es dann nicht für jeden Menschen selbstver-

ständlich, dass er danach seine Ruhe braucht, um sich innerlich wieder zu erholen? O Peter, was hast du mit mir gemacht? Was willst du von mir?

Wohin soll das führen? Jetzt begreife ich Bep, nun, wo ich das erlebe. Nun verstehe ich ihre Zweifel. Wenn ich älter wäre und er würde mich heiraten wollen, was würde ich dann antworten? Anne, sei ehrlich! Du würdest ihn nicht heiraten können, aber loslassen ist auch so schwer. Peter hat noch zu wenig Charakter, zu wenig Willenskraft, zu wenig Mut und Kraft. Er ist noch ein Kind, innerlich nicht älter als ich. Er will nur Ruhe und Glück.

Bin ich wirklich erst vierzehn? Bin ich wirklich noch ein dummes Schulmädchen? Bin ich wirklich noch so unerfahren in allem? Ich habe mehr Erfahrung als die anderen, ich habe etwas erlebt, was fast niemand in meinem Alter kennt.

Ich habe Angst vor mir selbst, habe Angst, dass ich mich in meinem Verlangen zu schnell wegschenke. Wie kann das dann später mit anderen Jungen gut gehen? Ach, es ist so schwierig, immer gibt es das Herz und den Verstand, und jedes muss zu seiner Zeit sprechen. Aber weiß ich sicher, dass ich die Zeit richtig gewählt habe?

Deine Anne M. Frank

Dienstag, 2. Mai 1944

Liebe Kitty!

Samstagabend habe ich Peter gefragt, ob er meint, dass ich Vater etwas von uns erzählen muss. Nach einigem Hin und Her sagte er Ja. Ich war froh, es beweist ein gutes Gefühl. Sofort als ich hinunterkam, ging ich mit Vater Wasser holen. Auf der Treppe sagte ich schon: »Vater, du verstehst sicher, dass Peter und ich, wenn wir zusammen sind, nicht einen Meter voneinander entfernt sitzen. Findest du das schlimm?«

Vater antwortete nicht gleich, dann sagte er: »Nein, schlimm finde ich das nicht, Anne. Aber hier, bei diesem beschränkten Raum, musst du vorsichtig sein.« Er sagte noch etwas in diesem Sinn, dann gingen wir nach oben.

Am Sonntagmorgen rief er mich zu sich und sagte: »Anne, ich habe noch mal darüber nachgedacht.« (Ich bekam schon Angst!) »Es ist hier im Hinterhaus eigentlich nicht so gut. Ich dachte, dass ihr Kameraden wäret. Ist Peter verliebt?«

»Davon ist nicht die Rede«, antwortete ich.

»Du weißt, dass ich euch gut verstehe. Aber du musst zurückhaltend sein. Geh nicht mehr so oft nach oben, ermuntere ihn nicht unnötig. Der Mann ist in solchen Dingen immer der Aktive, die Frau kann zurückhalten. Es ist draußen, wenn du frei bist, etwas ganz anderes. Da siehst du andere Jungen und Mädchen, du kannst mal weggehen, Sport treiben und alles Mögliche. Aber hier kannst du nicht weg, wenn du willst. Ihr seht euch jede Stunde, eigentlich immer. Sei vorsichtig, Anne, und nimm es nicht zu ernst.«

»Das tue ich nicht, Vater, und Peter ist anständig. Er ist ein lieber Junge.«

»Ja, aber er hat keinen starken Charakter. Er ist leicht zur guten, aber auch zur schlechten Seite zu beeinflussen. Ich hoffe für ihn, dass er gut bleibt, denn in seinem Wesen ist er gut.«

Wir sprachen noch eine Weile und machten aus, dass Vater auch mit ihm reden würde.

Am Sonntagnachmittag, auf dem vorderen Dachboden, fragte Peter: »Und hast du mit deinem Vater gesprochen, Anne?«

»Ja«, antwortete ich. »Ich werde es dir schon erzählen. Vater findet es nicht schlimm, aber er sagt, dass hier, wo wir so aufeinander sitzen, leicht Konflikte entstehen könnten.«

»Wir haben doch abgemacht, dass wir uns nicht streiten. Ich habe vor, mich daran zu halten.«

»Ich auch, Peter. Aber Vater hat es nicht geglaubt, er hat gedacht, dass wir Kameraden wären. Meinst du, dass das nicht geht?«

»Ich schon. Und du?«

»Ich auch. Ich habe auch zu Vater gesagt, dass ich dir vertraue. Ich verlasse mich auf dich, Peter, genauso, wie ich mich auf Vater verlasse, und ich glaube, dass du es wert bist. Ist es nicht so?«

»Ich hoffe es.« Er war sehr verlegen und rot geworden.

»Ich glaube an dich, Peter«, fuhr ich fort. »Ich glaube, dass du einen guten Charakter hast und in der Welt vorwärts kommen wirst.«

Wir sprachen dann über andere Dinge. Später sagte ich noch: »Wenn wir hier herauskommen, wirst du dich nicht mehr um mich kümmern, das weiß ich.«

Er geriet in Hitze. »Das ist nicht wahr, Anne! Nein, das <u>darfst</u> du nicht von mir denken!«
Dann wurden wir gerufen.

Vater hat inzwischen mit ihm gesprochen, er erzählte es mir am Montag. »Dein Vater dachte, dass aus Kameradschaft schon mal Verliebtheit werden kann. Ich habe ihm aber gesagt, dass wir uns beherrschen werden.«
Vater will nun, dass ich abends nicht so oft hinaufgehe, aber das will ich nicht. Nicht nur, dass ich gern bei Peter bin, aber ich habe gesagt, dass ich mich auf ihn verlasse. Ich will ihm das Vertrauen beweisen, und das kann ich nicht, wenn ich aus Misstrauen unten bleibe.
Nein, ich gehe hinauf!

Inzwischen ist das Dussel-Drama wieder vorbei. Er hat Samstagabend bei Tisch in schönen niederländischen Worten um Entschuldigung gebeten. Van Daan war sofort wieder gut. Dussel hat für diese Aufgabe bestimmt den ganzen Tag geübt. Sein Geburtstag am Sonntag verlief ruhig. Von uns bekam er eine Flasche guten Wein von 1919, von den van Daans (die ihr Geschenk jetzt geben konnten) ein Glas Piccalilly und ein Päckchen Rasierklingen, von Kugler einen Topf Zitronenlimonade, von Miep ein Buch und von Bep eine kleine Pflanze. Er hat jedem von uns ein Ei spendiert.

Deine Anne M. Frank

Mittwoch, 3. Mai 1944

Liebe Kitty!
Erst kurz die Neuigkeiten der Woche! Die Politik hat Urlaub. Es gibt nichts, aber auch gar nichts mitzuteilen. So allmählich glaube ich auch, dass die Invasion kommt. Sie können die Russen doch nicht alles allein erledigen lassen! Übrigens, die tun zur Zeit auch nichts.
Herr Kleiman ist wieder jeden Morgen im Büro. Er hat für Peters Couch neue Federn besorgt, also muss sich Peter jetzt ans Polstern machen. Begreiflicherweise hat er dazu überhaupt keine Lust. Kleiman hat auch Flohpuder für die Katzen besorgt.
Habe ich dir schon erzählt, dass Moffi weg ist? Seit vergangener Wo-

che Donnerstag spurlos verschwunden. Bestimmt ist sie schon im Katzenhimmel, und irgendein Tierfreund hat sich einen Leckerbissen aus ihr gemacht. Vielleicht kriegt ein Mädchen mit Geld eine Mütze aus ihrem Fell. Peter ist sehr traurig darüber.

Seit zwei Wochen lunchen wir samstags erst um halb zwölf. Am Vormittag gibt es nur eine Tasse Brei. Ab morgen soll das jeden Tag so sein, so können wir eine Mahlzeit einsparen. Gemüse ist immer noch schwer zu bekommen. Heute Mittag hatten wir fauligen Kochsalat. Es gibt nur Salat, Spinat und Kochsalat, sonst nichts. Dazu noch angefaulte Kartoffeln, also eine herrliche Zusammenstellung!

Seit mehr als zwei Monaten hatte ich meine Periode nicht mehr, seit Sonntag ist es endlich wieder soweit. Trotz der Unannehmlichkeiten und der Umstände bin ich doch froh, dass es mich nicht länger im Stich gelassen hat.

Du kannst dir sicher denken, wie oft hier verzweifelt gefragt wird: »Wofür, oh, wofür nützt nun dieser Krieg? Warum können die Menschen nicht friedlich miteinander leben? Warum muss alles verwüstet werden?«

Diese Frage ist verständlich, aber eine entscheidende Antwort hat bis jetzt noch niemand gefunden. Ja, warum bauen sie in England immer größere Flugzeuge, immer schwerere Bomben und gleichzeitig Einheitshäuser für den Wiederaufbau? Warum gibt man jeden Tag Millionen für den Krieg aus und keinen Cent für die Heilkunde, für die Künstler, für die Armen? Warum müssen die Leute hungern, wenn in anderen Teilen der Welt die überflüssige Nahrung wegfault? Warum sind die Menschen so verrückt?

Ich glaube nicht, dass der Krieg nur von den Großen, von den Regierenden und Kapitalisten gemacht wird. Nein, der kleine Mann ist ebenso dafür. Sonst hätten sich die Völker doch schon längst dagegen erhoben! Im Menschen ist nun mal ein Drang zur Vernichtung, ein Drang zum Totschlagen, zum Morden und Wüten, und solange die ganze Menschheit, ohne Ausnahme, keine Metamorphose durchläuft, wird Krieg wüten, wird alles, was gebaut, gepflegt und gewachsen ist, wieder abgeschnitten und vernichtet, und dann fängt es wieder von vorn an.

Ich bin oft niedergeschlagen gewesen, aber nie verzweifelt. Ich betrachte dieses Verstecken als ein gefährliches Abenteuer, das romantisch und interessant ist. Ich beschreibe jede Entbehrung in meinem Tagebuch wie eine Unterhaltung. Ich habe mir nun mal vorgenommen, dass ich ein anderes Leben führen werde als andere Mädchen und später ein anderes Leben als normale Hausfrauen. Das ist ein passender Anfang mit viel Interessantem, und darum, nur darum muss ich in den gefährlichsten Augenblicken über die komische Situation lachen.

Ich bin jung und habe noch viele verborgene Eigenschaften. Ich bin jung und stark und erlebe das große Abenteuer, sitze mittendrin und kann nicht den ganzen Tag klagen, weil ich mich amüsieren muss! Ich habe viel mitbekommen, eine glückliche Natur, viel Fröhlichkeit und Kraft. Jeden Tag fühle ich, wie mein Inneres wächst, wie die Befreiung naht, wie schön die Natur ist, wie gut die Menschen in meiner Umgebung, wie interessant und amüsant dieses Abenteuer. Warum sollte ich dann verzweifelt sein?

Deine Anne M. Frank

Freitag, 5. Mai 1944

Beste Kitty!

Vater ist unzufrieden mit mir. Er dachte, dass ich nach unserem Gespräch vom Sonntag von selbst nicht mehr jeden Abend nach oben gehen würde. Er will die »Knutscherei« nicht haben. Das Wort konnte ich nicht hören. Es war schon unangenehm genug, darüber zu sprechen, warum muss er mich nun auch noch so schlecht machen! Ich werde heute mit ihm reden. Margot hat mir einen guten Rat gegeben. Hör mal, was ich ungefähr sagen will:

»Ich glaube, Vater, dass du eine Erklärung von mir erwartest, ich will sie dir geben. Du bist enttäuscht von mir, du hattest mehr Zurückhaltung von mir erwartet. Du willst sicher, dass ich so bin, wie eine Vierzehnjährige zu sein hat, und darin irrst du dich.

Seit wir hier sind, seit Juli 1942, hatte ich es bis vor ein paar Wochen nicht einfach. Wenn du wüsstest, wie oft ich abends geweint habe, wie verzweifelt und unglücklich ich war, wie einsam ich mich fühlte, dann würdest du verstehen, dass ich nach oben will. Ich habe es nicht von einem auf den anderen Tag geschafft, so weit zu kommen, dass ich ohne Mutter und ohne die Unterstützung von jemand anderem leben kann. Es hat mich viel, viel Kampf und Tränen gekostet, so selbstständig zu werden, wie ich es jetzt bin. Du kannst lachen und mir nicht glauben, es macht mir nichts. Ich weiß, dass ich ein eigenständiger Mensch bin, und ich fühle mich euch gegenüber absolut nicht verantwortlich. Ich habe dir dies nur erzählt, weil du sonst glauben könntest, ich verheimliche etwas. Aber für meine Handlungen muss ich mich nur vor mir selbst verantworten.

Als ich Schwierigkeiten hatte, habt ihr, auch du, die Augen zugemacht und die Ohren verstopft. Du hast mir nicht geholfen, im Gegenteil, nur Ermahnungen habe ich bekommen, dass ich nicht so lärmend sein sollte. Ich war nur lärmend, um nicht immer traurig zu sein. Ich war übermütig, um meine innere Stimme nicht zu hören. Ich habe Komödie gespielt, anderthalb Jahre lang, tagein, tagaus. Ich habe nicht geklagt und bin nicht aus der Rolle gefallen, nichts von alledem, und jetzt habe ich mich durchgekämpft. Ich habe gesiegt. Ich bin selbstständig an Leib und Geist. Ich habe keine Mutter mehr nötig, ich bin durch all die Kämpfe stark geworden.

Nun, da ich es geschafft habe, will ich auch meinen eigenen Weg gehen, den Weg, den ich für richtig halte. Du kannst und darfst mich nicht wie eine Vierzehnjährige betrachten, ich bin durch alle Schwierigkeiten älter geworden. Ich werde meine Taten nicht bedauern, ich werde handeln, wie ich es richtig finde!

Du kannst mich nicht sanft von oben fern halten. Entweder du verbietest mir alles, oder du vertraust mir durch dick und dünn! Nur lass mich dann auch in Ruhe!«   Deine Anne M. Frank

Samstag, 6. Mai 1944

Liebe Kitty!

Gestern vor dem Essen habe ich meinen Brief in Vaters Tasche gesteckt. Nach dem Lesen war er den ganzen Abend durcheinander, hat Margot gesagt (ich war oben beim Spülen). Armer Pim, ich hätte wissen müssen, welche Wirkung diese Epistel haben würde. Er ist so empfindsam! Sofort habe ich zu Peter gesagt, dass er nichts mehr fragen oder sagen solle. Pim hat kein Wort zu mir gesagt. Ob es noch kommt?

Hier geht's wieder so einigermaßen. Was Jan, Kugler und Kleiman von den Menschen und den Preisen draußen erzählen, ist kaum zu glauben. Ein halbes Pfund Tee kostet 350 Gulden, ein halbes Pfund Kaffee 80 Gulden, Butter 35 Gulden das Pfund, ein Ei 1.45 Gulden. Für bulgarischen Tabak werden 14 Gulden je Unze bezahlt! Jeder treibt Schwarzhandel, jeder Laufjunge bietet etwas an. Unser Bäckerjunge hat Stopfseide besorgt, 90 Cent für ein dünnes Strängchen. Der Milchmann kommt an illegale Lebensmittelkarten, ein Beerdigungsunternehmen besorgt Käse. Jeden Tag wird eingebrochen, ermordet, gestohlen. Polizisten und Nachtwächter sind ebenso beteiligt wie Berufsdiebe. Jeder will etwas in den Bauch bekommen. Und da Gehaltserhöhungen verboten sind, müssen die Leute wohl oder übel schwindeln. Die Jugendpolizei ist dauernd beschäftigt. Junge Mädchen von fünfzehn, sechzehn, siebzehn, achtzehn Jahren und älter werden jeden Tag vermisst.

Ich will versuchen, die Geschichte von der Fee Ellen fertig zu machen. Zum Spaß könnte ich sie Vater zum Geburtstag schenken, mit allen Urheberrechten. Auf Wiedersehen (das ist eigentlich falsch, bei der deutschen Sendung aus England sagen sie »auf Wiederhören«, ich müsste also schreiben »auf Wiederschreiben«).

Deine Anne M. Frank

Sonntagmorgen, 7. Mai 1944

Liebe Kitty!

Vater und ich haben gestern Nachmittag ein langes Gespräch gehabt. Ich musste schrecklich weinen, und er auch. Weißt du, was er zu mir gesagt hat, Kitty?

»Ich habe schon viele Briefe in meinem Leben bekommen, aber dieser ist der hässlichste. Du, Anne, die du so viel Liebe von deinen Eltern empfangen hast, von Eltern, die immer für dich bereit stehen, die dich immer verteidigt haben, was auch war, du sprichst davon, keine Verantwortung zu fühlen. Du fühlst dich zurückgesetzt und allein gelassen. Nein, Anne, das war ein großes Unrecht, das du uns angetan hast. Vielleicht hast du es nicht so gemeint, aber so hast du es geschrieben. Nein, Anne, einen solchen Vorwurf haben <u>wir</u> nicht verdient!«

269

Ach, ich habe einen schrecklichen Fehler gemacht. Das ist wohl das Schlimmste, was ich in meinem Leben getan habe. Ich wollte nur angeben mit meinem Weinen und meinen Tränen, mich nur aufspielen, damit er Respekt vor mir hat. Sicher, ich habe viel Kummer gehabt, und was Mutter betrifft, ist alles wahr. Aber den guten Pim so zu beschuldigen, ihn, der alles für mich getan hat und noch für mich tut, nein, das war mehr als gemein.

Es ist ganz gut, dass ich mal aus meiner unerreichbaren Höhe heruntergeholt worden bin, dass mein Stolz mal angeknackst worden ist. Ich war wieder viel zu eingenommen von mir selbst. Was Fräulein Anne tut, ist längst nicht immer richtig! Jemand, der einem anderen, den er zu lieben behauptet, einen solchen Kummer zufügt, und das auch noch vorsätzlich, ist niedrig, sehr niedrig!

Am meisten schäme ich mich über die Art, in der Vater mir vergeben hat. Er wird den Brief in den Ofen werfen und ist jetzt so lieb zu mir, als ob er etwas falsch gemacht hätte. Nein, Anne, du musst noch schrecklich viel lernen. Fange erst mal wieder damit an, statt auf andere hinunterzuschauen und andere zu beschuldigen!

Ich habe viel Kummer gehabt, aber hat das nicht jeder in meinem Alter? Ich habe viel Komödie gespielt, aber ich war mir dessen noch nicht mal bewusst. Ich fühlte mich einsam, war aber fast nie verzweifelt. Ich muss mich tief schämen, und ich schäme mich tief.

Geschehen ist geschehen, aber man kann Weiteres verhindern. Ich will wieder von vorn anfangen, und es kann nicht schwer sein, da ich jetzt Peter habe. Mit ihm als Unterstützung <u>kann</u> ich es. Ich bin nicht mehr allein, er liebt mich, ich liebe ihn, ich habe meine Bücher, mein Geschichtenbuch, mein Tagebuch, ich bin nicht besonders hässlich, nicht besonders dumm, habe eine fröhliche Natur und will einen guten Charakter bekommen. Ja, Anne, du hast sehr gut gefühlt, dass dein Brief zu hart und unwahr war, aber du warst noch stolz darauf. Ich will mir Vater wieder zum Vorbild nehmen, und ich <u>werde</u> mich bessern.

Deine Anne M. Frank

Montag, 8. Mai 1944

Liebe Kitty!
Habe ich dir eigentlich schon mal was von unserer Familie erzählt? Ich glaube nicht, und deshalb werde ich sofort damit anfangen. Vater wurde in Frankfurt geboren, als Sohn steinreicher Eltern. Michael Frank hatte eine Bank und war Millionär geworden, und Alice Stern, Vaters Mutter, war von sehr vornehmen und reichen Eltern. Michael Frank war in seiner Jugend nicht reich gewesen, hat sich aber ordentlich hochgearbeitet. Vater führte in seiner Jugend ein richtiges Reicher-Eltern-Sohn-Leben, jede Woche Partys, Bälle, Feste, schöne Mädchen, Tanzen, Diners, viele Zimmer und so weiter. All das Geld ging nach Opas Tod verloren, nach dem Weltkrieg und der Inflation war nichts mehr davon übrig. Aber es gab noch genug reiche Verwandte. Vater ist folglich prima-prima erzogen worden und musste gestern schrecklich lachen, weil er das erste Mal in seinem 55-jährigen Leben bei Tisch die Bratpfanne ausgekratzt hat.
Mutter war nicht so reich, aber doch auch ganz wohlhabend, und deshalb hören wir oft mit offenem Mund die Geschichten von Verlobungen mit 250 Gästen, von privaten Bällen und Diners.
Reich kann man uns auf keinen Fall mehr nennen, aber meine Hoffnung richtet sich auf die Zeit nach dem Krieg. Ich versichere dir, dass ich keinesfalls auf ein so beschränktes Leben aus bin, wie Mutter und Margot sich das wünschen. Ich würde gern ein Jahr nach Paris und ein Jahr nach London gehen, um Sprachen zu lernen und Kunstgeschichte zu studieren. Vergleich das mal mit Margot, die Säuglingsschwester in Palästina werden will. Ich male mir immer schöne Kleider und interessante Menschen aus. Ich will etwas sehen und erleben in der Welt, das habe ich dir schon öfter gesagt, und ein bisschen Geld kann dabei nicht schaden!

Miep hat heute Morgen von der Verlobung ihrer Nichte erzählt, wo sie am Samstag war. Die Nichte ist eine Tochter reicher Eltern, der Bräutigam hat noch reichere Eltern. Miep machte uns den Mund wässrig mit der Beschreibung des Essens, das sie bekamen: Gemüsesuppe mit Fleischklößchen, Käse, Brötchen mit Hackfleisch, Horsd'œuvres mit Eiern und Roastbeef, Käsebrötchen, Moskauer Gebäck,

Wein und Zigaretten, und von allem so viel, wie man wollte. Miep hat zehn Gläser Schnaps getrunken und drei Zigaretten geraucht. Ist das die Antialkoholikerin? Wenn Miep schon soviel getrunken hat, wie viel wird sich ihr Gatte dann hinter die Binde gegossen haben? Sie waren natürlich alle etwas angeheitert. Unter den Gästen waren auch zwei Polizisten von der Mordkommission, die Fotos von dem Paar gemacht haben. Du siehst, dass Miep ihre Versteckten keine Minute vergisst, denn sie hat sich gleich Namen und Adresse von diesen Leuten notiert, für den Fall, dass etwas passiert und man gute Niederländer nötig hat.

Sie hat uns wirklich den Mund wässrig gemacht, uns, die wir zum Frühstück nur zwei Löffel Brei bekommen haben, denen die Mägen knurren vor Hunger, die wir tagein, tagaus nichts bekommen als halbrohen Spinat (wegen der Vitamine) und angefaulte Kartoffeln, die wir in unseren leeren Magen nichts anderes als Salat, Kochsalat, Spinat und noch mal Spinat stopfen. Vielleicht werden wir noch mal so stark wie Popeye, obwohl ich davon noch nicht viel merke!

Wenn Miep uns zu dieser Verlobung mitgenommen hätte, dann wäre von den Brötchen nichts für die anderen Gäste übrig geblieben. Wenn wir auf jenem Fest gewesen wären, hätten wir sicher alles geplündert und sogar die Möbel nicht auf ihrem Platz gelassen. Ich kann dir sagen, wir haben Miep die Worte aus der Nase gezogen, wir standen um sie herum, als hätten wir noch nie in unserem Leben von gutem Essen und eleganten Menschen gehört. Und das sind die Enkelinnen eines bekannten Millionärs! Es geht schon verrückt zu in der Welt!

Deine Anne M. Frank

Dienstag, 9. Mai 1944

Liebe Kitty!

Die Geschichte »Ellen, die Fee« ist fertig. Ich habe sie auf schönem Briefpapier abgeschrieben, mit roter Tinte verziert und die Blätter aneinander genäht. Das Ganze sieht jetzt hübsch aus, aber ich weiß nicht, ob es nicht etwas wenig ist. Margot und Mutter haben jede ein Geburtstagsgedicht gemacht.

Herr Kugler kam heute mit der Nachricht herauf, dass Frau Broks (eine frühere Mitarbeiterin) ab Montag jeden Tag hier zwei Stunden

Mittagspause machen möchte. Stell dir vor! Niemand kann mehr heraufkommen, Kartoffeln können nicht geliefert werden, Bep bekommt kein Essen, wir können nicht aufs Klo, wir dürfen uns nicht rühren und was es sonst noch für Unannehmlichkeiten gibt. Wir kamen mit den ausgefallensten Vorschlägen, um sie abzuwimmeln. Van Daan meinte, ein gutes Abführmittel in ihren Kaffee würde vielleicht reichen. »Nein«, antwortete Herr Kleiman, »bitte nicht, dann kommt sie überhaupt nicht mehr runter vom Thron!«

Schallendes Gelächter. »Vom Thron?«, fragte Frau van Daan. »Was bedeutet das?«

Eine Erklärung folgte. »Kann man das Wort immer benützen?«, fragte sie ziemlich albern.

Bep kicherte. »Stellt euch vor, sie fragt im Bijenkorf nach dem Thron! Sie würden sie nicht mal begreifen.«

Dussel sitzt täglich prompt um halb eins »auf dem Thron«, um den Ausdruck mal beizubehalten. Heute Mittag nahm ich beherzt ein Stück rosa Papier und schrieb:

Toiletten-Dienstplan für Herrn Dussel
Morgens 7.15–7.30
Mittags <u>nach 1 Uhr</u>
Ansonsten nach Wunsch!

Diesen Zettel befestigte ich auf der grünen Klotür, als Dussel noch darauf saß. Ich hätte leicht dazuschreiben können: Bei Übertretung dieses Gesetzes wird Einsperrung verhängt. Denn unsere Toilette kann man von innen und von außen abschließen.

Das ist der neueste Witz von van Daan:
Anlässlich der Bibelstunde und der Geschichte mit Adam und Eva fragt ein 13-jähriger Junge seinen Vater: »Sag mal, Vater, wie bin ich eigentlich geboren worden?«

»Na ja«, antwortet der Vater, »der Storch hat dich aus dem großen Wasser geholt, zu Mutter ins Bett gelegt und sie fest ins Bein gepickt. Deshalb hat sie geblutet und musste über eine Woche im Bett bleiben.«

Um es noch genauer zu erfahren, fragt der Junge auch seine Mutter:

»Sag mal, Mutter, wie bist du eigentlich geboren worden und wie bin ich geboren worden?«

Seine Mutter erzählt ihm dieselbe Geschichte, woraufhin der Junge, um wirklich alles zu erfahren, auch noch zu seinem Großvater geht. »Sag mal, Großvater, wie bist du geboren worden und wie ist deine Tochter geboren worden?« Zum dritten Mal hört er die gleiche Geschichte.

Abends schreibt er in sein Tagebuch: »Nach gründlichem Sammeln von Informationen muss ich feststellen, dass in unserer Familie während dreier Generationen kein Geschlechtsverkehr stattgefunden hat.«

Ich muss noch arbeiten, es ist schon drei Uhr.

Deine Anne M. Frank

P. S. Da ich dir schon von der neuen Putzfrau berichtet habe, will ich noch kurz hinzufügen, dass die Dame verheiratet ist, sechzig Jahre alt und schwerhörig! Sehr sympathisch im Hinblick auf eventuelle Geräusche, die von acht Versteckten durchdringen könnten.

O Kit, es ist so schönes Wetter. Könnte ich doch hinaus!

Mittwoch, 10. Mai 1944

Liebe Kitty!

Wir saßen gestern Nachmittag auf dem Dachboden und lernten Französisch, als ich plötzlich hinter mir ein Plätschern hörte. Ich fragte Peter, was das zu bedeuten hätte, aber er antwortete nicht mal, rannte zum Trockenboden, zum Ort des Unheils, und stieß Mouschi, die sich neben ihr zu nasses Katzenklo gesetzt hatte, mit einer groben Bewegung auf den richtigen Fleck. Ein lautes Spektakel folgte, und Mouschi, die fertig gepinkelt hatte, rannte hinunter. Sie hatte sich, um noch ein wenig katzenkloartige Bequemlichkeit zu empfinden, über einen Spalt auf dem porösen Oberbodengrund auf ein bisschen Holzwolle gesetzt. Die Pfütze lief sofort durch die Decke zum Dachboden und unglücklicherweise direkt in und neben unsere Kartoffeltonne. Die Decke triefte, und da der Dachboden auch nicht frei von Löchern ist, fielen einige gelbe Tropfen auch durch die Decke in das Zimmer, zwischen einen Stapel Strümpfe und ein Buch, die auf dem Tisch lagen.

Ich bog mich vor Lachen. Der Anblick war auch zu komisch, die geduckte Mouschi unter einem Stuhl, Peter mit Wasser, Chlorpulver und Lappen, und Herr van Daan am Beschwichtigen. Das Unglück war schon bald behoben. Aber es ist eine bekannte Tatsache, dass Katzenurin schrecklich stinkt. Das bewiesen die Kartoffeln gestern nur allzu deutlich, auch die Holzspäne, die Vater in einem Eimer herunterbrachte, um sie zu verbrennen.

Arme Mouschi! Woher sollst du wissen, dass kein Torfmull zu bekommen ist? Anne

Donnerstag, 11. Mai 1944

Liebe Kitty!

Etwas Neues zum Lachen!

Peters Haare mussten geschnitten werden. Die Haarschneiderin wollte, wie üblich, seine Mutter sein. Fünf Minuten vor halb acht verschwand Peter in seinem Zimmer und kam um halb acht wieder heraus, pudelnackt bis auf eine blaue Badehose und Turnschuhe.

»Kommst du mit?«, fragte er seine Mutter.

»Ja, aber ich suche die Schere.«

Peter half suchen und wühlte dabei in Frau van Daans Toilettenschublade. »Mach doch nicht so ein Durcheinander«, murrte sie.

Peters Antwort konnte ich nicht verstehen, sie muss auf jeden Fall frech gewesen sein, denn Frau van Daan gab ihm einen Klaps auf den Arm. Er gab ihr einen zurück. Sie schlug mit aller Kraft, und Peter zog mit einem komischen Gesicht seinen Arm zurück. »Komm mit, Alte!«

Frau van Daan blieb stehen. Peter packte sie an den Handgelenken und zog sie durch das ganze Zimmer. Frau van Daan weinte, lachte, schimpfte und strampelte, aber es half nichts. Peter führte seine Gefangene bis zur Dachbodentreppe, wo er sie loslassen musste. Frau van Daan kehrte ins Zimmer zurück und ließ sich laut seufzend auf einen Stuhl fallen.

»Die Entführung der Mutter«, witzelte ich.

»Ja, aber er hat mir wehgetan.«

Ich schaute nach und kühlte ihre heißen, roten Handgelenke mit etwas Wasser. Peter, noch an der Treppe, wurde wiederum ungeduldig. Mit seinem Gürtel in der Hand kam er wie ein Tierbändiger ins Zimmer. Aber Frau van Daan ging nicht mit. Sie blieb am Schreibtisch sitzen und suchte nach einem Taschentuch. »Du musst mich erst um Entschuldigung bitten«, sagte sie.

»Na gut, dann bitte ich dich hiermit um Entschuldigung, weil es sonst so spät wird.«

Frau van Daan musste gegen ihren Willen lachen, stand auf und ging zur Tür. Hier fühlte sie sich genötigt, uns erst noch eine Erklärung zu geben. (Uns, das waren Vater, Mutter und ich, wir waren gerade beim Abwaschen.)

»Zu Hause war er nicht so«, sagte sie. »Ich hätte ihm eine verpasst, dass er die Treppe runterfliegt (!). Er ist nie so frech gewesen, er hat auch mehr Schläge bekommen. Das ist nun die moderne Erziehung! Ich hätte meine Mutter nie so angepackt. Sind Sie so mit Ihrer Mutter umgegangen, Herr Frank?« Sie war aufgeregt, lief hin und her, fragte und sagte alles Mögliche und machte immer noch keine Anstalten, hinaufzugehen. Endlich trollte sie sich.

Es dauerte keine fünf Minuten, da stürmte sie mit geblähten Backen wieder herunter, warf ihre Schürze hin, antwortete auf meine Frage, ob sie fertig sei, dass sie kurz hinuntergehe, und sauste wie ein Wirbelwind die Treppe hinunter. Vermutlich in die Arme von ihrem Putti. Sie kam erst um acht Uhr herauf, ihr Mann kam mit. Peter wurde vom Dachboden geholt, bekam eine gehörige Standpauke. Schimpfworte wie Flegel, Bengel, ungezogen, schlechtes Vorbild, Anne ist ..., Margot macht ... Mehr konnte ich nicht verstehen. Vermutlich ist heute schon wieder alles in Butter.

Deine Anne M. Frank

P. S. Dienstag und Mittwoch sprach unsere geliebte Königin. Sie macht Urlaub, um gestärkt in die Niederlande zurückkehren zu können. Sie sprach von »Bald, wenn ich zurück bin ... baldige Befreiung ... Heldenmut und schwere Lasten«.

Eine Rede von Minister Gerbrandy folgte. Dieser Mann hat ein so nörgelndes Kinderstimmchen, dass Mutter unwillkürlich »och« sagte. Ein Pastor, der seine Stimme von Herrn Edel geklaut hat, beschloss den Abend mit einer Bitte an Gott, dass er für die Juden, die Menschen in Konzentrationslagern, in den Gefängnissen und in Deutschland sorgen möge.

Liebe Kitty!

Da ich meine ganze »Kramschachtel«, also auch den Füller, oben vergessen habe und ich sie in ihrem Schlafstündchen (bis halb drei) nicht stören kann, musst du jetzt mit einem Bleistiftbrief vorlieb nehmen.

Ich habe im Augenblick schrecklich viel zu tun, und so verrückt es auch klingt, ich habe zu wenig Zeit, um durch meinen Berg Arbeit durchzukommen. Soll ich dir erzählen, was ich alles tun muss? Also: Bis morgen muss ich den ersten Teil der Lebensgeschichte von Galileo Galilei auslesen, da das Buch zur Bibliothek zurück muss. Gestern habe ich damit angefangen, jetzt bin ich auf Seite 220. Es hat 320, also schaffe ich es. Nächste Woche muss ich »Palästina am Scheideweg« und den zweiten Teil von Galilei lesen. Außerdem habe ich den ersten Teil der Biographie von Kaiser Karl V. ausgelesen und muss dringend meine vielen Notizen und Hinweise auf die Stammbäume ausarbeiten. Und dann habe ich auch drei Seiten mit Fremdwörtern aus den verschiedenen Büchern herausgeholt, die alle eingeschrieben, aufgesagt und gelernt werden müssen. Nr. 4 ist, dass meine Filmstars schrecklich ungeordnet sind und nach Aufräumen schreien. Da das aber mehrere Tage in Anspruch nehmen würde und Professor Anne im Augenblick, wie schon gesagt, in Arbeit erstickt, wird das Chaos weiter ein Chaos bleiben. Dann warten Theseus, Ödipus, Peleus, Orpheus, Jason und Herkules auf ein gründliches Ordnen, da ihre verschiedenen Taten wie bunte Fäden in meinem Kopf durcheinander liegen. Auch Mykon und Phidias bedürfen dringend einer Behandlung, damit ihr Zusammenhang erhalten bleibt. Ebenso geht es z. B. mit dem Sieben- und dem Neunjährigen Krieg. Ich werfe auf diese Weise alles durcheinander. Ja, was soll man auch mit so einem Gedächtnis anfangen? Stell dir mal vor, wie vergesslich ich erst mit achtzig sein werde! Ach ja, noch was, die Bibel! Wie lange wird es wohl noch dauern, bis ich zu der Geschichte von der badenden Susanne komme? Und was war die Schuld von Sodom und Gomorrha? Ach, es gibt noch so schrecklich viel zu fragen und zu lernen! Und Lieselotte von der Pfalz habe ich ganz im Stich gelassen!

Kitty, siehst du, dass ich überlaufe?

Nun etwas anderes: Du weißt längst, dass es mein liebster Wunsch ist, einmal Journalistin und später eine berühmte Schriftstellerin zu werden. Ob ich diese größenwahnsinnigen (oder wahnsinnigen) Neigungen je ausführen kann, das wird sich noch zeigen müssen, aber Themen habe ich bis jetzt genug. Nach dem Krieg will ich auf jeden Fall ein Buch mit dem Titel »Das Hinterhaus« herausgeben. Ob mir das gelingt, ist auch die Frage, aber mein Tagebuch wird mir als Grundlage dienen können.

Cadys Leben muss auch fertig werden. Ich habe mir die Fortsetzung so gedacht, dass Cady nach ihrer Genesung das Sanatorium verlässt und mit Hans in Briefwechsel bleibt. Das ist 1941. Bald entdeckt sie dann, dass Hans zur NSB* neigt, und da Cady mit den Juden und ihrer Freundin Marianne großes Mitleid hat, entsteht eine Entfremdung zwischen ihnen. Nach einem Treffen, bei dem sie sich erst wieder versöhnt hatten, kommt es zum Bruch, und Hans bekommt ein anderes Mädchen. Cady ist tief gebrochen und wird, um eine richtige Arbeit zu haben, Krankenschwester. Auf Drängen von Freunden ihres Vaters geht sie in die Schweiz, um dort in einem Lungensanatorium zu arbeiten. In ihrem ersten Urlaub fährt sie zum Comer See, wo sie zufällig Hans trifft. Er erzählt ihr, dass er vor zwei Jahren geheiratet hat, Cadys Nachfolgerin, dass sich seine Frau aber in einem Anfall von Schwermut das Leben genommen hat. An ihrer Seite hat er erst gemerkt, wie sehr er Cady geliebt hatte, und nun hält er aufs Neue um ihre Hand an. Cady lehnt ab, obwohl sie ihn, gegen ihren Willen, immer noch liebt. Ihr Stolz hält sie zurück. Hans zieht daraufhin weg, und Jahre später hört Cady, dass er, mehr krank als gesund, in England gelandet ist.

Cady selbst heiratet mit 27 Jahren einen wohlhabenden Landbewohner, Simon. Sie fängt an, ihn sehr zu lieben, aber doch nie so sehr wie Hans. Sie bekommt zwei Töchter und einen Sohn, Lilian, Judith und Nico. Simon und sie sind glücklich miteinander, aber immer bleibt Hans im Hintergrund von Cadys Denken, bis sie eines Nachts von ihm träumt und Abschied von ihm nimmt.

Das ist kein sentimentaler Unsinn, denn Vaters Lebensroman ist darin verarbeitet.
Deine Anne M. Frank

* Nationalsozialistische Bewegung der Niederlande; A. d. Ü.

Liebste Kitty!

Gestern hatte Vater Geburtstag, und Vater und Mutter waren 19 Jahre verheiratet. Es war kein Putzfrau-Tag, und die Sonne schien, wie sie 1944 noch nie geschienen hat. Unser Kastanienbaum steht von unten bis oben in voller Blüte und ist viel schöner als im vergangenen Jahr.

Vater hat von Kleiman eine Biographie über das Leben von Linnaeus bekommen, von Kugler auch ein naturgeschichtliches Buch, von Dussel »Amsterdam zu Wasser«, von den van Daans eine riesige Schachtel, aufgemacht wie vom besten Dekorateur, mit drei Eiern, einer Flasche Bier, einem Joghurt und einer grünen Krawatte. Unser Glas Sirup fiel dagegen schon etwas ab. Die Rosen von mir riechen herrlich, im Gegensatz zu Mieps und Beps roten Nelken. Er ist ziemlich verwöhnt worden. Vom Bäcker sind 50 Törtchen gekommen, herrlich! Vater spendierte außerdem noch Kräuterkuchen und Bier für die Herren, für die Damen Joghurt. Alle waren zufrieden!

Deine Anne M. Frank

Liebste Kitty!

Zur Abwechslung (weil wir es so lange nicht gehabt haben) will ich dir von einer kleinen Diskussion erzählen, die Herr und Frau van Daan gestern Abend hatten.

Frau van Daan: »Die Deutschen werden den Atlantik-Wall inzwischen wohl sehr stark gemacht haben. Sie werden sicher alles tun, was in ihrer Macht steht, um die Engländer zurückzuhalten. Es ist enorm, wie viel Kraft die Deutschen haben.«

Herr van Daan: »O ja, schrecklich!«

Frau van Daan: »Ja-ah!«

Herr van Daan: »Bestimmt werden die Deutschen am Ende noch den Krieg gewinnen, so stark sind sie.«

Frau van Daan: »Das kann gut sein, ich bin vom Gegenteil noch nicht überzeugt.«

Herr van Daan: »Ich sollte lieber nicht antworten.«

Frau van Daan: »Du antwortest doch immer wieder, du lässt dich doch immer wieder hinreißen.«

Herr van Daan: »Aber nein, ich antworte wenig.«

Frau van Daan: »Aber du antwortest doch, und du musst auch immer Recht haben! Dabei stimmen deine Voraussagen längst nicht immer.«

Herr van Daan: »Bis jetzt haben meine Voraussagen immer gestimmt.«

Frau van Daan: »Das ist nicht wahr. Bei dir war die Invasion schon im vorigen Jahr, die Finnen hatten schon Frieden, Italien war im Winter schon zu Ende, und die Russen hatten schon Lemberg! O nein, auf deine Voraussagen gebe ich nicht viel.«

Herr van Daan (aufstehend): »Und jetzt halt endlich mal dein großes Maul! Ich werde dir noch beweisen, dass ich Recht habe. Einmal wirst du noch genug bekommen. Ich kann das Gezeter nicht mehr hören, ich werde dich mit der Nase auf all deine Hänseleien stoßen!« *(Ende erster Akt)*

Ich musste eigentlich schrecklich lachen, Mutter auch, und Peter verbiss es sich ebenfalls. O die dummen Erwachsenen. Sie sollten lieber selbst anfangen zu lernen, bevor sie so viel an den Kindern auszusetzen haben!

Deine Anne

P. S. Seit Freitag sind die Fenster wieder offen.

Wofür sich die Bewohner des Hinterhauses interessieren:
(Systematische Übersicht der Lern- und Lesefächer)

Herr van Daan: lernt nichts; schlägt viel im Knaur nach; liest gern Detektivromane, medizinische Bücher, spannende und belanglose Liebesgeschichten.

Frau van Daan: lernt Englisch in schriftlichen Kursen; liest gern Biographien und einige Romane.

Herr Frank: lernt Englisch (Dickens!), etwas Latein; liest nie Romane, aber gern ernsthafte und trockene Beschreibungen von Personen und Ländern.

Frau Frank: lernt Englisch in schriftlichen Kursen; liest alles, außer Detektivgeschichten.

Herr Dussel: Lernt Englisch, Spanisch und Niederländisch ohne nennenswertes Ergebnis; liest alles, urteilt mit der Mehrheit.

Peter van Daan: Lernt Englisch, Französisch (schriftlich), niederlän-

disch Steno, englisch Steno, deutsch Steno, englische Handelskorres-
pondenz, Holzbearbeitung, Wirtschaftslehre, ab und zu Rechnen;
liest wenig, manchmal erdkundliche Sachen.

Margot Frank: Lernt Englisch, Französisch, Latein nach schriftlichen Kursen, englisch Steno, deutsch Steno, niederländisch Steno,
Mechanik, Trigonometrie, Physik, Chemie, Algebra, Geometrie,
englische Literatur, französische Literatur, deutsche Literatur, niederländische Literatur, Buchhaltung, Erdkunde, neue Geschichte,
Biologie, Ökonomie; liest alles, am liebsten Bücher über Religion
und Heilkunde.

Anne Frank: lernt Französisch, Englisch, Deutsch, niederländisch
Steno, Geometrie, Algebra, Geschichte, Erdkunde, Kunstgeschichte,
Mythologie, Biologie, biblische Geschichte, niederländische Literatur;
liest sehr gern Biographien (trocken oder spannend), geschichtliche
Bücher, manchmal Romane und Unterhaltungsliteratur.

Freitag, 19. Mai 1944

Liebe Kitty!

Gestern war mir elend, übergeben (und das bei Anne!), Kopfweh,
Bauchweh, alles, was du dir nur vorstellen kannst. Heute geht es wieder besser. Ich habe großen Hunger, aber von den braunen Bohnen,
die wir heute essen, werde ich mich fern halten.

Mit Peter und mir geht es prima. Der arme Junge hat ein noch größe-
res Bedürfnis nach Zärtlichkeit als ich. Er wird noch immer jeden
Abend rot beim Gutenachtkuss und bettelt um noch einen. Ob ich
nur ein Ersatz für Moffi bin? Ich finde es nicht schlimm. Er ist so
glücklich, seit er weiß, dass jemand ihn gern hat.

Ich stehe nach meiner mühsamen Eroberung ein bisschen über der
Situation, aber glaube ja nicht, dass meine Liebe abgeflaut ist. Er ist
ein Schatz, aber mein Inneres habe ich schnell wieder zugeschlossen.
Wenn er jetzt noch mal das Schloss aufbrechen will, muss das Brech-
eisen schon stärker sein!   Deine Anne M. Frank

Liebe Kitty!

Gestern Abend kam ich vom Dachboden herunter und sah sofort, dass die schöne Vase mit Nelken auf dem Boden lag. Mutter lag auf den Knien und wischte auf, Margot fischte meine Papiere vom Boden. »Was ist hier passiert?«, fragte ich mit ängstlicher Vorahnung, und ohne die Antwort abzuwarten, betrachtete ich aus einiger Entfernung den Schaden. Meine Stammbäume, Mappen, Hefte, Bücher, alles schwamm. Ich weinte fast und war so aufgeregt, dass ich anfing, Deutsch zu sprechen. An meine Worte kann ich mich nicht mehr erinnern, aber Margot sagte, dass ich etwas von mir gab wie »unübersehbarer Schaden, schrecklich, entsetzlich, nie wieder gutzumachen« und Ähnliches. Vater brach in Gelächter aus, Mutter und Margot fielen ein, aber ich hätte weinen können wegen der verlorenen Arbeit und den gut ausgearbeiteten Anmerkungen.

Bei näherer Betrachtung war der »unübersehbare Schaden« zum Glück nicht so schlimm. Sorgfältig sortierte ich auf dem Dachboden die zusammengeklebten Papiere und machte sie los. Dann hängte ich sie nebeneinander an die Wäscheleine zum Trocknen. Es war ein lustiger Anblick, und ich musste dann doch wieder lachen. Maria de Medici neben Karl V., Wilhelm von Oranien und Marie Antoinette.

»Das ist Rassenschande«, witzelte Herr van Daan.

Nachdem ich Peter die Fürsorge für meine Papiere anvertraut hatte, ging ich wieder hinunter.

»Welche Bücher sind hin?«, fragte ich Margot, die gerade meine Bücher kontrollierte.

»Algebra«, sagte Margot.

Aber das Algebrabuch war leider Gottes doch nicht kaputt. Ich wollte, es wäre mitten in die Vase gefallen! Noch nie habe ich ein Buch so verabscheut wie dieses. Vorn drin stehen mindestens 20 Namen von Mädchen, die es vor mir besessen haben. Es ist alt, gelb, vollgekritzelt, durchgestrichen und verbessert. Wenn ich mal sehr übermütig bin, reiße ich das Drecksding in Stücke!

Deine Anne M. Frank

Liebe Kitty!

Vater hat am 20. Mai fünf Flaschen Joghurt bei einer Wette an Frau van Daan verloren. Die Invasion ist noch nicht gekommen. Ich kann ruhig sagen, dass ganz Amsterdam, die ganzen Niederlande, ja die ganze Westküste Europas bis Spanien hinunter Tag und Nacht über die Invasion spricht, debattiert, darüber Wetten abschließt und darauf hofft. Die Spannung steigt und steigt. Längst nicht alle, die wir zu den »guten« Niederländern rechnen, haben das Vertrauen in die Engländer bewahrt, längst nicht alle finden den englischen Bluff ein Meisterstück. O nein, die Menschen wollen nun endlich mal Taten sehen, große und heldenhafte Taten!

Niemand denkt weiter, als seine Nase lang ist, niemand denkt daran, dass die Engländer für sich selbst und ihr Land kämpfen. Jeder meint nur, dass sie verpflichtet sind, die Niederlande so schnell wie möglich zu retten. Welche Verpflichtungen haben die Engländer denn? Womit haben die Holländer die edelmütige Hilfe verdient, die sie so fest erwarten? Dass die Niederländer sich nur nicht irren! Die Engländer haben sich trotz ihres Bluffs bestimmt nicht mehr blamiert als all die anderen Länder und Ländchen, die nun besetzt sind. Die Engländer werden sicher nicht um Entschuldigung bitten. Sie haben geschlafen, während Deutschland sich bewaffnete, aber all die anderen Länder, die Länder, die an Deutschland grenzen, haben auch geschlafen. Mit Vogel-Strauß-Politik kommt man nicht weiter. Das hat England und das hat die ganze Welt gesehen, und alle, nicht zuletzt England, müssen schwer dafür büßen.

Kein Land wird seine Männer umsonst opfern, auch England nicht. Die Invasion, die Befreiung und die Freiheit werden einmal kommen. Doch England kann den Zeitpunkt bestimmen, nicht die besetzten Gebiete.

Zu unserem großen Leidwesen und zu unserem großen Entsetzen haben wir gehört, dass die Stimmung uns Juden gegenüber bei vielen Leuten umgeschlagen ist. Wir haben gehört, dass Antisemitismus jetzt auch in Kreisen aufkommt, die früher nie daran gedacht hätten. Das hat uns tief, tief getroffen. Die Ursache von diesem Judenhass ist verständlich, manchmal sogar menschlich, aber trotzdem nicht richtig. Die Christen werfen den Juden vor, dass sie sich bei den Deutschen verplappern, dass sie ihre Helfer verraten, dass viele Christen durch die Schuld von Juden das schreckliche Los und die schreckliche Strafe von so vielen erleiden müssen. Das ist wahr. Aber sie müssen (wie bei allen Dingen) auch die Kehrseite der Medaille betrachten. Würden die Christen an unserer Stelle anders handeln? Kann ein Mensch, egal ob Jude oder Christ, bei den deutschen Methoden schweigen? Jeder weiß, dass dies fast unmöglich ist. Warum verlangt man das Unmögliche dann von den Juden?

In Kreisen des Untergrunds wird darüber gemunkelt, dass deutsche Juden, die in die Niederlande emigriert waren und jetzt in Polen sind, nicht mehr in die Niederlande zurückkommen dürfen. Sie hatten hier Asylrecht, müssen aber, wenn Hitler weg ist, wieder nach Deutschland zurück.

Wenn man das hört, fragt man sich dann nicht unwillkürlich, warum dieser lange und schwere Krieg geführt wird? Wir hören doch immer, dass wir alle zusammen für Freiheit, Wahrheit und Recht kämpfen! Fängt jetzt noch während des Kampfes schon wieder die Zwietracht an? Ist ein Jude doch wieder weniger als die anderen? Oh, es ist traurig, sehr traurig, dass wieder, zum soundsovielten Mal, der alte Spruch bestätigt wird: Was ein Christ tut, muss er selbst verantworten, was ein Jude tut, fällt auf alle Juden zurück.

Ehrlich gesagt, ich kann es nicht begreifen, dass Niederländer, Angehörige eines so guten, ehrlichen und rechtschaffenen Volkes, so über uns urteilen, über das vielleicht am meisten unterdrückte, unglücklichste und bedauernswerteste Volk der Welt.

Ich hoffe nur, dass dieser Judenhass vorübergehender Art ist, dass die Niederländer doch noch zeigen werden, wer sie sind, dass sie jetzt und nie in ihrem Rechtsgefühl wanken werden. Denn das ist ungerecht! Und wenn das Schreckliche tatsächlich Wahrheit werden sollte, dann wird das armselige Restchen Juden die Niederlande verlassen. Wir auch. Wir werden mit unserem Bündelchen weiterziehen, weg aus diesem schönen Land, das uns so herzlich Unterschlupf angeboten hat und uns nun den Rücken zukehrt.

Ich liebe die Niederlande. Ich habe einmal gehofft, dass es mir, der Vaterlandslosen, ein Vaterland werden wird. Ich hoffe es noch!

Deine Anne M. Frank

Liebe Kitty!

Bep hat sich verlobt! Die Tatsache an sich ist nicht so erstaunlich, obwohl sich keiner von uns sehr darüber freut. Bertus mag ein solider, netter und sportlicher Junge sein, aber Bep liebt ihn nicht, und das ist für mich Grund genug, ihr von der Hochzeit abzuraten. Beps ganzes Streben ist darauf gerichtet, sich hochzuarbeiten, und Bertus zieht sie hinunter. Er ist ein Arbeiter, ohne Interessen und ohne Drang, vorwärtszukommen, und ich glaube nicht, dass Bep sich dabei glücklich fühlen wird. Es ist verständlich, dass Bep mit diesen Halbheiten endlich Schluss machen will. Vor vier Wochen hat sie ihm einen Abschiedsbrief geschrieben, fühlte sich aber noch unglücklicher, und deshalb hat sie ihm wieder geschrieben. Und jetzt hat sie sich verlobt.

Viele Faktoren spielen dabei eine Rolle. Erstens der kranke Vater, der viel von Bertus hält, zweitens, dass sie die Älteste von den Vossen-Mädchen ist und ihre Mutter sie neckt, weil sie noch keinen Mann hat, drittens, dass sie jetzt noch 24 Jahre alt ist, und darauf legt Bep viel Wert.

Mutter sagt, sie hätte es besser gefunden, wenn Bep ein Verhältnis mit ihm angefangen hätte. Ich kann das nicht sagen. Ich habe Mitleid mit Bep und verstehe, dass sie sich einsam fühlt. Heiraten können sie sowieso erst nach dem Krieg, da Bertus illegal lebt, und sie haben beide noch keinen Cent und keine Aussteuer. Was für eine triste Aussicht für Bep, der wir alle so viel Gutes wünschen. Ich hoffe nur, dass Bertus sich unter ihrem Einfluss ändert oder dass Bep noch einen netten Mann findet, der sie schätzt!   Deine Anne M. Frank

<u>Am selben Tag</u>

Jeden Tag was anderes! Heute Morgen ist unser Gemüsehändler verhaftet worden, er hatte zwei Juden im Haus. Das ist ein schwerer Schlag für uns, nicht nur, dass die armen Juden jetzt am Rand des Abgrunds stehen, auch für ihn ist es schrecklich. Die Welt steht hier auf dem Kopf. Die anständigsten Menschen werden in Konzentrationslager, Gefängnisse und einsame Zellen geschickt, und der Abschaum regiert über Jung und Alt, Arm und Reich. Der Eine fliegt durch den Schwarzhandel auf, der Zweite dadurch, dass er Juden versteckt hat. Niemand, der nicht bei der NSB ist, weiß, was morgen passiert.

Auch für uns ist die Verhaftung des Mannes ein schwerer Verlust. Bep kann und darf die Mengen Kartoffeln nicht anschleppen. Das Einzige, was wir tun können, ist, weniger zu essen. Wie das gehen wird, schreibe ich dir noch, aber angenehm wird es sicher nicht sein. Mutter sagt, dass wir morgens kein Frühstück bekommen, mittags Brei und Brot, abends Bratkartoffeln und eventuell ein- oder zweimal die Woche Gemüse oder Salat, mehr nicht. Das heißt hungern. Aber alles ist nicht so schlimm, wie entdeckt zu werden.

Deine Anne M. Frank

Freitag, 26. Mai 1944

Liebste Kitty!

Endlich, endlich bin ich so weit, dass ich ruhig an meinem Tischchen vor dem spaltbreit offenen Fenster sitzen und dir alles schreiben kann.

Ich fühle mich so elend wie seit Monaten nicht, sogar nach dem Einbruch war ich innerlich und äußerlich nicht so kaputt. Einerseits: der Gemüsemann, die Judenfrage, die im ganzen Haus ausführlich besprochen wird, die ausbleibende Invasion, das schlechte Essen, die Spannung, die miserable Stimmung, die Enttäuschung wegen Peter, und andererseits: Beps Verlobung, Pfingstempfänge, Blumen, Kuglers Geburtstag, Torten und Geschichten von Kabaretts, Filmen und Konzerten. Diesen Unterschied, diesen großen Unterschied gibt es immer. An einem Tag lachen wir über das Komische an unserer Untertauchsituation, aber am nächsten Tag, an viel mehr Tagen, haben wir Angst, und man kann die Spannung und die Verzweiflung auf unseren Gesichtern lesen. Miep und Kugler spüren am stärksten die Last, die wir ihnen machen, Miep durch ihre Arbeit und Kugler durch die kolossale Verantwortung für uns acht, eine Verantwortung, die ihm manchmal zu groß wird. Dann kann er fast nicht mehr sprechen vor unterdrückter Nervosität und Aufregung. Kleiman und Bep sorgen auch gut für uns, sehr gut sogar, aber sie können das Hinterhaus manchmal vergessen, auch wenn es nur für ein paar Stunden oder einen Tag oder zwei ist. Sie haben ihre eigenen Sorgen, Kleiman wegen seiner Gesundheit, Bep wegen ihrer Verlobung, die gar nicht so rosig aussieht. Und neben diesen Sorgen haben sie auch ihre Abwechslung, Ausgehen, Besuche, das Leben von normalen Menschen. Bei ihnen weicht die Spannung manchmal, auch wenn es nur für kurze Zeit ist. Bei uns weicht sie niemals, zwei Jahre lang nicht. Und wie lange wird sie uns noch drücken?

Die Kanalisation ist wieder verstopft. Es darf kein Wasser ablaufen, wenn, dann nur tropfenweise. Wir dürfen nicht zum Klo oder müssen eine Bürste mitnehmen. Das schmutzige Wasser bewahren wir in einem großen Steinguttopf auf. Für heute können wir uns behelfen, aber was ist, wenn der Klempner es nicht allein schafft? Die von der Stadt kommen nicht vor Dienstag.

Miep hat uns ein Rosinenbrot mit der Aufschrift »Fröhliche Pfingsten« geschickt. Das klingt fast wie Spott, unsere Stimmung und unsere Angst sind wirklich nicht »fröhlich«.

Wir sind ängstlicher geworden nach der Angelegenheit mit dem Gemüsehändler. Von allen Seiten hört man wieder »pst«, alles geschieht leiser. Die Polizei hat dort die Tür aufgebrochen, davor sind wir also auch nicht sicher. Wenn auch wir einmal … Nein, das darf ich nicht schreiben, aber die Frage lässt sich heute nicht wegschieben, im Gegenteil. All die einmal durchgemachte Angst steht wieder mit ihrem ganzen Schrecken vor mir.

Heute Abend um acht Uhr musste ich alleine nach unten, zum Klo. Niemand war unten, alle saßen am Radio. Ich wollte mutig sein, aber es war schwer. Ich fühle mich hier oben noch immer sicherer als allein in dem großen, stillen Haus. Allein mit diesen Poltergeräuschen von oben und dem Tuten der Autohupen auf der Straße. Ich fange an zu zittern, wenn ich mich nicht beeile und auch nur einen Moment über die Situation nachdenke.

Miep ist nach dem Gespräch mit Vater viel netter und herzlicher zu uns geworden. Aber das habe ich dir noch gar nicht erzählt. Miep kam eines Nachmittags mit feuerrotem Kopf zu Vater und fragte ihn geradeheraus, ob wir annähmen, dass sie auch vom Antisemitismus angesteckt wären. Vater erschrak gewaltig und redete ihr den Verdacht aus. Aber etwas ist hängen geblieben. Sie kaufen mehr für uns ein, interessieren sich mehr für unsere Schwierigkeiten, obwohl wir ihnen damit sicher nicht zur Last fallen dürfen. Es sind doch so herzensgute Menschen!

Ich frage mich immer wieder, ob es nicht besser für uns alle gewesen wäre, wenn wir nicht untergetaucht wären, wenn wir nun tot wären und dieses Elend nicht mitmachen müssten und es vor allem den anderen ersparten. Aber auch davor scheuen wir zurück. Wir lieben das Leben noch, wir haben die Stimme der Natur noch nicht vergessen, wir hoffen noch, hoffen auf alles.

Lass nur schnell was passieren, notfalls auch Schießereien. Das kann uns auch nicht mehr zermürben als diese Unruhe! Lass das Ende kommen, auch wenn es hart ist, dann wissen wir wenigstens, ob wir letztlich siegen werden oder untergehen.

Deine Anne M. Frank

Mittwoch, 31. Mai 1944

Liebe Kitty!

Samstag, Sonntag, Montag und Dienstag war es so warm, dass ich keinen Füller in der Hand halten konnte, darum war es mir auch unmöglich, dir zu schreiben. Am Freitag war die Kanalisation kaputt, am Samstag ist sie gerichtet worden. Nachmittags hat uns Frau Kleiman besucht und eine ganze Menge von Jopie erzählt, unter anderem, dass sie mit Jacque van Maarssen in einem Hockey-Club ist. Am Sonntag kam Bep und schaute nach, ob nicht eingebrochen war, und blieb zum Frühstück bei uns. Am Montag, dem zweiten Pfingstfeiertag, tat Herr van Santen Dienst als Versteckbewacher, und am Dienstag durften die Fenster endlich wieder geöffnet werden. So ein schönes, warmes, man kann ruhig sagen heißes Pfingsten hat es selten gegeben. Hitze ist hier im Hinterhaus schrecklich. Um dir einen Eindruck von den vielen Klagen zu verschaffen, werde ich dir kurz die warmen Tage beschreiben:

Samstag: »Herrlich, was für ein Wetter!«, sagten wir morgens alle. »Wenn es nur etwas weniger warm wäre«, sagten wir mittags, als die Fenster geschlossen werden mussten.

Sonntag: »Nicht auszuhalten, diese Hitze! Die Butter schmilzt, es gibt kein kühles Fleckchen im Haus, das Brot wird trocken, die Milch verdirbt, kein Fenster darf geöffnet werden. Wir armen Ausgestoßenen sitzen hier und ersticken, während die anderen Leute Pfingstferien haben.« (So Frau van Daan.)

Montag: »Meine Füße tun mir weh, ich habe keine dünnen Kleider, ich kann bei dieser Hitze nicht abwaschen.« Geklage von morgens früh bis abends spät, es war äußerst unangenehm.

Ich kann noch immer keine Hitze aushalten und bin froh, dass heute der Wind ordentlich bläst und die Sonne trotzdem scheint.

Deine Anne M. Frank

Freitag, 2. Juni 1944

Beste Kitty!

»Wer zum Dachboden geht, soll einen großen Regenschirm mitnehmen, am besten ein Herrenmodell!« Dies zum Schutz vor Regen, der von oben kommt. Es gibt ja ein Sprichwort, das heißt: »Hoch und trocken, heilig und sicher.« Aber es gilt bestimmt nicht für Kriegszeiten (Schießen) und Versteckte (Katzenklo!). Tatsächlich hat sich Mouschi eine Gewohnheit daraus gemacht, ihr Geschäft auf ein paar Zeitungen oder zwischen die Bodenritzen zu deponieren, sodass nicht nur die Angst vor Geplätscher, sondern eine noch größere Furcht vor entsetzlichem Gestank sehr begründet ist. Weiß man nun, dass auch das neue Moortje aus dem Lager an dem gleichen Laster leidet, dann kann sich sicher jeder, der je eine nicht stubenreine Katze gehabt hat, vorstellen, was für Gerüche durch unser Haus schweben.

Ferner habe ich noch ein brandneues Anti-Schieß-Rezept mitzuteilen. Bei lautem Knallen eile man zur nächstgelegenen Holztreppe, renne diese hinunter und wieder hinauf und sorge dafür, dass man bei einer Wiederholung mindestens einmal nach unten fällt. Mit den so entstandenen Schrammen und dem Lärm, den das Laufen und Fallen macht, hat man genug zu tun, um das Schießen weder zu hören noch daran zu denken. Die Schreiberin dieser Zeilen hat dieses Rezept mit viel Erfolg angewandt!

Deine Anne M. Frank

Montag, 5. Juni 1944

Liebe Kitty!

Neue Unannehmlichkeiten im Hinterhaus. Streit zwischen Dussel und Franks über die Butterverteilung. Kapitulation Dussels. Dicke Freundschaft zwischen Frau van Daan und Letztgenanntem, Flirten,

Küsschen und freundliches Lächeln. Dussel fängt an, Sehnsucht nach Frauen zu bekommen.

Van Daans wollen keinen Kräuterkuchen für Kuglers Geburtstag backen, weil wir selbst auch keinen essen. Wie kleinlich! Oben schlechte Laune. Frau van Daan erkältet. Dussel hat Bierhefepillen ergattert, wir bekommen nichts ab.

Einnahme von Rom durch die fünfte Armee. Die Stadt ist weder verwüstet noch bombardiert worden. Riesenpropaganda für Hitler.

Wenig Gemüse und Kartoffeln, ein Paket Brot verdorben.

Die neue Lagerkatze verträgt keinen Pfeffer, nimmt das Katzenklo als Schlafplatz und benutzt die Holzwolle zum Verpacken als Klo. Unmöglich zu behalten.

Das Wetter ist schlecht. Anhaltende Bombardierungen auf Pas de Calais und die französische Küste.

Dollars lassen sich nicht verkaufen, Gold noch weniger, der Boden der schwarzen Kasse ist schon zu sehen. Wovon werden wir nächsten Monat leben?   Deine Anne

Dienstag, 6. Juni 1944

Liebste Kitty!

»This is D-day«, sagte um zwölf Uhr das englische Radio, und mit Recht! »This is <u>the</u> day«, die Invasion hat begonnen!

Heute Morgen um acht Uhr berichteten die Engländer: Schwere Bombardements auf Calais, Boulogne, Le Havre und Cherbourg sowie Pas de Calais (wie üblich). Ferner Sicherheitsmaßnahmen für die besetzten Gebiete: Alle Menschen, die in einer Zone von 35 km von der Küste wohnen, müssen sich auf Bombardierungen vorbereiten. Wenn möglich, werden die Engländer eine Stunde vorher Flugblätter abwerfen.

Deutschen Berichten zufolge sind englische Fallschirmtruppen an der französischen Küste gelandet. »Englische Landungsschiffe im Kampf mit deutschen Marinesoldaten«, sagt der BBC.

Entscheidung vom Hinterhaus beim Frühstück um neun Uhr: »Dies ist eine Probelandung, genau wie vor zwei Jahren bei Dieppe.« Sendungen in Deutsch, Niederländisch, Französisch und anderen Sprachen um zehn Uhr: »The invasion has begun!« Also doch die »echte« Invasion.

Englische Sendung – in Deutsch – um elf Uhr: Rede von Oberbefehlshaber General Dwight Eisenhower.

Englische Sendung – in Englisch – um zwölf Uhr: »This is D-day.« General Eisenhower sprach zum französischen Volk: »Stiff fighting will come now, but after this the victory. The year 1944 is the year of complete victory, good luck!«

Englische Sendung – in Englisch – um ein Uhr: 11 000 Flugzeuge stehen bereit und fliegen unaufhörlich hin und her, um Truppen abzusetzen und hinter den Linien zu bombardieren. 4000 Landefahrzeuge und kleinere Schiffe legen unaufhörlich zwischen Cherbourg und Le Havre an. Englische und amerikanische Truppen sind schon in schwere Gefechte verwickelt. Reden von Gerbrandy, vom belgischen Premierminister, von König Haakon von Norwegen, de Gaulle für Frankreich, dem König von England und, nicht zu vergessen, von Churchill.

Das Hinterhaus ist in Aufruhr. Sollte denn nun wirklich die lang ersehnte Befreiung nahen, die Befreiung, über die so viel gesprochen wurde, die aber zu schön, zu märchenhaft ist, um je wirklich werden zu können? Sollte dieses Jahr, dieses 1944, uns den Sieg schenken? Wir wissen es noch nicht, aber die Hoffnung belebt uns, gibt uns wieder Mut, macht uns wieder stark. Denn mutig müssen wir die vielen Ängste, Entbehrungen und Leiden durchstehen. Nun kommt es darauf an, ruhig und standhaft zu bleiben, lieber die Nägel ins Fleisch zu drücken, als laut zu schreien. Schreien vor Elend können Frankreich, Russland, Italien und auch Deutschland, aber wir haben nicht das Recht dazu!

Kitty, das Schönste an der Invasion ist, dass ich das Gefühl habe, dass Freunde im Anzug sind. Die schrecklichen Deutschen haben uns so lange unterdrückt und uns das Messer an die Kehle gesetzt, dass Freunde und Rettung alles für uns sind. Nun gilt es nicht mehr den Juden, nun gilt es den Niederlanden und dem ganzen besetzten Europa.

Vielleicht, sagt Margot, kann ich im September oder Oktober doch wieder zur Schule gehen.   Deine Anne M. Frank

P. S. Ich werde dich mit den neuesten Berichten auf dem Laufenden halten! Nachts und am frühen Morgen landeten Stroh- und Schaufensterpuppen hinter den deutschen Stellungen. Diese Puppen explodierten, als sie den Boden berührten. Auch viele Fallschirmjäger landeten. Sie waren schwarz angemalt, um nicht aufzufallen. Morgens um sechs Uhr landeten die ersten Schiffe, nachdem die Küste in der Nacht mit 5 Millionen Kilogramm Bomben bombardiert worden war. 20 000 Flugzeuge waren heute in Aktion. Die Küstenbatterien der Deutschen waren bei der Landung selbst schon kaputt, ein kleiner Brückenkopf ist schon gebildet worden. Alles geht gut, obwohl das Wetter schlecht ist. Die Armee und auch das Volk sind »one will and one hope«.

Freitag, 9. Juni 1944

Liebe Kitty!
Mit der Invasion geht es oberprima! Die Alliierten haben Bayeux eingenommen, ein kleines Dorf an der französischen Küste, und kämpfen jetzt um Caën. Es ist klar, dass sie beabsichtigen, die Halbinsel abzuschneiden, auf der Cherbourg liegt. Jeden Abend erzählen Kriegsberichterstatter von den Schwierigkeiten, dem Mut und der Begeisterung der Armee. Die unglaublichsten Dinge passieren. Auch Verwundete, die schon wieder in England sind, waren am Mikrophon. Trotz des miserablen Wetters wird fleißig geflogen. Vom BBC haben wir gehört, dass Churchill die Invasion zusammen mit den Truppen beginnen wollte, nur auf Anraten von Eisenhower und anderen Generälen ist aus dem Plan nichts geworden. Stell dir mal vor, was für ein Mut von so einem alten Mann! Er ist doch sicher schon 70 Jahre alt.
Hier hat sich die Aufregung etwas gelegt. Trotzdem hoffen wir, dass der Krieg Ende des Jahres endlich vorbei sein wird. Es wird auch Zeit. Frau van Daans Gejammer ist kaum mehr zum Anhören. Nachdem sie uns jetzt nicht mehr mit der Invasion verrückt machen kann, nörgelt sie den ganzen Tag über das schlechte Wetter. Ich hätte Lust, sie in einem Eimer kaltes Wasser auf den Dachboden zu stellen!

Das ganze Hinterhaus, mit Ausnahme von van Daan und Peter, hat die Trilogie »Ungarische Rhapsodie« gelesen. Dieses Buch behandelt die Lebensgeschichte des Komponisten, Klaviervirtuosen und Wunderkindes Franz Liszt. Das Buch ist sehr interessant, aber meiner Ansicht nach wird ein bisschen zu viel über Frauen gesprochen. Liszt war zu seiner Zeit nicht nur der größte und bekannteste Pianist, sondern bis zu seinem 70. Lebensjahr auch der größte Schürzenjäger. Er hatte ein Verhältnis mit Marie d'Agoult, Fürstin Caroline Sayn-Wittgenstein, der Tänzerin Lola Montez, der Pianistin Sophie Monter, mit der Tscherkessenfürstin Olga Janina, der Baronesse Olga Meyendorff, der Schauspielerin Lilla ich-weiß-nicht-wie-sie-heißt usw. usw. Es nimmt überhaupt kein Ende. Die Teile des Buches, wo es um Musik und andere Künste geht, sind viel interessanter. In dem Buch kommen vor: Schumann und Clara Wieck, Hector Berlioz, Johannes Brahms, Beethoven, Joachim, Richard Wagner, Hans von Bülow, Anton Rubinstein, Frederic Chopin, Victor Hugo, Honoré de Balzac, Hiller, Hummel, Czerny, Rossini, Cherubini, Paganini, Mendelssohn und viele andere.

Liszt war an sich ein toller Kerl, sehr großzügig, bescheiden für sich, obwohl übermäßig eitel, half jedem, kannte nichts Höheres als die Kunst, war versessen auf Kognak und auf Frauen, konnte keine Tränen sehen, war ein Gentleman, konnte niemandem einen Gefallen abschlagen, gab nichts auf Geld, hielt viel von der Religionsfreiheit und von der Welt.

Deine Anne M. Frank

Dienstag, 13. Juni 1944

Liebe Kitty!
Der Geburtstag ist wieder vorbei, jetzt bin ich also 15. Ich habe ziemlich viel bekommen: Die fünf Bände Springers Kunstgeschichte, eine Garnitur Unterwäsche, zwei Gürtel, ein Taschentuch, zwei Joghurts, ein Glas Marmelade, 2 Honigkuchen (klein), ein Pflanzenkundebuch von Vater und Mutter, ein Doubléarmband von Margot, ein Buch von den van Daans, Biomalz und Gartenwicken Dussel, Süßigkeiten Miep, Süßigkeiten und Hefte Bep, und als Höhepunkt das Buch »Maria Theresia« und drei Scheiben vollfetten Käse von Kugler. Von Pe-

ter einen schönen Strauß Pfingstrosen. Der arme Junge hat sich so viel Mühe gegeben, etwas zu finden, aber nichts hat geklappt.

Mit der Invasion geht es immer noch hervorragend, trotz des miserablen Wetters, der zahllosen Stürme, der Regengüsse und der stürmischen See.

Churchill, Smuts, Eisenhower und Arnold waren gestern in den französischen Dörfern, die von den Engländern erobert und befreit worden sind. Churchill war auf einem Torpedoboot, das die Küste beschoss. Der Mann scheint, wie so viele Männer, keine Angst zu kennen. Beneidenswert!

Die Stimmung in den Niederlanden ist von unserer Hinterburg aus nicht einzuschätzen. Zweifellos sind die Menschen froh, dass das nichtstuende (!) England nun endlich auch mal die Ärmel hochkrempelt. Wie ungerecht sie argumentieren, erkennen die Leute nicht, wenn sie immer wieder sagen, dass sie hier keine englische Besatzung haben wollen. Alles in allem läuft das darauf hinaus: England muss kämpfen, streiten und seine Söhne für die Niederlande und andere besetzte Gebiete aufopfern. Die Engländer dürfen aber nicht in den Niederlanden bleiben, müssen allen besetzten Staaten ihren untertänigsten Dank anbieten, müssen Niederländisch-Indien dem ursprünglichen Eigentümer zurückgeben und dürfen dann, geschwächt und arm, nach England zurückkehren. Ein armer Tölpel, der sich das so vorstellt, und doch müssen viele Niederländer zu diesen Tölpeln gerechnet werden. Was, frage ich, wäre aus den Niederlanden und den benachbarten Ländern geworden, wenn England den so oft möglichen Frieden mit Deutschland unterzeichnet hätte? Die Niederlande wären deutsch geworden, und damit basta!

Alle Niederländer, die nun noch auf die Engländer hinunterschauen, England und die Alte-Herren-Regierung beschimpfen, die Engländer feige nennen, aber doch die Deutschen hassen, müssten mal aufgeschüttelt werden, wie man ein Kissen aufschüttelt. Vielleicht legen sich die verwirrten Gehirne dann in etwas richtigere Falten!

Viele Wünsche, viele Gedanken, viele Beschuldigungen und viele Vorwürfe spuken in meinem Kopf herum. Ich bin wirklich nicht so eingebildet, wie viele Leute meinen. Ich kenne meine zahllosen Fehler und Mängel besser als jeder andere, nur mit dem Unterschied, dass ich auch weiß, dass ich mich bessern will, mich bessern werde und mich schon sehr gebessert habe.

Wie kommt es nur, frage ich mich oft, dass jeder mich noch immer so schrecklich vorlaut und unbescheiden findet? Bin ich so vorlaut? Bin <u>ich</u> es wirklich, oder sind es nicht vielleicht auch die anderen? Das klingt verrückt, ich merke es, aber ich streiche den letzten Satz nicht durch, weil er wirklich nicht so verrückt ist. Frau van Daan und Dussel, meine hauptsächlichen Ankläger, sind beide bekannt als unintelligent und, spreche ich es ruhig mal aus, dumm! Dumme Menschen können es meist nicht ertragen, wenn andere etwas besser machen als sie selbst. Das beste Beispiel sind in der Tat die beiden Dummen, Frau van Daan und Dussel.

Frau van Daan findet mich dumm, weil ich nicht so schrecklich an diesem Übel leide wie sie, sie findet mich unbescheiden, weil sie noch unbescheidener ist, sie findet meine Kleider zu kurz, weil die ihren noch kürzer sind, und darum findet sie mich auch vorlaut, weil sie selbst doppelt so viel bei Themen mitredet, von denen sie überhaupt nichts versteht. Dasselbe gilt für Dussel.

Aber einer meiner Lieblingssprüche ist: »An jedem Vorwurf ist auch etwas Wahres«, und so gebe ich auch prompt zu, dass ich vorlaut bin. Nun ist das Lästige an meiner Natur, dass ich von niemandem so viele Standpauken bekomme und so viel ausgeschimpft werde wie von mir selbst. Wenn Mutter dann noch ihre Portion Ratschläge dazugibt, wird der Stapel Predigten so unüberwindlich hoch, dass ich vor lauter Verzweiflung, je herauszukommen, frech werde und widerspreche, und dann ist das bekannte und schon so alte Anne-Wort wieder da: »Niemand versteht mich!«

Dieses Wort ist in mir, und so unwahr es auch scheinen mag, auch darin ist ein Zipfelchen Wahrheit. Meine Selbstbeschuldigungen nehmen oft so einen Umfang an, dass ich nach einer tröstenden Stimme lechze, die alles wieder zurechtrückt und sich auch etwas aus meinem Innenleben macht. Aber da kann ich leider lange suchen, gefunden ist derjenige noch nicht.

Ich weiß, dass du jetzt an Peter denkst, nicht wahr, Kitty? Es ist wahr, Peter hat mich gern, nicht als Verliebter, sondern als Freund. Seine Zuneigung steigt mit jedem Tag. Aber was das Geheimnisvolle ist, das uns beide zurückhält, verstehe ich selbst nicht.

Manchmal denke ich, dass mein schreckliches Verlangen nach ihm übertrieben war. Aber es ist nicht so. Wenn ich mal zwei Tage nicht oben war, sehne ich mich wieder genauso heftig nach ihm wie zuvor. Peter ist lieb und gut, trotzdem, ich darf es nicht leugnen, enttäuscht mich vieles. Vor allem seine Abkehr von der Religion, seine Gespräche über Essen und noch andere so widersprüchliche Dinge gefallen mir nicht. Trotzdem bin ich fest davon überzeugt, dass wir nach unserer ehrlichen Abmachung nie Streit bekommen werden. Peter ist friedliebend, verträglich und sehr nachgiebig. Er lässt sich von mir viel mehr sagen, als er seiner Mutter zugesteht. Er versucht mit viel Hartnäckigkeit, die Tintenflecke aus seinen Büchern zu entfernen und Ordnung in seinen Sachen zu halten. Aber warum bleibt sein Inneres dann innen, und ich darf nie daran rühren? Er ist viel verschlossener als ich, das ist wahr. Aber ich weiß nun wirklich aus der Praxis, dass sogar die verschlossenen Naturen zu gegebener Zeit genauso stark oder noch stärker nach einem Vertrauten verlangen.
Peter und ich haben beide unsere Denk-Jahre im Hinterhaus verbracht. Wir reden oft über Zukunft, Vergangenheit und Gegenwart, aber, wie gesagt, ich vermisse das Echte und weiß doch sicher, dass es da ist!

Liegt es daran, dass ich meine Nase so lange nicht in die frische Luft stecken konnte, dass ich so versessen auf alles bin, was Natur ist? Ich weiß noch sehr gut, dass ein strahlend blauer Himmel, zwitschernde Vögel, Mondschein und blühende Blumen früher meine Aufmerksamkeit lange nicht so gefesselt haben. Hier ist das anders geworden. Ich habe z. B. an Pfingsten, als es so warm war, abends mit Gewalt die Augen offen gehalten, um gegen halb zwölf am offenen Fenster den Mond mal richtig und allein betrachten zu können. Leider führte dieses Opfer zu nichts, denn der Mond war zu hell, ich durfte kein offenes Fenster riskieren. Ein andermal, es ist schon ein paar Monate her, war ich zufällig abends oben, als das Fenster offen war. Ich ging nicht eher zurück, bis das Lüften vorbei war. Der dunkle, regnerische Abend, der Sturm, die jagenden Wolken hielten mich gefangen. Nach anderthalb Jahren hatte ich zum ersten Mal wieder die Nacht von Angesicht zu Angesicht gesehen. Nach diesem Abend war meine Sehnsucht, das noch mal zu sehen, größer als meine Angst vor Dieben und dem dunklen Rattenhaus oder Überfällen. Ich ging ganz allein hinunter und schaute aus dem Fenster vom Privatbüro und von der Küche.

Viele Menschen finden die Natur schön, viele schlafen mal unter freiem Himmel, viele ersehnen in Gefängnissen oder Krankenhäusern den Tag, an dem sie wieder frei die Natur genießen können, aber wenige sind mit ihrer Sehnsucht so abgeschlossen und isoliert von dem, was für Arme und Reiche dasselbe ist.

Es ist keine Einbildung, dass die Betrachtung des Himmels, der Wolken, des Mondes und der Sterne mich ruhig und abwartend macht. Dieses Mittel ist besser als Baldrian und Brom. Die Natur macht mich demütig und bereit, alle Schläge mutig zu ertragen.

Es hat so sein müssen, dass ich die Natur nur ausnahmsweise durch dick verstaubte und mit schmutzigen Vorhängen versehene Fenster sehen darf. Und da durchzuschauen, ist kein Vergnügen mehr. Die Natur ist das Einzige, das wirklich kein Surrogat vertragen kann!

Eine der vielen Fragen, die mich nicht in Ruhe lassen, ist, warum früher und auch jetzt noch oft die Frauen bei den Völkern einen so viel geringeren Platz einnehmen als der Mann. Jeder kann sagen, dass das ungerecht ist, aber damit bin ich nicht zufrieden. Ich würde so gern die Ursache dieses großen Unrechts wissen.

Es ist anzunehmen, dass der Mann von Anfang an durch seine größere Körperkraft die Herrschaft über die Frau ausgeübt hat. Der Mann, der verdient, der Mann, der die Kinder zeugt, der Mann, der alles darf … All die Frauen waren dumm genug, dass sie das bis vor einiger Zeit still haben geschehen lassen, denn je mehr Jahrhunderte diese Regel lebt, umso fester fasst sie Fuß. Zum Glück sind den Frauen durch Schule, Arbeit und Bildung die Augen geöffnet worden. In vielen Ländern haben Frauen gleiche Rechte bekommen. Viele Menschen, Frauen vor allem, aber auch Männer, sehen nun ein, wie falsch diese Einteilung der Welt so lange Zeit war. Die modernen Frauen wollen das Recht zur völligen Unabhängigkeit.

Aber das ist es nicht allein: Die Würdigung der Frau muss kommen! Überall wird der Mann hoch geschätzt, warum darf die Frau nicht zuallererst daran teilhaben? Soldaten und Kriegshelden werden geehrt und gefeiert, Entdecker erlangen unsterblichen Ruhm, Märtyrer werden angebetet. Aber wer betrachtet die Frau auch als Kämpferin?

In dem Buch »Streiter für das Leben« steht etwas, das mich sehr berührt hat, ungefähr so: Frauen machen im Allgemeinen allein mit dem Kinderkriegen mehr Schmerzen durch, mehr Krankheiten und mehr Elend, als welcher Kriegsheld auch immer. Und was bekommt sie dafür, wenn sie all die Schmerzen durchgestanden hat? Sie wird in eine Ecke geschoben, wenn sie durch die Geburt entstellt ist, ihre Kinder gehören schon bald nicht mehr ihr, ihre Schönheit ist weg. Frauen sind viel tapferere, mutigere Soldaten, die mehr kämpfen und für den Fortbestand der Menschheit mehr Schmerzen ertragen als die vielen Freiheitshelden mit ihrem großen Mund!

Ich will damit überhaupt nicht sagen, dass Frauen sich gegen Kinderkriegen auflehnen sollen, im Gegenteil. So ist die Natur eingerichtet, und so wird es gut sein. Ich verurteile nur die Männer und die ganze Ordnung der Welt, die sich noch nie Rechenschaft darüber abgeben wollten, welchen großen, schweren, aber zeitweilig auch schönen Anteil die Frauen in der Gesellschaft tragen.

Paul de Kruif, der Autor des Buches, hat völlig Recht, wenn er sagt, dass die Männer lernen müssen, dass in den Teilen der Welt, die kultiviert genannt werden, eine Geburt aufgehört hat, etwas Natürliches und Normales zu sein. Die Männer haben leicht reden, sie haben die Unannehmlichkeiten der Frauen nie ertragen müssen und werden es auch nie tun müssen.

Die Ansicht, dass es die Pflicht der Frauen ist, Kinder zu bekommen, wird sich, glaube ich, im Lauf des nächsten Jahrhunderts verändern. Sie wird einer Würdigung und Bewunderung für diejenige Platz machen, die ohne Murren und große Worte die Lasten auf ihre Schultern nimmt! Deine Anne M. Frank

Freitag, 16. Juni 1944

Liebe Kitty!

Neue Probleme! Frau van Daan ist verzweifelt, spricht von: Kugel durch den Kopf, Gefängnis, Aufhängen und Selbstmord. Sie ist eifersüchtig, dass Peter mir sein Vertrauen schenkt und nicht ihr, sie ist beleidigt, dass Dussel nicht genug auf ihre Flirtereien eingeht, sie hat Angst, dass ihr Mann ihr ganzes Pelzmantel-Geld aufraucht, streitet, schimpft, weint, beklagt sich, lacht und fängt dann wieder Streit an.

Was soll man mit so einer greinenden und verrückten Person anfangen? Von niemandem wird sie ernst genommen. Charakter hat sie nicht, klagt bei jedem und läuft herum: von hinten Lyzeum, von vorne Museum. Dabei ist noch das Schlimmste, dass Peter frech wird, Herr van Daan gereizt und Mutter zynisch. Was für ein Zustand! Es gibt nur eine Regel, die du dir gut vor Augen halten musst: Lache über alles und störe dich nicht an den anderen! Es scheint egoistisch, ist aber in Wirklichkeit das einzige Heilmittel für Selbstmitleid.

Kugler muss vier Wochen schippen gehen. Er versucht, durch ein ärztliches Attest und einen Brief der Firma freizukommen. Kleiman will sich bald einer Magenoperation unterziehen. Gestern Abend um elf Uhr sind alle privaten Telefonanschlüsse abgestellt worden.

Deine Anne M. Frank

Freitag, 23. Juni 1944

Liebe Kitty!

Hier ist nichts Besonderes los. Die Engländer haben den großen Angriff auf Cherbourg begonnen. Laut Pim und van Daan sind wir am 10. Oktober bestimmt frei. Die Russen nehmen an der Aktion teil und haben gestern ihre Offensive bei Witebsk begonnen, genau auf den Tag drei Jahre nach dem deutschen Einfall.

Beps Laune ist noch immer unter Null. Wir haben fast keine Kartoffeln mehr. In Zukunft wollen wir sie für die Einzelnen abzählen, dann kann jeder selbst entscheiden, was er macht. Miep nimmt eine Woche Urlaub. Kleimans Ärzte haben auf den Röntgenaufnahmen nichts gefunden. Jetzt schwankt er zwischen Operieren und Allem-seinen-Lauf-lassen.

Deine Anne M. Frank

Dienstag, 27. Juni 1944

Liebste Kitty!

Die Stimmung ist umgeschlagen, es geht enorm gut. Cherbourg, Witebsk und Slobin sind heute gefallen. Sicher viel Beute und Gefangene. Fünf deutsche Generäle sind bei Cherbourg gefallen, zwei gefangen genommen. Nun können die Engländer an Land bringen, was sie wollen, denn sie haben einen Hafen. Die Halbinsel Cotentin drei Wochen nach der Invasion englisch, eine gewaltige Leistung!

In den drei Wochen nach D-day ist noch kein Tag ohne Regen und Sturm gewesen, sowohl hier als in Frankreich, aber dieses Pech hindert die Engländer und Amerikaner nicht, ihre Kraft zu zeigen, und wie zu zeigen! Wohl ist die WUWA (Wunderwaffe) in voller Aktion, aber was bedeutet diese Art Katzenschelle anderes als etwas Schaden in England und volle Zeitungen bei den Moffen. Übrigens, wenn sie in »Mofrika« merken, dass die bolschewistische Gefahr jetzt wirklich im Anmarsch ist, werden sie noch mehr Bammel bekommen.

Alle deutschen Frauen und Kinder, die nicht für die Wehrmacht arbeiten, werden aus dem Küstenstreifen nach Groningen, Friesland und Gelderland evakuiert. Mussert hat erklärt, dass er die Uniform anzieht, wenn die Invasion bis hierher kommt. Will der Dicke etwa kämpfen? Das hätte er schon früher tun können, in Russland. Finnland hat seinerzeit das Friedensangebot abgelehnt, und jetzt sind entsprechende Unterhandlungen wieder abgebrochen worden. Was werden sie das noch bereuen, diese Dummköpfe!

Was glaubst du, wie weit wir am 27. Juli sind?

Deine Anne M. Frank

Freitag, 30. Juni 1944

Liebe Kitty!

Schlechtes Wetter oder bad weather from one at a stretch to thirty June. Ist das nicht gut? Oh, ich kann schon ein bisschen Englisch. Um das zu beweisen, lese ich »An ideal Husband« (mit Wörterbuch). Krieg hervorragend: Bobruisk, Mogilew und Orscha gefallen, viele Gefangene.

Hier alles all right. Die Stimmung steigt. Unsere Hyperoptimisten triumphieren, die van Daans zaubern mit dem Zucker, Bep hat ihre Frisur geändert, und Miep hat eine Woche frei. Das sind die letzten Neuigkeiten.

Ich bekomme eine ekelhafte Nervenbehandlung, noch dazu an einem Schneidezahn. Es hat schon schrecklich wehgetan und war sogar so schlimm, dass Dussel dachte, ich würde umkippen. Es hat nicht viel gefehlt. Prompt hat Frau van Daan auch Zahnweh bekommen!

Deine Anne M. Frank

P. S. Wir haben von Basel gehört, dass Bernd* die Rolle des Wirts in »Minna von Barnhelm« gespielt hat. Künstlerische Neigungen, sagt Mutter.

Donnerstag, 6. Juli 1944

Liebe Kitty!

Mir wird bang ums Herz, wenn Peter davon spricht, dass er später vielleicht Verbrecher wird oder anfängt zu spekulieren. Obwohl es natürlich als Witz gemeint ist, habe ich doch das Gefühl, dass er selbst Angst vor seiner Charakterschwäche hat. Immer wieder höre ich sowohl von Margot als auch von Peter: »Ja, wenn ich so stark und mutig wäre wie du, wenn ich so meinen Willen durchsetzen könnte, wenn ich so eine ausdauernde Energie hätte, ja, dann …!«

Ist es wirklich eine gute Eigenschaft, dass ich mich nicht beeinflussen lasse? Ist es gut, dass ich fast ausschließlich dem Weg meines eigenen Gewissens folge?

Ehrlich gesagt, ich kann mir nicht richtig vorstellen, wie jemand sagen kann »Ich bin schwach« und dann auch schwach bleibt. Wenn man so etwas doch schon weiß, warum dann nicht dagegen angehen, warum den Charakter nicht trainieren? Die Antwort war: »Weil es so viel bequemer ist.« Diese Antwort hat mich ein bisschen missmutig gemacht. Bequem? Bedeutet ein faules und betrügerisches Leben auch, dass es ein bequemes Leben ist? O nein, das kann nicht wahr sein! Es darf nicht sein, dass Bequemlichkeit und Geld so schnell verführen können. Ich habe lange darüber nachgedacht, was ich dann

* Cousin Bernhard (genannt Buddy) Elias; A. d. Ü.

wohl für eine Antwort geben muss, wie ich Peter dazu bringen soll, an sich selbst zu glauben und, vor allem, sich selbst zu bessern. Ob mein Gedankengang richtig ist, weiß ich nicht.

Ich habe mir oft vorgestellt, wie toll es wäre, wenn mir jemand sein Vertrauen schenkt, aber nun, da es soweit ist, sehe ich erst, wie schwierig es ist, mit den Gedanken des anderen zu denken und dann die richtige Antwort zu finden. Vor allem deshalb, weil die Begriffe »bequem« und »Geld« für mich etwas vollkommen Fremdes und Neues sind.

Peter fängt an, sich ein bisschen auf mich zu stützen, und das darf unter keinen Umständen sein. Auf eigenen Beinen im Leben stehen ist schwierig, aber noch schwieriger ist es, charakterlich und seelisch allein zu stehen und doch standhaft zu bleiben. Ich bin ein bisschen durcheinander, suche schon seit Tagen, suche nach einem ausreichenden Mittel gegen das schreckliche Wort »bequem«. Wie kann ich Peter klarmachen, dass das, was so bequem und schön scheint, ihn in die Tiefe ziehen wird, die Tiefe, wo es keine Freunde, keine Unterstützung, nichts Schönes mehr gibt, eine Tiefe, aus der es fast unmöglich ist, herauszukommen.

Wir leben alle, wissen aber nicht, warum und wofür. Wir leben alle mit dem Ziel, glücklich zu werden, wir leben alle verschieden und doch gleich. Wir drei sind in einem guten Kreis erzogen worden, wir können lernen, wir haben die Möglichkeit, etwas zu erreichen, wir haben Grund, auf Glück zu hoffen, aber – wir müssen uns das selbst verdienen. Und das ist etwas, was mit Bequemlichkeit nie zu erreichen ist. Glück zu verdienen bedeutet, dafür zu arbeiten und Gutes zu tun, und nicht, zu spekulieren und faul zu sein. Faulheit mag anziehend <u>scheinen</u>, Arbeit <u>gibt</u> Befriedigung.

Menschen, die nichts von Arbeit halten, kann ich nicht verstehen. Aber das ist bei Peter auch nicht der Fall. Er hat kein festes Ziel vor Augen, findet sich selbst zu dumm und zu unbedeutend, um etwas zu leisten. Armer Junge, er hat noch nie das Gefühl gekannt, andere glücklich zu machen, und das kann ich ihm auch nicht beibringen. Er hat keine Religion, spricht spottend über Jesus Christus, flucht mit dem Namen Gottes. Obwohl ich auch nicht orthodox bin, tut es mir doch jedes Mal weh, wenn ich merke, wie verlassen, wie geringschätzig, wie arm er ist.

Menschen, die eine Religion haben, dürfen froh sein, denn es ist nicht jedem gegeben, an überirdische Dinge zu glauben. Es ist nicht mal nötig, Angst zu haben vor Strafen nach dem Tod. Das Fegefeuer, die Hölle und der Himmel sind Dinge, die viele nicht akzeptieren können. Trotzdem hält sie irgendeine Religion, egal welche, auf dem richtigen Weg. Es ist keine Angst vor Gott, sondern das Hochhalten der eigenen Ehre und des Gewissens.

Wie schön und gut wären alle Menschen, wenn sie sich jeden Abend die Ereignisse des Tages vor Augen riefen und prüften, was an ihrem eigenen Verhalten gut und was schlecht gewesen ist. Unwillkürlich versucht man dann jeden Tag von neuem, sich zu bessern, und selbstverständlich erreicht man dann im Laufe der Zeit auch einiges. Dieses Mittel kann jeder anwenden, es kostet nichts und ist sehr nützlich. Denn wer es nicht weiß, muss es lernen und erfahren: »Ein ruhiges Gewissen macht stark!«   Deine Anne M. Frank

Samstag, 8. Juli 1944

Liebe Kitty!

Ein Vertreter der Firma war in Beverwijk und hat einfach so, bei einer Versteigerung, Erdbeeren bekommen. Sie kamen hier an, sehr staubig, voller Sand, aber in großen Mengen. Nicht weniger als 24 Kistchen für das Büro und uns. Abends wurden sofort die ersten sechs Gläser eingekocht und acht Gläser Marmelade gemacht. Am nächsten Morgen wollte Miep für das Büro Marmelade kochen.

Um halb eins: Außentür zu, Kistchen holen. Peter, Vater und van Daan poltern auf der Treppe, Anne holt warmes Wasser vom Durchlauferhitzer, Margot holt Eimer, alle Mann an Deck! Mit einem ganz komischen Gefühl im Magen betrat ich die übervolle Büroküche, Miep, Bep, Kleiman, Jan, Vater, Peter … Versteckte und Versorgungskolonne, alles durcheinander, und das mitten am Tag! Die Vorhänge und Fenster offen, lautes Reden, schlagende Türen. Vor lauter Aufregung bekam ich Angst. Verstecken wir uns wirklich noch? fuhr es mir durch den Kopf. So ein Gefühl muss das sein, wenn man sich der Welt wieder zeigen darf. Der Topf war voll, schnell nach oben. In der Küche stand der Rest der Familie am Tisch und pflückte Stiele und Blätter ab, wenigstens sollte das Pflücken sein, es ging mehr in die Münder als in den Eimer. Bald war noch ein Eimer nötig, Peter ging wieder hinunter zur Küche. Da klingelte es zweimal! Der Eimer blieb stehen, Peter rannte herauf, die Drehtür wurde geschlossen. Wir zappelten vor Ungeduld. Die Wasserhähne mussten zubleiben, auch wenn die halb gewaschenen Erdbeeren auf ihr Bad warteten. Aber die Versteckregel »Jemand im Haus, alle Hähne dicht wegen des Lärms, den die Wasserzufuhr macht« wurde aufrechterhalten.

Um ein Uhr kommt Jan und sagt, dass es der Postbote war. Peter rennt wieder die Treppe hinunter. Rrrang, die Klingel! Rechtsum kehrt. Ich horche, ob jemand kommt, erst an der Drehschranktür, dann oben an der Treppe. Schließlich hängen Peter und ich wie zwei Diebe über dem Geländer und horchen auf den Lärm von unten. Keine fremde Stimme.

Peter geht leise die Treppe hinunter, bleibt auf halbem Weg stehen und ruft: »Bep!« Keine Antwort. Noch einmal: »Bep!« Der Lärm in der Küche ist lauter als Peters Stimme. Dann rennt er die Treppe hinunter in die Küche. Ich schaue gespannt hinunter.

»Mach, dass du nach oben kommst, Peter! Der Wirtschaftsprüfer ist da! Du musst weg!« Das ist die Stimme von Kleiman. Seufzend kommt Peter herauf, die Drehschranktür bleibt zu.

Um halb zwei kommt Kugler endlich. »Oje, ich sehe nichts anderes mehr, nur Erdbeeren. Mein Frühstück Erdbeeren, Jan isst Erdbeeren, Kleiman nascht Erdbeeren, Miep kocht Erdbeeren, Bep pflückt Erdbeeren, ich rieche Erdbeeren, und wenn ich das rote Zeug loswerden will und nach oben gehe, was wird hier gewaschen? Erdbeeren.«

Der Rest der Erdbeeren wird eingeweckt. Abends: Zwei Gläser offen. Vater macht schnell Marmelade davon. Am nächsten Morgen: zwei Weckgläser offen, mittags vier. Van Daan hat sie nicht heiß genug sterilisiert. Jetzt kocht Vater jeden Abend Marmelade. Wir essen Brei mit Erdbeeren, Buttermilch mit Erdbeeren, Erdbeeren als Dessert, Erdbeeren mit Zucker, Erdbeeren mit Sand. Zwei Tage tanzten überall Erdbeeren, Erdbeeren, Erdbeeren. Dann war der Vorrat aufgebraucht oder hinter Schloss und Riegel in den Gläsern.

»Hör mal, Anne«, ruft Margot. »Wir haben vom Gemüsemann Erbsen bekommen, 18 Pfund.«

»Das ist nett von ihm«, antworte ich. In der Tat, es war nett, aber die Arbeit … puh!

»Ihr müsst am Samstagmorgen alle enthülsen«, kündigte Mutter bei Tisch an.

Und wirklich, heute Morgen nach dem Frühstück erschien der große Emailletopf auf dem Tisch, bis zum Rand gefüllt mit Erbsen. Enthülsen ist eine langweilige Arbeit, aber dann solltest du erst mal versuchen, die »Schoten auszunehmen«. Ich glaube, dass die Mehrzahl der Menschen nicht weiß, wie vitaminreich, lecker und weich die Schoten von Erbsen schmecken, wenn das innere Häutchen herausgenommen wird. Die drei gerade angeführten Vorteile kommen aber nicht gegen die Tatsache an, dass die Portion, die man essen kann, wohl dreimal größer ist, als wenn man nur die Erbsen isst.

Dieses »Häutchen abziehen« ist eine außergewöhnlich genaue und fummelige Arbeit, die vielleicht für pedantische Zahnärzte oder genaue Büroarbeiter geeignet ist, für einen ungeduldigen Backfisch wie mich ist es schrecklich. Um halb zehn haben wir angefangen, um halb elf setze ich mich, um elf stehe ich wieder auf, um halb zwölf setze ich mich. Es summt in meinen Ohren: Spitze abknicken, Häutchen entfernen, Fäden abziehen, Hülse werfen, Spitze abknicken, Häutchen entfernen, Fäden abziehen, Hülse werfen usw. usw. Es dreht sich vor meinen Augen, grün, grün, Würmchen, Fäden, verfaulte Hülse, grün, grün, grün. Aus Stumpfsinn und um doch etwas zu tun, quatsche ich den ganzen Vormittag allen möglichen Unsinn, bringe alle zum Lachen und komme fast um vor lauter Langeweile. Mit jedem Faden, den ich ziehe, wird mir wieder klarer, dass ich nie, nie nur Hausfrau sein will!

Um zwölf Uhr frühstücken wir endlich, aber von halb eins bis Viertel nach eins müssen wir wieder Häutchen entfernen. Ich bin fast seekrank, als ich aufhöre, die anderen auch ein bisschen. Ich schlafe bis vier Uhr und bin dann immer noch durcheinander wegen der elenden Erbsen.

Deine Anne M. Frank

Liebe Kitty!

Wir hatten von der Bibliothek ein Buch mit dem herausfordernden Titel: »Wie finden Sie das moderne junge Mädchen?« Über dieses Thema möchte ich heute mal sprechen.

Die Autorin kritisiert »die Jugend von heute« von Kopf bis Fuß, ohne jedoch alles, was jung ist, ganz und gar abzulehnen als zu nichts Gutem im Stande. Im Gegenteil, sie ist eher der Meinung, dass die Jugend, wenn sie wollte, eine große, schönere und bessere Welt aufbauen könnte, sich aber mit oberflächlichen Dingen beschäftigt, ohne dem wirklich Schönen einen Blick zu gönnen.

Bei einigen Passagen hatte ich das starke Gefühl, dass die Schreiberin mich mit ihrem Tadel meinte, und darum will ich mich dir endlich mal ganz offen legen und mich gegen diesen Angriff verteidigen.

Ich habe einen stark ausgeprägten Charakterzug, der jedem, der mich länger kennt, auffallen muss, und zwar meine Selbsterkenntnis. Ich kann mich selbst bei allem, was ich tue, betrachten, als ob ich eine Fremde wäre. Überhaupt nicht voreingenommen oder mit einem Sack voller Entschuldigungen stehe ich dann der alltäglichen Anne gegenüber und schaue zu, was diese gut oder schlecht macht. Dieses »Selbstgefühl« lässt mich niemals los, und bei jedem Wort, das ich ausspreche, weiß ich sofort, wenn es ausgesprochen ist: »Dies hätte anders sein müssen« oder »Das ist ganz gut so, wie es ist«. Ich verurteile mich selbst in so unsagbar vielen Dingen und sehe immer mehr, wie wahr Vaters Worte waren: »Jedes Kind muss sich selbst erziehen.«

Eltern können nur Rat oder gute Anweisungen mitgeben, die endgültige Formung seines Charakters hat jeder selbst in der Hand. Dazu kommt noch, dass ich außerordentlich viel Lebensmut habe, ich fühle mich immer so stark und im Stande, viel auszuhalten, so frei und so jung! Als ich das zum ersten Mal merkte, war ich froh, denn ich glaube nicht, dass ich mich schnell unter den Schlägen beuge, die jeder aushalten muss.

Aber darüber habe ich schon oft gesprochen, ich möchte zu dem Kapitel »Vater und Mutter verstehen mich nicht« kommen. Mein Vater und meine Mutter haben mich immer sehr verwöhnt, waren lieb zu mir, haben mich gegen die von oben verteidigt und getan, was Eltern nur tun können. Und doch habe ich mich lange so entsetzlich einsam gefühlt, ausgeschlossen, vernachlässigt, nicht verstanden. Vater versuchte alles, was nur ging, um meine Aufsässigkeit zu besänftigen, das half nichts. Ich habe mich selbst geheilt, indem ich mir das Falsche meines Tuns vorgehalten habe.

Wie kommt es nun, dass Vater mir in meinem Kampf nie eine Hilfe gewesen ist, dass es vollkommen misslang, als er mir die helfende Hand reichen wollte? Vater hat die falschen Mittel angewendet, er hat immer zu mir gesprochen wie zu einem Kind, das schwierige Kinderzeiten durchmachen muss. Das klingt verrückt, denn niemand anders als Vater hat mir immer viel Vertrauen geschenkt, niemand anders als Vater hat mir das Gefühl gegeben, dass ich vernünftig bin. Aber etwas hat er vernachlässigt: Er hat nämlich nicht daran gedacht, dass mir mein Kampf, hochzukommen, wichtiger war als alles andere. Ich wollte nichts von »Alterserscheinungen«, »anderen Mädchen«, »geht von selbst vorbei« hören, ich wollte nicht wie ein Mädchen-wie-alle-anderen behandelt werden, sondern als Anne-für-sich-allein, und Pim verstand das nicht. Übrigens, ich kann niemandem mein Vertrauen schenken, der mir nicht auch viel von sich selbst erzählt, und weil ich von Pim nichts weiß, werde ich den Weg zur Vertraulichkeit zwischen uns nicht betreten können. Pim bewahrt immer den Standpunkt des älteren Vaters, der zwar auch mal solche vorübergehenden Neigungen gehabt hat, der aber nicht als Freund der Jugend mit mir mitleben kann, so eifrig er auch danach strebt. Das hat mich dazu gebracht, meine Anschauungen und meine gut durchdachten Theorien niemals jemand anderem mitzuteilen als meinem Tagebuch und, ganz selten mal, Margot. Vor Vater verbarg ich alles, was mich berührte, habe ihn niemals an meinen Idealen teilhaben lassen, habe ihn mir mit Willen und Absicht entfremdet.

Ich konnte nicht anders, ich habe vollkommen nach meinem Gefühl gehandelt, egoistisch zwar, aber ich habe gehandelt, wie es gut für meine Ruhe war. Denn meine Ruhe und mein Selbstvertrauen, das ich so schwankend aufgebaut habe, würde ich wieder verlieren, wenn ich jetzt Kritik an meinem halb fertigen Werk aushalten müsste. Und das habe ich sogar für Pim nicht übrig, so hart das auch klingen mag,

denn ich habe Pim nicht nur an meinem inneren Leben nicht teilhaben lassen, ich stoße ihn auch oft durch meine Gereiztheit noch weiter von mir weg.

Das ist ein Punkt, über den ich viel nachdenke: Wie kommt es, dass
Pim mich manchmal so ärgert? Dass ich fast nicht mit ihm lernen
kann, dass seine vielen Zärtlichkeiten mir gewollt vorkommen, dass
ich Ruhe haben will und am liebsten sähe, er würde mich manchmal
ein bisschen links liegen lassen, bis ich ihm wieder sicherer gegenüberstehe? Denn noch immer nagt der Vorwurf von dem gemeinen
Brief an mir, den ich ihm in meiner Aufregung zugemutet habe.
O wie schwierig es ist, wirklich nach allen Seiten hin stark und mutig
zu sein!

Trotzdem ist es nicht das, was mir die schlimmste Enttäuschung bereitet hat. Nein, noch viel mehr als über Vater denke ich über Peter
nach. Ich weiß sehr gut, dass ich ihn erobert habe statt umgekehrt.
Ich habe mir ein Traumbild von ihm geschaffen, sah ihn als den stillen, empfindsamen, lieben Jungen, der Liebe und Freundschaft dringend braucht! Ich musste mich mal bei einem lebendigen Menschen
aussprechen. Ich wollte einen Freund haben, der mir wieder auf den
Weg half. Ich habe die schwierige Arbeit vollbracht und ihn langsam,
aber sicher für mich gewonnen.

Als ich ihn schließlich zu freundschaftlichen Gefühlen mir gegenüber gebracht hatte, kamen wir von selbst zu Intimitäten, die mir nun
bei näherer Betrachtung unerhört vorkommen. Wir sprachen über
die geheimsten Dinge, aber über die Dinge, von denen mein Herz voll
war und ist, haben wir bis jetzt geschwiegen. Ich kann noch immer
nicht richtig klug werden aus Peter. Ist er oberflächlich, oder ist es
Verlegenheit, die ihn sogar mir gegenüber zurückhält? Aber abgese-
hen davon, ich habe einen Fehler gemacht, indem ich alle anderen
Möglichkeiten von Freundschaft ausgeschaltet und versucht habe,
ihm durch Intimitäten näher zu kommen. Er hungert nach Liebe und
mag mich jeden Tag mehr, das merke ich gut. Ihm geben unsere Treffen Befriedigung, bei mir führen sie nur zu dem Drang, es immer
wieder aufs Neue mit ihm zu versuchen und nie die Themen zu berühren, die ich so gerne ansprechen würde. Ich habe Peter, mehr als
er selbst weiß, mit Gewalt zu mir gezogen, jetzt hält er sich an mir

fest, und ich sehe vorläufig kein geeignetes Mittel, ihn wieder von mir zu lösen und auf eigene Füße zu stellen. Als ich nämlich sehr schnell merkte, dass er kein Freund sein konnte, wie ich ihn mir vorstelle, habe ich danach gestrebt, ihn dann wenigstens aus seiner Eingeschränktheit herauszuheben und ihn groß zu machen in seiner Jugend.

»Denn im tiefsten Grund ist die Jugend einsamer als das Alter.« Diesen Spruch habe ich aus einem Buch behalten und gefunden, dass er stimmt.

Ist es denn wahr, dass die Erwachsenen es hier schwerer haben als die Jugend? Nein, bestimmt nicht. Ältere Menschen haben eine Meinung über alles und schwanken nicht mehr, was sie tun sollen oder nicht. Wir, die jüngeren, haben doppelt Mühe, unsere Meinungen in einer Zeit zu behaupten, in der aller Idealismus zerstört und kaputtgemacht wird, in der sich die Menschen von ihrer hässlichsten Seite zeigen, in der an Wahrheit, Recht und Gott gezweifelt wird.

Jemand, der dann noch behauptet, dass die Älteren es hier im Hinterhaus viel schwerer haben, macht sich nicht klar, in wie viel stärkerem Maß die Probleme auf uns einstürmen. Probleme, für die wir vielleicht noch viel zu jung sind, die sich uns aber so lange aufdrängen, bis wir endlich eine Lösung gefunden zu haben meinen, eine Lösung, die meistens den Tatsachen nicht standhält und wieder zunichte gemacht wird. Das ist das Schwierige in dieser Zeit: Ideale, Träume, schöne Erwartungen kommen nicht auf, oder sie werden von der grauenhaftesten Wirklichkeit getroffen und vollständig zerstört. Es ist ein Wunder, dass ich nicht alle Erwartungen aufgegeben habe, denn sie scheinen absurd und unausführbar. Trotzdem halte ich an ihnen fest, trotz allem, weil ich noch immer an das innere Gute im Menschen glaube.

Es ist mir nun mal unmöglich, alles auf der Basis von Tod, Elend und Verwirrung aufzubauen. Ich sehe, wie die Welt langsam immer mehr in eine Wüste verwandelt wird, ich höre den anrollenden Donner immer lauter, der auch uns töten wird, ich fühle das Leid von Millionen Menschen mit. Und doch, wenn ich zum Himmel schaue, denke ich, dass sich alles wieder zum Guten wenden wird, dass auch diese Härte aufhören wird, dass wieder Ruhe und Frieden in die Weltordnung

kommen werden. Inzwischen muss ich meine Vorstellungen hochhalten, in den Zeiten, die kommen, sind sie vielleicht doch noch auszuführen!   Deine Anne M. Frank

Liebe Kitty!
Nun werde ich hoffnungsvoll, nun endlich geht es gut. Ja, wirklich,
es geht gut! Tolle Berichte! Ein Mordanschlag auf Hitler ist ausgeübt
worden, und nun mal nicht durch jüdische Kommunisten oder englische Kapitalisten, sondern durch einen hochgermanischen deutschen
General, der Graf und außerdem noch jung ist. Die »göttliche Vorsehung« hat dem Führer das Leben gerettet, und er ist leider, leider mit
ein paar Schrammen und einigen Brandwunden davongekommen.
Ein paar Offiziere und Generäle aus seiner nächsten Umgebung sind
getötet oder verwundet worden. Der Haupttäter wurde standrecht-
lich erschossen.
Der beste Beweis doch wohl, dass es viele Offiziere und Generäle
gibt, die den Krieg satt haben und Hitler gern in die tiefsten Tiefen
versenken würden, um dann eine Militärdiktatur zu errichten, mit
deren Hilfe Frieden mit den Alliierten zu schließen, erneut zu rüsten
und nach zwanzig Jahren wieder einen Krieg zu beginnen. Vielleicht
hat die Vorsehung mit Absicht noch ein bisschen gezögert, ihn aus
dem Weg zu räumen. Denn für die Alliierten ist es viel bequemer und
auch vorteilhafter, wenn die fleckenlosen Germanen sich gegenseitig
totschlagen. Umso weniger Arbeit bleibt den Russen und Engländern, und umso schneller können sie wieder mit dem Aufbau ihrer
eigenen Städte beginnen. Aber so weit sind wir noch nicht, und ich
will nichts weniger, als den glorreichen Tatsachen vorgreifen. Trotzdem merkst du wohl, dass das, was ich sage, die Wahrheit ist, nichts
als die Wahrheit. Ausnahmsweise fasele ich nun mal nicht über hö-
here Ideale.
Hitler ist ferner noch so freundlich gewesen, seinem treuen und anhänglichen Volk mitzuteilen, dass alle Militärs von heute an der Gestapo zu gehorchen haben und dass jeder Soldat, der weiß, dass sein
Kommandant an diesem feigen und gemeinen Attentat teilgenom-
men hat, ihn abknallen darf.

Eine schöne Geschichte wird das werden. Der kleine Michel hat schmerzende Füße vom langen Laufen, sein Herr, der Offizier, staucht ihn zusammen. Der kleine Michel nimmt sein Gewehr, ruft: »Du wolltest den Führer ermorden, da ist dein Lohn!« Ein Knall, und der hochmütige Chef, der es wagte, Michel Standpauken zu halten, ist ins ewige Leben (oder ist es der ewige Tod?) eingegangen. Zuletzt wird es so sein, dass die Herren Offiziere sich die Hosen voll machen vor Angst, wenn sie einen Soldaten treffen oder irgendwo die Führung übernehmen sollen, weil die Soldaten mehr zu sagen und zu tun haben als sie selbst.

Verstehst du's ein bisschen, oder bin ich wieder vom Hundertsten ins Tausendste gekommen? Ich kann's nicht ändern. Ich bin viel zu fröhlich, um logisch zu sein bei der Aussicht, dass ich im Oktober wohl wieder auf der Schulbank sitzen kann! Oh, là, là, habe ich nicht gerade noch gesagt, dass ich nicht voreilig sein will? Vergib mir, ich habe nicht umsonst den Ruf, dass ich ein Bündelchen Widerspruch bin!

Deine Anne M. Frank

Dienstag, 1. August 1944

Liebe Kitty!

»Ein Bündelchen Widerspruch!« Das ist der letzte Satz meines vorigen Briefes und der erste von meinem heutigen. »Ein Bündelchen Widerspruch«, kannst du mir genau erklären, was das ist? Was bedeutet Widerspruch? Wie so viele Worte hat es zwei Bedeutungen, Widerspruch von außen und Widerspruch von innen. Das Erste ist das normale »sich nicht zufrieden geben mit der Meinung anderer Leute, es selbst besser zu wissen, das letzte Wort zu behalten«, kurzum, alles unangenehme Eigenschaften, für die ich bekannt bin. Das Zweite, und dafür bin ich nicht bekannt, ist mein Geheimnis.

Ich habe dir schon öfter erzählt, dass meine Seele sozusagen zweigeteilt ist. Die eine Seite beherbergt meine ausgelassene Fröhlichkeit, die Spöttereien über alles, Lebenslustigkeit und vor allem meine Art, alles von der leichten Seite zu nehmen. Darunter verstehe ich, an einem Flirt nichts zu finden, einem Kuss, einer Umarmung, einem unanständigen Witz. Diese Seite sitzt meistens auf der Lauer und verdrängt die andere, die viel schöner, reiner und tiefer ist. Nicht wahr, die schöne Seite von Anne, die kennt niemand, und darum können mich auch so wenige Menschen leiden. Sicher, ich bin ein amüsanter Clown für einen Nachmittag, dann hat jeder wieder für einen Monat genug von mir. Eigentlich genau dasselbe, was ein Liebesfilm für ernsthafte Menschen ist, einfach eine Ablenkung, eine Zerstreuung für einmal, etwas, das man schnell vergisst, nicht schlecht, aber noch weniger gut. Es ist mir unangenehm, dir das zu erzählen, aber warum sollte ich es nicht tun, wenn ich doch weiß, dass es die Wahrheit ist? Meine leichtere, oberflächliche Seite wird der tieferen immer zuvorkommen und darum immer gewinnen. Du kannst dir nicht vorstellen, wie oft ich nicht schon versucht habe, diese Anne, die nur die Hälfte der ganzen Anne ist, wegzuschieben, umzukrempeln und zu verbergen. Es geht nicht, und ich weiß auch, warum es nicht geht. Ich habe große Angst, dass alle, die mich kennen, wie ich immer bin, entdecken würden, dass ich eine andere Seite habe, eine schönere und bessere. Ich habe Angst, dass sie mich verspotten, mich lächerlich und sentimental finden, mich nicht ernst nehmen. Ich bin daran gewöhnt, nicht ernst genommen zu werden, aber nur die »leichte« Anne ist daran gewöhnt und kann es aushalten. Die »schwerere« ist dafür zu schwach. Wenn ich wirklich einmal mit Gewalt für eine Viertelstunde die gute Anne ins Rampenlicht gestellt habe, zieht sie sich wie ein Blümchen-rühr-mich-nicht-an zurück, sobald sie sprechen soll, lässt Anne Nr. 1 ans Wort und ist, bevor ich es weiß, verschwunden.

In Gesellschaft ist die liebe Anne also noch nie, noch nicht ein einziges Mal, zum Vorschein gekommen, aber beim Alleinsein führt sie fast immer das Wort. Ich weiß genau, wie ich gern sein würde, wie ich auch bin … von innen, aber leider bin ich das nur für mich selbst. Und das ist vielleicht, nein, ganz sicher, der Grund, warum ich mich selbst eine glückliche Innennatur nenne und andere Menschen mich für eine glückliche Außennatur halten. Innerlich weist die reine Anne mir den Weg, äußerlich bin ich nichts als ein vor Ausgelassenheit sich losreißendes Geißlein.

Wie schon gesagt, ich fühle alles anders, als ich es ausspreche. Dadurch habe ich den Ruf eines Mädchens bekommen, das Jungen nachläuft, flirtet, alles besser weiß und Unterhaltungsromane liest. Die fröhliche Anne lacht darüber, gibt eine freche Antwort, zieht gleichgültig die Schultern hoch, tut, als ob es ihr nichts ausmacht. Aber genau umgekehrt reagiert die stille Anne. Wenn ich ganz ehrlich bin, muss ich dir bekennen, dass es mich trifft, dass ich mir unsagbar viel Mühe gebe, anders zu werden, aber dass ich immer wieder gegen stärkere Mächte kämpfe.

Es schluchzt in mir: Siehst du, das ist aus dir geworden: schlechte Meinungen, spöttische und verstörte Gesichter, Menschen, die dich unsympathisch finden, und das alles, weil du nicht auf den Rat deiner guten Hälfte hörst. Ach, ich würde gern darauf hören, aber es geht nicht. Wenn ich still oder ernst bin, denken alle, dass das eine neue Komödie ist, und dann muss ich mich mit einem Witz retten. Ganz zu schweigen von meiner eigenen Familie, die bestimmt glaubt, dass ich krank bin, mir Kopfwehpillen und Beruhigungstabletten zu schlucken gibt, mir an Hals und Stirn fühlt, ob ich Fieber habe, mich nach meinem Stuhlgang fragt und meine schlechte Laune kritisiert. Das halte ich nicht aus, wenn so auf mich aufgepasst wird, dann werde ich erst schnippisch, dann traurig, und schließlich drehe ich mein Herz wieder um, drehe das Schlechte nach außen, das Gute nach innen und suche dauernd nach einem Mittel, um so zu werden, wie ich gern sein würde und wie ich sein könnte, wenn ... wenn keine anderen Menschen auf der Welt leben würden.

Deine Anne M. Frank

Hier endet Annes Tagebuch

Anne Frank mit einem Kaninchen in Amstelrust Park, Juni 1938.

Nachwort

Am 4. August 1944 hielt vormittags zwischen zehn und halb elf Uhr ein Auto vor dem Haus Prinsengracht 263. Ihm entstiegen der uniformierte SS-Oberscharführer Karl Josef Silberbauer und mindestens drei holländische Helfer von der Grünen Polizei, in Zivil, aber bewaffnet. Es ist sicher, dass das Versteck verraten wurde. Der Lagerarbeiter W. G. van Maaren wurde ernsthaft verdächtigt. Zwei Strafuntersuchungen führten jedoch zu keinen Ergebnissen, die juristisch für eine Anklageerhebung ausgereicht hätten.

Die »Grüne Polizei« verhaftete alle acht Untergetauchten sowie die beiden Helfer Viktor Kugler und Johannes Kleiman – nicht aber Miep Gies und Elisabeth (Bep) Voskuijl – und nahm alle Wertsachen und noch vorhandenes Geld an sich.

Nach der Verhaftung wurden Kugler und Kleiman am selben Tag ins Untersuchungsgefängnis am Amstelveenseweg gebracht und einen Monat später in jenes an der Weteringschans in Amsterdam überführt. Ohne Prozess wurden sie am 11. September 1944 ins Polizeiliche Durchgangslager Amersfoort verbracht. Kleiman wurde am 18. September 1944 aus gesundheitlichen Gründen entlassen. Er starb 1959 in Amsterdam. Kugler gelang erst am 28. März 1945 die Flucht, kurz bevor er zum Arbeitseinsatz nach Deutschland abtransportiert worden wäre. Er wanderte 1955 nach Kanada aus und starb 1981 in Toronto. Elisabeth (Bep) Wijk-Voskuijl starb 1983 in Amsterdam. Miep Gies-Santrouschitz lebt mit ihrem Mann noch in Amsterdam.

Die Juden kamen nach ihrer Verhaftung für vier Tage in die Haftanstalt in der Weteringschans in Amsterdam; dann wurden sie in das niederländische »Judendurchgangslager« Westerbork überführt. Mit dem letzten Transport, der von dort in die Vernichtungslager im Osten ging, wurden sie am 3. September 1944 deportiert und erreichten nach drei Tagen Auschwitz in Polen.

Hermann van Pels (van Daan) ist laut den (nachträglichen) Feststellungen des niederländischen Roten Kreuzes noch am Tag der Ankunft, am 6. September 1944, in Auschwitz vergast worden. Nach Aussagen von Otto Frank wurde er jedoch erst einige Wochen später, also im Oktober oder November 1944, kurz vor dem Ende der Vergasungen, umgebracht. Auguste van Pels wurde von Auschwitz über Bergen-Belsen und Buchenwald am 9. April 1945 nach Theresienstadt und von dort offensichtlich noch weiter verschleppt. Ihr Todesdatum ist unbekannt.

Peter van Pels (van Daan) wurde am 16. Januar 1945 in einem der Evakuierungsmärsche von Auschwitz nach Mauthausen (Österreich) verschleppt, wo er am 5. Mai 1945, nur drei Tage vor der Befreiung, starb.

Fritz Pfeffer (Albert Dussel) starb am 20. Dezember 1944 im KZ Neuengamme; dorthin war er über das KZ Buchenwald oder das KZ Sachsenhausen gekommen.

Edith Frank starb am 6. Januar 1945 im Frauenlager Auschwitz-Birkenau an Hunger und Erschöpfung.

Margot und Anne wurden Ende Oktober mit einem so genannten Evakuierungstransport in das KZ Bergen-Belsen in der Lüneburger Heide deportiert. Als Folge der katastrophalen hygienischen Zustände brach dort im Winter 1944/45 eine Typhusepidemie aus, der Tausende der Häftlinge zum Opfer fielen; darunter waren auch Margot und wenige Tage später Anne Frank. Ihr Todesdatum muss zwischen Ende Februar und Anfang März liegen. Die Leichen der beiden Mädchen liegen wahrscheinlich in den Massengräbern von Bergen-Belsen. Am 12. April 1945 wurde das Konzentrationslager von englischen Truppen befreit.

Otto Frank überlebte als Einziger der acht Untergetauchten die Konzentrationslager. Nach der Befreiung von Auschwitz durch russische Truppen gelangte er mit dem Schiff über Odessa nach Marseille. Am 3. Juni 1945 traf er in Amsterdam ein und lebte dort bis 1953; dann übersiedelte er in die Schweiz, nach Basel, wo seine Schwester mit ihrer Familie und sein Bruder lebten. Er heiratete Elfriede Geiringer, geborene Markowits, aus Wien, die wie er Auschwitz überlebt und Mann und Sohn im KZ Mauthausen verloren hatte. Bis zu seinem Tod am 19. August 1980 lebte Otto Frank in Birsfelden bei Basel und widmete sich dem Tagebuch seiner Tochter Anne und der Verbreitung der darin enthaltenen Botschaft.

Anne Frank
Geschichten und Ereignisse
aus dem Hinterhaus
Aus dem Niederländischen von
Edith Schmidt, Anneliese Schütz und Josh van Soer
Mit einer Einführung von Gerrold van der Stroom

Band 15777

In der Enge des Amsterdamer Hinterhauses, das die Familie Frank vor den Verfolgungen der Nazis verbarg, begann
Anne zu schreiben. Neben dem inzwischen weltberühmten
Tagebuch entstanden Geschichten, in denen sich Anne an
ihre Schulzeit erinnert, als sie noch leben durfte wie andere
junge Menschen. Sie erzählt von Lehrern, Freundinnen und
von Alltäglichem, das um so schwerer zu bewältigen ist,
wenn man in der ständigen Furcht lebt, entdeckt zu werden.
Neben diesen autobiographischen Texten schrieb Anne
Märchen sowie Geschichten, in denen sie sich fortträumt,
ihre Figuren reisen und Bekanntschaften schließen läßt und
die vor allem frei sind.

Fischer Taschenbuch Verlag

Willy Lindwer

Anne Frank
Die letzten sieben Monate
Augenzeuginnen berichten
Aus dem Niederländischen von Mirjam Pressler
Band 11616

Sieben jüdische Frauen, die Anne Frank und ihrer Familie nahe-
standen, berichten in diesem Buch von ihrem Leben vor dem Krieg,
von der Verfolgung, Verhaftung und Deportation und von ihrem
Überleben in den Konzentrationslagern. Manche, wie Anne Franks
Kinderfreundin Hannah Pick-Goslar (Lies Goosens in Annes Tagebuch) kannten die Franks aus der Zeit vor dem Untertauchen, andere lernten Anne erst auf dem Transport oder in den Lagern kennen, sahen sie noch Mitte März 1945, sprachen mit ihr. Willy Lindwer ist es zu danken, daß er diese Zeuginnen aufgespürt hat und
mit großer Behutsamkeit dazu brachte, von sich zu erzählen. Diese
Frauen haben das letzte, »ungeschriebene« Kapitel von Anne Franks
Tagebuch öffentlich gemacht.

Fischer Taschenbuch Verlag

Schoschana Rabinovici
Dank meiner Mutter
Aus dem Hebräischen von Mirjam Pressler
Band 15421

Die bewegende Geschichte eines jüdischen Mädchens,
das dank der Klugheit seiner Mutter den Holocaust überlebte: Klar, eindringlich und ohne Hass erzählt Schoschana
Rabinovici von ihrer Vertreibung aus dem Wilnaer Ghetto
und von ihren Leidensstationen in den Konzentrationslagern Kaiserwald, Stutthof und Tauentzin. Mit ihren Kind-
heitserinnerungen setzt sie ihrer Mutter Raja ein Denkmal,
ohne deren Stärke, Lebensklugheit und Willenskraft sie
diese Zeit nicht überlebt hätte.

Fischer Taschenbuch Verlag

Jacqueline van Maarsen
Ich heiße Anne, sagte sie, Anne Frank
Band 16286

»Es kann nicht genug Biografien aus dieser Zeit geben.«
Mirjam Pressler

Generationen von Lesern ist Jacqueline van Maarsen aus
Anne Franks Tagebüchern bekannt. Jetzt erzählt »Jopie«
selbst von ihrer Freundschaft mit Anne, die ihr Leben auf
tiefgreifende Weise beeinflussen sollte. Und sie erzählt die
Geschichte ihrer so unterschiedlichen Eltern, Eline und
Hijman, von ihren Kriegserlebnissen und wie sie selbst der
drohenden Deportation entkam.

»Heute, da uns täglich neue Bilder der Gewalt
gegen Wehrlose erreichen und die Sinnlosigkeit
der Kriege dokumentieren, scheint diese Flaschenpost
zur rechten Zeit einzutreffen.«
Süddeutsche Zeitung

Fischer Taschenbuch Verlag

fi 16286 / 1